Alabi's World

Also by Richard Price

Maroon Societies: Rebel Slave Communities in the Americas
(edited)

Saramaka Social Structure

An Anthropological Approach to the Afro-American Past
(with Sidney W. Mintz)

The Guiana Maroons: A Historical and Bibliographical Introduction

Afro-American Arts of the Suriname Rain Forest
(with Sally Price)

To Slay the Hydra: Dutch Colonial Perspectives on the Saramaka Wars

First-Time: The Historical Vision of an Afro-American People

Narrative of a Five Years Expedition against the Revolted Negroes of Surinam, by John Gabriel Stedman
(edited with Sally Price)

Two Evenings in Saramaka (with Sally Price)

Alabi's World

Richard Price

The Johns Hopkins University Press
Baltimore and London

This book has been brought to publication with the generous assistance of the National Endowment for the Humanities and is part of the Johns Hopkins Studies in Atlantic History and Culture.

The Johns Hopkins University Press
701 West 40th Street
Baltimore, Maryland 21211
The Johns Hopkins Press Ltd., London

The paper used in this publication meets
the minimum requirements of American
National Standard for Information Sciences—
Permanence of Paper for Printed Library
Materials, ANSI Z39.48-1984.

Library of Congress Cataloging-in-Publication Data

Price, Richard, 1941–
    Alabi's world / Richard Price.
        p.   cm. — (Johns Hopkins studies in
Atlantic history and culture)
    Bibliography: p.
    ISBN 0-8018-3862-2 (alk. paper). —
ISBN 0-8018-3956-4 (pbk. : alk. paper)
    1. Alabi. 2. Saramaka (Surinam people)—
Biography. 3. Saramaka (Surinam people)—
History—Sources. 4. Slavery—Surinam—
History—Sources. 5. Netherlands—Colonies—
America—Administration. 6. Surinam—
Biography. I. Title. II. Series.
F2431.S27A457   1990
988.3'3—dc20   89-15488 CIP

In 1978, the Saramaka elder Peléki voiced the greatest fear of all Maroons, prophesying that those times—the days of war and slavery—shall come again. In 1986, after two centuries of peace, they did. Great war *óbia*s that had lain dormant since the eighteenth century were dug from the earth and revivified. The blood of hundreds of Maroons—men, women, and children—as well as that of other Surinamers has once again stained the ground. And as this book goes to press, the end is not yet in sight.

Alabi's World, which recounts the way eighteenth-century Saramakas and whitefolks, at the end of a very long war, developed routines, rituals, and institutions that allowed them to live side by side in peace, is dedicated to the hope that the spiritual descendants of these parties will now have the courage to take up the same enormously delicate task once again.

Contents

Acknowledgments

It has become something of a fashion in the world of postmodern ethnography to acknowledge the assistance of a list of people and groups that resembles what is supposed to pass through one's mind in the seconds between jumping off a skyscraper and hitting the pavement. I choose here instead to thank those people and institutions who directly contributed to the production of this book, insofar as imperfect memory can conjure up faces and moments that stretch out over a period of some twenty years.

My major debt, and gratitude, is to the people of Saramaka. Many of those who worked with me on this book have since passed into the realm of the ancestors. My hope is that *Alabi's World* will stand as partial testimony to their lives, and that it will some day be read by their descendants and help enrich the meaning of their own lives.

A number of organizations have, over the years, provided financial support for some part of the research or writing: the Afro-American Program of Yale University, the American Council of Learned Societies, the Johns Hopkins University, the National Science Foundation (Grant BNS 76-02848), the Netherlands Institute for Advanced Study, the Netherlands America Commission for Educational Exchange, the Nederlandse Organisatie voor Zuiver-Wetenschappelijk Onderzoek, the U.S. Department of Education Faculty Research Abroad Program, the United States–France Exchange of Senior Scientists Program, and the Centre National de Recherche Scientifique (France).

I would like to thank those students (now professionals in their own right) who participated in seminars at Yale (1971 and 1972) or Johns Hopkins (1976), and whose papers or discussions helped point the way—in particular, Val Carnegie, Gene Galbraith, Ewa Hauser, Gary McDonogh, Roberto Melville, Scott Parris, and Rob Weller. The encouragement and criticisms of David Cohen, who sat in on the JHU seminar, were especially helpful. And my multifaceted association with Sidney Mintz has, during the period this book was in progress, contributed much to my general approach to the Afro-Caribbean past.

Harry and Ligia Hoetink offered hospitality whenever it was needed for this project in the Netherlands. Several colleagues in France helped make it possible for me to complete much of the writing there: Marc Augé, Kristin Couper, François Furet, Maurice Godelier, Françoise Héritier, Michel Izard, Patrick and Maryvonne Menget, and Aurore Monod-Becquelin. The final draft was completed while I was a guest of the Institute of International Studies at the University of Minnesota; an evening's discussion of *Alabi* at that university's Program in History and Society provided a number of especially useful criticisms.

I am grateful to Scott Guggenheim, Paul Sullivan, and particularly Ken Bilby for critical readings of the manuscript. And Bonno Thoden van Velzen kept me continually up to date by supplying clippings from the Dutch press (including his own acute analyses) about ongoing events in war-torn Suriname. I would also like to thank my long-time publisher, Jack Goellner, and long-time copy editor, Carol Ehrlich, for their continued support and sensitivity. It remains a special pleasure for me to work with the Johns Hopkins University Press.

Finally, the two women in my life both went out of their way to make this book far better than it would have been—Leah Price, through her unstinting literary counsel, and Sally Price, earlier acknowledged as "my most frequent, most generous, and toughest critic" (she still is), for continuing to be the Compleat Companion.

To all, *gaán tangí tangí f'únu.*

Prologue

> Ethnographic moments are never so piquant for
> the poetics of history as they are in the contact
> of natives and strangers. The compounded
> nature of histories, the self-images in the
> cartoons of the other, the processes of culture
> and expressed cultures are simply writ large
> in circumstances of extravagant ambiguity.
>
> —Greg Dening

About 1900, my grandparents emigrated as youths from the Old World, seeking their fortune in the Land of Opportunity. I was born in the 1940s in New York City, a third generation (Euro-)American. About 1680, Alábi's paternal great-grandparents, young enslaved Africans, were transported by force to the New World. Alabi (Ah-LAH-bee)—future tribal chief of the Saramakas, and their first convert to Christianity—was born in the 1740s in the Suriname village of Tímba, a fourth generation (Afro-)American. During the past twenty years, our lives have become closely intertwined.

Alabi's moment in time and space, however obscure at first glance, constitutes a privileged one for the exploration of Afro-American history and consciousness, and for that of the colonial experience more generally. *Alabi's World* concerns the kind of intercultural confrontation that must have occurred tens of thousands of times across the face of the Americas but which rarely bequeathed such rich traces to posterity. The available documents—the handwritten inscriptions of eighteenth-century missionaries and colonial officers and the oral testimonies of modern Saramakas—are focused precisely on the fundamental negotiation of meaning between Euro-Americans and Afro-Americans in relationships of differential power. Through these multiplex, ambiguous records, in German, Dutch, and Saramaccan, we are privileged to witness, deep in the rain forest of Suriname, the ongoing invention of culture.

In a previous book (*First-Time,* in which the young Alabi made a cameo appearance), I attempted to communicate the Saramaka past in Saramaka terms, drawing heavily on the forms they have developed to keep their own history alive. The present book, though it tries to remain equally faithful to Saramaka modes of historical understanding, adds several new layers of mediation and interpretation.

xi

Here, there is considerably more intersubjectivity, there are quicker shifts in perspective, there is more grist for the hermeneutic mill.[1] The reader is invited to participate more actively than is customary in the act of historical imagination. Through the use of multivocality and the presentation of large amounts of relatively raw materials, I make a conscious effort to evoke a past world rather than simply to represent it.

The three kinds of voices that I animate in this work deserve preliminary introduction, though a full understanding of their characteristics and perspectives will emerge only from close listening to their interaction.[2] Eighteenth-century Saramakas, German Moravians, and Dutch colonial officials had contrastive agendas, and this is reflected in the records each has unwittingly bequeathed to me.

For something over three years since 1966 I have lived in Saramaka villages, visiting most recently with refugees in French Guiana during the summer of 1987. My fascination with their collective knowledge of their ancestors' early years as maroons, hedged around as it is by extraordinary sacredness and secrecy, eventually resulted in *First-Time* (a book devoted, in part, to exploring the ways that Saramaka historical knowledge is embedded in ongoing social process). What Saramakas refer to as *fési-tén* ("First-Time"), their society's formative years whose end roughly coincides with the passing of Alabi—is an era that possesses overwhelming inherent power. It is the fountainhead of their collective identity. It contains the true root of what it means to be Saramaka. "If we forget the deeds of our ancestors," I once heard one man reminding another, "how can we hope to avoid being returned to whitefolks' slavery?" Or, as another man once told me, "This is the one thing Maroons really believe. It's stronger than anything else. . . . This is the greatest fear of all Maroons: that those times [the days of slavery and the struggle for freedom] shall come again." It is within the same complex web of epistemological, moral, and ideological concerns discussed at some length in the introduction to *First-Time* that the Saramaka voices who speak in *Alabi's World* were recorded and are here presented.

Two circumstances, in addition to the acknowledged difficulties of doing historical research in Saramaka, determine that the amount of direct Saramaka testimony about the events in this book is not still greater. First, I have lived exclusively with non-Christian Saramakas (who represent some 80 percent of the total population) and only visited occasionally, for several days at a stretch, in Christian villages, where my interest was at the time largely in observing differences from "standard" Saramaka life and thought. When I turned to studying the Saramaka past in the field, my own biases led me to be far less interested in what I tended to see as the routine and dreary history of missionization than in the possibility of reconstructing the heroic birth of the Saramaka nation. (I had not yet realized that the one might shed bright light upon the other.) Undoubtedly, too, I had a romantic sense—never fully lost—that non-Christian Saramakas were (as they

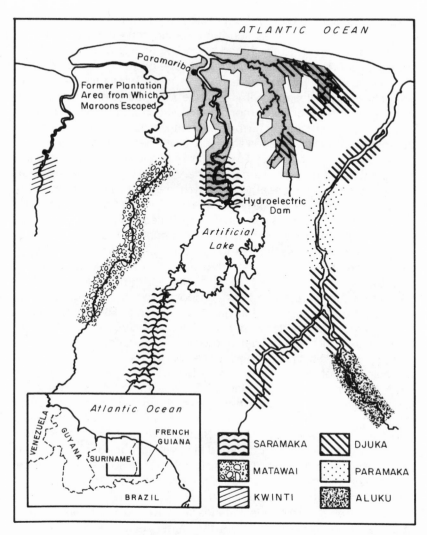

The Saramaka and Other Suriname Maroons. The Saramaka, today some twenty-two thousand people, are one of six Maroon (or "Bush Negro") groups in Suriname that together constitute well over 10 percent of the national population. Their ancestors were among those Africans sold into slavery in the late seventeenth and early eighteenth centuries to work Suriname's sugar plantations. They soon escaped into the dense rain forest—individually, in small groups, sometimes in great collective rebellions—where for nearly one hundred years they fought a war of liberation. In 1762, a full century before the general emancipation of slaves in Suriname, they won their freedom. (The English word *maroon* derives from the Spanish *cimarrón,* a term with Arawakan [Native American] roots that by the early 1500s had come to be used in plantation colonies throughout the Americas to designate slaves who successfully escaped from captivity.)

themselves see it) "real" Saramakas, with Christian Saramakas (again, as other Saramakas see them) being somewhere down the bumpy road leading to the hated but ambiguously alluring world of "whitefolks." And second, during the past eighteen months, when I have twice journeyed to Suriname or French Guiana to speak with Saramakas, the present civil war made it impossible to meet with those historical specialists among Saramaka Christians who might, at this stage, have provided further, final enrichment from a Saramaka perspective on the episodes that appear in these pages.

The German texts that appear in this book were, for the most part, produced systematically, as part of the worldwide Moravian master plan for converting the heathen. Missionaries were exhorted to keep a detailed record of their daily activities, with attention to both "outward and inward matters. . . . Such a diary, kept by the Missionaries, serves for the information, both of the direction of the Unity, and the deputation of the Missions, as to what has been done, and what is left undone, in order to assist them with their good advice" (Anon. n.d., 51). Thousands of pages of such diaries from Suriname, plus a number of letters and handwritten books recording congregational matters, are scattered in Moravian repositories at Herrnhut (now in the German Democratic Republic), Zeist and Utrecht (the Netherlands), Paramaribo (Suriname), and Bethlehem (Pennsylvania). Some of these materials have been published in German, most importantly the selection of diaries compiled by Bishop Staehelin in the period 1913–19, and some very selective English translations were published during the early nineteenth century in *Periodical Accounts,* intended for the edification of Moravians around the world. Moreover, one maverick missionary, Brother Riemer, after returning to Europe and leaving the Brethren, published his own account of his brief stay among the Saramaka two decades after the fact (1801). I have worked with these materials in various forms since the late 1960s; there is much that remains to be done with them.[3]

The written record of missionaries who lived in Saramaka villages stretches from 1765 to 1813, but the materials I have been able to consult are uneven because of the number of missing diaries, difficulties in deciphering crabbed handwriting faded or smudged by tropical conditions, the diarists' differential control of the Saramaka language (and hence their understanding of local affairs), and other mitigating influences, such as their current state of health. The texts, as will be clear from the many extracts presented here, were written at once for the Brethren back in Europe, as an inspirational record of missionary suffering and success, and as a personal confession to God, the strong sense of whose immanence emerges from every page. These rich, exotic Moravian texts pose a signal challenge to the interpreter seeking to comprehend the encounter between displaced Europeans and Africans in colonial America. For they address, however obliquely, some central processes of that encounter, what Taus-

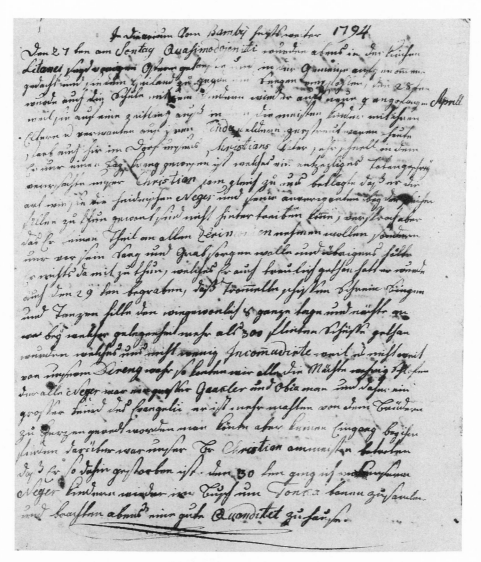

Moravian diary page from the Saramaka mission, 1794 (AEB). (For a page from a comparable Dutch administrative source, see p. 129.)

(For a page from a comparable Dutch administrative source, see p. 129.)

sig—writing of the confrontation of Indians and colonists near the headwaters of the Amazon—has glossed as

> new rituals, rites of conquest and colony formation, mystiques of race and power, little dramas of civilization tailoring savagery which did not mix or homogenize ingredients from the two sides of the colonial divide but instead bound Indian understandings of white understandings of Indians to white understandings of Indian understandings of whites. (1987, 109)

The Dutch texts that constitute the third voice in *Alabi's World* are, from a historian's perspective, the most conventional. Consisting largely of journals and letters written by the colonial officials charged with observing and reporting on Saramaka life (especially as it related to the security of the colony) and with carrying out the orders of the colonial Court of Policy in Paramaribo, these documents were intended to focus on political life. As such, they form an almost perfect complement to the contemporaneous Moravian records, as they deal largely with those apparently secular matters that least interested the otherworldly Brethren. The journals and letters of these Dutch "postholders" in Saramaka were written both for the members of the colonial Court, for whom they provided almost the only source of information about the collective behavior of the recently pacified Saramaka, and for the directors of the Chartered Society of Suriname in Holland, whose business interests were very much at the mercy of Maroon political decisions. Postholders, who were usually by training military men, were under specific orders to keep systematic journals—and there is strong stylistic continuity between the journals of the field commanders on military expeditions during the Saramaka wars (see R. Price 1983b) and the post-treaty writings of the postholders. As lone civil servants, stationed at distant posts, reporting back on their own activities to their superiors (who controlled their promotions, salary, and other emoluments), the postholders clearly had their own scripts, and—as with the Moravian documents and Saramaka testimonies—their records must be read with all of our critical faculties. Today, those postholder documents that survive (often in second or third generation manuscript copies, made by scribes in Paramaribo for shipment to the Netherlands) are to be found in the Algemeen Rijksarchief in The Hague, though a number of relevant volumes are not available for consultation because of physical deterioration.[4] Since 1969, I have worked with these materials intermittently, during three separate years spent in the Netherlands.[5]

The fourth and controlling voice in *Alabi's World* is my own, that of a self-styled ethnographic historian. (Though "ethnohistorian" might seem a simpler label, I worry that ethnohistory has all too often been understood as little more than "the history of the bare-assed"—and, as it happens, the only known depiction of Alabi, in a book by a Moravian, shows him in precisely this condition; see p. 198.) At its best, ethnography entails a special perspective, a way of seeing and writing that is equally appropriate for the study of a modern industrial corporation or a nonliterate hill tribe. The practice of ethnographic history, likewise, need know no geographical or typological boundaries: historical studies of "primitives" or "the civilized," Trobrianders or the British (and especially their respective interactions), come equally under its purview. But simply writing "social history" or reconstructing a past world, no matter how masterfully, would not qualify.[6] The endeavor must be animated by a constant attentiveness to meaning (teasing out the significance of experience and actions to the actors—a kind of ethnological hermeneutics), to the process of producing histories (the relations of power in creating and suppressing historical discourse, the social negotiation of historical knowledge, the relationship between the author and the historical observers upon whose records he depends), to relationships between the author and his historical subjects, to processes of knowing (maintaining the distance of others' categories), and to problems of form and "catching experience whole." To paraphrase Dening (1986, 1989), ethnographic history, shaped by the ironic trope in which things are never what they seem to be, would at its best be a thoroughly demystifying art (contrasting with "guilded history," which Dening reminds us tends also to be "gilded history").[7]

Historians, like anthropologists, are prime targets for the "if I were a horse" criticism, attempting, as they often do, to imagine themselves in another time or place and then interpreting the past accordingly. Yet, *pace* Geertz (1976), without such attempts at empathy, ethnographic or historical interpretation risks being empty and soulless. With no apologies, I aver that my own reading of the Moravian and Dutch documents, as well as Saramaka records about their own past, is deeply conditioned by my ethnographic experience in Saramaka (which included frequent interactions with twentieth-century Moravian missionaries and Dutch administrators). Throughout this book, I try hard to understand what the world of eighteenth-century Saramaka looked like, smelled like, and felt like, and the meanings that those who lived in it (whether Saramakas, Moravian missionaries, or Dutch postholders) attached to unfolding events and developing institutions. While taking the greatest pains not to read the present backward into the past, I nonetheless am constantly trying to understand the records left by the past in terms that are unavoidably colored by the present.[8] I know no other way, and the success or failure of the endeavor must be judged, ultimately, on grounds of plausibility, after taking into account every scrap of knowledge, written and oral, available to us. While my decision to present large, unadulterated swatches of observations by eyewitnesses is motivated in part by a wish to decenter the narrative, to fragment the power of the author's inevitable authority, and to draw the reader more directly into the process of interpretation, I would not pretend that the construction of this book is not a careful calculation or that the author is not always present, even when just off-stage.

James Boon, with only slight exaggeration, has characterized the traditional anthropological monograph as possessing

> a stylistic taboo on authorial viewpoint. . . . Its order of contents [was] physical surroundings firmly first, religion vaguely last, kinship and social organization determiningly at the core. . . . [Systematically omitted were] chapters on relations between a particular culture and others and on that culture's own sense of others . . . [as well as] chapters on the history of the tendency to conceptualize the population as a "culture" and on the ultimate fact

of fieldwork: the significance of a stranger's inserting himself into the routine context of a face-to-face population. (1982, 14–15)

In a very real sense, it is just these "taboos" and "omissions" that constitute the core of *Alabi's World,* even though the superficial organization of the book, as an alternation between narrative and descriptive passages, mirrors the form that standard travel narratives have taken at least since the sixteenth century (Pratt 1986): "On Thursday, I visited Mr. Smith, who showed me his hen Negroes. . . . The avocado is a pale green vegetable whose taste resembles the European peach, melting in the same manner in one's mouth, yet incomparably more delicious." Travel writers, wishing to describe their own experiences, to establish and maintain authorial authority, and to describe in natural history fashion an exotic world for their European readers, found it convenient to move back and forth, every few pages, between these master tropes. Though I cast this book in a biographical rather than an autobiographical mode, and though both my "narrative" passages (action descriptions) and "descriptive" portions (normative, cultural descriptions) are laced with observations made by others, in a general way I follow suit.[9] The body of *Alabi's World* consists of such narrative/descriptive alternation, with some explicit analysis thrown in. The extensive Notes and Commentary section, which is nearly as long as the main text, is composed of supplementary description that would have unbalanced the narrative/descriptive alternance of the main text, supplementary analysis (relegated to this section for similar reasons), and endnotes proper (discussion of sources). The whole is intended as, among other things, an ethnography of early Afro-American life, necessarily and unapologetically partial and idiosyncratic, but nonetheless texturally richer than any that has yet been attempted.

Since Saramakas display a strongly linear, causal sense of history (see R. Price 1983a), chronology seemed an appropriate dimension with which to vertebrate the narrative, permitting me to avoid the imposition of some other arbitrary analytic order. To evoke something of the texture of eighteenth-century life in Saramaka, it seemed especially important to eschew modern Western categories, such as religion, politics, economics, art, or kinship, as organizing principles. (My similar decision, despite the urging of several colleagues, not to make an index that encourages consultation along such ethnological lines stems from a growing conviction that such categories ultimately play a pernicious, obfuscating role in intercultural understanding.) Just as "religion" cannot be described by saying that the natives believe this or that, but can only be understood by describing and analyzing the connections between events, experience, social relationships, and the ways people represent these to themselves (Burridge 1975, 15), so too with any of these categories. Hence I attempt, by means of a variety of rhetorical devices, to focus attention on activities, encounters, and relationships through which may gradually emerge a partial understanding of a faraway past world.

This book, whatever its rewards, has been unusually tedious to write. (For more years than I care to recall, I have kept taped to my study wall—in Wassenaar, Oegstgeest, Baltimore, Paris, Anse Chaudière, and Minneapolis—an index card inscribed with a taunting Saramaka proverb, in esoteric language, *úzu úzu de a só lóbi* ["the way you've begun it, can you really finish it?"].) I have been constantly aware of the enormous weight of documents, fieldnotes, tape recordings, and previously published relevant tomes, each of which, while providing historical insight, in one way or another has circumscribed my freedom to choose particular written forms. This is one way that the practice of ethnographic history, like that of biography, differs fundamentally—because of the very great weight of the recorded past that must be taken into account—from that of the novelist.

> In a novel, the novelist knows everything about the hero or heroine. His characters are his own invention and he can do what he wishes with them. Novelists have omniscience. Biographers never do. The personages exist; the documents exist; they are the "givens." . . . They may not be altered. . . . The fancy of the biographer . . . resides in the art of narration, not in the substance of the story. The substance exists before the narration exists. . . . The biographer truly succeeds if a distinct literary form can be found for the particular life. . . . A writer of lives is allowed the imagination of form but not of fact. (Edel 1984, 13–17)

Nevertheless, like a good historical novelist, the ethnographic historian tries to penetrate existential worlds different from his own and to evoke their texture, by bridging, but never losing sight of, the cultural and semantic gulf that separates the author from the historical actors and from the historical observers (those who create the "sources," which themselves possess and represent complex prior histories— see Philipp 1983, Dening 1986). Philipp has written programmatically that "the primary aim of historical analysis is the recovery, partial though it must be, of the lived reality of people in their past" (352). As a statement of technical goals, I would accept this formulation. But as Whitten suggests (1986, 93), I also take a moral stance, insisting, with Saramakas, that "the horrors recorded and etched in their individual minds and collective psyche cannot be forgotten or left to a Western sense of history, as that which is only in the past." That the prophecy of my friend Peleki (see dedication page) has been chillingly realized in the present brutally collapses for him and other Saramakas Alabi's world and their own. With mine and yours as well. More than two decades of work on Suriname has taught me that in that particular postcolonial space (which has, ever since the conquest, been a prototypical "space of death," as Taussig [1987] has used the phrase), books as well as ideologies quickly take on a life of their own. My hope is that this book, about a moment of peace and reconciliation two centuries ago, may in some small way encourage the painful process of healing that must now be set in motion along the banks of the River Suriname.

A Note on Typeface

The four voices in *Alabi's World*—both in the text and in the Notes and Commentary—appear in different typefaces, to preserve their distinctive tones:

My own prose, as well as quoted passages from other scholars, is printed in Univers 45.

Materials taken from Moravian writings are printed in Trump Bold (intended by its heaviness to suggest German print).

Materials from Dutch (or other planter) sources are printed in Trump Bold Italics.

And words originally spoken by Saramakas are printed in Trump Italics, with ragged right margins, to emphasize their spoken nature.[10]

The reader who wishes to embrace this experiment fully might try to "hear" the Trump Bold passages in the accent of a working-class eighteenth-century German Moravian, the Trump Bold Italics passages in the Dutch accent of a bewigged colonial governor or his soldier-administrators, and the Trump Italics passages in the speech cadences of the elderly, dignified Saramaka men, some of whose portraits grace *First-Time* and *Alabi's World*.[11]

I   *Foreparents*

First-Time's Child

Whitefolks' Captivity

Through the proverbial mists of time, we strain to make out the opening scene, almost three hundred years ago to the day. A small Dutch Guineaman bobs in the roads off Paramaribo, tugging at her anchor chain, as the Atlantic tide sweeps up the broad River Suriname. She has lain there for a week already, slave cargo below decks in the fetid heat, as medical inspectors and insurance factors come and go, and the captain receives planters and bookkeepers, eager to get a leg up on buying strong bodies for their estates. From the bank, an Indian fisherman watches as a lighter, rowed by sweating slaves, moves out to the ship and ties on. The sounds of curses, cries, and whiplashes drift toward him, as the vessel disgorges a first batch of captive Africans. After the passage ashore, he watches them clamber up the bank, legs rubbery from weeks of lying chained in close and stinking confinement betwixt the decks. By late morning, after the lighter has been rowed out and back so many times the fisherman loses count, he watches as the sad and frightened group of men and women is herded along the riverbank toward the public market. With a scowl, the bookkeeper of Plantation Waterland watches his fastidious master poke, squeeze, and otherwise examine eight walking skeletons, and then sign the papers that give him legal possession. Leaving his master to attend to business in town, the bookkeeper loses no time in loading his cargo into a barge, rowed by experienced slaves, for the four-hour journey upstream. He is already late for the midday meal and his daily dalliance with one of the cooks.

Among the newcomers who huddle near the stern of that barge are two Twi-speakers who already call themselves brothers (whether by birth or by choice we do not know)—Lanu and Ayako.[1] Though

3

unsure whether they are being rowed upstream to be eaten by the whitefolks, melted down for fat, or simply worked to death like the slaves they see toiling at the oars, both are relieved to have felt solid earth under their feet at last and to be able, simply by dipping in an unchained hand, to taste once again the sweet grittyness of red-brown river water. Since having been captured by treachery, a continent away, they have suffered months of degradation, anger, and frustration, sliding almost imperceptibly during the Middle Passage into bored and nameless misery. Now life seems to be taking a new turn, and they silently thank their faraway gods and ancestors, begging for strength. Seeing the broad river and the forested banks re-awakens hope, the possibility of resistance and revenge, and perhaps even freedom.[2]

Since the founding of the colony three decades before, a unique plantation world had grown up alongside the Suriname. Ayako and Lanu had landed in a colony in early economic bloom. By this day in the mid-1680s, some seven hundred local Europeans, of diverse social backgrounds and national origins, were already living in considerable luxury off the labor of forty-five hundred enslaved Africans (of equally diverse social and ethnic origins). Small and relatively intimate plantations, using a mixed labor force of African and Amerindian slaves and white indentured servants, were rapidly yielding to large, factorylike estates worked by between one hundred and two hundred enslaved Africans. Planters, hellbent for quick prosperity, were busily creating a society that by the next century could claim to be "the envy of all the others in the Americas," producing more revenue and consuming more imported manufactured goods per capita than any other Caribbean colony. The everyday scenes described during the eighteenth century by Stedman—planters being served at table by nearly nude house slaves who also bathed their children in madeira, while on the porch of the Great House field slaves were being hamstrung and whiplashed for petty offenses—had not yet, perhaps, become mere commonplace, but Suriname had already earned a well-deserved reputation for its heights of planter opulence and cruelty and its depths of slave misery.

Within the elite world of Suriname whitefolks, Jews held a place apart. Refugees from religious persecution in Brazil, some two hundred Sephardim arrived in Suriname in the 1660s and were granted privileges that encouraged the formation of a relatively closed community, with its own religious, judicial, educational, and even military institutions, set firmly within the larger colonial structure. By the 1680s they owned about one-third of the colony's plantations, almost all along the Suriname River. Ayako and Lanu's new owner, Imanuël Machado, belonged to this special caste, managing both Waterland and a smaller plantation a few hours' walk through the forest to the east of the Suriname, along the Cassewinica Creek.

At Waterland, along with the other newcomers, the brothers were absorbed into the closed world of the slave village. Gradually, they

Plantation Waterland, 1708, only a few years after its driver, Ayakô, escaped. The drawing, by Dirk Valkenburg, is labeled, "This view of Waterland is seen by standing before the kitchen. 1 the mill and boiling house from the front. 2 the gallery on the river side. 3 the gallery on the land side. 4. the distillery. 5 a slave house" (Rijksmuseum Amsterdam, Rijksprentenkabinet).

regained their strength, both physical and moral, even while learning the new routines of what Saramakas today call "whitefolks' captivity"—up at dawn, work in the fields till dusk, whippings for protest. They discovered that Sééi, a married woman with two young children, spoke their language, and the three soon took to spending their evenings together. Despite bouts of loneliness, and frustration at their slowness in learning the new language (a creole with Portuguese, English, and African roots that had developed on the Suriname River plantations), Lanu and Ayako now had constant reminders of what life should offer: the smell of cookfires in the evening, the sounds of men and women chatting, even the laughter of the few children who chased each other between the tiny houses. With time, Lanu's gifts as diviner and healer brought him special respect, tinged with fear. Osíma, a fine-looking woman from Dahomey who worked in the white man's house, became his lover and would sneak him special treats from the kitchen. Ayako, a natural leader, became plantation *basya,* bossman or driver, in charge of a whole gang of Waterland slaves.[3] One day, while accompanying his master on a business visit to the Dombi Plantation, a few hours upstream near Jews Savannah, he, too, found a woman, Asukúme, and soon she was with child. Though they lived apart, Ayako got permission to visit on the Sabbath, and when the baby was born, they decided to call him Dabi (Dah-BEE), after a mother's brother far across the sea. Though the child would belong to the Dombi Plantation, Imanuël Machado was pleased to learn of the birth; he told Ayako of his special pride that one of his most trusted slaves had named his son in honor of the King of the Jews. Ayako, his face its usual mask, tied on the red silk neckerchief his master had proffered to celebrate the birth.

The rest of these particular beginnings, as they say, is (Saramaka) history, and it may best be told in the words of Tebini, Kála, and Otjútju—like Alabi, proud descendants of Lanu, Ayako, and Seei—who have shared some of their most precious knowledge with me.

Lanu's wife—I don't know if she was a girlfriend or a real wife—worked in the white man's house. Once she gave her husband a drink of water. ([whispering:] But they tell me it was really sugar-cane juice, because that was the "water" the white man normally drank.) Well, they saw that and said, "The woman gave Lanu sugar cane juice!" and they whipped her. They beat the woman until she was dead. Then they carried her to him and said, "Look at your wife here." Then they whipped Lanu until he lost consciousness, and they left him lying on the ground. Then, the spirit of his wife came into his head, and he arose suddenly and ran into the forest. The white man, seeing this, said, "Lanu's gone!" But his men said, "He won't live; he's as good as dead already."

When Lanu went into the forest, he ran this way and that, calling out to his wife, trying to find her. . . . He kept calling out and calling out until he got deep into the forest. Finally the apúku [forest spirit] named Wámba called out in reply. And Wamba came into Lanu's head, and brought him directly to where some Indians lived. These Indians welcomed him, took care of him, and gave him food. And he lived with them there.

Ayako had a sister [Seei] on the same plantation. One day she was at work, with her infant son tied to her back. The child began crying, but the white man didn't want her to sit down to nurse it. But it kept on crying. She kept working. The child kept crying. Then the white man called her. "Bring the child over here and I'll hold it for you." So she took the child off her back, handed it to him, and returned to work. He grasped the child upside down by the legs and lowered its head into a bucket of water until he saw that it was dead. Then he called the woman and said, "Come take the child and tie it on your back." So she did so. She returned to work until evening, when they released the slaves from work. The child was dead, stiff as a board.

Well, Ayako saw this and said, "What sadness! My family is finished. My sister has only one child left, and when she goes to work tomorrow, if the child cries, the white man will

Captain Kála (1967), holder of the
eighteenth-century Matjáu staff illustrated on page 148

*do the same thing again. I'll be witness to the final destruc-
tion of my family. Now when I was in Africa, I wasn't a
nobody. I will make a special effort, and see if since I left
there what power I had has been spoiled." Then he prepared
himself until he was completely set. And he escaped. He ran
off with his sister and her baby daughter [Yaya].*

   *When he got to the edge of the forest he called out his
praise name: "I'm the one, Okúndo bi okúndo.⁴ The largest
of all the animals. I may not have iron but I can still
raise my family!" Then he entered the forest and continued
till evening. All he carried was the Lámba gourd. Whenever
they were hungry, they simply ate from that [magical]
gourd. That was our food in those days. Lamba fed us.⁵*

*Ayako ran away to seek his older brother, Lanu. He found
him and saw that he had been well taken care of by the
Indians, that he had done well there. . . . Lanu had a serious
talk with Ayako, saying, "I shall never return to where
there are whitefolks, but if you wish to go take people, you
may. But never will I and the whites meet again. . . . Lanu
prepared Ayako to go back to the plantation, for he was a
great óbiama. From this trip, Ayako brought back a man
called Kwémayón, another great obiama who remained
thereafter always at his side.*

Otjútju (1978)

It was not long before Ayako, who roamed freely around the edges of the plantation region, succeeded in liberating Asukume and their infant son, Dabi, from the Dombi Plantation. Otjutju described what happened soon after.

> One day Ayako had gone off to scout the forest, "going hunting" as they called it in those days. But this was not hunting for animals; it was to see if the whites were nearby. Ayako had gone out searching when the whites arrived in Asukume's garden. She was there with her infant son. Divination told Ayako that his wife was in danger, that the whites were about to catch her. (In those days, if they came upon you with a child, they would catch you, because the child would cry and give you away.) Ayako prepared himself ritually and he warned Asukume. He was far away but he warned her by obia. He sang the obia song that instructed Asukume to throw the child into the reeds, where it would remain unharmed. . . . Well, that child was Dabi! The whites just passed by. She and the child were safe.[6]

Protected by their gods and *obia*s, as well as by friendly Amerindians, and joined from time to time by new runaways, Lanu, Ayako,

Seei, and the others who called themselves "Matjau-people" (in planter jargon, "Machado-slaves") made their gardens in an area at the very fringe of the plantation world, near a stream still called Matjau Creek today. It was from there that the brothers launched the attack that, more than any other single event, opened the hemorrhage that for the next seven decades would bleed the plantation society dry. Henceforth, what had been small-scale leaks in the system of slavery became a steadily widening river. And before long, fully 10 percent of the colony's African population would be with the rebels, building new Afro-American communities deep in the forest.

> *Lanu again prepared Ayako. There had been a great council meeting in the forest [at Matjau Creek]. You see, the white man who had whipped Lanu didn't own just one plantation. They decided to burn a different one of his plantations from the place where he had whipped Lanu because they would find more tools there. This was the Cassewinica Plantation, which had many slaves. They knew all about this plantation from slavery times. So, they attacked. It was at night. They killed the head of the plantation, a white man. They took all the things, everything they needed. And then they sacked the plantation, burned the houses, and ran. . . . They went and stood watch patiently, until they saw him. Then they killed him. And they set fire to the plantation.*

An eighteenth-century chronicler of Suriname life, David de Ishak Cohen Nassy, drew on then-extant Portuguese Jewish archives to write his own brief version of the event, which he described as Suriname's first true slave revolt.

> **There was in the year 1690 a revolt on a plantation situated on the Cassewinica Creek, behind Jews Savannah, belonging to a Jew named Imanuël Machado, where, having killed their master, they fled, carrying away with them everything that was there. . . . The Jews . . . in an expedition which they undertook against the rebels, killed many of them and brought back several who were punished by death on the very spot.**

Lanu and Ayako had made their first large mark on New World history. Seei's contribution, through her baby daughter Yaya and still-unborn son Adjágbò, was yet to come—Seei would one day be remembered as Alabi's father's mother's mother.

Within a few years of the Machado Plantation-burning, Ayako, Lanu, and the other Matjaus were joined by a group of runaways from Plantation Vredenburg, a large estate near Waterland, which the slaves called Watambii (watermill). And until the end of the nineteenth century, these Watambii people were to live side by side with the Matjaus in a single village, always under Matjau leadership. According to Saramaka historians, it was the Matjaus who sent word for

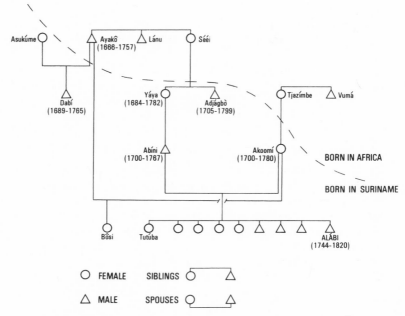

Some of Alábi's kinfolk

the Watambiis to follow them in rebellion. Asipéi, himself a Watambii, and the Matjau Otjutju describe their ancestors' joy at meeting in the forest, at Matjau Creek, setting the terms of their future relationship— Matjau priority in rebellion and Watambii relative subordination, balanced by the volitional aspect of the relationship, the fact that the Watambiis came to the forest with their own fire and, hence, potential independence.

> The great man [Ayako] was the first to come. The other one [Gúngúúkúsu, the Watambii leader] walked behind him. They had made an arrangement to go off together. But the person who's quicker will get started first. And the great man was the quicker of the two. My [Watambii] ancestors said that they didn't know if these two were mother's brother and sister's son, two brothers, African countrymen, or simply close friends. But they were something close. . . . When they finally met, they greeted one another. Then the Matjau invited the other to come and take fire. But he said no thanks, that he carried his own fire. Then he put his hunting sack on the ground, pulled out a flint, rubbed it kwákwákwá ví! He'd made fire! In other words, the great man hadn't "caught" him. They'd come as equals. And they remained special friends ever after.

When Gunguukusu fled to follow Ayako, divination led him to where Ayako was living. When he arrived at the edge of the camp, he didn't see Ayako. But he saw the woman, Seei [Ayako's sister]. He called out, "Ahúngwadja." She just stared at him. All she could see was a runaway. He said, "Awángamádesúsu." Because that man had come with a powerful obia and had been living for days at the outskirts of the camp. Every night he would come to see if his friend Ayako was there, and he lived by stealing Seei's chickens. Now, he had finally come by daylight. He knew that if he simply appeared in a strange camp, they would kill him, thinking he was bringing the whites. That's why he called out to her, "Ahungwadja." Three times he said it. She was silent. Then he said, "Awangamadesusu. Mi doro ko kadja." Which means, "I've arrived. Old woman, put your chickens in their baskets. It's me!" Today [on special occasions] people pour libations using these [secret] words. But it was Gunguukusu who first spoke them.

During the 1690s, while the maroons at Matjau Creek were gradually strengthening their forces at the edge of the plantation region, Suriname's sugar estates inexorably expanded, doubling the colony's population through massive imports of slaves. By 1700, Suriname's population stood at one demographic extreme among New World plantation colonies—in its remarkable preponderance of blacks to whites, slaves to free, recently arrived Africans to seasoned slaves (two-thirds had crossed the ocean during the past decade), Africans to Creoles, and African men to women, adults to children, and young adults to the elderly. Under such conditions, and with the rain forest growing up almost up to the doorsteps of the plantations, rebellion and escape were constant temptations. The problem of slave control and the fear of revolt had become central preoccupations of Suriname's whitefolks. The Jewish militia that for years had hunted down stray rebels was now strengthened; in 1698 the government increased its cash bounty for a captured maroon tenfold over the 1685 figure of five guilders. And the various "exquisite tortures" that for years had been used on recaptured runaways became routinized to include the standard removal of the achilles tendon for a first offense, and the amputation of the right leg for a second. Voltaire's emblematic Suriname slave, whom Candide "interviewed" some decades hence, was not off the mark, as many eyewitnesses attest, when he described how, in Suriname,

> when we work in the sugar mills and the grindstone catches a finger, they cut off the hand; when we try to run away, they cut off a leg. Both these things happened to me. This is the price paid for the sugar you eat in Europe.

Among the droves of Africans who near the turn of the century stepped ashore into this setting—what one European observer called "this Blood Spilling Colony"—were Vumá and his sister Tjazímbe, already visibly pregnant with the daughter who would one day give birth to Alabi. Saramaka captain Gome, a great historian and Tjazimbe's descendant, told me of his clan's beginnings.

Friend, listen well. Vuma came out from Africa. He and his sister Tjazimbe. Akoomí was born here, on the Suriname River. No one knows who her father was. He never left Africa. But when they came, and the child was born, Vuma said, "She has become mine" [A kó u mi], *and that's how Akoomi got her name.*

They had left Africa during a war. Vuma's wife had a great obia *called Madánfo. . . . When Vuma and Tjazimbe were loaded onto the ship, it wouldn't move. Vuma's wife didn't want him to depart. Well, she was the one who kept the* obia. *She was very ripe. But women can't use* obias *like men. Men are the ones who wander, who go to battle. Vuma was really ripe! With Madanfo he could walk in a wink from here to the river [two hundred yards], and walk right across it as if it were solid ground. He couldn't be followed. They say that Vuma could fly like a bird. But he was a human being. He'd prepare the* obia *till it was just right, push that ring onto the tip of his thumb, súúú, like this. That's what let him walk on water. Well, his parrot feather, specially prepared. He'd tie it to his belt like this—sááá. And he'd fly, vauu pííí! Until he alit. Then he'd remove the feather and put it in his sack, tjó.*

He told his sister, "Go. Go with these people. Don't be afraid. But expect me back. I shall return." Tjazimbe was very frightened. She didn't want to be without him. But he said, "Don't worry. I'll be back. I'm just going to take proper leave of my wife." Because they were running off. So he didn't get on the ship.

Well, that ship was finally ready to sail. But the wind wouldn't blow! It just sat there. Then the wind blew them out to sea but later blew them right back in again. Right back to Africa. It was Vuma who did all this. Then he killed his wife. If he hadn't killed her, he couldn't have come to rejoin his sister. His wife was ripe. She had "tied" him [to Africa] with the obia. *It's not that he knocked her with a stick or anything like that, but he managed to kill her somehow [with* obia]. *That's what allowed him to come to Saramaka [Suriname].*

So he went right to the place where the ship had left from, and it was still there. Then he walked right across the water onto the ship. He said, "Sister, I'm here." He had

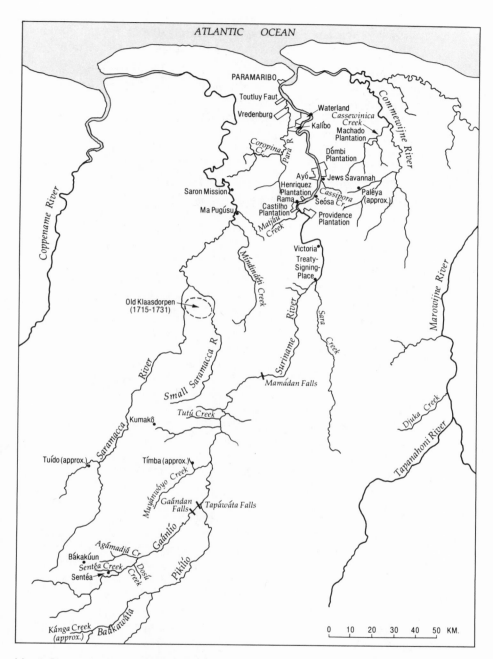

Map 1. Places mentioned in Chapter 1

taken the obia *from his wife, and he brought it with him.*
He'd prepared it just the way he wished, before he came.

Decades later that very *obia,* Madanfo, would become the center of the struggle for Alabi's soul, a pivot around which conversion, colonialism, and resistance all spun.

But meanwhile, the newly arrived Vuma and Tjazimbe have become slaves of a certain Tobias, near Plantation Toutluy Faut, just upstream from Paramaribo. And within just a few years of their landing they manage to escape, along with Tjazimbe's daughter Akoomi, toward the sizable group of runaways from the Nassy, Dombi, and Para River plantations that, under the leadership of Kaásipúmbu of Lángu, have been gathering force for a decade near the swamp called Ma Pugúsu (after the forest spirit that held sway there), to the west of Matjau Creek (see map 1). Already Lanu's Matjau group and the rebels at Ma Pugusu are exchanging intelligence, stolen goods, and sometimes members. Ayako, in fact, shows special interest in the young Akoomi and arranges with Vuma to take her as a second wife, once she comes of age.

The Nasis at Ma Pugusu had escaped very soon after the Machado rebellion, from plantations on the Cassipora Creek, the site of the first synagogue in the New World, just south of Jews Savannah. Yebá, their African-born leader, brought up his forest-born sons to be fighters; for decades the Nasis, led by the brothers Kwakú Kwádjaní and Kwakú Étja, were in the forefront of battles with whitefolks' armies. The Dombis, including Asukume's sisters, brothers, and mother, had marooned later, from the neighboring estate that had once been the center of the sugar empire of the colony's leading Calvinist cleric, whose title, "Dominee" (Minister), the slaves spoke as "Dombi." A "play" in the Dombi slave village, almost certainly with some of these very people present, was painted in 1707 by the plantation's bookkeeper, a Dutch artist. It was only three or four years later that these Dombi-people marooned, fleeing toward the growing group at Ma Pugusu, under the spiritual leadership of Kaasipumbu of Langu.

An incident in 1712 is emblematic, as Kaasi's powers saved the day (one account crediting Kaasi's *sóói-gádu,* a god that would play a major role in making the Upper Suriname River livable later in the century, another stressing Kaasi's special affinities to forest spirits). They were living in a village nestled between the swamp of Ma Pugusu and the large creek that feeds it. Tebini, perhaps the greatest living Saramaka historian, and Metisen, a descendant of Kaasi, described to me in elliptical fashion how they eluded a colonial army that archival records attest included seventeen whites, forty-eight slaves, and sixty-two Indians.

Kaasi used his "god" at this great swamp. And they were
able to pass! It was Kaasi who brought them across. . . .
There was a giant cayman who lived in this pool. It was just

Slave "play" on the Dómbi Plantation, 1707. Painting by Dirk Valkenburg. (Danish Royal Museum of Fine Arts, Copenhagen.) In the distance, one can see the planter's house (which is illustrated in a Valkenburg drawing reproduced in R. Price 1983a, 111).

Tebíni (1978). News of Tebíni's death
reached me while this book was in press.

> *waiting to eat them. But Kaasi "smoked" it with his*
> *special pipe. (There's a leaf called "*makóko tobacco.*"*
> *Well, Makoko is Kaasi's other name!) With the* makoko
> *leaf he smoked the whole pool. The cayman was so drunk*
> *it didn't know where it was. And they successfully crossed*
> *the pool. . . . At the pool, one man said to another, "Gwínzu"*
> *[an obsolete word for "man"]. The second one answered,*
> *"Gwinzu." The first said, "Gwinzu, the whites are getting*
> *close. When I* tjulú *you should* tjalá.*" The other answered,*
> *"No way, Gwinzu, I simply can't make it." The first said,*
> *"Gwinzu, just keep at it, and you'll succeed." Later, the sec-*
> *ond said, "I can't go on." The first said, "Just keep going,*
> *and little by little you'll win." And thus they passed*
> *the swamp. Captain Maáku of Kámpu used to tell us boys,*
> *"Gwinzu, keep at it and you'll succeed."*

Saramaka scouts had warned the villagers of the arrival of the
whitefolks' army just in time. The archives record that when the
expeditionary force reached the village, they found twenty-five
houses and a quantity of goats, turkeys, and other fowl, a great deal
of food (bananas, taro, corn, cassava, yams, sugar cane, oranges),
some cotton, and other supplies. After plundering and burning the
houses and ruining the surrounding gardens, the troops abandoned

the site. These Saramakas, meanwhile, were trekking toward their next homeland, deeper into the forest, along the Small Saramacca River.

In addition to Kaasipumbu's people and the large group at Matjau Creek, there was by the turn of the century a third major cluster of maroons—the Abaisa-people—who traced their collective identity to a major rebellion at Providence Plantation, the southernmost estate on the Suriname River, in 1693. This singular plantation was run by the Labadists (whom the slaves called Alabaisa or Abaisa), a utopian religious community that had fallen on hard times and seemed, according to contemporary Dutch observers, to be taking out many of its considerable frustrations directly upon its particularly ill-treated slave force. As twentieth-century Saramakas recount,

> *In slavery, there was hardly anything to eat. It was at the place called Providence Plantation. They whipped you there till your ass was burning. Then they would give you a bit of plain rice in a calabash. (That's what we [Abaisas] have heard.) And the gods told them that this is no way for human beings to live. They would help them. Let each person go where he could. So they ran.*
>
> *They were loading the boats to go. It was frantic. There were so many, it looked like a fish-drugging party. Well, the mother of Kaála [the female leader of the Abaisas during their early years in the forest] couldn't get to the riverbank fast because she was old. The man who is called Andolé, Kaala's husband, jumped into Kaala's boat and began paddling furiously out to midstream, to get across the river. Finally, the old woman got to the landing. Kaala's mother. Kaala begged her husband, "Look, my mother's there. Let's turn back and get her." But Andole refused. "How can you say that? Go back! That's my mother there," Kaala pleaded. (This is what our ancestors told us. We don't know if it's true or false.) Andole said he could not go back, and he continued to the other bank, where they fled into the forest. The mother of Kaala had to remain in slavery. . . .*
>
> *They continued walking upstream. Kaala said [thought to herself] that she would not punish her husband for the thing he'd done, but if the gods were her witness, Andole would surely get his due. They kept going upstream. They passed the mouth of Gaánkiíki, passed Mamádan, and passed Musumbá Island. But they hadn't gotten up to here yet. Then she left him because of what he'd done to her. She left him on the way upstream. And she took a new husband from the Nasi clan.*
>
> *Kaala had her divination. No one could measure them- selves against the likes of that woman. She was the ripest person alive! She would take her divining stick, and*

*they would all walk in the direction it indicated. That's
what told her to leave Andole.*

*Ma Kaala had a god that could talk with the water spirits.
Her* obia *could speak to the Mother of Waters. And it knew
the forests too! She was very ripe. She and her god were
the real warriors of the Abaisa.*

For many decades following their rebellion, these powerful Abaisa
maroons competed directly with the Matjaus for landrights and other
prerogatives, and their village cluster south of the plantation area—
known to whitefolks as the Papa Dorpen—was a redoubtable barrier
to the colonists' attempts at military penetration of the forests. The
Abaisas' mid-eighteenth-century leader, Samsám (whom some Saramakas believe was the son of Ma Kaala), periodically challenged his
Matjau counterparts over claims to be Chief-over-All, Saramaka
gaama. And this sharp, often violent interclan rivalry, which plagued
Alabi's father, Tribal Chief Abini, during the final years of his life, was to
continue well into Alabi's own political manhood.

Guerrillas

During their stay at Matjau Creek (while fomenting new rebellions
among slaves they had known when in whitefolks' captivity and conducting periodic raids on vulnerable plantations), Lanu, Ayako, Seei,
and the other Matjau-people were engaged in the everyday process
of building new lives in the unfamiliar forests—forging anew everything from horticultural techniques to religious practice, building on
their diverse African memories as well as their New World experience with both transplanted Europeans and local Amerindians. As
they prepared their fields for planting, they encountered local forest
and snake spirits whom they had to learn, by trial and error, to befriend and pacify; a Watambii mother of twins inadvertently discovered, via a monkey, the complex rituals that would forever thereafter
be a necessary accompaniment to the birth of Saramaka twins; and
newly found gods of war joined those remembered from across the
waters in protecting and spurring on Saramaka raiders when they
attacked plantations for guns, pots, and axes, as well as to liberate
their brothers and, particularly, sisters still in bondage.[7]

During this period, about a decade after the Machado plantation-
burning, Yaya—who had fled to the forest with her mother Seei as a
child—gave birth to a son, Abini, in a small hut near Matjau Creek. A
leader of the first generation of men born in the forests of Suriname,
Abini would one day play a central role in the making of peace with the
whites and, soon after, would meet his death in attempting to maintain that peace. But, before these heroics, he would break with his
Matjau kinfolk over a woman, and as a result, Alabi would be born.[8]

The Matjau group took a decade and a half to trek southward from

Matjau Creek, which by 1715 was becoming too vulnerable to attacks by colonial militias and armies, to the area that they still call their home, along the Pikílío, the eastern tributary of the Suriname on which the tribal capital is located today. Lanu, Ayako, and Seei, as well as Seei's children Adjagbo and Yaya, and the latter's son Abini, set out together on this migration ever deeper into the forests, along with tens of others whose names have been forever lost from Matjau collective memory.

But early on, Abini, then in his late teens, split off from this group of Matjau migrants. His "grandfather," Ayako, had already taken the young Akoomi as a wife, by prearrangement with the girl's African-born mother's brother, Vuma. Yet relations between the Matjaus and Vuma's people had become strained. Ayako accused Vuma, a renowned *obia*-man, of witchcraft, and, at a large meeting in the forest, the Matjaus pledged not to have any more to do with Vuma's people. Meanwhile, Abini and Akoomi (who, some say, was pregnant with Ayako's child) fell in love. As one of their descendants, the aged Captain Gome, told me excitedly (using a characteristic Christian Saramaka metaphor),

> This is very secret! Ayako was a man's man! Abini was a real man too. Ayako was powerful. He was Abini's elder. Both were very powerful, with obias. But Akoomi loved Abini more than Ayako. Ayako was already getting old when he took Akoomi. You yourself must have heard this: the bell doesn't ring so loudly any more, not loudly enough to go to church! My mother's brother didn't hide this from me, but he told me it was secret. If I speak it, my ancestors may kill me. Ayako was a real man. When all this happened, Abini's wife's people, the Awanas, didn't throw him out. They held him close. That's why Ayako couldn't get the better of him. That's why Abini came to live with the Awanas. While his kinfolk went upstream, he stayed down with the Awanas.

The Matjau Otjutju complemented this version.

> Abini had been sleeping with Akoomi, and they had run off to the east, toward the Tempati, to hide from Ayako. Akoomi told Abini that she was pregnant with Ayako's child, and as the pregnancy progressed, he became afraid that the whites would find them, so they crossed the Suriname River and settled across from the mouth of the Sara Creek, where a daughter [Bôsi] was born.

Captain Gome added that

> Abini raised the child. She always called him "father." You'd never guess it wasn't his child. Her lineage gave her to him to raise.

During the next two and a half decades, Akoomi bore Abini—who remained living with her people—five girls and four boys. Though Gome preserved memories of the exploits of each (many of whom we will meet in the course of these pages), there were two whose names brought sparkling tears to his eyes—the first-born girl, Tutúba, who was captured in battle by the whites and placed in slavery, and the last born of all, Abini's favorite son, the future *gaama* of all Saramaka, Alabi.

The Matjaus trekked on without the young Abini, reaching the confluence of the Pikilio and the Gaánlío around 1730, apparently without having been attacked by whitefolks' armies along the way. As the southernmost vanguard of Saramakas, these Matjaus were constantly staking out new territory, and many of their descendants' traditions regarding this period concern their making peace with local gods and spirits and making the Upper River region truly their own. This cycle of migration stories ends with a dramatic descent by Ayako's inseparable companion, a strange African named Kwemayon, who served as his personal *obia*-man, into the depths of the Suriname River, where he found legitimacy for the Matjaus' settlement of the creek called Baakawata, far up the Pikilio.

> *There at the confluence of the two rivers [the Pikilio and the Gaanlio], Ayako "cut" the reeds, claiming the Pikilio forever for Matjaus, as Kwemayon "smoked" the whole area with his ritual apparatus. Then, as they crossed the river at Pikídan, just below the falls, the river "took" Ayako's protective armband. It fell in the river there. So he swore, he prayed to the Great God, he prayed to the river god. He had "paid," he could now have his way.*
>
> *It was then that Kwemayon descended into the river. He slept right there, underwater at the foot of the falls. The African! He slept there at Túlíobúka underwater until he came out and said, "Wherever you can find a suitable place, we can stay there." . . . Divination told them, "Only at Baakawata will you be able to hide people successfully." And that's the way it finally came to pass.*

At Baakawata, where the Matjaus remained through much of the eighteenth century, they hosted not only the Watambiis but other latecoming clans as well—the Papútus, who arrived on the eve of the Peace, the people who today live in Asáubásu, and others. It was in Baakawata that the Matjaus celebrated the Peace of 1762, and from Baakawata that Ayako—during the 1740s and 1750s—held sway over all of Saramaka, as "forest" (unrecognized by the government) *gaama*, tribal chief. The great historian Tebini, in telling me of this period, explicitly linked the Matjaus' ongoing survival as a group to Wamba, the forest spirit that had been in Lanu's head at the time of his escape from whitefolks' slavery and that now (after his death sometime during the early 1740s) had passed into the head of his sister's daughter Yaya.

Well, they lived there [Baakawata]. And they hid. All kinds of people came to live with them there. It hid them all! Well, the god [Wamba] that was in Mama Yaya's head. It hid them so well. The apuku *[forest spirit]. [At first] if you went to get water at the river there, it was not fit to drink. You could not eat the food from the forest [without getting sick]. As soon as newcomers arrived, the forest [gods] would trouble them. But Yaya's god fixed that! So everyone decided to make Ayako tribal chief, to put him above all other people. And then they cut footpaths, from Bakakuun to Agámadjá, from Agamadja to Sentéa Creek, and from Sentea across to Baakawata.*

Matjaus retain numerous memories of their decades at Baakawata. None are richer, in terms of the human relations and incidents they depict, than the accounts of how Yaya's brother, Adjagbo, found his beautiful wife, Paanza. As Tebini tells it, drawing on a telling he heard at the beginning of the present century from the famous female captain, Maaku,

Avó [grandfather] Ayako had been in the forest for a very long time. He'd been living at Baakawata, he and his brother Lanu. They had brought Adjagbo there as a youth. Well, they lived there until he took someone else's wife, Maaku said. Then they [the people of the wronged husband] came to try to kill them [the Matjaus]. Well they lived . . . until he once again took someone's wife, and those people came to try to kill them. By then Ayako was ready to kill him too! But before he could, Lanu said, "Don't kill him. Leave the child to me." He called him over and said [gently], "What's wrong? What is doing this to you? You go to one woman, you screw her, then you go to the next, you screw her, but you stay with none. If you don't stop this, Ayako will really kill you." Adjagbo said, "Mother's brother, it's because I had someone I loved, when we were on the coast, in the savannahs at Djúgoón [near Matjau Creek]." "What do they call her?" "Paanza." "Paanza, huh? You and she loved each other?" "Yes. That's the problem. I keep thinking of her. I can't see another woman without thinking of her." "Is that what's really bothering you, then?" Lanu asked.
  Lanu called his brother [Ayako] and spoke with him. He said, "So that's what he said?" Ayako asked [sarcastically], "Well, does he think he is going to be able to get her himself?" Lanu said that he would do it. Lanu called a council meeting. He prepared everyone [ritually] as fully as he wished. In those days they didn't travel by canoe. Then

he set out . . . all the way to the Kasitú Plantation, on foot.
(My father used to raise his hand when we were on our
way downstream to the city to point out the plantation, right
there upstream from Rama.) There they were cutting rice
in the great field, the savannah field, just cutting and cutting
that rice. . . . He kept watching for Paanza until suddenly
he saw her clearly. He "took" her. He called her. The woman
was bending over, arranging the harvested rice. He had
"boiled" her.[9] *In a flash he was standing next to her. She ex-*
claimed, "What's this?" "I have come to take you away,
to give you to that lover of yours called Adjagbo. He's not
dead. He's in the forest. Let's you and I go together." She
hesitated, "What am I to do?" He said, "Let's get going." She
was acting as if she didn't know how she could just pick
up and leave. He said, "What's this? We're leaving!" She con-
sented. Then she turned around, picked up the rice in
one motion, and they were off. The others were eating. When
they returned they didn't see her. They searched high and
low for Paanza. The white man's daughter! The whites
entered the forest, for they heard she had been taken away.
They searched and searched. But Paanza was already in
Baakawata. Avo Adjagbo took her in an instant.

Paanza, the daughter of a Jewish slave master named Moses
Nunez Henriquez (whom Saramakas remember as "Hendilíki") and a
slave woman, bore Adjagbo the children who became the Saramaka
clan still called "Kasitu," after the owner of the plantation from which
she was liberated. A report from the governor of Suriname, now in
the Dutch national archives, helps to place the event firmly in whitefolks' time and space; it describes how, shortly before 28 October
1739, a troop of maroons attacked the upper Suriname River plantation of Joseph Castilho, killing one white man and taking with them
the few slaves he owned. The girl whom the youthful Adjagbo had
known while he roamed the plantation periphery from the base camp
at Matjau Creek had finally become his. And, for the next four decades, they lived together at Baakawata and along the Pikilio, as Adjagbo became a leader of the Matjau group, gradually taking on the
responsibilities and powers that had once been held by his two mother's brothers, Lanu and Ayako.

Meanwhile, the sizable group that Abini had joined remained physically closer to the plantation area, periodically adding new recruits

Paánza's plantation, "Plantation 'the two good Friends,' or on the general Map
called 'Steenbergen' belonging to R. de Castilho." Watercolor by J. H. Rotke. This
lovely watercolor depicts the "Kasitú" plantation just seven years after Paánza's
escape to join the Saramakas (CETECO, Diemen, Netherlands). *Facing page.*

from the estates. After the 1712 battles with the whites around Ma Pugusu, Kaasipumbu had led this Langu/Nasi/Dombi/Awana group some miles to the south to the Small Saramacca River, where they remained until 1730. In that year, the colonists discovered their location and sent at least eight separate military expeditions against them, finding more than 440 houses spread among five villages and capturing some twelve Saramaka adults, who were brought to Paramaribo for punishment, "in the hope that it would provide an Example and deterrent to their associates, and reduce the propensity of slaves to escape." Their terrible sentence, pronounced by the Court of Policy and Criminal Justice in Paramaribo, would have been known within days by Abini and his fellows, through their clandestine contacts with plantation slaves all along the Suriname River, though they remained powerless to respond directly:

The Negro Joosie shall be hanged from the gibbet by an Iron Hook through his ribs, until dead; his head shall then be severed and displayed on a stake by the riverbank, remaining to be picked over by birds of prey. As for the Negroes Wierrie and Manbote, they shall be bound to a stake and roasted alive over a slow fire, while being tortured with glowing Tongs. The Negro girls, Lucretia, Ambira, Aga, Gomba, Marie, and Victoria will be tied to a Cross, to be broken alive, and then their heads severed, to be exposed by the riverbank on stakes. The Negro girls Diana and Christina shall be beheaded with an axe, and their heads exposed on poles by the riverbank.

Kaasi and his people abandoned their villages on the Small Saramacca in the wake of the bloody battles of 1730–31. Indeed, a map drawn by one of the members of the expeditionary force graphically depicts the whites' use of attack dogs on Saramakas who were fleeing, carrying what they could in their arms, from their burning villages; Saramakas using spears and bows-and-arrows to defend their homes; and Kaasipumbu himself, wounded, being borne toward the south in a hammock by his Saramaka followers. As one of Kaasi's descendants told me,

In those days, they might just be sitting down to eat a meal when . . . "Hurry! The whites are coming. Run for your lives." They would find a night's campsite and be ready to sleep when divination advised that the whites would surely find them if they stayed. So they'd trek onwards. Until, finally, they got to that hill [Kumako], where they found "a couple of days" of rest.

By 1732, after decades of wanderings and battles, Kaasi and his followers settled the massive village of Kumako, atop a stone mountain that rises abruptly from the forest, halfway between the Saramacca and Suriname rivers. There they finally found, as their descendants put it, a few days of rest. But Kaasi himself soon moved on, with his Langu people, seeking greater security in the distant forests to the south. The other diverse groups already at Kumako—Dombis, Awanas (Vuma and Akoomi's people), Nasis, and Biítus[10]—stayed on, wishing to be able to continue raiding the coast, as necessary, and hoping they were far enough inland to prevent the whites from following. Yeba of the Nasi clan became their chief; his sons Kwaku Kwadjani and Kwaku Etja, who become powerful chiefs after the 1762 Peace, were among the foremost warriors. Saramakas still preserve memories of the raids conducted from Kumako.

> *[During this period] women, weapons, and ammunition were our most pressing needs. And the Nasis were especially masterful bush scouts.*

> *The Nasis were famous fighters. They killed the whites near Seósa, at the creek we call "Red Creek" because of all their blood. That's why Nasi people have a taboo on going to that place, until today. Kwadjani and his brother Etja. That is where they fought it out with the whites, alongside their father Yeba.*

> *They raided the plantations, fighting great battles at Kalíbo, then at Paléya. When they left Paleya they fought in the savannahs across from Ayó.*

Contemporary archives confirm the violence of these activities; for example, in 1738–39, the slaves of Manuel Pareyra (whom slaves called "Paleya"), encouraged by raiders from Kumako, successfully revolted, and a Jewish military expedition sent after them returned with no less than forty-seven prisoners plus six hands of dead maroons. Today, Saramakas continue to stress the size and diversity of Kumako. As a Dombi told me,

> *Everyone met there—Dombis, Nasis, Biitus, Awanas, [a few] Paputus. That was Kumako. There were seven battles at that village before it was finally taken [by the whites]. They lived there a long time.*

The Battle of Kumako, in October 1743, remains etched in Saramaka historical memory, though the whitefolks' archival accounts and those of modern Saramakas, not surprisingly, stress different aspects of the experience. The elderly David Cohen Nassy—longtime leader of the Jewish militia, whose relatives had kept Yeba and his Nasi companions as slaves a half century before—emerged the military victor. It was in the month of August that he set out,

> **with 27 civilians, 12 soldiers, 15 Indians, 165 slaves and 65 canoes, following a plan he had formed and presented to the Council on July 1, 1743. After having followed the Suriname River and having passed several cataracts . . . he began his**

march, and the enemies were attacked on the day of Kippur, or of Atonement of the Jews; and without any regard for this sacred day, he pursued the enemies, put their cabins to the torch, utterly ruined their village, tore their crops from the ground by their roots, took fourteen prisoners, and killed a large number.

Descendants of the Saramaka participants (whose voices are heard more fully in *First-Time*) recall a number of personal details.

An old woman foresaw the battle. She was lying in her hammock. She said, "The whites are coming, they're already on their way." And it was true, it happened that way.

The attack on Kumako occurred while a corpse was laid out [preparatory to burial]. The men had gone off hunting for the funeral rites. Papá Kuná was the dead man. They had to flee at night, leaving the corpse unburied.

It was the Long Dry Season. All of the men had gone to the Small Saramacca River. It was the tenth moon [September/ October], and water was gone from the forest floor. The men had gone to hunt fish in the pools left in the dry creek-beds. That's when the battle began.

The whites used the gun called "kwantákwalá" at Kumako. If it's shot here, it lands across the river [four hundred yards]! Its shot is spread over a broad area.

Yeba, the leader of Kumako and the father of Kwaku Etja and Kwaku Kwadjani, was killed in the battle. Some people say he was captured, but he was really killed. We don't like to say it. It was only because the able-bodied men were all absent when the whites attacked. They'd gone to the Small Saramacca River to hunt. The old man was resting up against a tree when the whites started shooting at him. The hail of bullets was so intense, it actually felled the tree. Just think, the father of Kwadjani and Etja!

The slave who brought the whites, who showed them the way, must have known Maroon customs. He told the soldiers to line up on either side of the path outside the village, and he called out at the top of his voice, "Fóódênde, Fóódênde" [this is the call when wild boars have been killed]. The young people came running out of the village, thinking pigs had been killed. And the soldiers tried to grab them. The children who were in the lead shouted, "Wóóóó, white people! Kids, run for your lives!" But the soldiers caught a young Dombi woman, Kokóóko.

Among the thirteen other Saramaka prisoners that day, returned by the soldiers to the colonial authorities to live out their lives in whitefolks' slavery, was Abini and Akoomi's oldest daughter, Tutuba, whom we will meet many years later, when her brother Alabi—who had never known her in freedom—finally succeeds in negotiating her return to Saramaka.

After the battle of Kumako, its inhabitants moved south into the area of the great creek called Muyánwóyo ("Wet Eye"). The Awanas (accompanied by Abini) established a village with the Dombis on one of its tributaries, Timba Creek, and the Nasis and Biitus settled along the mother creek itself. Saramakas preserve poignant memories.

> *After the battle, people fled in different directions. The Awanas went to Timba, in Muyanwoyo Creek. The soldiers stayed a long time at Kumako, but when they finally left, people came back to get their belongings. A man named Pítayánfaasú, a Paputu, was the husband of the [Dombi] woman whose daughter was captured at Kumako. He was returning from Timba to get his belongings. His wife had been separated from him in the battle and had run off in the direction of Matawái [west]. Later, she saw that she was pregnant, and she set out for the old village of Kumako, in search of her husband. And they were reunited there, at the ruined, abandoned village. Together they came to the new village at Timba.*

Saramakas also connect that moment to the arrival of one of their greatest First-Time *obia*-men, Kúngoóka, who gave the group of Dombis that eventually settled in the village of Dáume (which they named after Kungooka's African birthplace, Dahomey) the *obia* that sets bones as if they were new, cures gunshot wounds, and helped engineer some of Saramakas' final battle victories over the whites.

> *Kungooka was a lone runaway. The first group he met up with were the Biitus, and he tried to find a wife there. But they said he was too ugly, and they denied him a wife. Then he went to the Mísidjáns, the Dombis. At the other place they'd made fun of him, taunted him. But the Dombis gave him a wife. Well, they had been so generous with him that he said, "Brother-in-law, catch a chicken and bring it to me." He did. "Now break its leg and put it under that basket there. Then go bring . . . [leaves and other secret ingredients]." He also went and gathered ingredients himself. Then he prepared it all until he was satisfied. He said, "Brother-in-law, watch carefully." And he applied the medicine to the chicken. Every day for seven days. Then they lifted the basket. The chicken ran off tjá tjá tjá tjá! It didn't run tíngo tíngo tíngo! Then he said, "To express my thanks for your generosity, this obia is now yours."*

And as of 1980, the mission hospital at Djumú had never seen a broken bone or gunshot wound, though its medical staff had treated tens of thousands of cases of illness and accident, and though many such cases occur each year in Upper River Saramaka; all continue to be handled by the keepers of Kungooka's *obia* at Daume (or by a functionally similar but historically separate *obia* in another Saramaka village, considerably downstream).

But, from the perspective of future Saramaka historians, the most important event at Timba involved Akoomi and Abini. Just as Tjazimbe had carried Akoomi in her womb from Africa to the Americas, Akoomi herself was heavy with child at the moment the whitefolks attacked Kumako. As Captain Gome's spare words framed the moment,

> *She carried Alabi in her belly all the way from Kumako to Timba. And that's where Alabi was born.*

Or, as another aged descendant of Alabi further collapsed these events,

> *When they reached Timba Creek, she began to feel the pains, and just before daybreak she bore Alábi Pantó.*

Toward Freedom

Akoomi and her lastborn son, along with the others at Timba, did not stay longer than two or three harvests. Whitefolks' armies had been getting dangerously close, and the Langu leader Kaasi had already sent word of his new, seemingly invulnerable fortress high up in the mountains, called Bakakuun (Behind-the-Hills), known to some Saramakas as the House of the Wind, far to the south. Kaasi and his people had left Kumako even before the great battle there, traveling to the southwest along the Saramacca River to the large village of Tuido, already settled by maroons known as Matawais. In 1747 (after Kaasi had already moved on to his hilltop retreat), this westernmost of Saramaka villages received the brunt of the largest whitefolks' army yet sent against Saramaka. And this battle at Tuido (which the whites knew as "Loango-dorp," after the African birthplace of Kaasi) was the first of the major military encounters in which the tide of war finally began to turn in the rebels' favor.

Alabi's "grandfather," Adjagbo, played the central role in this complex incident. Part of a Saramaka raiding party that, betrayed by a "faithful" slave, was repelled with considerable losses from a coastal plantation in 1747, the wounded Adjagbo was captured by a white bounty hunter. Upon "interrogation" in Paramaribo, he agreed to lead a whitefolks' army to "Loango-dorp," and some two hundred fifty men, in twenty-five canoes, eventually reached Tuido, from which the inhabitants, forewarned by their scouts, had managed to escape to the forest only moments before. In what became the first of a number of abortive peace attempts on the part of the colonists, the white commander was persuaded by Adjagbo to send him as a messenger to the main Saramaka villages, over the mountains, to carry an offer of peace. But Adjagbo, "in spite of the promises he had made to be faithful to the whites," never returned, instead organizing a massive Saramaka ambush that caught the whites on their way downstream and thoroughly defeated them.

By this time, Akoomi and her family had abandoned Timba and joined the large agglomeration of people on Kaasi's mountaintop. But even the village cluster at Bakakuun proved vulnerable. In 1749, the governor of Suriname decided that the only way to eliminate what he liked to call the maroon "Hydra" was

> **to divide them [the various groups] and, insofar as possible, deal with each in turn. . . . [We should begin by mounting] one massive expedition and, even after conquering one or more villages and inflicting a crushing defeat, make peace, as the saying goes, with sword in hand.**

And he sent an expedition numbering hundreds of troops, which managed to pillage and burn over four hundred large houses. Saramakas retain strong memories of the final battle, during which they valiantly defended their hilltop fortress.

> *They were living on the mountaintop. And they dug a trench running from the very bottom up to the top. It was the only way to get in or out of the village. They cut big logs, just the width of the trench, and many men together rolled them to the top. When the whites came up the path, they did not know that things would come pouring down the trench to kill them. They came up and up until they were close. They could see the blacks. Then they [the Saramakas] released the logs. Well, there was no way to run fast enough to avoid them! They were mashed to a pulp. No way to escape alive.*

> *Bakakuun! That's where they rained down those stones upon the whites.*

> *The village was not on the very top of the mountain but on a plateau. There was only one entrance, along a depression. But they had not dug it out. Water, rushing down the mountain had made it, not men. At the top, they poised boulders, all kinds of stones. When the whites approached, they released the stones and finished off the soldiers.*

> *Bakakuun. The whites' guns were useless there. They killed those whites like nothing. The big ditch. In order to get up the hill, you had to walk in it. They rolled the tree stumps down there, zálálátjé, all the way down to the bottom. So many were killed!*

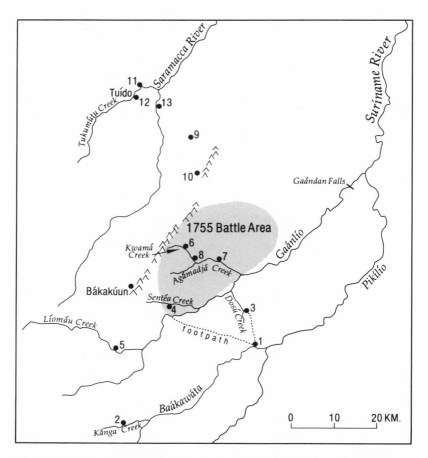

Map 2. Main village locations, 1750s (approximate). (1) Matjáu-Wátambíi. (2) Kasitú (and later, Papútu). (3) Nasí-Bíitu. (4) Awaná-Dómbi-Agbó. (5) Abaísa. (6) Lángu (Kaapátu). (7) Lángu (Kadósu). (8) Kwamá. (9) Lángu. (10) Lángu. (11) Matawái. (12) Matawái. (13) Matawái.

Yet the whitefolks' army managed to wreak considerable devastation on Saramaka villages and gardens, and, according to the governor's plan, the white commander succeeded in getting the Saramaka leaders (who told him that their own supreme chief, Ayako, was too old to come and negotiate personally) to agree to a provisional cease-fire, with plans to sign a definitive treaty of peace—marked by the transfer of a long list of goods to the Saramakas—a year hence.

Once the colonial troops finally left, most of the people who had been living on the mountain moved down into the watershed of the Gaanlio, into an area where many had already established gardens.[11] On the basis of evidence in both whitefolks' documents and Saramaka songs, place-names, and fragments of oral history, I can construct a map of the way that Saramakas, after the battle of Bakakuun, had by the 1750s spread themselves over the landscape. Alabi, still a child, lived in his mother's village of Sentea, where his father, Abini, served as headman. But he seems to have spent the bulk of his time during these early years in informal fosterage with his paternal grandmother Yaya, who lived for long stretches in that village, where she had a husband.

In 1750, a few months after the cease-fire, the delicate balance between war and peace was tipped by the ongoing rivalry of Matjaus and Abaisas. As Saramakas remember it, Ayako and Samsam were the larger-than-life protagonists, with Abini playing his characteristic role as peacemaker. The occasion was the whites' follow-up to their recent proposal of permanent peace. Five months before the agreed-upon date for meeting the Saramakas to seal the peace, the whites sent a small delegation to again "sound out their sentiments": three white military men and some twenty slaves bearing a small quantity of gifts set out for Saramaka. But the expedition was never heard from directly again. Some of Saramakas' most dangerous historical memories surround what happened.

> *Abini met them [the whites, as they were coming upstream] at the mouth of the Sara Creek. He warned them not to go further [as it was not yet the proper time], saying, "If you go now, you'll meet with evil. Let me go instead." But they insisted. . . . They didn't listen to his advice. . . . Well, they got to where Samsam was.*

> *Ayako told Samsam, the Abaisa, that he was "going hunting" [that is, going to scout out the whites]. Ayako left Samsam to take care of the village and went upstream. In the meantime the whites arrived. Samsam told them to unload the goods while he went to fetch Ayako. But he warned them that Ayako was a very fierce man who might decide to kill them. "If you hear me hitting the tree roots [buttresses] with my machete on my return, run for your lives! It will mean Ayako is coming to kill you."*

> *So they brought ashore all the goods intended for the peace-making. Every single one! Then Samsam went off a bit. And he began hitting the tree trunks, búnguung, búnguung, búngun, búngun, over and over. When he came in sight, he yelled, "For God's sake, run for your lives. I went to those people, but they were so hostile that if you meet them, evil! Please run!" And they ran. Well, that was the end of that! Their canoe smashed over Gaandan Falls.*

> *After the sinking at Gaandan Falls, the whites decided they weren't going to come to the Gaanlio [to make peace with the Saramakas] any more.*

Peléki (1978)

And it was not until 1755 that whites and Saramakas again confronted each other directly, in the area around Sentea.

This time it was a most unusual African-born slave, the man whom John Gabriel Stedman later referred to as "The Celebrated Graman Quacy . . . one of the most Extraordinary Black men in Surinam, or Perhaps in the World," who played the colonists' hand against the aged but still redoubtable Ayako, himself supported in these events by Wamba, the god that had once been in his older brother Lanu's head and was now controlled by his sister's daughter Yaya. I have described the psychologically complex drama in detail elsewhere: how Kwasi arrived in Saramaka pretending to be a new recruit from the plantations, used his powerful ritual knowledge to befriend Ayako, and *almost* became privy to the ultimate secrets of Saramaka invulnerability, with Wamba—speaking through Yaya—warning Ayako that Kwasi was in fact a spy; how Ayako set a trap and allowed Kwasi to escape back to the whites; how Kwasi returned the next year at the head of a colonial army of hundreds of men; and how, during the final battles around Agamadja Creek, the Saramakas were able to claim their sweet revenge. And no set of wartime incidents so well expresses First-Time ideology. It was just after telling me some details of this highly secret and dangerous story that Peleki, a Matjau descendant of Ayako, remarked,

> *And that's why, Friend, Maroons do not trust Creoles [non-Maroon Afro-Surinamers]. . . . Because of what happened to our ancestors. If you take one of them as a* máti *[formal*

*friend], that's what they'll do with you. You must not trust
them with a single thing about the forest. City people! They
fought against us along with the whites. Like you. I must
not [am not supposed to] tell you anything! It isn't good.
Because whites used to come fight them. Well, Kwasi was
a Creole, and he joined up with the whites to bring them
here. . . . But if you teach an outsider something, well,
little by little he'll use it to come kill you. . . . Well, they
didn't trust him [Kwasi] fully. They didn't teach him all of
their knowledge. And that's why he didn't triumph in the
end. That's why we say, if you teach a Creole or a white person, that's what they'll do with you. This is the one thing
Maroons really believe. It's stronger than anything else. . . .
This is the greatest fear of all Maroons; that those times
shall come again.*

During the mid-1750s, it was above all the Matjau leader Ayako who
epitomized these wartime values of fierce independence. And it was
his sister's daughter Yaya, with her god Wamba, who held open the
door to eventual peace.

After more than six decades of war, and with the whites making
intermittent peace overtures to them, Saramakas had now become
divided about their conduct toward the whites. The oldest generation, men like Ayako whose whole adult lives had been devoted to
war, remained wedded to First-Time ideology and turned their backs
on compromise. Yet the generation coming to power, men like Abini
who were then in their fifties, foresaw a brighter future through negotiation and, eventually, peace. Yaya, in the generation between the
two, seems to have sensed the momentum of contingent events. As
Saramakas remember this moment,

*It was at Baakawata. [It's as if] I wanted us to make peace;
you didn't want us to make peace; that man over there
didn't want us to make peace; that other one wants us to
make peace. That's how we disputed the thing!
    Avo Ayako had said he couldn't [stand to] see outsiders
[bakáa]. Whitefolks [wéti sèmbè], he simply couldn't stand
them. Then they asked [themselves], "If the whites want
peace, how will we respond?" It was as part of this discussion that Yaya said "that thing" [her famous pronouncement].
It was she who had the god [Wamba, in her head]. She
said that they should not be hostile to the whites any more.
She said, "The person to whom this is unacceptable
[Ayako] is the oldest of us all. When he is no longer here,
well, peace will come."*

*She said, Tei u tei huena, vunvu sa fúu tjéni pôtò. [Little
by little, the hummingbird fills up the sugarcane cauldron.]
Then the old man, it wasn't too long before . . . he died.*

And, in fact, it was Ayako's death, sometime between 1756 and 1758, that set the stage for the final rush toward peace.

Free at Last

The final pre-treaty years also saw Alabi moving out of the world of women and children, which as a prepubescent boy he had hitherto occupied, into that of men. Until Ayako's death, when he was about thirteen, Alabi divided his time between his maternal group—his mother Akoomi, her mother Tjazimbe, and his older sisters and brothers—and his paternal grandmother, Yaya, alternating between gardens, village, and river. Having reached his teens, he began to spend considerable time with his father, Abini, and became his favorite. And it was probably at this time that, before the ancestor shrine in his paternal village at Baakawata, Alabi's father's clan gave him his first *kamísa,* the breechcloth that symbolized his coming-of-age.[12]

Alabi, by Abini's side, witnessed a flurry of political activity during these several years. Ayako's funeral, still remembered as one of the most lavish ever staged in Saramaka, provided the stage for the incident that Saramakas today think of as the proximate cause of peace. Tebini once gave me the bare essence of the story.

> *[After Yaya's hummingbird speech] it wasn't long before the old man died. Then they accepted the Peace. It was during his funeral rites that Wii [an important Langu ancestor] went into the forest. He went all the way to Djuka. And he saw the whites. He said, "What are you doing here?" They said, "We came to you [Saramakas], but you killed us, so we went back and never came again." Then they gave him the Peace. "Take it," they said. The old woman [Yaya, back in Saramaka] said, "Hasn't it happened exactly as I told you it would?" They all said, "Yes."*

Richer Saramaka versions describe how Wii, who was married to one of Ayako's daughters, had been found by divination to be the cause of Ayako's illness; how Ayako, feeling himself dying, had privately instructed his son Dabi to perform an ordeal during his funeral to determine if Wii in fact had killed him by witchcraft; and how, during this ordeal, in which Dabi shot a specially prepared musket ball at the suspected witch, Wii disappeared into the forest, where after days of travel he found refuge with the Djuka Maroons, far to the east. Documentary sources confirm that Wii, who had taken refuge with the Djukas in the late 1750s, told colonial government officials who had been engaged in making peace with the Djukas that the Saramakas too wished to end hostilities. In early 1762, a delegation of Saramakas, led by Abini, traveled to the already "pacified" Djukas, at Djuka Creek, to meet with colonial officials and discuss arrangements (including the enormous quantity of goods to be given the Saramakas as tribute) for concluding a definitive peace.

By September 1762, the Dutch negotiator had installed himself (without the tribute gifts, which had not yet arrived from Holland) at the agreed-upon Treaty-Signing-Place across from the mouth of the Sara Creek, on the new frontier between whitefolks' and Saramaka territory. Over a period of days, large numbers of Saramakas arrived: Abini, accompanied by his son Alabi; the Langu leader Wii and his sister's son Antamá; the Nasi headman Kwaku Etja; and a number of other headmen plus some two hundred Saramakas, "almost all with snaphaunce muskets, of which several had four or five." After difficult negotiations, centering largely on the quantity of gunpowder and shot to be given to the Saramakas, the agreement was finally sealed on 19 September 1762.

> *They took earth and water, and each chief placed a child or youth from his own family in front of him, calling on God Above and the Earth as witnesses. Then they swore, with considerable ceremony, that anyone who violated any of the articles would perish with his people, giving a little of the mixture to the youths to consume.*

From a Saramaka perspective, the highlights of the treaty were that the whites had granted them unconditional freedom "with forgiveness for all that had passed," access to Paramaribo and the coastal region for purposes of trade and commerce, and the periodic distribution of large quantities of tools, gunpowder, and other necessities, which they considered as tribute. In return, they had formally agreed to turn back all future runaways from whitefolks' slavery (in return for a bounty), with the whites retaining the right to inflict capital punishment on such returnees, and they agreed also to cooperate with the whites in punishing any Saramaka, including a chief, who harbored new runaways.[13]

Immediately following the treaty-sealing near Sara Creek, Abini and some of the other Saramaka chiefs journeyed to Paramaribo with the Dutch negotiator for the first time as legally free men and were officially received by the colonial Council. A day of public thanksgiving was proclaimed in all the churches to celebrate the signing of the Peace and "to ask Him to assure that the Peace be permanent and prosperous." And before sending them home, the Court of Policy bought the chiefs 120 florins-worth of presents and designated a flag and a drum for the elderly Dabi, who had remained in Saramaka, and whom Abini had told them was their Chief-over-All.

But though the actual treaty was signed at Sara Creek and ratified in Paramaribo, it was the arrival of the official government emissary at Sentea later that year that, for Saramakas, marked the real end of the war and sparked a celebration still remembered with joy today. (When a public meeting is really large, Saramakas say, "It's as big as the one at Sentea!") And in modern Saramaka consciousness, all history tends to be measured against "the day they celebrated the Peace at Sentea," as either "before" or "after."

In mid-October of 1762, the newly appointed government "post-holder," Ensign J. C. Dörig (a former antimaroon soldier), left Para-maribo for the journey upstream, accompanied by an escort of twenty-seven Saramakas. After an often-frightening three-and-a-half-week canoe trip to the Upper Gaanlio (punctuated by the bellicose but largely empty threats of Samsam), Dörig made his historic entry into Sentea on 3 November, the first peacetime visit of a white man to a Saramaka village. Even he was impressed by the reception he received.

> *At 6AM we set out [up river] passing several stony rapids, until at 8 o'clock I heard a horn blowing. Not knowing what it meant, I asked about it and was told that it was a signal that they were ready to receive me. At about 8:30 at a creek on the right hand side going upstream, at Dabi or Abini's landing-place, I heard some musket salutes being fired and I saw Abini and some Negro men and women standing there to offer a warm welcome. Among others they included an old Negro woman painted completely white with a plantation-slave ma-chete in her hand [the blade of] which she held in her [other] crooked arm, pacing back and forth making a racket, babbling in her language which I could not understand. The other nearby Negro women appeared very frightened and went to stand behind the men, using them as a barrier. After I had a talk with Abini, he had all my goods carried off, and at 9 o'clock we set off together accompanied by the sound of the horn and the firing of their muskets. At 10 o'clock as we ap-proached their village, the first [person] we saw was an old Negro right in our path, holding a calabash of water and a siebie siebie [scoparia dulcis] or wild plant in his hands, using it as a brush to sprinkle us with the water that was in the calabash, in accordance with their pretences [that it serves] against the evil spirits and further because of their religiosity. The second [person] who we met as we proceeded was an old Negro wearing a tall red hat who gave me his hand with the words, "Greetings, Master. If you curse me, I'll curse you back. That's the way this Peace works. . . ."*
>
> *During our March, the other Negroes who accompanied me from Paramaribo walked one behind the next, and we were all sprinkled by the old Negro with water from his calabash. This continued right up to [our arrival at] their shed which they call Gran Cassa. There, while we sat on low blocks of wood, the horn was blown and muskets fired with tremendous shouting and noise, clapping hands to the mouth and with [regular] handclapping. The spectacle was curious.*

After being subjected to further "exotic" rituals, Dörig listened to a public speech of welcome from Abini and began to answer politely in kind; but he was interrupted by

> *a great handclapping with other gestures toward both Heaven and Earth, and clapping them [hands] to the mouth. The horns were blaring and I was honored with the firing of several salutes. When the ceremony had ended, I was conducted from there by the whole company to my lodgings, having asked Abini if I could rest, being weary from the tiring journey.*

But Dörig was unable to get to sleep.

> *All the Negro men and women came and made an unbelievable uproar with muskets, and stayed for a long while near me, until Abini finally chased them away. [But there were] howling and shrieking figures shooting off guns the whole night.*

Saramaka memories of the occasion, preserved in songs still sung for the entertainment of the First-Time ancestors at occasional rites in their honor at the Pikilio shrine of Awónêngè, stress simple but immense joy.[14] As Tebini describes the culmination of that night's events,

> *They had finished praying; it was the dead of night. The women said it was time to dance—until morning! The men said, "Let's dance. Let's celebrate. Peace [freedom] has come!" Then they sang out:*

Fií kó, —— kó dén-de fií —— o. —— Kó dén-de,

Peace has come. Kó dénde, Freedom. Kó dénde, Peace.

> *Peace had come . . . Then they said, "Well women, it's time to show off [strut your stuff], to dance aléle." And they sang out:*

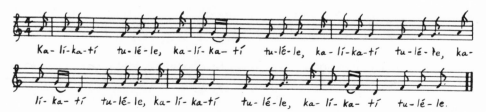

Ka-lí-ka-tí tu-lé-le, ka-lí-ka-tí tu-lé-le, ka-lí-ka-tí tu-lé-te, ka-

lí-ka-tí tu-lé-le, ka-lí-ka-tí tu-lé-le, ka-lí-ka-tí tu-lé-le.

> *Then the women danced gilin gilin gilin [intensifiers]. The men danced, moving their hips. . . . The house . . . the whole village was going "zzzz . . ." [with excitement]. Well, that night they played alele . . . all night long, gbele, gbele, gbele.*

Everyone was dancing it! They played alele *at Sentea.*
Then they went [another day] and played it at Baakawata!
That's what they did when the Peace came.

When they finished this celebration, . . . one woman
said to another, "Child [term of affection], with the size
of our celebration at Baakawata, with that fantastic alele,
how come you didn't show up!" [The other] said, "Oh!
The man [my husband] locked me up and left me in the
house [because he was jealous]. That's why I didn't come."
Then the first woman sang out [composing a new song,
still sung today]:

Diítawéndjèmánu [the woman's play name], Why didn't you come to the aléle?
Hóókóó [expression of joy]. [Expletive] Kwasí didn't want me to come. Hóókóó.

As Postholder Dörig settled in for his restless sleep, who would
have been bustling about the village of Sentea? From the official's
journal we know that Abini and Dabi were his primary hosts, and that
Samsam had made a special point of being absent. We can surmise
that Abini's elderly mother Yaya, and Akoomi, Tjazimbe, and their
Awana relatives were supervising the cooking. Alabi and his brothers
would have been helping with practical arrangements, as well as
attending to the scores of young girls who had flocked to Sentea from
throughout Saramaka. The inseparable Nasi brothers, Etja and Kwadjani, Wii's sister's son Antama, Kaasi's son Alando, Musínga and Bekú
from Tuido in Matawai, the Dombi Dóndo Kasá, and Adjagbo (with his
beautiful wife, Paanza)—all soon to be recognized as captains—would
have been in attendance. Kungooka would undoubtedly have been
supervising ritual activities. And many others would have been there
as well—some of their names known to us from later events, some
still invoked in rituals at Saramaka ancestor shrines today, but most
now lost forever as individuals. But there was one final group whose
presence weighed heavily on the celebrants that night: those men
and women who did not live to see the Peace, but upon whose
sacrifices and heroism it was built. Among those names invoked
earlier that evening at the ancestor shrine of Sentea would have been
many now familiar to us—Lanu, Ayako, and Seei, Kwemayon, Gun-

guukusu, Kaala and Andole, Kaasi and Yeba, Vuma, Gweunga, and so many others. But now the night is given over to celebration. From village to village—from Sentea to Baakawata, from Dosú Creek to Tuido—women dance the *alele*. *Fii ko*. Peace has come at last. A new chapter of Saramaka history is about to begin.

II   *In the Wings*

Two — *The New Politics*

With the euphoria of the Sentea celebration still fresh, Saramaka captains and other elders wondered how they could best maintain their collective momentum in dealing with whitefolks. To Abini and his men, two concerns (which were to retain their central symbolic valence for the rest of the century) quickly emerged from their initial post-treaty encounters with colonial authority: keeping a maximum stream of "tribute" flowing in their direction and assimilating as many newly arrived brothers and sisters from the plantations as possible. Their chief adversary on the colonial side was Postholder Dörig, the soldier-turned-peacemaker, who defined his own central tasks as the restriction of "presents" from the whites to the Saramakas and the "repatriation" of "slaves" being harbored by the Saramakas in violation of the terms of the treaty. Alabi, then eighteen years old, occupied an especially privileged vantage point for observing this post-treaty jockeying for position, for he served during the four years following the Great Day at Sentea as his father Abini's almost constant companion.

Ensign J. C. Dörig was the first of the four military men who occupied the office of postholder in the two decades following the Peace. Commenting on his 1762 appointment, the Chartered Society of Suriname made it clear that they would have preferred a "capable, moderate, and sensible Political [civilian] man" to a soldier, but, as had been the case two years earlier when the first postholder to the Djuka was appointed, the members of the planter-dominated Court of Policy "opposed such a [civilian] appointment . . . [arguing that] the expenses involved would be too high . . . that it was more difficult to find a capable man, or even someone who could write at all, among the civilian population; and that the work was dangerous."[1]

Postholder Dörig's official 1762 instructions were rather general: to monitor adherence to the treaty, to keep tabs on individuals and villages and on their movement, and to keep a regular journal. Special additional instructions were sent out by the Court from time to time—for example, for him to prevent communication between Saramakas and Djukas, to interdict contact between Saramakas and the Berbice rebels in 1763, and so on—but the bulk of the postholder's interactions with Saramakas involved just two issues: the distribution of whitefolks' goods to the Saramakas and the returning of post-treaty newcomers in Saramaka to the whites. A close reading of the historical record makes it clear that neither side in these negotiations saw the other as fully human, that each was persuaded of its moral superiority, and that each had its own very different understandings of the agreements outlined in the peace treaty.[2] Not surprisingly, matters of prestige—the symbolic balance of domination and dependence—took on enormous significance for both parties. And throughout the second half of the eighteenth century, this balance remained delicate and easily upset.

Dörig's first tour of duty in Saramaka, which spanned the four months following the Sentea Celebration of November 1762, witnessed many of the modes of interaction that were to characterize dealings between postholders and Saramakas during the succeeding decades. For example, when Dörig (following specific instructions from the Court) tried to cajole the Saramakas into returning some Indians they had captured in a raid on a Moravian mission post just prior to the treaty, he "got the answer that most of them were already dead and the rest were divided among them . . . [though] the chiefs . . . would do all that was possible to have them returned on condition that the [Saramaka] owners get a bounty as compensation" (which Dörig was unable to promise), and the matter was temporarily dropped.[3] When Dörig, again on special orders, tried to argue the chiefs out of their receiving "gunpowder, lead, and muskets" as part of the goods already promised by the treaty (suggesting instead that "since they [now] had no enemies to fear, it might be better for them in place of ammunition to accept goods of a household nature"), they said "they could never agree to this but absolutely insisted on gunpowder and lead"—at which Dörig backed down and said that "it had only been a proposal."

Reciprocally, when one of the Saramaka chiefs "helpfully" suggested to Dörig that perhaps the whites should now abandon the colonial military post on the Lower Saramacca River, "since there was [now] peace, [and] the soldiers ought to be allowed some rest . . . [Dörig] replied [testily] that this depended on the Governor, who did not let [just] anybody tell him what he ought to do." And when "[Captain] Samsam sent two Negroes to me with the demand that I come to him . . . I refused, reminding him that I was a white man and he a Negro; that he was obliged to come to me first and that I would come to him only afterwards." Throughout this stay, Dörig was drawn into internecine disputes among the Saramaka captains, and though he argued to them "that I and the whites do not care what quarrels they have among themselves, taking no sides in them," he was repeatedly frustrated by his inability to operate effectively without becoming engaged in Saramaka factionalism.

Dörig's first tour of duty also included the tense weeks during which the Saramakas learned of their compatriot Wii's murder at the hands of the Djukas and prepared seriously for intertribal war, before finally accepting the advice given by the Djuka chief to Abini and making peace with one another. "Why," the Djuka chief had asked rhetorically, "should blacks fight blacks? The whites would gladly give us sufficient powder and lead, and would then just sit back and laugh about it!" During the culminating days of this intertribal crisis, Dörig played no part. Remarkably, Tribal Chief Abini had ordered him to be placed under stringent house arrest in a village a day's walk from Sentea, and the postholder—deprived of his liberty for two full weeks—meekly accepted.[4] Clearly, a whole new political relationship was being forged, and both sides were involved in a complicated dance of threats and retreats, demands and acceptances, posturing, flattery, and self-effacement.

Dörig's September 1763 distribution of whitefolks' goods to the Saramakas became the next public setting for this developing drama. Article 13 of the treaty had specified a major distribution of "tools, etc., which they [the Saramakas] have requested and which were granted according to the appended list," but it was only now that the bulk of these goods had finally arrived from the Netherlands.[5] In August 1763, Chief Abini, his sons Alabi and Jan, the Saramaka captains, and a large number of other men ritually readied themselves to journey downstream to Sara Creek, right on the border between their territory and the land of the whites, to receive their hard-won tribute, which Postholder Dörig had gone to the city to prepare (having left his white assistant, Hintze, in Saramaka during his absence).[6]

The symbolic meaning of these varied goods clearly differed for colonists and Saramakas. Were they to be conceptualized as "presents," freely given by the whites to needy subjects, or were they "tribute," exacted from the whites by the victorious Saramakas as a kind of war damages? The whites understood very well what was at stake in these contrasting definitions. One planter wrote, with considerable discomfort, of

> *the weakness of the government of Suriname when they offered them [the Saramakas] freedom . . . and submitted to conditions so humiliating for us and so glorious for them. . . . It is they who demand and receive our homage in the form of annual presents . . . a kind of annual tribute under the name of presents which, at base, is nothing less than the public recognition of their superiority.*[7]

The periodic transfer of these goods became, along with the transfer of the whites' "slaves" in the other direction, the pivot upon which the whole issue of political dependence was symbolically balanced. (Indeed, the government consistently tried to link the granting of "presents" to the returning of "slaves.") Dörig clearly believed that it was his natural prerogative to try to trick the "child-like" Saramakas, and he described with apparent glee (on 16 September) how "I arranged all the shares [of goods] in such an attractive way that they [the Saramakas] would think that there was three times as much as there actually was"; yet he seemed indignant and angry when these same Saramakas showed that they were not fooled and subjected him to some characteristic rhetorical whiplashing. In their own language, Saramakas called these goods *"fri,"* their word also for "peace," "freedom," and "peace treaty." Saramakas clearly saw them as a *right,* an earnest of the new relationship that the whites desired with them; for them the goods were tribute. Yet, for the Saramakas, these goods were also far from being mere symbols; they were sorely needed supplies for a people whose access to Western manufactured goods was otherwise limited.

Postholder Dörig, recently promoted from ensign to second lieutenant, described the central events of this first general gift distribution in his 1763 diary. Some excerpts may demonstrate the ways in which independence and domination, sovereignty and paternalism were being actively negotiated during these highly theatrical confrontations—all of which Alabi watched with fascination at his father's side.

Dörig's initial dealings were with Tribal Chief Abini and his political allies.

[13 September, Sara Creek] I bade the piper and drummer begin to play. Shortly thereafter I saw six canoes full of Negroes, all armed. Then Abini came up to my landing place and all the others followed him. . . . After I welcomed them with a drink of rum . . . they asked to see the goods and afterwards left me silently.

[14 September] Early in the morning all the same Negroes came to me with happy faces, and after having talked with them about one thing and another, I asked them about the four Negroes [recent runaway slaves whom Abini had brought back with him from the peacemaking expedition to Djuka in 1762] they had taken with them from Djuka, for the whites had a right to them. The chiefs answered that they did not know anything about it, and then asked to have a[nother] look at the goods. . . . The first thing they checked was the powder kegs; they asked whether these were all the presents that had been promised them, and I answered Yes. Then all the Negroes began to speak of their surprise and dissatisfaction, grumbling and saying that they could now see that the whites meant them

no good, for many more goods had been promised them and these were hardly enough for a single village, and if they did not get any more they would not accept one piece of these goods, and said that I must immediately send an express messenger to the city to fetch more goods. I tried to refute them tactfully, but it did not help, and they continued to rage. . . . They left me with the same anger [but] said I must likewise come visit them. . . . At ten o'clock the same morning I went by boat to their camp. They received me with ceremony, in their way, with gunshots, drumming, and other baljarden.[8] Noticing some dissatisfaction in them, and after having some conversation with them about matters of no importance, I asked them again about the [four] Negroes they took with them [from Djuka]. . . . Received the same answer and then left them. . . . After I had been in camp for half an hour, the seven chiefs came to me to make a rigorous inspection of the goods—and they insisted on the right to demand more later. It was possible to read anger in their eyes—I saw it. Then they began to act like devils and reiterated their previous proposition, that the whites meant them no good. I even heard them mumble that if it was going to be like this, they would rather break the peace, because they had been promised so many goods that they would not be able to get them all into their canoes and that [now] three more ships would have to come from Holland with goods for them. Whereupon I again refuted their argument, saying that they must wait until the goods are unpacked and that we certainly did not need to lose our heads about this.

Later that day, Dörig opened negotiations with Captain Samsam and those captains most closely allied with him. Ever since the 1750 sinking of the white emissaries at Gaandan Falls, Samsam had been at odds with Abini and his allies. And since the treaty-signing, this enmity had become still more pronounced, with Samsam disputing Abini's claim as most powerful chief. During his first tour of duty as postholder, Dörig had spent a good deal of time trying to patch up this relationship—trying to keep Samsam satisfied with his own treatment while not interfering with the whites' key relationship with Abini, the official tribal chief. At the 1763 tribute distribution, Samsam was directly competing with Abini for Dörig's favor.

At six o'clock Samsam came with 12 canoes full of armed Negroes, accompanied by drum, horn, and flute, and when they neared my camp he had his people arrange themselves into two groups. Samsam sat down before me and welcomed me. He had 30 to 40 shots fired off, then had drum and horn played, and had his people go through strange exercises [grimaces] with guns and swords. When it was over, Samsam said it had been done in my honor, for which I thanked him. Likewise, I had him greeted with three salvos. After this, Samsam asked me to let him see the presents. I brought him to the storehouse and showed them to him. He said it was good, and that because he was tired from his journey he would go to his camp, which he did, provided that I would also come visit him tomorrow.

[15 August] At eight o'clock in the morning I went to Samsam in a canoe he had sent to fetch me. When I neared the landing place, I found Samsam and his people standing there to receive me. As I set foot on land, Samsam grasped my hand and led me to his hut, which was about the distance of a musket shot from the shore, to which a path had been cleared. His people stood in two rows, all well-provided with guns, bows, and arrows. I had to sit down beside him and he ordered that the horn be blown and the drum beaten and, in between, the flute played. After sitting for some time, Samsam had three Negroes with guns come before me to shoot, and this went on until they had shot nine salvos of three shots apiece. Then Samsam apologized that he had not honored me with salvos by his entire force: the reason was lack of gunpowder. I thanked him nevertheless for the honor done me. . . . [Samsam] asked me to be allowed to have a white man to stay with him [in Saramaka], to write letters whenever anything happened, and to give out passes whenever they wanted to go to the city. And . . . I asked him [about the four Negroes taken from Djuka]. . . . He told me that they were divided among Abini's people.

Dörig next paid a courtesy call on Abini, to clear up any lingering contretemps from the previous day, but reserving a confrontation over Abini's alleged slave-harboring until Samsam was also present.

I got to Abini's camp at 10:30. . . . I spoke with them [the chiefs] about their mumblings yesterday, namely to break the peace, saying that they must not come to us with threats and that we were not in the least afraid, and that if I were to write about this to the Court they would be very offended. They answered in one voice that they knew nothing about it, and that such a thing could only have been said in casual talk among the common men, for they, on the contrary, were well pleased with the peace treaty provided they got the goods that were promised them. . . .

[16 September] This morning early, our friends arrived to get the presents from me. . . . Before starting, I asked about the hostages and said that I had to have them before laying a finger on the distribution. They answered that they could not give the children before they had seen the distribution of the presents, or had they sold their children to the whites? I replied, No! they had not sold them, "But that is your own oath which you swore with us, and you may be sure that if the children are not given to me, you will have a long wait before I divide up the goods."

They replied in turn, "We shall give our children as soon as we have received the presents, and we will not give more than two children [instead of the four specified in Article 13 of the treaty], for among us that is as valuable as if we had given ten, for they are our own flesh and blood, and we do not want to give more." "Come on, then," said I. "Give the two children! I'll see how I can square it with the Court." They gave me the children, one from Chief Abini [his son Jan] and the other from Chief Samsam [his son Christoffel].9 I went on to ask them where the four Negroes [slaves] were now, whom they were keeping among themselves. "I must know whether they are with Abini or Samsam." Abini replied, "I don't know anything about any Negroes who are supposed to belong to the whites." Samsam's Tromp interrupted him to say: "Don't you know, Abini? The three Negroes you took with you from Djuka . . ." Then all of Samsam's retinue shouted in chorus, "That's true, you've got the slaves. Were you trying to pin the blame on us?" Abini, seeing he was defeated and contradicted by such a large number of witnesses, immediately confessed to having the Negroes under him, but [said] that these had [simply] followed him, that they belonged in Djuka, and had [simply] wanted to visit their family members [in Saramaka], so they had gone with [his people]. I could not resist trying to persuade them still further, and said to all who stood by, "You people! Listen to this! There are four foreign Negroes with Abini, and they don't belong to the Djuka but to us whites, and I must have them back. That is according to Oath and Duty." Abini wanted a way out of this dispute and said, "When I get to my village I will investigate it carefully, and if I find that these Negroes belong to the whites I shall return them to where they came from, namely to Djuka." Abini's contrariness made it necessary for me to show him clearly that he would not take the Negroes back to Djuka but return them to us, which he then promised he would do when he returned to his village.

After finally distributing the goods to the representatives of each of the ten villages, Dörig said,

"Well, friends, look there! Isn't there more there than you had thought?" Samsam spoke for the whole gang: "There isn't enough." I replied at once, "Well, Samsam, I see they have put you up to saying that, because you have never appeared so contented as during the past two days." Chastened, he remained silent. Then Abini began to complain, saying, "Come on, I'll say what we need and what was promised us [in the document appended to the treaty]. Namely: 53 kegs of gunpowder, 13 long muskets, some light guns, then some cotton, earrings, beads, cowrie shells, hot African peppers, copper belts, hats, jackets, and trousers, staffs with silver knobs." (N.B. I

answered that these were being prepared.)[10] After they listed all this, I asked if that was all, and they answered in unison, "Yes!" . . . They wanted to give me several Negroes as an escort [for the trip to the city] to take their pleasure at the fort at Government expense, but I refused. Then they took the goods after having thanked the Honorable Court with handclapping,[11] as well as thanking me for my efforts, for they were certainly pleased about the division of the goods and again asked me to ask the Court if they might have the [additional] goods listed. . . . Finally, all departed in good harmony after the division of the goods. The agreements back and forth had taken from 7:30 in the morning until 3:30 in the afternoon. More than an hour afterwards, they returned with all their guns, all kinds of instruments and baljarden to show their gratitude and satisfaction about the distribution of the presents, and thus until evening they spent the time shooting, drumming, blowing the horn, playing the flute, and [conducting] many other ceremonies, until at last they took their leave.[12]

The upstream journey from the tribute distribution was capped by a great celebration, this time strictly for Saramakas.

When they got back safely to their villages, they fired many salutes for the people who had waited at home. These people came to the riverbank singing, to escort them ashore. They played drums, danced, blew African trumpets, and sang, danced, and celebrated the whole afternoon until nighttime and the whole night until morning. In the morning, they took a piece of white cloth and they raised a white flag to the Great God in the heavens. Then they all touched their knees to the ground and gave the Great God thanks for all that he had done for them and for the strength that he had given them against the many hardships they had encountered in the forest. Moreover, the Great God had helped them and given them strength in the forest to fight and win a major war against the whites. Now the whites themselves were bringing them peace and many goods. And for that, everyone knelt down on the ground to give the Great God thanks. They put all their children with their bellies to the ground, and even many of the adults threw themselves with their bellies to the ground to show the Great God respect and to give him thanks for the good things that he had done for them. Then they got up, took their guns, and shot many salutes for the Great God, to honor him. And finally, they were finished.

Then they raised another flag with a black cloth. This they did to honor the former warriors, those who had fought and won against the whites. Then they all came together under the flag; this was also to give thanks to the warriors

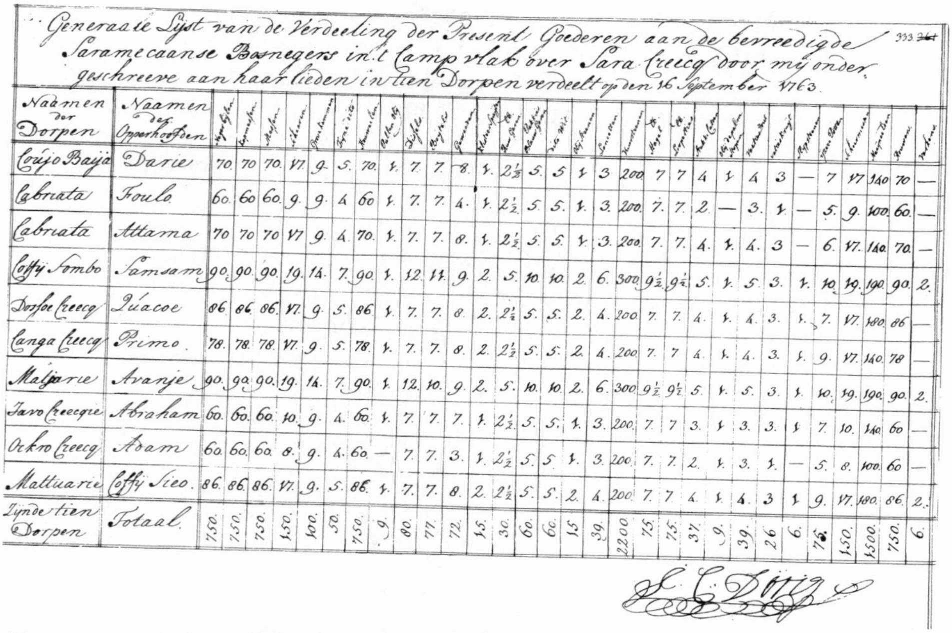

Generaale Lijst van de Verdeeling der Present Goederen aan de bevreedigde Saramecaanse Bosnegers in 't Camp vlak over Sara Creecq door mij onder geschreeve aan haar lieden in tien Dorpen verdeelt op den 16 September 1763. 333.

Naamen der Dorpen	Naamen der Opperhoofden	[illegible]	[illegible]	Messen	Scheeren	[illegible]	Fyne dito	[illegible]	[illegible]	[illegible]	[illegible]	Geweeren	[illegible]	[illegible]	[illegible]	dito Wit	[illegible]	Lancetten	[illegible]	Hagel	[illegible]	[illegible]	[illegible]	[illegible]	[illegible]	[illegible]	[illegible]	[illegible]	[illegible]	[illegible]	[illegible]
Coujo Baija	Darie	70	70	70	17	9	5	70	1	7	7	8	1	2½	5	5	1	3	200	7	7	4	1	4	3	—	7	17	140	70	—
Cabriata	Foulo	60	60	60	9	9	4	60	1	7	7	4	1	2½	5	5	1	3	200	7	7	2	—	3	1	—	5	9	100	60	—
Cabriata	Attama	70	70	70	17	9	4	70	1	7	7	8	1	2½	5	5	1	3	200	7	7	4	1	4	3	—	6	17	140	70	—
Coffij Sombo	Samsam	90	90	90	19	14	7	90	1	12	11	9	2	5	10	10	2	6	300	9½	9½	5	1	5	3	1	10	19	190	90	2
Dorsoe Creecq	Quacoe	86	86	86	17	9	5	86	1	7	7	8	2	2½	5	5	2	4	200	7	7	4	1	4	3	1	7	17	180	86	—
Canga Creecq	Primo	78	78	78	17	9	5	78	1	7	7	8	2	2½	5	5	2	4	200	7	7	4	1	4	3	1	9	17	140	78	—
Maljarie	Avanje	90	90	90	19	14	7	90	1	12	10	9	2	5	10	10	2	6	300	9½	9½	5	1	5	3	1	10	19	190	90	2
Javo Creecqie	Abraham	60	60	60	10	9	4	60	1	7	7	7	1	2½	5	5	1	3	200	7	7	3	1	3	3	1	7	10	140	60	—
Ockro Creecq	Adam	60	60	60	8	9	4	60	—	7	7	3	1	2½	5	5	1	3	200	7	7	2	1	3	1	—	5	8	100	60	—
Mattuarie	Coffij Sieo	86	86	86	17	9	5	86	1	7	7	8	2	2½	5	5	2	4	200	7	7	4	1	4	3	1	9	17	180	86	2
Zijnde tien Dorpen	Totaal	750	750	750	150	100	50	750	9	80	77	72	15	30	60	60	15	39	2200	75	75	37	9	39	26	6	75	150	1500	750	6

J. C. Dörig

"General list of the distribution of the tribute goods to the free Saramaka Bush Negroes in the camp just across from the Sara Creek by me, the undersigned [J. C. Dörig], to the people of ten villages on the 16th of September, 1763." For each village, this document lists the name of the headman and the amount of axes, knives, muskets, cloth, needles, etc. received (SvS 320, 16 Sept. 1763, 333. See also R. Price 1983b, 236–38, 243).

and to honor their name and to blow African trumpets, which the Africans had made out of wood in Africa, and which they loved to blow whenever they went off to battle and with which they talked to one another. These First-Time people who lived in the forest really loved to blow those trumpets! Whenever they blew such a trumpet, they would shoot many salutes, play drums, sing, dance, and play sangáa *drums. And the adults would* sangaa *all over the place. . . . And they played drums so! When they were finished, they would bring a bush drink that they made from sugar-cane juice. . . . They would pour a libation on the ground. That was to give thanks to the Great God and the ancestors. After that, they would play for the* obias *and for the other gods who had helped them fight.*[13]

Soon after his celebratory return to Sentea from the tribute distribution, Abini and his advisers settled on a strategy for dealing with Dörig's continuing pressure to return the several runaway "slaves" who—everyone now knew—were living in his villages. Rather than turning in these people, who were already becoming assimilated into Saramaka society, he would offer the whites some newly found runaways, with whom he did not yet have strong ties. With Dörig still in the city attending to the aftermath of the tribute distribution, Abini asked Dörig's white assistant, Hintze (who had been left in Saramaka in his stead), to write Dörig stating that Abini now had fourteen "prisoners" (belonging to plantations Boxel and LaRencontre) to turn in and needed pairs of "hand and foot shackles" for each; and in the succeeding weeks, both Abini and Samsam sent further messages to this effect, in case the first had not been received. The Court reacted positively to this flurry of news, resolving that, once the slave transfers were effected, Abini and Samsam each be given "silver snuff boxes with the arms of the colony engraved upon them."

Dörig spent the better part of March and April 1764 in Saramaka, mainly taking care of these slave returns, which were—this time—conducted with little apparent acrimony on the part of the Saramaka captains. Abini and Samsam were openly competing for the whites' favor, and most of the slaves in question had not yet become "Saramakas." Yet, even so, the chiefs managed the affair in such a way that the bulk of the Boxel and LaRencontre runaways remained with them in Saramaka: the two slaves whom Samsam had chained up at Dörig's request "escaped," chains and all, during a funeral in Samsam's village and were not recovered; two of the slaves whom Dörig was transporting to the city (with guards supplied by Abini) escaped "because they were not sufficiently well-bound"; and Dörig in the end arrived in Paramaribo with only five. The chiefs got their silver snuffboxes and the whites' good will; the "slaves" from Djuka plus the bulk of the new runaways remained to become part of Saramaka families and villages.

But there is a darker side to the story, and it was very much on Saramakas' minds. Turning back *any* slaves made a person ideologically suspect: Dörig witnessed a Djuka visitor to Samsam's village telling the chief how he would lose face enormously with his Djuka brothers if he went ahead and turned in the two slaves he had just chained up (whom Samsam, in fact, later permitted to escape). Moreover, there was strong perceived danger to anyone who turned in even an unknown other; upon the slave's death, he would almost certainly become an avenging spirit, wreaking his vengeance eternally upon the lineage of the person who committed the act. And, finally, there were the brute facts of how the colonial judiciary dealt with turned-back slaves: three of the people brought back from Abini by Dörig were condemned to be hanged (and the others may have been executed soon after as well), and Saramakas were bitterly cognizant. Three years before, the Djukas, after witnessing their own first batch of post-treaty returned runaways being executed in Paramaribo, told the whites "that they had found it sickening and that it was not at all what they had expected [to happen]." And, perhaps aware of Article 5 of the treaty (in which the whites reserved the right of capital punishment in such cases), the Saramakas several times during the succeeding years, when turning in a runaway, pleaded openly with the whites not to exercise that option.[14]

For the government, much more was at stake than the economic value of these new maroons themselves. The slave system, to perdure, simply could not tolerate an open door of this kind, a way out for the massive labor force that supported the foundation of the colony. Saramaka chiefs (like the Djukas caught in the same dilemma), faced with tremendous pressures from the whites, devoted a great deal of time and energy during the second half of the eighteenth century to delaying, dissimulating, and beclouding the issue and, in general, managed to turn back only occasional newcomers. After the turning-in of several more Boxel and LaRencontre runaways in late 1764 by Samsam and the Baakawata Matjaus (who were also vying with Abini for Dörig's favor)—for which they received axes, adzes, chisels, and a number of days' holiday in the city at government expense—no more than a handful of others were turned in during the rest of the decade. And for each of the ones that was turned back, a number of others were quietly assimilated. For example, in 1767 Kwaku Etja (at the time aggressively seeking to win the whites' support for his candidacy for the office of tribal chief) made a great show of turning in a single slave, telling Postholder Dörig: "Master, here is a Negro who has run away from the whites. I had six of them but the other five escaped." Not surprisingly, in 1774 we encounter one of these latter "escapees" happily married to Kwaku Etja's own sister.

Three   *Soldiers of the Bloody Cross*

Toward the end of 1765, three Saramaka captains and the official deputies of seven others, accompanied by kinsmen and friends, paddled downstream to the Sara Creek in order once again to receive their shares of whitefolks' tribute from the hands of Postholder Dörig.[1] But at this second major distribution, Dörig brought them, in addition, a surprise: three strange white men, black-suited Moravian missionaries, the vanguard of a group that would play a signal role in Saramaka life for the next two centuries.[2]

The Moravian Brethren were hardly just another evangelical eighteenth-century church.[3] Dörig, no doubt unwittingly, had brought the Saramakas as singular a group of European whitefolks as could at the time be found anywhere on earth. The Brethren considered themselves the world's oldest Protestant church, tracing their origins to the fifteenth century. They had experienced a strong revival during the 1720s, after settling on the estate of Count Nikolas Ludwig von Zinzendorf und Pottendorf in Saxony, where they founded the community of Herrnhut, converted Zinzendorf (who became bishop and spiritual leader) to their particular brand of New Christianity, and probably sent more missionaries per capita to far-off lands than any other contemporary church.

Zinzendorf's personal theology and social theories, which dominated the church during much of the eighteenth century, had their roots in German Pietism but went well beyond dissident Protestant belief and practice of the day. While still a youth, Zinzendorf had created tiny societies for Christian prayer and edification, bearing such names as "The Slaves of Virtue" and "The Order of the Mustard Seed." And as his ideas developed, he increasingly located the seat of religious experience firmly in the heart, arguing, in a deeply anti-rationalist spirit, that

1. Westindisches Compagnie Haus in Amsterdam 2. Lichter 3. Abreisende 4. Begleiter und Absied nehmende.

Moravian Brother Riemer (no. 3 in the engraving), bound for Suriname, bidding his co-religionists adieu in front of the West India Company building, bastion of power and wealth (Riemer 1801, 19).

> **faith has its seat not in speculation, not in thought, but in the heart. . . . There is nothing more dangerous or useless than a little brain, filled with thoughts about theology, trying to penetrate the godhead. . . . [Salvation depends less] on the truth in ideas than the truth in sensation.**

His was a true "Theologie der Konkretheit," a theology of the concrete. For Zinzendorf,

> **the trademarks of the Shepherd-Redeemer-Become-Flesh were corporeality, palpableness, realism, and perceptibleness. Zinzendorf followed this path—in his sermons, liturgy, and songs— all the way to its logical conclusion . . . [wanting] to hold aloft . . . the concreteness of God's salvation through Christ before peoples' very eyes.**

The sufferings of Christ on the Cross constituted the central image through which God was to be apprehended. Zinzendorf and his followers held a relentlessly Christocentric view of the Passion, deeply sensual and heavily baroque. Indeed, toward the mid-eighteenth cen-

Count Zinzendorf, in middle age (Weiss 1911, facing p. 32).

Early view of Herrnhut (Archives of the Moravian Church, Bethlehem, Pa.).

tury, the Brethren's spiritual concerns became focused almost exclusively on the blood that was left on the cross and on Christ's five wounds—especially the much-beloved side wound, or "sidehole."

The *Litany of the Wounds,* written in 1747 at the height of the Moravians' *Sichtungszeit* ("Sifting Period"),[4] in a florid, baroque, and sensual style, represented the epitome of Zinzendorf's theology, celebrating Christ's wounds by such terms as "worthy, beloved, miraculous, powerful, secret, clear, sparkling, holy, purple, juicy, close, long-suffering, dainty, warm, soft, hot, and eternal." By this time, Moravian texts were "centered on constantly varying images of the body, using metaphors of betrothal, kisses of love, and the marriage bed to express the sensual fusion of the community with the mystic lamb." Zinzendorf's 1748 *Hymns Composed for the Use of the Brethren,* translated from German, offer some taste of the imagery that the missionaries who traveled to Suriname carried in their hearts and minds. (These missionaries, both men and women, envisioned themselves as "brides of Christ" whose father was God and whose mother the Holy Ghost. In this imagery, the church was born in the Savior's side wound, betrothed to Christ on the cross, and married to Christ in Holy Communion, making it the daughter-in-law of both God the Father and the Holy Ghost.)

Tune: *Brought to the Birth, &c.*

We kiss each other in the Side Of our beloved Spouse, Which is ordain'd for his dear Bride Her everlasting House. The Lamb, the Husband of our Souls, Hath got indeed more Wounds and Holes, Yet is the bleeding lovely Side The Chamber of the Bride. 2 Our Husband's Side-Hole is indeed The Queen of all his Wounds; On this the little pidgeons feed, Whom Cross's Air surrounds. There they fly in and out and sing, Side's Blood is seen on ev'ry Wing, The Bill that picks the Side-Hole's Floor, Is red of Blood all o'er. . . . 4 Blest Flock in th' Cross's Atmosphere, You smell of Jesu's Grave, The Vapours of his Corpse so dear Are the Perfume you have. It's Scent is penetrant and sweet; When you kiss each other and greet, This Scent discovers that you were To Jesu's Body near. 5 With thy Side's Blood quite cover me, And wet me thro' and thro'; For this I pant incessantly, And nothing else will do. The Blood-Sweat in thy Agony Come in full Heat all over me. Thy Body stretch its Breadth and length O'er me, and give me Strength. 6 A Bird that dives into the Side, Goes down quite to the Ground, And finds a Bottom large and wide In this so lovely Wound. A Side-Hole's diver will I be: O Side-Hole! I will sink in Thee. . . . 7 To live and work and sleep therein, I'm heartily inclin'd. As a poor Dove myself to screen, Is my whole heart and Mind. O Precious Side-Hole's Cavity! I want to spend my life in Thee.

Tune: *What does a Bird, &c.*

My dearest, most beloved Lamb! I, who in tenderest Union am To all thy Cross's-Air-Birds [the privileged birds that fly near the Cross] round, Smell to and kiss each Corpse's-Wound; Yet at the Side-Hole's Part, There pants and throbs my Heart. I see still, how the Soldier fierce Did thy most lovely Pleura pierce, That dearest Side hole! Be prais'd, O GOD, for this Spear's Slit! I thank thee, Soldier, too for it. I've licked this Rock's Salt round and round; Where can such relish else be found? In this Point, at this Season, The Side has stole my Reason. . . .

Ye Wounds! You all I greatly prize, But yet this one attracts my Eyes. . . . On my Lambs Corpse the favourite Part, 'Tis mine, 'tis mine! Yes, mine thou art! How shall I call thee? Thou Rock-Grott in the lamb so dear! Side, Where a thousand Beauties are; Here are my Meals both first and last, I eat and drink a full Repast, Till all my own Excellence, Is in one Side's-Consistence.

Lovely Side-hole, dearest Side-hole
  Sweetest Side-hole made for me,
O my most beloved Side-hole,
  I wish to be lost in thee. . . .

I saw from out the Lanced Side,
  The Streaming Blood and Water;
There all my Happiness I spy'd,
  With Joy and Holy Rapture. . . .
O Let my Soul sink deeper,
  In the Blood's unfathomed Ocean!
My Pasture-Ground is always green,
  I feed upon thy Passion.
Till once I can the Nail-holes kiss,
  And greet with Bride's Affection,
And close embrace upon my knees
  these Seals of my Election. . . .

And let me then with Juice of Blood,
  Thy scars uncounted Numbers
Pourtray before the Brotherhood,
  With all thy dying Members. . . .

Pierc'd thro' Wound-Hole-Sluices,
  Scratches, Bruises, Mangled Members,
Where I have my Dwelling-Chambers.

Happy, happy, happy are,
  Who in the Blood-streaming Wounds
of the Saviour
  quite buried are.

"We stick," insisted the Brethren at midcentury, "to the Blood and Wounds Theology. We will preach nothing but Jesus the Crucified. We will look for nothing else in the Bible but the Lamb and His Wounds, and again Wounds, and Blood and Blood." "We stick," they further declared, "to the Lambkin and His little Side-wound. It is useless to call this folly. We dote upon it. We are in love with it. We shall stay forever in the little side-hole, where we are so unspeakably blessed."

The profound antirationalism of this *Sichtungszeit* led to the formation in Herrnhut and other Moravian communities of societies such as "The Order of Little Fools," "Little Worms," "Baby Chicks," and "Little Bees, 'who feel at home in the Sidehole and crawl in deep.' " The members of such societies were said to have no heads but only hearts, since, as Zinzendorf contended, God had revealed His will not to wise men but to babes. Thus, the Moravians "were not to use their own brains; they were to wish they had no brains; they were to be like children in arms; and thus they would overcome all their doubts." But even during periods of lesser religious intensification, eighteenth-century Moravian communities—which were by design "closed," insofar as possible, to the outside world—were organized according to radical social principles: for example, the secular family was subordinated to a system of "choirs" that grouped people (for purposes of socialization, residence, work, and worship) by age, sex, and marital status; couples engaged in "militant marriage," with spouse selection done by the community and women seen as official "helpmeets" to their husbands, sharing whatever position the latter occupied; and all important community decisions were mediated by divination ("the lot").[5]

Soon after becoming spiritual leader of the church, Zinzendorf began making arrangements for a missionary presence abroad. "It grieved [him] to hear of so many thousands and millions of the human race, sitting in darkness and groaning beneath the yoke of Sin and the Tyranny of Satan." Before long, more than 10 percent of the men from the community of Herrnhut were serving in the missionfields in Greenland, Lapland, Armenia, Persia, the Danish Virgin Islands, Suriname, and elsewhere. Moravian missionizing strategy emerged directly from Zinzendorf's general theology. Without offering "the minds of the heathen" any other preparation, the missionaries "at once declare unto them *the record God gave of his Son.*"

In preaching the Gospel to the Negroes, and to all other Heathen nations, the Brethren endeavor to follow the example of the apostle Paul, who was determined to know nothing among them, save Jesus, and him crucified. They have experienced how little is effected by first endeavouring to enlighten their reason. . . . [P]lain testimony concerning the death and passion of Jesus Christ the Son of God, together with its *cause* and happy *consequences*, delivered by a Missionary touched with an ex-

perimental sense of it, is the surest way of enlightening the
benighted minds of the Heathen, in order to lead them afterwards, by degrees, into all truth.

For the Moravians, conversion became "a sensual, even an erotic,
persuasion." Their intent was to effect a slow but complete awakening of each convert's heart, to be followed by baptism, with considerable further instruction preceding admission to the Lord's Supper.

By these means, Zinzendorf's "theology of the concrete"—his belief that salvation should be tastable, graspable, palpable—quickly
"spread out from Herrnhut over Western Europe and from there via
the missionaries over the whole world." As a 1753 hymnbook put it:

Es geh uns allen wohl	May all be well with us
in JEsu Wunden-Hohl	in Jesus' wound-holes
in Europa druben	From Europe
bis an den Norder-pol	to the North Pole
in Indien hieruben;	here in India;
und in Asia und in Africa	and in Asia and in Africa
sey uns JEsus nah.	may Jesus be near us.

The influence of Zinzendorf's personal theology, which declined
gradually after 1760 in Herrnhut, nevertheless had great staying
power in the missionfields. In spite of attempts by many later church
historians to underplay the significance of the *Sichtungszeit* (and
even to destroy archives pertaining to it), its central text, the *Wunden
Litaney,* "had a tremendous influence on the Brethren and Sisters in
the missionfields until late in the century." And in Suriname, its influence extended well into the 1800s. For example, one of the Brethren
who served in Saramaka wrote a Sranan-Tongo hymnbook (written in
1803, first printed in 1820) which "is strongly filled with the theology
of Zinzendorf-of-the-forties . . . the sidehole, a very strong [general]
stress on Jesus' blood and wounds, and on the Crucified Jesus—
straight out of the homilies of the *Wunden Litaney* of 1747."[6]

O heddi nanga wonden	[Oh head with wounds
en brud na kruis janda;	and blood on the cross (there?)
O heddi hufa dem tai ju	Oh head how they have tied you
nang krone va makka.	with a crown of thorns.
Na fossitem dem fredde	At first they feared
va lukku ju Glori;	to look at your Glory;
Jusnu wi si joe dedde.	Now we see you dead.
Wi takki joe grangodi.	We bring you our greetings.]

Oh Head so full of bruises,
So full of pain and scorn,
'Midst other sore abuses,
Mocked with a crown of thorn!
O head, e'er now surrounded
With brightest majesty,

The congregation at Barby (near Herrnhut) bidding good-by to a missionary departing for Suriname. The original caption translates: "Chapel in Barby, (1) liturgist, (2) his [communion] table, (3) bishop and elders, (4) female elders, (5) community of Brethren, (6) same of Sisters, (7) the departing one" (Riemer 1801, 14).

> **In death now bow'd and wounded,**
> **Saluted be by me![7]**

And a Saramaccan-language version of the *Wunden Litaney* was a true staple of the liturgical diet at the Saramaka mission throughout its eighteenth-century history.

> **On the 18th [September 1772] we decided upon the future schedule of our services: on Sunday morning, every two weeks, we will read the Litany, and on alternate Sundays preach a sermon. Afternoons there will be the Liturgy . . . and in the evenings we will read from the translated portions of the four Gospels and have our evening service. Monday and Wednesday evenings, there will be choir practice. As usual, we will hold our evening as well as our morning service each weekday. Friday evenings, we will have the Liturgy of the Blood and Wounds, but not with all the verses that we enjoy at the Lord's Supper.**

"First Fruits," the *Erstlingsbild,* painted by Johann Valentin Haidt (Heydt) in 1747 at Herrnhaag, at the height of the *Sichtungszeit,* and now at Zeist. It represents the first baptized heathens from the missions in Persia, Greenland, Armenia, the Caucasus, and South Africa, and among North American Indians and the slaves of the American South and the Danish Virgin Islands. The Lord, seated on a cloud and surrounded by angels, prominently displays the five wounds on his hands, feet, and side. In this iconography, the side wound clearly holds pride of place. The text held aloft, from Revelation 14:4, reads, "These have been redeemed from mankind as first-fruits for God and the Lamb."

The Suriname mission was initiated through Zinzendorf's Dutch connections, dating from his student days at Utrecht. In 1734, his deputy Spangenburg met with the directors of the Society of Suriname in Amsterdam, and the following year the first three missionaries were sent out from Herrnhut, with specific instructions "to investigate whether amongst the Savages [Indians] and Moors [Africans] there might be any souls to save." The first three decades of Moravian proselytizing in Suriname, largely among Amerindian populations, were—in the understated judgment of one Moravian historian—"not very successful." Indeed, by 1765, only two small Indian mission posts remained, operated by six missionaries.

The impetus for a Maroon mission seems to have come from the colonial government, as part of its general pacification efforts. In 1759, Governor Crommelin floated the possibility in an interview with Moravian Brother Ralfs, just before the final signing of the Djuka treaty; his real motives shine through the missionary's trusting prose:

On 2 November ... the Governor called me to him ... and asked whether our congregation would want to send Brethren to those negroes called Free Negroes. ... He truly wants Brethren

to go live with these negroes so that they can spread the word of Christ. He also wants our Brethren to maintain a correspondence with the Governor so that they [the colonists] are able to follow events there. . . . He was very friendly toward us, and I must have spent two hours with him.

But it was only in the spring of 1765 that the Moravian leadership in Europe finally sent out three Brethren to open a Maroon mission (now expected to be among the more recently pacified Saramakas): Ludwig Christian Dehne, Rudolph Stoll, and an Englishman, Thomas Jones. These men came from backgrounds typical of the eighteenth-century Moravians sent out to the Suriname missionfield, who counted among them tailors, shoemakers, bakers, weavers, sailmakers, cabinetmakers, wigmakers, musicians, and a clockmaker. The artisanal bias was not accidental:

> Besides the indispensible requisite of personal piety, and love for the service in which they engage, the qualifications deemed essential to a missionary in the Brethren's Church, consist in a ready knowledge of the scriptures, and a good natural understanding, in some degree improved by education, combined with a kind and affable disposition, calculated to conciliate the affection of the heathen. No stress is laid on profound erudition. Long experience has taught the brethren, that the habits of a student do not, in general, qualify a person so well, for the laborious life of a missionary, as those of a mechanic.

Brother Dehne, uniquely experienced, with two and a half decades of previous mission work among Guianese Indians, was a German-born tailor, and the initial leader of the group.

On the eve of their departure from Holland for the New World, all three wrote parting letters back to the Moravian Directorate in Germany. That of Jones, written in English, is representative in its heavy emphasis on Jesus' blood and wounds and its quasi-commercial conception of salvation:[8]

> Zeyst, May the 8. 1765.
> My dear Brethren. I will write you a few lines before my departor from hear and let you know that j am chirffull happy and well and wait with longing to proceed on our journey. The time appointed that we go abord is the 18. of the month. The reason why we could not go with the first ships was because our troncs were not come. My dear Brethren, I have not much to write, but that I feel that my dear Saviour and his wounds is my one and all and that I will go on my journey with a happy reliance on him, for I am his. . . . I felt when I came away from Herrnhuth the whole congregations heart was with us and blessed us; the deep impression of which I feell still in my heart and I believe will follow me through this my pilgrimage and often times will comfort my heart. I don't doubt but the dear Lamb will out of

these Blaks gather a smart reward for himself. for all souls are his and the purchase of his Blood. I shall now conclude with recommending myself and my two Brethren to yours and the whole congregation. . . . P.S. Amsterdam May the 23. Tomorrow we shall go on bord the ship Catering Cornele, all 4 happy and well and salute you once more by Jesus wounds.

On 27 July 1765, the new Brethren arrived in Suriname. To their discomfort, Governor Crommelin seemed insistent on viewing them as potential government agents, and several times tried to coopt them with promises of material help for the new mission. The Brethren, however, were wary,

as this might in a sense make us obligated to them [the governor and the Court], and what we need is to have complete freedom to preach the gospel among them [the Free Negroes].[9]

The newcomers' attempt to disengage themselves from worldly politics was specifically sanctioned by Zinzendorf's teachings, which counseled his missionaries "to get involved as little as possible with the politics or commerce of the colonists." "Do not," he wrote in a personal letter to a missionary, "work against the police, or regard the government with suspicion. . . . Do not interfere between employers and employed [master and slave]; do not play any part in party politics." For the missionaries in Suriname, these teachings implied strong support for the status quo, including acceptance of the slave system. And as we shall see, they participated in it actively as slaveowners.[10]

Brother Dehne, just three days after landing in the colony, was summoned by the governor, who pressed him hard about providing incidental intelligence;[11] four days later, he was called to a meeting with both the governor and Postholder Dörig. Dehne was then informed that the Moravians would be granted permission to live among the Saramaka, but in return for a promise to keep a watchful eye and to report anything (politically or militarily) out of the ordinary. The governor added a friendly caution

that we would have very hard times there, especially when the heathens held their entertainments, because at such times they get very drunk and act insane, and we would have to keep a very low profile until such festivities were over. I replied that it would be nothing strange for us to find ourselves among wild heathens.

As it turned out, Dehne and his colleagues would not only find the "wild heathens" stranger than they had expected, they would be forced to conclude that the experience of living among them in "the tangled pestilential forests" represented "a foretaste of what Hell must be like." Indeed, years later, a Moravian historian concluded that "of all the stations, occupied by our missionaries in South America, this may justly be deemed the most difficult." However, the beginning of the mission was a time of great expectations, and the initial encounter between Moravians and Saramakas seemed to hold promise for all involved.

Postholder Dörig introduced the three Brethren to the Saramakas on the very day of the 1765 tribute distribution, a moment of high (and positive) emotional pitch;[12] tying the missionaries' arrival to this event may well have eased their provisional acceptance. Brother Dehne described their introduction:

> As soon as he told them that we were coming to live in their presence, they said that they were very pleased. . . . The gifts were then set aside for each separate village, and the delegates received them. Mr. Dörig spoke on our behalf and said, "These missionaries are not soldiers but come to you out of love. They are not required to stay in any one place, and you must treat them well, so that they treat you well, and this will give me great comfort. However, if you treat them badly, I shall consider it as done to myself." After hearing this, they each wanted one of us. But he immediately rejected this idea, saying "they are Brethren who want to remain together, but they will come and visit each of you."[13]

Brother Dehne's account of the upriver trip includes a revealing incident in which one of Tribal Chief Abini's men prevented the newcomers from going ashore at Captain Samsam's, as they had planned.

> On the 15th, Thomas [Jones] and I departed upriver, each in a separate canoe. Rudolph [Stoll] remained behind [to follow several weeks later] since some of the necessary provisions had not yet arrived. A total of ten canoes set out. Mine was truly tiny and was filled with ten negroes and so many provisions that I had a very difficult time maneuvering in it, and was not able to remain dry at any time during the trip. There are a great many large waterfalls, and there are very sharp stones that cause great pain on the feet because one has to get out of the canoe and carry everything over the rapids. At the same time, it takes real skill to remain standing since the water rushing through the stones is so strong, and nothing remains dry. Finally, everyone gets back into the vessel. If the falls is too high, we have to lay down pieces of timber and haul the canoe over the ledges. Once we get across, we have to reload, which takes a great deal of time. . . . On the 20th, in the evening, we met up with the canoe carrying Thomas [Jones], but on the 21st, we again lost sight of each other, not to meet again until the evening of 1 January, when he came to me [at Sentea].
> On the 24th of December, we landed at the appointed place [Samsam's], and were told to walk to his village on foot; Mr.

> Dörig's white assistant [Hintze] said I should accompany him to Samsam. But the deputy of Abini, who was also with me, said, "I will not let that happen. I must bring you myself to my chief, so that I can be properly compensated for having brought you all the way alive and well." They argued heatedly about this but the white man finally had to let the deputy have his way, and I continued on to Abini.

Soon after, Samsam tried to intercept each of Dehne's confreres to keep them in his, rather than in Abini's, village.

> Samsam, who was a chief, and with whom Brother Jones had traveled, kept him by force. Nor was this the effect of any particular regard or attachment he had conceived for the missionary, but solely of ambition, that he might likewise have an European residing with him, which the negroes esteem an honor. January 1st, 1766, Brother Jones found an opportunity of disengaging himself from his ungracious host, and rejoining his fellow-missionary, Dehne, on the Sinthea Creek [Abini's village].

> [Several weeks later] Stoll asked Samsam to send him to his brothers [Dehne and Jones, at Sentea], but Samsam refused, saying that the others should instead come to him. After continuous requests and bickering, however, he finally relented and gave him a negro guide. On 2 February, Stoll arrived at Abini's.[14]

Dehne's description of his own arrival at Sentea, on Christmas Eve 1765, highlights initial Saramaka and Moravian concerns: Tribal Chief Abini's wish to be the one (rather than his rival, Captain Samsam) to host the missionaries; his central interest in getting the missionaries, as the first resident whitefolks, to teach Saramaka children to read and write; and his immediate decision that their house site should be close to his own, for purposes of observation and control. And on the missionary side, there was an immediate attempt to proselytize, to spread "the central message with which eighteenth-century Herrnhut was trying to blanket the whole world."

> That afternoon at two o'clock we came to the village where Abini lives. The forceful shouts of joy made by the women and children, as well as the gunshots from the men's muskets, lasted fully until we were inside the large open shed which adjoins the chief's house. After the most respected men were assembled, I was brought to them. The most powerful of the men [who had been on the upriver trip] stepped into the center and proceeded to recount all that had happened with me, including his strange encounter with the above-mentioned white man [Dörig's assistant, at Samsam's landingplace]. All were satisfied and thanked him. Then, when everyone else had departed, Abini came to me, gave me his hand, and said that he was very pleased that we had come to him and wished us a friendly welcome. I then told him

> that I really loved the negroes, and that I wanted to tell them the Word of their Creator who had shed His blood for them and for all mankind, the Creator who loved them but about whom the negroes remained ignorant. "Ah," he said, "Is that the Gran Gado?" "Yes," said I, "It is the God above us, the God whom all men, yes, every creature in the heavens and on earth must revere and respect."

But Abini quickly turned the conversation to a subject of greater interest to him and other Saramaka men:

> Abini then asked if we would not teach their children [to read and write]. And I replied to him that we would.

Then, taking Dehne firmly under his wing, so he could observe, protect, and control him,

> Abini then took a walk with me, first pointing to a [temporary] house [for me], and then leading me to a place where he thought we could [later] construct a house. Frankly, I thought it was a bit too close to them [the Free Negroes] but I had to agree to it because he said, "I would not want you to be too far away from me, because I want to visit you frequently and give you advice whenever you need it."

Saramakas seem to have perceived two main potentials in the newly arrived missionaries. First, as whites clearly allied with the government, the Moravians appeared to be a fairly direct conduit to power. Just as rival groups of Saramakas, and rival leaders, jockeyed for position through the postholders, the possibility of getting on the right side of the Moravians—getting one's own version of an incident accepted, with the expectation that this would be passed on to the government—was, at first, a powerful draw. The desire of so many villages to have the Moravians come live with them (specific requests from at least five are mentioned in the documents) seems to have had less to do with some notion of gaining prestige than it did with gaining an avenue to the white power structure in the city, and thus a competitive advantage in matters of tribute, and so forth.

Second, as those whites most closely associated with books, the Moravians were seen as a potential entree into the mysterious and hitherto forbidden world of reading and writing. Indeed, it is a painful fact that from 1765, when Saramakas were first reported to request a way of learning these prototypically "white" skills, right through the time of our own arrival in Saramaka precisely two hundred years later, the *only* means Upper River Saramakas had of learning reading, writing, and arithmetic was via Moravians. And the toll exacted over the centuries for this privilege remained constant: intense pressure to renounce "heathen" ways and to break off relations with non-Christian family and kinfolk. Saramakas then as now were caught in this terrible bind, knowing that literacy was a password to an understanding of the outside world and the key to being able to manipulate it, but also knowing that its acquisition entailed what was, for them, a truly Faustian bargain, the willingness to sell their souls.[15]

The arrival of whites as permanent residents posed countless and complex dangers for the Saramaka nation. And the gods and ancestors reacted swiftly.

During the night [Dehne's first in Sentea], there was a tremendous noise coming from nearby Abini's house. It [turned out to have been made] . . . by a negro who usually lived along the Saramacca River but had been here for some time. The next morning, the causes were investigated [by divination], and finally the answer was found: the gods were unhappy and Abini must give a feast in their honor to placate them.[16] Thus, on the 27th, it was announced out loud[17] that a festival for the gods would be held in three days, and that each person should bring whatever he could to help placate them.

On the 30th, after a horn was blown, a feast was begun on a hill a good quarter hour from the village. The sacrifice consisted mainly of sugar-drink. Once everyone was gathered together, a small mound was decorated with fresh palm leaves and fenced-off, except for a small entrance for the priest, so that no one else could enter. Then a man and a woman began to dance about, soon followed by all the women, shouting loudly, and gamboling and singing with wondersome gestures. Then the priest entered and fell to his knees, followed by all the menfolk. The women and children, who stood apart, fell down with their faces touching the earth. The priest prayed: "Our gods, listen to us! Listen to what we have to tell you, and look at what we are bringing for you [as offerings]. Please be satisfied with us. We want to give you everything we have." At this point, the others chimed in, saying, "Listen to us, our *Massera*, (Lord)." During this prayer for food, drink, and health, the women and children repeated, pleading, "Listen to us!" After the prayer, everyone stood up again. Then they brought all the offerings to the priest, who poured them on the hillock, saying, "Behold, this is what we give to you, to make you pleased with us." When most of the sacrificial goods had been used, the priest turned to the others and said "The god says he has had enough." And with this, the menfolk drank up what was left. After this, a pot with a solution of ash-grey earth and water was brought out and, first, sick people came and the priest smeared this liquid onto their heart and breast, then the healthy people came with their wives and children, and the liquid was smeared onto their faces. Then everyone showed their joy by a great deal of gun-shooting, and all returned home satisfied that the gods had been appeased and were no longer angry with them. As for myself, my heart be-

Some of Abíni's descendants performing a similar ritual in 1968. The kneeling woman is being washed with medicinal herbs from the *óbia*-boat.

came extremely melancholy and I sang "My God, do you see them?"[18]

In Brother Dehne's melancholy observation of what was, in fact, an *awaínza* ceremony, designed to placate the gods and ancestors on the occasion of his own arrival in Saramaka, he alluded to many characteristics of major eighteenth-century Saramaka collective rites: the blowing of African-style wooden signal horns; libations of sugar-cane juice; prestations of food; the smearing of kaolin solution first on the sick (and probably the pregnant), then on the healthy; special postures for addressing the Sky God (*Gaán Gádu*); men and women dancing and speaking in possession states; and the joyous firing of salutes. Around the *awainza* hillock, ringed with *azang*-palm fronds, Abini's people had sung, spoken, and danced to their gods and ancestors, to tell them once again (as they had upon Dörig's 1762 arrival) of the dawning of a new day. In 1978, the Saramaka elder Tebini offered his interpretation of what had happened on that faraway day two centuries before.[19]

> *That hillock they made there, that was an* **awainza**. *It's like a "transmitter" direct to the Sky God. Whatever you say there, it goes straight to the heavens. They sang out*

Fiï kó, ——— kó dén-de fiï——— o.——— Kó dén-de,

Peace has come. Kó dénde, *Freedom.* Kó dénde, *Peace.*

> *They told their gods,*

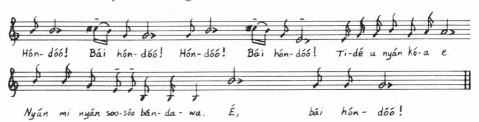

Hón-dóó! Bái hón-dóó! Hón-dóó! Bái hón-dóó! Ti-dé u nyán kó-a e.

Nyán mi nyán soo-sóo bán-da-wa. É, bái hón-dóó!

"Joy, shout out 'Joy'! / Today we celebrate peace / I am eating meat bándawa! */ Shout out 'Joy'."*

> *They flattened themselves belly to the ground [in a gesture reserved] for the Great God. . . . They said, "Let the Great God send it [peace] to us as is really fitting. Let him continue to give us more." And they prayed to him:*

A - bí- ti   a - bí- ti   mu-lê- lê————   dá mi   a - vó.————

Mbéi mi sú- su—— Gbá- na-mbé- mbu.   Un sê   mi sa fé- ni mu-lê - lê?

"A few stars for my ancestors. . . . But how will I ever reach the stars?"

> *"The Great God has caused us to emerge from the forest*
> *undergrowth to receive the peace. Let's celebrate it and go*
> *still further. Let it go on and on."*
>   *Then they danced in a circle [with upraised arms, stepping*
> *sideways] as they sang* Fii ko! *joyously again.*

That day at the *awainza,* Tebini recounted, Abini's people also
spoke with special feeling to their kinfolk who had given their lives
during the wars. For, it was especially such as these—Ayako and
Vuma, Seei and Kaala, Kaasi and Yeba—who "couldn't see [tolerate]
whitefolks," whose hearts had to be cooled by collective supplica-
tion, upon the arrival of the Moravians.

> *They spoke to them: "Those people who didn't live to see*
> *the Peace, they must not be jealous. Their hearts must*
> *not be angry. There is no help for it. When the time is right,*
> *we shall get still more freedom. Let them not dwell on*
> *what they have missed. Let us and them be on the same*
> *side together, those First-Time people! It is to them we*
> *are speaking."*

Mbéi-u án sáa môò un pèê dá wi e.——— Mbéi-u án sáa môòun pèê dá

wi e.—— Mbéi-u án sáa môòun pèê dá wi o. Ké, mbéi u án   sáa

môò un pèê   dá- wi.   Wè téé———   di tén kí- si

un sa kó a wi o.   Mbéi-u án sáa môò un pèê dá wi.

"[Ancestors,] Let's not be sad any longer, come 'play' for [with] us. . . . Well, when
the time is right, you can come to us."[20]

Almost immediately after the *awainza* ceremony, even before the three Moravians were finally assembled together in Sentea, physical sufferings began to dominate their lives—a pattern that was to continue throughout the history of the mission. Brother Dehne described how, two days after the ceremony,

> **on 1 January 1766, to my joy, Thomas Jones came to me. On the 3rd he was still in good spirits, but on the 4th he complained of headache and chills. On the 7th I let a negro bleed him, which went well;[21] because nosebleeding occurred, I had high hopes.[22] I also had the fever.**

A correspondent in Paramaribo continues the story, based on letters he had received from upriver:

> **On 2 February, Brother Rudolph arrived at Abini's, but he found Thomas so weak that he could not get up from his hammock, and Dehne barely able to crawl. He himself also felt sickly. However, they thanked the dear Savior for the joy of all being back together once again. On the 7th, our Thomas fell asleep in the arms and lap of Jesus.**

Dehne then reports that

> **Abini himself made the coffin out of cedarwood, and on the 8th we laid his earthly remains to rest. . . . My own health continues very weak. . . . I would have a great deal more to write down but the pain in my foot, which has a gaping hole in it and which allows me no rest at night, simply does not permit this. Please have patience with me. . . . Toward the end of the month, I was afflicted with the white runs [dysentery] which was very persistent and left me very weak. I thought that the time might have come for me to go home [to Jesus] as did my Rudolph, as this sickness was [also] calling many negroes out of time. But the Savior was merciful and helped me once again.**

As another missionary in Suriname wrote home that year, "Our plans are large and our strength small." Or, as the leader of the Suriname Moravians concluded soon after in a letter to the directorate in Germany,

> **As regards what you should say to those people who are considering service among the negroes [here in Suriname], it is important to stress to them that they must not value their own lives too highly.**

Throughout the eighteenth century, the specter of Death absolutely haunted the Saramaka mission. Perhaps fortunately for them, the Moravians considered "falling asleep in the arms and lap of Jesus" (which they also referred to as "being called out of time") a signal privilege. Of the thirty-nine missionaries who served in Saramaka between 1765 and 1813,[23] at least thirty were devastated by an initial attack of "the seasoning fever," and eleven perished—like Brother Jones—within days of their arrival.[24] Brother Riemer, who arrived in Saramaka in 1779, left a graphic description of this ubiquitous and violent fever (almost certainly caused, in most of the cases described, by malaria of the falciparum variety).

> Already that morning [the ninth day in Saramaka] I arose from my hammock with an attack of fever. . . . Soon I realized that this was the same sickness contracted by most European newcomers, namely a putrid or nerve fever, which can be very dangerous and flare up most dramatically in these hot climes. . . . This very dangerous sickness completely robbed me of my consciousness for several days, and there was little hope that I would survive. Soon, a baptized negro took the sad step of building my coffin with cedarwood, and he had to work very hard since it is necessary in this hot climate to bury a corpse no later than 24 hours after a person has died. . . . The aftermath of this grave illness was extremely melancholy, leaving me with severe weakness in my chest and lameness in my nerves, and this made me incapable of doing any of the things I would normally have done. Even the smallest things that one holds with one's hands I simply let drop, and I was also left with a skeleton-like figure.

With their friend Jones buried, the Brethren Dehne and Stoll—the first suffering greatly from his infected foot, the second from a debilitating fever—gratefully accepted Abini's help in moving themselves and their few possessions from their temporary lodgings, "a small miserable hut, near the dwellings of two old negroes . . . [where they] suffered great hardships and poverty," to the new house that Alabi and his brothers had been building for them nearby.

> The erection of a new house is the work of a few days, and requires comparatively little labour. Nine posts are driven into the ground, and the spaces betwixt them filled up with a kind of palm leaves, very large and thick; and these also serve for the door. These leaves are plaited and tied together by means of a plant called *bushtau* [or woodrope] which twines itself round large trees frequently attaining the length of twenty or thirty feet, and is easily split so as to become as fine as a thread. The roof is covered with the leaves of another tree, called *Tassi*. Thus the whole edifice is completed without lime, or mortar, or a single nail; and yet such a building will stand several years without needing any repairs.[25]

Almost in spite of themselves, the Moravians became aware of the bustle of activities going on around them.

> The friendliest conversations among the inhabitants of a negro [Saramaka] village take place in very noisy fashion in the midst

of their dwellings, which are built close upon one another. Men and women, when they wish to speak with the inhabitants of other huts, stay at their own doorsteps, and the women who, here as everywhere, gossip a great deal with each other, keep up a savage chattering and babbling in loud tones that can truly deafen you. To be sure, in this type of conversation no secrets can be kept.

But not yet knowing much of the language, and both quite sickly, Dehne and Stoll spent the first part of 1766 making the slow adjustment to living among people whom the latter characterized as "to be sure, a horrible race." (Soon after, another early Moravian stalwart referred to "those of us who are living here alone in the wilderness, and serving a people who can truly be called ugly and frightening," adding that "the most repulsive among them are the women.") And together they prayed:

May the Lord and his Spirit continue to ignite our hearts with his fire and warm us daily with his Blood, so that our activities will never decline and that we may relate His death until our lips grow cold.

At this time, the missionaries in Saramaka could hardly have been farther from being able to heed Zinzendorf's personal advice:

Teach the heathen by your example, to fear God and honour the King. . . . The right way with savages is this: you must set them such a dazzling example that they cannot help asking who made these delightful characters.

During this early, melancholy period of the mission, Tribal Chief Abini (whom Dehne characterized as "a dear and understanding man") and his sons, especially Alabi, remained the Moravians' main direct link with the Saramaka world.[26] Indeed, a Moravian historian with access to documents that I have not seen claimed that sometime in 1766, Abini formally

presented his son (the present Johannes Arabini [Alabi, who was then twenty-two years old]) to the missionaries [presumably as a kind of companion/helper], with words to the following effect: "That he did not know what sort of people the Brethren were, nor the cause of their stay, but believed God had sent them."[27]

In August, the missionaries reported that "a son-in-law of Abini named Kodjo [-Maáta] brought his twelve-year-old son Skipio to us, saying that he wished to give him to us, to live with us, so that we could teach him to read and write," and soon after Brother Dehne described him as "a capable lad who is able to learn."

Abini, during the year since the tribute distribution and the arrival of the Moravians, had been gradually consolidating his political power. When the most powerful chief of the Saramacca River villages died (in late 1765), Abini took those villages—now headed by captains Musinga and Beku—more directly under his authority. And the four Suriname River villages over which Abini's rival, Captain Samsam, claimed control (at least according to the missionaries) now drew closer to the five more closely allied with Abini's "politics of peace." In 1765, shortly before the tribute distribution, Chief Dabi—the elderly son of the great wartime leader, Ayako, who had been Samsam's greatest nemesis—died at Sentea. And the death of Dabi, who had been Abini's mentor throughout the final peacemaking process, seems finally to have permitted a thawing of relations between Samsam and Abini. The governor of Suriname, immensely relieved by the apparent amity between these perpetually feuding Saramaka leaders, wrote happily to the directors of the Society of Suriname in Holland:

> *Between Abini and Samsam there now exists complete harmony, all of which has come about since the death of Dabi.*

And in early 1766, the Court resolved to obtain from the Netherlands two identical sets of special gifts, one for Captain Samsam (despite the fact that he was said to be "often drunk") and one for Tribal Chief Abini: "a hat with a Spanish peak and a white plume, a saber and scabbard, and a ceremonial gorget."

III   *Center-Stage*

Four   The Whole Land Shook

On 18 October 1766, around midnight, Tribal Chief Abini was roused from his conjugal hammock by the sound of excited voices. A messenger had just arrived to announce that Captain Musinga and his men from Matawai—the westernmost Saramaka village—had despoiled four whitefolks' plantations. The Peace that Abini had fought so hard to achieve, and then maintain, was again in jeopardy. With Postholder Dörig absent in Paramaribo, Abini had Alabi recruit Brother Stoll to serve as his amanuensis for an urgent letter (written in German) to His Excellency the Governor. After briefly reporting news of the raid, Abini's letter emphasized that

> **"I have always forbidden Musinga and all the negroes from Matawai to use any route other than the one through my village [and down the Suriname River] when they wish to go to the fort [Paramaribo] or to the whites, in order always to know what is happening. But now I have learned that Musinga has, clandestinely and without my knowledge, used the Saramacca River instead."**

Abini further described how, at the emergency council meeting that he had convened, his people had resolved to send a commando to catch Musinga on his return journey and cut him off, but that since hearing that troops were to be sent out from the city, he was hoping that the two groups could catch Musinga in a pincers movement and ruin his village. Abini begged the whites to act fast and to send powder and shot for his troops (as they had used up that given in the last tribute distribution for hunting). And he ended by noting that "Your Excellency will clearly see what faithful allies we are." In Paramaribo, where a hastily organized commando had already gone after Musinga's retreating raiders but had returned without success, the

Court was now organizing a full-scale expedition, to be led by Dörig; their orders called for 160 white soldiers, 65 free mulattoes and blacks, and 120 slaves.

The particulars of Captain Musinga's "raid" speak volumes about the continuing fragility of Saramaka-whitefolks relations. It seems to have started in all innocence, as an attempt by Musinga to bring some trade goods to the coast via the Saramacca River—the only really practicable route from his village. (Article 10 of the peace treaty had guaranteed Saramakas the right to use this route, though Musinga had been interfered with whenever he had tried it.)[1] On 1 October, Musinga and his men, on their way to the coast, had stopped off at the Moravian Indian mission post of Saron, on the Lower Saramacca River. They were hardly on the warpath. Two different missionaries at Saron described how,

> **on the first of October, a group of Free Negroes arrived. They were very friendly toward us and begged us to come to where they lived. . . .**

> **The two captains Beko and Massingo from the Upper Sara-macca [River], with about thirty men, visited us during the autumn in Saron and were very friendly. They had asked that two of our Brethren come live with them, just as they do with Captain Abini.**

Three days later, the missionaries learned that these friendly visitors had, on the night of October 2/3, apparently "stolen" some one hundred fifty slaves from four plantations on the Coropina Creek, in the nearby region of Para. Captain Musinga, nearly a year later, gave his own version of what had occurred the day they left the missionaries.

> **"I went to Mr. Planteau [the owner of Plantation Sonderzorg] and requested permission to pass through on the way to Paramaribo, having brought along canoes we had made to sell, and wanting to buy goods there in return. Mr. Planteau replied [angrily], 'Musinga, I have made no peace with you or other Bush Negroes! Go deal instead with those who made your peace, the Governor and the Honorable Society!'"**

Musinga then describes how he told Planteau that he and his men would, in any case, need to spend the night there, before moving on; and how that evening, Planteau, unbeknownst to Musinga, arranged to borrow powder from a neighboring plantation and then doled it out to his slaves, with orders to fight Musinga. Indeed, before Musinga and Planteau had parted that day, there had been more angry words, with Planteau even threatening that "the head of a chief [captain] that I bring to Paramaribo would fetch me a fine price!"[2] That night four (some sources say five) adjoining plantations on the Coropina Creek were engulfed in flames—those belonging to Planteau, Letterman,

Dumare, and the widows Picolet and Papot. By morning, some one hundred fifty slaves, men and women of all ages, were fleeing through the forest with Musinga's men toward freedom in Saramaka.

In the village of Sentea, Abini and his captains, including Samsam and others who had often been at odds with Abini, resolved as one to enforce the treaty and do battle with Musinga. Abini's letter to the governor had been expressed by canoe, accompanied by a delegation of eight men that included his son Alabi. In all the villages of Saramaka, great war *obia*s that had lain dormant since the Peace were reawakened, and, under the direction of elderly priests, men of fighting age now washed in heavily scented ritual baths and otherwise steeled themselves for the expected military encounter. On 7 November, a full month after Musinga's "raid," Dörig's commando finally left Paramaribo, with "14 punt-boats, 22 canoes, one officer (Lieutenant Larcher), three sergeants, 55 privates, 63 mulattoes and free blacks, 15 slave soldiers," and a number of slaves; supporting troops and provisions—28 canoes-worth at one time, and "a captain, a lieutenant, an ensign, 3 sergeants, 3 corporals, 2 surgeons, 61 privates, and 53 slave soldiers" at another—joined Dörig's forces later. Their orders were to capture and bring back the one hundred fifty slaves who were with Musinga and to despoil his village and gardens, rendering the area uninhabitable. After two weeks of difficult travel upstream, in which some lives as well as provisions were lost in the rapids, Dörig—still on the Lower Suriname River—met canoes sent downstream by Abini and Samsam to greet him.

After several days of meetings about strategy, with various chiefs participating, Abini and Samsam finally suggested "joining hands together" and summoning the Matawai chiefs to discuss a peaceful solution to the crisis. Two Saramaka messengers were sent to try to contact Musinga, while Dörig's expeditionary force and some scores of Saramaka warriors, along with many of their wives and children, waited in a large encampment by the Suriname River.

During this lull, Dörig reports various examples of what were becoming almost routine dramatic confrontations with Saramaka chiefs about "presents" and "slaves." For example, Captain Kwaku Etja, "looking very thin and quite sick," came and said, "Good day, Dörig. Where are the guns you promised to bring me?" Dörig replied that he "had not had time and, besides, had forgotten." Etja: "Have you really forgotten? No problem. Then I also haven't time to go with you to fight Musinga! You can go alone. I have also forgotten to bring food supplies for you. And you must not think that a single man from your commando shall set foot in my village without my firing at him." Dörig: "Go right ahead, they will shoot back—and quite straight— right at you. Nor do my troops have any need of your village." But Dörig did send to the city for Kwaku Etja's promised guns and, some weeks later, after the arrival of his reinforcements, actually handed them over to the pleased captain, with the reminder that he must help return any of the whitefolks' slaves still in his village. During this lull, while Dörig and the Saramakas waited for the messengers to return from Matawai, they amused themselves in other ways as well: one day, Captain Kwaku Kwadjani brought "30 negroes—men, women, and children—for entertainment," and in the evening they held a "play [dancing, drumming, singing] which they truly enjoyed."

On 14 December, Abini's messengers returned from Matawai with the news that Musinga wanted a peaceful settlement. Indeed, he denied having stolen any slaves at all, saying that the Para slaves had rebelled on their own and then simply followed his men to his village. He expressed pleasure that Abini and Samsam were now willing to intervene on his behalf with the government and asked them "to make a good arrangement for giving back the slaves to the whites, so that everyone may continue to live together in good friendship." Dörig's reaction, apparently prompted by his original orders, was mixed. "Once I have received all the whites' slaves, I still must deal directly with the wrongdoers and, finally, must destroy Musinga's village and see that no one lives on the Saramacca River side any more." He told the chiefs that he and his troops were not leaving Saramaka until all of this had been accomplished.

After further meetings and indecision, Chief Abini came to Dörig with startling news from Matawai: Captain Antama had just returned from a visit to the village of Musinga,

> *who has completely changed his mind and will no longer keep his word, and would not listen to Antama's reasoning. When Antama called the Para slaves together [in Musinga's village] and said to them, "Come, friends, I will divide you up, so we can take some of you with us [to Saramaka]," these negroes said to Antama, "We will not be divided but will stay right where we are. If the whitefolks really want us all back, then Mr. Planteau himself will have to come get us here, because he treated us in such an unheard of and unconscionable way— which is the only reason we are here [i.e., ran away] in the first place." Though Musinga refused to discuss the matter further with Antama, Musinga's wife came to him and said, "My husband is as changed as day and night and [now] will absolutely not turn in the Para slaves."*

Abini's reaction to this news, undoubtedly discussed at length with his captains, was to change tactics. He told Dörig,

> *"Master, I call on the Great God as my witness that I have tried to do everything in my power to get the Para slaves turned back to you, but you have seen and heard what a brutal man he is. . . . Look, Master, let us now attack with all our force."*

Dörig, still ambivalent about fighting, suggested that a delegation consisting of Tribal Chief Abini and some senior captains—Samsam, Kwaku Etja, Antama, and Kwaku Kwadjani—be sent to Musinga for one last try at a peaceful solution. But Abini is reported to have argued, "No, Master. It would be better to go with all the troops, because the message Musinga sent via Antama is a true insult. Let's lose no time in attacking." Dörig and the chiefs finally agreed to this advice and decided to go after Musinga with all their forces. At their final muster, Abini counted seventy-three Saramaka warriors, all of whom were given ammunition by Dörig. His own sons Alabi and Kinke,[3] and his son-in-law Kodjo Maata, served throughout the expedition as advance scouts.

On 2 January 1767, after several days' difficult march, Dörig recorded that

> *Abini called his people together and said, "Well, friends, we're drawing close to Musinga's, and I have no doubts that we will all show real bravery against Musinga-the-Peacebreaker, and prove our fidelity to the whites. For myself, as long as my eyes remain open, I will always try to do this. What do you all say?" Whereupon, the Bush Negroes replied that they would all follow his example steadfastly.*

The next day, Alabi and Kodjo Maata returned from scouting to say that Musinga's village lay close by. The troops marched

> *the whole night with candles and torches in our hands, with great difficulty. [The next morning] Day broke around third-cock's crow from Musinga's village. . . . I warned everyone to be silent, to array themselves to the right and left, to surround the village.*

And then, the denouement:

> *But Tribal Chief Abini, who was truly furious, fired prematurely at the house of Musinga, whereupon the whole commando abandoned their orders and, bravely, fired this way and that.*

This continued until, just at the moment that Dörig had ordered his men to cease fire and attack the houses saber in hand, he

> *heard a frightening noise from the Bush Negroes. When I got there, I learned that Tribal Chief Abini had been shot dead. . . . The chiefs Samsam and Etja, and other elderly Negroes came to me, saying, "Master, let us return . . . home. . . . Musinga is in a [ritual] state to kill us all, without our being able to harm him. . . . Don't you see that we have lost our Tribal Chief Abini in the battle? . . . Please come away with us, so we can properly bury Abini."[4]*

After burning and pillaging the now-abandoned houses in Musinga's village, the Saramakas placed Abini's corpse in a hammock and, with a detachment of Dörig's troops fore and aft, set off in the direction of Sentea. And that evening, deep in the forest, *the deceased Abini was buried, wearing a long-sleeved shirt which I [Dörig] provided, and with his cotton cap on his head. And I expressed my deepest sympathies over this man's death. Before wrapping him in a shroud, they cut some hair off Abini's head and nails from his fingers and toes. Then, after dressing him, they buried him at half past six, and asked me permission to fire salutes in his honor. He was thus laid to rest, with considerable pomp and circumstance.*[5]

Back in Saramaka, the news of Abini's death spread from village to village like wildfire. As Captain Gome, the octogenarian leader of Alabi's clan, described it two centuries later: *kôndè séki,* "the whole land shook." As the men returning from Matawai entered Sentea, carrying the cloth packet containing the dead chief's hair and nails, piercing mourning shrieks rang out from women in every corner of the village. To alert the ancestors, Alabi and his brothers fired three gunshots into the air,[6] as the elders carefully suspended the hair-and-nails packet from a beam of the village council house. Since Abini had already been buried, albeit summarily, the elders decided to hold an elaborate *nyanyántúè* (food offering) in place of the funeral.

Although the missionaries are silent about the specific aftermath of Abini's death (being quite sick themselves during the period), they described this type of "large spectacle for the deceased's pleasure" on several other occasions. For example,

On the night of the 26th through the evening of the 27th [January 1773], we heard terrible shouting, drumbeating, and dancing. It was a sacrificial feast, which was being held in the neighborhood. The reason for it was the following: a local negro had been quite sick. They asked the Obia, a type of oracle, the cause of the illness. It, or rather the deceiver who they call the Obia, said that the deceased sister of the sick person has made him ill because he had promised her some Dram [(libations of) rum] after her death but had not given it to her. After this, the deceased was begged solemnly to make her brother healthy again. They wanted to hold a feast for her with eating and drinking, and they wanted to do this as soon as the [other] people had come back from Paramaribo. As the sick person became better, some cooked up a drink from sugarcane, some hunted wild boars, some hulled rice, and a day was chosen for the sacrifice. Part of the food was set at the grave of the deceased. Amidst prayers and many flintlock salutes, the dogs eventually ate up the meal, the drink was poured on the earth, and the rest, as long as any was left, was eaten by the guests.[7]

A week before the day of the great feast, Alabi, his brothers, and a dozen other young men went hunting *a duumí mátu,* "sleeping in the forest" far upstream from the inhabited area for several days, while they sought game and fish for the ceremony. After building a rough shelter and praying to the god-whose-place-it-was for a safe and productive stay, they set to work. Just before dusk, the men set bowtraps for paca and basketry fishtraps for *nyumáa* and *patáka* (*Hoplius* spp.); during the days, while some hunted for game, ranging from peccary, small deer, and turtle to bushfowl and wild turkey, others drugged nearby streams for fish. The two or three women who accompanied them tended the fire over which fish and game were smoked on a rack, day and night, in preparation for the feast. After several days, they all paddled downstream in canoes heaped with the meat and fish to be cooked for villagers and visitors, and for the food offering itself.[8]

From every village people flocked to Sentea. As the landingplace had been jammed with canoes four years before, when Abini triumphantly welcomed the white emissary to conclude the Peace at Sentea, once again it was blackened with craft from throughout Saramaka, this time carrying angry mourners. The chief who had guided them to Peace had been slain.

Abini's aged mother Yaya, Alabi's maternal grandmother, mother, and sisters, and other village women were at the center of a swirl of activity: cooking, brewing, and otherwise preparing festive offerings for the deceased and for the living celebrants who had come to honor him. Meanwhile, male elders were organizing the ritual appeasement of the gods and ancestors whose world was so seriously shaken by this event. At dusk, the day before the feast, the senior captains poured libations from a calabash, right in front of the council house where Abini's hair-and-nail packet was hanging. Invoking Abini's ancestors, one by one, as well as various war leaders and other important dead Saramakas (Lanu, Ayako, and Seei, Vuma, Kaala, Kaasi, and many others), they told each and all of the terrible events in Matawai, reciting the formulaic "there's no help for it" and begging them—and Abini—to join the living "with pleasure" the next day for a special feast in their honor. And later that evening, Saramakas from Abini's "mother's village" of Baakawata, from the Nasi village at Dosu Creek, from Kánga Creek, Agamadja, and the other villages that comprised the Saramaka world all joined together to honor their late chief with a "play"—singing, drumming, and dancing the whole night through: *papá* drumming and singing (the Saramaka music of death) from Dahomey, *nagó* drumming from Yorubaland, *luángo* music from the Kongo, and *komantí* rites from the interior of the Gold Coast.[9]

After having caught a few short hours of sleep, some of the older women gathered in an open shed to finish cooking the festive meal. Giant pots—most of earthenware but a few of iron (liberated from whitefolks' plantations or received by the village as tribute)—were soon bubbling with rice, fish, fowl, and game. Meanwhile, men, slower to arise from their hammocks, began loading their muskets with black powder for the traditional salutes. By mid-morning, scores of calabashes filled with cooked food had been placed on the cleanswept earth in front of the village council house, and women stood before a massive pot calling children, and anyone else who wished, to come "burn their hands"—to dip their hands quickly in a calabash of cool water and then receive a steaming double handful of peanut rice to gobble before the official ceremony began.

Soon men carrying their stools strolled over to the council house, sat down before it, and bantered lightly until one of the older captains began washing his hands in a calabash and pouring water on a banana leaf for the ancestors to do the same, as he invited them to join the living for the feast. "You, old people, don't you see? We've prepared a little food for you today. Accept this food!" After mentioning his own close ancestors, he spoke to Abini, "You who so recently left us," recalling with affectionate familiarity the good times they had passed together and asking his special help in the difficult times that lay ahead. As he spoke, periodically interrupting his conversation with Abini to call on other ancestors, he slowly loaded up a large wooden rice-winnowing tray, placed on the banana leaf, with bits of food, carefully including some of each delicacy laid out in the women's calabashes. When the tray was fully heaped, and as he continued to speak quietly to the ancestors, the old man took a bit of each kind of food from the plate—a piece of cassava cake that he had dipped in broth, some white rice, peanut rice, meat, and fish—and with his cupped hands tossed it onto the banana leaf for the ancestors to eat. Then, rising, he took double handfuls of peanut rice and distributed them into the waiting hands of Yaya, Alabi, and other seated relatives and dignitaries, finally calling on the village children to take their turn: in a mad melee, they rushed for the still-heaped tray, scrambling to grab whatever tidbits they could find. A woman next poured some palm oil into the remaining rice on the tray and rubbed the mixture onto the bodies of those who shared Abini's *nêséki,* his tutelary spirit.[10] The captain then took a calabash of sugar-cane juice and poured a libation, asking Abini and the other ancestors to accept what they had been offered and to protect them in the future. The tray was turned over on the banana leaf and, after a few seconds, tapped three times with a stick and righted once more. The food offering was over.

But the village quickly sprang alive with a celebration in honor of Abini and the ancestors: the missionaries heard "incessant drumming, singing, and the firing of salutes." Finally, by mid-afternoon, the public part of the ceremony had ended, and the visitors to Sentea began to disperse. At dusk, a tired group of elders carried their tiny stools back to the feast site, where they poured one last libation (this time a sequence of water, then cane juice, then white rum) to Abini and the ancestors, informing them that they would hold the "second funeral"—the largest and most spectacular of Saramaka public events—in a year or so, at Abini's "mother's village" of Baakawata, home of the Matjau clan, where the chief's hair and nails would symbolically be laid to rest.

Though many Saramakas now drifted back to their villages and gardens, the captains and other elders stayed on for some days in

A twentieth-century Alúku Maroon food-offering for the ancestors (Hurault 1961, facing p. 162).

Sentea, attending to their own central concern: the complex interrogation of the dead man's spirit to determine their future course vis-à-vis both whitefolks and the Matawai, and to decide who would succeed Abini as tribal chief. By the middle of the eighteenth century, Saramakas had already developed a whole series of special procedures to deal with unusual deaths, including those of children, pregnant women, people who had drowned, and people who had died while away from home.[11] Though the carrying of a coffin on the heads of two men, to interrogate the spirit, was a part of all standard funerals, the occasional substitution of a hair-and-nails packet, tied to a paddle, was also routine at certain moments (since carrying the coffin was always a heavy job).[12] In Abini's unusual case, the packet of hair and nails could now be used as an all-purpose substitute. The carrying of the cloth packet (further wrapped in a banana leaf and tied

"Heathen Funeral on a [Suriname] Plantation" (1840s). Chromolithograph by Petit after a drawing by Theo Bray (Atlas van Stolk, Rotterdam).

to a paddle on the heads of two men), to interrogate Abini's spirit, went on intermittently over several days. Many of the political events of the past few years were discussed. Describing a similar event—the funeral of an old woman—a few years later, a missionary wrote:

> **Two negroes carried the corpse on their heads, and the relatives, and anyone else who understood the arts of sorcery, danced and drummed and fired musket salutes. The corpse was asked, for example, if any individual was responsible for the death, if the village in general was in a good state, who would die in the near future, and so on. They believe that a movement of the coffin gives them the answer. . . . They wanted to carry the corpse to the grave but suddenly stopped and then went running through the bush and thorns, and all over the place. In great haste they arrived back in the village, bumping with the coffin against the doors of houses, where the owner of each house had to throw either a handkerchief or piece of cloth onto the coffin. This lasted till late at night. . . . I cannot describe how horrifying I found these activities.[13]**

With Abini's hair-and-nail packet, the interrogation focused less on the past than on the future (though there was undoubtedly some discussion of why the *gaán óbia*s had failed them, permitting the Matawais to slay Abini).[14] Should they pursue Musinga, seeking vengeance but risking further bloodshed, or should they make peace and present a united front against the whites? And, most important, who should succeed Abini, receiving his staff of office, his stool, his authority? During the course of several days' interrogation, under the guidance of Abini's spirit, a political compromise seems to have been reached: Alabi, his favorite son and close companion, would succeed him as village captain, but a decision about revenge on Musinga as well as the choice of a new tribal chief would be delayed.[15]

The selection of Alabi was unusual—but so were the circumstances. By mid-eighteenth century, Saramaka succession had already taken on its present matrilineal cast.[16] Normally, a younger brother or a sister's son succeeded a deceased captain. But in this case a unique constellation of pressures made Alabi's selection appropriate. First, Abini, though a member of the Matjau clan, had been living for years with his wife's people, the Awanas, and functioning as their village headman. (At the Peace of 1762, the Matjaus had received two other captain's staffs, while the Awanas received none at all, except for that of their affine Abini.) So, by the appointment of a son instead of the more usual sister's son, the Awanas effectively held on to this staff, making it their permanent possession. Second, the elderly Yaya, Abini's mother and the most powerful of living Matjau women, had herself raised Alabi during his boyhood. As the medium for the forest spirit Wamba, who had already protected the Matjaus for some eighty years, Yaya's explicit wishes that Alabi succeed her son must have effectively quelled nascent Matjau jealousy. And third, Alabi—who had accompanied his father throughout the peace negotiations of the late 1750s and early 1760s and had been his closest aide on the side of maintaining solidary relations with the government and the Moravians right up till the end—was uniquely placed to carry forward his father's mediating role. "The only objection," as Brother Dehne wrote in 1767, "might be that he is too young." Saramakas temporized: they accepted the spirit's designation of Alabi as the successor to Abini's office of captain (village headman), but they did nothing for the moment about the issue of his successor as tribal chief.

Having dealt, at least partially, with the business of choosing Abini's successor, the captains and elders dispersed to their villages to await further developments. Meanwhile, under the care of Yaya and her Matjau kinfolk, Abini's widow Akoomi—hemmed in by numerous ritual prescriptions and prohibitions—was taken from Sentea to Baakawata to serve out her mourning period there; she would be permitted to emerge only after the "second funeral," many months later.[17] The same Matjau delegation taking Akoomi to Baakawata also carried the relics of her dead husband, Abini's hair-and-nail packet, which they would hang from the beams of one of Abini's houses there until the "second funeral," after first removing the whole woven-leaf front of the house, thereby transforming it into a *kèê-ósu* ("house of wails," or "house of death").[18]

In the village of Sentea, finally quiet after months of turmoil, Alabi and his close male kin began preparing to voyage to Paramaribo to meet with government officials, so that he could receive official recognition as captain in Abini's stead. A few weeks before, at his mother's behest, he had formally been given the symbols of office that Dörig had intended for the late Abini—a "fancy hat, ceremonial gorget, and saber and scabbard."[19] Now, for a full week, each man washed in herbal baths, avoided contact with women, and otherwise prepared for the always dangerous visit to whitefolks' territory as his "mothers' brothers" and "fathers" had taught him. For their protection, Alabi and his brothers called on the Matjau and Awana *obia*s that had carried their kinfolk through decades of warfare—Afiima, Masa Lamba, Akwadja, and Madanfo.[20]

Alabi and his eight companions (accompanied by Brother Dehne on their downstream trip) spent about two weeks in Paramaribo, and another four traveling the river. During this June visit, Alabi was duly recognized by the colonial authorities as his father's rightful successor as village captain, and he received as well permission—required by the 1762 treaty—to put into action his plan to move his people down below some of the fiercest rapids, closer to the whites and farther from his father's old political rival Samsam, who was now also at loggerheads with him. In Paramaribo, Alabi did everything he could to please and flatter the whites, as he had already been doing in Sentea, following in the footsteps of his father, who—in the words of Brother Stoll—"had always showed great kindness and love for us."

> **Old Abini's son and his family—in all nine negroes—have come here [to Paramaribo] to seek permission from the authorities to take over his father's position as captain. Nothing was more painful to me [a newcomer in Suriname] than not to be able to speak to them.**

> **The eldest son of Abini . . . is a reasonable man who is loved by all. . . . He calls himself Arrabini [Alabi] and loves us dearly. He has also given a favorable report about us [Moravians] which has truly amazed the Government authorities here.**

Alabi, in his attempt to please, had also engaged in some wishful thinking, telling the Moravians in Paramaribo that his mother—Akoomi, the priestess of Madanfo and a powerful opponent of Christianity—especially wanted some female missionaries to come live with her.

But his major personal concern, while in Paramaribo and throughout this period, was what posture to adopt toward his father's killer, Musinga, the peace-breaker. Though the whites at this time above all wanted peace, Alabi felt that Musinga deserved double punish-

1. Missionairs   2. Freÿneger.

Saramakas visiting the Moravians in Paramaribo. Note the key, apparently considered necessary to avoid any possibility of confusion (Riemer 1801, 97).

ment—first, for breaking the treaty, and then for murdering his father. The governor of Suriname summed up the information reaching him, via the Court of Policy, in a letter to the directors of the Society of Suriname in Amsterdam:

> *There seems to be a serious conflict going on between him [Alabi] and those allied with Samsam, as these latter do not seem eager to avenge the death of Abini and pursue Musinga.*

Having returned from Paramaribo in mid-July, Alabi seems to have taken a private and radical decision—he would prepare himself with Madanfo *obia* and avenge his father himself. In 1978, Awana captain Gome recounted this two-hundred-year-old event:

> *The others didn't want him to [seek vengeance]. So he left secretly and prepared his* obia *until it was just right. Madanfo. He came right down to here [Tutú Creek]. Right here, where you see the church building [today], he made a shed. That's what my mother's brother told me. Alabi was alone. The* obia *had a rule: no one else could be there [while he washed in it]. He made his shed and a ritual enclosure. Then he sought the necessary leaves. And he washed in them! He washed and washed. When he went to get water at the river, no one was allowed to see him— that was the rule of the* obia. *Women couldn't be anywhere near by. But he saw that canoes were passing by on the river, so he left there. And he went to a place a bit inland from here called Lánga Amaná. There he could get water from a creek and people would not be able to see him.*

In August 1767, the Moravians reported that Alabi and some close family went to Tutu Creek "where they are felling trees and brush" in preparation for a new settlement there.[21] It was during this time, unbeknownst to the missionaries, that Alabi was preparing himself for battle, convinced that Madanfo would permit him to avenge his father's death and bring Musinga's people back into peace with the whites.

The older Saramaka chiefs had become increasingly concerned about Alabi's behavior. Samsam and Kwaku Etja, who had been great warriors and were now the two most powerful Saramaka captains, had spent the months between the departure of Dörig's abortive expedition and Alabi's quiet leaving for Langa Amana in a series of delicate negotiations. With the whites, they had tried to appear faithful and conciliatory, promising to try to persuade Musinga to return the one hundred fifty slaves he had captured and to accept once more the terms of the 1762 Peace. Toward Musinga, they seem to have felt considerable solidarity and sympathy, and they tried to help him figure out how to get the most from the whites while giving up as little as possible. Throughout, they petitioned the whites for more time to work out a quiet solution, all the while continuing to shield Musinga

The Whole Land Shook   93

from possible white vengeance. The persistent rumors that Alabi was
ready to go fight Musinga threatened Samsam's and Kwaku Etja's
developing plans. And they were coming to feel that Alabi's generalized zeal to please the whites had, somehow, to be curbed. The old
chiefs palavered and came to a decision, and a delegation was dispatched to intercept Alabi at his ritual shed at Langa Amana.

Six men of the Dombi clan, including their chief Dondo Kasa,[22]
accompanied by the Nasi chiefs Kwaku Etja and Kwaku Kwadjani,
found Alabi at Langa Amana preparing himself with Madanfo, to do
battle with the Matawais.

> They called out to him: "Panto! Alabi!" He answered. They
> said, "Your father's death hurt us all. He did not go to
> Matawai with an evil heart. Yet they killed him, treach-
> erously. The Matawais remain at war [with the whites]. Now
> you intend to go do battle. They've already killed one [of
> our leaders]. And they would kill more. They would best you
> if you went. So, on behalf of all the people, we have come
> to take you away." And together they brought him to a cer-
> tain place and "sat him down."

The details of this "sitting down" are today told by Saramakas in a
series of related images, involving three lines of political influence.
The powerful Nasi clan possessed a special jacket that they had
obtained from the whites during the 1740s under somewhat obscure
circumstances, but which was widely understood as a symbol of pan-
tribal authority. The small village led by Alúbutu (later to become the
Kwama clan) possessed a ceremonial stool given them some fifteen
years before by the great Matjau war leader and unofficial tribal chief
Ayako, after Alubutu had saved his life. And the Matjaus, who had
been the politically preeminent clan throughout the Peace-making, of
course had the staff and other symbols of office that had belonged to
their own man, Abini. All of these were now brought to bear in pleading formally with Alabi, to prevent him from reopening the war with
Musinga.

Together, near Tutu Creek in September of 1767, Saramaka leaders
who had fought in the wars and some of whom were old enough to
be Alabi's grandfather made him an offer he could not refuse: to
become tribal chief when he truly came of age, that is, when the
office *next* became vacant—after a chief who they would soon designate had himself died. Alabi is reported to have wept copiously, as is
appropriate for a newly designated officeholder and, in the end, to
have accepted. The future tribal chief—he in fact acceded to that
office in 1783—was now but twenty-three years old. The senior chiefs
had bought considerable time to pursue their own policies.[23]

Alabi seems for a time to have turned inward, choosing largely to
ignore the ongoing political maneuvers of the older chiefs in regard to
Musinga and the colonial government. During the final months of
1767 and the early part of the new year, his main preoccupation was

the imminent move of his people from Sentea to a new village at Kwama ("Bamboo") Creek. In the years following the Peace, Saramaka villages moved frequently—perhaps every five or six years on average. The overall flow was in a downstream direction now that the wars were finally over, in order to make transportation to the city less onerous. But individual village moves—which meant the construction of new houses and the clearing of new gardens—were usually motivated by collective crisis, most often repeated sickness and death. As one of the missionaries wrote,

> **Should two or three people die in quick succession, they immediately leave the place even if the land they have been using is [still] fertile, because they believe that the god-who-owns-the-land is angry and has killed them.**[24]

Abini's killing and its attendant supernatural consequences would probably have been sufficient to cause the breakup of Sentea, but political tensions—the wish of individual captains, such as the Dombi leader Dondo Kasa, to have a village of their own—seem also to have played a part. Alabi took an active role in constructing the new village at Kwama Creek (often called by Saramakas Fínu Kwamá ["Thin Bamboo"]; see map 3), and by February 1768, Sentea was abandoned, except for "four old negroes" and the missionaries, who stuck it out for another year, teaching the several boys who had been brought to them for schooling, before finally joining the others at Kwama in the spring of 1769.[25]

During this period, these schoolboys had been—with the exception of Alabi—the missionaries' main contact with the Saramakas who surrounded them. Alabi's sister's son Skipio, the first of the Moravians' pupils, was soon joined by two others.

> **On the 21st of June [1768] while we were picking coffee, two boys, one of whom was called Grego, came to us from the neighboring village and spoke to us of a great fright they had experienced the previous night. When we asked why they had been so afraid, they answered that the elders had told them that a Gado [probably a snake or jaguar god] wanted to kill them all. Moreover, this animal had actually entered their homes that night in order to get chickens, and all of the people had screamed. When they heard the screaming, they thought that the Gado had come to kill them. We told them that God, who had created us and them and all mankind, loved them and wanted to save them, and that they must pray and promise Him to live in His way. Yes, we told them, He would take them into his arms and make them safe from all harm. When they heard this, they became happy and made marvelous gestures with their hands and wanted to begin to pray in their own manner. We told them, however, that they should pray in another way that would bring them greater happiness. We told them that if they would come**

this evening, we would show them how to pray. They really did come, and we told them more of our beloved Savior and His love for them and for all mankind. On the 23rd, the two boys came again and begged us to pray with them. We prayed on our knees both for them and for the entire [Saramaka] people.

Although one of these new boys never came back "because his mother did not allow him to come to us anymore," Skipio and Grego stayed on. Missionary and Saramaka priorities, however, remained at odds.

On the 28th [June 1768], we accepted Grego for instruction in reading and writing, for which he showed great desire. Although he does not show much talent for this, we can take the opportunity to teach him about our Savior, which is, after all, our real purpose here.[26] His aunt is the great priestess of the idol, yet she presents no obstacles to his instruction. On July 2, we had a blessed discussion with Skipio and Grego about the battle in Gethsemane. The former was moved to tears.

Saramaka men, particularly important men, continued to present their boys for instruction, convinced that reading and writing were key tools for successful interaction with whites on the coast.

On the 3rd [July 1768], a negro brought his son Witta and asked us to instruct him. Captain Antama has asked that we do the same, and we took the boy willingly to see if the Dear Savior will not transform one or another of these lads into a payment for His suffering. On the 4th, another lad came whose name was Thoni, and he asked us if we would instruct him. We told him that we indeed wished to take him on but that he would first have to speak with his parents and have them bring him here and promise that they would not be an obstacle to his learning. . . . On the 5th, his eldest brother brought him back, in the name of his parents who were unable to come themselves, and he promised us all of the above. On the 9th, the stepson of Captain Kwaku [Etja] was brought and we were asked to teach him. We took him on without any difficulty because it was promised that he could remain with us. . . . We have now taken on five children for schooling, at the request of their parents, who have all promised that they will not place obstacles in their path. . . . There are two among the five [Skipio and Grego] who are not insensitive when one tells them about the Dear Savior. . . . On 2 August, another father brought his son to us for schooling . . . and on 10 August, still another was brought to us.

Since the Saramakas expected schooling, not proselytization, it is not surprising that these "agreements" and "promises" were not kept, once the exclusivistic tone of Moravian "education" became clearer.

Letter written in Dutch, in his own hand, by Étja's stepson, one of the Moravians' pupils. The text reads, *"My father Itja requests for himself four guns one jar cooking oil four jugs powder four lengths of linen four jars rum three pairs earrings two barrels of salt some machetes some hoes[.] Johannes [Alabi] arrived on 30 December 1768 at the plantation [village of] Kwama. [signed at] dossukriki 10 January 1769 [by] Gemmis, the son of Itja"* (Hof 79).

For example, the recently arrived Brother Kersten reported in 1770 how Skipio

> was called by his father early in the morning to be smeared with Obia, because he was going with him to Paramaribo. He did not want to have this done to him, but out of fealty to his father nevertheless did so. However, immediately afterward, he went to the stream to wash it all off.[27] On the 3rd, Grego was also supposed to undergo the Obia, but he categorically refused.[28]

As we shall see, such temptations for the (potential) Christians to "backslide," often in the wake of tremendous family pressure expressed through religious sanctions, were very great, and they form a recurrent theme in the missionary accounts.

But, in general, the Moravians remained optimistic about their small group of schoolboys, reporting continued "progress."

> During the last few days [September 1768] Skipio developed a large hole on his foot, and he wrote the following on his writing tablet: "Jesus, meki mi foette kom boen!" which means "Jesus, make my foot be healed again."

A few days later, Brother Stoll, again writing of Skipio, reported that

> one of the boys with whom we have begun a school has become a real convert. My daily wish and prayer is: Oh Dear Savior, see to it that you open their hearts, and have mercy for them as you do for all mankind. . . . The students are a diligent lot and they are learning to read and write, because we are treating them with love and gentleness, so that they trust us and love us as well. The old people, namely their parents, realize that their sons are happy and are glad they are learning so well, but as far as they are concerned, it does not occur to them that they too should be converted. I would like to have a few conversations about this with them.

And four months later, in 1769, Brother Stoll expressed his ultimate hopes concerning the boys:

> Oh how happy we will be if one or two of them will truly enjoy the life given us by Jesus' death and actually become baptized. It is to be sure a horrible race but the blood of Jesus also screams out for mercy for them. . . . And our Creator loves them and would like to take them in His arms so that they can enjoy eternal bliss. We have one lad [Skipio] who is with us day and night, and he even attends the morning and afternoon services with us. It is, to be sure, a good sign that his parents have allowed us to take full responsibility for him.

The schoolboys represented the sole bright spot in what had otherwise been a very trying period of adjustment for the Moravians.

> Their situation was often rendered extremely unpleasant by the
> wild and rude behaviour of the inhabitants, who frequently
> spent whole weeks in rioting and drunkenness, especially when
> there was a sacrificial feast or a funeral.

In mid-1767, Brother Stoll complained that

> it brings me great pain that I cannot make the Savior's presence
> more meaningful to these poor people. . . . Until now, they have
> not expressed any longing to become aware of their Creator or to
> have their souls saved. . . . But I have the blessed faith that . . .
> the Holy Ghost will have mercy on them and take them from
> out their Darkness and make them Children of Light. Only then
> will the external freedom that they abuse through many thou-
> sands of superstitious things come to its proper exercise.

Brother Nitschmann, who arrived in Saramaka at the end of 1767, also
underlined the lack of spiritual development he found among his
hosts.

> They are truly idolatrous in their ways, in fact it seems to be
> ever-increasing. But we shall await with patience the proper
> hour to reveal to them the teachings of the Savior. . . . I sustain
> myself meanwhile through the teachings of the Lord and by his
> Bloody Reconciliation.

And in their 1767 year-end report, the missionaries noted that

> our situation is even more dangerous than we are aware of; but
> we depend on Him, who is the sure defence of his servants, and
> is mightier than all. If it please him, we are willing to make a
> sacrifice.

In their daily interactions with Saramakas, the missionaries were
gradually realizing that they confronted a whole new moral system.
And for them this confrontation was both confusing and painful. In
February 1768,

> Brother Rudolph [Stoll] went to Samsam, who had asked him
> several times to come, to read him the letters from his son [an
> official "hostage" in Paramaribo], but also because we had some
> baggage that had remained at Samsam's village and that needed
> to be brought to us. When he arrived there, Rudolph saw that
> our trunks had been broken into and most of the contents re-
> moved, but he remained silent about it. While he was reading
> the letters out loud, Samsam would often take his hands and
> press them against his breast as a sign of happiness. And he
> would say, "You speak well with us." Brother Rudolph replied,
> "We love you and all the other negroes. And the Brethren who
> remain in Europe have written to greet you and send you their
> love, too." Samsam replied "Gran Danki" [thank you] and

added, "Well, if they love me as much as you say, why don't they send me a fine musket so I can see their love for myself?"

Samsam was not simply "puttin' on ol' massa" (as U.S. slaves glossed this form of wit). In Saramaka ideology, love and material generosity went hand in hand, and the act of not-sharing demarcated clear social boundaries. Differing missionary and Saramaka notions regarding property and its role in social relations served as a privileged symbolic idiom in the negotiation of power throughout the history of the mission.

A few months later,

on the 19th [July 1768], the above-mentioned negro brought our remaining cargo from the city, and we asked him what we could pay him for his efforts. We offered him gunpowder, and re-minded him that he knew full well that we did not engage in productive work. Then we offered him a double salary. But he would have none of this, and said spitefully only that he would return the next day to take by force whatever he desired. We answered, "If you attempt this, we will not be able to prevent it. But God in heaven, who sees all, will find you out." On the 20th, he came very early in the morning and, though we tried to appeal to his kindness, nothing would work. He took his ma-chete and struck the little chest he had brought and took what-ever he wanted. Then he left us, showing off the things he had taken to four old negroes who dared not say a word.[29]

And a month later,

Thoni [one of the schoolboys] asked us for permission to accom-pany his father to Paramaribo, to which we assented. When we told the other boys that Thoni was going to the city, they were very pleased. But when we asked them the cause of their happi-ness, they said that he had told them to steal and had secretly taken away various things himself.

As we know from countless examples elsewhere in plantation Amer-ica, slaves—as whitefolks' property—themselves conceptualized other of massa's belongings as fair game. One could "steal" from a fellow slave but only "take" from a white. And today in Saramaka, older people, especially, still speak in such terms. The eighteenth-century missionaries, with experience, not only learned to accept the existence of this "other" moral system but even, at times, tried to work within it, drawing further fine distinctions.

On the 2nd of June [1782], we were the victims of a robbery for the first time since being here [in the village of Bambey]. As it turned out, we received the stolen goods back from the woman who had done it. The [Christian] villagers were of the opinion that we should punish her. For, even though it was not consid-

View of the Town of PARAMARIBO, with the Road & Shipping, from the opposite Shore.

London Published Dec.r 1 1794 by J. Johnson, S.t Paul's Church Yard.

**ered a sin for them to steal from whites, it was not good to take
something from us.**[30]

Alabi spent the whole second half of 1768 in Paramaribo, along
with a number of Saramakas of different clans. Most were village
chiefs or other important men, trying to cajole whitefolks' goods from
the government—in particular, extra gunpowder and muskets. Alabi
himself seems to have been largely occupied with assembling the
diverse Western goods that would be expended early the next year
for his father's "second funeral"—traditionally the largest kind of public event in Saramaka life.[31] He and the others had brought newly
made canoes, as well as all sorts of garden produce (rice, peanuts,
cacao) and processed foods (cassava cakes, peanut butter, dried fish
and game) to sell or barter for gunpowder, flints, cloth, pots, tools,
rum, molasses, and other Western products.

After years of war in the forest, Saramaka men found the attrac-
tions of a stay in Paramaribo exciting enough to outweigh the risks it
entailed. They slung their hammocks, in large groups, either in government sheds near the fort or with freedmen friends and relatives
(carpenters, blacksmiths, or shoemakers) on the outskirts of town.
With slavery still in full swing, they could parade their hard-earned
freedom, always carrying their staffs of office or cardboard passes
from the postholder to prove their freedom, and enjoy some of the
pleasures of the town—indulging in Western foods and drink, watching the local militia go through its drills, and ogling the opulence of the
town-dwelling whites. Alabi's eyes would have framed many of the
same scenes witnessed five years later by that other visitor to Paramaribo, John Gabriel Stedman, though their meanings to the two
men would have been worlds apart: slaves being marched off the
ships to be sold at market, planters and their entourage arriving for
lavish balls and entertainments at sumptuous townhouses, and gruesome public tortures and executions in the city square.[32]

The Saramakas also got into minor scrapes with town dwellers—
accusations of stealing by slaves, altercations with shopkeepers. Especially in the evenings, Paramaribo took on the look of a brawling,
cosmopolitan port. As Stedman described one contemporary incident,

a general hub bub took place [and] . . . A Mob now gathered and a
riot ensued, before Mr. Hardegens Tavern at the Waterside while
hats wigs. bottles and Glasses flew out at his Window[.] the Mag-
istrates were next sent for to no purpose and the fighting continued in the Street till 10 OClock at night, when I with my friends

"View of the Town of PARAMARIBO, with the Road & Shipping, from the opposite
Shore" (Stedman 1988, 235). The drawing on which this engraving is modeled
was made less than a decade after Alábi's 1768 visit. *Facing page.*

fairly keep'd the field, having knocked down several Sailors, planters, Jews, and Overseers and lost one of my Pistoles which I
threw after the rabble in my Passion . . . after which we all sat
down and drank away the night till the Sun rose the next morning.

And during this 1768 visit, Alabi's famous "grandfather" Adjagbo
(soon to become a Matjau captain) tangled with a white soldier: a
certain Ensign Verster de Balbian, later judged to have been under the
influence of drink, shot and wounded Adjagbo, was arrested and
required to pay damages to the Saramaka, and was then stationed to
a "distant post."

By December, Alabi and his kinsmen had finished getting together
the funeral goods and, accompanied by his brother, the official "hostage" Jan Abini, who was reluctantly permitted to return to Saramaka
for his father's "second funeral," set out for home.

After a two-week-long canoe trip, running the always dangerous
gauntlet of plantations along the Suriname River, Alabi arrived in
Kwama on 30 December and visited Sentea on New Year's Eve—in
time to celebrate with the missionaries and, apparently, just in time to
save the Brethren Stoll and Nitschmann from possible mischief.
Christmas and New Year's were the only calendrical celebrations observed by eighteenth-century Saramakas—Christmas as a time when
all sorts of evil spirits were abroad, New Year's as a time of drunken
festivity and thanksgiving.[33]

This year, in the absence of their protector Alabi, these holidays
had brought the missionaries threats and fright. Saramakas from
Kwama and nearby villages had given their hostilities free rein.

**On the 28th of December an old negro who had always been
very friendly to us warned us that we should not so much as step
out of our door that evening, even if we were called. And if we
did step out, we should do so only with a loaded musket. Apparently there was more danger than we knew. . . . On the 29th,
another negro came to us and warned us to be careful, and he
added that we did not realize what might happen.**

But Alabi's arrival was opportune, and no violence occurred.

Meanwhile, in the giant Matjau village along Baakawata Creek, a
long day's walk from the Sentea-Kwama region, New Year's found
Abini's matrilineal kinfolk busy with their own preparations for his final
celebration, his "second funeral" (called by Saramakas *uwíi limbá*
["hair purification"] and *adjú paayá* ["ghost chasing"]). Adjagbo, Alabi's

"Sea Captains Carousing in Surinam," painted in 1758 by John Greenwood, an
American who spent nearly six years in Suriname (St. Louis Art Museum).
Facing page.

"grandfather," had already returned from the city with a canoe filled with Western goods for the ceremony and, with the help of *obia* performed by Kungooka of Daume, had recovered from the gunshot wound he had suffered there. When word reached them that Alabi and his brother Jan, the hostage, had finally arrived in Kwama, the Matjau captains decided the time had come to consult Abini's hair and nails to set a general date for the second funeral. Abini's spirit agreed that it was time for the young men of the village to go hunting *"a duumi matu,"* as had been done by Alabi and his friends for the food offering two years earlier at Sentea. And after they had spent a week of hunting and fishing in the wilderness upstream, the successful youths were welcomed back by the whole village of Baakawata, who helped unload the quantities of dried meat, fish, and fowl for the coming feast. That evening, the elders again raised the hair-and-nail packet on a paddle to consult Abini's spirit and set a final date for the ceremony—a week hence. Four active men were chosen as "over-seers" for the ceremony (as Saramakas say that nothing can get accomplished without someone officially taking charge), and they quickly sent messengers from village to village, by footpath and ca-noe, to alert the whole Saramaka world that their chief was finally and fully to be ushered into the world of the ancestors.

Almost precisely two centuries afterward, I overheard a Saramaka man, eagerly anticipating arriving in a village for a "second funeral," say joyfully to another, "We Saramakas have two 'gods' [supreme pleasures]: nubile women and second funerals!" And, judging from everything I have been able to learn about eighteenth-century Sara-maka, this *bon mot* would have been equally apt at that time. From all over Saramaka, men and women converged on Baakawata, having paddled as far as the path on the Gaanlio that gave access, after a half-day's walk, to the village itself.

On the first day of the ceremony, the men of Baakawata arose at cock's crow to cut sugar cane in their gardens, which they carried back to the village, where Alabi and his brothers joined them in crush-ing it in a hand-mill, amidst lively banter and joking—setting aside the juice and then further mashing the canes in large mortars. In a giant pot, they boiled the crushed canes, adding the juice and some river water until they agreed, after lively disputation, that the taste was just right for *apínkusu,* one of the characteristic drinks of "second fu-nerals," much appreciated by the ancestors. Finally, they poured the whole potful through a sieve into an old canoe—now become the "cane boat"—commandeered and hauled ashore near the council house for the occasion.

Meanwhile, a group of women—Yaya, Abini's sisters and daugh-ters, and other close relatives—busied themselves with great pots in an open shed, cooking up quantities of *madjáma wáta*—the meat, fish, and fowl broths that every visitor to the second funeral would have at least to taste that evening. And they collected and stacked high the cassava cakes that they had baked on the previous days and that formed the obligatory accompaniment to this special dish.

The four overseers directed the cleaning of the whole village, with special attention lavished on the paths leading into Baakawata from the river and the forest, which were first widened by men wielding machetes and then hoed and swept by women. The *azang*-palm barriers under which all visitors walk were replaced by new green fronds, and the cane trash left over from the sieving process was strewn in a line underneath, creating a further symbolic frontier to the village. And all through the day, from all over Saramaka, groups large and small arrived in Baakawata, carrying presents and slinging their hammocks with friends and relatives in the village.

In mid-afternoon, the purification process was again taken up. While most of the village relaxed, a small group of elders ceremoniously lifted Abini's hair-and-nails packet down from its perch and carried it to a hastily dug shallow grave, alongside the path to the Baakawata cemetery, where they quietly buried it, with no coffin and little comment. Upon their return, and on the orders of the four overseers, three boys—sixteen or seventeen years old—set off briskly through the village in single file, each bearing on his head an earthenware pot filled with white *obia* solution from which, with a branch of a medicine plant, he sprinkled a few drops on the front of each house as he strode by, purifying the whole community from the pollution caused by Abini's death. When they had finished their rounds, just after sunset, with the western sky still faintly glowing pink, village elders and important visitors, stools in hand, gathered in front of Abini's house for the opening libations of the great feast.

For a good fifteen minutes Mbutí, the senior Matjau captain, dribbled first water, then *apinkusu,* and finally white rum from a calabash onto the ground, as he spoke to Abini and to literally scores of other ancestors by name, inviting them to come celebrate with the living and to protect them from danger for the duration. Once all had solemnly clapped their hands and chanted the obligatory "great thanks," a ragged line of some fifty younger men, standing to one side and facing west, pointed their muskets skyward and fired an uneven barrage of salutes, the flashes from their powder intermittently lighting up the gathering darkness, while Akoomi and other close female relatives, sitting nearby, added shrieks of mourning to the tumult. As soon as the last of the several hundred salutes was fired, the *papa* musicians set to work just outside Abini's house, facing west, with an energetic ten-minute burst of drumming and singing to *púu tjína* ("remove the prohibition").[34] With everyone's appetite whetted for more, they abruptly stopped and pulled their drums partway into the house, as the hundred or so spectators slowly dispersed to their houses or wandered around the village.

Torches illuminated the scene; the atmosphere was festive. Men strolled about in their finest—special double-width breechcloths, either bare tops, fancy capes, or storebought European nightshirts, and cloth or knitted caps. A few sported "whitefolks' hats" from Paramaribo, and all had earrings, finger rings, and *obia* jewelry (from jaguar-tooth or brass-blade necklaces to iron rings for their biceps). Most carried, in addition, shiny machetes or sabers, deerskin over-the-shoulder hunting sacks, and umbrellas or carved staffs of office. Women complemented their finest skirts and waist ties with many sorts of beaded jewelry, gold and silver earrings, and fancy hairdos, and they took special pleasure in what one missionary dourly described as "showing off in dress-up clothes." Young teenage girls, meanwhile, showed themselves off by sporting only an Amerindian-style *koyó,* "a cloth two hands wide with which girls cover themselves [in front]."[35] The aroma of perfume, made from palm oil and other forest ingredients, pervaded the air. In the open doorway of Abini's house (from which the whole front had been removed soon after his death), small boys beat on the idle drums, while some men sat by torchlight playing *adjíbóto,* a game brought by their African foreparents and closely associated with funerals.[36] As the crowds of visitors wandered about Baakawata, greeting, visiting, and chatting, local women made the rounds bearing steaming bowls of *madjama wata* and pieces of cassava cake, which people consumed on the spot.

As the cool of the night set in, around 9 or 10 P.M., young girls, soon joined by their older sisters, began "playing" informally in the open area before Abini's house—singing, dancing, handclapping—as visitors and villagers, hearing the music, drifted over to join them. Before long, more than five hundred people had formed a rough circle, into which first one and then another performer jumped for a few moments of flashy footwork or solo singing, as the crowd chorused the response. Youths manned the drums and, in the course of the next few hours, no kind of current secular music was ignored. Large numbers joined in dancing to the popular *adunké* and *luango* songs; specialists did acrobatic stilt and pole dancing, to the appreciative hoots and handclapping of the crowd; singers who for months had been spontaneously composing songs while in their ricefields or paddling the river now tried them out in public; dancers who had been practicing in private now had the crowd eating out of their hands with stylized imitations of a hummingbird sucking pollen or an anteater raiding a nest. The four overseers, each with a paddle in hand as sign of authority, tried vainly to hold the crowd back as it pressed in for a better view. Intermittent musket salutes added to the commotion. And periodically, one of the overseers would enter the ring to scold the performers and spectators good-humoredly, shouting out to one and all that the elders had poured a really big libation and had invited all the ancestors to attend: "Do you think this is a 'play' for just anyone? You'd better heat it up, and fast!" And the crowd responded with ever-hotter music and dancing. For much of the night, another overseer moved through the crowd passing around calabashes of sweet *apinkusu* from the nearby "cane boat." Meanwhile, couples slipped off into the darkness of the largely abandoned areas of the village; second funerals were a favorite opportunity to meet lovers.

An hour or two past midnight, as the play finally began to cool down, the eight or ten Matjau-clan *papa* specialists made their appearance—middle-aged and older men, easily Abini's contemporaries, with their heads tied with triangular cloths. They stoked up the ritual fire that burned just before Abini's doorway and soon were deep into *papa*, the haunting but energized Saramaka music of death that they played inside Abini's house—the lead drummer on a "long drum" (played horizontally, with two hands, between the legs), a second on a small constant-rhythm drum, played with one stick and one hand, and a third striking a hoe blade with the blade of an old knife.[37] While most villagers returned to their hammocks to catch a few hours' sleep, the *papa* men drummed, sang, and drank the night away, imbibing large quantities of *apinkusu* and white rum and inhaling large quantities of liquid snuff,[38] their words evoking people, battles, and domestic incidents of years long since gone by. Soloists and chorus interwove their melodies subtly but with vigor, in syncopated alternation; for many songs, the solos were taken first by one, then another singer. As each man stepped forward almost to belt out his part, he gestured with clenched fists, in a punching motion, to accentuate his words. For *papa* aficionados, this was the ultimate: highly spirited but esoteric music, the meaning known only to initiates, being hurled right into the face of Death.

Well before cock's crow, not long after the *papa* men had settled down to work, more than a dozen local women had dragged their mortars into a space near the council house and began pounding the large quantities of rice needed for the morning's *nyanyantue*—the large food offering for Abini and the ancestors. Lying in their hammocks, villagers and visitors now heard the complex, fluid rhythms of the *papa* drums joined by the steady thumping of the women's pestles. Soon after cock's crow, the drummers switched to *adugbá,* the second of the three rhythms of second funerals, which they would continue till after dawn. The women pounded on, three pestles to a mortar, urging each other on. Until the rice was fully hulled, the next stage of the ceremony could not begin.

As the sky began to lighten, the women finished their task, and people throughout Baakawata arose from their hammocks and made their way to the river for morning ablutions. Once the sun rose, it was time to "bring the play outdoors," and the *papa* men played the special song that signals the transition. Pulling their drums out in front of the house, and taking a bit of a mixture of white clay and rice, provided by the women, to dab between their first and second toes as protection, the *papa* men prepared to play *adju*—the final and wildest part of the night's ceremony, in which Abini's ghost, and every other imaginable kind of evil, would be chased forever from the village, in a climactic *sangaa*.[39] With the addition of an *apinti* drum to the battery,

Twentieth-century Alúku Maroon drummers at a funeral (Hurault 1970, 42).

for the *adju* leader to play, the new rhythms began, as people from all over the village converged once more on the house of death. Abini's kinswomen from Baakawata set down a basket in front of each *papa* man, while they played, and then filled them with the "payment" for their all-night services—raw coconuts, lengths of cloth, peanuts, dried fish, bundles of rice, hulled rice, bottles of palm oil, and special oval cassava cakes baked only for second funerals. As the play heated up once more, men stepped forward to pour rum down the throats of the sweating drummers, and women danced up to wipe their faces and chests with cloths.

Soon, from the edges of the village, through the narrow spaces between houses, scary-looking *adju* men appeared, dancing their way into the space before the drummers. White, red, and black dyes stain their faces and much of their bodies; many wear nothing more than a slim breechcloth; some have made obscene-looking diapers stained deep brown around the anus. They dance bent over, stalking, with sticks representing guns, mimicking wartime raiding parties hunting whitefolks, threat-dancing at the spectators who press around. Suddenly, other figures appear—horrifying *básikaánus*—masked creatures whose bodies are totally covered with cloth and leaves tied with vines, so that not an inch of skin is visible to attest that a human is inside. Many of their masks are carved from wood, painted red, black, and white, and decorated with jaguar skin; some are made from calabashes or gourds; many have grotesque protuberances; some smoke giant cigars. The dozen or so *basikaanus* and the similar number of *adju* men dance at each other in stylized postures, the former lurking and springing, the latter stalking them as if they were their prey. Women join the melee, as snake-god spirits come upon them. Some men, possessed by *komanti* warrior gods, begin to play with the fire in front of Abini's house.

The *adju* men become more violent, bursting through the crowd and returning moments later with "gifts" for the drummers: they drag in palm fronds, broken baskets, old umbrellas, whatever they can get their hands on in the village, creating a giant refuse pile. There are minor altercations, when people see their own possessions being dragged into the ring and try to wrestle them back from the *adju* men. A couple of masked figures begin to copulate wildly with two drums that are lying idle; some *adju* men pull them off and take over the game, and then mime buggering the *basikaanus*. Other *adju* men run into Abini's house and poke violently at the roof and walls with their sticks; one clambers up on top and actually jumps right through the roof. The crowd constantly shifts position as *adju* men and *basikaanus* run at them in one direction and then another. Possessed *komanti* men are the most violent of all, and the drummers play a few minutes of special *komanti* rhythms in their honor, as they grab at a drinking glass and chomp it, pick up burning sticks and rub them over their bodies, try to climb up thorn palms, and slash about with machetes. Other men chase them, trying to wrestle dangerous items from them, while at the same time calming their spirits. One *komanti* man stops the show for a moment by turning suddenly to confront a man trying to calm him. From somewhere, he produces an egg and, like a magician doing a parlor trick, shows how, by weighing it in his hand, he can tell whether it's cooked or raw. Possessed women, some with snake gods, others with the ghosts of ancestors in their heads, walk dreamily about, strewing white rice from calabashes; *komanti* men violently sprinkle rum and *keeti* all about. The drumming reaches a climax.

Three *adju* men dance into the center, each with a stem of bananas, which they slash at with a machete until the ground is strewn with the remains. Some possessed women throw rice chaff and stalks of rice all around, while others smash green calabashes on the ground—offerings to the usually invisible gods and spirits that they can now see. Likewise, possessed *komanti* men sprinkle rum and offer *apinkusu* trash to the spirit familiars now visible to them. The drums take up a final song, calling for the ritual cleansing of the area, and the crowd slowly disperses.

Three women from Abini's family each knock the back of a reed broom on the ground three times and then begin to sweep the dance area, carrying the refuse in palm-tree dustpans on their left shoulders to a special disposal place—the spot where the village dead are washed before being placed in a coffin. Likewise, two men carry the "cane boat" filled with the rest of the trash from the ceremony to the same place, but tilting it to the left, with all people present hurrying to be on the right as they pass. The *papa* men line up their drums and gong, and these are cleansed with rum. Finally, the leader of the *papa* men lines up all the sticks in the ritual fire with their burning ends to the east, and, as all present face west and cover their eyes with their hands, he douses the fire with a calabash of water. An elder steps forward and pours a libation in front of the fire: water, *apinkusu,* and then rum. Finally, a turtle is brought and butchered, some blood dripped on the ground as an offering, and its meat set back into its shell and left there. At long last, the *papa* men and the others who have been going nonstop for hours could relax. It was time to go to the river and bathe.

The evening's *nyanyantue,* held around sunset, was a family affair, in front of Abini's house. But many of the visitors who had celebrated all through the previous night were still in Baakawata, and they came to pay their respects. The feast was much like that in Sentea two years before, but this time, because of the crowd, three winnowing trays were placed on the banana leaves and, as was customary at second funerals, turtle meat was the central offering. The following morning, the same group joined Alabi's Baakawata relatives for a final libation in Abini's doorway: water, *apinkusu,* and rum to announce that the ceremony was over. Mbuti, the Matjau captain, also threatened Abini rhetorically, as he poured the drinks on the ground: "If people die, you're the one who'll be blamed! Doesn't the *gaama* have the final word in everything? Akoomi must live! All your kin must live! Please stand up tall to protect us." Then the captain took some pieces of cassava cake and dipped them into a calabash of hot chocolate (made from home-grown cacao and cane sugar)—one of Abini's favorite drinks—and laid them on the ground, begging the dead chief once more, with the crowd rhythmically clapping their approval, "Great Thanks."

For a week, Alabi and his relatives from elsewhere lingered in Baakawata, as young people continued the celebration each afternoon or evening, playing drums, singing, and dancing with whatever energies they could muster. And then, on the seventh day after the wild *adju paaya,* the chasing of the ghost, the play was literally *túè a wáta,* "thrown in the river." In the afternoon, "playmen" of all ages took the celebration around the village, first playing before a newly set ritual table in front of Abini's house (laden with hot chocolate, dried bread brought from the city, and rum), then stopping in front of the houses of the captains and other village elders for a few minutes of drumming, song, and dance. At each stop, the captive hosts offered soap, candles, beads, or other notions as "payment." And then, after *keeti* had been sprinkled on the shoulders of each of the young drummers, they carried the drums they had been using all week to the river, accompanied by a large crowd. Loaded into a canoe, the drummers played their way noisily to midstream, as the crowd shouted approval, and then violently rocked their own boat until it "sank," soaking them all. As the *deindein* drum, the smallest of the battery, floated out of the canoe, a man on shore "shot" it with a load of harmless powder. Salutes rang out all along the shore; women hooted their approval. And suddenly it was over. The drummers bailed out their canoe, rescued their drums, and returned to shore. And from Baakawata to the northernmost villages of Saramaka, far downstream, no one was allowed to use the river for the rest of the day.

By the next morning, the pollution that had lain so heavily on Baakawata (and the now-abandoned Sentea) since the death of *Gaama* Abini was finally raised. Alabi and his relatives could feel proud that they had succeeded, as the Saramaka dictum prescribes, in burying him "with joy" (*ku pizíi*). And the gods and *obia*s that had been placed in a state of dormancy for the interim could now be revived in full. Akoomi, after two difficult years of mourning, was able to accompany Alabi and his sisters back to Kwama, to take up a normal life once again.[40]

Soon after returning from the second funeral, Alabi turned his energies to helping the missionaries move to join him and his kinfolk at Kwama—building houses for them, helping them cut gardens, and so on. But the Moravians, despite their Panglossian outlook, continued to suffer seriously, with but little to show for their efforts. In October 1769, Brother and Sister Kersten arrived to join the Brethren Stoll and Nitschmann (Dehne having left the previous year for Europe, where he died). As Sister Kersten described their arrival, years later,

We set out [from Paramaribo] October 5th, and in a fortnight reached the place of our destination, after encountering much danger and fatigue. When we arrived within a few miles of the place, the negroes who traveled with us, fired their pieces to give notice of their arrival, the report of which soon brought a great number of people together, who welcomed us with hideous noises. Our sensations on this occasion cannot be described, for the power of darkness reigning among these heathen, oppressed our spirits beyond conception. When we entered the house, we found our two Brethren in a most pitiable condition. Brother Rudolph Stoll endeavored to come out to meet us, but fainted in the attempt. Yet he was so overjoyed to see us, that his fever left him. Brother Johann Nitschmann was quite lame, and departed to eternal rest some months after.

Her husband provided somewhat more detail.

On the 17th of October, both of us arrived in a very weak state. We quickly saw that we had come to a land in which suffering and misery were everywhere.... We found our two Brethren sick: Brother Joh. Nitschmann had a frighteningly bad foot, and Brother Rud. Stoll, who can truly be regarded as a martyr in regard to what he has suffered internally and externally in this land of misery, lay there with a malignant fever.... Thus we were to remain together until the end of October, when I came down with a horrible fever, accompanied by day after day of terrible vomiting. Then my dear wife also became ill with this awful sickness, which lasted twelve days before subsiding. I next came down with a terrible case of the white runs, accompanied by some painful attacks of side-pain and pain in my stomach. And my wife suffered during this period as well.... Our dear beloved Rudolph [Stoll] had a difficult time with us three sick ones.... Since the beginning of November, we have not had any healthy days.... Brother Nitschmann's foot is still very ugly and swollen; his ankle is so large that one cannot cover it with a whole outstretched hand. The ankle is still open and much putrid liquid runs from it, so that it is hard to be in his presence. However, the heel is healthy now, healed in the negro manner by applying dry powdered herbs, and Brother Rudolph hopes that the ankle can be cured likewise. He has been sitting for three full months now in great pain. Brother Rudolph, too, has gotten terrible pain in his feet from the little bugs called sandflies [chigoes]. One has to dig out twenty or more daily, and the wounds are filled with an awful noxious liquid.... All three of us have great difficulty getting as far as the kitchen because of the great pain. It is really terrible to see us in such a condition. None of the necessary work for planting our gardens can be done.... God help us!

Meanwhile, two years of negotiations involving the older Saramaka chiefs, Musinga, and the colonial government had reached a turning point. (Alabi was conspicuously absent from these affairs, which concerned his father's killers.) In the spring of 1769, just after Abini's second funeral, Postholder Dörig finally sealed a definitive peace treaty with Musinga, who turned over to the whites a couple of dozen of the escaped slaves he still held. The course of the negotiations had been tortuous.

The senior Saramaka captains, such as Samsam and Kwaku Etja, had posed throughout the period as the whitefolks' trusted allies, ostentatiously interceding with Musinga to persuade him (at least publicly) to agree to turn back his slaves. Only six months after Musinga's "raid," three old Matawais drank an oath with Samsam and a Matjau captain—and with Postholder's Assistant Hintze, who was cajoled into participating—swearing eternal peace between whites and Matawais, and the return of the runaway slaves. And a few months later, Musinga and his men again assured Hintze that they would return them all and proposed beginning at once with three slaves—at the same time asking the whitefolks for quantities of guns, powder, cloth for their wives, and other things to replace what had been ruined by the Dörig-Saramaka expedition against Matawai. The Saramaka chiefs joined their own urgent requests with those of Musinga: Samsam wanted various presents, as did Kwaku Etja, for their help in bringing Musinga around—guns, swords, fancy hats, and so on. The documentary record of these 1767 negotiations reveals the terrible strains between those turning back slaves and the victims; the grotesque jockeying for favor in the eyes of the whites by the various chiefs; the awful dependence of the chiefs on the whites for guns and powder; and, in their final laconic request upon finally turning in a handful of the Matawai slaves, the full horror of their situation: "All the captains of Saramacca and Suriname [i.e., Matawai and Saramaka] humbly request of Your Excellencies that none of the Para slaves be executed."

Within a year of Musinga's "raid" on Para, though the Matawais had turned back only a few of the one hundred fifty slaves they were harboring, they had managed—with the assistance of the Saramaka chiefs—to persuade the whites of their good intentions. During the following year, the Matawais informed Hintze that they had passed many of their slaves along to Samsam, to be turned in to the whites, and Kwaku Etja traveled to Paramaribo to assure the whites that they need not worry about receiving these same slaves: he, Etja, had already been given eight of them by Samsam and would turn them in shortly. With everything apparently calm, Dörig decided to visit the Matawai himself, and in April 1769, he officially renewed the Peace that had first been sealed in 1762. As part of this agreement, the Matawais turned over some thirty of their slaves directly to Dörig, who brought them to the city. And soon after, Musinga himself turned in another twelve slaves—the last record I have seen of a large-scale return.[41] The Moravians, who usually understood internal Saramaka politics only dimly, seem right on the mark about these mass slave returns (in which the very great majority of the newcomers were, nonetheless, kept secreted in Saramaka): "They only return those who are useless to them, and they keep the best ones for themselves. . . . It is a very strange type of peace, and the less said about it the better." (A nineteenth-century historian, basing his analysis on diverse documents, wrote more generally, "The Bushnegroes were willing to turn in [only] the wrongdoers, murderers, and sorcerers.")

Musinga's 1769 Peace served to shift the burden of returning the remaining one hundred or so Para slaves from the Matawais—who now claimed that they had given back all they still had in their possession—onto the other Saramakas, to whom the Matawais had in fact quietly transferred most of these liberated slaves during the previous two years. Henceforth, the Matawais tended to deal with the government autonomously, without the mediation of the Saramaka chiefs,

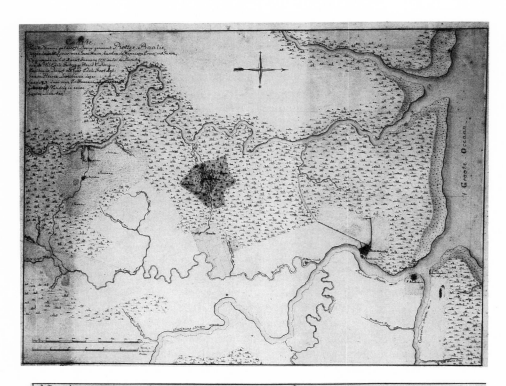

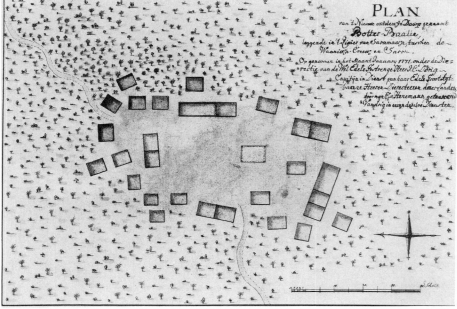

Map and Plan "of the Recently Discovered Village Named Botter-Baalie," by Christoph van Henemann (ARA, Leupe 2125, 2126). The relative locations of Paramaribo, Plantation Osembo, and Boterbalie (in the shaded area) are clearly visible on the upper map.

and after their separate Peace, they had their own official postholder. Indeed, by 1770, the Matawais had devised a strategy not otherwise used by Saramakas but to which they would resort repeatedly in the coming years: they became runaway slave-catchers themselves, discovering a "new" village of maroons and reporting it to the government, in return for material favors. The first such village that they found, on the Boterbalie Creek in Para, was only two hours from Plantation Osembo and had twenty solid houses plus "1 gado huis" (shrine). Dörig himself led the expedition that destroyed "Boterbalie," and he took along a cartographer, who drew several plans of its location. At Musinga's special request, two of the captured inhabitants—Quamina and Ula—were declared free. The court rewarded Dörig with a gratuity of two hundred florins.

But in spite of their apparent fidelity to the whites, the Matawai were, as usual, selective in turning in those Boterbalie people they had personally captured. As one Moravian noted,

> **Since they [the Matawais] had only recently made peace with the Europeans, Masinga, their captain, offered to turn in to the Government the negroes he had captured [at Boterbalie] in return for a bounty. However, he deceived them by only turning in half of them.**

Indeed, there are indications that the Boterbalie people whom Musinga kept were soon transferred to Saramaka where they became known, because of the site of their island village, as Paáti-nêngè (Island People), the ancestors of the people who today live in Asaubasu. In any case, Musinga had found a dangerous but efficacious way to placate the government without giving up any more of "his own." Just three years later, the son of Matawai chief Beku was killed in a battle with new runaways on the Lower Saramacca River; on this occasion his Matawai comrades brought in three hands of their victims to claim their bounties. And the Matawais continued such activities for years.[42]

For other Saramakas, who did not engage in bounty-hunting, serious pressure to turn in slaves was just beginning, and Alabi was caught very much in the middle. Months after presiding at his father's second funeral, he was still expressing his personal outrage that the whites should have allowed the Matawais to make peace, receive whitefolks' goods, and suffer no sanctions for Abini's death.

> *Musinga . . . has sent messengers [to Paramaribo to warn] that Alabi . . . has evil intentions and that people are on guard against him. The [Saramakas] are in discord about Musinga's Peace but till now have been unable or unwilling to take action against him.*

Alabi found himself to be doubly isolated—jealous and vengeful toward Musinga at a time when other Saramaka chiefs as well as the colonial government were expressing solidarity with him, and wishing to please the whites by returning the remaining 1766 slaves at a time when the other chiefs were doing their best to incorporate these very people clandestinely into their villages and families. And throughout the period, Alabi had been edging ever closer to the missionaries, serving as their most constant companion and protector, and helping them to spread their message. By early 1770, the Moravians noted with pleasure:

> **We are especially aware that the sufferings of Jesus have made a great impression on Arrabini [Alabi] and that he has been truly moved . . . his heart is taken with the Gospels.**

A personal crisis was building.

Five	To Be a Christian and a Man

In February 1770, a serious fight broke out between Alabi and his sister's husband Kodjo, each supported by his brothers.

The enmity reached such a pitch that they all grabbed their muskets and two shots were exchanged, though without damage. [Our schoolboy] Skipio and his older brother asked their father Kodjo, with tears in their eyes, if he would please calm his rage. But he struck the latter in the leg with his machete and pointed his musket at the other, threatening to shoot him if he did not immediately leave. . . . Kodjo and his brother [Zan] felt that . . . there was no way out, that either they or Alabi would have to die.

Such fights, in eighteenth-century Saramaka as today, have only one cause: "woman trouble" (*muyêè toóbi*). As the missionaries recognized,

Marriage is looked upon very seriously by this nation . . . [and] adultery often has the gravest consequences.

And from the scant information available, it appears that Alabi must have been caught in a hammock with Zan's wife.

In this case, Zan would have had two choices: with the support of his wife's matrilineage, to seek material compensation and formal apologies from Alabi, or to defend his honor against Alabi in a *tjánga-féti,* public hand-to-hand combat with winner-take-all (that is, the wife).[1] The missionary Riemer, who spent but several months in Saramaka, presented an idealized (and somewhat Teutonic) picture of the fighting option that Zan and his people seem to have chosen.

A day is set aside for this [duel], and regular seconds are assigned to each of the parties. Their task is to see that the duel, or fistfight, does not become fatal. The combatants place thick iron or brass rings on their fists, and in an open space in the village they strike at one another in the presence of their seconds and several observers, uttering atrocious curses, until their heads are bloodied. Hatred and fighting are often so fierce that the seconds, who had been engaged as observers, instead get involved in the fracas, and it can easily happen that a murder occurs unless the observers remind the seconds of their duties. Such fisticuffs often last several days, until one of the combatants gives up, either voluntarily or by force. The stronger one then carries off the woman as his booty and keeps her. [Riemer adds a footnote: Again it is the right of the strongest! How strange that a nation of people who are in general so honest and have so many noble principles in this case so poorly protect the rights of the insulted and leave the outcome up to relative strength. What is the point of officially authorized marriage if the woman is simply given to the one who is stronger? Thus, the woman who wants to get rid of her husband needs only to boldly choose a lover whom she knows to be stronger than her husband. . . .] Others then seek to comfort the loser, and this business is finally done with. However, some negroes who are the losers in such situations seek, after a long period of time, to avenge themselves in a treacherous fashion.[2]

But though Zan seems to have chosen to fight Alabi in a *tjanga-feti,* it appears (as often happened) quickly to have gotten out of hand and degenerated into a free-for-all that had to be stopped by onlookers. In that case, the combatants would have been persuaded to reconcile their differences publicly, with Alabi paying compensation and offering formal apologies to Zan to end the affair. Brother Riemer again provides a generalized description:

The village captain summons his Council of Elders plus the guilty woman and her husband, as well as the guilty man. He [publicly] accuses the two guilty parties of their crime and admonishes all to be reconciled with one another. If he finds them all disposed to this, he turns to the accused man and requires him to beg the injured man forgiveness for his wrongdoing, and requires him to give the wronged man presents so that the latter will have no cause to avenge himself. Then the assemblage forms a circle. The guilty man falls on his knees in the center, grasps the other man's feet with both hands, kisses them, and humbly begs his pardon. He wipes his feet with one or more new handkerchiefs and then gives them to him. In the meantime, the husband takes a jug of water and delivers a speech, interrupted by many pauses, during which he intermittently pours water on the earth, and promises to forgive the guilty negro as well as his own wife, and forget all. He then calls upon the assemblage to act as witnesses and they then urge him to take seriously those words of forgiveness spoken before them.

Not long after the termination of this incident, Alabi and Kodjo were reported to be close companions again.

Alabi's fight with Kodjo was his final expression of violence. And it seems to have been his last fully Saramaka manly act. Very soon afterward, his thoughts and behavior began bending strongly to missionary pressure, and he rapidly developed a distinctive new persona.[3]

On the 13th [May 1770], Brother Stoll preached for the first time in the Sarameca language; a great number both old and young attended, and their silence and devout behavior surprized the missionaries. In the evening they returned, and requested to hear more of the word of God. Brother Kersten then addressed them with power and the demonstration of the spirit. The powerful effect of the gospel of Jesus Christ was particularly manifest in Arabini. He earnestly sought the fellowship of the Brethren, and the work of the Holy Spirit effected within him a real change of heart.

On the 16th of May [1770] when Arrabini came back from the hunt, Brother Kersten asked him whether he had thought about Jesus's words while hunting. "Oh, yes," he said, "I can never forget them. I sobbed the whole night to Jesus and begged that He would take me. Then I suddenly felt as if He were saying to me, 'I want to take you, so you shall be mine.'"

Two weeks later, on a visit to his wife's village at Agamadja, Alabi proselytized with the special enthusiasm of the newly awakened:

He addressed them in a very passionate way, saying that they had previously only served the Devil and did not realize what they had been doing, but that the best thing for them would be to serve the true God and to love Him the way He truly loves them.

It was soon afterward that Alabi committed the first of several closely related acts that finally pushed him beyond the point of no return:

The obia [Madanfo]. Alabi said, "The whites have brought a church. I will test it to see which is stronger. At Sentea Creek [where the obia shrine still stood]." That day, he took the obia pot. He took his machete. He took his gun. He aimed his gun right at the pot which was on the head of the obia-post. He said, "If you're stronger than the church, the gun won't fire." The pot there was the Madanfo pot!

*That's what they fought with in the forest. [With it,] Snakes
can't bite you. Nothing in the forest can harm you. You
can walk on top of water, go right across the river. Water
can't sink your canoe. "Well, if you're stronger than
the church they've brought, the gun won't fire at you."
It shot the pot* bím! *waaaa [sound of the water running out].
He said, "So! That church of mine is stronger than you!"*[4]

A few days later, Alabi carried his dangerous experiment still farther.

He took his kokotí *[obia staff]. It was spiraled round with
vines. The obia's walking stick. Madanfo. Alabi would
walk with it in the forest. He prepared himself until he was
all ready. His whole body was white with kaolin chalk,
and he was covered with herbs. He made a big fire. He said,
"So. If the church they brought here is false, fire won't
burn you. Because I walk with you right through fires when
we 'wash obia.' We dance in the midst of the fire until
we can't be seen! We don't get burned. Well now I'll see
which is stronger, the church or Madanfo." And he took it
and threw it into the fire. The big, big fire. Until . . . it
turned right to ashes!*[5]

More than two decades later, Alabi himself reminisced about this
moment. A missionary reported his saying, in the course of a speech
to baptismal candidates:

**"I used to be a fierce person, and engaged in every dubious
activity. I was so blind that I knew nothing. Once I went to
Masra Rudolph Stoll and saw something colorful [a depiction of
the crucifixion] hanging on his wall. I asked, 'What is that?' and
he said, 'It is a representation of the Great God, the Creator of
the heavens and the earth, who came down and out of love for us
became a man upon the earth, allowing himself to be executed
to redeem our sins. Now God wants you to give Him your heart,
and He wants you to do this so your sins will be forgiven.' . . . I
said, 'In my whole life I have never committed sins and have
been a good man.' Brother Rudolph asked, 'What is that you
have in your hand?' I said, 'That is my Gado stick' (symbol of
the idol). Brother Rudolph took the stick in his hand and saw
that it was full of parrots' feathers and all kind of magical things
and that I considered it my guardian angel. He then said, 'Arrabini, I tell you with certainty that this is nothing but a stick
made by human hands and not a god at all. With this magical
thing, the Devil is certainly playing with you, and this is but one
of his tricks. You tell me that you are good and have no sins, and
yet you believe in such idolatry. You serve the Devil with such a
stick, and you turn your back to the true and living God.' I went**

home completely distraught because Brother Rudolph had so insulted my Gado. I tried to conciliate my Gado, begging him not to blame me for what had occurred since I could not help it if the wicked white man chose to speak so evilly of him. I could not sleep the whole night, and the words kept recurring to me that God had been willing to die for my sins and had shed His blood because of me. I thought that I might have heard the truth. In the morning before daybreak, I went again to Masra Rudolph to ask him if what he had said to me the previous day was true, or whether he was really trying to trick me. Because I was truly uncertain. He reassured me in a most certain manner, and told me still more about the blood of Jesus. When I returned home, I took my Gado stick and said 'Now I want to test you. I will place you in the fire. If you really are a god, you will not burn, and then I will trust in you. However, if you do burn, then I will not believe in you.' My Gado was soon turned to ashes,[6] and soon after that I destroyed all my other idolatrous things. Eventually I learned that I had truly been a great sinner, and I felt the strength of the blood of Jesus in my heart, and I continue to feel it daily."[7]

With the great *obia* Madanfo apparently destroyed, Alabi immediately took out after the most powerful purely local god, who lived in the form of a cayman in the creek that flowed by Kwama. The missionaries left two descriptions:

[On 15 June 1770] he went . . . with a loaded gun to the river, where the crocodile or alligator, who was said to be the god of the village, used to have his haunt. On seeing the creature, he addressed it thus. "I mean to shoot thee. Now if thou art god, my bullet will do thee no harm, but if thou art a creature, it will kill thee." He then fired his piece and killed it.

Arrabini shot a large crocodile (which the negroes consider a Gado of the local creek), but it was not wounded mortally. Soon, it came to, and then Skipio shot and killed it. His mother immediately ran out and was enraged with him because he had killed their Gado. Grego's father did not even want to admit that his son had touched the animal, because he might therefore turn the same colors as the crocodile.

Alabi's desecrations did not go unanswered, though the missionaries were largely oblivious to the bustle of Saramaka ritual activity that must have been going on. (Indeed, it was at this time that the missionaries decided "to declare five negroes as Baptismal Candidates": Alabi, his brother-in-law Kodjo Maata, his sister's son Skipio, the schoolboy Grego, and the elderly Yanki.) Two days after killing the sacred cayman,

Saramakas "pouring water"—making a libation—at their local ancestor shrine, 1968

Arrabini was forced to "pour water," a type of sacrifice intended to placate his deceased father.[8] . . . Because one of his sisters had fallen ill today, her husband had gone to the Obia man, who found [by divination] that her sickness was caused by her dead father. . . . [Alabi] was very embarrassed about his relatives and told us that people were saying that we Brethren were seducers who only wanted to confuse them.[9]

The following week Alabi was summoned to a stern discussion with the "Priestess of the Idols"—his grandmother Tjazimbe, whom the missionaries described at that time as an "idolatrous old woman, whose opinions were venerated as of divine inspiration, [and who] was a sworn enemy to the mission."[10] And there must have been innumerable such signs of Alabi's guilt/responsibility and discussions of its consequences during this period, whenever people in the village became ill or met other misfortune.

Alabi himself was absent for most of the next month, traveling to the Sara Creek to participate, in his role of village captain, in the government's third general tribute distribution and to return his brother Jan—who had been in Saramaka since before Abini's second funeral—to the whites, as official "hostage." Once he returned to Kwama, Alabi quickly set to work helping the missionaries clear a garden and preaching on their behalf whenever he found listeners. Sometimes, like the missionaries, he was mocked or ignored:

> A local priestess of the idols, who is very much against the Word of Jesus . . . tried to persuade Arrabini to abandon the Word of God, but he told her that she was merely a slave of the Devil. At which she replied angrily to him, "I am already quite accustomed to this manner of slavery!"[11]

This woman and her heathen sisters soon got their own, when Alabi suffered a severe hernia:

> One day Arrabini went into the forest to get a large piece of timber and injured himself so severely that we anticipated his end. This created a sensation because, according to the pronouncement of the priestess of the [cayman] god which he had killed, he would die.

> Arrabini suffered such terrible fever and convulsions that the people all doubted he would recover. . . . [Three days later] we felt the strong power of darkness around us. This took the form of a deceiver who pretended that he had a Gado [i.e., was possessed]. He led the people in procession to the creek and asked them to call Skipio so that they could pray and sacrifice a fowl to the god accompanied by the shooting of a musket. These supposed gods are two crocodiles which Arrabini and Skipio had shot. They want to appease their gods because they believe that the fever and sickness were caused by them.[12]

Before long, the missionaries had cause for rejoicing; Alabi

> was soon perfectly restored. The heathen and their lying priestess were thus put to shame, and could do nothing but sacrifice a cock to appease the wrath of the pretended deity.

But Saramakas kept up fierce pressure on Alabi and the other potential Christians. Locally, the missionaries reported great ritual activity and excitement. "The people have become very impassioned about a woman who has received [been possessed by] a god."[13]

Larger-scale activity was under way as well: Captain Antama, one of the most powerful of all Saramaka *obiama,* was busy building a new shrine for his god in a village an hour's walk from Kwama.

> **He pretends that he is revering the Great God there and that the whole village must be absolutely silent. Nor may anyone enter it with a tobacco pipe, axe, or musket.**

Antama, remembered today by the epithet Antama-of-the-Obia, was building a new shrine to *tone,* the great river god.

Antama was a major figure on the eighteenth-century Saramaka stage. The son of Wii's sister, and the official successor of Wii (the Langu leader who "brought the Peace" to Saramaka), Antama considered himself entitled to more than the usual captain's prerogatives. Only five days after Abini's death, he boldly asked Postholder Dörig to appoint him *gaama* in the dead chief's place. In 1768 he sent a delegation to Paramaribo to request on his behalf "four muskets, four jugs gunpowder, five jugs rum, one crate of candles, a short sword, and a hat with a silver or gold [medallion?]," and he explicitly told them to say that these were in gratitude for the services performed by his uncle, "Wiel." His posture toward the whites always tended toward the confrontational; the postholder noted that he

> *comes to no political meetings [with the whites]; says he has nothing to do there; says that when whites distribute gifts he's grateful; he is [by character] impatient.*

And a message from Antama to the postholder, "ordering him to come see him in his village," caused the white official to reply, "You chiefs are always summoning me. Do you think I am a slave or a dog with nothing better to do than run through the forest at your bidding?"

When Antama's pan-tribal political ambitions seemed stymied, as first Abini and later Kwaku Etja (Abini's eventual successor) found greater general support for the office of tribal chief, he turned increasingly to the realm of ritual, though always maintaining his position as village captain. For this, too, he had excellent credentials. Antama's father was Gweunga of the Biitu clan, the African-born priest of the *tone* cult whose most famous feat was "bringing down the rains" and "sinking" a large detachment of colonial soldiers during an important battle in the 1740s. *Tone* priests, who control the rains, maintain the strictest taboos against contact with tobacco, fire, and steel (iron), in order to maintain the power of their *obia.* In response, then, to Alabi's shooting of Madanfo and the local gods, Antama decided to use the knowledge learned from his father to construct his second and most powerful *tone* shrine. And for the next twenty-five years he remained the bane of the missionaries, exerting a magnetic power to gather all but the very staunchest converts at a moment's notice to his dramatic *tone* ceremonies.

Alabi was keenly aware of these developments, as he had spent the several weeks during which Antama was preparing his new

A Saramaka *tonê* shrine, 1968

shrine in his own wife's village and gardens at Agamadja, which like Antama's belonged to the Langu clan. Saramaka customs firmly required men to reside separately from their wives, to build a house for each wife in her own village, to cut gardens for her there each year, and to visit her periodically.

> **The young man is obliged to build [his wife] a new house either near the dwelling of his parents-in-law or near her [other] close relatives. He is also under obligation to provide labor for his parents-in-law and to hunt and fish for them. . . . The woman does not leave her family but instead the husband must come and live with her family. This is a law amongst them.**

After Alabi's public break with Saramaka tradition—desecrating Madanfo and killing the cayman god—his periodic visits to his wife's village became markedly uncomfortable. Not only was Antama's new god in ascendance, but Alabi's wife was herself an especially strong devotee: "Really she only stood in his way because she was a great servant of the idols and was opposed to his behavior." Alabi decided to flout custom and persuade his wife to leave her kinfolk to come live with him by the missionaries' side. But though he was the father of her daughter, and a captain (and therefore an especially good provider), Alabi-the-nascent-Christian was not quite what she had bargained for, and she coldly refused.

Alabi now determined to go all the way. On New Year's Day 1771, one of Alabi's brothers, Bambo, paid him the traditional holiday visit.

> **[In the evening] there was a frightening noise made by drums and shouting. Abini's widow [Alabi's mother, Akoomi] was calling their Gado. When he [the Gado] came, it had Arrabini and Bambo summoned. The two were at that time with us, and they did not want to go because, as they themselves said, they no longer wished to have anything to do with sorcery. The people were very upset with us over this. Our great advantage is that they do not wish to use force against us. Otherwise, we would have been compelled to flee long ago.[14]**
>
> **On the 5th, we held a blessed meeting in which it was decided *that we would baptize Arrabini. . . .* We immediately called him to tell him the good tidings, and he was very joyful. We asked him if he knew a name which he would like to be called, whereupon he said Johannes (after the Baptist).**

On January 6, 1771, Alabi was baptized Johannes by Brother Kersten, after making

> **a happy and fundamental confession before the assembled people, to our complete satisfaction. "Jesus Christ," he said, "can and wants only to help us. I believe in Him, and I foreswear with all my heart the works and service of Satan, and wish until the end of my days only to be with Jesus."**

The reaction from other Saramakas was swift and predictable:

> Soon after the service, Captain Antama, accompanied by another negro, arrived in great anger, holding a musket in one hand and a saber in the other. The captain, with great passion, asked us if we did not know to whom this land belonged and what we thought we were doing with Arrabini, or was it our intention to kill him? He feared that the gods would kill Arrabini. They had different gods from the whites, and each must remain true to his own. We allowed him to speak his mind, but when he had finished we related to him the Truth. Finally, in the presence of Johannes Arrabini, we spoke to his heart and he gradually calmed down. . . .
>
> We can clearly see and feel that as the light becomes stronger in one person, the others become darker and more bitter. One person said that it would not have hurt him any more had Arrabini's own father killed him, since what we had done was to take away his soul.[15]

Other Saramakas responded similarly, and Alabi (Johannes) spent considerable time explaining his actions to them. The next day, for example,

> our Johannes spoke from the heart to one of his brothers-in-law who, after he had heard him out, laughed at him. [Johannes] then said to him, "Oh, this is nothing to laugh about! I assure you that he who does not believe in God's message and does not want to convert . . . will find naught but ill!" In the afternoon Johannes' father's brother [probably "Okro"] came, he whom the local family called "Father." Straight from the hunt he came to our place, angrily asking what we had done with Arrabini in his absence and why we had not told him about this beforehand.

During the next two weeks, "the village was very restless," as the dead Abini was brought into the chain of explanation surrounding Alabi's conversion: "Abini's brother was planning a large spectacle for the deceased's pleasure." This "spectacle" was a *nyanyantue,* a "food offering"—the most important ritual in honor of an ancestor, performed periodically, whenever divination revealed that ancestor's discontent (see Chapter 4). To placate the dead Abini, whom divination had revealed to be unhappy about his son's conversion, Alabi was formally summoned to preside at this ceremony. "But he rejected the idea and the others finally gave up on him." Alabi had burned yet another bridge behind him.

Other Saramakas correctly understood Alabi's conversion as part of a more general threat to their cultural integrity. Acceptance of the whitefolks' god clearly went hand in hand with acceptance of whitefolks' authority.[16] Alabi's forceful urging of other captains to turn slaves back to the whites during this period—and their angry refusal—left little doubt. In terms of taking sides, there seemed to be no possibility of compromise. And the great bulk of Saramakas chose resistance. Antama's god became a focal point.

> *On the 24th [Jan. 1771], a woman got her god, at which the Negroes asked the god about another woman who was pregnant. Would the child come happily into the world? The god said that he would not reply as long as they remained friendly with the whites and trusted them, and until they stopped this, he would say no more. When the Negroes heard this, they began to implore the god saying to him that he had better be satisfied, that they would no longer believe the whites but only him, that he would be their master, and that they would believe only in him. He began to say that he would tell the truth, but if from that day on they ever again listened to the whites, he would never speak again. He said that he would see to it that the child came into the world well, but he said that they must pray to him, which they did. Then he said to them, "Now it is good. It shall go well." Five days later, the woman had a miscarriage.*

> On the 10th of March [1771] we were truly inconvenienced by the frightening shouting which the local people made in the midst of their heathen service to their idols. The Devil is surely very busy trying to make Captain Antama his special servant and a leader among his people.

> *Here in Kwama [27 March 1771], a woman had a miscarriage and Captain Antama came to her to say that a god must be summoned or else she would have nothing but repeated miscarriages. But if she paid [him] he could "make" [domesticate] this god. The poor heathen, knowing no better, let him talk on, and the god was "made." Antama had some hopes for his payment, but whether she will be punished like the one on the 24th of January or whether the Dear God will open her innocent heart and liberate her, only time will tell.*

In fact, Antama seems to have used his god so forcefully during that spring of 1771 that his old political rivals felt called upon to clip his wings. In May, Captain Kwaku Kwadjani publicly accused Antama's god of having killed his wife, and Antama had to propose that they "drink the oath"—that if his god really did it, the potion would kill him but if it did not, the potion would kill Kwadjani.

Alabi felt under constant pressure. The gods, whenever consulted, seemed to hold him individually responsible for the ills not only of his village but of his kinfolk elsewhere. The majority of captains—who were struggling to give the hated whitefolks as little as possible while maximizing their own benefits in the ongoing negotiations about returning slaves and receiving tribute—were often displaying direct hostility. (Captain Samsam, for example, included Alabi in a list of those whom he publicly threatened to kill by sorcery that March—and soon

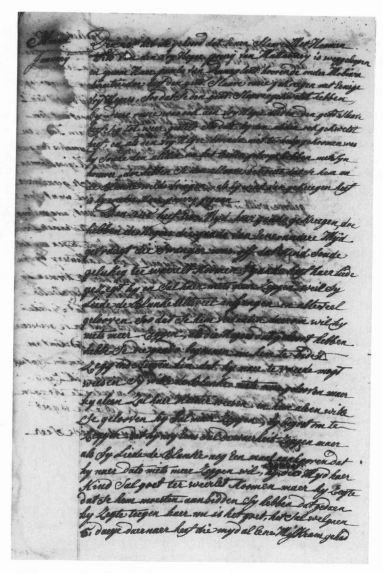

Archive page from Daunitz's journal, including the full entry of 24 January 1771, translated here. (My notes on this page, now ten years old, say it represents a rare "ethnographic" passage and is in an unusually clean and clear script.) (Hof 84, 25 October 1771.)

after, he was reported to have actually attempted to carry out some of these plans.)[17] And Alabi's relations with his "idolatrous" wife and her kinfolk were at a nadir.

In March 1771, Alabi made one last attempt to persuade his wife to come live with him and the missionaries at Kwama, and when she refused he made arrangements with her kinfolk for divorce. In eighteenth-century Saramaka, men rarely initiated divorce—but then Alabi had not been behaving "normally" for some time.[18] Divorce usually occurred because of a husband's apparent infertility, a wife's adultery, or simply a wife's wishes.

> **During the course of the first two years of marriage, if his wife has been unable to bear him a child, the blame is usually placed on the man. In this case he is looked upon as being useless, and his wife and parents-in-law take formal leave from him in front of the village captain. He is told dryly that he can now go wherever he desires, that is, whence he came. If he refuses, they can chase him off. Of his property, he is not allowed to take anything besides his musket, hammock, machete, axe, and bow and arrows. Afterwards, another man takes over his [other] possessions including the woman.**
>
> **It is often the case . . . that a woman will chase away her husband. In this case, she keeps the house and all the children for herself.[19]**

The complications of Alabi's unusual divorce must have been compounded enormously three weeks later when his (ex-)wife died suddenly, after a very brief illness. Among Alabi's other burdens, he was now required to mourn publicly, as a standard way of showing his lack of guilt. And he must have been extremely vulnerable to the accusations of the gods and spirits that were consulted during the long funeral at Agamadja, which he attended.[20]

Having buried his wife, Alabi turned back to political activities—the complex preliminaries for the October/November tribute distribution.[21] In the months preceding the ritual preparations for their departure downstream, the Saramaka captains were busy drawing their battle lines with the new postholder, Ensign Daunitz.[22] Several times, Etja and Alabi confronted Daunitz on behalf of all Saramakas: they wished to be sure that the distribution of goods would include "sufficient powder and guns, all kinds of tools, earrings, beads, and forms in which to cast bullets." Moreover, "each chief should have a white person in his village [presumably to ask for further goods and other favors], each chief should receive a large kettle in which to boil drinks, and each should get butter, saltmeat, coffee, and sugar, as well as enough salt." They also transmitted special demands: "[The Matjau] Djáki would like a doctor" to come live in his village, and so on. And other chiefs also accosted the postholder with diverse demands: Captain Folú, for example, had lost his official staff on a visit to Paramaribo and wanted a replacement. Daunitz, meanwhile, replied according to his orders from Dörig, citing the latest relevant resolution of the Court, that *if* all slaves were returned, there would henceforth be an annual distribution of twelve kegs of powder, twelve guns, and a quantity of flintstones. (To this particular resolution, Etja responded that the captains indeed wanted "powder and guns, but that twelve kegs and twelve guns is not enough, and that they need also various kinds of cloth, beads, fine earrings that are not too long, good machetes and knives, salt, and rum.") Meanwhile, three Matjau chiefs—Kristofel, Djaki, and Sentea—visited Daunitz frequently to demand that they be formally recognized as captains by the whites; he consistently replied that he did not have the authority to confer captaincies.

The tribute distribution itself witnessed the eruption of many of the ongoing tensions between Saramakas and the colonial government. Alabi was right in the thick of things, at once urging moderation in dealing with the whites (as opposed to the explicit hostility of many of the other captains) and pressing his personal opposition to the whites' continued courting of the Matawais through gifts.

Dörig, accompanied by soldiers and slaves, had left Paramaribo with the goods on 20 October, expecting to meet Daunitz and the Saramaka captains at Victoria, a plantation-turned-military post several hours below the "Treaty-Signing-Place" across from Sara Creek. But when the Saramakas let him know that they adamantly refused to change the rules of the game as spelled out in the treaty, and that Dörig would have to come to them at the Treaty-Signing-Place as usual, he decided to pay them a visit "to reason with them." He was greeted by

> various Bush Negroes with guns standing on a sandbank, and on going ashore, I found Etja in his hammock, near the bank, and with him Kristofel, Sentea, Djaki, Mbuti, and Kasa, all with guns in a circle around him. No one said a word. When I said "Odi, Etja" . . . the chiefs answered, "Odi Dörig" very brutally. I said to Etja, "What more do you want? Here I am now. And why didn't you come to me at Victoria?" To which they answered, "That is not the Treaty-Signing-Place which is [here] at Sara Creek."

Immediately following this initial confrontation, Dörig was approached by "the three chiefs Sentea, Kristofel, and Djaki . . . who must not imagine," said Dörig, that he "recognizes them as chiefs." The three insisted angrily that he owed them three guns, two bottles of powder, and ten jugs of rum, plus whatever the other captains received at each distribution. When Dörig reiterated that these men were not captains as far as he was concerned,

> the Neeger Kristofel sprang from his hammock in great anger, shaking and trembling, and said, "Don't you know me? I certainly know you. And we insist on getting [our goods]. And if you don't give us the same as the others, we'll leave and get our young [fighting] men and then you'll see what we can do." [Dörig then tried to calm them with talk about all the presents. But] . . . they answered: "There is not half enough for us all." At that point Chief Mbuti sprang from his hammock, with his

pipe in his mouth and his hat on his head . . . in a full fury . . .
and came right up to me and said, "And you, Dörig. What is it
you said? . . . If I hadn't held myself in check, I would have
given you a punch in the face!" All the while he threatened me
with his fist. I wished I could have sunk down into the ground,
and I took a step or two backwards, raising my cane, and said
"Neeger, who gave you permission to try to hit me and to treat
me in such a brutal manner? Do you think that I'm scared of
you just because I'm alone here?"23

Back in Victoria, on 29 October, Dörig received four delegates from
Matjau captain Mbuti with the message that Kristofel, Djaki, and
Sentea must get the same size shares as he. Numerous other individual requests arrived: a Langu chief, Bákisipámbo, asked for special
presents for having served as intermediary with the Matawais about
turning back the 1766 slaves, and he also requested to be recognized
as an official captain and receive separate goods for his village; a son
of Wii asked for special presents because of his father's having
"brought the Peace" from Djuka; the Langu captain Agósu Danyéi
asked for the bounties still due his recently deceased predecessor for
having turned in slaves; and so on—to all of which Dörig answered
that he would take the requests up with the Court. Finally, on 31
October, Captain Mbuti himself arrived at Victoria, and Dörig replayed
his humiliating Sara Creek encounter, only this time his way.

[After hearing that Mbuti had arrived] I went inside and
smoked my pipe in my hammock [just the way Mbuti had
received him] . . . Mbuti requested permission to enter . . .
[and] said to me roughly, "Give me a light" and "Where should I
sit?" I answered, "I am not about to give you a light, and you
can go sit on the ground or stay standing, just as I had to do at
your place while you lay in your hammock." Whereupon he,
with wonderment, said "If you won't offer me a light, that's all
right, Massa," and he sat down on a crate. I asked him why,
when I visited him, he had wished to punch me in the face. He
answered that I well knew that they weren't getting sufficient
presents

but then he "admitted," Dörig wrote, that he had acted in haste. Three
days later, Alabi came downstream to Dörig on behalf of all the Saramaka captains with an ultimatum: if the goods now at Victoria were
all the whites intended for them, they would leave at once without
them—at which Dörig said that two could play that game, threatened
to leave himself, and reminded Alabi that the Saramakas should be
"grateful" for the presents the whites had brought them and spend
less time complaining.

The mounting tension was broken somewhat by the arrival of a
letter from the Court, reporting a resolution dated 31 October: at

Dörig's request, "Kristofel, Djaki, and Sentea, who had acted as captains since the Peace, would now be recognized as such, but that no others would be [in future], and that these three would now receive a full share of goods." The Saramaka captains then made a final attempt to persuade Dörig that he should give them all more goods, by asking Postholder Daunitz, who had been in their villages recently, to confirm to his superior that "the people he [Dörig] had known as children [at the time of the Peace] were now grown men, and that the young men's greatest pleasure was in firing guns." The issue of *where* the Saramakas would receive their goods also remained unresolved.

Etja came to Victoria looking like a just-freed hunting dog, raging and howling at me, with his whole face and body painted up like a bush-devil. . . . He asked why I wouldn't come to Sara Creek so he could receive his presents, since his god had said that this would happen. I said that whether or not his god had said that, I would stay here.

But the Saramakas, after an unsuccessful attempt to get Dörig to meet them halfway, finally agreed to come down to Victoria. And on 9 November, after further dramatic scenes—Mbuti, "angry as a devil," being restrained from breaking up the ceremony because he was receiving a jug rather than a barrel of powder, Alabi complaining about the size of the gifts Musinga had been receiving from the whites—Dörig and the Saramaka captains ritually resealed the treaty, and the goods were at last distributed.[24]

During the rest of 1771 and throughout the following year, sickness reigned in Saramaka. Measles, influenza, and other epidemics swept from village to village, and funeral obligations occupied much of Alabi's time. As the postholder wrote, "Serious illness and many deaths are everywhere." Among the victims were Alabi's father's sister, Ayábe, and her daughter, at Baakawata. The village of Kwama was not spared:

> Because the measles are everywhere in the neighboring villages, an Obia man was called here in the middle of the month to make an Obia so that sickness, which the negroes so fear, would not come. He filled two pots with earth and herbs and the people washed themselves every day with them. They had been doing this for four or five days when the sickness broke out among them. . . . A very bad cough has lately held sway in all of the villages, sending several people to the grave. Then came the measles, and though the people did many Obia- and Gado-things, this proved no help at all, and everyone became despairing.

It was during this troubled period that a man named Kaána, an Awana-clan companion of Alabi who had at first accepted the shooting of Madanfo as a *fait accompli* and been sympathetic to the missionaries, decided to act. Divination had revealed that

> *the* obia *[Madanfo] was what was troubling them now.*
> *So Kaana said, "This* obia*. It has the power to fix up [purify]*
> *the forest. It has the power to fix up water. I shall leave*
> *the church." And he went back to Sentea Creek. He cleaned*
> *up the old* obia *house until it was all ready. And then he*
> *called the* obia*. (Alabi wasn't with him; he wasn't interested*
> *in these things any more. Kaana and Alabi had been the*
> *very first ones to go to the church; they were the ones*
> *to whom the whitefolks had given the hymnal and the*
> *primer, before they moved from Sentea to Kwama. What*
> *Alabi had done to the* obia *had hurt Kaana. Because the* obia
> *had always helped them. So he went back. He knew all*
> *about it [from former times].) . . . When Kaana went back*
> *to Sentea, it wasn't done in secret. People made a very*
> *big fuss when that happened! It was a very big thing! Alabi*
> *and Kaana had been friends and had "taken" the church*
> *together. Now, Alabi had shot the* obia *pot. They became ene-*
> *mies! Kaana, when he "awakened" the* obia*, he gathered*
> *all the leaves, the* biyôngòs*. (It wasn't just one pot. There*
> *were several. If one broke, they could use another.) He*
> *put everything in a pot. He fixed up the post that the pot*
> *had been shot on [by Alabi]. He ritually removed the taboo*
> *[pollution] of the gun. Then he prepared himself. He had*
> *parted with Alabi. He had left the hymnal to Alabi. Alabi*
> *was not with the* obia *any more.*[25]

Loud "heathen festivals" led by this "New Priest of the Idol" were reported by the missionaries during the early months of 1772, and in June,

> **the new priest of the idol summoned all the people on this side**
> **of the Suriname River for a spectacle. All the local negroes went**
> **with the exception of Johannes and one negro, and the two boys.**

Madanfo, the god brought from Africa seventy years before by Alabi's grandmother Tjazimbe, had found a new lease on life.

Alabi now continued his sacrilegious course with a vengeance. The very evening of Kaana's great Madanfo spectacle, Alabi returned from his prayers with the missionaries to find an anaconda in his house. "A Boma [anaconda] is the largest type of snake and lives as much in water as on land. It is an idol of the negroes. He killed it." (In Saramaka logic, the killing of sacred caymans or anacondas involved the most serious consequences for one's kin. Indeed, the accidental slaying of such creatures was, in the Saramaka system of explanation, perhaps the major source of evil in the world. These gods were viewed as living, responsive beings.)[26] Soon after Alabi killed the snake, a village woman expressed community opinion after having heard that a duck she owned had been killed by another anaconda:

> She went to the creek and addressed herself to the Gado. "You did not do right when you killed my only duck. I have always served you faithfully. To those people who have more and who want to kill you, you do nothing. Is that fair?" She meant us [the Moravians] by that.[27]

Later, Alabi reported yet more direct family pressure about his sacrilege, indicating incidentally that his kinfolk—once all else had failed—were even willing to consider conciliating him. But he remained intransigent.

> Six of his sisters who had been living here sent two of his brothers to him with the following request. They knew that they did not share his opinion as to the proper way of life, but since they followed a different path, would he please allow them to continue living the way they had been, and no longer shoot their gods, namely the large snakes and crocodiles? He had them told again that he felt truly sorry that they did not want to see in the bright light of day but that he, thank God, realized that those are not gods but malicious animals that he tried to get rid of so that the children will not be harmed when they bathe in the river.

By this time, even the missionaries were wondering, in their own self-interest, whether it might not be prudent to curb their convert's excessive zeal. Brother Kersten described how,

> on the 26th, I talked with Johannes about whether it would not be better to allow these animals, which the negroes take to be gods, to go their way instead of aggravating matters.

But it appears that Alabi, at this stage of establishing a new persona, really needed these repeated acts of destruction as continuing proof of his freedom from what he now viewed as overwhelming and oppressive Saramaka religious obligations. During this period, he is reported to have "often said":

> "In my previous life, I never had quiet. First, I would feel that I had to feed my 'soul,' then that I had to pacify my Gado, then that I had to placate someone who had recently died so that he would not kill me, then that I had to make an Obia and purify [myself with it]. But now, I am free from all these burdens, torments, and fears."[28]

And shooting sacred caymans and anacondas to prove his new invulnerability to their powers was, ironically, a most characteristically Saramaka means for Alabi to deal with his new situation. After this period, however, we hear no more about Alabi's committing acts that, in non-Christian terms, would "automatically" harm his non-Christian kinfolk. Rather, he began to stress a new, more personal form of piety, as in this speech to his brother Bambo, reported by Brother Stoll:

> "[It's as if] you had made a canoe and brought it to Paramaribo [to sell], but it was stolen [on arrival] and you got no payment for all your toil and trouble. This would really hurt you. Thus it is with us. We owe a payment to the Savior for His toil and pain on our behalf. If we do not pay Him, it hurts Him greatly, for He loses His reward, and we bring ourselves true misery."

And Alabi especially focused his spiritual attentions on the Passion.

> At our evening meeting [19 July 1772] . . . Johannes Arrabini again requested that something be read from the story of Christ's Passion.

It seems that Alabi and his non-Christian kinfolk were moving toward an uneasy, still-hostile modus vivendi.

Alabi spent much of the second half of 1772 far downstream, at the chosen site of his new village, Gwafu, called by the missionaries Bambey.[29] Conflict, sacrilege, death, and sickness had made Kwama an unsuitable place for people to live. As Saramakas today recall:

> [The gods of] that place were not ready for the church.
> There was an apuku [forest spirit] who lived near by. It used
> to growl ominously. Divination revealed that it was because
> the church-people didn't respect its taboos. So they had
> no choice but to leave.[30]

Alabi and his kinsmen devoted the month of August to felling trees in the new gardens, the most dangerous and difficult of horticultural tasks.

Groups of three or four men worked together, first carefully "examining the site" (*lúku goón básu*), walking for several hours through the area scouting ecological hazards and potentials: Was the soil moist? sandy? heavy? Were there large boulders or silk-cotton trees that might house *apuku*s, termite nests that housed fierce spirits, or the telltale holes of snake-gods, all of which had to be given a wide berth? When they had settled on a potential site for a garden, one of the older men balanced a palm-frond device on two quickly cut short poles and prayed to the god-who-has-the-place to permit them to make their gardens there. Then, retiring for the night, they ate cassava cakes and fish broth, served by the women who had accompanied them, before slinging their hammocks in the open sheds they had constructed near the river. The next morning they returned to see if the palm frond was still in place, signaling that the god was at ease with their plans.[31] During the next several days they cleared the underbrush with machetes before settling down to the heavy axe-work. Working in pairs, often balancing on precarious platforms built

Twentieth-century Maroons engaged in tree-felling (van de Poll 1959, 83).

around a thick trunk high above the folded buttresses of a forest giant, Alabi's brothers swung in alternating rhythm at the hard trunks, singing melodically complex call-and-response axe-songs that at once boasted of their own strength and prowess (giving them the courage to continue) and spoke directly, by name, to the forest spirits, begging their assistance in the dangerous task at hand.[32]

After several weeks of labor, Alabi and his companions paddled upstream, returning again in October to set fire to the then-dry fields and to continue clearing the site for their new village. At the same time, Alabi and his kinsmen made a garden for the missionaries, for which they were paid. Once the rains came, during the final two moons of the year, planting—carried out for the most part by the women—took place in earnest, and before New Year's most crops were in the ground: rice, cassava, plantains and bananas, peanuts, sugar cane, maize, sweet potatoes and a variety of other root crops, capsicum, okra, watermelon, pineapple, and various others.[33] With the planting of fruit trees—oranges and papayas, limes and coffee—brought down by canoe, on the site of the new village itself, Alabi and his people had completed much of the work needed to make their new home three days downstream from Kwama.

When he was not engaged in preparing the new village site and gardens, Alabi was attending to political affairs—witnessing the official enstoolment of his Matjau "grandfather" (his father's mother's brother) Adjagbo as a captain, participating in deliberations about a knotty double-murder case, and helping to deal with an equally complex sorcery case that was finally settled by a public execution. But he remained in daily touch with the missionaries and, a year and a half after his baptism, was finally admitted to the Lord's Supper. Soon after, Alabi also served as catalyst for the second adult baptism—an old man named Yanki who was baptized Simon on New Year's Day 1773.

Simon Yanki, whose wife and brothers-in-law were "faithful devotees of the idol," was subjected to the same kinds of family pressures that Alabi had come to know—for example, being requested by his kinfolk to make a sacrifice to his own "soul."

> The conditions surrounding such a sacrifice are the following: the negroes believe that the soul of the deceased lives on either in a newborn child or in a beast. . . . They have a post in their houses on which they have a small figure in the shape of a weaver's shuttle, made from a piece of wood, in which they believe their soul lives. In order to stay healthy, they believe it necessary from time to time to cut a chicken in the gullet and throw it on the ground.[34] If it falls on its back as it dies, they clap their hands with joy and say "Gado, aoma hem," meaning God has taken it on or God is pleased with it. After this, they prepare it with some tasty greens and place it with a drink for the soul for whom it is intended underneath the post, and they pray to it that their bodies be healthy and happy. Then their friends come and eat together with the soul.
>
> On the 20th [August 1773], Simon told us that his mother-in-law had gone to the Obia to ask about the cause of the sickness of his little child.[35] The Obia, or rather the deceiver, answered as follows: "The soul of Simon is making the child sick. He must therefore sacrifice to his soul and pray to it. Only then will the child regain its health." He [Simon] answered to her, however, that he no longer believed in such things. Because he now knew better that his soul could not do damage without his willing it.[36]

Alabi had recently gone through a similar experience, but with Madanfo, not his "soul," as the agent:

> On the third of May [1773] the child of a man who usually came to our meetings died. And the Obia priest gave this [his attending church] as the cause of the child's death. Thus the man in question stopped coming to our services for four weeks, and began again to pray to the idols. The women put the blame [for the death] on our Johannes because he no longer wished to serve their gods. He spoke very earnestly to these women, who were his biological sisters and relatives. But they stuffed their hearts and ears out of malice, and told him freely that they did not want to hear anything about our God.

Soon afterward, Alabi and the missionaries had further proof of their powerlessness to influence most Saramakas, even within Kwama.

> On the 27th [June 1773], the oldest man in the village died. He had been honored as a father, but apparently had a dubious moral character and had been a great obstacle to Johannes. It weighed very heavily on our hearts that his funeral caused so many people from other villages to travel here and spend eight days, and that not one soul would listen to a word about the Creator. Most of the people here are dead set in sin, and others stuff up their hearts and ears out of contrariness.[37]

During this period, Yanki (Simon) and Alabi seem often to have given each other solace by discussing their joint isolation.

> On the 20th [February 1773], Simon came home after completing his work. He and Johannes came to our house in the evening and spoke about what it would be like if all the Europeans here were forced to leave because of a war with the whites. The first one said, "I could not remain here. I would have to go with them, even if it meant as far as Europe. Because I cannot do without the presence of the Brethren." To which Johannes replied, "That isn't the only reason, because we also need to hear the words of the Savior and we could easily lose our way without His presence, and eventually go back on the path to sin, which would be worse than never having encountered the Savior in the first place."

At some time during this period—the diaries are silent on the matter—Alabi married for a second time, choosing Sialoto, a young woman who, as a child, had been one of the last plantation people to have been liberated by Saramakas before the Peace.[38] When she arrived with her mother Sofí, at the age of six or seven, they seem to have been taken in by Alabi's people, and it was there that she grew up until she was ready to be given the skirts of womanhood. Missionary evidence suggests that she was living with Alabi by the beginning of 1773.

Alabi spent much of that year preoccupied about relations between the Saramaka chiefs and the colonial government, which had again reached a critical stage. The government, fighting an all-out war against the new Aluku/Boni Maroons in the coastal area and facing a serious economic crisis in the colony, had decided to play it much tougher with the Saramakas. In March 1773, the Court issued a new set of orders to Daunitz (who had come to Paramaribo for consultation, after an apparent Saramaka attempt to poison him), written as a precaution in French. As the postholder was traveling upstream to deliver these government ultimatums to the Saramaka captains, he met a canoe carrying Alabi and one of the Moravians coming down. Alabi explained that he was going to the government to renounce his captaincy and to seek permission for his family "to come live near the whites as Christians leaving heathenism behind once and for all," and that he had had his fill of Saramaka politics and serious threats against the Peace. Daunitz, realizing that Alabi could be his strongest ally,

> *responded to Johan Arabi in the presence of his mentor the Herrnhuter that I was surprised [by his plan] but if he wanted to carry it out, he had no need to go to Paramaribo. Instead, he should return with me and help me at the council-meeting, because there would be harsh words exchanged there, as I was carrying very tough letters from the Court. . . . "If your people do not turn in all the slaves, you will be considered to have broken the Peace. . . . I therefore ask you to accompany me, to persuade the others to listen to the letter from the Honorable Court."*

On arrival in Saramaka, Daunitz and the chiefs fenced for several days about setting a date for the council meeting—Daunitz pressing and threatening, the chiefs obfuscating and procrastinating. Then, after a preliminary meeting with some of the chiefs on 4 April,

> *on the 5th, Kwaku [Kwadjani], [Kwaku] Etja, and Mbuti arrived—Kwaku and Etja as mad as the devil—but it was only to try to scare me. Once they saw that I too was angry, and had tough words to say to them, Etja asked if this place [where we were standing] was mine or his. I said, "I have more rights to this land than all of you. Don't you know that this land belongs to the Honorable Society [of Suriname] and that I am their servant while you are just outlaws? And that therefore I have more rights to it than you?" Having heard this, Etja said to me that he was just kidding . . . and it ended with their giving me promises of cooperation. Thus it is with the Bush Negroes: we must not speak kindly with them. If we wish to keep the peace, the tougher our demands and responses the better, as it makes them have a certain fear of the whites. . . . [Otherwise,] in their*

brutal arrogance, they will imagine that "the whites are afraid of us," and when we give them rights to a finger they'll want the whole body.

The major council meeting was held on 6 April, with Daunitz reading the Court's ultimatums: If the Saramakas did not turn in the 1766 slaves they still held within three weeks, the river would be sealed off at Victoria and their access to the coast blocked; they must shoot any slaves who try to escape from them (for whom they would still receive the full bounty, as long as they showed the corpses to Daunitz); all pending requests for powder, guns, and so forth would be considered only after the matter of returnees was settled—indeed, there would be no further gift distributions until that time; any Saramakas who "corrupted" plantation slaves would be hanged without mercy;[39] and finally, the Court resolved to separate completely the administration of the Matawais, who would henceforth have their own official postholder, from that of the other Saramakas. And Daunitz—after presenting a long string of arguments to persuade the Saramakas that the Court was giving them this "last chance" out of "the great goodness of their hearts," despite consistent bad behavior by the Saramakas—told the chiefs that he must have their agreement or refusal,

not in a palaver lasting three days and a night like the last time, but with a final yes or no at this meeting, without waiting till morning.

The captains, as was standard council meeting procedure,[40] left Daunitz and retired for two hours of private discussion at the forest's edge. When they returned,

Johan Alabi spoke, on behalf of the captains on this side [of the river], to say that although those on the other side were not fully willing to declare themselves, those on this side—Alabi, Mobiara and Antama [both of Langu], Folu's successor [of Kwama], and Kasa [of Dombi] had no intention of breaking the Peace—quite the contrary—and that they would turn in the couple of slaves that they still held. . . . Etja [representing the captains "on the other side"—the Nasi, Abaisa, and Matjau clans] then said, "We have heard and understood all the letters and arguments of the great whites, and we will do our best."

Negotiations about the slave returns—often quite heated—continued with particular captains for many days. Throughout, Alabi served as a central mediating force, often slipping Daunitz key information about what the Saramaka chiefs were saying among themselves. Nevertheless, Daunitz became increasingly frustrated, and the chiefs often reminded him, in subtle ways, of his ultimate powerlessness. Sometimes the Saramakas even subjected him to lectures about why the whites had problems with their plantation slaves in the first place.

Etja came to visit and said that I must inform the Honorable Court that it is not in their interests to question the slaves under duress [torture]. And that whenever any of them [Saramakas] go to Paramaribo and pass plantations [on the way home], many slaves beg them to take them back to their land with them, saying that they are black like them too, and that each day with their masters is filled with anger and sorrow and that they cannot take it any more. He also said that if the slaves hear that the Peace is in jeopardy or will be broken, that they will all run off. But I [Daunitz] said that they won't run off if they have no place to go [i.e., if the Saramakas won't receive them]. He then said that the whites should not treat their slaves so brutally, that they would be perfectly able to do their work with cool hearts, that they ought not have to suffer so much melancholy because of their masters and directors, and that if they are treated so cruelly and have the opportunity to run away, they would, and then the plantation would suffer a great loss, and the Bush Negroes would no longer enjoy goods and other things from the whites, so that there would be a real loss on both sides.

Frustrated by his inability to get results despite what he considered heroic efforts on his own part, Daunitz finally decided to go on a hunger strike.[41]

Seeing that those on the other side of the river had little interest in turning back slaves, I thought to myself, "I shall try another tactic," and I began to show my extreme melancholy . . . and ate nothing offered by any of them, nor in my own house. . . . I explained that this was because they would not turn in their slaves. . . . Two days later, the chiefs sent for me and said that I should eat, that they would do their best to return the slaves.

And, to show their "good will," the Saramakas did turn in a handful of slaves—largely those who, for one or another reason, they no longer wanted living among them.[42] One such turn-in was accompanied by a practical argument to support the humane treatment of the slaves concerned.

Just at this instant, Captain Samsam has asked me to report that they [the Saramakas] beg the Honorable Court with great thanks not to execute the slaves they are turning in but instead to let them live. Otherwise, if they hear that they have been hanged, they will be afraid to turn in others.

The outcome of these dramatic 1773 confrontations was thoroughly equivocal—the whites believed that their get-tough policy was vindicated, the Saramakas believed (I think correctly) that they had succeeded in maintaining the favorable status quo. Daunitz, mean-

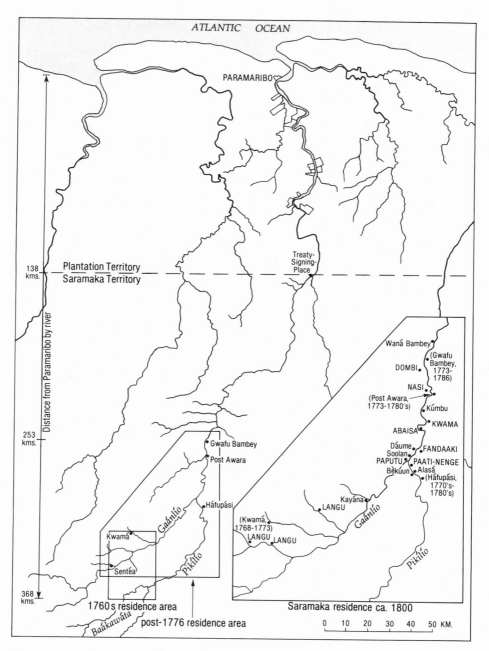

Map 3. Saramaka residence ca. 1800. My use, in most cases, of clan rather than village names stems from the transitoriness of most late eighteenth-century villages. During this period, each clan (-segment) moved frequently, but usually within a very small area.

while, was given a "douceur" of five hundred florins by the Court for his part in these transactions.

The government at last seemed to believe that the Saramaka captains "meant well," and the Court gave permission for various villages that had occupied the Upper Gaanlio since the years of war to move closer to the city—Alabi and his Awanas to Gwafu Bambey, the Nasis to Saanga, the Dombis to Wánganía, and so on. Over the course of the next three or four years, during the mid-1770s, Saramaka village geography was forever altered, and by the end of the decade, the inhabited territory had taken on the shape it would retain until the next large northward expansion in the middle of the next century.[43]

In November 1773, after eight years at Sentea and nearby Kwama, the missionaries reluctantly departed the Gaanlio, unhappy about having to leave behind "houses, tables, benches, coffee trees, and gardens which . . . in the new place we will have to start again from the very beginning." And just before leaving, they reported a final sacrificial rite by the heathen Saramaka to the local deity whose fortunes had become so intertwined with their own, the cayman god of Kwama Creek.

Six   On to Bambey

With the move to Gwafu Bambey in late 1773, Alabi found himself more embroiled than ever in Saramaka politics. Since the whites had decided to get tough about the issue of slave returns, Postholder Daunitz, who was a friend and supporter of the Moravians, had become increasingly dependent on Alabi for advice in his negotiations with other Saramakas. Finally, at the beginning of 1774, Daunitz resolved to stay at Bambey as Alabi's guest indefinitely—or until he could effect a definitive solution to the runaway issue, which was threatening to drag on. The negotiations continued to be marked by dramatic posturing and threats, as an interchange in May between Daunitz (who was accompanied by Alabi) and Captain Kwaku Etja (whom Brother Stoll described as "one of the most respected captains and most famous Gado- and Obia-men in the entire land") vividly illustrates.

> *30 May [1774]. . . . Etja said "Am I the only one who has 'slaves' that you always complain about this to me? I will not hand them over now." Then I said to him, "Then I shall not come live near you."* [N.B. Etja, to reinforce his claims on the gaamaship, very much wanted Daunitz to establish his permanent post across from his new village]. *At which the boy [Etja was then in his eighties!] became so fresh that he slapped me and said "If you utter another word, I'll kill you on the spot." And he ordered me off exactly as if I were a mad dog. I also became angry but I didn't back down. I stood right up to him while he was threatening me with death and I said "Here I am. Kill me if you have the guts. I won't flee from you!" But he didn't carry it any further and I said to Alabi . . . "Let's go home, and let this crazy keep railing as long as he wants."*

Daunitz, after exchanging further threats with Etja, went to wait at the riverbank for Alabi, who remained in Etja's village to complete some other business. There he mused that he had been sorely tempted to fight Etja,

> *as I would have bested him because he is not very strong. [Then,] Etja came to me by the river bank . . . and said, "Daunitz, do you really want the 'slave' Kodjo? Then go to my sister, who is his wife, and argue the matter with her." I answered that I had no orders to argue with women.*

But Daunitz did go back into the village and entered Etja's house.

> *Etja had his sister summoned. [Kodjo] brought his wife, that is Etja's sister, on his shoulder because she is lame in one leg and cannot walk without being carried. . . . Etja said to his brother-in-law, "Kodjo, this is the white man who is so hungry to turn you in. Take a knife and fight him. If he is stronger and beats you, that is all right. But if you succeed in killing him, that is also good. He deserves it." When I heard this, I was truly despairing but at the same time I thought of God who helps me with all my needs. . . . When Etja saw that the slave Kodjo was not coming after me with a knife, Etja went right up to him and hit him, saying "You bastard! Why don't you ever do as I tell you?" The slave began to cry and came to me weeping, saying, "Massa, if the whites will kill me, it's their money [they are wasting], but if they let me live, I'd accept that too." When I heard this from the slave, I gave him my hand and said, "Kodjo, as long as you don't withdraw your hand from mine, you have no need to fear. I shall ask the Court to spare your life." But the obscenities that his wife then uttered I cannot write down. This slave then put his wife on his back and carried her back to her house.*

Others soon came carrying muskets, hearing that there was a fight, and threatened Daunitz. Etja finally offered him a conciliatory drink but he refused, fearing poison.

During this period, Etja used various arguments to justify not returning the two (some documents say three) slaves he was allegedly harboring. For example, he once asked, "Why should I give up my three 'slaves' when Samsam still has a whole village full?"; at other times, he claimed that the two slaves were a substitute for the husband of his crippled sister, who had been killed by the whites;[1] on still other occasions, he stressed that one of the slaves was married to his sister.[2] To my knowledge, neither Kodjo nor the other(s) were ever returned.

The negotiations of 1774–75, intended by Daunitz to be final, in fact led to few new slave returns. Indeed, after the government-provoked "crisis" of 1773, Saramakas never turned back more than a handful of these newcomers, successfully practicing vis-à-vis the whites what might be characterized as a politics of mass confusion.[3] During these negotiations, the Saramaka chiefs relentlessly demanded goods of the most diverse kinds—which the whites consistently tried to tie to the return of runaways. In 1775, for example, when Matjau captain Mbuti "demanded to know the whereabouts of the captain's staff that was promised him at Victoria," he was told that "the captain's staff is ready but its delivery will be delayed until the further turning in of slaves."

Meanwhile, Saramakas were expressing boisterous and self-righteous indignation over a 1775 government gift distribution to the Matawais. Since the Matawais had received their goods even though they had not turned in their runaways, argued Captain Kwaku Etja, Saramakas would now refuse to turn in theirs as well. Captain Samsam, who was under particular pressure to turn in runaways at this time, as his tribute goods were in fact being withheld, arranged an apparent intelligence coup by releasing the names of seventy-four 1766-vintage slaves still allegedly held at Matawai, in the hope of buying himself out of his predicament. (In fact, however, few of these people were still at Matawai;[4] most were hidden with the Matjaus or in Samsam's own [Abaisa] territory.) Alabi requested "patience" from Daunitz regarding a slave who had been with him but who had allegedly fled back to Matawai.[5] And Daunitz was forced to continue devoting the great bulk of his time in Saramaka to trying, unsuccessfully, to figure out which slaves were where, and to jockeying for position with the chiefs on this issue.

On balance, the negotiations of 1774–75 must be seen as a remarkably successful smokescreen, set up by the Saramakas, which permitted them finally to assimilate the one hundred-odd slaves that the Matawais had clandestinely passed on to them five years before. After 1775, pressures from the government and its postholders on this score waned markedly: Saramakas clearly maintained the upper hand. Saramaka oral history provides a decisive complement to the evidence contained in the documents, revealing that during the early 1770s, most of the slaves liberated by Musinga on his famous 1766 "raid" became the Fandaakis, an important Saramaka clan. When subjected to a close reading, the archival documents make it clear that the Nasi, Matjau, and Abaisa clans were the main initial hosts for these illegal immigrants. And Saramaka oral history faithfully traces the Fandaakis' path from Matawai, over the mountains to the Langu villages and on to the Nasi village of Dosu Creek, next across the forest to the Matjau region of Baakawata (where they lived with the Paputus—another relatively new group under Matjau tutelage)[6]— and, finally, to their own village built on land provided by the Abaisas, just below the confluence of the Pikilio and the Gaanlio.[7] Tribal Chief Agbago, in a whispered, guarded discussion with me in 1978, demonstrated that his father's clan had carefully preserved the story of its origins, despite its relatively nonheroic heritage.

Matjáu captain Dangasí (Kála) in 1978, holding his silver-headed staff originally made for Mbutí, which is inscribed "GENT. BOUTI, Kapitein van de bevredigde Saramaccanders" and crowned with the arms and motto of the House of Orange. Kála stands before Dángogó's newly refurbished ancestor shrine, for the first time fenced with poured concrete.

Peace had already been made. My father's clan [the Fan-
daaki] came very, very late. They had no forest. They had no
land. Until they went to live with the Abaisas, right where
you see them today. They paid for the creek. Two creeks.
Those great men [he names three]. They brought up my
father. They said they [their clan] hadn't come early. They
came and mixed with other people. That's the way it hap-
pened. They had no land of their own. [R.P.: Where did
they live in slavery?] They lived toward the Saramacca River,
on a creek with a branch going to the Saramacca. They ran
away to Matawai. . . . Beku and Musinga brought them. They
had wanted more people to add to their strength. . . . But
then things didn't go well for them with Beku. So they
came over to this side [the Suriname River watershed]. There
was a rule: every last person who arrived in peace-time—
If you were already here, you had to turn that person in!
That was the law! Well, that Beku, with his "brother"
Musinga, they made an agreement with the whitefolks.
They would catch them for them. But there were others
[in Matawai] who didn't want to have anything to do with
the catching. Let's say they might even have been family.
So they arranged for them to cross over to this side here.
. . . Beku and Musinga had an agreement with the white-
folks. And they gave them some of them! But it wasn't
most of them. Then they told the others to go to Saramaka
to safety. . . . Now, when they crossed over, they met
with those people . . . Agosu Danyei [the Langu clan].[8]
And they lived with them. Agosu said to them, "Stay
with me. If war comes, I will help you." . . . The Fandaakis
had heard about some frightening negotiations. It sounded
as if the whitefolks might find them and take them back.
But the Langus said, "No way. They'll never find you here.
One doesn't take one's own wife and give her to someone
else! The child that you and she have together, you can't
take it and give it to someone!" That's what they said. . . .
That's why Kayana [Agosu's village] and Fandaaki are
like one clan. But Kayana was there first. At that time,
Fandaakis were in a subservient status.[9] *But now, they're*
just like anybody else [any other clan].[10]

Meanwhile, the postholders—arrogant, condescending, and confident of their racial superiority—remained largely unaware of their
ultimate powerlessness and ignorance regarding the shell game Saramakas had been playing with the new runaways. In the early nineteenth century, one postholder illustrated this mystification when he
summed up decades of administrative experience on this issue with
the assertion that

> *the [Saramaka] Bush Negroes are exceptionally jealous, hateful, and vengeful, which is why they are unable to protect many new runaways—since one of them will easily betray the next in return for a small gift from the postholder.*

For the Saramakas, the 1770s assimilation of the slaves freed on Musinga's raid—who became the Fandaaki clan—had been a dangerous game indeed. But it was one from which, on balance, they emerged as victors.

By August 1774, postholder-Saramaka relations were deemed to be sufficiently calm to allow another general tribute distribution. Captains Alabi, Kwaku Kwadjani, Kwaku Etja, Kasa, Mbuti, and Kristofel journeyed downstream to attend; five others sent deputies in their stead. As usual, there was a great deal of political maneuvering on both sides. Dörig and Daunitz, on behalf of the Court, read the Saramakas a number of ultimatums. Henceforth, no captains, other than "the eleven of past years" (and their lawful successors), would be recognized by the whites. Other current "pretenders" (eleven are named) would be dealt with on an individual basis. For example, the Matjaus Djaki and Sentea would—by special dispensation—continue to be treated as if they were captains in terms of the personal gifts they would receive, out of recognition for the special services they had performed during the Dörig-Abini expedition against the Matawais, but upon their deaths these gratuities would cease.[11] The Langu men, Agosu Danyei and Bakisipambo (each, in fact, soon to succeed to captainships), would each be given—on a one-time basis only—a gun, a jug of gunpowder, and a jar of rum. And the general goods would henceforth be distributed once every three years instead of every two (with a proportional increase to assure equity). The goods actually distributed for each village, designed to last three years, included "1 barrel gunpowder; 25 [————?]; 1 gun; 6 jars rum; 1 barrel salt; 12 machetes; 40 sailor's knives; 40 flints, 3 pieces cotton cloth; 3 pieces *platille* cloth; 3 pieces *dobbelsteen* cloth; 6 iron pots; 12 axes; 12 billhooks; 6 adzes; and 1 small grindstone."

The whites were also interested in getting Saramaka agreement to a long laundry list of proposals redefining their relationship, but, as with other such one-sided "agreements," actual practice developed in far less rigid ways.[12] The whites now wished, for example, to wipe the slate clean in terms of continuing, persistent, and (for them) confusing Saramaka claims for past gifts not properly received; to end the practice of giving "mourning goods" to Saramakas upon the death of a captain;[13] to end the practice of helping Saramakas repair their guns (requiring them, instead, to do so at their own expense); to permit Saramakas to buy shot and flints at Paramaribo only with a letter from the postholder; to establish a more formal "pass system" for Saramakas going to Paramaribo, who would henceforth need a letter from the postholder; to forbid anyone but a captain himself from carrying the staff of office when walking around Paramaribo; to punish any Saramaka who showed impudence to a white person; to turn in any Saramaka who "corrupted" a slave; to reduce the bounty awarded to Saramakas for turning back a new runaway to thirty florins plus a gun and a bottle of gunpowder; and, finally, to require Etja—"in spite of his pretences about having 'lost' two of his men—to turn in his two 'slaves.'" At this tribute distribution, Alabi and his main man, Kodjo Maata, were singled out for special recognition "for their faithful service performed for postholders Dörig and Daunitz," and they were given new guns and powder. Captain Samsam's share of the goods was, meanwhile, withheld, pending his cooperation in turning back slaves.[14]

Returning from this 1774 distribution, Alabi as well as other captains came under severe pressure from other villagers regarding the equitable distribution of goods. Since the end of the wars a decade earlier, Saramaka population had increased so fast that many villages were now on the verge of fission.[15] As new leaders emerged, with the wish to head their own villages, they began agitating for independent shares of goods from the government, and they often claimed that the current captains were not distributing the goods properly.[16] Much of the problem was built into the system itself: once the village (or captain) had been chosen by the whites as the unit for receipt of goods, gross inequities were inevitable. For example, in 1774, Captain Antama's village, which, according to Daunitz's census, had only 14 men, received the same share as the Matjau village of Baakawata, which was said to have 150 men. Jealousy and charges of favoritism haunted Alabi and the other captains during this period.[17] Samsam's people accused him of hoarding whitefolks' goods; Adjagbo and the Paputus who lived in his village were constantly at odds over the issue of equity; and by 1777, Alabi actually went to Paramaribo with the intention of renouncing his office over this issue because he feared for his life. As reported in the governor's journal,

> **There is real trouble with the Free [Saramaka] (quasi-Christian) Jan Arabini [Alabi], because his people have threatened his life (or so he says) because he receives too few presents, including powder and guns, considering the size of his village. He wishes to renounce his captaincy.**

During this same period, the Saramaka chiefs, under continuing pressure from the whites, finally agreed to name an official successor to Tribal Chief Abini. Rivalry among the most powerful clans (Matjaus, Nasis, Langus, and Abaisas), as well as collective advantage in being able to treat with the whites individually, had encouraged procrastination, once Alabi had been temporarily shunted aside (see Chapter 4). But now, after a decade of developing peacetime politics, the Saramakas apparently felt sufficiently secure to designate a new *gaama*.

Sometime during the mid-1770s, they chose Kwaku Etja, the elderly Nasi captain, to be official chief of the Saramaka nation, and he was duly recognized by the whites.[18]

There was one other major political issue during this period that, understandably, preoccupied the whites considerably more than the Saramakas—the ways in which the latter could be used to help the whites in their continuing wars against the Cottica Rebels (recent, unpacified maroons) led by Boni. Unsure (with good reason) of the fidelity of their Djuka "allies" in these wars, the whites hoped to use at least the threat of Saramaka force as a guarantor of Djuka military aid. The archival reports reveal a complex strategic game. In 1773, Postholder Daunitz was so worried about a Saramaka-Djuka conspiracy against the government that he questioned the "faithful" Alabi on the subject at some length. (And it seems that the bellicose Saramaka captain Samsam may indeed have been planning an attack on the whites with some Djuka friends.) But the next year, the Djukas were complaining to their postholder that Saramakas had been receiving payments of goods for cutting a secret path to Djuka, so that they could join up with government troops coming from the north in a pincers attack. Meanwhile, Colonel Fourgeoud (the leader of Stedman's famous "five-years' expedition"), apparently fearing a pan-Maroon alliance, treated separately with the Saramakas on several occasions. In 1776, he sent two of his officers to Bambey to meet formally with Alabi, Kwaku Etja, Kwaku Kwadjani, and the other chiefs as a friendly gesture. And the Saramakas responded in kind: a postholder's letter to Fourgeoud reports, "Chief Etja sends Your Excellency [with this letter], some prepared Pinda [peanuts] with the hope that Your Excellency will consume it with pleasure." Two years later, Alabi and the other chiefs were still bickering about the gifts that Fourgeoud had promised to send to them—by this time, Alabi and six others had each received "a hat with gold tassels and a sword."

If "Bambey" indeed meant "patience" (as some Moravian sources suggest), the name proved unfortunately apt, as far as the missionaries were concerned. Their move to the new village had been intended as a new beginning. Thenceforth, they expected to be more on their own, surrounded by sympathetic Saramakas and better insulated from "the heathens."[19] As they wrote on the eve of their departure from Kwama, "Our longing . . . is to move with those who believe and want to convert to Jesus, so that we can live with them there [at Bambey] alone."[20]

When they were not ill, the Moravians at Bambey set about building, for the first time, a small mission complex, "facing a little waterfall, with excellent air, and an outstanding view"; Brother Stoll "worked very diligently in planting the garden as well as in building houses and a kitchen"; Brother Kersten soon helped him make "tables, benches, and beds"; and, despite various interruptions for illness, the two men continued "going off into the forest to split cedar boards to bring back home." At this time, the missionaries also in-augurated their "new house of prayer, which is ten feet wide and fifteen feet long," and Brother Kersten wrote enthusiastically that

> we now have one kitchen, two living houses [one for Brother and Sister Kersten, the other for the Brethren Stoll and Rothe], and a chapel, all standing side by side on the bank of the Suriname, twenty paces from the river. Behind us, on a hill, we have a hen house[21] and workshed. The buildings are fenced off to form a closed-off courtyard. In front of us, we have planted coffee trees[22] and, on one side, we have a beautiful banana ground.

During these early days at Bambey, the missionaries even seemed optimistic about their food supplies (which had often been a serious problem at Kwama),[23] though they knew they remained dependent on the good will of Saramakas and on the vagaries of river transport.

> We seldom lack meat because people from other villages bring it to us, and we give them gunpowder in return. Unfortunately the [smoked?] meat is often quite dry, and we are therefore forced to eat bread to satisfy ourselves.

> On the 11th [June 1774], we received some clothes, housewares, books, and letters from Paramaribo. But that was all [i.e., no sugar, salt, vinegar, flour, etc.] because the canoe had sunk and its contents were lost.[24]

But despite their naive optimism and their several special advan-tages—a supply line to the coast, the use of domestic slaves, the ability to barter gunpowder for food with Saramakas—the mission-aries adapted only imperfectly to their physical and social environ-ment, and soon after the founding of Bambey, they were once again suffering badly.

In January 1774, Brother Stoll (accompanied by Brother Rothe) traveled to Paramaribo to marry the widow of a recently deceased confrere. In their absence,

> Ensign Daunitz [the postholder] moved into the house of the absent Brethren. [The next day] I (Kersten) became quite ill, as did my wife, and this lasted all through February and March. Throughout, Mr. Daunitz faithfully attended us, serving often as our cook, doctor, and surgeon.[25]

Soon after Brother Stoll's return to Bambey with his bride, he wrote:

> On the 1st of August my dear Rosine suffered a fainting spell and attack of chills. We brought her to bed, and after the usual remedies had been administered, she became burning hot with intermittent chills and convulsions, and lay in bed for days. Her heart was of great comfort to me . . . because she remained in the power of the dear Savior the whole time and she bore her pains with great patience, often saying to me, "If the dear Savior

wants to take me, then that is all right with me. I will go home to Him; there is no ill feeling between Him and me. If He wants to leave me here a little while longer, then I will stay here by you for a time." That gave me hope, but on the 13th our dear Savior thought it fitting to take her to His side.

Brother Kersten noted, as an epilogue, that

she is the first of us to pass away in this new place [Bambey], and now some of our Brethren and Sisters are resting in each of the places [the others being Sentea and Kwama] where we have lived.[26]

Alabi and the Moravians received another blow when Simon Yanki, who had become the second baptized Saramaka on New Year's Day 1773, fell seriously ill. His "heathen relatives" (who some months earlier had been so forceful in preventing the baptism of his son and then blamed Simon's "soul" for the child's illness and subsequent death—see Chapter 5) now prevented his move from Kwama to Bambey.

On the 30th [May 1774] the negroes returning from a visit to Kwama told us that Brother Simon has now become even sicker. It really pains us that he was unable to come with us [when we moved] because his family plagued him so much with their superstitious ways of healing. They have, of course, blamed us and Johannes [Alabi], because they believe that we seduced him. They have also proclaimed that should he die from his illness, they will shoot me and Johannes, since I baptized him. There are now so many malicious lies floating about that our few listeners are truly frightened. However, we are not afraid of the threats to kill us because our dear Father will protect us as His Son's ransom.

Not long after, Simon died. The missionaries received a report of his funeral which they considered "favorable" but which corresponds, in Saramaka terms, more to the way a convicted "witch" or other outcast is buried than to a Christian ceremony:

Some negroes from Kwama reported that . . . his family did not make any sacrifices after his death but buried him in silence. . . . He is now at peace and is the first of the local negroes who is actually seeing for himself what he believed.[27]

Only months later, the Moravians suffered another serious misfortune.

On the night of the 24th to the 25th [March 1775], the Suriname flooded so quickly that soon after midnight, Brother and Sister Kersten realized that their beds were already under water. Brother Kersten carried their possessions from the water, and

Brother Stoll brought them to a dry place till daybreak, when some negroes could lend assistance. We moved to another spot, hoping to find safety there but the water rose so fast that on the 28th we had to abandon it. Johannes [Alabi] and Grego cleaned out our two houses but the rain continued, and the Brethren Kersten and Stoll still could not find any dry land. We are amazed and thank the Savior in a child-like manner that we remain healthy in the midst of such awful weather. . . . On the 3rd of May we had the first day in a long time without rain, and with the help of the negroes we placed the house in which the Brethren Stoll and Rothe live onto its new site, three feet above the high-water mark. . . . Since the house of Brother and Sister Kersten was still higher up the hill, we again moved our dwellings on the 18th. On the 14th and 15th of June, the church and chapel were moved a bit higher on the hill, and we had a Lovefeast in which we gave the Savior heartfelt thanks.

Even in the promised land of Bambey, the missionaries' material subsistence became a constant struggle. They seem especially fortunate to have been able to believe:

We have never really suffered from want, because even the slightest amount of food eaten with love and contentment tastes far better than the most costly meal eaten with the opposite seasonings.[28]

And by Christmas 1775, despite the flood and other misfortunes, their diary reports that "we can honestly declare that we have never celebrated a more blessed Christmas in the bush."[29]

The spiritual progress of the Moravians at Bambey paralleled their material difficulties, though, again, they tried always to look on the bright side. Alabi remained the true rock of the mission, its only unwavering support. Except for Simon Yanki, who died upriver soon after the establishment of Bambey, the next converts were Alabi's brother-in-law Kodjo Maata ("who was the right hand of our Johannes and, in his absence, took his place as captain") and Kodjo's son Skipio and his friend Grego who, by 1775, were "the only two who remained with us of the eight schoolboys we had with us at Sentea." In 1779, five years after settling Bambey, a Moravian summarized the state of the missionizing enterprise:

(1) Brother Johannes Arrabini is in close contact with the Savior, and his heart lives in the sufferings of Jesus. His ways are unreproachable and whenever he gets the opportunity, he preaches unwearily to his countrymen.

(2) Christian [Grego] comes closer each day to self-awareness and knowledge of the Savior, and the Holy Ghost increasingly opens his heart to what God has done for him.

(3)   Our own negro Abraham [their slave] goes his own quiet way and one can be happy about him. These three are the communicants.

(4)   Joshua [Kodjo Maata] is baptized, and seems to be improving. He is less concerned than previously with Obia-things, and we are now beginning to have high hopes for him.

(5)   David [Skipio, Kodjo Maata's son] continues in his old [heathen] ways but there is still a small spark that we hope will ignite his heart. We hope he will think of the Savior and give himself unto Him.

There are, in addition, two baptismal candidates here and, as far as I can ascertain, they are ready to leave the heathen life, and they give us hope.

Even the generally optimistic Moravians had to admit that the fruits of a decade and a half of mission work appeared, at this time, to be rather meager.

Although I [Brother Schumann] thanked the Savior with humble heart for the blessing during these holidays [in 1778], it was at the same time very painful to me that among our churchgoers there was not to be seen a trace of Jesus's suffering, death, or Resurrection.

And Brother Wietz complained,

There are some people here who have been coming for so long to our meetings that they might appear to be true Brethren, but in fact they are hypocrites and lead a life of sin. In sum, there are about twelve who attend our public meetings. . . . I am happy here and I love the negroes. To be sure, I must look at them with compassion because they are so devoted to their sorcery and deceptions. However, they do come to church, and one never knows when their hour will strike. I am always comforted by this hope.

No more than a tiny handful of converts, of whom only two seemed "reliable," plus from one to four missionaries and one or two domestic slaves, imported from the coast: such was the composition of the Bambey Christian community during the 1770s.

In 1775 Alabi, constantly mediating between missionaries and Saramakas (and, in so doing, trying to shore up his own faith), took the occasion of his son's birth for a public show of piety.

On the 8th of March, a little son was born to our Johannes. He asked us: "How shall I thank my dear Lord for all the faith and trust He puts in me? . . . The people [here] have always said, 'Those who are baptized will not have any children since they

cannot make Obias.' Now, they will see that just the opposite is true—though they will remain as obstinate as before."

On the 9th, in the evening, Johannes requested that his new son be baptized, as he appeared to be ill. When the Brethren Kersten and Stoll went to see the child, they found a few young and inexperienced women bathing him in cold water in order to refresh him. Nonetheless, he slept gently. We told Johannes that there was no immediate danger, and we gave him and the women a little lesson in the proper handling of newborns.[30]

On the 12th, Johannes spoke at Holy Communion about his passionate desire that the child be baptized. Because we could see that he spoke from the heart, we sent the Brethren Kersten and Stoll with him to the house, and the latter baptized the child with the name Isaak. During the night, the Savior took the soul of tiny Isaak to Him. The father was very consoled because the child had received Holy Baptism.[31]

Presumably, Alabi's wife Sialoto and other relatives were less "consoled" and remained more convinced than ever of the dangers of converting, or of consorting with converts. The "tiny Isaak," under the care of his mother's mother and her "heathen" friends, was buried according to the special procedures used for children.[32]

The death shrieks rang out, and our hearts were terribly melancholy. The corpse was carried completely naked in front of our house to its grave. And when we asked why they did not clothe the corpse, they answered that if they were to do this, the parents would not receive any more children. For this reason, children are buried naked. A good hunting dog, in contrast, would be laid in his coffin all dressed up![33]

Increasingly, encounters about spiritual matters between Moravians and Saramakas brought fundamental cultural differences to the fore. Even after a decade and a half of mission work, deep misunderstandings marked almost all Moravian-Saramaka religious interchanges. Saramakas remained interested in "practical religion," in such here-and-now problems as sickness, misfortune, and crop loss. Moravians, meanwhile, remained heavily otherworldly in their orientation, seeing themselves as "a small band of pilgrims on their way to a better world. They were in this world but not of it." Brother Stoll's complaint during the mission's second year still held true for almost all Saramakas:

Until now, they have not expressed the least desire to become aware of their Creator and save their souls. They know that they have an eternal soul but they are not primarily concerned with its fate after death.[34]

In 1775 at Bambey, the ever-optimistic missionaries reported a characteristic encounter.

> **On the 21st [August], we were holding our evening service and a few unfamiliar negroes were sitting outside on a bench. Brother Johannes [Alabi] tried to talk to them about the true God who because of His love for us had been resurrected. Brother Kersten then talked in greater detail about these same matters. One of these negroes came back on the 23rd and told how he had lost his hunting sack the day before yesterday and, despite long searching, was unable to find it. Yesterday, he again looked in the forest, and because he wanted to believe what we had told him, he prayed to God saying "Great God, thou great Lord, I wish to believe the story that I have heard, so be good and see to it that I find my sack." Soon thereafter he found the sack, and that gave him the wish to hear more about how God became a man so that He could die on the cross and arise for us all. He listened to the story again with great interest and asked fundamental questions.**

But this Saramaka never, apparently, returned to the missionaries.[35]

The Moravian insistence on "confession" was another frequent stumbling block to intercultural understanding. Saramakas, then as now, were taught from early childhood to nurture a self-image that was generous, kind, and, above all, upright; the finding, by divination, that a person's heart was not pure indicated that he was a witch who must be executed. Conflicts based on such divergent cultural assumptions of Moravians and Saramakas dot the diaries for this period.

> **Once a sick old man visited us and told us over and over what a good man he was. I asked him whether he knew the Creator. "Yes," he said, "I know Him, but not as well as you Europeans do." "Do you know," I continued, "that He was resurrected because of your sins?" "Oh, no, no. I have no sins! My heart is pure. That He surely sees, which is why He has let me live so long. . . . The others who escaped with me to the forest are all already dead. If I had any sins, He would have killed me long ago. But He knows that I am a good man, and I show Him this each morning and pray to Him, 'Look here, nothing that I do is bad, please allow me to live.'"**

As one Moravian aptly remarked, "by nature these negroes would rather die than confess their sins."

Saramaka and Moravian cultural logics clashed in other ways as well. Even Saramakas sympathetic to the missionaries demanded results and found the missionaries' passivity confusing.

> **I have often heard [nonbelieving] negroes ask: "Why should we start to go to church if those who already do live in worse ways**

than we do? And if your cause were true, why would [some of] those who have already taken it up leave again and return to us?"

On the 21st [July 1783] a child died once again. We heard frightening shouts and shrieks among the people and Brother Wietz went to them and said "You dear people, listen to me please. You are crying but you are not crying about the child who died. Really, you are crying about yourselves and your children who are still alive. Please think how God has sent us to you Saramaka negroes, to show you the true path of life. You are no longer ignorant but still you resist the Merciful God who has sent you His Word. How will you excuse yourself before God's throne of judgment? God takes away these innocent children for his eternal security, so that when they get older they will not become Satan's servants." They all recognized this—one could truly see that. But their hearts and ears remained closed.

And other Saramakas, thinking about the way their own gods and ancestors behaved, were even wondering whether the missionaries' strange insistence on regular and lengthy prayer might not backfire.

When we came together for our evening service, a negro visiting from a neighboring village said to another one, "The people here pray every single day. Won't their god be angry at them because they burden him so?"

By the mid-1770s, Alabi stood alone among his countrymen in trying to bridge the cultural gap and make sense of the Moravians' message in Saramaka terms.

In July 1777, the missionaries witnessed two spectacular public executions of Saramakas who had been convicted of witchcraft.[36] Alabi, as village captain, presided at the decisive council meetings and participated fully in these events.[37] Because the Moravians considered such proceedings primarily political and juridical, rather than religious, they seem not to have been overly concerned that Alabi was playing a central role. For them, *wisi* meant "poison," not "witchcraft" or "sorcery" (as it did to Saramakas). The Moravians seem to have thought that some Saramaka *wisi* accusations were well founded, while others were trumped up—as in any system of criminal justice.[38]

Two famous priests of the idols were burned alive during this period. It had been discovered that (as they themselves admitted) they had, at the request of their gods, poisoned a number of children because their gods would only eat human flesh. One of them had such horrible fear and anguish as he watched the illness of the children he had poisoned, that he himself confessed his deeds. We had hope that this poor soul could be spared and asked Brother Johannes [Alabi], who served as captain at this trial, whether he would not be able to speak to this poor slave of Satan about the love and the compassionate heart of God, and to proclaim Salvation to the whole world through the Savior's Passion and Death, and to assure him that his own redemption was still just as possible as that of the Savior. Johannes did this on the night before the execution. However, the criminal gave him no response and the conversation did not hinder him from screaming out to *his* god as he was dying. This situation awakened among the negroes an indescribable lust for vindication and revenge. They were so filled with hatred that it was a heavy burden for us to hold meetings.

Brother Riemer, who arrived at Bambey two years after this event, left a more detailed description, based on the graphic account given to him by Alabi himself.

This is the frightening story of a young negro who believed that he had so angered his god, a big Boma [anaconda] snake, that the snake could only be reconciled to him if he killed three innocent children. . . . This negro knew a family with three small boys, the oldest being five and the youngest a year-and-a-half old. These he chose as the sacrificial victims of his idolatrous craze. Since this negro was well-known in the house, he entered on some pretence and took the occasion to offer the oldest child a fruit which contained strong poison [Alabi would probably have said, "prepared with witchcraft-medicine"], from which the boy died the following day. Afterwards, he watched with care to see where the father had buried his dead son, and the next day, unnoticed, he took the body from the grave to bring to his idol as a sacrifice. He then let some time pass, after which he gave the second child a piece of very tasty fruit which also contained strong poison, and from which his death quickly followed. The death of one healthy child so soon after another aroused suspicions among both the parents and relatives. But they knew no one who might be suspect. The sad father went with bleeding heart to bury this child beside the first. But he noticed that the body of the first child was missing, and his suspicions grew. After a few days, the murderer came to take the body of the second child and sacrifice it to his idols.

Next came the turn of the third little innocent. The monster, after several vain attempts, finally found a means to get this year-and-a-half-old child in his clutches, and once they were alone he gave him a piece of poisoned fruit. As he must not have eaten that much fruit, he did not die as quickly as his two brothers, and had to suffer for many days before he succumbed. During his long battle against death, this extraordinary adventure was much discussed in the neighboring villages. People came from far and wide to comfort the despairing parents.

"Execution of the Child Murderer" (Riemer 1801, pl. 9).

Among these was the murderer, who came to show the father his grief. But he was to pay a price for his duplicity. The sight of the tiny, innocent child suffering so severely moved the rest of those human feelings he still possessed, so that he was unable to leave the baby's side. And, finally, when he managed to force himself to leave, he found himself returning soon after. His exterior, and facial expression, betrayed so much fear and anxiety that people, with sound suspicions, finally placed him in chains and forced him to stay by the child's bedside for an uninterrupted period of time, so that he would witness the child's sufferings. During this time, the poisoner's agitation grew to such an extent that the relatives called the captain and some elders to arrest this man. Some queried him about his anxiety and agitation, to which he replied that he did not wish to submit to the Kangra [kangáa] ordeal of the Obia man but instead would make a free and open confession.[39] But the murderer trembled and quaked; his tongue seemed paralyzed and he was silent. Meanwhile, the captain urged him to confess. Finally, he pulled himself together and confessed his horrible deed.[40] Soon thereafter, the long-suffering child passed away.

After the burial, during which time the murderer remained in chains, a Grang-Kruttu [gaan kuutu, tribal council meeting] was called. The tribal chief [Riemer means Alabi, not Etja] opened the council meeting by relating the gruesome series of events, after which the murderer was led in and confessed his crimes without hesitation, in the presence of all the relatives of the poisoned children. Thus, no extensive Kangra ordeals were necessary. The tribal council condemned the criminal to death and presented him to the parents for their decision as to how the execution should be carried out, for they should not lack their well-deserved revenge.

The execution of this negro is supposed to have been one of the most frightening and monstrous ever carried out by this nation. They tortured the offender for each murder, one day at a time, and gradually mutilated him completely with the choicest tortures. They cut the limbs off his body and, finally, on the third day of torture they allowed him slowly to fry to death at the stake.[41]

If the missionaries did little to interfere with Alabi's participation in these witchcraft executions, this may also be because they themselves were once again suffering mightily and were hardly in a position to exert authority. (Brother and Sister Kersten had returned permanently to Paramaribo in 1776; and Brother Stoll, who had been one of three founders of the Saramaka mission twenty-two years before, had died in Bambey in early 1777.) Brother Schumann, recently arrived in Bambey, describes this trying period for the Moravians.

Brother Lehmann and I are all alone here. Brother Lehmann has for some time hardly been able to move hand or foot because of his painful illness. Since the 6th of August [1777], I have had a heavy fever and have had to endure great pain and suffering. I have also been terribly inconvenienced, and even our negro slave has had it and can do nothing. On the 10th of August, when the negro Brethren and others had returned from the forest, they were frightened to see our terrible situation, and decided to leave one of them with us, so that he could take care of us and at the same time make a coffin for Brother Lehmann, who had become very weak. . . .

On the 13th of August, we two sick men and Brother Johannes [Alabi] enjoyed Holy Communion together, but we also had a melancholy feeling which is difficult to describe. That same evening, Johannes returned to [his gardens in] the forest, and on the 14th, the negro who had stayed behind to help us followed him as well, since he had finished making the coffin. Thus, in the whole village there was no one left besides us and one negro and his family, who had never taken too much of an interest in us. . . . On the 16th . . . the Savior freed Brother Michael Lehmann from his long and difficult suffering. . . . On Sunday the 17th, after a speech about how Jesus ransoms the blessed death of redeemed sinners, he was buried by his hut. Although I was very weak mentally and physically, I gave a sermon, feeling the strength of God close by, which comforted and strengthened me a great deal. . . . I have become so saddened about the departure of my deeply beloved Brother Lehmann, which left me all alone on this difficult post. Nonetheless, there are also joyous and thankful tears in my eyes because I know that the Savior has helped him and will help us in these difficult circumstances. Thus, I give myself up voluntarily and entirely to the care of the Lord. . . .

On August 29th, my pains increased, and a terrible rash broke out all over me, from my skull to my feet, leaving me with sleepless nights, as if lying on broken glass or being grated by a big knife. I lay completely alone and sleepless the whole night. In addition to that sickness, there followed others, and day and night there were terrible stomach cramps. Strong hours of temptation of a different kind bore down upon me. It was particularly painful to me that the preaching of the Gospels has had no effect here [in Saramaka], and I have shed many tears because of this. I have asked the Savior to continue spreading His word and I have gotten patience and endurance from Him. . . . On 9 September and the following days, I became so weak that it appeared I would return home [to the Savior]. . . . Toward the end of the month and the beginning of October, our situation looked rather grim. My feet and hands, and even my fingers, were full of ulcers, and I could hardly walk or even touch things for several weeks. . . . On the night of 10 October, I fell asleep with a high fever, and a whole horde of ants filled the house. I awoke and found myself completely covered by them. I ran from my bed as best I could and retired to another house. But the biting of the ants and the inevitable infection of the sores and wounds increased my pain to an extraordinary degree. In addition, I got terrible chills. In these conditions, I found comfort and strength. . . .

It looks rather bad here not only because of the heathen negroes but also because some of our old listeners have now left us completely, since (as they say) death reigns in our house. Since then, I have had to listen to the most unpleasant truths and bitterness about this. How happy they are that we are all dying out and that we have to suffer such pain and, because of this, that our Brethren are afraid to come here. Nevertheless, the Savior's mercy continues to comfort me here.[42]

Very soon after Brother Schumann's recovery from smallpox, two new missionaries arrived to help him out. But without success, for they "were both called out of time, not more than a month after their arrival, and within six days of each other." Brother Schumann describes how

[on 3 March 1778] Brother and Sister Hans seemed happy and alert, with real enthusiasm about learning the local language. But already on the 23rd, Sister Hans had succumbed to a fever with periods of unconsciousness. . . . On the 25th her sickness became worse and, on the 30th, she was unable to get up at all. Brother Hans's wife felt certain that she would soon be called home [to the Savior], and she requested in all compassion that she be given Holy Communion. After this, she bid farewell to her husband, and on the 3rd of April she departed in a very gentle way. By this time, her husband was himself so weak that he could hardly take notice, and was unable to participate in her burial on the 4th.

On the fifth, Brother Schumann himself felt quite weak with fever and wrote that his slave was also ill. Then,

on the 9th, the Savior took Brother Hans to Him, and in the afternoon we held his funeral. I shed many tears but could not say a word and succeeded only in singing a few verses. The next several days I went about in great weakness and could do nothing but weep over the terrible events that the Savior had visited upon us, which now left me here completely alone. . . .

Today [12 April] was extremely difficult for me because a group of Free Negroes [Saramakas] returned from Paramaribo bringing the beds and clothing destined for the late Brother and Sister Hans plus some things for our household. But they refused to give them to me because I had not yet paid them, and their price was so high I could not meet it. I pleaded with them through gentleness but they left with the goods. The next day, when I was home all alone with no one nearby, the whole group returned with the goods and—as I still could not meet their request—they began to plunder the house and bitterly mocked us Brethren and made terribly damaging remarks against our Lord. They claimed to want to see if our God would punish them! He may have sent us to this land (they said) but he could not protect us here. Instead of answering them, I prayed in silence to the Savior, saying "This is a matter for you, Lord Jesus Christ, honor or shame!" And the Savior helped me so that I could give them some compensation and make them set aside their demands. Afterwards, it became apparent that this whole affair had been instigated by a hostile negro, and that something even worse had been planned for me. During Holy Week, we read the story of Jesus's Sufferings every day. On the 18th, I held Holy Communion [alone] with Johannes Arrabini. On Easter morning, the 19th, we prayed the Easter Litany and thought with melancholy feelings about the four Brethren who had passed on in the last thirteen months here in Bambey. . . .

Since the death of Brother Hans and his wife, the enmity of these hostile people has become so unabashed that they don't even hesitate to vent their hatred, mockery, and devilry openly. The tools of the Devil make clear that they see what is happening here as a victory over the true God. . . . On Whitsuntide we celebrated at a service with the only three negroes we can still regard as baptized. . . . In this [last] time, I have had to undergo a great many trials and tribulations.[43]

Perhaps the most remarkable of all Moravian achievements at Bambey was Brother Schumann's compilation of a Saramaccan-German dictionary, during the precise nine-month period that included his terrible illnesses and ended with the abortive arrival of Brother Hans and his wife. Alabi played a central role: "With the help of Johannes, I have now revised and corrected it in depth." By any standards, it is a fine piece of work, showing considerable sensitivity to Saramaka lifeways; considering the circumstances, its compilation seems little short of miraculous.[44]

Three months after the death of Brother Hans and his wife—with Brother Schumann still alone and barely able to cope—the Moravian leaders in Paramaribo decided that it was time to cut their losses in Saramaka. Schumann writes that

On July 25 [1778] I received a letter from Brother Kersten [who was now posted in Paramaribo, in administrative charge of all Suriname missions], in which he reported that our budget for Bambey was being discontinued, at least temporarily, and that I was to return to Paramaribo, with our pair of slaves and with a portion of our possessions. Consequently, during the next few

days we had much work to do. . . . Among the negroes here it was apparent that our departure was viewed not without pleasure.[45]

On 3 August 1778, Brother Schumann, his two slaves, and the small children of one of them boarded a canoe and set off downstream for Paramaribo. The Bambey mission, opened amidst much missionary optimism, was—for the time being—abandoned as a failed experiment.

Seven   *Ringer of Bells*

"You can well imagine," wrote Brother Heydt (who was sent out from the city to reopen the Bambey mission in early 1779), "what a settlement in the forest looks like after it has been left alone for five months." He found, to his dismay, that

> **the rats have eaten up the entire main building and have done fearful damage to our bedding. All the books which Brother Schumann had kept in a trunk have been completely ruined by the wood lice. Not one book is fit to be used, though the Bible is in a semi-proper state. When I visited the church, I discovered that the large ants had taken over and had thrown up large heaps of earth. The bats live under the roof, which was true in the other houses as well. Weeds have grown up so high, both in front of and behind the house, that they have choked half the coffee trees.**

But to Brother Heydt's joy, Alabi greeted him with unrestrained enthusiasm.

> **When they [the Christian Saramakas] saw me they uttered a wild cry of joy. Brother Johannes Arabini was so enraptured that he said "I could eat you up out of joy!" All day long he had felt as if his heart was to experience true joy, but he had not known from whence he could expect it. But now he saw it with his own eyes and kissed me.**

During the time that the mission was closed, two political events of note had occurred. The first, deceptively simple at first glance, sheds new light on the familiar issue of whether runaways were to be returned: Musumba, a Matjau who would later succeed to a captain's staff, turned back a slave.

The documentary background dates from at least 1774, when a certain "Kokroko," described as a Matjau, was reported to be harboring two slaves belonging to "Snijder," a man and a woman. (Musumba's full name, as spoken at ancestor shrines by Matjaus today, is Musumba Kokoko.) Four years later, the postholder confronted Musumba about this couple and was told that, in return for extra presents—a jug of gunpowder and some cloth, in addition to the usual cash bounty—he would consider turning in the man, but not the woman. (Another Saramaka eloquently presented a disingenuous supporting argument, which clearly irritated the postholder, that the 1762 treaty actually required that only *male* slaves be returned.) And shortly thereafter, in October 1778, Musumba finally returned the male slave to the whites.[1]

Musumba's turning in of this slave is one of the few such cases actively preserved by Saramakas today. It proved to be one of the most resistant nuggets of history I encountered in the field, for it both encapsulates a politically explosive "secret" and involves a "murder" with supernatural consequences. The secret: the segment of the Matjau clan that today lives in Asindóópo, the Saramaka capital, is in fact descended from Musumba and the newly arrived slave woman (and is therefore not really Matjau at all).[2] The "murder": Musumba, who coveted this wife of the recently arrived slave man, turned the husband back to the whites so that he could marry the woman (creating, after the whites executed the slave man, an avenging spirit who fiercely continues to haunt Matjaus to this day). A Matjau man, whose older brother was at the time being gravely sickened by the avenging spirit in question, finally shared with me Saramaka memories of what had taken place two hundred years before:

> *It happened at Djántipakía, at Bèdótilíba [under what is now the artificial lake]. Adjagbo [a Matjau captain] saw them there. The woman and her husband. Well, those "Negroes" [recently escaped slaves] were trying to find a place to settle in the forest. They said they wanted to come back [to Saramaka] with him. He said, "Well, come. I have land for you." So they came. And they lived well together until. . . . Well, Musumba coveted the man's wife. The woman said, "No way. If my husband finds out he'll kill you." Musumba said, "Yes." Now, whenever the man went hunting, he always had his knife. He and his knife never parted. He wasn't someone to fool with! So, [one day] when he came back with some game, they [Musumba and his people] said, "Give us the knife and we'll skin the game for you." So, he took it and gave it to them. Well, he no longer had any protection! So they grabbed him and tied him up. . . . That's the origin of A—— [the avenging spirit].[3]*

The late Matjáu elder Dooté in 1978, during the period when he was repeatedly sickened by the avenging spirit unleashed by his ancestor Musumbá, two hundred years before. Dooté had recently cut gardens on a site once used by Musumbá.

There is a touching epilogue to this story. An elderly Matjau described to me how he was once in Paramaribo with a group of Saramakas, during the early twentieth century, when A—— possessed B—— (its normal medium at that time). A Creole from the Para region, who happened to be present and heard the avenging spirit "recount its name," said that A—— was an ancestor of his, and that the descendants of the Para people who had stayed in slavery still preserved knowledge of his running away, but that until that moment they had never known what had happened to him.

Musumba's solution to the general problem of "female shortage" in this polygynous society was not unique. In 1778, the postholder's reports record that another Matjau man had "caught" a slave couple, but that Captain Mbuti claimed that the man had subsequently escaped and, despite Matjau searches for him, had not been found. And oral accounts dating to this period record several murders of the man in newly "found" couples.[4] Other Saramaka men sought different solutions: in 1776, the postholder reported that "the chiefs as well as ordinary people have asked for permission to buy slave women, saying that they are just as free as the Djukas who already buy slave women," and three years later Tribal Chief Etja registered a complaint, on behalf of the Matjau quasi-captain Djaki, that he had been denied permission for too long to purchase a slave woman for himself.[5]

There was a second political event—a brief potential crisis—during the period when the mission was closed, when the explosive news reached Tribal Chief Kwaku Etja that his favorite son, Gau, had been killed, allegedly by accident, while visiting relatives in Djuka. Although we do not know the immediate Saramaka reaction, we do know that only a short time later a peaceful delegation of eight Djukas was visiting the Saramaka tribal chief's village to discuss the case and to try to preserve friendly intertribal relations. And Kwaku Etja quickly dispatched two of his other sons to Djuka, to investigate further.

Gau must have been in his early sixties at the time of his death, which Saramaka investigations showed had, in fact, occurred accidentally, during a peccary hunt.[6] He formed but one link in a complex network of kinship and friendship between the Saramaka Nasi and Kasitu clans and the Djukas. We know that, at this time, yet another son of Kwaku Etja (who is called "Adgije" in the documents) was married to a Djuka woman and living most of the time in her village, and that Kwaku Etja was gaining considerable intelligence (e.g., regarding the whites' refusal to distribute tribute goods to the Djukas because of their current harboring of runaways) from this son's frequent visits back and forth. But, in addition, one of Kwaku Etja's own "sisters" was married to Djuka captain Kofi Tjapanda.[7] (Indeed, it was this latter whom Gau was visiting at the time of his fatal accident.) And just two years after this incident, Kwaku Etja sent four of his children off to Djuka on a friendly visit to their "uncle," Kofi Tjapanda. Saramaka-Djuka solidarity, which had already withstood the severe tensions surrounding Wii's murder in 1763, proved by this time to be too strong to be damaged by an accidental death, even that of the son of the tribal chief.[8] Another potential crisis had been averted.

Two months after the reopening of the Moravian mission, another new missionary, Brother Wietz (accompanied on his upriver journey by Alabi), replaced Heydt—who then returned to Paramaribo—as the sole missionary at Bambey. After a long and painful bout of "inflammatory bilious fever," accompanied by the construction of a coffin for him, Brother Wietz had the good fortune to recover, though he found himself "quite alone, among a strange nation, unacquainted with and unexperienced in every thing." By July, Brother Wietz had written that

> **of course it has been very difficult for me to take this on all by myself as I really do not yet know the language of the Free Negroes that well, and do not have the skill to tell the story of the dear Savior in it. He is, however, very close to me with His suffering and death, which is my sole text. . . . I very much hope that the [other] Brethren who are supposed to come to Bambey will arrive soon!**

The brother who in fact arrived to join Wietz in September, Johann Riemer, was something of a maverick among the Moravians. Of all the eighteenth-century missionaries to the Saramakas, it is he who left the fullest written record. Though he stayed barely half a year in

Bambey, he much later wrote a book based on the experience. And though he was apparently less well fitted to the missionary vocation than his confreres—indeed, he left the Brethren not long after returning to Europe—this former linen weaver had a keen ethnographic eye. Racist, romantic, self-involved, and very blunt, Brother Riemer in many respects more resembles Captain John Gabriel Stedman, his adventuring contemporary in Suriname, than his Moravian colleagues.[9]

Like every other visitor to Saramaka until the mid-1960s, Brother Riemer traveled upstream by canoe, utterly dependent on his Saramaka boatmen. Every missionary arrived by river; some traveled along it many times; and those who survived the rigors of mission life to return to Paramaribo made that final journey by canoe as well. Of the many descriptions of river trips left by visitors, Brother Riemer's account of his first upstream voyage is perhaps the richest. Though the trip was unusually uneventful (there were no serious accidents or losses of cargo) and lasted only seven days (the typical trip to Sentea or Kwama covered twice the distance, took two weeks, and included many times the number of rapids), Riemer's prose brings the more general river experience to life and reveals a good deal about just what kinds of people—slaves and masters, missionaries and Saramakas—made up Alabi's world. Because of its richness, I cite his report *in extenso*.

> The day of my departure [from Paramaribo] for the [land of the] Free Negroes (21 September 1779) approached. The previous day, Akra—who was the leader of the boatmen—came and asked me if I was ready to begin the trip and if I was in good spirits. I assured him, in all sincerity, that I was. He immediately explained that he and his traveling companions had finished with their local business and were ready to leave . . . and that we should now agree to a specific time, since a Free Negro never breaks his word. With this he gave me his hand and took his leave, saying, "Massra, tomorrow evening at midnight in the presence of the little heavenly lights, the stars, we will begin our voyage. Take courage and everything will go well." . . .
>
> The following day toward evening, my things were placed in the Free Negroes' canoe . . . and after everything was put in order I stepped into it and sat at the indicated place, which was one ell long and a half ell wide—a wooden plank placed exactly in the middle of the canoe and held fast to either side. The edge of the canoe was three fingers higher than the place where the board was fastened, and when I held my hands on either side they could feel the water to the right and left. When such a boat is filled to capacity, the sides are only two fingers above the water. This kind of canoe is made out of a single piece of hollowed-out tree.[10] . . .
>
> As evening descended, I prepared my departure from the lo-

cal European congregation, who held a Lovefeast for me, and toward midnight we all took Holy Communion. . . . I truly felt strengthened in body and soul. At midnight, I decided to leave for Bambey, in the land of the South American Free Negroes, and my local friends all accompanied me to the river.

Black clouds dominated the heavens, and we could not see the beautiful starlight. It finally became so dark that it was only by the light of a lantern that I could find my seat in the boat. . . . [Finally] the blacks untied the boat and *Akra* began the shout of the Gado or "songs-for-the-gods." Four of his helpers joined in while paddling.[11]

The negroes like to travel the river best at midnight, because the water is at its calmest and, in such a narrow canoe, they feel most safe. They must use such simple vessels because they are safest in the difficult rapids and falls that lie on the [middle and upper] Suriname River. A boat that was made from many pieces of wood would split asunder in the falls and rapids.

Akra now began to breathe easier and gaily knocked down a glass of *Dram*. "Massra," he exclaimed, "We are back again in our own element." By which he meant this forest. "And [referring to himself] from now on you'll see more cheerful people around you. Although the second half of our return-trip will be difficult and dangerous, we will never be without courage. You shouldn't be surprised if most of the whites we meet on the plantations seem to fear or hate us. Experience will teach you that we do not merit this, as we are honest folk." While he was talking about all this, he was very good natured in his manner and, although I had to interrupt him frequently to ask him questions, since I didn't know the language, he never became impatient but repeated what I could not understand until I had caught the meaning. He and his fellow negroes wanted to wait for moonrise at this place but because of a heavy rainstorm they had to continue the journey through the dark night. Since they always stay close to the bank, especially at night, my face and hands were wounded by the overhanging thorny bushes.

An hour before daylight, the rain became so heavy that we found it necessary to seek shelter in a creek. . . . As soon as it dawned, the rain stopped and the negroes bailed out the canoe and set off once again. I was completely drenched but had no opportunity to change my clothes and had to dry them gradually right on my body.

When we arrived at a large sugar plantation at seven that morning, I became aware of all the wounds I had received from the overhanging foliage. Also, my clothes were ripped and torn and my face covered with blood. However, the negroes had not suffered any such wounds, because their skin is so firm and strong that the thorns do not affect them.[12] The director of the plantation[13] was very happy to discover that I was a recently arrived European. I had hardly entered his house, when his Missi—a very charming mulatto girl—brought me coffee and other quite welcome refreshments.[14] When this man heard that I had grown up in *Berlin* and had only recently left there, he tried to make me stay through midday. But I had to decline his offer because I knew that my Bush Negroes were anxious to leave. In the interim, however, there came the to-me welcome discovery that our canoe had suffered serious damage on the trip that morning and that it would be necessary to repair it. As this would take several hours, all the cargo would have to be unloaded. This was as unpleasant a piece of news for the people who were accompanying me as it was welcome news for me and my friendly host. He gave the negroes some jugs of *Dram* and other refreshments in order to cheer them up. He also asked me to tell them that he would appreciate their not coming onto the plantation itself but staying by the riverbank in a small hut that was there until they had finished their work.[15]

In my discussions with the director, I found out that he too was from Berlin, and that he had originally come from a French family that had settled there.[16] He also said that he had a brother there from whom he had not heard a word in several years. When I told him that I in fact knew his brother, who was alive and well, and that I even knew the family and could tell him the baptismal name of his brother's son, with whom I had gone to high school, the good man cried tears of joy, and we spent much time together reminiscing. Because of this pleasant conversation, all of my terrible memories of the morning's adventures were cast aside. After the midday meal, I realized how badly I needed some quiet and rest, and since my negroes had not yet finished their repairs, my very thoughtful host gave me a hammock where I could sleep. And he ordered a *Futteboy*—negro slave—to swing it back and forth. By this pleasant and comfortable movement not only are people who wish to nap able to get some cool breeze in the great heat but also the hundreds of shameless mosquitos are thus able to be chased away.[17] During my noonday rest, the director prepared his [tent]boat at the shore so that it could take me to the next plantation where I could visit the next director.

At two o'clock my negroes were ready to travel. . . . My host took me in his boat, which was covered over, which I certainly appreciated, as the sun was truly burning. He had eight slaves as rowers, and although both craft set off at the same time, my negroes were soon out of sight and reached the distant plantation an hour before us, though we had not traveled slowly ourselves. The director of the plantation was already standing at the shore, since my negroes had told him of our imminent arrival. His friendly reception included the advice that I warn my blacks not to come ashore at his plantation because a planter

"Representation of a Tent Boat, or Plantation Barge." Anonymous engraving after a drawing by John Gabriel Stedman made only four or five years before Riemer's voyage (Stedman 1988, 93).

and some white women from Paramaribo were visiting, and the latter were very frightened of Bush Negroes. I then told him that his worrying was uncalled for as the negroes were already waiting for me at the shore, and a longer stay at his plantation would make them unhappy. We left without further delay.

Then followed one of the most difficult experiences in all my travels. We voyaged between high forest. Not a breeze stirred. The most burning sunbeams shot directly down on me. . . . I felt miserable and had a very powerful desire for the shade of European trees. I imagined them incessantly, but no shade was in sight, and in these latitudes the sun remains king from its rising until its setting every day. . . . Even had I possessed an umbrella to shield me from the sun, it would not have helped, as it would have been very dangerous, since the negroes are used to paddling extremely fast and, when we passed over a stone or submerged tree, I could have cut off their view. . . . I had suffered one very long hour from this indescribable heat when finally the heavens had mercy on me and some dark clouds appeared, accompanied by a very powerful wind. Then suddenly, some thundery weather and heavy rain came, and this set the current in motion so that with each stroke of the paddles, the water streamed into the canoe from both sides, and one negro had to bail continuously. After all that heat, getting wet was actually a comfort to me.

At sunset, we arrived at the coffee plantation where my negroes had decided to spend the night. Just as we stepped on land,
we saw a most dreadful sight, which left me with scarcely
enough composure to be able to give appropriate greetings to the
director of the plantation, who was hurrying toward me in a
friendly way. Near the shore lay two unfortunate negroes who
that afternoon had received the so-called "Spanish Bok." (This
torture is given to slaves who run away from their owners. One
ties these unfortunates to a kind of apparatus so that they cannot make the smallest movement. In this position, they receive
such a brutal whipping on their flanks that their entire skin is
ripped off. If they recover from this barbarous chastisement,
they often receive an iron collar with long spikes on it in order
to discourage any further attempts to escape.) Apparently, these
two slaves had been captured in the forest by a military commando and brought back. Here they lay just as they were left
after their tortures, on their stomachs, without being able to
help themselves. And they languished, suffering, until the evening, when they were allowed to be carried back to their huts.[18]

My negroes felt again, when they beheld this sight, how
much their own freedom meant. *Akra* shook his head with
visible repugnance, and went to the victims to offer a drink of
Dram. He displayed care and concern, and he said to his fellows,
"Look at me and don't say a word." It was clear that the planter
as well as his director were very uncomfortable and ill at ease at
our arrival today, and when I had dinner with them, I also saw
this. . . . I took the opportunity to try to talk to them about the
horrible ways that they had used to punish the negroes. . . . I
believe that the planter was a man of compassion; but the director appeared to have abandoned his human feelings a long time
ago. Yet even he showed an indescribable fear of the Free Negroes and could not understand how I could be so stupid, to risk
my life among these fearsome and odious people. Certainly, it
was only out of fear that he often asked his mulatto girl how my
canoemen were doing and ordered that they be treated in the
best manner possible.

How comfortable it was for me to spend the evening at this
well-equipped plantation, especially since I had spent the previous night completely sleepless. The next morning at four
o'clock, my negroes had the plantation watchman wake me up,
and we continued our trip by the bright moonlight. When my
hearty canoemen came to the first pause in their lively morning
song, I asked Akra why he had forbidden his followers to speak
to the people on shore, and he replied, "The behavior of the
whites seemed so low that I didn't even think it merited our
observations and comments in their presence. I of course did my
duty by trying to refresh the poor people who had suffered these

"View of the Jews Savannah" (ca. 1800). Anonymous engraving after a drawing by J. H. Hottinger, itself after a painting by J. A. Kaldenbach (Atlas van Stolk, Rotterdam). This depiction shows many of the same buildings that appear in the better-known anonymous engraving made after Stedman's 1770s drawing (Stedman 1988, 545).

Ruins of the synagogue at Jews Savannah, 1970s (Centraal Bureau Luchtkartering, Suriname).

inhuman tortures, and by so doing criticized more effectively by action than by words the behavior of our white brothers."

At eight in the morning, we arrived at the small town of *Jews Savannah*, which lies on the Suriname. It is a well-built place whose inhabitants are mostly Portuguese Jews, who have many plantations and a large number of negro slaves. They have the privilege of maintaining their own system of justice and their own ways. *Akra* led me to the most respected Rabbi, who received me in a friendly way and showed me the local sights, especially the very beautiful synagogue. He entertained me with refreshments and then accompanied me to the riverbank. There, once again, I saw a frightening example of the horrors I had seen the day before. Three negroes who had received the Spanish Bok several days before were lying on their stomachs on the riverbank. I was truly horror-struck by the sight, but my sense of compassion did not allow me to come closer to them. Meanwhile, before my arrival, my negroes had given them a refreshing drink. They told me how maggots were running around in the pus-filled wounds of these poor tortured negroes, which is not rare among the negroes here because of the terribly hot climate and the negligence of the plantation doctors. Actually, one must say that the custom of the negroes here is to allow those wounds and lacerations received from whippings to dry out in the hot sun.

Towards midday we arrived at one of the largest sugar plantations. The director knew *Akra* well, and he came to the riverbank, where he welcomed us in a very friendly manner, showed my traveling companions where they could stay, and took me to a meal which various guests were enjoying in a large room in the plantation house. All of the guests sat at a table filled with refreshments, even though the real noonday meal was supposed to be eaten later. The owner of this plantation, a friendly and lovable person, was entertaining some visitors from Paramaribo. On my whole trip [to Suriname] I really never met his equal. After an hour and a half, *Akra* sent word that he was ready to leave. The director, who wanted to continue having my company at table, was not happy with this. As he was acquainted with my black commodore, he himself went to the riverbank and, without my knowledge, spoke with him and told him that my negroes should all go to the next plantation where the slave negroes were holding a big celebration that day, and should allow me to remain behind until evening when he himself would accompany me to this place. *Akra* decided to follow these instructions, which is quite out of character for a Free Negro, but he decided not to travel until he had spoken personally with me.... "Massra," he said, "I have promised your brothers in Paramaribo to care for your life and not to let you out of my sight for the entire trip. However, since this Massra, who I know as a good man, has offered to take my place for the time being and promises to take you to *Rama*, I will go there with peace of mind and await you, and I will expect you there in the evening."

I was certainly satisfied with the way these crude savages [*rohen Naturmenschen*] reasoned, and I went back with the director to the company. Everyone was very pleased to see me again, especially once I had explained that I could remain for a longer stay in their company and did not have to depend on the arbitrariness of my Bush Negroes. In the meantime, the table was set in the dining room and there were twenty different dishes. The table was waited on by young mulatto girls who were very attentive and who seemed to know their way around so well that one would have to assume that such princely meals were served every day. The style of china and linens, and the different kinds of food and wines, not to mention the overall neatness, were all part of Dutch cuisine, just as I have seen it in the homes of the foremost Amsterdam merchants. To be sure, in such a prosperous setting, the afternoon hours sped by quickly. . . .

After we had spent the night at Rama, which was a military post, we arrived on the afternoon of the following day at a large sugar plantation. It lies in one of the most beautiful and fertile regions of the country and has lovely meadows and fields. The director, who was born in Switzerland, has established a cattle-breeding ranch here with the permission of the planter, which in just a few years has become so successful that he now has the best meat in the whole Paramaribo region. The owner of the plantation is a Portuguese Jew who was present when I arrived. Both received me in a friendly way and were most hospitable to me as well as to my negroes. . . . Just as we were sitting down to eat our lunch, *Akra* sent word that he was ready to leave. I had to accede to his request because the negroes wanted to reach a plantation that was a considerable distance from here by night-fall.

The heat on this trip was unbearable, and the reception that we had at this next plantation was not nearly as fine as the one we had at midday. Neither planter nor director, both Portuguese Jews, were there to greet us. But some of my negroes knew these gentlemen from previous transactions and, without further ado, went to the owner's house, where we found both carousing with bottles in their hands. The director, to be sure, stood up to greet us, but he fell down immediately and it was difficult for him to pick himself back up and once again get on his chair. As little as I liked it here, my negroes loved it because, in their drunkenness, these gentlemen gave my negroes a large bottle which contained four Dresden potfuls of Dutch gin for their refreshment. And that is how these gentlemen struck their Achilles heel. . . . I spoke to these gentlemen about their drunkenness in a very earnest tone, and warned them against it. These gentlemen's Missis were not even present. Because *Akra* felt at home at this plantation,* he immediately got one of the domestics to bring him and his fellows a quarter of a roasted pingo—wild pig meat. After spending two hours here, my negroes got into the canoe again, half drunk. Thank God, both *Akra*, out of pride, and the youngest negro, because he had listened to me, drank in moderation, so that they were in a proper condition to maneuver the canoe. In contrast to them, the three other negroes often jumped into the river, but this brought them no danger; in fact, little by little they gradually sobered up.

With sunset, we arrived at *Victoria*, the last plantation on the Suriname, where they gather together all the costly timber to be sold for Europe.[20] . . . The very rude watchman who stood on the bank called out to us roughly. We answered in kind, but a noncommissioned officer received us politely and accompanied us to the military commander. Even he received us in a friendly and hospitable way. He immediately said that my negroes should take up their quarters in the barracks and told the guards that they should watch over our things in the canoe, so that the plantation negroes would not steal anything.[21]

The lieutenant in command here is a German, and he immediately asked me my plans and where I was born. He told me that on this plantation were the last Christians that I would meet for a long while, and that I would have no protection for the next few days and nights except for the heavens above, and that there would be hordes of wild animals all around. Therefore, he wished to make my hours here as pleasant as possible. At dinner we had all kinds of intimate discussions, reminiscing about our fatherland. It appears that this officer, whose name was *Neumann*, had studied in *Berlin* for a whole year and had actually been my schoolmate. To be sure, the situation of my friend, at this faraway isolated military post, does have the disadvantage that he rarely has the opportunity to converse with white people. . . .

Before my negroes retired for the night, *Akra* came to me accompanied by a noncommissioned officer and confessed that he had decided to leave at four in the morning. He advised me to get to sleep early so that I could enjoy the last night we would spend in a sheltered place. Then, the officer brought him back to his comrades. The well-intentioned advice of the negro could

---

*The Free Negroes bring rice from their land and exchange it for dram and molasses and sugar syrup here. The rice they deposit at the plantations on their way to the city, and on their return they pick up the dram and molasses to take home.[19]

not prevent us from continuing our conversation, and *Neumann* assured me a number of times that he had not had as enjoyable an evening during his whole stay here. Finally, at midnight, we both went to rest, and already at three o'clock my hospitable host woke me up himself and had already seen to it that breakfast was prepared. Then he gave me a whole bunch of ripe bananas and two loaves of army bread, which came in very handy as it later turned out. He accompanied me to the river, where the Bush Negroes awaited me, and he advised them to paddle with care. And then, after a most impassioned farewell, he left with tears in his eyes, and returned to his quarters. . . .

[On the 25th of September] at four in the morning, we left Victoria under bright moonlight. My negroes, who had been treated to fine hospitality at the order of the lieutenant, were in a very good mood and they paddled while singing their songs-for-the-gods in unison. . . . The different prayers that they sing to their gods while setting out on a trip are so persuasive and purposeful that one is truly moved by them, and they seem truly incongruous with their brainless concepts of the Godhead. They also have the custom, before drinking a glass of liquor, to pour a bit of it on the ground for their Gado.[22] . . . We proceeded along the river, as they paddled powerfully and sang their song. After I repeatedly admonished them to take care, I received the cold-blooded reply: "We are now in the forest, and things will be much more difficult than before. From now on, you are the one who will have to take care."

After an hour had passed, the moon set and all we could see was thick clouds. As it was the dead of night, and the Suriname was walled in by tall trees on both sides, it was so dark that I could not even make out the negroes who were sitting ahead of me in the canoe. But they remained undaunted by the darkness until suddenly our canoe hit a fallen tree with such force that I was thrown into the air and would have fallen overboard had not the negro sitting behind me grabbed me and held me in. Because of this event, the paddlers became more cautious. . . .

When dawn finally shone through the thick clouds, gradually driving away the darkness, I heard in the distance a hoarse roar, which became louder and louder. I became scared and asked my negroes where this was coming from. They immediately answered, "Fear not, Massra." However, it was clear from their anxious movements and incredible silence that there was impending danger, and I became still more frightened. Suddenly, the river streamed toward us sideways, and we were face to face with a rocky wall. Quicker than a wink, all my negroes, without saying a word, sprang into the water, two of them landing on the rocks and holding the canoe steady from the front, while the strongest of their comrades climbed higher onto the ledge holding the vine rope in his mouth. The final two negroes held the

"Massa! Fear not!" (Riemer 1801, pl. 6).

Twentieth-century Alúku Maroons hauling a canoe through the rapids (Hurault 1970, 30).

canoe steady from either side. . . . Alone and lonely I sat at my place and had to be patient about what was going to happen, and could hardly open my eyes because of the heavy spray. Suddenly, I noticed the negro who had climbed up onto the upper surface. He stood with half his body in the water, and pulled with the rope. He also called to his comrades to help him push the canoe forward, but to me he cried out "Fear not, Massra." He called this out several times in a heartfelt manner. In this way our canoe finally came to rest on the edge of the rocks and was pulled free from the rushing, plunging water. The water kept rushing forward and sideways into the canoe, but it all ran out too, because of the slanted angle at which it was leaning. Just when we were finally set to leave this dangerous waterfall, at six in the morning, the sun broke through. . . .

After completing this difficult work, the negroes called a short halt, during which the canoe was drained of all the excess water, and they asked for a glass of dram as compensation. Before each drank, he poured a bit onto the earth as his *Gado*'s share. Not one bit of my clothing remained dry through all of this. Laughing, *Akra* said, "Do you see? Our skin is dry and your clothes are still dripping! We certainly have the advantage over you whites!"[23] But my own discomfort was only short-lived as the hot, bright rays of the early morning sun dried my clothes within an hour. At eight o'clock we again passed one of these waterfalls and all the above-mentioned precautions were again undertaken. Once again my clothes became soaked, and again the heat of the sun dried them. However, the heat became so unbearable, especially for my head, that by the time noon approached, all of my courage had left me. Finally, a lucky idea came to mind that would lessen my suffering. Namely, I took a large handkerchief, folded it in eight, dipped it into the water, and then placed it on my hat, and thus the power of the sun became very much reduced. To be sure, however, I had to re-enact this procedure every quarter of an hour. As we will see, I had to undertake this type of difficult trip on the Suriname four times during my stay, and each time this precaution was of great help.

At noon we passed the highest and largest waterfall thus far, and upon this occasion I almost lost my life, due to the carelessness of the youngest negro. After we had successfully mounted the waterfall with the canoe, the negroes stopped on one of the many small wooded islands in the middle of the river. They tied the canoe to the base of a tree and gave the young negro the order to watch over it while the other four went to cool off in the water. Because our situation did not permit me to come ashore, I had to remain sitting in the canoe, and because the heat of the sun is much stronger when one is sitting quietly in the boat than when it is moving, I had to endure it silently, along with the negro left on watch. However, the heat became so unbearable for him that he finally left his post and went with the others to cool himself in the river. Completely alone, I remained in the canoe, as it strained back and forth in the current, held by a thin vine rope. I saw nothing except, from time to time, a negro head which was jutting up from the water, and I felt completely helpless. . . . The boat remained in constant motion and the rope, which had apparently not been well enough secured, little by little loosened.

All of a sudden the current captured the canoe and sent it with unbelievable speed toward the above-mentioned waterfall. In this frightening instant, when Fate had the upper hand and I was almost destined to meet my end, heaven and water disappeared from view, wrapped in darkness, and I was almost unable to shout for help. However, a hoarse cry finally rang out through my terror and alerted the watchful *Akra*, who had swum back down a bit. My eyes then turned to heaven, and just then I saw my faithful companion jump toward me from the above-mentioned rocky ledge. He quickly grabbed the forward part of the canoe with his hands, just as the rear part began to slide down the waterfall, and he allowed himself to be dragged along the surface of the rock, endangering his own life, so that he could hold the canoe onto the rock and not let it fall over. Without this help from the negro I could never have been saved. In the meantime, the other negroes jumped up and emptied the canoe of all its water, and carried it with much effort back upstream. *Akra* was wounded all over by the sharp stones, especially on his knees.

This event caused a great deal of strife among the negroes, as they hauled the boat over the falls, and the negligent one would undoubtedly have been badly mishandled, had I not spoken out on his behalf and tried to quiet the others and prevent them from doing anything to him. It was most difficult to speak of reconciliation to *Akra*, and he said in a very feeling manner that the behavior of this youngest negro was not at all fitting for a Free Negro, and that it was totally against their rules to be so disobedient. However, he said that because of my pleas he would not, this once, take the proper action of punishing his colleague. At that moment he requested for himself and his companion a glass of dram. This time, however, he poured almost half on the earth for his *Gado*, because he believed that, on this occasion, he had had his help. Thenceforth, not a word was ever said about this.

After an hour, we again ascended a waterfall with the canoe, where we expected to eat a noonday meal consisting of some of the bananas that we had received as a gift in Victoria. However, the accident had brought about their loss, which we had not noticed at the time. Because of our lack of time, it was impossible for the negroes to fish or hunt, so they contented themselves with some turtlemeat and cassava cakes that they had brought along. (*Cassabi* or *Cassaba* is the substitute for bread that is eaten by the slaves as well as the Free Negroes, and by many whites as well, because it is much cheaper than wheat bread, which is extraordinarily expensive in this country. . . .) Fortunately, we had the luck not to lose the loaves of army bread, which they left for me, saying it would only give them stomach cramps. I was very pleased about this and ate a piece dipped in molasses, with great gusto.

During the afternoon, we again had to cross some waterfalls, but we successfully overcame all difficulties. Gradually, I got more used to the dangers of such travel. My chief enemy, however, remained the ever-increasing and oppressive heat of the sun. Shortly before sunset, *Akra* shot a *Bavis* [*Powisi*, crested curassow], a large black bird, on the riverbank, and it served as a fine evening meal. Soon thereafter, we arrived at the place where we were to spend the night, which had three small huts that my negroes had built on their trip to Paramaribo. In the middle one of these huts, they quickly hung my hammock. I made immediate use of it, since one does not like to touch the ground unless absolutely necessary because of the many little bugs that generally live near the shore.

As soon as my companions came ashore, *Akra* made a serious speech, according to their custom, welcoming me as a fearless white to our first evening in the forest. Then the negroes divided up the preparation of the evening meal: some plucked and cleaned the *Bavis*, some took care of the fire and the boiling water in which they were going to cook it. And all this took place so quickly that within an hour I received my portion in a calabash. Although the meat was too tough for me to enjoy, the broth in which I dipped some of the cassava had a strong and pleasant taste. The fire used to cook the meal became increasingly strong and stayed lit, and eventually an individual little fire was placed under each hammock. A bright fire in front of the huts burned the entire night. The reasons the negroes use these fires are two: first, they serve to keep the wild animals from approaching, and second, they help warm the negroes, who sleep naked in their hammocks, as it usually gets cold in the evening because of the strong dew that falls at night.

Even though I was quite tired from the heat of the sun and all kinds of other adventures, no sleep came to my eyes in this new and for me unfamiliar night camp. To pass the time, I played my flute and expressed my mournful mood by melancholy fantasies. The negroes listened in amazement, and even for me these tones—with which the waves of the nearby river harmonized sonorously—had something new and attractive. But what a horrible noise interrupted my soft melodies! A great many wild animals which had heard us approached our quarters and raised their voices in such frightening noise that it was impossible to bear. Among these, the howler monkeys especially distinguished themselves. This accompaniment was hardly pleasant and brought my Arcadian music to an end. I asked the negroes to fire their guns so that the beasts would leave, and slowly but surely their shouting ceased. As soon as this was over, a new plague arrived. Toward midnight a breeze blew up which the negroes saw as the harbinger of thunder storms. The smoke from the night fire, which came from a greenish-type wood from fruit trees, was then blowing right toward my hammock, and I felt as if I were being smoked alive. This bothered me so much that I had to leave the hut, and I decided to hang my hammock outside in the fresh air. But no sooner had I done this than a big storm broke and, before the negroes were able to bring me and the hammock back to the hut, I was thoroughly drenched. With this, my health—which had gradually been getting better—suffered a severe setback. Because of this incredible rain, the negroes had so much work keeping up the fires that they were robbed of sleep, but this did not seem to bother them. Only after several hours did the rain abate and the moon shine through with its full glow.

I had hardly slept an hour when the negro on watch woke me to have some coffee and continue our trip. At 4:30 on the 26th of September, we left by moonlight and, accompanied by the usual Gado song, we soon arrived at a very dangerous waterfall. It was comprised of a sort of street about a hundred paces long, lined with boulders and as wide as the river itself. The whole river was divided up into small streams which pressed very forcefully through the different stone passages. The negroes could not immediately go around this, so they tied the canoe to a low portion of the rock and then unloaded it, bit by bit, to bring it up above the falls. Since the path among the dry rocks was sometimes very deep, a negro carried me up through this passage on his back. Despite his great caution, he fell down once, and we both became wet though we did not injure ourselves. On the next ledge we saw a broad space of stone which the negro said was for me; he also remained with me till another could come and bring my saber and musket. . . . For the next several hours we found good, navigable waters and probably traveled two German miles. I saw my first tapir—a kind of Satyr [because of its enormous penis?]—which was swimming across the Suriname River. Although a negro tried to shoot it, the muskets had not been kept dry during the night's heavy rainfall and would not fire. And the tapir continued on his way unhindered. After this good stretch of river we hit some very difficult ones, and the heat of the sun became more and more unbearable for me.

Towards afternoon the canoe again had to be unloaded and the things carried along a surface of exposed rock until we could find navigable water. Since I was really suffering from the heat, I simply allowed myself to be led along by the people accompanying me. And I waded up through different watercourses even though I had received a wound on one foot, which the negroes believe was caused by a bite from a large fish called Haymann.[24]

. . .

After a while we made our midday halt at a small wooded island in midstream. But unfortunately we lacked all provisions, so my negroes had to go hunting and fishing. While they were thus occupied, I shot a rather large, magnificently colored bird on the island and expected to make a fine meal of it. But I was disappointed, for when the negroes returned and I happily showed them the bird they became distraught and showed their anger, and they reprimanded me violently: *"Massra bi dedde wan Gado,"* that is, "Massra has killed a god."

I stood there aghast, but on the advice of one of the negroes who understood a little German I quietly put aside the bird so as not to entertain their natural repugnance any longer. Soon, they

"Masra bi dedde wan Gado!" (Riemer 1801, pl. 7).

calmed down and their unfriendly regards once more became friendly. In less than half an hour, these black fishermen made such an enormous catch that all of us had a full lunch, and there were even considerable leftovers. . . . After we had eaten, the negroes went into the water for a few minutes to cool off, while I—who could not, to my great regret, swim at all—simply sat there, longing for a European evening breeze.

Our afternoon's voyage was similar, except that the negroes themselves now complained about the great heat. As it turned out, our route took us increasingly closer to the oppressive heat of the sun, and further away from the fresh pure air of the ocean. . . . In this distress, the repeated moistening of the hand-kerchief in the water gave me comfort, and without this I would more than likely never have been able to bear the sun. Neverthe-less, I truly felt numb much of the time, and I could not distin-guish whether I was in America or Europe, and I probably would not be wrong in assuming that many Europeans who travel under similar circumstances to Suriname experience the same sufferings but never return, instead finding their grave there. . . . At sunset, we came to the largest and most dangerous water-fall of the whole trip, which the negroes call *Sissabo* [Mama-dan].[25] This waterfall is distinguished by its two high shelves, following one upon the other. It was surely very difficult to ascend in the usual manner, though when the river is high it is quite easy to descend.

The negroes were so tired from paddling the canoe and un-loading it that they felt it necessary to settle here for the night. The roaring of the falls was so loud and unrelenting that one could hardly hear the hefty voices of the negroes. The ham-mocks were slung from trees in the open air. Then the negroes prepared the lizards they had shot for dinner. They tasted so good to them that they forgot the hardships which they had to endure. Because of the relentless noise of the river no sleep came to my eyes. Meanwhile, my negroes slept peacefully, to the ac-companiment of the roaring waters and the howler monkeys. However, they were soon awakened by a frightening thunder-storm with strong rain which shook the trees on which the hammocks were hanging. I crawled under my blanket, which had been covered with an oil-soaked cloak to protect me from the rain. While I lay there, a lightning bolt split a very large hardwood tree, just a few paces from us. My negroes lept with a shout from their hammocks, and the one who had been serving as guard, by the fire, lay there for several minutes, totally dumb-struck. But he pulled himself together and was able to collect his wits, with the help of his comrades. They had all become frenzied, but my ears were protected by the cover under which I had crawled. The fire was set again, and finally sleep was able to comfort us until morning.

When day broke [on the 27th of September], the negroes brought their supplies back to the canoe. . . . That morning we had good, navigable water for the first two hours and in this short time were able to travel some two and a half German miles. But the rest of the day went very slowly because of all the waterfalls. Our breakfast today consisted mainly of the previous night's lizards, and it seemed to me that they tasted better cold than hot. During the entire day my negroes held very animated conversations with one another, all dealing with the same theme: what type of ceremonies they wanted to carry out upon arriving at their villages.[26] The thought of being once again among their own kind appealed to them greatly and allowed them to endure the very difficult and painful journey. . . . Until sunset, we passed through difficult stretches of river, which the negroes overcame with great skill, never allowing the difficulties to destroy their peace of mind. Then, finally, the river became navigable again, and we paddled by the light of the stars for some three hours, covering a couple of miles before, as usual, setting up our night shelters in the open air. Instead of resting, as they had done during the previous evenings, they sat together with the man on watch and discussed with light hearts the reunion with their families and their festive entrance into *Bambey*. In contrast to my negroes, I slept more peacefully than at any time during the whole journey.

At three in the morning on September 28th, my companions awakened me and gave me a calabash of coffee, and by three-thirty we began our onward trip by the bright moonlight. Never was the Gado song of the negroes sung with greater inspiration than on that morning. It dealt mostly with praise and gratitude to their gods for having spared them on their difficult trip, and they raised their voices in very melodious song. When they were not singing, they engaged in animated conversation, and the trip went so fast that we moved quicker than the best horseman could have managed. And the negroes thought neither of refreshments nor breakfast as long as the water was this navigable.

When day broke, we arrived at a high and ten-minute-long rapids. I tried my best, as I was becoming increasingly experienced, to overcome the dangers on my own, but it took me a good half hour to get through it, and the negroes found it difficult as well to unload the canoe and carry it through. But they remained all the while in their joyful mood.

After another half hour, they stopped and I thought they wanted to have some breakfast, but actually my high-spirited negroes only wanted to give me a surprise. They told me that we would arrive at *Bambey* at three that afternoon, though I had no idea we had already reached their land. . . . Each of them opened his travel-basket, and in it were the different pieces of apparel which they wear when in Paramaribo or for ceremonial occasions. And they dressed themselves in the best manner they could. Our proud commodore, *Akra*, was particularly distinguished in the strange manner in which he dressed. By his bartering in Paramaribo, he had gotten a splendid colored nightshirt that had been made at Zitz, and for which he had been charged fifty guilders. He wore it tied together with a dagger, and he had a hat with tresses on it. In this ridiculous attire he ordered his comrades about, and I had a difficult time suppressing my laughter. When our muskets were finally charged with double loads [of powder without shot], the negroes, with pride in their splendorous dress, continued the trip in a most uncommon silence.

We had hardly been traveling for a quarter of an hour when a negro gave me my musket and asked that I shoot it with them. The salutes were soon answered from a nearby Pinda [peanut] garden. When we arrived at the shore, a whole lot of negroes were gathered with their women and children. They gave very wild shrieks of welcome accompanied by drum and fife, and this lasted as long as I remained in the canoe. Once we had landed, the women and children surrounded me, the women flooding me with enormous numbers of questions, each wanting her own to be answered first. Meanwhile, others shouted out *Hodi Massra!* (Welcome, Master!). Because I did not yet know the language, I was unable to answer the women and they therefore assumed that my hearing was poor. Soon, one after the other came very close to me in order to shout her question in my ear, and the only provision I had was patience and gentleness, which I used to rid myself of these curious creatures, little by little. The younger negro, who knew a bit of German, helped me out in this predicament.[27]

In the meantime, those negroes who were in the peanut gardens filled their muskets with double loads and surrounded me in order to tell me about their joy and the honor that they wanted to accord me. One stepped behind and the other in front of me, and both placed their muskets between my feet. Whereas the other ones positioned themselves around me and held up their muskets cross-wise above and beside my head. A pistol shot was the signal, finally, for the firing of these overloaded muskets, and the sound was deafening, with the shots reverberating from the hills back to the huts, to which the crowds of people led me amidst continuous shouting by the women and children.[28] When I finally sat down in one of their huts, in order to catch my breath, they again all pressed forward to me, so that I almost lost my reason. Although their forwardness distressed me, I realized that their hearts meant well, and they even brought all of their medical provisions with them so that I could be strengthened. Meanwhile, my negroes had unloaded the canoe and brought with them a large bottle of dram obtained on the plantations, as well as half of our pingo meat, as a gift. Everyone soon got busy with the preparation.

As soon as I had recovered a bit and had decided to leave the hut, they gathered round again. They all welcomed me and gamboled to fife and drum music, singing while clapping their hands, and for some time continuing to dance around me. Then they led me into another hut where many of them were preparing food according to their custom. All of the negroes sat down on very low stools in order to eat the food, which stood in calabashes on the ground, and my negro brought a little stool from our canoe for me, so that I could sit and eat.

After the women and children had, as a group, stepped back from the men's hut, we could partake of our meal, which consisted of banana pudding—which is rather like mashed potatoes—and peanut broth.[29] (According to the old custom which the negroes have brought from their fatherland, Guinea, the male and female sex eat separately, so that a husband never takes a meal in the presence of his wife. The Europeans believe that the reason is this: those negresses who live in freedom generally rule over their husbands, work very little, and pay little attention to their husband's business. But even among them, there are some reasonable women who work hard and maintain a clean and orderly household.) The negroes eat with their fingers, taking the food, dipping it in broth, and then placing it into their mouths. True, this does not look appetizing, but I must confess that the negroes carefully wash their mouth and hands before eating. And often they repeat this each time a new dish is served. I asked them why their womenfolk do not eat with them, as we Europeans believe it is more pleasant to take our meals together. They were very surprised and one of them answered, in a rather apathetic manner, "Well, they prefer to eat by themselves, as well."[30] . . .

After the meal, my negroes brought in at least ten Dresden pots full of dram. All were immediately consumed. My negroes felt strengthened by this breakfast but, unfortunately, three of them were so drunk they had to be led away. It was our luck that the leader of the canoemen, *Akra,* who is known as a big drinker, remained stone sober, and the youngest one in the group, out of respect for him, also stayed sober. After remaining here for a good two hours, my negroes made their preparations to go on.

Some of the local people here decided to travel on with us in order to participate in the arrival celebrations at *Bambey.* They took two of the drunkards in their canoe, the third remaining in ours, and thus the trip continued, accompanied by the joyful noise of drums, fifes, and human voices. By ten in the morning, the beams of the sun were indescribably oppressive; toward noon we reached a second peanut garden, where our arrival had already been announced by a messenger who had preceded us, to assure that the negroes would all be there, ready to receive us, on the riverbank. Large and small, they all joined in, shouting with joy as the music played, with a great deal of excitement.

I would have loved to remain simply sitting in my canoe, without the bright glare of the sun. However, they did not notice my reluctance, amidst the general jubilation, and without hesitation they took me from it and placed me right in the middle of a crowd of black people, and I had hardly stepped ashore when the shots of the men, and the joyful cries of the women and children, rang out, and the festivities that had taken place before were again resumed in this new location, lasting without pause for a quarter of an hour. The women, especially, were so excited that they had tears in their eyes. There was something really dangerous about the ceremony of welcome: they fired their mostly-overloaded muskets either right next to my head or right between my legs. Under these circumstances, my headache became much stronger. As had been the case before, each of these gentle, harmless people asked to speak to me alone. This I granted them, as best as my uncertain tongue permitted. No matter how much I wished that our ceremony of arrival would remain simple, this was not to be the case. Here, also, they led me to their garden huts where, according to negro custom, they had prepared a fine meal. The negroes sat around me in an orderly fashion and ate, as soon as the women had left. In order not to offend them, I ate a bit of rice pudding while, in contrast, my two sober negroes ate a hearty meal. For the drunkards, strong coffee was brewed. After they had drunk it, they went swimming and became so sober that when it came time for us to leave, they were already at their places in the canoe. To close the entertainment, my negroes again produced a large bottle of dram, and people drank—as had already taken place that morning—to the health of the Bakkramanns, who are the negroes who have come back to their land from Paramaribo. I would hardly have believed that *Akra* and the youngest negro could drink so much, after having already drunk so much before. Yet they held it well. I tried to motion to *Akra*, by signs, that he should take care not to drink too much, but he called over the other negroes and asked them to testify that he, in fact, would have to drink a great deal more before he would be drunk, and they all agreed that this champion drinker would need six times as much dram as he had consumed that day before he would lose his reason. Finally, he himself tried to calm me down, saying, "You know, Master. Today, I still have to carry out an important mission: to persuade Master Wietz in Bambey that you are truly the person he should take on as his colleague. And for that I will need a clear head." At my request, the noon-day meal was soon ended, and we once again prepared to set out.

Four boatloads with negro men and women left here in order to accompany us, so that the whole caravan now consisted of seven fully loaded canoes, one of which was filled with musicians playing instruments.

After a half hour, we arrived at the third and final peanut garden. All the inhabitants had gathered on the riverbank, and our arrival was accompanied by their musket shots and shouts of jubilation, and the huzzahs of our companions. Because I was feeling very tired and my headache got worse every minute, my negroes asked the local negroes if we could please not land, because of my condition. Though we did not go ashore, our group got larger, because some additional canoes joined us there. Among those people coming with us to Bambey there was not a single idle spectator. Each person did whatever he could to help make this entry into Bambey as spectacular as possible. If I could only describe to my readers the confusion of so many busy blacks, in their natural simplicity, making an unbelievable uproar with their voices and instruments, with the noise echoing a thousandfold between the walls of high forest, with the river rushing in between. . . .

A half hour below *Bambey* we stopped. *Akra* had all the canoes come together, and he ordered that everyone load his musket with a double charge. Then he instructed everyone about how they should behave during the entrance to Bambey, and this meant that all the canoes would have to remain silent as they approached *Bambey*.[31] As soon as the village came in sight, all the muskets were fired at once, and immediately all the voices took on their previous strength. This alerted the inhabitants of Bambey, who were truly excited, and by the time our vessels approached, they were fully prepared to receive us in a festive manner. The men fired salutes, the women and children gave their shouts of joy, and music accompanied us.

Deacon Wietz was standing there with some baptized negroes. In each hand he held a loaded pistol. And his [Saramaka] colleague blew some melodies into a European hunting horn, which one really could not hear because of the powerful shouts of jubilation from the crowd.[32]

When I stepped ashore, *Wietz* fired a pistol over my head into the air and embraced me, in the presence of all the well-meaning blacks, with tears in his eyes. At that same moment, the women and children of Bambey pressed me with their hands and welcomed me with the words, *Hodi Massra! Hodi Massra!*, which were repeated more than ten times by each. Wietz led me to our dwelling place and all the inhabitants of the village followed while congratulating us. They also gave refreshments to those negroes who had accompanied us, and they voiced their gratitude to them for having been so kind to do this. . . .

On the following morning, the 29th of September, the ne-

"Hodi Masra!" (Welcome, Massa!) (Riemer 1801, pl. 8).

groes who had accompanied me here took their leave in a most
moving manner, and *Akra*, especially, said a very solemn good-
by. I must admit that I was truly moved as I said farewell to my
faithful companions, who left for the different villages in which
they live. When they reached home, they told their neighbors
about the new European they had brought with them to Bambey—among other things that he had an instrument that resem-
bled their Tutu but played many different notes. This especially
piqued the curiosity of the women, so that already, on my first
afternoon here, a large canoe filled with women arrived. They
asked if I would play the flute for them. It was very important
for me to be hospitable and thus to win their trust, since previously it was the womenfolk who had most strongly resisted our
mission and had been most mistrustful of us. These negresses
were all Creoles [born in Suriname] who in their whole lives had
perhaps never seen a healthy European and, therefore, seemed
much taken with me. After I had satisfied their curiosity about
the flute, some of them asked Deacon Wietz if my complexion
and the rest of my physique was natural. And after he assured
them that it was, they asked for permission to touch me. Once
they had satisfied their curiosity about this, they left, contented.

  As soon as these women left, two canoes full of negro women
from another village arrived, and they visited in a similar way
before leaving. On the following days similar visits took place
which bothered me enough that I let them know, through the
good services of my colleague Wietz, the only missionary I
found in Bambey, that I would be unable to take care of my daily
obligations if I had to constantly play my Tutu. But I promised
that I would play it on Sunday at the church service.[33]

  The curiosity of these women has to be excused because they
had never left their land, as traveling back and forth would be
much too dangerous for them and is mostly a matter for men.
They only very occasionally get a chance to see those few
whites who live in their land, and it fascinated them to see the
contrast between a young, healthy, newly-arrived European and
the haggard looks and pale complexions of those who have lived
here for some time.

Brother Riemer's healthy good looks quickly paled before a violent
attack of first-shock fever. For several weeks he hovered between life
and death, and, as with several of his confreres, Alabi took the precautionary step of constructing a cedarwood coffin for him. During this
time, Brother and Sister Moser (who had accompanied Brother Riemer on the ocean voyage to Suriname) arrived in Bambey, with characteristic enthusiasm, to join the mission.

  They found me lying in my hammock. . . . My own joy at seeing
  my traveling companions safe and sound before me was fully
  matched by their great sadness at seeing how much I had

"What a Change!" (Riemer 1801, pl. 11).

changed in such a short time. They both stood there weeping and exclaimed, *What a change!* as our scene of mutual welcome, which should have been filled with such happiness, became instead a tearful scene of grief.

On Brother Moser's firm insistence, Brother Riemer, despairing of ever recovering his health at Bambey, undertook an immediate return trip to Paramaribo.

Although I was not aware of it at the time, my confreres gave instructions to the negroes about what to do with my corpse, in case I should die on the voyage. . . . But within three weeks [of arriving in Paramaribo] I felt completely healthy.

On 30 December 1779 Brother Riemer once again boarded a canoe in Paramaribo to journey to Bambey, this time for his final stay of six months. Alabi seems to have been the leader of the canoemen who brought him upstream.[34] Within days of this second arrival in Bambey, Brother Riemer found himself "completely alone at the mission post, abandoned to my fate," Brother Moser having already died from "the fever," and his widow and Brother Wietz, who was also quite ill, having left—the latter only temporarily—for Paramaribo. In this situation of relative isolation, Brother Riemer came more and more to depend on Alabi.

The baptized negro captain Johannes Arrabini helped me every day, even hourly, with difficult work. I was so grateful for his presence! . . . He helped build a new chapel which I was able to consecrate.

One day, Alabi accompanied Brother Riemer into the forest, to show him a garden that Riemer's slave had prepared for rice-planting.

We armed ourselves in the usual way and set off. On the way, a large tyger appeared, dignified and courageous, but as soon as he saw us he stood still, looked at us imperiously, and listened. My companion, who had been hoping for some time to provide me with a piece of fur and some teeth from such an animal, took the opportunity and told me to ready my musket in case something unexpected were to happen. Very quickly he aimed at the animal and, as it happened, on this occasion the unthinkable occurred: the powder burned harmlessly in the pan without a shot. Excitedly he encouraged me and, while he was reloading with fresh powder, I aimed at the tyger with my musket. But just at the moment I was about to fire, his well-trained hunting dog ran at the animal. The tyger was not fatally wounded by my shot and grabbed the dog in his jaws and shook him back and forth. The embarrassed Johannes aimed a second time and was lucky enough to kill the tyger, but the dog was badly mangled and we had to pry open the tyger's jaws with a piece of iron to

"Courage! Courage! Massa." Alábi and Riemer aiming at a jaguar (Riemer 1801, pl. 13).

free him. Unfortunately, this faithful dog, who had saved our lives, died a few days later from the wounds he had suffered. Soon thereafter, Johannes brought me a piece of fur and some teeth from the dead tyger, and to this day [twenty years later, in Europe] I have the fur and teeth, which I display as a souvenir.[35]

Besides being terribly lonely, except for the time he spent with Alabi, Brother Riemer also had intermittent health problems. His description of a cutaneous mycosis is among the most graphic of Moravian accounts of illness.

A terrible sickness came on because I had innocently talked to a visiting negro who had the sickness called ringworm. (This is an awful irruption which attacks Europeans, so long as they remain in these latitudes, though it is less virulent among the negroes.) By chance, the man had come to my house and sat down in my usual place. As soon as he left, I happened to sit down in this still-warm place without the slightest suspicion and, a few days later, I found that my whole body was itching terribly all over. . . . We examined my body and found, underneath my clothing, that there were little red rings, the size of sixpence coins, all over me. From that moment on, my [previous] fever left me, but instead of that I was itching day in and day out. The spots grew each day, and by full moon they were the size of a four-Groschen coin and they became raised up over their whole surface. It looked like scarlet fever and gave off a liquid. I was itching all over, and day or night never had peace. The sleep that would normally have given me comfort never came, and even though I tried to tie my hands together at night so I would not scratch, I could never sleep for more than half an hour at a time. The only way I could find relief was by disrobing and throwing myself into the Suriname River, but I had to keep constantly moving so that I would not be attacked by the piranhas. During the waning of the moon, the rash dried up and became paler, but the itching continued and I never ceased scratching. Over a period of three months, I must have ruined six pair of linen underclothes because of my scratching.

Other Saramakas were quick to sense Brother Riemer's aloneness and cultural vulnerability, and, characteristically, they set about testing him whenever Alabi was temporarily absent. Brother Riemer describes one such incident that seems especially revealing of Saramaka assumptions and attitudes about whitefolks, as well as of his characteristic colonial attitudes toward his "charges."

One day when all the male negroes, including the captain [Alabi], were away in their gardens and thus absent from the village, all the women got together to put me, a newcomer, to the test. It should be noted that the bartering that the whites have always maintained with them to procure foodstuffs is standardized, with the price of each item permanently fixed; and I had in my possession a complete list, which they did not anticipate. On this early morning one woman after another came to trade foodstuffs with me for such things as beads, sewing needles, Camissa (a piece of cloth), and other such goods. When I proposed to exchange the proper articles for these [foodstuffs], she would not agree but responded smilingly, "No, No! Master Wietz and all his predecessors all gave us more for that! You are still new and inexperienced with us, and that is why I have to teach you this!"

When I stood firm with my offer, she said, begrudgingly, "All right, here is a calabash with all of the goods our husbands told us to bring you, so that you wouldn't suffer any need [in their absence]. So here, take this, even if you do not give us more. Even if you are giving us far less than your predecessors always have, take the calabash with the provisions anyway. Because I am going to report to them just how stingy you are! And nothing more will be brought." No sooner had this person gone out the door, than a second one came in, with the same goods to barter as the first had in her calabash. She, too, got all excited, clapping her hands, turning her back to me, and leaving in a huff. After this one followed a third, and then a fourth, until about twenty women with similar vessels filled with rice, corn, eggs, peanuts, sweet potatoes, and suchlike had come into my dwelling, with a great deal of noise, and complained in common that I had been too stingy in my dealings.

Had I not already been warned about such goings on and had a complete price list in hand, the women's threatening and stormy impertinence would have truly frightened me. Only my courage saved me from harm. I realized that kindness would only be to my disadvantage, and they were shouting so madly at me that I was unable to hear my own words. In any event, my patience was at an end. In a threatening tone, I ordered them to be silent, and I then took my saber from the wall, removed it from its sheath, and asked if they did not know that I was master in my own house and would not tolerate such treatment any longer. No sooner did they see my shining sword than they ran off with such speed that they tumbled over one another to reach the door, leaving behind the containers with all the provisions. I waited several hours for their return, but in vain. Finally, I sent my negro slave to their houses to let them know that they should return to pick up their calabashes. The negro returned without any message from them. They had sat and listened to his words without giving the smallest response.

After a short while those people who had brought the very first goods arrived, and they excused themselves for their previous misbehavior and graciously explained that it was the other women who had goaded them to this behavior. Then they sought out their baskets of chicken eggs, and accepted in all humility the same payment for their goods that they had previously refused as too small. They were followed by all the other negro women, who each excused herself for her previous bad behavior—something I had not asked them to do. Once this had taken place, from then on they were always happy to accept the amount that I was ready to pay for their goods, and they never left me in need. The real instigator of this whole experiment was the wife of a baptized negro [probably Kodjo's "heathen" wife], who told my slave girl that it was a mystery to her how I had known how much each of the goods should cost, since my experienced compatriot Wietz was so far away. . . . As for myself, I did not find this behavior so surprising, as I had already become accustomed to their cowardice. But to prevent any further misunderstandings, I related these events in every detail to some of the negro men who visited me the following day, and found that this was the first they had heard of it, even though their own wives had been the participants. They not only approved my behavior but asked me, in similar circumstances in future, to do the same, since according to their traditional ways they must concede so many privileges to their wives that these latter end up paying them no heed at all.

The Saramaka attitudes toward missionaries, expressed in this encounter, had been shaped by the dual experiences of slavery and warfare, as well as by Saramakas' continued, if qualified, economic dependence on the plantation society. Whenever Saramakas sensed weakness in a Moravian's character, they took advantage—toying with him, humiliating him, and misleading him in countless ways. Testing of the sort Riemer describes was a common ploy, to see just how far they could go. While hostile Saramaka men more often affected an ironic, Sambo-like self-deprecation (never understood as such by the missionaries), women seem to have taken the lead in direct taunting.[36] By this time, both had become standardized styles of cultural performance. Some of this testing, especially when it involved property, was undoubtedly motivated by a belief that the missionaries were holding out and were feigning poverty. After all, most of the whitefolks that they had seen or heard about were enormously wealthy, in terms of consumer goods.[37] But, in addition, basic cultural ideas about property and compensation were often at stake, and neither side fully understood the other's assumptions.

Shortly after his encounter with the women of Bambey, Brother Riemer had a yet more serious confrontation, with Tribal Chief Kwaku Etja, in the wake of another Saramaka test. The description, once again set down in Brother Riemer's colorful prose, reveals a vivid picture both of Kwaku Etja and of his relationship with Captain Alabi, his eventual successor as tribal chief.

One day when I was down with a fever, a baptized man came to
me with the report that a famous witch doctor or so-called Obia
man was making a spectacle of his magical arts at the other end
of the village, attended by a crowd of people from various villages. I asked him if such conjuring was common in Bambey,
and he said that it had been a very long time now since a sorcerer
had thus performed his art in the village, and that it was happening now only because it was known that I was a newly arrived white man and had been left completely alone amongst
them.

Despite my fever, I immediately left my hammock and, machete in hand according to local custom, went to the appointed
place. In an open space, I saw the conjurer, who had fiery red
hair (which is most unusual among the negroes), in the middle
of more than fifty curious negro men and women. The latter
listened attentively to every word that this idolater, on purpose,
barely stammered, giving their complete attention to him and
believing that whatever he said was infallible prophecy. The lad
seemed very well versed in the arts of deception, as if he had
been trained in them from his early youth, and he seemed to
have the ability to feign inspiration well in his control. His face
was twisted around almost facing his back and, because he was
straining himself in this way, the veins on his face and neck
were almost ready to burst. As soon as he saw me he suddenly
fell silent.

I spoke to him, breaking the heavy silence, in the loudest and
most forceful tone I could muster, saying, "You miserable deceiver! To be sure I do not know your name nor whence you
came, but of one thing I am sure: the people of this village did
not summon you here. Yet you wish to deceive these innocent
people with your miserable spectacles. In the name of our captain [the absent Alabi], I order you now to board your canoe and
return whence you came, and never again set foot with your
deceptions in this place." Although these harsh words were spoken very slowly, because of the fever and my weakness, there
was a solemn silence when the people heard them. And even the
silent witch doctor changed his posture and took on his natural
shape. He seemed truly happy when I ended my speech, and
without saying another word or threatening me, he ran to his
canoe at the shore and left in shame without receiving any kind
of compensation from the auditors. (To be sure, he would have as
compensation a quantity of foodstuffs had I not interrupted him
and chased him off, since the only reason these people partake in
deceiving their brothers is so that they can secure a fat income,
and live as comfortably as possible, and avoid the difficulties of
manual labor.)[38]

This encounter had a very strong influence on the spectators
at this conjuring performance, especially those of the female

sex. And it is almost certain to have an effect on their morals, and to begin a trend in which the word of the magician is not given as high a status as before. They were certain that I would encounter some terrible misfortune because of the abilities of the Gadoman, who in their eyes was extremely exciting and powerful. And they sent representatives to me all through the day, until late at night, to observe me and see what would happen, to see in what way the Gadoman would take his secret vengeance on me. But when they saw that I remained unharmed . . . they lost their faith in the wonderworker and his powers, while their trust in me increased greatly. . . .

On the following day, the local village captain [Alabi] returned with the other elders, all of whom were baptized, and they entered my dwelling to show their gratitude that I had sent away the sorcerer in their absence, and they voiced the opinion that my decisiveness would have a good effect, since some of the women had already said that the gods of the white people must certainly be more powerful than those of the Gadoman, as he had run off with shame and cowardice after the white man chastised him. . . .

Some days after this incident with the sorcerer, the Government postholder visited me. He had come from the Upper River where he had had a serious argument with the tribal chief, because of a well-known Gadoman or sorcerer whom he had prevented from demonstrating his art and prophecies in the postholder's village [the administrative post of Awara, an hour upstream from Bambey]. At first, the captains of the place tried to prevent him [the postholder] from doing this [interfering with the sorcerer], and they gave protection to the sorcerer. They even went to the tribal chief to complain about the way the postholder was acting. After a very sharp exchange of words, it was decided that the sorcerer was never to conduct these ceremonies in front of the postholder's house again. The postholder came to me, then, to tell me that he, too, had had a run-in with the same sorcerer, for he had heard that I had had one as well. He wanted me to know also that this man was a close relative of the tribal chief and that he had complained to him about my having chased him away by force. Out of friendship, this Government official had come to tell me this, in order to prepare me for any encounter that the tribal chief might wish to have with me. . . . He then wished me luck and said that he could send me some military personnel should I want them, and that they could arrive in a few days. Though I did not accept the offer, I was grateful nonetheless. . . .

[Some time later,] The famous Tribal Chief [Kwaku Etja], along with the local village captains and all the elders, came to my dwelling. With various gesticulations and a strong "Hodi Massra!" he stepped into the middle of my room, stroked his long fire-red beard and, at my solemn invitation, sat down but said nothing for a long time. During this pause, the postholder decided to leave, as he did not trust the chief's intentions regarding the Peace. I accompanied him to the door before returning to my usual place. The silence lasted still longer. Since it was hard for me to bear, I began to speak, asking the black leader in a pleasant and open voice the purpose of his visit. He stood up and stepped before me, saying with great seriousness, "Master, now you are alone among us negroes, and I have some weighty words to tell you in the name of the Grang Kruttu (Supreme Council) of our free negro nation." While saying this, he stuck out his index finger, placed it on my forehead, and then sat down again, stroking his beard constantly.[39] He continued to talk in a slow, grave manner. "I am talking to you for the first time in my life. How I had hoped that the first occasion to talk with you would be a pleasant one—but it is not. As the leader of my nation I must talk gravely and seriously with you. By your sharp tongue, you have not only troubled one of our most respected Obiama when he presented some Great Words to the people of Bambey, but you have also insulted his numerous family. This insulted Obiama and his closest relatives have asked me to call a general council meeting, as he has serious complaints both against you and the local elders, and he would like this council to consider the case publicly, so that they can reach a judgment. Master and elders! I would therefore like to begin by asking two questions, which I expect you to answer. First of all, why did you, Master, send this Obiama away from Bambey in such a demeaning manner? And second, why did the elders of this village not protect this man from such miserable treatment?" While asking these questions, he solemnly stood up, but afterwards sat down and was silent.

I then began to speak and told the tribal chief that we whites had come to the land of the Free Negroes to direct his people away from their pernicious errors and to lead them along the path of salvation to the Great God. I told him that we had received encouragement from many negro captains, who had helped us by their authority to sustain our mission. I reminded him that his own Governor [of the colony of Suriname], with a handshake and a solemn promise, had lent his support and did not bother to ask us troublesome questions, as he had just done. And that neither I nor my colleagues were prepared to answer such questions, or to use force to teach his people the ways of our Lord. Nor would we tolerate the Gado people from other villages coming to practice magic publicly in our neighborhood.

With that, Captain Johannes [Alabi] stood up and said with pronounced boldness, "Tatto! (Father!) The answer to your second question is my affair. You have been designated by the Great master [the colonial governor] in Paramaribo as our tribal chief.

From you we should expect such orders as we can obey without the slightest qualms of conscience. But Tatto, think carefully how far you have deviated from the correct paths of your office!" He then took the old man by the hand and said to him in a gentler tone, "Tatto! I beg you to choose a dearer and better way, and even though at first you might have no inclination to accept the teachings of Christ but would rather remain in darkness and choose that over the Light, please do not disturb us in our faith, or let us be disturbed by such deceivers and magicians. Tatto, you are already very old and have had much experience with life, and thus it is only fitting that the whole nation looks upon you with the greatest respect. But as long as your ears remain deaf to the teachings of the Great God, and as long as you support the seduction of our people, then I must tell you that, in terms of wisdom, you remain a child."

Now the patience of the old man was at an end. In anger he said "Arrabini, I order you to hold your tongue!" Then turning to me, in a friendly manner, he gave me his hand and said his farewells: "Master, I leave you now with the assurance that no Gadoman will ever, with my will or knowledge, set foot in your village again, nor will you ever be disturbed in your undertakings."

After a few days, I again received a visit from the Government postholder who told me that yesterday the tribal chief had come to him of his own accord and told him in a friendly manner that he would now see to it that no Gadoman would ever come close to his dwelling place again.

It would be an error to conclude, with Brother Riemer, that Tribal Chief Etja simply capitulated before the combined force of missionary and postholder moral suasion. Etja's speech is nearly identical in tone to those made to me by twentieth-century Saramaka captains, at moments when I inadvertently showed disrespect toward a Saramaka or transgressed an unspoken law. *Gaama* Etja, simply by convening his council meeting, made clear first and foremost his authority and power. He took the opportunity forcibly to scold the white man in public (undoubtedly saying a great deal that Brother Riemer, still new in Saramaka, did not understand, about the collective sins of white-folks), and then, from his position of authority and control, he graciously deigned to permit the whites to remain, unmolested. Clearly, he had little patience with Alabi (again, speaking to him in a tone very much like that which would be used by a traditional Saramaka captain today addressing a proselytizing Christian Saramaka). Through (non-Christian) Saramaka eyes, the whole incident would have been seen as an insult to a respected priest by a white guest, as a ritual scolding of the offender, and—once it had been clearly demonstrated who held ultimate authority—a gracious and generous compromise.

In the midst of these confrontations, and despite frequent missionary illness, death, and rapid turnover of personnel, by early 1780 the Moravians had finally begun to make spiritual inroads—at least among Alabi's kinfolk. Shortly before Brother Wietz left for a visit to Paramaribo in February 1780, he noted in his diary that

> Johannes' biological [*leibliche*] sister [Bebi], who has always been very hostile to us, now comes often to our meetings. Once, she told me that a dream had made her very uneasy. She had dreamed that after a negro she knew had died in Paramaribo, he appeared to Brother Kersten with the request that Johannes go to his brothers and sisters to tell them that they should make the effort to learn the teachings of the true God and thus be set on the path of righteousness. Johannes, who listened to her account, seized the occasion to tell her and everyone present, "I will not be remiss in doing this, and am never so happy as when you will listen to me." And then he turned to the others and gave them an emphatic sermon, in which he told them the parable of Lazarus and the rich man. We truly believe that the Savior has been responsible for these events.[40]

And soon after,

> on the 30th of January [1780] we had a very important day, both for us and for the negroes. . . . The following negroes were all baptized: Kwakú [the husband of Alabi's sister Bebi], who was named Andreus, our domestic slave Jamina, who was named Johanna, and her four-month-old baby [whose father, Abraham, was also a slave of the Moravians] named Joseph. They were baptized into the death of Jesus, after having answered their questions with joy. So many negro men, women, and children were present that our church could hardly hold them.

Some weeks later, there was a further report about Bebi:

> Our Johannes' biological sister, who was from the very beginning hostile to us, has—ever since her husband's baptism—become quite embarrassed about her former ways and visits our meetings regularly, which has earned her many enemies among the other women.

On 21 March,

> two negroes and two negresses became baptismal candidates [today]. The first two are the oldest men in the village [Kwakú Óbia and Fortuin, both born in Africa]; the two women are Johannes' wife and his sister [Bebi], who is the wife of our baptized Andreus.

On 18 June,

two men, [renamed] Stephanus and Simeon, and Charlotte [Sia-loto], Johannes' wife, as well as her child [with Alabi] Helena were all baptized. All the spectators were very moved by this. Some of the strangers said, "Oh, we live like cattle in the bush without even once realizing that we are true human beings." Others said, "Who would have thought that this fellow (one of the baptized who had led a very disorderly life and had been the butt of many jokes) could change his ways like this!"

Meanwhile, it seems that Alabi's sister Bebi, who at first had been such a nemesis of the Moravians and was now a baptismal candidate, had postponed her own baptism out of concern for the wishes of her mother, Akoomi. For, within months of Akoomi's death, in September 1780, Bebi too was finally baptized, as Rebecca. By this time, there were (including Alabi) eleven baptized Saramakas, at least six of whom were Alabi's close relatives.[41]

During this period of active proselytizing among his close relatives, Alabi dictated a letter in Saramaccan to Brother Wietz, who took it down in German, addressed "to all the Brethren in Europe." Despite its compositionally corrupt form, it gives some hint of the way he was thinking about himself at the time.

"I, Johannes, send you warm greetings. It brings me great sadness that God has taken Brother Moser to Him, because we will now also lose Sister Moser [who, as a single woman, was about to leave Saramaka territory permanently]. I know not why God did this; we do not understand it. Perhaps, we are meant to see from this that just as many of those who have come to us have died, we, too, should think of how we shall go home to the Savior. I thus beg that you Brethren will not tire [of the task] and that you will not give up, and that you will send a new brother and sister who will not go home right away. The Savior truly struggled to help us sinful people, and that is the way it has to be amongst us, His people. Whatever you do, you do for His sake.

You probably know that when the first Brethren came to us I was the most simple person in the whole world. I have to cry when I think how dear the Savior was to me and how He showed me mercy and blessed me through your work. Of course, I have greatly bothered Him since then and given Him much cause for complaint and many reasons to abandon us—but He will not forsake us! I have a great deal to say because my heart thinks a great deal. Naturally, I am not really dissatisfied that the Savior has allowed Sister Moser to leave, since He has at least made her healthy again.

We cannot see each other, which is why we must talk to each other by means of paper. When we receive the Savior, we will be able to thank him for all the things He has done for us. Now I am

sending all of the Brethren and Sisters my greetings. I am very
happy when I hear that there are so many Brethren [in Europe]. I
beg them all, on behalf of the Saramaka Negroes, that the Savior
will open up many more eyes and hearts because so many of
them remain in darkness. When I have the opportunity of
speaking to someone about the Savior, I cannot keep my mouth
quiet. Normally, the negroes come to me [in my role as captain]
when they are in disagreement with one another, and I have to
judge and decide who is right. Often I become very tired of this.
I bid my dear Brethren and Sisters farewell."[42]

Soon after Alabi wrote this letter, in April 1780, his aged mother
Akoomi died. Conceived in Africa, carried in Tjazimbe's womb to the
New World, this octogenarian Priestess of Madanfo was, at the time
of her death, among the most powerful of Saramaka women. During
her final illness, Alabi's personal intervention on behalf of the missionaries seems to have shifted the balance, if only temporarily, toward a
new openness among local Saramaka women to conversion. Brother
Riemer noted that

soon after the funeral of the old woman, many began to attend
our services and different women had themselves baptized,
among the first of whom was the daughter-in-law of the deceased [Alabi's wife, Sialoto],

soon to be followed by Akoomi's own daughter, Bebi.

Akoomi's spectacular funeral made a vivid impression on the two
relatively green missionaries who witnessed at least parts of it.
Brother Wietz, who by this time had spent less than a year in Saramaka and still knew the language and culture only poorly, wrote:

At the end of the week we had two very sick women in our
neighborhood. The first [Akoomi], who was the oldest in the
village, was visited by Johannes [Alabi] and Joshua [Kodjo] [her
Christian son and son-in-law]. They told her a great deal about
the right and true God. But, to their chagrin, this had no effect
on her; in her great pain she continued to tell the other women
never ever to get involved with the church.[43] . . .

On the 3rd of April, the famous old [Tribal] Chief Etja came to
pay a visit to the sick. He had decided not to pay us a visit, as a
precautionary [ritual] measure, but he sent us friendly greetings. . . . On the 7th, the old woman died. While she was on her
deathbed, she begged all the people who gathered round her not
to become friends with us after her death. Because the dying
words of such a Mama have such strong effect on the people
here, Johannes and Joshua tried to counteract her statements.
The men seemed affected by what these two said but the women
paid no attention. Two hours after her death, the racket that
accompanies death began, with shooting, weeping, howling,
and drumming. This lasted as usual for eight days and nights,[44]

and one can hardly look back on it without shuddering at the way Satan knows how to profit from such occasions. When this tumult had continued for several hours, the musket of a negro who had fired three salutes split open, damaging his hand so that two fingers had to be amputated with shears. The next day the funeral took place with countless spectacles. After this had been going on for a while, Johannes tried to put an end to the ceremony and talked to the people about yesterday's unhappy events. The men were affected by his statement but the women were not, and they went back to their noise and carrying on.

Brother Riemer, whose Saramaka experience was at this time only half of Brother Wietz's, waited some twenty years before writing his own account of the funeral:

During my stay at Bambey, the biological mother of the captain [Alabi] died at the age of four score years and odd. She was recognized not only in her own village but throughout the entire land as the most accomplished sorceress and beloved Grang-Mama.[45] She was particularly respected by the members of her own sex but was held in reverence by all. Just as it was chiefly the women who most resented the missionaries' attempt to convert people, it was this Grang-Mama who distinguished herself in preventing her compatriots, particularly the women, from having contact with the missionaries. Still dissatisfied about this during her final illness, she called all the women in her neighborhood to her, and extracted the promise from them that they would never enter our church or, even worse, become baptized. To lend even greater solemnity to this oath, she had each woman shake her hand and promise to keep the oath after the old woman's death. And she called upon all her own friends, relatives, and children to see that the promise would be kept.

One of the negro women who was present reported this to her husband, who was a Christian, and he in turn reported it to the captain of the village [Alabi], her son, who was also a Christian. The captain was terribly frightened by this, knowing that a promise of this type, carried out by a Grang-Mama amidst handshakes, would be looked upon as holy by the negro women, and observed by them to the letter. He felt that this oath might have dire consequences for the furtherance of Christianity among his nation, and he realized that the only way out was to get his mother to rescind the handshake oath herself. As she was still alive, though very weak, he asked me to accompany him, in order to get her to take back the handshake oath. Although I did not expect much to come from this visit, I felt it my duty to accompany the captain to the dwelling of the old woman.

We found the front and back rooms packed with the followers of the ailing woman, so that it was hard to get through. The sick woman presented such a frightening picture, with her face and whole body covered by different colors and countless Obia herbs. Her son stepped up to her hammock and began in a friendly way by saying that I had come to her to see how she was feeling. The sick woman was weak but still retained her faculties and understood the real purpose of our visit. She turned over, showing us her back, without deigning to reply to her son. In vain he tried to bring her to speak to us. Finally, he ordered that all present leave so that we could remain alone, which as captain he could do.

As soon as they had left, he delivered a speech filled with pathos to his mother, imploring her to recant her culpable oath, and telling her that there was still time. Among other things, he said to her, "You have taken away their natural freedom. The highest God will punish you unless you give it back to them." His expressions were so moving and heart rending! He called upon me periodically as a witness, saying repeatedly, "I'm washing my hands in innocence."[46] In the end, his imprecations had their effect on the old woman. Our purpose did not go unachieved. The ninety-year-old heathen[47] was moved by his constant entreaties. She not only gave her son her hand, but also gave it to me and asked softly that all the women who had been with her that morning return to her so that they could rescind that solemn and ridiculous oath, and so that their freedom would not be put in jeopardy. This event made a strong impression on the collectivity of black women. . . .

On the morning after the Grang-Mama had passed on, an extraordinary silence reigned for one full hour in the village: not one of the inhabitants or strangers present said a single word. But during this silence the negroes set about filling their guns with a double load. All were then fired together, some 60 or 70 in all, so the neighboring villages and the whole nation would know that there had been a death. In those villages, in turn, similar salvos were fired so that news of the death passed quickly all along the Suriname River. With the firing of salutes arose a frightening death shriek, in which the women in particular distinguished themselves. Both young and old made every effort to express their mourning through wild howling. This endless, strange performance made my own dwelling seem too small. I walked through the village to get some fresh air and saw all the families standing before their huts as if in trance, their hands behind their necks and their faces turned toward heaven. Their tragic excitement and poses were so extreme that they hardly noticed me, though they rolled their eyes back and forth. What most amazed me was that both adults and children had tears rolling down their cheeks, attesting to the sincerity of their bereavement, though it seems impossible that all these peoples' bereavement could come from the heart. In this situation, the houses of the baptized were distinguished by the fact

**that one saw only women and children in front of them, since
their men had come to our house and had been accompanying
their death-celebration with fife and drum for over an hour,
when I found them upon my return.[48]**

The octogenarian Akoomi—as priestess of Madanfo, widow of
Gaama Abini, and mother of Christian captain Alabi—had earned the
respect of all Saramakas, however much they might otherwise dis-
agree about religion or politics. Her funeral was the largest public
occasion ever to take place in Bambey.[49] When death took her during
the night, she was surrounded by her children—Alabi, five of his six
sisters, and two of his three brothers[50]—as well as older relatives and
friends. After closing her eyes and covering her with a shroud, they
wrapped her in her hammock and laid it on three banana leaves on the
ground. Then, wet-eyed, they sat reminiscing about moments they
had shared with her, evoking playful incidents that emphasized
Akoomi's individual wonts, or major events that revealed her generosity. Some of her friends spoke to her directly, recalling things they
had done together and begging her to intercede in a child's illness or
some other personal concern. Repeatedly, Akoomi's children were
told to cease their crying and to abandon any wish they might have to
go join their mother. They must go on with life, even if they now felt all
alone. Only when daylight came did they begin the formal preparations for the funeral, as word spread through the village that Akoomi
had finally departed.

As men loaded their muskets and tied ritually protective *maziga-
zigá* grass around their guns, elders rushed to embrace Alabi and his
sisters and brothers, draping cloths over their shoulders and speaking
to their *akaa*s ("souls"): "You must not die! You must live!" A few old
men walked over to the village ancestor shrine and poured a libation
of water, speaking to the ancestors by name to inform them that
Akoomi was coming to join them, to invite them to participate in the
funeral, and to ask their assistance and protection in the days ahead.
Youths—late teenagers and men in their early twenties—tied their
heads with deep blue or red kerchiefs, twisted to a point in front, tied
lengths of *mazigaziga* grass around their waists, and began gathering
near Akoomi's house: they would compose the gravediggers' sodal-
ity, the *baákuma,* who would rule the village with an iron hand for the
next eight days. In front of Akoomi's house, the firing of scores of
salutes, which alerted people in the Dombi village of Wangania and
the Nasi village of Saanga (who in turn passed the news along upriver), also signaled the commencement of women's piercing mourning wails, which continued intermittently all day, as visitors streamed
into the village.

While some of the gravediggers pulled the woven front off Akoomi's house, transforming it into a house of death (*ke-osu,* "house of
wails"), others went to the river to cut the bottom out of her old
canoe—a piece some six by two feet, which would serve as *bungulá,*

proxy coffin, at various points in the funeral rites. Once they had returned, they placed her on the canoe-bottom, still wrapped in her hammock, and set off, carrying their burden on banana leaf head-pads. Several elders, men and women, accompanied it to the place, beside a path at the edge of the village, where the dead are washed. Some carried baskets filled with cloths, hammocks, and hammock sheets. Kaana, the priest of Madanfo, and one of the older women presided over this complex procedure, amidst banter from onlookers about the proper way to complete this or that detail. Two hundred years later, washing the dead (as well as other funeral procedures) remains a cardinal occasion for heated—and much appreciated—argument about ritual details; at a time when some of those present had firsthand memories of one or another African way of doing things, such loud discussions must have been especially memorable. ("There are no burials without argument," approvingly runs the modern proverb.)[51]

The men took Akoomi's corpse off the canoe-bottom and sat it on a bed of banana trunks in a quickly dug lozenge-shaped hole. Women built a fire, on banana-trunk "hearthstones," to heat water in Akoomi's own black iron stewpot. As the pot was placed on the fire—and when it was later removed as well—Kaana and his female assistant performed a delicate ritual dance: each held his side of the pot with a foot and the opposite hand while his partner did the reverse, and then they switched, and finally switched back (with the pot going on and off the fire three times at each end of the procedure). Kaana and the woman, holding a calabash of cold water in their left hands and a calabash of hot in their right, began pouring cold water over Akoomi's head, as Kaana prayed, "Akoomi, we give you cold water, water from the stream you loved." They washed her thoroughly, using rags torn from a new white cloth. Kaana took a razor and shaved off a bit from her hairline, rubbing the shavings onto a cloth that would later be "carried" in divination on the canoe-bottom; this constituted the hair that would be periodically consulted until final burial at the second funeral. Then the wooden door of Akoomi's house, which had been brought for the purpose, was laid over the washing hole, and her body was seated naked upon it for the dressing-of-the-corpse. They began with a new home-woven cotton waist string (the only "clothes" of Saramaka children, said to distinguish humans from "animals") and a scanty breechcloth, but dressing her as well in a half-dozen layers of skirts and capes, a similar number of beaded necklaces, and gold earrings. Then Akoomi was wrapped, mummylike, in layer upon layer of hammocks and hammock sheets, leaving only her head and feet exposed, and her head was tied vertically and horizontally with two pieces of white cloth. Suspended by strips of cloth slung under the rigid wrapping, Akoomi was borne by six of the onlookers back to her house, where she was laid out on a planked platform that had been constructed while she was being washed. All those who had touched the corpse or the utensils used in the rites thus far stepped forward as Kaana poured rum over their hands and then passed around what was left in the bottle to drink.

While several men went off to seek boards from which to construct the coffin, the gravediggers set out to begin their dangerous job, carrying Akoomi's paddle, plus a couple of live fowls and some cassava cakes, and blowing wooden trumpets as they strode through the village and out onto the forest path. When they arrived at the cemetery, a half-hour away, the oldest among them poured a libation to announce to the ancestors why they had come and who they were going to bury. After clearing a gravesite in the virgin forest, they marked off the grave-space with a *pempé* reed that they had measured against the corpse. Using the same stewpot and calabashes that had been used to wash the dead, the youngest gravedigger killed and began to cook the fowls, which they would all eat with heavy doses of hot pepper—a strict taboo of the dead, and therefore a reassuring protection that they were eating alone. The digging was strenuous, and teams of young men moved in and out of the growing hole every few minutes. Akoomi's grave was twelve feet deep and side-vaulted; after being lowered to the bottom, the coffin would be inserted sideways to its final resting place under a thick roof of earth.[52] In late afternoon, with their preliminary task complete, the gravediggers "swept their bodies" (*baí sinkíi*), with their leader dusting them twice down and once up with handfuls of fowl feathers, as they faced east at the edge of the grave. "The evil must go to the ground, the good to the heavens." Without turning back, they headed toward the village, many sporting a chicken feather—to show what they had feasted on—in their hair.

Back in the village, the gravediggers poured a libation of rum at the doorstep of Akoomi's house and then raised the canoe-bottom on two of their heads, for divination. Speaking to Akoomi's spirit, they discussed the recent rash of sickness in the village, the amount of witchcraft that had threatened them all during these past months, and the reasons for her death. Her material possessions—as considerable as those of any Saramaka woman—were one by one distributed by her spirit to her daughters: her pots, her stools, her paddles, her clothes. When they had finished this work, the gravediggers returned the canoe-bottom to its place next to the corpse and began the most cherished part of their role: licentious and otherwise outlandish pranks to which villagers and visitors had to submit without complaint. Some gravediggers strapped long wooden penises around their waists and went in search of teenage girls to startle; others appropriated fruits and cooked foods, without so much as asking, from people's houses; still others caught villagers' chickens and brought them to the shed near Akoomi's house where they were going to cook that night; and some held a noisy wrestling match in front of Akoomi's doorway.

While the gravediggers were off in the forest working, another group of men—some thirty in all—had been busy, at the edge of

A twentieth-century Alúku Maroon coffin (rather simpler than contemporary Saramaka ones) being raised for divination (Hurault 1970, 36).

the village, constructing Akoomi's coffin. By mid-morning, leaning against a tree, there were ten rough-hewn planks, each a dozen feet long, several of which had been brought to Bambey by Matjau visitors, on behalf of the late Abini. Tasks were quickly divided: some men sharpened tools on whetstones, others began sawing, others planing. A small table was set up at the head of the coffin, as it began to take shape, and a glass and a bottle of rum were placed on a tablecloth. Some men began singing *papa,* the music of death, accompanied by a hoe blade-knife blade gong. Once the end pieces were set on the sides and bottom, a libation of rum was poured at the coffin's head. "Akoomi, we give you rum. Not one of us wanted you to die! But now that you have gone, all of us want to bury you with joy."

And using hot chocolate, freshly brewed from local cacao by the women, they poured a libation from a teakettle onto some bits of cassava cake at the coffin's head. Slowly, over many hours, the giant coffin took shape. With its steep gables and complex angles, a Saramaka coffin is an awesome object to behold. Every step of its construction is surrounded with prescriptions and prohibitions. And by the time the top of Akoomi's coffin was ready to be fitted, in late afternoon, and they had purified themselves from the dangerous task, the coffin makers felt exhausted but exhilarated: they had made a resting place that befitted the *gaama*'s widow.

Brother Riemer's account of that busy day describes how,

> **after a few hours, the relatives of the deceased, and other negro men and women who wished to participate in this scene of bereavement, began arriving from neighboring villages. There was a constant stream of canoes, each with three or four people, coming downstream, and by nightfall, there were some five hundred visitors in Bambey. With the setting of the sun, the formal death music, with fife, drums, and musket salutes began. More than a hundred human voices accompanied the music, and this incredible noise lasted the entire night till dawn. It should be mentioned that heavy drinking and gluttony abounded during the night, as each visitor had brought a full supply of Dramm. In the morning, they lay about like flies in their huts, during which time an ever-increasing number of negro men and women streamed in from distant places, until Bambey began to resemble a populous European market town.**

By nightfall on that first day, Gwafu Bambey was indeed packed with visitors. Matjau-clan in-laws, carrying presents of cloth, rum, and rice, had been arriving throughout the day. And friends of Akoomi from all over Saramaka had come bearing burial gifts, to pay their last respects. Soon after dark, the gravediggers fired a series of salutes and began to play their drums, and before long, scores of young people were gathering in front of Akoomi's house to sing and dance the evening away. It was only after midnight, when the recreational "play" had run its course, that the Matjau *papa* men arrived, to give Akoomi the proper send-off to the land of the dead. With their drums inside Akoomi's house, right next to the corpse, the *papa* men drummed and sang nonstop till dawn, when they went to the river to wash and then to their hosts' houses to catch a few hours' sleep in their hammocks.

Brother Riemer again picks up the story:

> **At nine in the morning the funeral commenced. First the corpse was laid in a coffin built of cedar wood, in front of the deceased's hut so that people could pay their respects. Then all the female sorcerers arrived in pairs, led by the person who was to fill the position that had been held by the Grang-Mama. She held in her**

hand a scepter made from tree-shoots. With this scepter, she consecrated the deceased, amidst grimaces and rites, and then danced three times around the coffin with amazing skill, considering her age, accompanied by fife and drums. The most remarkable aspect of her death dance was that she could move about without her feet ever leaving the ground, while every part of her body moved in perfect time to the music. As she danced, she also consecrated several of her companions with the scepter. Before she finished, her next companion began to dance, and this continued till all were dancing, and then they all danced together.[53] After a solid hour, this painful dance of death was over. This is such a strenuous dance that one can see every muscle of the naked negro bodies moving. It is not surprising that, after a short while, all had broken out in a sweat. While this dance was in progress, the relatives were dragged [from the corpse?] by certain leaders, and they made it seem as if, in their melancholy, they could not move one step alone.[54]

While a few of the gravediggers went to check their previous day's work (bailing out any water that had seeped in, shoring up the sides), back in her house Akoomi's corpse had been laid into the coffin, where it rested on a number of hammocks and hammock sheets and was surrounded by scores of other cloths offered by kinfolk, affines, and friends. Extra earrings were placed near her ears, extra necklaces on her chest. Then Bosi, one of her daughters, stepped forward, and all were asked to avert their eyes as she placed Akoomi's "wrestling belt" (the erotic beaded belt that she had worn while sharing her husband's hammock) across her middle and quickly covered it with a cloth. Carried outdoors (and then back in, and out again, three times), the coffin was sealed with nails and then "dressed" for the occasion, with a dozen neckerchiefs pinned to the front and skirt-length cloths and hammock sheets draped around it. Finally, a long rope of cloths, tied end to end, was used to wrap the coffin like a giant package— three vertical ties that encircled the whole, plus one running the length of the peak and one around at each end, to hold the whole taut. The massive construction was lifted onto the heads of two men, on banana leaf head-pads, and carried to the ancestor shrine for a silent parley between Akoomi and those she was going to join. Then, in front of her house, Akoomi's coffin was set down for the rituals of separation (*paati*)—from her close kinfolk, from her neighbors, and from those who shared her gods.

With drums playing *adunke* rhythms as well as special Madanfo music, older women consecrated the coffin with white *keeti* powder and danced around it carrying sprigs of *sangaáfu* plants. The *paati* rites—what Brother Riemer calls "the ceremony"—consisted of each participant holding a sprig of *sangaafu,* whitened on one end and extending over the coffin, by the "good" (white) end as she stood facing sunrise, back to the coffin, and Kaana slicing it in two with a machete, leaving the good end in the woman's hand. Meanwhile, Kaana intoned that the good must stay, the evil must go. "Akoomi, Don't take it badly! We're simply separating you from your snake god." And a woman holding half a *sangaafu* branch would hurry away from the scene. Or, "Akoomi, it's time for you and your Madanfo to be parted. Don't be angry." And another woman strode off with another piece of whitened *sangaafu*.

Brother Riemer continues:

The funeral procession itself began at ten o'clock.[55] The twelve Grang-Mans [elders] designated as pallbearers placed six folded old cloths under the coffin and it looked like it was almost floating as they carried it. First they carried the corpse three times around its former dwelling so that she would never find the place or disturb her friends again.[56] Then, the firing of fifty salutes gave the signal to begin the burial procession, and then commenced enough wild drumming and fife playing and screaming and howling to terrify and horrify any European.

The corpse was carried all about the village in the already mentioned manner.[57] Upon arrival at the burial ground,[58] the grave digger took one of the three white chickens that were to be used as sacrifices and threw it alive into the grave, so that its blood sprayed all over. Then, they lowered the coffin, leaning it in its proper place, opened the cover, and by means of cedarwood boards formed a type of arch over it which they covered with green leaves. After each of the close relatives threw a shovelful of earth onto this arch, the gravedigger walked over to the grave and spoke in the name of all the relatives for the last time with the deceased, saying, "Mama, all of your close male and female friends trust you to rest easily in your grave without disturbing them with a visit. I bid you, in their name, to greet all their friends at the place where you now are, and also to bring about the pregnancy of the young women so that they may happily bear children. In addition, may great herds of Pingo come from distant places, and may we always be fortunate in our hunting and fishing. And also may no one lose his life in the river. Etc."[59] After this speech, the grave was closed, accompanied by music and dirges,[60] and then all returned to the house of mourning.[61]

The two other sacrificial chickens, which had been tied to the grave, were brought back by the gravedigger to the house of mourning, where they were slaughtered and prepared for the deceased, so that she could take part and enjoy the feast of mourning at the same time as the living. Before the feast began, some men were sent with these cooked chickens and with a container of hand-washing water to the grave, where they placed these things and then quickly fled. The dogs running about in large numbers made good use of this meal. This food and hand-washing water had been sent by the negroes to the deceased so

that she could take part and enjoy the mourning feast, and would not attempt to return [to the village] and personally take part in it.

On the evening of Akoomi's burial, and on into the night, Bambey staged a massive "play," with almost every kind of recreational song, dance, and drumming. The next day, the gravediggers tried their luck at hunting, and in the evening poured a libation followed by three gunshots in front of Akoomi's house to invite her and the other ancestors to the "first feast" (*fési nyanyán*) the next day. That evening, there was more drumming, singing, and dancing, but the crowds had thinned. The gravediggers as well as Alabi's non-Christian siblings had meanwhile slung their hammocks in Akoomi's house, where they slept each night until the "last feast" (*báka nyanyán*) a week later. On the morning of the "first feast," there was another libation in front of the house, and then the gravediggers purified themselves and their tools with a fire built at the site where Akoomi's body had been washed the day after death. Leaving axe, shovels, machetes, and stewpot in the fire, they jostled joyfully to get the maximum exposure to the purifying smoke. The afternoon's ancestral feast was much like that for Akoomi's husband, a dozen years before, though turtle was not appropriate since this was not a second funeral. When the winnowing tray was overturned, but before it was "knocked" with a stick three times, three gunshots were fired. Then came a long libation of water and rum, after which the crowd of several hundred dispersed for dinner. In the evening, for the first time during the funeral, a score of people gathered by torchlight in front of Akoomi's doorway for a few hours of lively riddling and tale telling. African exploits of Anancy the Spider Man rubbed shoulders comfortably with stories of Suriname slavery and creatures of the deep bush.[62]

And so it went for a week, with "plays" or tale telling, and sometimes both, each evening, and the gravediggers keeping up a spirit of festivity all day long—commandeering rum from older men, stealing chickens from old ladies' henhouses, blowing their wooden trumpets, staging spontaneous wrestling matches, and chasing young girls. On the morning of the "last feast" (which was preceded, like all *nyanyantue*s, by libations the preceding evening), the gravediggers formally ended their reign, first throwing their hammocks out of the house of mourning and then, apparently, breaking down the whole structure.[63] For the first time since they had taken on their role, they could (like living people but unlike the dead) once again eat salt. And the village of Bambey, along with Akoomi and the other invited ancestors, sat down together in front of Akoomi's doorway for the "last feast."

The next morning, Kaana and the other elders of Bambey, Alabi's non-Christian relatives, and those visitors still present brought their stools before Akoomi's doorway and sat down for the longest libations of the whole week. Speaking largely in proverbs and elliptical

Saramakas dancing *sêkêti,* 1980 (Photo, Terry Agerkop).

metaphors, the elders called on Akoomi, Abini, and large numbers of other ancestors by name to take responsibility for particular problems and people. Sometimes Akoomi was gently threatened: "If sickness comes to the village, we'll know who to blame!" Sometimes, she was cajoled: "Alabi's whitefolks are ruining us. With the help of Madanfo you are our only hope!" When they had finally finished, the gravediggers came forward and gave presents of soap and candles to each of Alabi's sisters. In return, Alabi's brothers gave a new length of cloth to each of the gravediggers, as thanks for their help during the week. The jug of rum from which the libations had been poured was still largely full, but it did not last long as the men relaxed together, talking about hunting and the weather and preparing to return to their normal pursuits. While awaiting the second funeral, a year or so later, the villagers of Bambey could feel justly proud that they had buried Akoomi, their Grangmama, "with joy." Meanwhile, Alabi and the Christian congregation stayed very much at the edge of these noisy goings on, having in their own terms done their part to commemorate Akoomi's death in a manner befitting their new beliefs.

Brother Riemer summed up these same "heathen" events from his perspective.

This type of mourning ceremony for a distinguished personage takes eight full days and nights without interruption. The great quantity of edibles and strong drink, which the visitors are themselves obliged to bring, is completely consumed. The relatives, too, expend as much gun powder as possible, as the Government in Paramaribo gives them gifts of powder in such situations.[64] By means of singing, drumming, and fife playing, the negro men and women are able to unwind, and during the entire period there is never a quarter hour of peace, either day or night.

After the mourning period is over, the grave digger fills a vessel with river water and then sprinkles and cleans the paths over which the corpse was carried. After this, he loads a tray with firewood, edibles, and a cooking pot, and takes it to the other side of the river, where he unloads it at a convenient place in the forest and announces in loud tones to the deceased that this will be her new dwelling place and presents her with the objects he has brought. Then he rushes away, screaming wildly, toward the village, and by firing several salutes, announces to the village that the death feast has ended.[65]

During the months before his mother's death, Alabi had tried hard to grant her one long-cherished wish—to see again, in freedom, a daughter whom the whites had enslaved some forty years before. In 1779, Tribal Chief Kwaku Etja, accompanied by Alabi and Kodjo Maata, had pressed Postholder Weinhold to write a letter to the Court on their behalf. Etja told Weinhold how Tribal Chief Abini's daughter (with Akoomi), Tutuba, had been taken captive during the wars and was still a slave on a plantation owned by the Society of Suriname. In requesting that the Society set her free, they noted that the mother of the Saramaka "Andries" (who had also been captured in wartime) had already been freed,[66] and that the freeing of Tutuba would be especially appropriate "since Abini had offered his life for the whites." The Court, during its deliberations, outlined the background:

> She is the daughter of Chief Abini, who was shot dead in the 1766 expedition against the Negroes of Musinga, and who went to lend us assistance. She is thus a sister on the father's side [but also on the mother's] of the present chief Johannes Abini [Alabi] who has been baptized by the Moravians. She was captured after being shot about 30–40 years ago in an expedition against the then-hostile Saramakas, and purchased by the Society. She is now a grizzled and of-no-practical-service Negress. She has three children: a son named Jan, a slave carpenter; a slave daughter named Jacoba; and a mulatto daughter named Betje, who herself has two mulatto sons.

Though I have not seen whitefolks' documents regarding the final disposition of Alabi's request—Alabi was still petitioning the government for her release in 1781—Saramakas preserve vivid memories of what happened. When I mentioned Tutuba's name to Captain Gome, the elderly chief of Alabi's clan, in 1978, his eyes filled with tears of joy, and he sang out:

> Tutúba, Tutúba u mi o, mmá   Tutuba, my Tutuba, [little]
>   momma
> Miíi o, u o míti a goónlíba?   Child, oh. Will we ever meet
>   again on this earth?

And Gome excitedly told me:

> This is what Alabi's mother used to sing as she pined for
> her stolen daughter. Alabi learned his sister's name from his
> mother [i.e., he never knew her]. Tutuba, Alabi's sister. The
> child the whites caught and carried off! . . . My mother's
> brother once told me, "The story of Tutuba. You must not
> forget it as long as you still breathe. The sister of Alabi. They
> captured her in battle, took her to the city, and put her in
> slavery. Well, her name was Tutuba.". . . They say she wasn't
> "red" [light-skinned]; she was absolutely black! She died
> here, on the Upper River [after she was returned to Alabi].
> She died before her brother.

Tutuba's story is a further testimony to the intense family feelings among eighteenth-century Saramakas, and to the terrible pain brought by forced separation, even after they had won their freedom. Though Akoomi did not live to see her final wish granted, we know that her daughter did return to live out her days with Alabi and other members of her family. Somewhere in *dêdè-kôndè,* the land of the dead, Akoomi's spirit must have rested easy.

Sometime during this period (the diaries I have seen are silent on the matter) Alabi's mother-in-law Sofi also died. Never baptized, Sofi is remembered by Christian and non-Christian Saramakas alike as both a leper and—because her daughter founded, with Alabi, an impressively large lineage—a woman of prestige. For modern Saramakas, memory of her illness is preserved in the name of the creek across from Gwafu Bambey, just below the modern Suriname government post at Debiké: Sofí Creek. As a Dombi elder recounted two hundred years after the event:

> Now, Alabi was living at Gwafu. And while he lived there,
> his mother-in-law died. Well, his mother-in-law was sick
> with leprosy. So they took her to be buried at the mouth of
> the creek there. Now, the woman's name had been Sofi.
> That's why the creek is called Sofi Creek.[67]

A few years later, in 1785, the missionaries reported the birth of Alabi and Sialoto's fourth child, whom the parents named Sofi.

At about the same time, Alabi's brother-in-law Kodjo Maata became host to a small group of "fellow Indians," who remained to become assimilated into the Ingi Pisi ("Indian Quarter") segment of the Awana clan. Kodjo, born in the early years of the century and himself part Indian (whence his sobriquet, Maata [mulatto]), was apparently a refugee from the group of mixed African maroons and Indians who lived to the west of the Saramacca River. One day in the early 1780s, not long after the founding of the village of Kumbu by Alabi's father's sister's son, the Matjau Djaki, some mysterious Indians appeared. As Basia Bakaa of Bótópási described it to me in 1978,

> *They were at Kumbu. Djaki and his brother Awoyo. One day they saw an* awáa *[palm] pit land in front of them, on the ground. After a moment,* vi pém!, *another. Djaki said to his brother, "This thing. Human beings! People are doing it." And he circled around [behind the village]. He saw three Indians, two women and a man. He caught them and brought them to his house. . . . Now at that time Alabi had an Indian named Kodjo Maata living with him. When the three Indians arrived [at Kumbu], no one knew how to talk with them. But they knew Alabi had an Indian so they sent for him. So that they could talk, Indian with Indian* gbêgêdê! *[ideophone for "pure," "the real thing"]. The Indians said they came in peace. And then they lived there with the Matjaus for a while. Then they went to the Awanas [where Kodjo lived]. They're still with the Awanas today![68]*

In addition to his other concerns during the early 1780s, Alabi continued to devote a substantial portion of his time to politics. Rare is the report of a meeting with the government postholder that lists him as absent. Routine rather than new issues dominated relations between Saramakas and the government, the sole exception being difficulties stemming from the Boni Wars, including contretemps between the whites and the Djukas, for which Saramakas agreed to lend a conciliatory hand. In July 1780, Postholder Weinhold announced to the assembled Saramaka chiefs that the government considered itself in a state of enmity with the Djukas, because the latter were refusing to turn in two children of the rebel maroon chief Boni, whom they had captured.[69] For a full hour, the chiefs "stepped aside" (*bendi a se*) for a confidential consultation, in standard council-meeting procedure, and then Tribal Chief Etja, speaking on behalf of the others, asked Weinhold to plead with the Court for clemency for the Djukas. Etja offered a remarkably detailed and sympathetic accounting of the difficulties experienced by the Djukas because of the wars between the whites and the Bonis (disruption of Djuka agricultural routines, and so on). The Saramakas promised, and later sent, a mediating delegation to the Djukas, which seems finally to have helped settle the difficulties.[70]

But there were other, more serious Djuka-Saramaka difficulties.

When the elderly Nasi-clan war hero, Captain Kwaku Kwadjani, died suddenly, divination revealed that a Djuka man was responsible, by witchcraft. The Moravians report that

> **on the twenty-fifth [July 1781] we heard the news that a chief of a village two hours from here had suddenly died. All the negroes [from Bambey] went there in order to take part in the funeral. The negroes there believed that the deceased had died because of poison [sorcery], and the corpse was examined [through divination], revealing—according to them—that a certain Auka [Djuka] Negro was the perpetrator. A canoe was immediately dispatched with deputies in order to capture him and bring him here. . . . As it turns out, the poor man was burned to death on the 15th of September.**

The Moravians report further that the execution was attended by several Djukas, as official witnesses. On the day following the burning at the stake,

> **four Djukas visited us, one of whom was a captain. They were very friendly and humble and recommended that we . . . help see to it that the peace between them and the whites not be broken.**

Saramakas retain more detailed memories of what happened.

> *Kwaku [Kwadjani] and the Djuka were* mati *[formal friends]. The Djuka came here [to Saramaka] simply to visit. But [after a while] he began to want Kwaku's wife![71] The Djuka dug a spot under the woman's hearthstones, right where she cooked for Kwadjani, and he buried something there. That's what killed him! When they raised his coffin [in divination] that's what it indicated. It [the coffin] went right to that spot and "knocked" it. They dug and everyone saw it. "Who put it there?" they asked the coffin. "His* mati *from Djuka who came to visit," was the reply. [Tribal Chief] Kwaku Etja [the brother of Kwadjani] left there and went all the way to Djuka! To get the person. To bring him to Kambaloa [the Nasi-clan village]. Then they held a council meeting. But suddenly, they didn't see Etja any more. No sign of him. Until . . . at dusk he returned to the council meeting. And then, until morning, they didn't see him again. He had been going off to cut firewood across the river! He cut it until there was really a lot, and he piled it into a great heap. Then in the morning, he took fire and kerosene and poured it all over until the fire was roaring. Well, when he disappeared from the council meeting, it was to see if the fire was really blazing. Finally, the fire was just as he wanted it. He came back to the council meeting, went up to the Djuka man, and tied him up. He dragged*

him along, shrieking all the way to the fire. And they burned him. Right there at Puúma Sándu [behind Kambaloa].[72]

In October 1781, the governor of Suriname recorded in his journal that Tando, the successor to Kwadjani, had come to the city to be officially recognized as captain and to request "mourning goods" for Kwadjani's ("second") funeral; he noted also that the Saramakas believed Kwadjani to have been "poisoned" by a Djuka.[73]

Other than this flurry of intertribal activity, the period was dominated by politics as usual—negotiations and disputes about returning "whitefolks' slaves" and receiving the now-triennial tribute goods. The government, through the postholder, tried to maintain pressure regarding slave harboring, both by threatening not to give goods to particular offenders and by more general discussions of the law.[74]

> *I [Postholder Weinhold] asked [Matjau captain] Kristofel what response he had concerning Bakki [a runaway he was harboring]. He replied that he hadn't come here to have an argument about slaves, and that we whites didn't seem to have anything better to do than to bother them about slaves. I told him that we whites also had far too much to do to spend our time bothering about [the Saramakas'] presents, and that, besides, these were our slaves.*

Saramakas, meanwhile, continued lobbying for more goods, both individually and collectively. For example, Captain Kwaku Kwadjani, the oldest of Saramaka chiefs and the brother of the *gaama,* only months before his death,

> *will leave me [Postholder Weinhold] no rest until I write Your Excellencies requesting for him a jacket . . . of the type given out to plantation slaves at New Year's, for which Kwaku thanks you one hundred times over.*

And, before the tribute distribution of 1781, the chiefs joined to ask for an increase in the proposed quantities of "cooking oil, 'African' peppers, earrings for their wives, scissors, and 'African' cooking oil." At the actual distribution of 1781, the eleven captains collectively received, on behalf of their villages, "40 muskets, 40 barrels (plus some extra) of gunpowder, 52 barrels of salt, 97 iron pots, 34 plates [*platiljes*], 46 pieces *vriesbont* [cloth], 11 ditto osnaburg linen, 48 ditto cotton cloth, 200 [quantities] of beads, 800 [quantities] of shot, 2300 flints, 2200 sailor's knives, 554 machetes, 202 axes, 67 adzes, 102 hoes, 34 canoe adzes, 34 shovels, 380 jars of dram [rum], 23 packs of sewing needles, 23 packs of blue and white embroidery thread, and 13 grindstones."[75]

Meanwhile, the tension between Christianity and Saramaka religion continued to occupy Alabi actively. His daily rounds placed him in the frequent position of mediator, and he played an important role in effecting compromises that permitted a modus vivendi between the tiny Christian community and the large number of "nonbelievers" in Bambey who surrounded them. In effect, Alabi was serving as an active agent in the ongoing, if still very limited, process of syncretism between Christianity and Saramaka religion (which ultimately affected the nascent Christian community but had little effect on other Saramakas).

In early 1781, for example, Alabi confronted a set of beliefs that Saramakas considered simply common sense: that children born with certain unusual characteristics (e.g., albinism, polydactylism) were gods, whose mortal lives required special treatment.[76]

> **During the night of February 11, a child was born. Because it had six fingers on each hand, a great shriek was heard in the village, for they wanted to make the child into a god. We were summoned and told them that the extra fingers could be cut away without harm. Johannes seized on the occasion to warn his brothers about their blindness and horrid idolatry, and told them that should it continue they would certainly anger the one and true God. . . . He went on to say, "If the true God were to withdraw the protection He was granting you, and leave you in the hands of your self-made idols, how would you fare then?" They sighed at this but said nothing.**

By the time the missionaries next describe such a case, in 1783, a compromise seems to have been worked out.

> **On July 8, a four-month-old child, who had been revered as a god, died. When such children die, they are thrown into the water amidst all kinds of spectacles. Our Johannes tried to prevent this from occurring. However, they did manage to bury the child so close to the river that the grave would from time to time be overrun by water.**

Such ritual compromises, in which Christian sympathizers retain part of the outward Saramaka rite that still holds meaning for them, continue to characterize that brand of Christianity practiced by Christian Saramakas to this day. (Ancestors continue to be worshiped, but privately rather than at public ancestor shrines; god-children continue to be treated as such, but are buried near, rather than in, the river.) But during the eighteenth century, the compromises worked out under Alabi's influence in Bambey, whether among baptized Christians or their non-Christian relatives, affected only a very small group of Saramakas. Beyond the special village of Bambey, in which Alabi was captain, very little direct attention was being paid to these local modifications of Saramaka practice.[77]

Alabi did occasionally help the missionaries branch out beyond the small world of Bambey by leading one or another of them on a proselytizing trip to other villages, but such visits provided only superficial contacts. In 1781—to cite but one example—Alabi and Brother Wietz made such a trip, traveling up the Suriname River to the village of Kaapatu on the Gaanlio, partly to visit Alabi's kinfolk there. On the way, they stopped at the village of Kofi Creek, just below the confluence of the Pikilio and the Gaanlio, where Alabi introduced Wietz, if only for a moment, to one of the greatest of all Saramaka *obiama,* Kungooka of Dahomey,

> an old captain[78] who is the most respected servant of the idols and with his sorcery produces the greatest deceptions. One can actually see the evil spirits in his eyes. He and his people acted very strangely toward me. I could not but look at them with melancholy in my heart.

Later, in the Langu village of Kaapatu, where one of Alabi's brothers lived, Alabi introduced Brother Wietz to his aged grandmother—Yaya, mother of Abini and medium of the great Matjau *gadu* Wamba, who had raised Alabi.

> She was an elderly woman who was regarded as a grandmother by the entire village. She had raised our Johannes. I told her that I had undertaken this trip to acquaint her with her God and Creator who would make her eternally happy. She answered that she had already heard this ten years before from the late Rudolph Stoll in Kwama, and she then began to relate everything that she had heard about the Creation, the Fall of Man, and the Redemption that we had received through the Savior. She seemed to be not without feeling.

Outside of these two encounters, the report of this trip contains little of interest except that many of the women and children in Kaapatu were extremely curious about Brother Wietz, as they had never seen a white man, and that the village men were surprised that Brother Wietz would eat with them from the same calabashes, as no white person had ever done this before.

Back in Bambey, Alabi continued to serve as the missionaries' buffer against the non-Christian Saramakas who surrounded them in the village.

> Just as we were about to hold our meeting, the people of the village began a large spectacle. Johannes immediately went outside to beg them to cease their drumming and singing until we were finished with our service, to which they agreed.

Clearly, for the great majority of people in Bambey, the missionaries were, at best, merely tolerated. Non-Christians complied, when it suited them, with missionary admonitions regarding sobriety, dress, and demeanor in the immediate neighborhood of their meeting house. But they made few other concessions. One lively woman could have been speaking for many of the residents of Bambey when she told the Moravians:

> "I still love the spectacles of the negroes. I love to dance and I cannot hear any story about the Great God just now because if I were to convert, I wouldn't be able to dance any more."

And even the few converts wrestled constantly with conflicts between Moravian and Saramaka personal style.

> On the first of January [1777] we wished one another, and all of those Christians among us, a Blessed New Year. Our listeners came and congratulated us. We had been telling the people in the village for some time that when they came to bring us New Year's greetings, they should not make noise and fire muskets in front of our houses, as we wished to celebrate the holiday in the company of our God, the Father, the Son, and the Holy Ghost. They behaved themselves accordingly and remained quiet.

A similar conflict occurred whenever a canoe returned from the city, and the missionaries rarely got their way.

> During the subsequent days, the village was restless, as everyone was drunk from the liquor that the negroes had brought back with them. We thus had to cancel the sermon that was to be held on the 16th. In the evening, during choir practice, the Brethren and Sisters were asked not to take part in the [other] negroes' orgy of food and drink but instead to stay close to the Savior.

Except for the ill-fitted Brother Riemer, the intrepid Moravians showed little true sympathy for their Saramaka charges, even for children; their rigid ideas of right and wrong behavior, imported from Herrnhut, rarely bent. A poignant confrontation occurred when old Simeon, a very recent Moravian convert who had for years taken care of the children in the village, died.

> The children he had cared for came to us [the Brethren Wietz, Wiesner, and Randt] and asked if we would not permit them to make a shriek of mourning, because they had all loved him dearly. We told them that this was most repulsive to us and that Christians did not do this. And it was left at that.

Non-Christians in Bambey, despite their frequent conflicts with the mission, did sometimes take advantage of church meetings for entertainment—as an occasion for singing, showing off their appearance, and meeting members of the opposite sex. New Year's was a favorite moment.

> On the first of January 1781 we held our first sermon in our new church and Johannes invited many strangers so that 70 listeners were present.

> Many people visited us—men, women, and children—in order to congratulate us on the New Year. At the sermon were many

strangers who do not normally come to church. Many just came to show off their finery.[79]

Throughout, Alabi—not only as village captain but as the missionaries' eyes, ears, and hands—remained at the very center of Bambey life. Years later, back in Europe, Brother Riemer penned a retrospective word portrait of Alabi-the-Christian in 1780, when he was thirty-six years old.

[Alabi] had such an extraordinary memory that he remembered all the biblical phrases he had heard years before when the first missionaries came, and little by little these had been incorporated into the impoverished native language. He not only knew them all by heart but also tried constantly to inform himself about the true content of these religious phrases, so that he could communicate this better to his negro brethren. He was so humble and whatever he did for me and for the mission he carried out in a most assiduous way, looking upon it as edifying in itself. Because of all this, he had to take care of his own domestic duties only after the evening prayer service, which took place by moonlight. Yet he was always the first at the morning service. He also took special pleasure in being responsible for the ringing of the bells for Sunday services. For this duty he usually appeared in his honorary uniform, provided by the colonial government—a jacket, a vest, trousers of the finest striped linen, a hat with golden tassels, a lace shirt with cuffs, and a captain's staff made from cane and topped with a large silver and heavily-gilt ball. With all this finery, he nevertheless went barefoot.[80]

Eight   Chief-over-All

On 5 July 1783, Postholder de Vries wrote to the Court in Paramaribo to report the death of Tribal Chief Kwaku Etja.

The postholder, having reported the death of Tribal Chief Etja . . . and understanding that the Court must now appoint a [new] tribal chief, suggests that no one is as qualified as Johannes Arabie, son of Tribal Chief Abini who was killed in 1766 [sic] in the expedition against the Matawais and in whose place he [Alabi] was named village captain, making him [now] one of the senior councilors.

Five months later, in December 1783, the colonial governor formally announced the appointment of "the Saramaka Free Negro Johannis Arabie to become *'algemeen opperhoofd'* in place of the deceased Etja." The promise made by the senior chiefs sixteen years earlier at Langa Amana, where Alabi was preparing to do battle against his father's slayers, had at last been fulfilled.[1] For the next thirty-seven years, until his death in 1820, Alabi served as *gaama*—Chief-over-All of the Saramaka nation.

Alabi's *gaama*ship spanned a period during which Saramaka society was turning decidedly inward. The frequent and dramatic confrontations with white colonial authority that marked the first two decades of peace had, by Kwaku Etja's death, become largely a thing of the past. Saramakas and the government had established a political modus vivendi that was to remain relatively stable until well into the nineteenth century.[2] In contrast to the twenty years following the Peace of 1762—which were truly formative in terms of political relations with the government, relations with missionaries and Christianity, and internal peacetime political arrangements—the thirty-seven years of Alabi's *gaama*ship were marked by the gradual and less dramatic consolidation of Saramaka institutions.

Available historical sources reflect these realities. Postholders' journals, reports, and letters become scarce early in the period and soon disappear almost completely, as the government decided that Saramakas no longer posed a sufficient threat to require close administrative supervision; the Moravians' journals and letters become strongly routinized and less voluminous than during the early years of the mission;[3] and modern Saramakas' oral accounts are far sparser for this period of consolidation than for the preceding periods of war and institution-building.

As *gaama,* rather than simply village captain, Alabi devoted increasing time to tribal politics and the administration of justice—even though beyond Bambey, Saramakas turned to him as a leader far less than they had to Abini or to Kwaku Etja (or would, in later decades, to his non-Christian successors). The Moravians themselves rarely mentioned that Alabi was *gaama.* Indeed, in the documents I have examined, they recorded nothing about his formal installation and continued to write of him almost solely as Alabi-the-Christian, mentioning his official duties only in those rare cases when they posed a direct conflict (that the Moravians happened to understand) with his congregational life. Because of missionary and postholder reticence during this period, we know relatively little about the official side of Alabi's life.

In late November 1783, Alabi left Bambey for Paramaribo, to receive his ceremonial uniform and the governor's official congratulations.[4] For the governor's information, Postholder de Vries wrote a detailed memorandum summarizing what he viewed as the key outstanding issues between Saramakas and the government. They comprise a familiar and dreary litany: problems surrounding the distribution of whitefolks' goods by Matjau captain Adjagbo to the Paputu-clan people who lived in his villages; problems about continued requests for special gifts and for permission to buy slave women by the Matjau quasi-captain Djaki; problems between Pieter Soni (who had split off with some people from Bambey) and Alabi over tribute goods; problems about gift distributions within the Abaisa clan; problems regarding the turning in of slaves by the Matawai; problems between Suriname River planters and Saramakas, prompting the postholder to suggest that a trading post be set up at Victoria so that Saramakas could do their business there rather than coming all the way downriver into the plantation area; the postholder's personal complaint list, including his pressing need for soap, candles, vinegar, cooking- and lamp-oil, powder and shot, tools, nails, and medicine; and, finally, a tangle of problems involving Djuka captain Kofi Tja-panda, whose Saramaka kin and in-laws were involved in the accusations of sorcery being brought against him in Djuka.[5] Meanwhile, Alabi, soon after arriving in Paramaribo, responded point by point to de Vries' report: he wished to have nothing to do with the vicious conflict between the Paputus and Adjagbo; he promised to take care of the Abaisa and Soni problems; he expressed real concern about the Kofi Tjapanda incident, which seemed potentially explosive; and so on. In addition, he formally requested the services of "an assistant, because the [governing] work in the forest [in Saramaka] is too heavy [for one person]"; he asked that "his [first] wife's mother, Welkom, who is in Paramaribo . . . receive some support"; and, finally, he asked that at the next tribute distribution, each captain receive an extra gun.

Alabi's subsequent political activities, insofar as they are visible in the reports of the postholder and missionaries, present few surprises. In 1785, he journeyed to Victoria for the first time as *gaama* for the triennial tribute distribution, where the standard ritual renewal of the 1762 Peace was accomplished: each captain was asked by the postholder whether he pledged to maintain the Peace, and each answered in Sranan, "Jaa." Then,

> *Arabie and [the Matjau quasi-captain] Djaki made a small incision on the hand of each of us, and Djaki took from each chief a little blood on some cotton, and squeezed it out in a glass of white wine. We reminded each other of the oath, and the sanctions on breaking it. . . . Alabi then took the glass and said that if anyone does, or allows to be done, any harm to the whites, may the Great God visit punishment upon him and his descendants. . . . He then took a bit of the blood and wine mixture and knocked it down. Each of the other chiefs followed suit.*

As *gaama,* Alabi (or occasionally his delegate) was to repeat this ceremony, at roughly three-year intervals, for the next thirty-five years.[6]

In 1797, Alabi characteristically avoided dealing with a judicial case so as not to compromise his Christian principles. (The adjudication of almost all Saramaka legal conflicts involved, at some stage, divination and other non-Christian practices.)

> **On the 27th [January 1797] a delegation sent by the elders of the Aucaners [Djukas] who live on the Marowijne, eight days from here, came to our Johannes in order to bring a law case before the local judiciary. It concerned a negro whom they suspected of having poisoned [killed by sorcery] another negro. Since this type of case requires all sorts of sorcerer's tricks and deceptions, Johannes sent them to another village in order to have an old woman there administer the ordeal-by-fire.**[7]

In his role as Chief-over-All, Alabi seems to have chosen to exercise his pan-tribal office largely in a ceremonial manner, with most of his actual authority confined to Bambey and several of the nearby villages.[8]

Several times each year, when problems required formal council meetings, Alabi participated—with, or more frequently without, the postholder, and sometimes in upriver villages, to which Alabi traveled. The Moravians often simply note such meetings, without mentioning their content; when they do allude to specific political problems, these tend to be familiar: nonreceipt of government tribute goods, accusations by the whites of slave-harboring, and so on. Only three times are there hints of serious conflict. In 1790, when Langu-clan captain Alando was accused of harboring slaves, a number of other captains tried to persuade Alabi to join them in a confrontation with the whites, but after a big meeting at New Bambey, Alabi convinced them to keep the Peace by returning these new runaways. Then, in 1792, there are indications that Captain Antama, the great *obia* priest of the Langu region, was trying formally to wrest the *gaama*ship from Alabi.

> Grang Adama [= Great Antama, his sobriquet throughout the late eighteenth century] is a captain but like all other captains is subordinate to Johannes, to whom the Government gave this distinction as well as extraordinary presents because of his fidelity and truly great services to the country. Grang Adama now believes that *he* should be Chief-over-All and, because he was denied this or that thing which he had requested from the Government, the other captains have succeeded in convincing him that Johannes—whom the others consider their enemy—is responsible. In earlier days [at the time of Alabi's baptism], Grang Adama was so agitated that he actually wanted to shoot Johannes. However, little by little he has had a change of heart and now wishes to extend to Johannes the hand of friendship.

Antama, for complex reasons, lost this battle (see below), and Alabi maintained his hold on the office. Finally, in 1800, the government again brought pressure on Saramakas because of slave-harboring. Alabi helped Brother Wietz, who was doubling as postholder at the time, to carry the day.

> On the 19th [December 1800] we received letters from the Government in which it was announced that two Saramaka Free Negro captains and their people, according to the terms of the Peace Treaty, would be forbidden to travel to Paramaribo until two runaway slaves who were hidden with them had been returned. Brother Wietz immediately informed them and told them the consequences if they refused to obey. Three weeks later, they passed through here [New Bambey], on their way to bring the slaves to Paramaribo, and Brother Wietz gave them a letter to the Government to accompany them.

But though the details of Alabi's political activities as *gaama* remain obscure, it is clear that he suffered from the burdens of office. Squeezed between, on the one hand, his private ideological commitment to Christianity, pacifism, and accommodation with whitefolks and, on the other, the widespread traditional Saramaka confrontational stance toward outside authority, Alabi had little room for maneuver. In 1792, under pressure from Captain Antama and his allies and in utter frustration at his inability to carry out his duties effectively, he actually attempted to abdicate.

> On the second of February, Johannes left for Paramaribo with the purpose of giving up his position as first captain [tribal chief], to whom all the other captains in the land are subordinate. It has been a very difficult period for him lately, because the other captains have been fighting incessantly among themselves as well as with the Government in Paramaribo. Lots of people from many different parties have grown distrustful of him. And he realizes how much his heart has suffered because of his official duties.

Alabi, however, was persuaded to keep his position, which he maintained in the ambiguous marginal role to which he had become accustomed, until his death.

If we know little of Alabi's formal political activities as *gaama,* we are nonetheless privileged to share a good many of his concerns as the leader of the Christian congregation at Gwafu Bambey. The first involved the local villagers' growing wish to abandon the site of the village of Bambey against the missionaries' wishes, and this conflict dragged out over several years. Already in 1782, when the deaths of several children occurred in quick succession, there had been talk about a move.

> Since they could think of no other reason, the sorcerers said that [the deaths were because] the local ground had become tainted, and thus there was a great deal of talk here about moving away.

The next year, in the wake of more children's deaths, there was a great deal of "sorcery and confusion" and further talk of a move.

> On the 22nd [July 1783] Johannes [Alabi], Joshua [Kodjo], and Andreas [Kwaku] came to us [the Brethren Wiesner and Wietz] and told us that the local negroes wanted to leave here. Some had even begun to make preparations for the move and were ready to leave with their children for a place that was an hour away. They asked whether we might not be interested in moving too. This was a very difficult decision for us to make, as our buildings here were in excellent condition, and it would be a tremendous effort to move to a new place and rebuild, and begin making gardens again. And it especially hurt us that the move was prompted by superstitious fears, as the negroes believed that the local ground had been tainted by poison [sorcery], and that a certain old woman was killing off the children in this way.[9]
> We felt that we needed some time to think about this and

wrote to our Brethren in Paramaribo to ask their advice. We received an answer on August 9, saying that we should not move with the negroes, since disease and death were in the hands of God, and could come at one place as easily as another. Thus we resolved not to move to the new place; in any case, our strength was sapped. However, we could not prevent them from moving should they choose; we could only try to persuade them against it. Our baptized ones, who really did not want to leave us, were very perplexed by the situation. But we were helpless as well.

The Moravians soon began cultivating their gardens at Bambey (as it was the beginning of the planting season), and this seems to have tipped the balance temporarily. For,

when the people saw that we were serious about remaining here, they also began once again to cultivate their gardens.

Soon, the Brethren Wiesner and Wietz became privy to evidence about what local Saramakas had decided was the real reason they had to move—serious hostility toward the Moravians and their "sacrilegious" acts—though they understood it all only dimly. As the missionaries explained:

On October 9, the people made preparations for a sacrifice behind our house, near a tree that we had felled the previous year. This tree was considered to be a great god, and our felling it the cause of so many children having died. As a sacrifice, they slaughtered some chickens and presented them to the god, praying that he not hurt them any longer. For it had not been *their* fault, they said, but that of the wicked Europeans and their baptized people. He would better kill *them*.

On December 2, many local heathen negroes gathered with their children at this same tree, kneeling down before it and begging it for life and for health, for them and their children, and they again sacrificed four chickens. Brother Wiesner, who had also come there, spoke to them about their folly, and ordered them to leave, at which point one negro became so angry that we were quite lucky no mishap occurred.

The following day two children died, and the people became nearly crazed. As practically all of our baptized people were in Paramaribo [where Alabi was receiving formal recognition as *gaama*] . . . we were in a very ticklish situation, and the heathens tried to annoy us in every possible way.

In 1978, I asked the elderly Captain Gome, Alabi's Awana-clan descendant, whether he knew anything about such a tree. In a deep, firm voice, he told me:

Silk-cotton! [katu] *That's what the white man felled. It [that act] was absolutely finishing off the people of that village. A silk-cotton tree! When they cut off the chicken's*

head, kúkú *[sound of cutting off the head], the last time,
it ran* kpákpákpákpákpá *right up to the riverbank. The
site had chased them! What did you hear about that tree?
[expressing amazement I had heard anything at all.] It
was a silk-cotton. That's why they left [Bambey]. . . . The
final chicken they killed to decide whether they could
stay there. They asked it, "The thing we did here, the tree
we felled here, if you want us to stay with you. We'll kill the
chicken. Its blood will pay you, as it falls on the ground."
And they cut it [the head] off. And it ran* kpákpákpákpákpá
*right down the path, all the way to the river. Well, to leave:
that was all there was to do. The place expelled us. It
jumped all along that path! My mother's brother told me.*

In Saramaka, two species of forest giants—*kankantíi* and *katu* trees—
frequently serve as homes for *apukus* (forest spirits), and under no
circumstances may they be felled.[10] When the forest is cleared for
gardens, a wide margin is left around such a tree, for should it be
singed or otherwise disturbed by horticultural practice, the *apuku*
becomes an eternal avenging spirit for the lineage of the offender.
Because of the missionaries' (and their Christian helpers') act, the
apuku was taking revenge and killing off the children of Bambey. As
far as Saramakas were concerned, there was now no choice but to
move and to hope, over time, that they could succeed in cooling the
angry spirit's heart.

For many months the Brethren Wiesner and Wietz persisted in
refusing to move, though further "signs" were raining down on the
villagers:

On the 18th [December 1784] there was a great uproar in the
village. Several nights before, a sorcerer had dreamed that the
Great God wanted to ruin them and let them perish. He thus
demanded that all the negroes pray to their deceased forefathers
to ask God in Heaven not to destroy them. Our Johannes took
this opportunity to warn them to come to church where they
could hear about God and, the next day, the church was indeed
so full during the sermon that many listeners had to stay outside. . . .

Then, on the afternoon of the 29th of December, we had a
very powerful earthquake, lasting a full minute. Everyone in
the village ran to us in great fear, and then Johannes told them
that they would do better to run like this straight to church
where they could hear about their Creator and Redeemer. . . . At
the end of the year, we were again all alone [i.e. with few Sara-
makas]. To be sure, it has been a most difficult year for us—both
externally and internally.[11]

By early 1785, with almost everyone except Alabi, Christian Grego,
and a handful of others unwilling to make the trip to the nearly aban-

doned village of Gwafu Bambey to attend Sunday services, the Moravians reluctantly concluded that "in time, we may eventually have to do their bidding," and move. In August, Alabi helped the missionaries select a new site near the village where the Bambey people had moved, in case they should decide to follow. By the end of the year, the missionaries—Brother Wiesner, Brother Wietz, and the latter's new wife—were feeling nearly abandoned in Bambey, with the jungle gradually taking over.

> **During November and December we were largely alone again. . . . Our neighborhood has now become a wilderness and is overgrown with all kinds of bush, and harmful animals are taking over. Our few chickens have almost all been lost. The bats come at night and suck out their blood, and during the day large birds of prey and snakes attack them. Our dwelling place is becoming more and more unhealthy because the rapid growth of the bush prevents the air from circulating.**

Finally, in early 1786, the three missionaries decided that they

> **could no longer go on living here alone but would have to follow the negroes to their new place. We thus left on the 25th [February 1786] to find a place for our future dwelling. It will be on a cliff, a musket shot's distance from the river, and surrounded by land for planting. Our negro Brethren and Sisters were very happy upon hearing that we would join them.**

After striking a bargain with Alabi and some of the other converts to pay them in exchange for some already-cleared gardens at the new village,[12] the Moravians

> **on 13 April held our last communion meal in Bambey. Soon afterwards, we left for our new place. Sister Wietz was so ill that she had to be carried. . . . On the 7th of May we consecrated our new church.**

The Saramakas called their new home Wana, after a nearby creek (itself named to commemorate a hunting incident of fifty years before); the Moravians called it New Bambey.

Before long, the missionaries were able to write:

> **Our [new] dwelling place is healthy and completely cleared of forest. It is situated on a higher level, so that the lovely north and northeast winds waft through. Also, we have planted a good number of coffee trees around it, as well as bananas, rice, corn, cassava, napi, and so forth. . . . We also have lots of chickens and squabs . . . so that we do not suffer from hunger. . . . [Our main house is] very beautiful, decidedly better than the old one in Bambey but [like it] made by weaving the walls . . . according to the local custom. . . . We also planted a whole alley of orange trees stretching from our house to the river.**

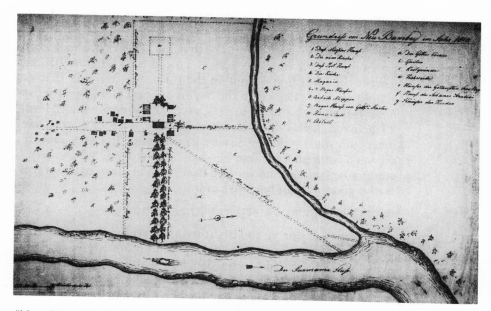

"Map of New Bambey in 1810." The indications in the legend point to the central grouping of missionhouse, church, kitchen, storehouses, and postholder's office; the houses of the baptized Brethren just to the left (with Alábi's house marked *f*); the houses of the heathen vaguely delineated at the extreme left; and the cemetery (near the top) and gardens in the open spaces to the right, bordering the Waná Creek (reproduced from Wekker 1986, 184; original source unknown).

The mission complex continued to grow, and the Moravians and their house slaves eventually built a "pasture fenced off by lime-tree hedges" in which they kept cows and sheep. A decade after the move to New Bambey, a Moravian visitor from Paramaribo waxed idyllic about the good life there:

> **The dwelling place [of the Brethren] is perfect for the health because it is fully open and situated on a height. The drinking water from the Wana Creek is excellent. The Brethren purchase all kinds of delicious fish, as well as game, from the negroes. Bananas, rice, corn, and all kinds of root crops they cultivate themselves. They also have various domestic animals and poultry, as well as a pen for turtles. . . . I have tasted these turtles and they are—especially their liver, when fried in fat—a true delicacy.**

But in spite of the physical charms of the place, New Bambey did not prove very hospitable for the missionaries, and the early years brought them their accustomed share of personal hardships. In late August 1787, Brother Randt (who had served for two years at Bambey, five years earlier) arrived with his new wife to join the Brethren Wiesner and Buchner at the mission.

In September we all became sick. Brother Wiesner caught the fever, and was bothered by his old leg problems. Brother Randt also had the fever—so strongly that his wife expected him to pass on, though thank goodness he did not. On the 9th, she caught the fever herself and on the 16th . . . when told that she should abandon herself to the Savior . . . said "Oh, I really cannot!" But then she began to pray, saying, "Ah, dearest Lord Jesus, all beloved Savior. Is there then no help for me? Please have mercy on me!" And the Savior was helpful: her eyes and lips changed immediately, and her hands grew cold. When we put compresses on her, she showed that she had given up the spirit, to the great pain of her husband.

A month later Brother Randt described how he

was awakened during the night by a bat which bit me in three different places so that I lay in a pool of blood. This also happened to our slave girl, who slept up in the loft. The peculiar thing is that one does not wake up immediately from the bite, and thus one can lose a dangerous amount of blood.

Soon, after Brother Buchner had returned permanently to the city, Brother Randt was writing that

we two Brethren, Randt and Wiesner, become sick rather frequently, one after the other. Nonetheless, we try to carry out our work.

And his frustrations at opposition to his proselytizing caused him on occasion

to become truly melancholy about the blindness of these people. I broke into bitter tears and sobbed at my complete helplessness, crying in the presence of the Savior and begging for new strength.

In spite of himself, this brother clearly found the Saramakas repulsive:

It is indescribable how uncomfortable it is for me, on such a trip, to lodge with the negroes in their huts. Not only do they live in a very disagreeable manner, which stems from their heathenish customs . . . but their begging is a strenuous business. If one begins to eat even the most meager meal, they immediately stand all around and will all try to get a taste, and one really does not know what to do in such situations.

But Brother Randt's difficulties were hardly over. Having lost his first wife so quickly, he tried remarriage, arriving with his new bride at the mission in April 1789, greeted "with happy shouts and the firing of muskets." Soon,

Sister Randt was very busy putting our household in order and getting to know the negro women, by whom she was much

loved. But on the 27th she fell ill and her fever increased daily.
. . . On the 8th of May she seemed to be somewhat better. . . .
On the 2nd of June, while she was sitting at table with us, she
fainted dead away. Very slowly, she came to herself, but on the
3rd in the evening, the Savior took her. We cannot describe how
melancholy her husband felt.

During this same period, the Brethren Randt and Wiesner were
also suffering from severe problems with their domestic slaves, upon
whom they were dependent in many ways.[13]

On the 22nd [November 1789] our own negro [slave] Abraham
had the misfortune of falling into the river while fishing and was
unable to save himself. The situation was such that no one
could come to his aid. For us, this was a terribly painful event—
not only in itself but because he was a very loyal negro and we
needed his services greatly. We will miss him in every way. Soon
thereafter there appeared among our negro [slave] girls, who
cook and wash for us, the signs of that evil and pernicious Suriname negro leprosy. One does not want to come too close to a
person who has it so as not to become infected. And it should be
easy to imagine with what appetite we now ate our food. It is
not quite clear what the Savior is trying to tell us with all of this.
We are truly having a difficult time here in [New] Bambey but
He will put an end to all temptation, so that we can praise Him
and say Amen. Our motto for these days has been: Is there a
misfortune in the town which the Lord does not bring about?

Soon, Brother Randt, visiting Paramaribo, complained that the New
Bambey mission was now without the services of all four of its
slaves.

We now have no one to help out domestically, that is to wash,
cook, clean house, carry water, and suchlike. Nor do we have
anyone to do heavy labor like clearing the cassava gardens, or
planting Napi [and] taro.

And two months later, Brother Wiesner noted in the mission diary
that

our household looked terrible because our domestic [slave] was
suffering from a very serious fever and was too sick even to take
care of cooking and the wash. Some [Christian Saramaka] negroes came to help with household chores but they really did
not help much. During the month, the [slave] girl was sent to
Paramaribo to be cured to the extent it was possible. Fortunately, on the 9th of March Brother Randt returned [from Para-
maribo]. During the succeeding days both of us were sick. Neither of us much felt like cooking, so it was just as well that
neither felt like eating either. Johannes called a meeting and
said that people should help us, and thus sent his wife to care for

our household. She was very willing but her gout pains began to bother her and thus she was unable to continue. After she left, we were helped somewhat by the children of Johannes and David [Skipio].

In 1792, Brother Wietz—already a veteran, with a decade of Saramaka mission experience behind him—summed up the first six years at New Bambey:

As for the progress of our congregation here, I can neither report anything very happy or very sad, because things go along much as usual. Some people have been found, but there is as yet little conviction, only good intentions. It is very important to our [Christian Saramaka] people that their countrymen convert. However, the local inhabitants as yet have little desire. . . . It is now rice-harvest time and the negroes do not respect Sundays. Even our church people have to be reminded repeatedly about the Sunday holiday.

Missionary illness and death also continued apace. As Brother Wietz wrote some years later,

In spring, 1793, Brother Randt returned to Paramaribo; and my wife and I were left again alone. In the sequel, we got a faithful assistant in Brother Trabant, but this pleasure did not last long; for it pleased our Lord, in August, 1794, to take him home to Himself. Now we were again in our solitary situation, with the care of all the external and internal concerns of the Mission committed to us, amidst frequent indispositions and illnesses. Our Saviour was our only comfort and support.

In the year 1795, Brother and Sister Horn, and the single Brother Mahr, arrived with us from Europe: but Sister Horn, soon after her arrival, departed happily; and her husband, being in a poor state of health, went to Paramaribo, where he also soon departed this life. Brother Mahr was likewise ill for a long time; so that I was almost continually employed in nursing the sick.

By this time, there was a little church community, better organized if not more pious than before, and it included a sufficient number of children so that the school that had operated during the first years at Sentea and Kwama could now be reopened. Holidays were now celebrated together with the fourteen baptized adults and five children who comprised the congregation—almost all close kin or affines of Alabi:

On Christmas Eve we held a beautiful Lovefeast with the baptized, and we ate peanut cakes made by the three negro sisters, Rebecca [Alabi's sister], Charlotte [Alabi's wife], and Frederica. The children received little candles which were stuck into

limes, and they went about the village with these things and were very happy. On the 31st we celebrated New Year's Eve in the church in a very solemn manner.

In 1793 they were divided into four "choirs," according to the more general Moravian system—one each for married and unmarried men, one for women, and one for children—and these tiny groups held separate meetings on Sundays.

Alabi never faltered in his efforts to persuade his heathen country-men to join the Brethren, no matter how resistant they proved to be.

[In the Langu village of Kayana, in 1788] Johannes spoke with the many heathen people who had come to make sorcery for his sick daughter [who lived there], trying to stop them by saying that he would have nothing to do with their heathen ways and that he had another God whom he really believed in. Although these poor people felt trapped, they could not resist joining a woman who was possessed by a Gado, and who already had a great many followers kneeling around her.

In 1792, the Moravians formally constituted a "national [missionary] brotherhood" in Saramaka, under Alabi's direction, to proselytize be-yond Bambey, where the Moravians rarely ventured. Besides Alabi, this special group consisted of his wife Sialoto, his sister Bebi Re-becca and her husband Kwaku Andreus, and Christian Grego. (The missionaries referred to these people as "assistants" or "Native Help-ers.")

Nor did Alabi tire of shoring up the faith of his Christian brothers and sisters when it seemed fragile. He had frequent opportunities, for at New Bambey both non-Christians and the baptized seem rou-tinely to have participated in "heathen" rituals.

On the 10th of December [1786] the village was very restless because a woman had decided to hold a spectacle for her dead husband. It began on Saturday and lasted the entire Sunday. It was accompanied by incessant drumming, singing, and shoot-ing, and such things make a tremendous impression on the baptized, and they come away having participated in evil goings on.

On the 12th of September [1788] and the subsequent days, we were very upset because a memorial service was taking place in honor of two people who had died. Many of our Brethren and Sisters took part, because they did not want it to appear that they did not love the deceased. Afterwards, however, they con-fessed that they were very unhappy for having taken part, and they begged for forgiveness.

Alabi found himself spending a great deal of time trying, with only partial success, to keep his co-religionists on the straight and narrow.

At the beginning of the year [1788], it pained us to learn that one of our baptized men, Joshua [Kodjo], had again been lost to heathen superstition. Soon after that we heard the additional unfortunate news that the widow of our Simon [Yanki], who was a heathen, had died. We soon heard the frightening death shrieks, drumming, and shooting. During the burial, our Johannes came to them and said that they should not engage in the customary practice of asking the dead person who had killed her. But someone had secretly cut off some of the deceased's hair and, as soon as Johannes and the others [Christians] had left, they immediately commenced their conjuring, in order to find out who was responsible for the death. The blame fell on a very old man, and someone suggested that they kill him. But others suggested that he was half dead anyway, and that it would be senseless, so he was spared. In all these horrors, not only one of our baptismal candidates but two of the baptized actually took part.

On the 14th [July 1789], a woman died who had been a great priestess of the idols. As she had been closely related to our Johannes, he ordered that she be buried without the usual spectacles and without the usual [divination] procedures to determine responsibility for her death. But since he was not for the moment present, the people claimed that the dead woman [when her coffin was lifted] refused to be moved, and that she had to be asked why. Thus they commenced the questioning. Johannes, however, appeared and said that she could indeed be carried off, and she was in fact buried without further delay, and the sorcerers were shamed.

On the 19th, our people were reprimanded not to take part in any further heathen activities, since they had recently participated in a nine-day funeral celebration, visiting the house of mourning and participating in all the activities. Johannes repeated this warning to them, and on the next day most of them returned to their work. The heathen negroes, of course, were quite upset by this turn of events. At the end of the funeral celebration, on the 9th day, people came from all the different villages and we harbored the hope that they might abandon their heathen ways. We held our meetings regularly but no one other than the usual churchgoers came. Indeed, it seems that the other negroes are becoming more and more hostile.

In 1791 a woman pretended, that she had repeatedly dreamed, that a man came to her with a fire-brand in his hand, which she interpreted as a sure indication, that he was a sorcerer and poison-mixer, and consequently ought to be burned. A council was convened to decide the fate of this unfortunate man. Arabini, (who, as captain of the village presided at this consultation,) with the unanimous approbation of all the councillors, declared: "They could pay no attention to such absurdities, and if no other evidence of the guilt of the accused person could be adduced than foolish dreams, no one should dare to do him the least injury."

On Easter-Monday [1794] we had a meeting with all the baptized and candidates for baptism, at which a lively conversation took place. When a wish was expressed by some, that more of their countrymen might be converted, Johannes Arabini observed, that especially the heathen women were excessively hardened in idolatry and other abominations, and wished that the baptized women might in all things give them a better example, by forsaking even the slightest remnant of superstition. Afterwards, I addressed them together, and declared, that I firmly believed, that our Savior had thoughts of peace over this nation. He had now permitted the gospel to be preached here for a great number of years. Many a missionary had ventured his life in this service, and the word sown had been watered with innumerable tears. Nor can we deny that our Savior has gathered a small flock in this wilderness, who may be called living members of the Body of Christ. Yet there were some things amongst them, about which we could not be quite satisfied. Old prejudices ought not to prevail, and superstition of every kind was a disgrace to the children of God. From these things, as from all sin, the Blood of Jesus alone can cleanse us. We then kneeled down and prayed the Lord not to be weary, faithfully to keep and lead this poor, small congregation, which he has purchased with his most precious Blood, as he has done hitherto; and not to let any soul here present have any rest, till he had obtained his whole aim with it.

Sometimes the missionaries had to take sterner measures with their own, formally "excluding" from the congregation those who had "lapsed." Moravian mission practice, worldwide, was insistent about enforcing "Christian" behavior among the converts.

Every thing also that is accounted decent and virtuous among Christians is [to be] inculcated into the minds of the people. Drunkenness, adultery, whoredom, sorcery, theft, anger, and revenge, and all other works of the flesh, enumerated by our Lord and his Apostles, as proceeding from the heart, being plain proofs that a man is altogether unconverted, or, relapsed into Heathenism and idolatry, it follows of course, that any one guilty of these things is put away from the congregation, and not re-admitted, before a true and sincere repentence is apparent, and the offence done away.

In New Bambey, at least ten members of the congregation (including one of Alabi's own daughters) were excluded at one time or another.

We have had some painful business these last days [1793]. After a special meeting with the baptized and baptismal candidates, at which we explained the expectations for a member of the congregation and that those who disgraced Him would have to be excluded, the Native Helpers came together and this was further discussed. Two persons were summoned who had fallen into grave sin, namely Simon, a communicant, and Alexander, a communicant-candidate. When we told them that they had truly fallen back into sin, and were no longer in the congregation, Simon was completely devastated and wept. Another brother spoke with him and tried to persuade him to return to the Savior with an open heart.

On the 12th of July [1789] one of the communicant-Brethren who had recently been excluded confessed, with great regret, that he had participated in the [heathen] events of earlier that day, and he was reprimanded.

As to others of our small congregation [in 1809], especially some of the excluded, who always come to church, and call upon us, (a proof of confidence we are pleased to see and encourage), we perceive, alas, too little knowledge of themselves, as sinners that need conversion.

Apparently, such people's sins consisted largely of occasional participation in "heathen" rites, in treating Christianity as if it could simply be added on to Saramaka religious practice. The Moravians felt strongly about what they called "the discipline." Saramakas, meanwhile, continued to feel that religion need in no sense be exclusivistic.

The believing Negroes are not suffered to go to any place where the Heathen meet for the sake of feasting, dancing, and gaming, &c. and the usual plea of not entering into the sinful part of these diversions is never admitted, as the least step toward vice and immorality generally plunges them, by degrees, into gross sins. The hankering after the vain traditions of their forefathers is already considered as a falling off from [the] love to the Lord Jesus.

Upon the whole, the pagan inhabitants of the village [of New Bambey], though they showed no disposition to be converted, lay no further impediments in the way of their believing countrymen, but evinced a spirit of toleration and liberality, and were even ready to assist them, when preparing for any religious solemnity. They, however, expected the same liberality from the christian Negroes, and expressed displeasure when they refused to assist them in their idolatrous festivities.

And even Alabi, despite his genuine and profound conversion, faced frequent temptations to continue certain fundamentally Saramaka practices that the Moravians considered incompatible with Christian conduct.

> **On the 29th [January 1788] a messenger arrived from the noto-
> rious Captain Beku (who was the [Matawai] leader of the attack
> on the Saron Mission in 1761), to beg our Johannes to make some
> sorcery, as he was suffering from a fatal illness. Unable to rid
> himself of the messenger, Johannes finally brought him to us to
> seek our advice about this whole business. We told him that the
> truly faithful refuse to have anything to do with sorcery. In the
> end the messenger did get help from a great sorcerer, but this did
> not prevent the death of the captain. We must add that though
> our Johannes could be tempted, because he is [tribal] chief, to
> return to heathen ways, he continually comes to us and in all
> honesty tells us everything on his mind and asks our advice.**

Since Beku was the "brother" of the man who had slain Alabi's father, the messenger must have been desperately begging the son to hold a feast for Abini (who, as avenging spirit, was now killing Beku), asking his forgiveness and pity. Alabi's refusal, in effect, publicly signed Beku's death warrant. And though there certainly was no love lost between Alabi and Beku, Alabi's decision to refuse this common courtesy was—though the missionaries only dimly perceived it as such—a remarkably defiant gesture on the part of the tribal chief, another sign of the steadfastness of his decision to be a Christian's Christian.[14]

Meanwhile, beyond the narrow purview of the missionaries, Saramaka life was flourishing as never before. With the gradual postwar equalizing of the sex ratio had come a considerable population expansion, and new villages were frequently splitting off from old and filling in the spaces between the Upper River villages (along the Pikilio and the Gaanlio) and Wana Bambey (the northernmost of Saramaka settlements, closest to the city). Modern Saramakas preserve a number of events from this period, in songs and rites, as historical precedents for current interclan relations. Several bear repeating here, though they do not appear in contemporary whitefolks' documents, as a reminder of the vibrant cultural activity taking place beyond the rather dour confines of Bambey.

The first dramatic incident involves Alabi's rival, Captain Antama, and the origin of the Agbo-clan segment that lives in the Langu-clan village of Bundjitapa, far up the Gaanlio. (The Agbo-clan woman about whom the story revolves may have been related to Alabi's wife Sialoto, though I cannot specify the link.)[15] The speaker is Metisen of Langu, who was brought up in his father's village, Bundjitapa, in Langu.

*A man at Malobí [the name of the modern Biitu-clan village,
which is substituted here for its eighteenth-century prede-
cessor] took an Agbo-clan wife from Guyába [likewise,*

*Guyaba is substituted here for Wana Bambey]. But the
woman wanted him only for herself. It seemed to her that
he didn't love her enough. So she begged an elder of the
village, a Biitu-clan person, to make an* obia *for her. So that
her husband would love only her. But the man made the*
obia *with witchcraft-medicine! He prepared it with the taboo
of the village! He cooked it up for her. Then he told her
that when her husband returned from the coast—he had
been in whitefolks' territory—she must be the very first person to cook something for him. And when she had cooked
the food and it was ready, she should put the* obia *in it
and feed it to him. Then, he would really love her. (But he
[the* obia-*man] was tricking her, in order to kill the husband
[because he wanted to sleep with the wife].)*

*Finally, the husband returned from whitefolks' territory.
The woman peeled some very ripe plantains and cooked
them until they were just right. Then she mashed them with
peanuts, and while she was mashing, she threw the* obia
*in with them. Then she added palm oil. If you saw it, you
just knew it would be sweet! The man came ashore and
said he'd go back [to the canoe] to unload. She said, "You
know? Why don't you eat before you go?" He said, "No,
I'm not hungry. I'll get the baggage." She said, "No. Please
eat a little first." Finally, he sat down, and she brought
him the plate of plantains and a spoon. As soon as he'd
taken the first bite, his belly roared* huun! *And it began to
hurt him terribly. People made medicines and performed
rites till they were weary. All night! And then, around five
in the morning, he breathed his last. He was dead. So they
performed divination and it pointed to the woman. It
said she had killed her husband. But they decided not to
say a word to her. They went off and built a coffin—big
enough to hold two people! They would put the woman in
first and then put the man in on top of her. They would
say, "The way she wanted him so much, now she'll have
him!" They would put them both in the coffin. In the morning they went to cut timber. But it took two days because
there had to be so many planks for the size of that coffin.*

*That evening, Antama—returning from whitefolks'
territory—stopped to spend the night on his way upriver
[to Langu]. He had a* mati *[formal friend] at Biitu [Malobi].
And his* mati *didn't like what was happening. So he told
Antama the whole story. And he begged Antama to help,
saying that he couldn't bear to see this double burial. "The
living with the dead in one coffin, it's no good," he said.
Antama told him, "Don't worry, I'll help." And they slept.
Till midnight. Antama went and called the woman. He
talked with her. He said she must come with him or they*

*would kill her. "The size of that coffin, it's for you too! Get
up at once!" Well, the woman had a girl she was raising,
an adolescent. The two of them went to the river with
Antama and set out upstream. In the morning, no one went
to ask the woman how she'd slept because they were punishing her [by not being normally polite]. Until perhaps nine
o'clock. Then they called her but didn't see her. So they
assumed she had gone into the forest to kill herself. So they
thought, "the thing is finished." But at that very moment,
after paddling all night, Antama was passing Fandaaki [not
far below the confluence of the Pikilio and the Gaanlio].
He saw a canoe headed downstream. So he sent a message.
"The woman the people of Malobi think is lost isn't dead.
She's with me." At Malobi, night fell. They still hadn't found
her. By the time word reached them, there was nothing
left for them to do but bury the dead. And that's how the
Agbo-clan segment came to Bundjitapa.*

The elderly Antama, nevertheless vigorous, fathered two daughters
and three sons with the younger of his two wards, and their descendants still live in this southernmost of Saramaka villages, Bundjitapa
on the Gaanlio, today.

A second incident, preserved by modern Saramakas because of
the interclan relations it defined among Matjaus, Paputus, and that
segment of the Dombi who live in the village of Soolan (and who
are called Agbos), bears witness to tensions relating to population
growth at the same time that it illustrates ongoing cultural efflorescence. As Tebini recounted,

*The Paputus [a late-coming clan] were living near Baakawata
[at Kanga Creek, under Matjau protection]. Ngweté [who in
some versions is depicted as Ayako's wife's brother, in others
as her son] had married a Paputu woman and had brought
them to live at Kanga Creek. When the Paputus left [years
later] to build Gaan Djumu [at the confluence of the Pikilio
and the Gaanlio], Ngwete said he would not live with the
Matjaus any more. He would go live with his wife's people.
The Matjaus warned him. They begged him to stay. "Don't
go. Please stay and live with us." He said no, he was going
to live with them, and [this was the crux of the matter for
Matjaus] take with him the children of Ayako [i.e., his
matrilineal siblings and sister's children].*

The fact that, three decades after Ayako's death, his wife Asukume's
resident kinfolk had difficulties with his own kin should not surprise;
deprived of his protection, these "clients" were in a delicate position,
and their decision to leave would not have been unexpected. But this
does not lessen the sense of loss suffered by the Matjaus. The climax
of the tale came not long after the move to Djumu, and it involved
Ngwete and one of the sons of Ayako and Asukume, Abaánsi.

In those days, when they played adunke *music, the women danced and danced. Until, at a certain moment, a man would take his gun. He'd load it up [with powder, not shot] until it was just right. Then, at the proper moment, the male dancer and the female dancer. He would fire, gbóó! Shoot again, gboo! The smoke [from the powder] would completely envelop them. It would hide them!*

Well, it happened at Djumu. They were dancing. A big adunke *dance. There was a beautiful Paputu woman, Adjéuwensé. They say she was more beautiful than any woman! The man she was dancing with, Abaansi. He was famous. Everyone loved him. Then an evil man took Abaansi's gun and loaded in a ball. When the moment came and Abaansi fired at the woman, she died!*

Abaansi and his kinfolk, who had been framed, tried to return to their Matjau "fathers," who paid a large indemnity to the Paputus in this case. But Adjeuwense became an avenging spirit for the descendants of Asukume, and the Paputus are said to have prevented their departure by force and to have built the village of Soolan right next to the new village they established for themselves in the wake of this incident, just across from Djumu. Thenceforth, the groups would be bound together by the ritual dependence stemming from the homicide.[16]

The Matjau clan preserves the contemporaneous story of how three forest spirits (*apuku*s) miraculously appeared to their ancestors on the same day (which, using geographical and genealogical information, I can date to about 1790). This triple apparition explicitly marks the passing of one historical era and the dawning of another: the Matjau *apuku* Wamba, which had been at the center of their battles against the whites and which had been in the head of Alabi's grandmother Yaya, was now replaced by three new *apuku*s, who were to take over the tutelary role of the former god for Matjaus. The great Matjau god of war was now replaced by three gods of peace.[17] The speaker is Peleki, whose own source is his "mother's brother," the late Matjau Kositan.

They were living at Bekuun [on the Lower Pikilio]. One of them [a Matjau person] . . . was at the place upriver called Kwáminangóto. That's where it came into someone's head. Another person was at Hafupasi [the site of present-day Dangogo]. Well, that person was "possessed" there. On the same day, at the same moment! Well, the other person was at Bekuun. And the god possessed him. On the same day at the same time. All by itself. Well, the one that was at Bekuun said, "I'm not the only one there is! One like me 'came' at Kwaminangoto. One like me 'came' at Hafupasi. I'm not the only one who 'came.'" Well, the one that came at Kwaminangoto said, "I'm not the only one there is! One like me 'came' at Bekuun. One like me 'came' at Hafupasi. I'm not the only one who 'came.'" And the one that came at Hafupasi said, "I'm not the only one there is! One like me 'came' at Kwaminangoto. One like me 'came' at Bekuun. I'm not the only one who 'came.'" On the same day at the same time they came.

Then the one at Kwaminangoto said, "Take me to the others of me, at Hafupasi and Bekuun." The one at Hafupasi said, "Take me to the others of me, at Kwaminangoto and Bekuun." The one at Bekuun said, "The two others like me, at Kwaminangoto and Hafupasi, will come to me!" Then they took the one at Kwaminangoto and brought it down. When they arrived just above Dangogo, where Doote [the speaker's brother] has his gardens [today, in 1976], then the one at Hafupasi said, "The other one of me is nearby; it's already arriving!" Then the gods met and talked. They said, "Let's go to the other one at Bekuun." So they brought the two of them to meet the other one of them. The one at Bekuun said, "The others of me are coming!" And they met there. They [the gods] held a meeting. They said they hadn't come for any particular reason. It was not that someone had [badly] cleared gardens [desecrating their forest domain]. [Rather,] they had been sent by the Sky God to be ready when they were needed. "Like the apukus who fought alongside you people during the wars. Now, our own time has come, so here we are. There is no other special reason. But we will show you that all we're saying is true. Wait until the Long Dry Season, and then call us to come into your heads, and we'll come.

Well, the Long Dry Season arrived. So they called them all, to come into their heads. They said, "Well, just as you asked us to, we are calling on you today." And they [the gods] said, "Well, the thing we told you. Go clear three garden-sites until all the trees have been felled. Then come back and tell us." Time passed. They cleared the gardens until there were no trees left. The gods said, "No problem. You see those three garden-sites? Burn them. And then come tell us." They burned all three garden-sites. They called the gods who said, "Now, forget about those gardens. Don't go into them." Harvest time came. So they went to look at the gardens. Every crop that people had ever heard of was ripe there! Without anyone having planted them! The gods said they had done it to show that something really real had come down that day.

These three protective *apukus*, who assisted the Matjaus during the final years of the century, were called Tjímba, Kátamatjímba, and Songiánvula. Less than two decades after their appearance, the most important—Tjimba—was itself replaced, in a similar process of renewal, by an *apuku* called Sáa, who was to play a central role in determining the succession to the office of *gaama,* upon the death of Alabi.

The man who became Alabi's chosen successor, the Matjau Gbagidí (also known as Gbagidí Adaníbasu, Gbagidí Gbagó, or Záda) was the protagonist in the story of Saa's discovery. Born at the time of the Peace, two decades after Alabi, Gbagidi was genealogically his younger "brother" (Alabi's father's mother's sister's daughter's son). When still in his twenties, Gbagidi had gone to Djuka and returned with a wife, with whom he had several children who were to play important roles in Matjau history (and who, with their many descendants, were to assure his lasting fame among twentieth-century Saramakas).[18] And it was Gbagidi who had angrily intervened with his Djuka affines when they marched into Saramaka territory playing the drum made from the skin off Tata A-ke's back (see Chapter 7, note 73). By 1800, Gbagidi was already emerging as an important leader within the large Matjau clan, and he is referred to as an official captain in documents of the period.[19] Indeed, during the first two decades of the nineteenth century, the final years of Alabi's life, Gbagidi served as de facto *gaama* for the Pikilio region that comprised well over a third of the Saramaka population.[20] But it is the coming of the god Saa that present-day Saramakas remember as the real beginning of his glory.[21]

One day while hunting on the Upper Pikilio, near Kwaminangoto (the site of Tjimba's coming a decade and a half earlier), Gbagidi discovered a mysterious swamp surrounded by tempting bananas, wild rice, and various other crops. After cutting samples and setting out for home, he was horrified to see his favorite hunting dog being swallowed up by the swamp's quicksand. He called out to the god of that locality (whose identity he did not know) that he would give it anything it desired if it would only spare the dog. The animal emerged immediately, unscathed. As Gbagidi, paddling downstream, neared his village, he heard shouts and commotion. His sister Yaya (a sister's daughter's daughter of Abini's mother Yaya) had just been violently possessed by a previously unknown *apuku.* As Gbagidi arrived, the god (speaking through Yaya) proclaimed, "My name is Kokobandá-mama or Saa," and it recounted in detail how Gbagidi had taken its bananas, rice, and other crops and how he had promised obedience; it then demanded that Gbagidi wash it immediately with an entire demijohn of rum. This done, the god demanded Gbagidi's gun and broke it. In the course of a few minutes, the god had summoned to it all of Gbagidi's possessions and had destroyed them all. Saa then instructed Gbagidi to construct a canoe and go to the city. In Paramaribo, Gbagidi was miraculously given a whole boatload of every kind of whitefolks' goods by city merchants. With Gbagidi's triumphant arrival back in Saramaka, the extraordinary powers of Yaya's god were confirmed.[22]

The supernatural succession of Wamba to Tjimba to Saa represents a rich metaphor for ongoing changes in eighteenth-century Saramaka life. A generation after the official Peace, the time was ripe for Wamba, the god of war, to be replaced by Tjimba, whose attributes were linked to agriculture and the assurance of plenty in a time of population expansion and cultural efflorescence. The death of Wamba's long-time medium Yaya, who had been one of the final links to the years of war, prepared the way for a new focus on internal Saramaka growth and development. But Tjimba's replacement by Saa, a scant two decades after its first appearance, also marked a major shift in Saramaka perspectives. For Saa, above all, appears as a god who brings Saramakas whitefolks' riches. While Wamba's gift was to defeat whites in battle, and Tjimba's to bring miraculous harvests, Saa was the harbinger of cargo from the coast. With her help, Matjau men could be assured of returning from their increasingly frequent trading trips with canoes laden with whitefolks' goods.

Alabi must have been actively involved in the aftermath of all of these incidents. Antama's new wife was said to be a close relative of his own. The Paputu homicide was closely tied to deteriorating relations between Alabi's father's brother, Matjau Captain Adjagbo, and the Paputu village that had been under his charge for years. And the triple *apuku* descension replaced his grandmother's famous god and set up the coming of another who, upon his death, would determine the identity of his successor as *gaama.* But the available documents are mute on Alabi's direct role in these issues.

The final decade of the eighteenth century brought a flurry of (at least quasi-) Christian activity in the far-off villages around Kayana, in the Langu region of the Gaanlio. Moravians have referred to this as the Great Awakening, and modern anthropologists as a "prophetic movement." Although I believe that, ultimately, it was neither, it did—paradoxically, perhaps—sound the death knell of eighteenth-century Saramaka Christianity, by temporarily appropriating fragments of it, as just another cult, into ongoing Saramaka religious life.

The central figure was Puli, who first appears in the missionary diaries during Brother Randt's mid-1788 visit to Kayana.

> **On the 17th [July] I came to Kayana, where I stayed a week in order to get to know the people better. I saw a negro [Puli] whom we could look upon as a baptismal candidate if he were living a bit closer to us. Others realize that they are not following the path of the righteous, but they prefer worldly rewards to the sufferings of Christ. There are others who gladly listen to the Word of God but end up following the heathen ways of the others anyway. The majority live in the most abominable idolatry and sin.**

When Puli visited Bambey a few months later, it is clear that he had made a decision to convert.

On the first of December, the negro came from Kayana. We had seen him there and had hoped he would become a baptismal candidate, to which he now agreed with all his heart. He told us that there were a couple of other negroes who sometimes came to him to speak about the Savior. The [Kayana] unbelievers told him that if he was to abandon their god in favor of the Great God, then his former god would kill him. He told us that he had answered them, "Should I die in that way, then I will know I am serving the true God."

The next year Brother Randt again visited Kayana, where baptismal candidate Puli welcomed him to his home. And by 1790, Puli seems to have been proselytizing in his own region with some success, for several people from there visited Bambey seeking further instruction. Puli's conversion affected his fellows particularly because he had been unusually active in Saramaka rites, the medium of a god that Captain Antama had "put in his head for a lot of money" and for whom he had built an impressive shrine. Now, in 1790, Puli was demanding immediate baptism.

On the 9th of April, the baptismal candidate Puli came back . . . and after greeting us immediately said "I will not have peace of mind until my Savior has washed my sins away with His blood!" And on the 10th . . . he was baptized into the death of Jesus with the name Paulus. There were many strangers [to Bambey] who watched. Because the baptized man had been a sorcerer and had often gotten the Gado in his head and even built a house for it, these people could not understand why he had become a Christian. For them, it was a puzzle. However, he was so happy to receive grace that his whole face shone. In his honor, we read Christ's Passion once more, and we had very interesting conversations with him practically every evening.

Some weeks later, a woman from Kayana who had received the same god as Puli from Antama exclaimed to the missionaries,

How amazing that Puli has abandoned his god and shrine yet the god does not come into his head and destroy him! Now that he is baptized, the god doesn't bother him in the least!

No doubt because of his past activities, Puli was awakening considerable interest in his heathen neighbors during the period immediately following his baptism. In August 1790, the missionaries report on a visit by some Bambey Christians to the Gaanlio.

Some of our people visited the villages in the Upper Region and brought me many greetings, as well as the request that I visit them soon. Charlotte [Alabi's wife] told some members of her sex about the Savior, and she said that it interests them greatly. Christian [Grego] said that he had never before had such pleasure when he visited the Upper Region, because every day people would visit him in order to hear about the Savior. Even the great sorcerer Grang Adama [Captain Antama] wanted to hear about Him, and he even said that he had the intention to convert to the Savior—although he would want to continue his sorcery as well.

A year later, a "biological brother" of Antama, Pikinkoyo, came to Bambey seeking baptism, and he reported that "there would be others following him because in the Upper Region there were now many who wanted to hear about God." Though Puli was clearly gaining power at the expense of Antama, there is little indication that he was trying to bypass the missionaries to become a prophet in his own right.[23]

Several months later, Brother Wietz visited the Upper Region to check on the progress of the Awakening. His lengthy report implies that a number of people were indeed impressed with the potential powers of Christianity. If almost none were willing to use it as a substitute for their own religion, many were nonetheless interested in exploring whether or not it might offer certain useful powers.

I first visited [the Kayana negroes] in their homes and spoke with many of them individually, and then spoke with a group that had gathered in a house. One of the biggest idolaters showed me his sorcery apparatus with which (as he himself admitted) he had already deceived many people, and among which was a bundle of feathers from a black cock, to which the Free Negroes attribute great power. He explained that he planned to cast all of these away, and then went from house to house inviting people to the meeting. We found a goodly number of people gathered together and, since there was not sufficient room for them all in the house, I held the sermon outdoors by the clear moonlight. They all sat around on the earth to hear me. Afterwards, Christian [Grego, who was traveling with Wietz] took up the word and enlarged upon what I had said from his own experience, with a great deal of compassion, which seemed to make a great impression on them. . . .

On the 3rd we arrived at the place where Paulus lives, and he was delighted to see me. He remains in close contact with the Savior, but I had to warn him not to be overzealous in his desire to convert others, and not to forget the admonition to know thyself. Though he means well, he is apparently too forceful in trying to prod others, and when they refuse to listen, he flies into a passion about their idolatry.[24] In the afternoon we came to Kwama Creek and the village of Captain Grang Adama. Previously, Satan's throne had held sway here but now it is beginning to totter. We soon received many visits from the men and women, some of whom felt truly awakened. In the evening, we held a meeting outdoors with many listeners, and the Savior gave me the courage and joy to preach. Afterwards, when I had gotten into a conversation with them, I noticed that they were not understanding everything. Christian then added "If the teacher had told you worldly stories, you would have understood him fully, because he speaks good Saramaccan. But since he has told you about God, who created you, and out of love for you became a man, and was willing to die on the cross for your sins so that you would believe in Him and find forgiveness for your sins, your ears are deaf to this, and the Devil, whom you have served hitherto, has hardened your heart. But God is stronger than him, and if you turn to Him, He will free you from the Devil, etc." They asked me the next day to preach to them again, which I did on the 4th. However, my sermon was frequently interrupted. One said, "Teacher, today we understand your words." Another, "What you say is the truth." A third, "I see that our Obia men (sorcerers) have deceived us." A fourth, "I believe that the Great God is the one and only God and that there are no other gods," and so on.[25] ...

In the evening when I preached there were a great many listeners. Meanwhile, at the other end of the village there was drum-beating and dancing, with the noise there intended to disturb us. My listeners, however, came up close to me so they could hear everything correctly, and some repeated every word. They begged me to sing to them and to teach them how to sing, saying that Paulus had sung a great deal with them but they had never really understood how to do it, which I can easily believe, because Paulus really knew no verses and even less of the melody. I taught them a few verses and explained their meaning, and they were very eager to learn. Some of the women prayed to God in a very moving manner, making gesticulations with their hands, and most of them promised to devote their hearts to Him. . . . I found much cause to thank the Savior for the new receptiveness to the gospel amongst these people because, when I made my first trip to the Upper Regions ten years ago, I found not a single soul ready for the blessing, and now in all the villages I find open ears.

Few people were at home in the village of Captain Alando [which Wietz visited on the fifth] nor were there many at the two other small villages nearby, but some who knew me from my previous visit did come to greet me. They were most attentive when I told them how I had come in the name of God to spread His word. While I was talking to them, a young negro arrived and said that his mother had heard I was here and wished me to come to her. I found her to be a most considerate woman. She said, "Master, I have always wanted to speak with a Bambey teacher and hear the Truth. For these last seven years, I have been lying here ill and have tried to avail myself of everything that might help. I have summoned all the gods and made many sacrifices to them. These three here (there were three water pots) I have made myself at great expense, yet they have not helped me at all. Now, a dream has really frightened me: someone shows me two paths, one leading to the Great God and His holy place, and the other to a place filled with evil spirits. Now, please, give me wise counsel because I am very afraid and do not know which path I will take when I die." I answered, "I am no dream-interpreter but I can preach you the Holy Writ. When you look at your body, you see what a miserable state it is in. But if you look at your soul, you will see that it is in an even more miserable state. Your body feels nothing once it is dead, but with your soul it is a different story." I thus praised the love of God in Jesus Christ to her, and she, as well as those who were listening around her, was moved and all wanted to hear more. Christian added that they should not delay in thinking about this further, as there was no other way except to have faith in the Savior. At our departure, the people begged us to visit them again without delay as they truly wanted to hear more of the Great Story.

In the evening we came to Kwama Creek where I held a farewell meeting. I found I had to warn these people again as they were once more slipping into idolatrous ways. I told them that this was not the true path and that we were praising the love of Jesus to them. . . . They listened and asked that we come to them again. . . . Early in the morning on the 6th we traveled and on the 7th in the evening arrived safe and sound in Bambey. I can truly hope that this visit resulted in more souls being blessed.

The aftermath of Wietz's trip was recorded in a diary entry of January 1792:

On the 21st, our Paulus arrived from the Upper Region, on his way to Paramaribo, to the general joy of our congregation. Johannes took him under his wing and had a long talk with him, finding that he was still in a state of grace and remained faithful. He asked for more information and gladly accepted our criticisms, and we recommended him into the grace of the Holy Ghost so that he may serve as a beacon to his people. Apparently, since the last visit of Brother Wietz to the Upper Region, many more people wish to know the path of Salvation, and they plead for another visit, so we resolved that Brother Randt should visit them as soon as possible.

In March 1792, Brother Randt (soon to leave the Saramaka mission permanently) made his trip, designed to keep the Awakening alive.[26]

On the 6th we came to Kwama Creek, where Captain Grang Adama lives. This visit, like the last one of Brother Wietz, occurred while the captain was away, which he does not like at all. However, although he is a big priest of the idols, some of his family wish to hear the gospel, and it is much less troublesome when he is not here. His brother, Pikinkoyo, had got news of my arrival and was standing on the shore when I arrived, and received me with great joy. Because the village lies at some distance from the river, we shot our muskets, whereupon Paulus and some others immediately came to meet us. My belongings were carried into Pikinkoyo's kitchen, which was to be my dwellingplace and where I held all my meetings, while in the meantime they cooked. Soon, both the healthy and the sick arrived, cripples and the blind, and I was constantly surrounded by people who wanted to hear about the Savior. I was especially pleased by a couple of old grandmothers. One was quite blind but clamored each time to be let into the meeting. The other is the mother of Simon, who was baptized by Brother Kersten in 1773, and who soon after his baptism departed in bliss.

After I had been here a few days, many people became quite candid, which is not their usual way. One told me that when he has done something evil, he feels uneasy about it. "Once I did something," said he, "and I became so fearful, but then I thought, 'Why am I so afraid? No one saw me do it.'" Those sinful ones were then told about the Bloody Redeemer who took on the sins of the whole world, and who is the only one who can cleanse and purify them. Once, one of the above-mentioned grandmothers said to me, "One of my sons went to study with Meister Rudolph [Stoll] in school but became very sick, and when I took him back he got better. But another of my sons went to church and was baptized by Masra Kersten and then got sick and died. I then became angry and refused to send any of my children, or to allow any of my children's children, to go to church. But now that I myself am on the same path, I am sorry that I held them back." She is already a great-grandmother but still hale and healthy, and she cannot hear enough about the Savior, and many of her descendants feel likewise. We are noticing that the harvest of tears of our predecessors, who suffered so much among these people, can now for the first time be reaped. May the Lord help this continue and advise us how we can serve them according to His heart, as there are still divers difficulties here. For the time being it does not seem possible for them to come to [New] Bambey, and they keep asking if a brother might not come live with them here. . . . At last I spoke with them about the possibility of building a small church here, and in response to my question as to whether Grang Adama would allow this, Pikinkoyo responded, "My brother has his heart and I have my own."

It was here that I met the father of our Christian [Grego], who had always been a big enemy of the gospel but was now beginning to think otherwise. He said, "There is no story more certain and true than the one the Brethren tell us, and when Grang

Adama comes home I will speak with him about it." After this, he had a long discussion with our Paulus. Another time, he came to me and asked about the correct way to pray to the Great God, and if one could also use musket shots. This is their custom, especially when they pray to the spirits of the dead.

Soon after Brother Randt's trip, a man arrived in Bambey from the Upper Region with further news of the power struggle between Antama and the nascent group of Christians.

We learned from him that Grang Adama is now very angry that no one will help him repair his damaged god. Three times, he asked an old lady, who had always been very useful to him in these matters, to help out, but she never appeared. When asked why, she said, "I never want to deal with these evil idols again because their deceptions are the work of the Devil. I now believe in the great and true God who made me, and I want to serve Him because He can help me, and when I die I will go to Him, and this is what I tell you once and for all." He then went to our Paulus, who lives there, seeking his help and saying, "You evil person, you are responsible that my people have become ruined, and you have told so many lies that they have made my god angry." Paulus answered, "I cannot help this because *I* am not responsible, rather God has done it. You do not understand this, which is why you talk as you do."

Other Upper Region people continued to visit New Bambey, to hear more of what Paulus and Pikinkoyo were preaching, and a delegation of New Bambey Christian women visited the Upper Region in August 1792, to "sing verses" and "set good examples for their heathen relatives." Very soon after, Alabi himself journeyed into the area of the Awakening, partly on political business but largely because "I have often thought I should go there, and have often prayed to the Saviour that He send us there . . . to see what I can do." The "marvelous report" of Alabi's trip describes some the interaction between the tribal chief and Captain Antama, his greatest political rival.

Grang Adama still intends to keep peace with Johannes. When asked whether he would hinder his people from believing in the Great God, he said he would not, though he himself could never do so. He was a respectable man and would serve his gods according to their own beliefs. Many of his people had become rebellious and had embraced the European God, and he would not get in their way, because the European God might kill him. During our conversation, the people who had been awakened to the faith gathered together, and Christian [Grego] read to them from the Passion of Christ, and then spoke about it. They got together several times in similar fashion and both Brethren [Alabi and Grego] were unstinting in their praise of the gospel. Once, Grang Adama organized a dance with lots of drumming and singing, but the people said "Let us rather go further in the faith and pray to God; that is better than the 'play.' " Then they went to the place where the faithful were gathered with the two Brethren. Paulus wanted to chase them off, and he said, "Evil people do not belong in the meeting because they still serve the Devil." But Johannes and Christian restrained him and said, "The Savior did not do things like that, because even the worst of people could be converted if they truly became serious." All of them then held a very fine meeting.

Several months later, Christian Grego made another trip to the Upper Region, reporting "great hunger for the word of the Lord," and at the end of 1792, Alabi also made a visit. On his return to New Bambey, Alabi

could not speak enough about how eager he had found the people to hear the Word of God. They had sat up past midnight with him, and were there again in the early morning. The old women, who used to be our hard-hearted enemies, were now especially interested.

By 1798, when Brother Mahr, Alabi, and Kwaku Andreus visited the Upper Region—apparently the first missionary visit in several years— they found a kind of stabilization: some villagers were integrating certain outward aspects of Christianity into their Saramaka religious repertoire.

On the 27th we reached the village of Kayana and were received with acclamations of joy. The day following, we visited in the houses and in the evening held a meeting which was attended by more than thirty people. On the 29th there were yet more listeners, including the captain of the village [Antama], who was a noted idol-priest. When he heard the end of my sermon, which dealt with the life, sufferings, and death of Jesus, as well as his resurrection and ascension, he said "The story is for the most part true." Johannes replied to him that it was not *for the most part* but *altogether* true, and the Holy Scriptures are for your Salvation." . . . As we saw the next day, this village contains many souls who are concerned for their salvation . . . to whom we preached Christ crucified with warmth of heart. . . . They would willingly live at Bambey but the captain will not permit it. . . . [Several days later,] we met with one of our baptized and with a baptismal candidate, whom we admonished to remain faithful to the Lord. The baptized man said my admonition was very necessary, for they lived, as it were, among ravenous tygers.[27]

And finally, in 1801, Brother Wietz (just before leaving Suriname forever)

undertook yet another a trip to the Upper Region and found many attentive listeners. . . . [In Kayana] it appeared as if some glimmering of knowledge, like the light of the morning dawn, had penetrated the night and darkness of superstitious ignorance. . . . But because those people who are awakened to the faith cannot free themselves from their heathen ways and draw themselves to the Brethren, for the time being it appears that nothing more can happen.

And nothing more did. The Awakening died with the closing of the Saramaka mission several years later. (Puli himself died in 1807.) Even during the later nineteenth and the twentieth centuries, when many of Alabi's descendants again embraced Christianity, the people of the Upper Region and their descendants, the spiritual children of Antama, remained resolutely "heathen."

What was the true nature of this temporary Awakening? Available documentation, all written by Moravians, leaves considerable room for speculation. Part of the changes taking place in Saramaka by the end of the century involved the waning power of those who had actually known war and the rise of new generations to positions of influence. Antama's (or Etja's, or Samsam's) actively militant brand of antiwhite ideology, nurtured during the wartime years, was losing its direct relevance and gradually passing from the scene.[28] At the same time, Alabi's defiantly conciliatory stance toward whitefolks and their culture was confined to a tiny minority of Saramakas who actively chose to reject much of their own way of life in favor of Christianity. Most Saramakas, meanwhile, were choosing a middle path, integrating highly selective aspects of whitefolks' lifeways into their own while maintaining a general disdain for all the rest.

The Awakening might best be seen in this broader context of ongoing cultural change. Some Upper Region Saramakas, reacting in a very normal kind of Saramaka way to the longstanding and sometimes oppressive power of Antama's god by embracing a rival cult, temporarily took aspects of Christianity to add in to their daily religious life. For them, this appropriation of certain external aspects of Christianity—praying directly, for example, to the Great God—in addition to maintaining their cults of ancestors, *obia*s, and so on, was part of a standard process of renewal. Saramaka religion, like many of its African precursors, had from the first been additive and agglomerative. Except for Puli (and perhaps Pikinkoyo), who experienced the first really radical conversion since that of Alabi, participants in the Awakening seem not to have been interested in giving anything up; their Awakening involved no fundamental changes in conduct or belief. One might almost say that from the culturally available repertoire of cults and shrines, they simply stopped (at least some of the time) choosing what Antama had to offer and chose parts of the missionaries' product instead. But with no local support system to maintain, interpret, or integrate these bits and pieces of Christianity into their daily lives, they soon moved on to other things.[29]

The several more or less detailed accounts of conversion left by the Moravians during this period help flesh out some of these ideas. They also underline, to anyone who is familiar with the complex chains of explanation that are revealed through Saramaka divination, the extent of the missionaries' ignorance of what the actual motivations for conversions might have been. The first case involves Domósi, a woman who had been on the periphery of the tiny Christian community from the very beginning.

> On the first of May [1790] two new people, a man and a woman, came to church. The latter's name was Domosi, and she told us that her first husband [Simon Yanki] had been baptized by the Brethren.[30] This took place in 1773 and he died in 1774. She had been against his baptism and had given him much difficulty because of it. After his death she was afraid to come into the church because she believed that his spirit was still present and might seek vengeance upon her. Now, however, she had changed her mind. She had remarried with a man who had at one time been a raving enemy of the Brethren and had often said, during the days of Brother Kersten, that he hoped all the Brethren would fall in the river and drown. But this man now comes to church regularly.
>
> Several days later, Johannes told us that Domosi had asked for some food from his wife [Sialoto], which was most unusual since heathen negroes do not normally accept food from our sisters because they have wholly abandoned certain superstitious customs which the [other] negro women observe every four weeks.[31]
>
> On Ascension Day, which was on the 13th, the sisters remained after the meeting for two hours and spoke in a very loving manner with Domosi. She said, "If only my dear Savior will receive me, then I will be satisfied." ...
>
> After Whitsuntide [she] ... became quite ill. Brother Randt visited ... and Domosi exclaimed, "Masra, I do not want to hide anything from you but rather to tell you everything about me. You know that we have many gods who come into our heads and speak through us. You also know that I never used to go to church, nor did I ever enter your houses, and I never set foot in the house of Johannes or Andreus or any other baptized person, because it would have offended my god. But now I have been in the church several times, I have been in your house, and I have been in the houses of the baptized and have eaten with them. Because of this, my god has become angry with me and has made me so sick. He has also told me that even were I to go into the church ten times I would never be baptized. ... Now I have

no idea what I should do. I do not really trust myself to enter the church, and I am equally afraid to go inside my own Gado house. I am truly confused, and everything frightens me." We told her in a very sensitive way that she should follow the path of Jesus Christ and give up all of her heathen ways.

On the 13th, Brother Randt visited . . . her. Domosi is still struggling because she cannot completely renounce the Devil and his ways.

It is not for another decade that Domosi again appears in the diaries.

On the 4th of March [1799], the assistant Andreus brought us the joyful news that a sick old woman was deeply concerned for her salvation, and begged that Brother Wietz would visit her. He went immediately and found her full of sorrow and penitence because of her sins. After she had confessed them with deep humility, Brother Wietz preached to her with a warm heart the great love of Jesus to sinners, referring her to the example of the thief on the cross. Upon this, she exclaimed, "O that God would but show me the same mercy also!"

Sister Wietz visited on the 5th and found her quite comforted. She said that since the visit of yesterday, her heart had been greatly relieved, and she could now believe that our Savior had forgiven her all her sins. She then exhorted her two adult daughters to give up their hearts entirely to the Saviour, and she made them promise in future to frequent our church and to continue to do so as long as they lived; which promise they made rather reluctantly but with tears in their eyes. The patient also put away from her person every thing belonging to idolatry and sorcery, that they might not, according to her own expression, stop up the way between her and God. She warned her children also against that idolatry, to which she had herself been so long addicted, and by which the devil had deceived her; and exhorted them on the contrary, to seek the way to the true God, with whom alone help was to be found, &c. Our assistants visited her often, and expressed great joy at the grace which the Lord had shown to this soul. Rebecca was day and night with her. And the patient having repeatedly declared unto them, how much she longed to be baptized; Johannes was directed by us to visit and speak solidly with her on that head, after which, we could no longer refuse to grant her request. Accordingly, on the 6th, she was baptized into the death of Jesus, and called Maria, in the presence of all the Missionaries, and the greater part of the negroe-congregation. . . . The newly baptized woman declared, that she now wished immediately to depart and be with our Saviour. Her former name was Domosi. She is the widow of our late Brother Simon Yanki, who departed happily at Kwama in the year 1774. He was the first Suriname free-negroe who departed in reliance upon the merits of Jesus. . . .

> On the 9th. the hour of her dissolution arrived. . . . On the
> 10th. in the forenoon the corpse was borne by some Brethren
> into our church, and at four in the afternoon was the interment;
> at which Brother Wietz delivered a discourse from the words
> *The wages of sin is death; but the gift of God is eternal life.* The
> hearers could not all find room in the church, but many were
> obliged to stand without. They were all still and attentive; and
> at the funeral itself every thing went on in good order, which we
> mention, because it is unusual.

Domosi's deathbed renunciation of her idolatry—in particular, a god
put in her head by Antama—in favor of her late husband's faith undoubtedly involved a chain of explanation completely beyond the ken
of the Moravians, who saw only the outward results.

Three related cases involve deathbed conversion and, again, the
converts are people who had always been on the periphery of the
Christian community, attached to it by close ties of kinship.[32] The first
involves Djemi, the mother of the late Simon Yanki.

> On the 6th of January [1793], our helper Johannes and his wife
> and Christian [Grego] and Andreus all came together and . . .
> we held the Holy Baptism. . . . The baptized included the old
> woman Djemi, who was named Elizabeth. . . . She had formerly
> been a very famous priestess of the idols but now she announced
> to everyone the grace that had befallen her, and all could see the
> change that she experienced. One of her sons had been baptized
> by Brother Kersten in 1773 and named Simon, but he died soon
> after. At that time, she believed the gods had killed him because
> he had abandoned them, and she therefore prevented any other
> of her progeny from following the church. But now she, as well
> as most of her children, have taken the Savior to their hearts.

The second case involves David Skipio, one of the original schoolboys at Sentea Creek and among the first three converts, who had
later been excluded from the church for heathenism.[33] In 1799, he
apparently decided to die a Christian.

> Christian [Grego] brought us the account that *David*, previ-
> ously called *Skipio*, who had been cast out of the church . . .
> now lay an hour from here, very ill of the pleurisy. Because we
> were unable to visit him the next day, as it was Good Friday, he
> was brought hither the following day early in the morning. He
> recognized us and folded his hands as if to pray but he could not
> speak a word. With sorrowful hearts and tears in our eyes, we
> commended this poor soul, now in the agonies of death, to the
> faithful friend of sinners, and an hour afterwards he departed
> this life. This was a very painful event for us. The deceased was
> a son of our old Brother Joshua [Kodjo], who, even before he
> himself belonged to us, had given him into the care and instruc-

tion of the late Brother Rudolph Stoll. In the sequel he had sought and found grace through the merits of Jesus, and was admitted to the Lord's Supper; but not being faithful to the grace received, he fell into deviations, and would not hearken to our entreaties and representations. We therefore came under the necessity of excluding him from the Lord's Supper. After this he remained uneasy in his mind and suffered several misfortunes. . . . We had a great deal of compassion for him as we could see the uneasiness of his heart. During his final illness, the Negro Brethren visited him frequently, and directed him to the Savior, who has compassion even upon the disobedient and backsliding, when they again seek his face. The assistant Christian, his former school-companion, was more especially attentive to him, and to whom he confessed his sins with pain and sorrow. The day before his departure, he said to Christian, "My mouth cannot speak much but my heart cries out to God my Savior." His death has given us an opportunity of declaring salvation in Jesus with confidence to several souls.

The third case concerns Agudon Cornelius, one of Alabi's sister's sons, whose parents were Bebi Rebecca and Kwaku Andreus, and whose younger brother was also a convert. For some years, he had wavered radically, first becoming a baptismal candidate, then "returning to the slavery of sin," then becoming "anew awakened, and fervently desiring to be delivered from the dominion of Satan," and finally once again becoming "overcome and seduced to sin." In 1794, Brother Wietz described the climax of this drama, a cautionary tale that makes sense in both Moravian and Saramaka cultural logics.

August 30th, the negro *Cornelius*, who had been out a hunting, was brought home very ill. He was yesterday bitten in the leg by a rattlesnake and suffered very great pain, the swelling having spread beyond the hip. In the following days the poison spread further, and the offensive smell, occasioned by its effects upon him, rendered it very unpleasant to be with him. September 16th, he sent for me, being in great torment both of body and mind. He seized my hand with eagerness, and held me fast; confessed that even since his baptism he had frequently committed sin, and declared that he now felt forsaken of god, and expected soon to be cast out into everlasting darkness.

His parents, and younger brother, who are baptized, and the former assistants in the Mission, were present and exceedingly affected. I encouraged the patient to turn with confidence to Jesus, our compassionate Savior, who has received gifts for men, yea, for the rebellious also. But he seemed to refuse comfort, and accused himself before all who visited him without reserve, as a miserable perishing sinner, adding, that the Lord could not now receive him, as he had behaved too bad.

On the 18th, he again sent for me, and was in the same state of despondency. He entreated me and all the negroes present to pray for him, that he might receive mercy, which we did, kneeling around his bed, and he himself prayed most fervently and incessantly. When I visited him the day following, he received me with joy, and testified that he had obtained forgiveness for his sins, and felt the peace of God in his heart; and that he now greatly desired soon to depart and to be with Christ. He then addressed the company present to the following effect: "Ah, my friends, abide in Jesus; give him your whole heart; do not turn again to the ways of sin; look at me and consider how things have gone with me! I am a great sinner, but I have obtained mercy and pardon! yea, most assuredly, every thing has been forgiven me; I have obtained mercy! Ah! join me to praise and thank our Savior!" On the 26th, he departed this life rejoicing, and a large company attended his funeral.

This man was the eldest son of our assistant Andreus, and was under strong convictions when a boy. The best hopes were entertained of his prosperity, and in 1784, he was admitted to the class of the candidates for baptism. However he departed from the path of truth, and got entangled in the snares of sin. God then made use of various extraordinary means to bring him to reflection. As he was fishing in the Sarameca, he was stung by a poisonous fish, and it was with difficulty that his life was preserved. For some time he showed signs of repentance, which however, were not lasting. Some time after he was attacked and bit by a wild boar, and again lay dangerously ill. He then confessed it to be a chastisement for his unfaithfulness, and seemed willing to forsake his heathenish connexions, and turn with his whole heart to the Lord. But, alas! by degrees all his good resolutions again vanished away. Last year, as he was hunting in the woods, a tyger sprang upon him, and tore him in a most shocking manner. However, to our great astonishment, he recovered. He now was brought to more solid reflection, and expressed a great desire to be truly converted. January 6th, he was baptized, and for a short time appeared to be seriously awakened. Yet he did not remain faithful to the grace received, but seemed gradually falling into his former habits. When therefore the above-mentioned accident happened, he immediately cried out: "This is of God, and a just judgment, which will cost me my life." His departure and the circumstances attending it, made a deep impression upon the minds of the negroes, especially of the young people, and on the same day, an old companion of Cornelius, who had also been excluded on account of his bad conduct, came and entreated me to take him again under our care.

Despite these and occasional other conversions, and in spite of the enthusiasm engendered by Puli's Awakening, the end of the century brought general discouragement among the local Brethren. In 1794, Brother Wietz reported that

> during the last week of February, the village was all in an uproar, the heathen being employed in making a new set of idols; on which occasion there is no end of drumming, dancing, and shooting. Notwithstanding all this noise, the peace of God was felt amongst us in all our meetings, and we prayed fervently, that the time might soon come, when these poor blind and idolatrous people shall receive and believe the gospel of our Savior.

There was time, during this period, for nostalgia—a sentimental journey to the site of (Old) Bambey, abandoned more than a decade earlier.

> We arrived about nine o'clock, and had to climb up a very steep bank, cutting our way through the thicket, with which the hill is overgrown, since our Brethren left the place. Brother Wietz [who had lived there] pointed out every thing to us, and we could well discover the situation of the houses. Several posts of the old garden-fence were still standing. The burying-ground was quite covered with brushwood, and could only be known by the large pieces of rock which were rolled on the graves of six European Brethren and Sisters, whose remains lie interred here: viz. the Brethren Stoll, Lehman, Hans, Moser, and the Sisters Hans and Stoll. Having cleared the ground a little we could not but contemplate with awful sensations, the resting-place of those servants and handmaidens of Jesus. We took six of the best bushes of benanu, which we found growing in the old garden-ground, to transplant at New Bambey in memory of the dead, and at half past eleven returned home.[34]

In 1798, a diarist admitted that

> we have often been concerned about this mission and the slow progress made in it, especially when we compared it with the other missions of the Brethren, where the blessing of the gospel spreads so abundantly.

For the end-of-the-century missionaries, Alabi's faith remained the central beacon of hope.

> On Sunday, October 1st [1797], we had a meeting with all the children of baptized parents; the latter, as likewise the assistants being present, I reminded them of the privilege they enjoyed to be born of christian parents, baptized into the death of Jesus, and educated in the fear and admonition of the Lord, and entreated them to give their hearts unto Him who made and bought them with His precious blood. When I had finished,

The site of Gwafu (Old) Bambey, seen from the river, 1978

Johannes Arabini rose, and addressed them in a very suitable manner, explaining what I had spoken, in a way more intelligible to their capacities, and like a tender father besought them to devote themselves in their early days to the Lord Jesus.

In the evening-meeting [3 August 1800], the fourth and fifth chapters of the second Epistle of Paul to the Corinthians were read and expounded. After it was over, Johannes Arabini, Joshua, and Andreus, our oldest negroe Brethren, sat down on the bench before our house, and immediately entered upon a spiritual conversation. Brother Wietz sat down by them, and heard them with tears of gratitude, thanking the Lord for what he has done in the hearts of some of this most idolatrous nation. . . .

Johannes Arabini said. . . . "And what has not our Saviour done for us! I was the leader at every dance and merriment, as you all know. You also know, that, as heathen, we indulged in every abomination, in gluttony and drunkenness. I was the chief drummer, and you, Joshua, and you, Andreus, were the chief singers and noise-makers. Our women and children danced with us, and thus we spent whole nights in every kind of profaneness and wild uproar. We also carved idols in wood, or formed them of clay, consecrated them, put victuals and drink

before them, commended ourselves to their protection, and fell
down with our children prostrate before them, addressing them
with great earnestness, and mentioning to them our desires and
wants, which, however, all regarded only earthly enjoyments.
We thought we were doing right, but we were worshipping the
devil. And yet God had mercy upon us. He would not, that we
should be lost eternally." The other two Brethren confirmed all
this, and exclaimed,—"O, merciful Lord! receive thousand
thanks and eternal praises, that thou hast sent teachers unto us,
or we should have yet been in the same darkness." Johannes
added, "which of us then thought, that we should be one day
sitting on this bench, singing unto the Lord." He then began to
sing several verses, treating of the unmerited grace of Jesus.
This loud singing brought more brethren and sisters and children together, who stood around us. Andreus said: "Our Saviour
sweated bloody sweat on the Mount of Olives for us. He has
delivered us from sin and eternal judgement. O, let us love him
with our whole hearts, and no more grieve him as we have done.
O. how I mourn, that I am still so far behind."

Johannes then began to sing the verses

Thy blood so dear and precious
Love made thee shed for me!
O, may I now, dear Jesus!
Love thee most fervently, &c.

May in my hearts recesses
Thy name any cross alway, &c.

Andreus then gave out some more verses; and the conversation
continued afterwards for a long while upon the fall of man and
his redemption through Christ Jesus.

Andreus, one of the mission's true stalwarts, was soon, however,
"called out of time."

On the 4th [March 1801], it pleased the Lord to put an end to the
sufferings of the negroe brother Andreus by a happy departure
out of time. He was baptized in 1780 at Old Bambey, two years
after admitted to the Communion, and was faithful and blessed
in the execution of his office as assistant, which was committed
both to him and his wife, and for which he had a particular gift.
In the year 1799, he attended Brother Mahr on a visit in the
Upper country [= Langu, on the Gaanlio], and proved very useful, particularly in the village of Kayana, his native place, in
making his poor straying countrymen acquainted with our Saviour. . . . The truths of the gospel, which filled his heart, and
became more and more clear to him, the nearer he approached
to his latter end, preserved in him a cheerful mind, and comforted him also in his last painful illness, called here boasia, a

corroding kind of leprosy, so that he bore his heavy sufferings with almost unexampled patience, and, without ever complaining, was resigned to the will of the Lord, till his happy departure. He will always remain in blessed remembrance with us.

By 1803, the state of the New Bambey mission was officially considered problematical.

Indeed, the Missionaries have, at present, a difficult post among the free-negroes at [New] Bambey. Few of them will listen to the gospel, and join the believers, so that there is but a very faint prospect of increase. The unhealthiness of the climate, the late removal of so many valuable servants of Christ into eternity, by means of the dreadful seasoning fevers, and the great blindness and profligate idolatry of the heathen, are very discouraging circumstances; and we, therefore, the most earnestly recommend this Mission to the constant fervent prayers of all the Lord's people.

The following year Brother Wied, then visiting Bambey, reported that

wherever one looks, one finds traces of the most foolish superstitions. Streets, houses, and people are draped with amulets and protective idols.

The 1805 diary makes it clear that the missionaries themselves felt truly embattled.

A man having died in a neighboring village, several of our people went to attend the funeral. We are always anxious on these occasions, lest by the craft and power of the enemy, and the seducing arts of their heathenish acquaintance, they should be led astray; nor were our fears imaginary; for a drunken negro, having fired a musket, though only charged with powder, at the foot of Christian's son, and wounded him severely, Christian was so much incensed, that he could not refrain from using very violent language; and another of our people had almost carried his resentment farther still, and would have fired at the offender, had he not been prevented in time.

On the 18th, we spoke very earnestly with all our baptized and communicants concerning this affair, and represented to them, that indifferance and inattention to the word of God was the beginning of every deviation; and as thereby their hearts became cold and uninfluenced by the love to our Saviour, it was no wonder, that they were so easily drawn into things, quite inconsistent with His pure and holy will. . . .

October 7th, we met uninterruptedly, and had attentive hearers in the church, but in the evening, the heathen negroes began their amusements, and during the whole succeeding week, there was, by night and day, a most hideous noise and riotous revelling in the village. . . .

Some of our young people having given offence by their laxity, we spoke very seriously with all the baptized, and represented to them, that, by a walk not conformable to the gospel, they put obstructions in the way of the conversion of their countrymen, which was a great sin. One of Johannes Arabini's daughters had even suffered a heathen sorcerer to apply his art in her concerns, and we were obliged to exclude her.

And they prayed, at the end of the year that

notwithstanding the many imperfections which will always exist in a congregation of free negroes, and sometimes perplex and distress us, He will maintain His cause, and deliver yet many of the poor heathen negroes from the galling yoke of Satan, and the deeply-rooted idolatrous habits to which they are subject, and make them happy members of His family on earth.

By 1807, a discouraged diarist reported that

the hope that reigned from time to time that more of the heathens would come to hear the word of God has now disappeared. . . . The hearts of the poor heathen Saramaka Negroes, so steeped in superstition, are still hardened and indifferent to the sweet message of the gospel, and members of the congregation, especially the younger ones, unfortunately follow the bad example of their heathen relations, causing great discomfort to their teachers, who become very discouraged.

For the first time since the mission opened, forty years earlier, the Moravians seemed ready to admit that the battle for souls was going very much against them.[35]

In 1806, Alabi—who himself was "old and bent . . . but still a fervent believer"—had lost his closest friend, Joshua Kodjo, who had returned to the Christian fold in 1791, after a several-year hiatus.[36]

On the 3rd of April, our dear old *Joshua* Kodjo died. In his younger years he had been one of the bravest leaders of the negroes in the wars against the whites. He was also an excellent provider, and helped the first of the Brethren who came here. . . . Kindled to the faith of Christ by the good works of his brother-in-law Johannes Arabini, he was for years a problem child for his teachers because he was very passionate and undisciplined, but this slowly improved through the grace of the Savior. For the last twelve years his path has been correct and with every expression he proclaimed his sinfulness and could not give sufficient thanks to the Savior that He had not let him die in his heathen state. He had probably attained the age of 100.

In 1810, the last year for which I have seen diary entries, the missionaries described Alabi's attempts to turn back the incoming tide of heathenism.

Two Saramaka ritual figures—what the Moravians called "Idols"—collected by
M. and F. Herskovits in 1929/30 (Hamburgisches Museum für Völkerkunde).

[In July we] asked all the negroes who were at church to stay after the sermon so that the Native Helpers could talk with them. Johannes Arabini spoke with his children and grand-children and then with the other negroes. He asked them to choose between water and fire, using terms familiar to them, and told them the choice was completely their own. All of them chose water and promised that they would follow the path that leads to eternal bliss, where there is comfortable, cooling air, so that they would not have to end their days at a place filled with glowing heat. On the night of the 22nd and 23rd of September, the village was very noisy because the heathens were finishing making new idols and they were drumming and singing. The noise lasted a long time because the idols were not sure whether they wanted to have four chickens sacrificed or not.... The local Free Negroes continue to be steeped in superstition, and even the old heathen negroes are amazed by this. Previously, only two protective idols were in the village [of New Bambey] but now almost every home owner has his own protective god. Previously, only one or two local women were possessed by the Gado but now his powers are felt even among many of the young people.

And several letters, written shortly thereafter from Paramaribo to Moravian headquarters in Germany, dramatically sum up the situation.

We lament, that [the mission] among the free-negroes at Bam-bey seems to be on the decline. Heavy clouds seem to rise in that part, and threaten its destruction. If ever the power of satan was anywhere manifest, it is among the free-negroes at present. He exerts it by a host of diabolical emissaries, by sorcerers and old witches, with their lying fables and predictions, and by other heathen who, having been excited to enmity against the govern-ment, seem determined to expel the Missionaries out of their country, because they are appointed to transact affairs between the negroes and the government [i.e., to serve as postholders]. If it thereby becomes necessary to give up their agency, by which, hitherto, the post has been [financially] maintained, we cannot much longer support a Mission in that wild country. The rebel-lious spirit now prevailing among the free-negroes, has also more or less influence upon our small flock of christian negroes, and we can find but few, and those chiefly among the old people, who are to be depended upon as sincere and faithful to their convictions. Johannes Arabini is their leader, but even as cap-tain, finds his power and influence unequal to the overwhelm-ing torrent of wickedness and rage of the enemy. Nothing but Almighty power can do this, and overcome and cast out satan. O that we all might be earnest in prayer, and possess that courage, which true and living faith alone gives to the followers of Jesus.

We can do nothing but lie at His feet, and implore his help and protection. May He grant, that His cause may yet triumph, in defiance of all the machinations of the devil. . . .

But the most lamentable of all is, the disposition among the few negroes belonging to [the congregation at New] Bambey to act without any control, and not to regard the influence of the Spirit of God. The young people particularly, are wholly averse to any restraint, and reject good advice. O that the Lord would arise and beat down Satan under our feet, among this deluded nation; for here the prince of darkness seems to maintain his throne, fortified by every evil work, superstition, and horrid idolatry.

This revival of non-Christian religion within New Bambey itself was the note on which the mission ended. The "very sad situation" described in 1810 dragged along into 1812, when Brother Mahr (who was by then a twenty-year veteran of the mission) presented "a mournful report of the state of the free-negroes" in the "wild region" of New Bambey. The following year, Brother Mahr's "yearning to leave" was finally approved by the Moravian authorities in Germany. The full weight of preserving Christianity among the Saramakas fell upon the frail shoulders of Alabi and those of his kinfolk who shared his faith.[37]

Epilogue:
Alabi's Legacy

In 1820, when the aged Alabi—surrounded by his innumerable children, grandchildren, and great-grandchildren—breathed his last at Kambalóagoón, the nation he had ruled for four decades was in full flower. What had been, at the time of the Peace, a handful of villages far up the Pikilio and the Gaanlio, deeply preoccupied with their defense against whitefolks, had become a populous, flourishing nation that stretched from those faraway sites all the way to Gingee Bambey, only a week by canoe from the capital.[1]

While Alabi was buried as a Christian rather than a Saramaka *gaama,* the installation of his successor was carried out with the full panoply of Saramaka royal ritual. (And with one brief exception during the 1870s-1880s, Christianity never again played a major role in Saramaka affairs of state.) Earlier, Abini's enstoolment, lasting several weeks and including countless separate ritual acts, had been supervised by the Matjau *apuku* Wamba (in the head of Abini's mother, Yaya); now, that of Alabi's Matjau successor, Gbagidi, was closely overseen by Wamba's successor god, Saa (in the head of Gbagidi's sister, also called Yaya). When Gbagidi died almost immediately after his installation as *gaama,* it was Saa who sanctioned the transfer of the office to Yaya's husband, the Nasi Kofi Gbosuma. And in 1835, it was once again Saa who brought the office back to the Matjaus, for Yaya's son Wetiwoyo to begin his lengthy reign as *gaama.*[2] Today, *Gaama* Agbago, the centenarian Matjau, occupies the stool once held by Wetiwoyo, and by Alabi and Abini before him.

Slavery persisted in coastal Suriname for four decades after Alabi's death, and the special tensions it engendered between Saramakas and whitefolks—confrontations about returning new maroons and

Gaamá Agbagó (Abóikóni), 1886–1989,
who died while this book was in press
(photo 1978)

about relations between Saramakas and plantation slaves—continued right up to the eve of emancipation in 1863. So too did the more
global confrontation between the ways maroons and whitefolks
viewed themselves and the world. An emblematic encounter from
the period is still remembered in a historical narrative recounted on
the coast of Suriname; it concisely captures some of the tone of the
ongoing confrontations between German Moravians and Afro-American maroons.[3]

Those folks [the maroons] had been off in the forest for quite a
while when the whites decided to make peace with them [in the
early 1860s]. So they sent out a missionary. This preacher was
supposed to try to catch those folks. Well, he went. The preacher
had a couple of Creoles with him. They were going to teach those
folks how to sing psalms, those psalms that the whitefolks
brought here, with the church following along right behind.

At the time the preacher arrived, they were beating the *agida*
drum. But the preacher went right up to them and said, "My loving
brethren and loving sisters, this is not a good kind of thing. The one
you call *man* drum, smash it and throw it away. The one called
apinti drum, put it aside. It's not good. You must learn how to
become Christians. You must learn how to become Christians. You
must learn how to cast aside all of those idolatrous things, none of
which is good!

But there was a woman in the village who had a god-of-the-
earth in her head. The preacher said, "As soon as you stop that
music, I will teach you a beautiful psalm that assures that when
you're dead you'll come back to life and go up to Heaven. [He
sang:] *"Ao yayayayaya* [repeated twice more]. *Ao ya."*

There was an *obia*-man who was off in the forest. When he heard that thing he called his kids and said, "What's that I hear there?! The good-for-nothing whiteman's come to bug us? Bring the *agida* drum, quick!" Then they sang to their god-of-the-earth: *"A go na liba Tobosi go na liba* [repeat] / But when someone gives me food [good things] I'll give him work [worship], *go na liba* [repeat]." The man called out to them, "Play that *agida* still harder!" [They sang:] *Agida kon masi agida* [repeat twice more] / The agida's captain is surely coming / *Kon masi agida o.*"

The missionary was still there! An old fellow came up to him and said, "Massa, listen here. You taught us *your* psalm, but now I'm going to sing you *my* psalm." He sang, "Since my master's death / not a single white would buy me. / Since my master's death / not a single white's come to buy me. / Finally, later, massa's come to buy me. / But not a single person can buy me [any more]. / Only Death can buy me."

Massa preacher man is still singing his psalm. He says, "That's not good work, sister. That's evil. This idolatry is evil work. You must cast aside those gods. Leave them. These are not true gods. The true God is in Heaven. These pieces of wood that you worship aren't gods. Split the *apinti* drum, set fire to the long drum, smash the *apudya,* throw away the *kwakwa* board."

"Massa, I'm supposed to throw away my *kwakwa* board? I have to split my *apinti?* I must burn my long drum? . . . Son, tilt that drum and start playing!" [He sang:] *"Yenge yenge yenge yenge fia yenge / yenge mayongo / yenge yenge yenge yenge suma dadi / yenge mayongo."* Which means [in Kromanti language], "Perk up your ears. They went and took our foreparents out from Africa. They beat them, they spoke to them roughly. We ran away into the deep forest. Look at how his face is white! Look at his ears! And he comes here saying he's going to bring the church to us. Chase him right out of here! Then let him try to tell us to smash our long drum!"

Or, to make the same point differently, I might refer to a chapter of breathtaking simplicity and beauty in which Dening describes the coming of Aoe (outsiders, strangers) to the Marquesas (whose inhabitants called themselves Enata, "the Men"). To cite a characteristic paragraph:

> Enata knew who they were from their own unique roles and rituals. In the way they smelt, in their sense of beauty and their postures, in the way the spent their days, they knew their proper persons. Aoe came with different definitions of what it was to be a man or a woman. With Aoe's coming, a woman with two husbands became unnatural, sacrifices to the gods murder, a woman's waistcloth immodest, coconut oil on the body rancid, tattooing savage. Beauty, propriety make the man. In making what was beautiful ugly and what was good bad, Aoe remade the Land. (Dening 1980, 64)

But in eighteenth-century Suriname, though the confrontation involved very similar stakes, Saramakas—with few exceptions—said,

The Moravian Church at Ganzê (the village of Alábi and Sialôto's descendants)
ca. 1965, as it sank forever beneath the waters of the Suriname, behind the hydro-
electric dam built by the colonial government to supply Alcoa's smelter with
cheap electricity (Walsh 1967, facing p. 30).

"no thanks." And their general refusal to redefine themselves according to whitefolks' images of them has led to a contemporary landscape that looks quite different from what it would have been had
Alabi's minority views won the day.

By the 1980s, a rough estimate might place only some forty-four
hundred of a total of twenty-two thousand Saramakas as nominal
Christians, living almost exclusively in villages peopled by their co-
religionists.[4] (In addition, I believe that a disproportionate number of
Christian Saramakas have now settled in the city or migrated to the
Netherlands, though no precise figures are available.) And, as in the
days of Bambey, these Christian villagers partake of an in-between
lifestyle. To mention just a few examples (and ignoring, for present

purposes, village-to-village variation): there are no traditional drums (but people drum on wooden crates); there are no ancestor shrines (so people pour libations and speak to their foreparents inside their houses); though horticultural taboos are the same as elsewhere, there are no public ceremonies for forest spirits, snake gods, and so forth (but Christians still have such gods in their heads, "calling" them for purposes of divination and curing inside people's houses, and visiting neighboring non-Christian villages when their gods need specialized attention); crimes against persons still lead to the creation of avenging spirits (but they are placated by offerings made inside houses); polygyny is frowned upon (but tolerated), with men who have more than one wife forced to sit on the back bench in the church; as in Bambey, burials are quick and take place in cemeteries near the villages—contrasting strongly with those of other Saramakas; and city influence, via the frequently present Creole minister and schoolteachers, means that Christians often speak a Srananized version of Saramaccan as well as some Dutch, that women cook city-type sweets, that city dress is much more common, and that people celebrate Emancipation Day (a major city holiday without historical significance for Saramakas).

First-Time memories, however, die hard: while hurrying one day to get to the city stadium in time for a soccer match, I heard one urbanized Christian Saramaka chide another, "What's the rush? *Ná a bakáa féti u nángo!*" ("It's not that we're going to a battle-against-white-folks!") And today, while the Christian descendants of Alabi—school-teachers, civil servants, office workers—are among the leaders in the Netherlands of the political resistance to Suriname's military regime, many of Alabi's non-Christian descendants have spent the last two years washing in *obia*s and carrying shotguns in the same cause.[5] For many Upper River Saramakas, Alabi and Sialoto's Christian descendants are hardly Saramakas at all; and for most of these latter, other Saramakas are "heathen." Nonetheless, the recent civil war may well have brought them closer together, as joint victims of state repression, just as these same events have forced Saramakas to recognize, more than in normal times, their common cause with Djukas, Paramakas, and Alukus. As Thoden van Velzen has recently observed (in the best overview to date of the civil war and its implications), the Suriname government—by its politics of collective reprisals, by cutting off captains' and other officials' emoluments in the interior—has done much to solidify what is becoming a Maroon "state-within-a-state" (Polimé and Thoden van Velzen 1988, 124–26).

If it is difficult to conclude with a happy ending—Thoden van Velzen, just back from a visit to Maroon villages in Suriname, observes that "the future of the Suriname Maroons appears to be far from rosy" (ibid., 123)—we can nonetheless express guarded hope. (As *Gaama* Agbago likes to say, *"Sondí án dê a múndu án sa seeká"* ["There's nothing in the world that can't be fixed up"].) Dribbling some rum on the earth, we might—as on the dedication page—pray that the spiritual descendants of Kwasimukamba and Ayako, of Daunitz and Etja, of Brother Kersten and Alabi, now have the courage to take up the enormously delicate task of negotiating an agreement that allows *all* Surinamers to live together in peace and justice. The period known as First-Time involved raw fighting, but it also involved the more subtle interethnic negotiating skills that were finely honed in Alabi's world. And perhaps it is this repertoire of mediating skills, this capacity to balance between the world of Maroons and that of whitefolks, that constitutes Alabi's ultimate legacy. May all this now be brought to bear once more, and this time forever. *Gaán tangí.*

Notes and Commentary

Prologue

1. All authors are firmly grounded in their time and place, yet also engage in the constant process of staking out their own ground from one book to the next. I feel considerable ambivalence regarding my temporary elevation (on the basis of *First-Time*) to the ranks of anointed postmodern ethnographers (Clifford 1986). For inclusion by others in a school or movement can easily deflect attention from what an author thinks he is up to. It is partly because of such concerns (which, ultimately, may come down to matters of taste) that I have written this book in such a way that—in contrast to a number of recent works in what is becoming an increasingly fashionable field—within these pages the reader will search in vain for casual allusions to Mikhail Bakhtin or Walter Benjamin.

2. As Clifford reminds us, " 'Culture' is always relational, an inscription of communicative processes that exist, historically, *between* subjects in relations of power" (1986, 15). Or, as Boon puts it, "Cultures meet indirectly, according to conventional expectations of the cultures themselves. . . . A 'culture' can materialize only in counterdistinction to another culture" (1982, ix).

3. One of the most delicate challenges in writing *Alabi's World* has been to present Moravian realities empathetically and in the round. While Westerners are equipped with plenty of ready-made categories that mold conceptualizations of foreign peoples who are, say, darkskinned and bare-breasted, they may be rather less well prepared to come to grips with cultural distance when the Others involved are Europeans. I would not be disappointed if the initial passages about Moravians evoked in readers as much of a sense of the exotic as those concerning Saramakas. But, as with unfamiliar aspects of Sara-

maka life, I would also hope that the more seemingly exotic features of Moravian existence (whether their lurid theological preoccupations or their militantly androcentric constructions of gender roles) would, over the course of the book, become sufficiently contextualized to permit empathy and understanding. In allowing the missionaries to speak at length in this work about themselves, about others, and about their relations with their Maker, my intent is to permit the reader the same degree of appreciation of their human predicament as those of any other "Other" about whom historians or anthropologists choose to write. (See, for further comments on this issue, Beidelman 1982, Ranger 1987.)

4. Occasional Dutch quotations—perhaps 5 percent of those used in this book—are found uniquely in such officially "sealed" volumes, some of which I was permitted to examine briefly during the 1970s. For these materials, in contrast to those that served as sources for the great bulk of the Dutch translations that I present, I have been unable to double-check the accuracy of my original notes.

5. It may be worth putting on record my differential degree of selectivity regarding the three kinds of sources in this book. With both the Moravian diaries and the Saramaka oral accounts, I actually present a very large proportion (perhaps 80 percent) of the nonredundant materials I possess that deal with the second half of the eighteenth century. In contrast, I use the Dutch sources far more sparingly, selecting only that small percentage of texts for presentation that bear directly on the concerns of the book.

6. Rosaldo's (1986) critique of *Montaillou* suggests a number of reasons why not. The delicate challenge facing the ethnographic historian who wishes to carve out a new way of seeing and writing consists in part in not "abdicat[ing] to conventional social-historical narrative . . . to do[ing] social history, just as a historian might" or to "treat[ing] ethnographic experience and the theoretical apparatus derived from it as merely complementary information on a par with journals, letters, censuses, and other documents" (Marcus and Fischer 1986, 96).

7. Fortunately, Stuart Schwartz's apt characterization of ethnographers as "the tribe that hid from history" (1986, 6) no longer applies. Among those who, like myself, seem actively to practice what would otherwise be the oxymoronic trade of ethnographic history, I would list David William Cohen, Greg Dening, Rhys Isaac, and Renato Rosaldo, as well as a growing host of anthropologists and historians of the generation of our students.

8. In this same vein, I intersperse throughout the text photos of twentieth-century Saramakas (and sometimes other Suriname Maroons) engaged in activities relevant to the adjoining text—drumming, praying, tree-felling—not because these images *document* details of eighteenth-century practices (which they surely do not, given ongoing cultural change), but because in my view they may legitimately be used to *evoke* those practices (given the very real cultural continuities

that exist, side by side with dynamism, in this society—see also S. and R. Price 1980). All field photos, unless otherwise credited in the captions, were taken by R.P. or S.P.

9. My narrative mode, however, remains a world away from the teleological narrative sometimes attributed to "traditional history" (Philipp 1983, 347). Like most social historians, I am specifically interested in the way that "certain happenings are turned into events . . . [become] invested with dramatic or symbolic power . . . become markers of social meaning" (346), and I keep my eyes wide open regarding my own role in this process. In telling a story that unfolds over many decades, I draw repeatedly on what Philipp calls "event statements created in the past by historical actors trying to locate or explain themselves" (ibid.).

10. When there are reports of direct discourse, I retain the typeface of the person *reporting* the speech, placing the spoken words in quotation marks. Rarely, there is a more complicated case, for example when Tribal Chief Abíni asks Moravian Brother Stoll (probably in Sranan, Abini's second language, which Stoll speaks) to pen a letter for him to the colonial governor, which Stoll writes out in German; but the document that I have seen is a Dutch translation of the letter Stoll wrote, placed in the colonial archives. Though nonliterate Abini's name is at the bottom of this thrice-translated letter, I print it here in the "German" font, using quotation marks to indicate that this is a Moravian's version of a Saramaka's words.

11. Some comments on translation and pronunciation deserve placement here:

On Translation.   This book includes translations from Saramaccan, Sranan (the creole language of coastal Suriname), French, Dutch, and German. With the first three of these languages, I have made the translations myself. With translations of Dutch documents dated prior to 1764, I draw on my previous collaboration with Barbara Blair (see R. Price 1983b, 222–23, passim); for those postdating that moment (which occurs in *Alabi's World* toward the beginning of Chapter 2), I have made the translations myself. Dutch-English conventions developed during the preparation of R. Price 1983b are continued here: "runaways" for *wegloopers,* "Bush Negroes" for *Boschnegers,* "Negroes" or (depending on context) "slaves" for *neegers,* "ensign" for *vandrig,* "garden" for *kostgrond,* "barrel" for *vat,* "keg" for *vatje,* "jug" for *stoop,* "jar" for *pul,* "case" for *kelder,* and "rum" for *dram* (though what is meant is always white rum or "kill-devil").

The German translations have a longer and more complicated history, as this was not a language I controlled at the outset of the project. During the early 1970s, I selected passages from Staehelin 1913–19 for rough translation, which was done at sight into a dictaphone by a Ph.D. student in Yale's German department, Steven Cerf, and then typed out in English. Over the years, as I worked over particular passages, I returned to the originals, much-thumbed dictionary in hand, occasionally getting help from one or another native speaker, as I refined and corrected the English.

In 1987–88, able by this time to understand far more than I had fifteen years earlier, I painstakingly retranslated all passages that appear in the book, marking residual problems and questions. With the generous assistance of Professor Heidrun Suhr, who was visiting the University of Minnesota from Germany, I was able to clear up and check all problematical passages and to feel that the translations are fully adequate for present purposes. Ultimately, much of my efforts became devoted to matters of style, as I tried to catch accurately those phrases peculiar to eighteenth-century Moravian discourse ("being baptized into the death of Jesus," "falling asleep in the arms and lap of Jesus," "being called out of time," and so on). I was fortunate to have some scores of pages of nearly contemporary English translations from the very same Suriname diaries that were reproduced by Staehelin or of which I have photocopies in manuscript, in the form of the *Periodical Accounts* now at the British Library. I have tried hard to follow, insofar as is reasonable two centuries later, the conventions used by these English Moravians who translated the diary passages from Suriname soon after they were written. For example, I generally use lowercase "negro," "tyger" (rather than "jaguar") for *Tiger,* "witch doctor" for *Hexenmeister,* "spectacle" or "performance" for *Gaukelei,* "conjurer" for *Gaukeler,* and so forth (but have also tried to keep in mind that there was real variation between both diarists and eighteenth-century translators). For a number of passages, I have been able to draw directly on *Periodical Accounts,* permitting the reader to confront firsthand the English prose style of the eighteenth- and early nineteenth-century Brethren.

On Pronunciation and Orthography. My orthography for Saramaccan is a modified version of that proposed by Voorhoeve (1959). Vowels have "Italian" values except that è = ɛ (the vowel in English "met") and ò = ɔ (the vowel in English "all"); vowel extension in speech is indicated by vowel repetition in writing; a nasalized vowel is indicated by V*m* before labial consonants and by V*n* before nonlabial consonants; single prenasalized consonants are indicated by *mb, nd, ndj,* and *ny.* Both *kp*(= *kw*) and *gb*(= gw) are single consonants. High tones are indicated by an acute accent; low tones are unmarked. However, with the dual goal of making this book maximally accessible to an English-speaking audience while at the same time preserving full pronunciation information, I have chosen to use diacritics only upon the first occurrence of each Saramaka word or name in the text, as well as in all illustration captions. (My working definition of "first occurrence" assumes that the reader interrupts his or her reading of the text to read the Notes and Commentary in the order signaled by the superscripts in the text. So, a first appearance can be either in the text or in the Notes and Commentary.)

As a handy guide for nonspecialist readers who may wish to pronounce some of the Saramaka personal names, place names, and concepts that appear most frequently in these pages, I list them alphabetically (but otherwise promiscuously) with a rough English-based equivalent. (For purposes of pronunciation reference, I also include in this listing, with their diacritics, all Saramaka words and names that appear more than once in the text.)

Abaánsi, Abaísa (Ah-BUY-sah), Abíni (Ah-BEE-nee), Adjágbò (Uh-JAHG-baw), Adjéuwensé, adjíbóto adjú paayá, adugbá, adunké, Afíima, Agámadjá, Agbagó (Ah-gbah-GO), Agbó, A-gébófo, Agósu Danyéi, akáa, A-ké, Akoomí (Ah-koh-MEE), Akra (Ah-KRAH), Alábi Pantó (Ah-LAH-bee Pahn-TOH), aladá, Alándo (Ah-LAHN-doh), Alasá, aléle, Alúbutu, Alúku, Andolé, Antamá (On-tah-MAH), apínkusu, apínti, apúku (Ah-POO-koo), Asáubásu, asêmpè, Asindóópo, Asipéi, Asukúme (Ah-soo-KOO-may), awáa, Awáa Creek, Awaná (Ah-wah-NAH), awaínza, Awóyo, Ayakô (Ah-yah-KAW), azang, Baákawáta (Bah-kah-WAH-tah), bakáa kôndè, Bákakúun (bah-kah-KOON), Bákapáu, Bákisipámbo, Bambey (Bahm-BAY), bandámmba, basiá, básikaánu, Bébi (BAY-bee), Bekú, Bèkúun, Bêndêkôndè, béndi a sê, Bentóla, Biítu (BEE-too), Bôsi (BAW-see), Bótópási, Bundjitapá, Dabí (Dah-BEE), Dákwama, Dangasí, Dángogó, Dáume, dêdé kôndè, Djáki, Djankusó, Djánti, Djuká (jew-KAH), Djumú, Dómbi (DOME-bee), Domósi, Dóndo Ainsá, Dóndo Kasá, Dosú Creek, Dungí, duumí mátu, Fandááki (Fahn-DAH-kee), Folú, Foola, gaamá (Gah-MAH), Gaándan Falls, Gaánlío (Gahn-LEE-oh), gaán óbia, gádu (GAH-doo), Ganzê, Gáu, Gbagidí, Gódo, Góme (GO-may), Gúngúúkúsu, Guyába, Gwafu, Gweúnga, Gwínzu, Háfupási, Íngi-písi, Kaála (KAH-lah), Kaána, Kaa-pátu, Kaásipúmbu (KAH-see-PUM-boo), Kabálo, kabiténi, Kadósu, Kála, Kambalóa, Kámpu, kándu, Kangáa, Kánga Creek, Kasitú, Kayána, keéti (KAY-tee), Kodjo Maáta, Kofí Creek, Kofí Tjapánda, komantí, Kositán, Kudébaku, Kumakô (Koo-mah-KAW), Kúmbu, Kúngoóka (Koong-GO-kah), kúnu, kuútu, Kwakú Étja (Kwah-KU EY-cha), Kwakú Kwádjaní (Kwah-KU Kwah-jah-NEE), Kwamá, Kwáminangóto, Kwé-mayón, Lánga Amaná, Lángu (LAHN-goo), Lánu (LAH-noo), lô, lôndò, luángo, Madánfo (Mah-DAHN-foh), madjáma wáta, Mafúngu, Malobí, Mamádan, Ma Pugúsu, Mása Lámba, Masiá, Matawái (Mah-tah-WHY), máti (MAH-ti), Matjáu (Mah-CHOW), Mbutí, Mètisên, Mus-ínga, Musumbá, Muyánwóyo, nagó, Nasí (Nah-SEE), nêséki, Ngweté, nyanyántúe (nya-nya-TOO-way), nyumáa, óbia (OH-bee-uh), óbiama, Otjútju (Oh-CHOO-choo), Paánza (PAHN-zuh), Paáti-nêngè, papá (pa-PA), Papútu (Pah-POO-too), patáka, Peléki (Puh-LAY-kee), Pempé, Pikílío (Pee-kee-LEE-oh), Puli (POO-lee), Sáa, Saánga, sabá, Samsám (Sahm-SAHM), sangáa, sangaáfu, Sasaaku Creek, Sééi (SAY-ee), seéka, Sentéa (Sen-TAY-uh), Sialôto (Syah-LOH-toh), siliê, Sofí, sóói-gádu, Soolán, Tandó, tási, Tebíni (Tay-BEE-nee), Tímba, tjánga-féti, Tjazímbe (Cha-ZIM-bay), Tjímba, Tobiási-nêngè, tonê (tow-NAY), Tuído (tu-EE-doh), Túlíobúka, Tutúba (Too-TOO-bah), Tutú Creek, Vumá (voo-MAH), Wámba (WAHM-buh), Waná, Wánganía, Wátambíi (Wah-tom-BEE), Wíi (Wee), wísi (WEE-see), Yáya (YAH-yah), Yebá, Záda.

One: First-Time's Child

Many of the facts, ideas, and images in Chapter 1 (as well as in the first few pages of Chapter 2) may be found somewhere in my previous writings, in particular *First-Time, To Slay the Hydra,* and *The Guiana Maroons.* But here, I have reoriented these materials toward the life of Alabi, focusing on his specific ancestors' arrivals in Suriname and their life on the plantations, their escapes and early years in the forest, and finally Alabi's own birth (in 1744) and childhood, spent by his father Abini's side, during the years that the latter (the chief peacemaker for the Saramakas) negotiated the final settlement of 1762. That climactic moment—the coming of peace, after a century of slavery and war—marks the chronological ending of *First-Time* as well as the opening of Chapter 2 of *Alabi's World.* Readers familiar with *First-Time* may choose to read lightly in this first, introductory chapter, to arrive more quickly at the qualitatively different colonial encounters that characterize the world of the rapidly maturing Alabi, who is eighteen years old when Chapter 2 begins.

Sources for the quotations in this chapter, in order of presentation, include: for the claim of Suriname-envy, Nassy 1788, 1:56; for the per capita statistics, Nassy 1788, 2:40; for these Stedman scenes and others, 1988 [1790]; for Saramaka versions of Lánu's and Ayakô's escapes, Dabí's story, and the great raid, R. Price 1983a, 43–54; for Nassy's account of the Machado revolt, 1788, 1:76; for Wátambíi beginnings, R. Price 1983a, 54–61; for bounties, "exquisite" and other tortures, and the Voltaire reference, R. Price 1976, 24–26; for the "Blood Spilling" citation, Stedman 1988 [1790], 472; for Góme's account of his clan's beginnings, R. Price 1983a, 112–113; for Nasís and Dómbis in slavery and after, R. Price 1983a, 101–5, 108–11; for Tebíni and Mètisên on Kaasi's exploits, and for the corresponding archival accounts, R. Price 1983a, 77–79, 82; for the Abaísa escape, R. Price 1983a, 70–73; for Abini's split with the Matjáus, R. Price 1983a, 115–16; for the Matjaus' southward trek, R. Price 1983a, 62–68; for their stay at Baákawáta, and Paánza's story, R. Price 1983a, 127–34; for Kaási's movements and the battles of 1730–31, R. Price 1983a, 75–88; for Kumakô, R. Price 1983a, 106–7, 116–19; for Timba, R. Price 1983a, 120–21; for Tuído, R. Price 1983a, 92–95; for the battle of Bákakúun and its aftermath, R. Price 1983a, 135–36; for the sinking at Gaándan Falls, R. Price 1983a, 140–43 and 1983b, 21–26, 43–84; for Kwasí's gambit and the battle of 1755, R. Price 1983a, 153–59 and 1983b, 26–34, 85–124; for Yáya's prophecy, R. Price 1983a, 160; and for the sources for "Free at Last," R. Price 1983a, 167–81 and 1983b, 34–40, 125–217.

1. I cannot be absolutely sure that Ayako and Lanu were from the Akan area (in what is now Ghana), but I have sufficient indications, in oral fragments attributed to them and in related proverbs, to make it seem likely. Very few ships reached Suriname with Gold Coast cargoes prior to 1700—perhaps only 2 percent of all slavers (R. Price

1976, 13–14)—so Ayako, Lanu, and the others who arrived together would have been very much a linguistic and cultural minority in their new home.

2. Dear Reader, already we abut a delicate issue that had best be confronted at once. When a distinguished historian of slavery (who had just read the first two paragraphs of this chapter in manuscript) learned that I was unable to footnote the name of the Guineaman, the exact date, the presence of the Indian, and the source for Ayako's and Lanu's reactions to stepping ashore, he was, simply, incredulous. I attempted to explain myself, as I shall again here. *Alabi's World* is based, like any serious work of history, on a great many bits of evidence about the past. I use every single scrap of evidence known to me, after some twenty years of work with Suriname materials, that can enlighten the issues addressed. But at certain moments in the text—and these opening paragraphs are the most startling example— I permit my educated imagination to construct probabilities. Half a dozen paragraphs into the chapter, when my "historical data" become firmer in a conventional sense, I shift directly to Saramaka sources, and I remain largely within the bounds of Saramaka, Dutch, and German sources for the duration. (At those rare moments in the text when I do conjure up events that are, in the absence of specific documentation about these particular events, "educated reconstructions," I take pains to signal them clearly in the Notes and Commentary [see, for examples, chapters 4 and 7].) Thus, I would note here that the Indian on the shore is artifice, but from my knowledge of who might have been standing on the shore that day, quite plausible artifice. Lanu and Ayako, however, were as real as you or I. If, like my historian friend, you are made uncomfortable by the juxtaposition of these two kinds of people in the same passage, consider that it is solely my orneriness to make the only truly fictional characters in this whole book appear in the first paragraph: the Indian and the bookkeeper. Likewise, my attribution of particular thoughts and feelings to these newly arrived Africans is a very rare venture, from the perspective of the rest of the book. From here on out, *Alabi's World,* with all its quirks, is ethnographic history, and the Notes and Commentary (particularly the long lists of sources in the initial note of each chapter) are intended to satisfy the appetite of the most footnote-hungry positivistic historian. Ultimately, I would stand squarely with Clifford Geertz in asserting, first, that ethnographic or historical facts *are* facts and, second, that serious ethnography consists not simply in compiling such facts but in an imaginative way of seeing through experience. "The facts are *made out,* not *made up"* (Shweder 1988). Precisely, I would add, as in our mutual straining through those proverbial mists to make out the opening scene.

3. In Suriname, at least, black drivers or overseers were far from being simply the lackeys of the whites. Hoogbergen, on the basis of extensive work in the archives, argues persuasively that the plantation *basya* was, rather, a leader among his slave peers, chosen by

them as an intermediary with the white power structure (1985, 49). It was he who, while responsible to the whites for the completion of a particular task, would decide who worked when and how hard, who should be excused because of illness, and so forth. And, as Hoogbergen argues, it was he who most directly interacted with maroons on the plantation periphery, permitting them access to food and other plantation resources and not infrequently joining with them to plan an uprising. Since the eighteenth century among Saramakas, the office of *basiá*—assistant to the headman or captain (*kabitén̄i*)—has been invested with that same combination of secular and ritual authority as have the offices of tribal chief (*gaamá*) and *kabiteni*. Matjaus continue to express pride that Ayako served as Waterland's *basya*.

4. *Okundo bi okundo* is the verbal form of the drum slogan still played on the *apínti* (talking) drum to summon to council meetings the important village officials known as *gaán* (big) *basia,* a title that derives etymologically from Sranan (coastal Suriname creole) *basya,* Ayako's plantation job.

5. Mása Lámba was a Matjau "great *obia,*" part of a complex of war *obia*s that included the *agó óbia* Akwádja (closely associated with the forest spirit Wamba). Today, Masa Lamba's drum rhythms are still played and danced at rarely held rites for the First-Time ancestors, to commemorate the *obia*'s role in confusing the enemy and making themselves unfindable. During Lanu's and Ayako's early years in the forest, it is said, the whites would hear the Masa Lamba drums and follow, but always in the wrong direction.

6. The story of the infant Dabi's miraculous escape from danger, and its accompanying *obia* song (see R. Price 1983a, 53–54), have been preserved for nearly three hundred years in the lore surrounding the great Matjau war *obia* called Afíima (sometimes Kafíima). During the final years before the Peace of 1762, Dabi—as we shall see—followed in his father's footsteps, serving as unofficial tribal chief.

7. As I have argued in *First-Time* (and elsewhere), Saramakas have from the first been specially attuned to living *in* history, both sharply aware that their own lives have been affected by the actions of others in the past and conscious of their own accountability toward their descendants. Likewise, their physical world, within which time unfolds, has always been highly particularized and personalized. To a remarkable degree, events are catalogued, recorded, and remembered through their associations with particular sites; geography in Saramaka becomes a major repository of historical traditions. The initial experience of taking over a new land, conceptualized through tales of coming to terms with local gods and spirits, remains a central text of those First-Time years. As Saramakas created their social and cultural institutions, during their years of nation building, they were also possessing an unfamiliar environment. And this process is also reflected, in interestingly different ways, in Saramaka *kóntu,* the folktales that are told at wakes and that frequently have as a theme this

same appropriation of a previously unknown and menacing environment (see R. and S. Price 1990).

8. In Matjau historiography, the same motivation that causes the collective "forgetting" of the names of early Matjau men's fathers—neither Adjagbo's nor Abini's father is remembered today—causes the collective insistence that Matjau men themselves fathered particular sons (Ayako begetting Dabi, Abini begetting Alabi). In the former case, the convenient forgetting of a father renders Matjaus dependent on no other group; in the latter case, the remembering makes some other group (the son's matrilineal clan) dependent on the Matjaus for having "made" a son for them. Thus, part of Awaná captain Gome's willingness to share his clan's First-Time lore with me stemmed from the fact that I was considered a guest of the Matjaus in Saramaka, and the Matjaus' greatest gift to the Awanas was begetting Alabi for them. Gome's discussions with me, in one form of Saramaka calculus, formed a partial repayment of a major debt.

9. The technique of "boiling" a person was one of a number of ways used by Saramakas to gain control over their enemies. As a Matjau friend explained to me, "They prepare the *obia,* call your name, put the *obia* pot on the fire. [Said in a tone used for praying:] " 'You see now, Lisáti [R.P.]. You're the one we've put in the pot here. You're the one we're boiling. As we boil you here, you're dizzy, you're so confused you can't walk. Your strength is sapped. You're the one we're boiling here.' " He then described boiling a plantation manager to put him to sleep during the whole time a group was raiding and taking supplies. "The watchman would be boiled too. He'd leave the door of the plantation house wide open."

10. The Nasis, almost from the first, traveled with the much smaller Biitu group, who came from a neighboring Jewish plantation owned by a man named Britto. While the Nasis retained their reputation as the predominant warriors, the Biitus, through their African leader Gweúnga, made a different contribution: in the eighteenth century, as today, they owned the powerful *tonê obia,* which controls the rains via the *tone* gods who dwell in rivers. An incident during the years of guerrilla activity is emblematic. As Tebini told me,

> *Wherever the Kwadjanis [Nasis] had walked, the Biitus walked with them.* **Mati ku mati** *[friends with friends]. The Kwadjanis had been battling all over the forest. The Biitus just stood to one side [supported them]. Finally they got to Muyanwoyo. . . . The whites followed them to there. Then the Biitu man called Gweunga said to them, "Now it's your turn to stand aside. I will help you fight." And he brought down the rains! He brought them down until . . . the whites were completely encircled by rain. They were stuck right in the middle. It sunk those soldiers, finished them off completely. He did that thing, Gweunga.*

11. Kaasi's Langu people had been the first in the area; the other clans had come in their wake. Saramakas encapsulate this priority in stories about how Kaasi (or his son Alándo) used his Loango-god to transform the Gaanlio, which had been unfit for human use, into the clear stream it remains to this day (R. Price 1983a, 98–99). And today, the whole watershed of the Gaanlio is simply called by Saramakas "Langu."

12. I do not have direct reports of Saramaka coming-of-age ceremonies during the eighteenth century. But for as long as the oldest living Saramakas in the 1960s could remember, or had ever heard of, both boys and girls had gone through these formal rites under the supervision of their father's clan at the village ancestor shrine (see, for twentieth-century descriptions of female coming-of-age ceremonies, S. Price 1984, 15–20).

13. The full treaty is presented, in English translation, in R. Price 1983b, 159–65.

14. The final song cited here illustrates the way Saramakas use songs to keep alive once-topical events, even ones dating from more than two centuries ago. The preservation through song of a transient domestic squabble that happened to take place on the greatest day in Saramaka history seems to me to epitomize a prototypically Saramaka way of at once humanizing (or individualizing) and celebrating their distant collective past.

Two: The New Politics

Sources for this chapter, in approximate order of use, include: for the Society's comments on Dörig's qualifications, SvS 100, 23 Mar. 1763; for the comparable Djuka materials, de Groot 1977, 15; for Dörig's general "instructions," SvS 154, 20 Nov. 1762; for his special instructions, SvS 155, 13 Mar. 1763; for Dörig's first tour of duty as postholder, SvS 155, 20 Apr. 1763, translated in English in R. Price 1983b, 165–96; for the planter's comment on "tribute," de Salontha 1778, 5–6; for the meanings of *fri*, Schumann 1778, s.v. *fri*; for Dörig's military promotion, SvS 155, 22 Sept. 1763; for Dörig's full journal of the first general tribute distribution, SvS 155, 15 Nov. 1763, translated in English in R. Price 1983b, 196–216; for Abini's request for shackles, SvS 156, 9 Jan. 1764; for Abini and Samsam's confirming messages, Hof 69, 13 Feb. 1764; for the Court's snuffbox resolution, Hof 69, 13 Feb. 1764; for the escape of turned-in slaves, SvS 156, 17 May 1764, 22 June 1764, which seem unclear about whether Dörig arrived with five or six; for the Djuka's speech about Samsam, SvS 156, 22 June 1764; for the slave sentences and executions, SvS 156, 29 May 1764, SvS 205, 15 Dec. 1764; for the Djuka comments on executions, SvS 205, 9 Apr. 1761; for a plea by Saramakas not to execute, SvS 333, 16 Nov. 1767; for Samsam's and the Matjaus' turn-ins, SvS 156, 5 Nov. 1764; for Etja's single turn-in, SvS 331, 28 Mar. 1767 [9 Mar. 1767]; for Etja's sister-in-law, Hof 90, 5 Aug. 1774 [30 May 1774].

1. The members of the Court in Paramaribo were also that much closer than the directors of the Society in Holland to what they perceived as the ongoing threat of renewed military action by the recently "pacified" Maroons, and they capped their argument by remarking, "Whereas it is the military man's duty to remain at his post in case of trouble, a civilian could leave if things became 'too hot for him'" (de Groot 1977, 15). The directors of the Chartered Society of Suriname exercised their political control from afar via the governor, whom they appointed; the Court of Policy, though appointed by the governor, was selected from lists drawn up by the planters and represented their own local interests. These two parties clashed throughout the colonial history of Suriname.

2. The Dutch characterized the Maroons as "vermin," "pernicious scum," "a crowd of monsters," and "parasites," symbolically placing them—with considerable justice—beyond the boundary of what they saw as the proper colonial order; yet, to the colonists' dismay, the Maroons remained near enough to prey constantly upon them, like a "chronic plague," a "gangrene," or a "Hydra." The Saramakas, meanwhile, tended to describe their colonial adversaries with the more direct but equally disdainful *"ná sèmbè"* ("not human"), because of what they—again, with considerable justice—saw as severe moral lapses that placed the colonists well beyond the pale of fully human behavior.

3. These Indians had been captured by Musinga and his people (who lived in the westernmost Saramaka village of Matawai, on the Saramacca River), in a 1761 raid. In the late 1750s, Moravian missionaries, who had been working with Arawak Indians in the colony of Berbice (to the west of Suriname), had moved to the Lower Saramacca River, bringing some thirty Indians with them and establishing the mission post of Saron. During 1760, a number of more warlike Carib Indians moved in; these same Caribs were active participants in bounty-hunting for escaped slaves. While the Caribs were temporarily absent, in January 1761, the Saramakas from Matawai—who needed free passage down the Saramacca River for easy access to Paramaribo—attacked the mission, killing two Indians, wounding ten, and carrying off four women and four (or possibly seven) children (see, for sources, St 2, pt. 1, 103–4; Wolbers 1861, 784–85, 788). At news of the raid, the government sent an unsuccessful following commando, then established a military post, "The Seven Provinces," nearby (Bubberman et al. 1973, 70). Dörig's official instructions had been to "negotiate for the return of the Indian women and children who were captured from the Moravians, that is 4 women and 7 children, if they are all alive; and if this does not work, as a last resort offer them [the Saramakas] a small present such as beads [in order to persuade them]" (SvS 154, 20 Nov. 1762).

Dörig took up this issue again on his first personal visit to Matawai. On 26 January 1763, he told captains Musinga and Beku about his instructions from the Court regarding the "Herrnhuters' Indians." The chiefs made him a novel proposal:

They answered me that they had obtained them by fighting and the possessors did not want to give them up, neither for a bounty nor for gifts of beads and cotton cloth, but that in order to show [us] that we were doing business with reasonable people, they would exchange them for Negroes, man for man, woman for woman, child for child. The remaining Indians totalled six persons. I could not agree to this proposition but did manage to persuade them to take into consideration the proposal that they take the Indians along to Sara Creek when they come to fetch the goods, where it would still be possible to make an agreement about this. (SvS 155, 20 Apr. 1763 [26 Jan. 1763])

In these several exchanges about the captured Indians, one can read considerably less urgency on the part of the government than in the case of harbored slaves. The reason seems clear: the system itself was not here at stake. To my knowledge, none of these Indians was ever returned (except the dying "Johann Gottfried"—see Chapter 4, note 41). In 1770, a missionary visiting the Matawai reported that, "of the Indians stolen nine years ago from Saron, only two girls and a lad survive, but these three have completely assimilated themselves into the ways of the Negroes" (St 3, pt. 1, 143). And in 1788, another missionary noted that "two of the Indians who were captured at Saron" were living in a Saramaka village on the Gaanlio (St 3, pt. 2, 213).

4. The first postholder among the Djuka, Sergeant Frick, was similarly dependent upon his reluctant hosts and was subjected to parallel trials.

In one of his letters (August 1762) he complains about the difficulty of capturing and confining runaways; these were usually armed and offered strong resistance. So he was asking for handcuffs. The letter ends with a pathetic cry of distress, asking for more help to be sent with the regular provisions and stores. These latter the Maroons were willing to fetch only if they were paid more than he could afford. "I cannot believe that it is your Honours' intention to let me go to the dogs here, to put it bluntly, without clothes, and without powder and shot." He ended up being so unpopular with the Maroons that they forbade him to send any letters setting forth their wishes and complaints to Paramaribo at all, "as they did not help anyway," and once even imprisoned him and his two soldiers, confiscating all his possessions. Although he was soon released, the Maroons and he no longer trusted each other and he asked to be relieved. (de Groot 1977, 151)

Postholders' letters and reports from Saramaka are filled with plaints of penury and dependence. For example, in 1773 Postholder Daunitz pleaded with the Court to send "some delicacies which might help him tolerate his loneliness" (SvS 165, 30 July 1773); in 1780 Postholder Weinhold beseeched the Court to send him "a crate of candles, as I cannot see without light, and I must write everything by night, as by day I do not have a free instant" (Hof 111, 22 Aug. 1780; see also Hof 115, 7 Dec. 1781, passim); and in 1783, Postholder de Vries begged for "a crate of soap and one of candles, a jar each of cooking oil, vinegar, and lamp-oil, 3 jugs of gunpowder, a bottle of shot and one of bullets, 8 jars of rum, a machete, 2 axes, a shovel, a hoe, nails, writing materials, and medicines" (SvS 175, 17 Dec. 1783).

5. For the full list of 1763 goods, see p. 51, and for comparisons to lists from other distributions, R. Price 1983b, 236–38.

6. In early 1762, Abini and Louis Nepveu, at Djuka, had negotiated the list of goods to be given to the Saramakas at the treaty-signing. But by September, when the Peace was sealed, the bulk of these had not yet arrived in the colony. At the September treaty-signing, preliminary goods were distributed (except to Samsam and the Baakawata Matjaus, who were absent and received extra portions in 1763), and provisional "hostages" (children of Saramaka chiefs)—who were sent back to Saramaka in December 1762—were turned over to the government (Hof 66, 19 Sept. 1762, translated in English in R. Price 1983b, 159–65; SvS 154, 9 Dec. 1762).

7. During the several decades following the treaties, it seems to have been a standard part of planter discourse to refer to them as a "shameful capitulation" on the part of the colonists (see, for example, Stedman 1988, 510).

8. *Baljarden* was the common eighteenth-century colonial term (< Portuguese *bailar*) for slave or Maroon secular dance/drum/song performances—what Suriname slaves called *banja* and Saramakas *pèê* ("plays").

9. These children, like the Djuka "hostages" who were also raised in Paramaribo at government expense, attended school there with the "Mulatto Schoolmaster" (SvS 155, 25 July 1763; see also Wolbers 1863, 285). Jan seems, eventually, to have become a member of the Dutch Reformed Church (St 3, pt. 2, 140).

10. Just before Dörig left Paramaribo to distribute the goods, the Court had written the directors in Holland requesting twenty-four silver-headed staffs of office, to be distributed later to the chiefs (SvS 155, 30 May 1763).

11. Such rhythmic handclapping, which is quiet and slow, is unlike Western applause. It is used in contexts of giving formal thanks, prayer, and asking a favor.

12. The following day, as the whitefolks' downriver voyage began, one of their boats "overturned and a soldier was drowned and 16 guns lost with all the tools. The other 15 men, who all fell overboard, were saved and brought to the riverbank by the [Saramaka] chiefs," who later received compensation for bringing up the guns and other materiel from the bottom of the river (SvS 155, 15 Nov. 1763 [17 Sept. 1763]). It may well be this incident that is commemorated by the

modern place-name Brokopondo: a report from ca. 1828 refers to the place as "Brokoponto, that is broken *pont* or boat, because once a government *pont* with goods sank there" (ARA, Coll. J. van den Bosch 145).

13. This description comes from a literate nineteenth-century Matawai, Johannes King (ca. 1830–1899), who witnessed such post-tribute distribution celebrations (which lasted till 1849) during his youth (King 1979, 302–3). King's description of *sangaa* activities is presented in Chapter 4, below.

14. It was only during the 1780s that the government ceased executing runaway slaves turned in by the Saramakas and the Djukas (see Hoogbergen 1985, 394).

Three: Soldiers of the Bloody Cross

Sources for this chapter, in approximate order of use, include: for the youthful Zinzendorf's edification societies, Rupp-Eisenreich 1985, 130; for his antirationalist argument, Gollin 1967, 10–11; for his theology of the concrete, van der Linde 1956, 66–68; for his florid characterizations of the wounds, Gollin 1967, 12; for Moravian body imagery, Rupp-Eisenreich 1985, 137; for the familial conception of the church and Christ, Hutton 1909, 275; for the hymns and hymn fragments, *A Collection . . .* 1748, 16–17, 19, 28–29, 32, 54–55, 88–89, and *Hymns Composed . . .* 1749, 6; for the "stick-to" stance, Hutton 1909, 276; for the headless societies and Zinzendorf's view of brains, Gollin 1967, 12, and Hutton 1909, 274; for the heathens' "yoke of Sin," *A Concise Account* 1776, 1–2; for Moravian missionizing strategy, Holmes 1818, 466, and *PA* 1:7–8; for the sensual angle, Rupp-Eisenreich 1985, 136; for the spread of Zinzendorf's theology, van der Linde 1956, 68; for the 1753 hymn, *Londener Gesangbuch;* for the destruction of *Sichtungszeit* records, Gollin 1967, 230; for the continuing influence of the *Wunden Litaney,* van der Linde 1956, 72, 182; for the schedule of Saramaka mission services, St 3, pt. 1, 181; for the iconography of the Erstlingsbild, van der Linde 1956, 66–67; for the instructions regarding Savages and Moors, St 1:7; for the "Moravian historian," St 3, pt. 1, 7; for Ralfs's interview with Crommelin, St 2, pt. 3, 145–46; for the missionaries' artisanal bias, Holmes 1818, 470 (cf. *A Concise Account* 1776, 3); for Jones's letter, St 3, pt. 1, 9–10; for the Brethren's "wariness," St 3, pt. 1, 11; for Zinzendorf's political advice, van der Linde 1956, 39, 86, and Hutton 1909, 177 (see also St 3, pt. 1, 58); for Crommelin's continued pressure, St 3, pt. 1, 12; for Crommelin's "caution," St 3, pt. 1, 13; for the "pestilential forests" quotation, Hamilton 1900, 273; for the "foretaste" quotation, St 3, pt. 1, 198; for the "difficulty" of the mission station, Holmes 1818, 287; for Dehne's description of the tribute distribution, St 3, pt. 1, 24; for Dehne's upriver trip, St 3, pt. 1, 24–25; for Jones's stay with Samsam, *PA* 2:415–16; for Stoll's run-in with Samsam, St 3, pt. 1, 31; for the Herrnhuters' "blanketing" strategy, van der Linde 1956, 168; for Dehne's arrival at Sentea, St 3, pt. 1, 25–26; for the *awainza* ceremony, St 3, pt. 1, 26–27; for Dehne's description of Jones's arrival, St 3, pt. 1, 27; for Jones's death, St 3, pt. 1, 28, 31; for Dehne's near-death, St 3, pt. 1, 28, 31; for the "other missionary's" comment, St 3, pt. 1, 42; for the letter to Germany, St 3, pt. 1, 33–34; for Riemer's illness, St 3, pt. 2, 204–5; for the missionaries' first hut, *PA* 2:416; for house-building, Holmes 1818, 281; for "no secrets," St 3, pt. 2, 273; for the denigrating comments about Saramaka character, St 3, pt. 1, 92, 186; for the missionary prayer, St 3, pt. 1, 139; for the "delightful characters" quote, Hutton 1923, 177; for Abini's character, St 3, pt. 1, 30; for Abini's presentation of Alabi, *PA* 2:416; for reports on Skipio, St 2, pt. 1, 79, 3, pt. 1, 82; for village political realignments, St 3, pt. 1, 28; for the governor's comments, SvS 328, 1 Feb. 1766 (see also SvS 157, 2 Dec. 1765); for Samsam's drunkenness, St 3, pt. 1, 28; for the chiefly gifts, Hof 73, 29 Jan. 1766, SvS 328, 1 Feb. 1766.

1. I have never seen Dörig's official report on this tribute distribution, but I have encountered various references that it will "soon" be submitted to the Court (e.g., SvS 205, 6 Dec. 1765, Hof 73, 21 Dec. 1765).

2. The Moravians' arrival was not a complete surprise for all the Saramakas present. On 12 August 1765, Dörig claimed he "told the negroes that Brethren will come to them and remain with them," and the Moravians reported that Dörig "was surprised that they had heard so much about us and were so ready to welcome us" (St 3, pt. 1, 13). And it was Saramaka canoemen who actually served to transport Dörig and the missionaries from Paramaribo up to the tribute-distribution site (ibid.).

3. The Moravian Brethren are often referred to, alternatively, as the "Moravian Church," *"Unitas Fratrum,"* "Unity of the Brethren," "Herrnhuters," or, in Suriname, *"Evangelische Broedergemeente"* and (in Sranan-Tongo) *"Anitri."* There is an extensive literature, in several languages, on the Brethren. Those works I have found most useful as background include Gollin 1967, Helman 1968, Holmes 1818, Hutton 1909, van der Linde 1956, Oldendorp 1987 [1777], *Periodical Accounts,* van Raalte 1973, Rupp-Eisenreich 1985, Staehelin 1913–19, and various hymnals, particularly *A Collection* (1748). Their religious ideas are said to have had a significant influence on Schleiermacher, Lessing, Herder, Goethe, Novalis, Kierkegaard, and even Bismarck (Rupp-Eisenreich 1985, 126).

4. The *Sichtungszeit,* or "Sifting Period" (the Moravians' own term), generally designates the years 1738–52 and derives from Luke 22:31, "And the Lord said, Simon, Simon, behold Satan hath desired to have you, that he may sift you as wheat."

5. Zinzendorf, like many contemporary Pietists, himself "carried his Lot apparatus in his pocket; he consulted it on all sorts of topics. (It was a little green book, with detachable leaves; each leaf contained some motto or text; and when the Count was in a difficulty, he pulled out one of these leaves)" (Hutton 1909, 274). "To me," Zinzen-

dorf wrote, "the Lot and the Will of God are one and the same thing. I would rather trust an innocent piece of paper than my own excited feelings" (cited in Hutton 1923, 173). But "the systematic employment of this practice [the lot] in both public and private affairs, so characteristic of eighteenth-century Moravian settlements," focused especially on two kinds of situations: decisions about individuals' suitability for particular roles (e.g., leadership, missionary activity, marriage to a certain person, baptism) and decisions about communal policy (whether to move a settlement, close a mission station, etc.) (Gollin 1967, 50–58). The frequent use of the lot was documented among Moravian missionaries in Jamaica, who consulted their apparatus before proceeding with baptisms:

> A number of scriptural texts were written on strips and jumbled together, and if a candidate pulled out one which could be interpreted favourably, this was a sign of Divine approval. If he failed, he had to wait until the next crop of candidates came up. (Furley 1965, 107)

And in Paramaribo, the lot was used to assign leadership roles within the congregation (van der Linde 1963, 105). For the Saramaka mission, there appear to be allusions to the use of the lot several times (e.g., St 3, pt. 3, 139), but I have not encountered direct descriptions, possibly because its routine use was simply assumed (see Gollin 1967, 237).

6. I have not examined the several eighteenth-century Saramaccan language manuscript liturgy- or songbooks in various archives. See, for an inventory, Voorhoeve and Donicie 1963, 106–9.

7. This appears to have been Zinzendorf's favorite hymn (Hutton 1909, 179); Bach used it in his *Passionsmusik* According to St. Matthew ("O Haupt voll Blut und Wunden, voll Schmerz und voller Hohn!"). The Sranan translation was made at least by 1803 (van der Linde 1956, 183–84). The English translation of this Sranan version, in brackets, is my own. The eighteenth-century English version is from *Liturgic Hymns* (1793).

8. Moravian doctrine stressed that "it is the Saviour who has made God accessible to man, and it is through Christ's suffering on the Cross that the ransom for men's sins has been paid" (Gollin 1967, 11). An 1832 Moravian primer in Sranan is still more explicit: *"[J.C.] ben bai wi, nanga hem santa broedoe"* ("[J.C.] bought us with his holy blood") (*A.B.C. Boekoe,* cited in van der Linde 1956, 174–75). It does not seem implausible that the lurid Moravian imagery of blood and suffering would have been more appealing to slaves than to Saramakas, which may help explain the missionaries' relative success among them (Rupp-Eisenreich 1985, 152).

9. During the final years of the century, the missionaries actually served the colonial government directly, officially taking over the postholder's duties for some sixteen years, with unfortunate results for the mission (St 3, pt. 3, 105, 139; see also van Raalte 1986, 46). Brother Wietz described, retrospectively, the Moravians' motives.

> It was about this time [1795], that, with the consent of the Elders' Conference of the Unity, the office of [postholder], in the country of the free-negroes, was committed to me by the Government of Surinam. . . . Though I thought myself incapable of this station, yet, in reliance on the help of God, I accepted it; especially as the salary came in aid of the Mission. (*PA* 3:387)

During this period, Moravian support for government policies was such that the governor of Suriname wrote, "Their mission is worth more to me than a whole regiment of soldiers!" (van Raalte 1973, 160).

10. During Zinzendorf's 1739 visit to the Danish Virgin Islands, he had told the slaves that they should promise to

> remain faithful to your masters and mistresses, your overseers and bombas [drivers], and [to] . . . perform all your work with as much love and diligence as if you were working for yourselves . . . for the Lord has made everything Himself—kings, masters, servants, and slaves. And as long as we live in this world, everyone must gladly endure the state into which God has placed him and be content with God's wise counsel. . . . God has punished the first Negroes with slavery. The blessed state of your souls does not make your bodies accordingly free, but it does remove all evil thoughts, deceit, laziness, faithlessness, and everything that makes your condition of slavery burdensome. For our Lord Jesus was himself a laborer for as long as he stayed in this world. He was a craftsman pursuing His craft until a few years before His departure from this world. . . . As for myself, I was born free, but my Savior has taught me day and night to work joyfully for others. (Oldendorp 1987, 363)

Another Moravian authority explained that

> the teaching of our Savior Jesus Christ prescribes the duty of Christian slaves toward their masters clearly, emphatically, and completely and that this duty proceeds from motives that are independent of the character of the master and his conduct toward his servants, be it harsh or generous. These teachings make it a duty for the slave who practices them to serve his master with the same fidelity and submissiveness that he feels obliged to exercise in the service of Jesus Christ, his Redeemer. (Oldendorp 1987, 229)

And in 1776, Brother Kersten, who was at the time director of Moravian activities in Suriname, reiterated that

> the conversion of a slave to Christianity is a matter of the heart which does not directly affect the external relationship between master and slave. (Cited in van der Linde 1963, 103)

11. At this meeting, the governor asked that Brother Jones, who spoke English, be sent to the Djukas, since Djuka captain Boston could read and write that language (see R. Price 1983b, 232). But the three missionaries were able to persuade the governor of their need to stay together.

12. The frequency of tribute distributions was not, at first, definitively spelled out, and it became a point of considerable argument during the course of the eighteenth century. I have examined records attesting to such distributions in 1763, 1765, 1770, 1774, 1777, 1781, 1783, 1785, and 1788, but there were certainly others during this period (St 3, pt. 2, 84, 132; SvS 155, 15 Nov. 1763; SvS 205, 6 Dec. 1765, St 3, pt. 1, 21–24, 140; SvS 207, 23 Aug. 1774, 15 Sept. 1774; SvS 208, 24 Feb. 1778; SvS 208, 16 Mar. 1781; SvS 376, 26 Aug. 1782). In 1774, the government announced that the gifts would thenceforth be distributed every three years, rather than every two (with proportional increases to maintain equity), and by the late 1770s, the institution seems to have been thus regularized (Schumann 1778, s.v. *fri*, and SvS 167, 23 Aug. 1775, Hof 90, n.d. [mid-1774], Hof 94, 16 June 1776). However, in 1788 the distribution was said by one source still to be "yearly" (St 3, pt. 2, 132). The distributions continued until the middle of the nineteenth century (see von Sack 1821, 2:117, who claims they were "annual," and, for the interesting details of the ending of this tradition among the Djukas, de Groot 1977). The literate Matawai Johannes King set down this personal remembrance of nineteenth-century tribute distributions, the last of which he witnessed in 1849.

> *The Government said that if they [the Maroons] honored the [peace] agreements, every three years they would send many goods. . . . Every three years they had to drink an oath all over again. The whites did indeed hold to the agreement and the oath. . . . Even up to my, Johannes King's, lifetime, when I was a little boy, the Government kept sending presents. . . . By the time I saw the distribution of presents for the second time [i.e., ca. 1842], I was already pretty big. They again drank an oath. That was the last time the whites and Bush Negroes drank a blood oath. After that the Government again sent goods to distribute . . . [but] the whites and Bush Negroes [simply] gave each other their hand; they shook hands together to make peace; it was over. And the whites gave presents which the Bush Negroes received with joy. (King 1979, 302)*

13. Brother Stoll wrote a letter describing these same events but adding that "the gifts were presented, which took place according to heathen customs in a very quiet manner" (St 3, pt. 1, 22)—likely glossing, in this fashion, the "blood oath" that had become a standard part of this transaction, and which whites as well as Saramakas,

Christians as well as heathen, accepted as a central symbolic expression of their new political relationship. One might almost say that, just as the whites succeeded in symbolically possessing the Saramakas by means of writing, the Saramakas succeeded in possessing the whites by means of the blood oath and similar rituals to which they subjected them.

14. A Moravian historian, drawing on letters or diaries not available to me, added that

> Samsam continued for some time to be very troublesome to them, by insisting on having one of them as resident in his house; and when he found them resolute in their purpose of dwelling together, kept back their goods left with him, and either applied them to his own use, or suffered them to spoil in the wilderness. They felt this loss very severely. (*PA* 2:416)

15. In 1804, the missionaries reported a Saramaka folktale that comments on this tension.

> A negro from the Upper Country [from upstream] called here on the 28th, on his journey to Paramaribo. He said, he came to tell us a story he had heard from his parents, and to ask whether it was true. They had an old tradition, that the great God in heaven, after he had created heaven and earth, made two large chests, and placed them near the dwellings of mankind, on the coast. The black people, on discovering the chests, ran immediately to examine them, and found one locked, and the other open. Not thinking it possible to open that which was locked, they contented themselves with the other, which they found quite full of iron ware[?] and tools, such as hoes, axes, and spades, when each seized as much as he could carry, and all returned home. A little while after, the white people came also, and very calmly began to examine the locked chest, and, knowing the way to open it, found it filled with books, and papers which they took and carried away. Upon which God said, "I perceive, that the black people mean to till the ground, and the white people to learn to read and write." The negroes, therefore, believe, that it thus pleased the Almighty to put mankind to the proof; and as the blacks did not show so much sense as the white people, he made them subject to the latter, and decreed, that they should have a troublesome life in this world.
>
> We heard him patiently, and gave him the needful information concerning the difference of rank and status[?] amongst men, and then described to him the love of God. . . . We told him, that now He invites all men, black as well as white, to come unto Him, that they may obtain the forgiveness of, and deliverance from sin, and life everlasting, through His blood-shedding and death. (*PA* 3:425–26)

For discussion of this tale—which has seventeenth-century African antecedents and, in slightly different form, is widespread in Afro-America—see R. and S. Price 1990.

16. A missionary, inadvertently revealing how little the Moravians grasped of the workings of Saramaka religion, added that

> the number of their *gado*s is almost incalculable, every person choosing one according to his own fancy. Some fix on a large tree, a heap of sand, stones, a tiger, a crocodile, a serpent, &c. for their *gado;* and others make use of an image, or a stick, decorated with the teeth of some ferocious animal. Before these idols they perform their devotions with great reverence. However, they are not scrupulous in reproving their *gado*, if they think he has done them a mischief. (Holmes 1818, 275)

17. This "announcement" was a *basiá bái* ("assistant headman's call"), a stylized and dramatic African-derived speech act still practiced today for important community-wide announcements. The *basia,* holding up a palm frond (or simply using his cupped hand) against his mouth for greater voice projection, calls out *"Un haíka! Un haíka-ééé!"* ("Everyone listen! . . .") and makes his announcement, repeating the call at several places around the village. In some villages, *basia*s used to give their calls from the branches of a centrally located tree, and until recent decades, they sometimes made their announcements on wooden signal horns. (Saramaka elders had a "horn name" as well as a "drum name," both of which were used to summon them on ceremonial occasions.)

18. Years later, Brother Dehne wrote a summary account, which includes some revealing observations, of these same events.

> At first we were received by them with much friendship. We told them the reason of our coming to live with them, which was to instruct them in the knowledge of the only true God, their Creator and Redeemer; upon which the negroes began to set up a most prodigious and pitiable howling, believing that there idol was dissatisfied with them, and, on the 29th of December, they endeavoured to appease him, by appointing a great feast. Our hearts were greatly distressed by what we saw of the effects of our first address to them. . . . [But] He comforted us, and we confidently trusted to his power to destroy the works of Satan, even here in this wilderness. (*PA* 1:334–35)

19. When I read Dehne's *awainza* description to Tebini in 1978, he exclaimed, laughing with pleasure, "So, the missionary saw the hillock but had no idea what it was! Well, that was our 'prayer' (*bégi*). A real African-style *begi!*" During the 1970s, I saw decorated *awainza* hillocks outside two Saramaka villages, the Langu-clan village of Bundjitapá and the Nasi-clan village of Kambalóa.

20. When I read Dehne's *awainza* description to Awana captain Gome, in 1978, he gave an alternative interpretation:

They were praying to the [local] god-of-the-earth. The
apuku *[forest spirit]. They did not [contrary to Dehne's*
description] put their knees on the ground. They put their
bellies to the ground. And the [god-of-the-] place answered
them. It heard *them. I've heard that. The god-of-the-river.*
That's the only one they begged in that way. To say: "White-
folks have come. We and they must eat together [in peace]."
The way they put their bellies to the ground there, they
were praying, great thanks, may the god-who-has-the-forest
not kill them. At the base of the hillock, they made the
medicine. They made that **awainza,** *raised the flags there [for*
the ancestors]. With the **azang-***palm leaves.*

21. It is not clear whether this "negro" was a slave of the Moravians or a Saramaka. The missionaries' extensive use of domestic
slaves is discussed in Chapter 8.

22. It may be worth noting that the practice of "bleeding," which
was widespread among Europeans during the eighteenth century,
was particularly harmful for malaria victims, since anemia is a frequent concomitant of the disease, and the body needs all of its blood
(Curtin 1961, 101). According to Curtin, a typical initial bleeding for a
fever in the eighteenth century might have released twenty to fifty
ounces, with more later, for a total that could exceed one hundred
ounces; sixteen ounces is the standard amount taken from healthy
blood donors today (ibid.).

Unlike bloodletting, there was another widespread technique of
eighteenth-century "heroic medicine" that the Saramakas, too, may
have practiced—intestinal purging. Enemas were a constant presence among Europeans on Suriname plantations. At Providence, the
Labadist plantation on the Suriname River from which the ancestors
of the Abaisa clan escaped, one chronicler described dramatically
how "clyster upon clyster" failed to unblock the fourteen-day con-
stipation of one of the Labadist sisters (Dittelbach 1692, 57). The 1762
Saramaka "request list" for tribute included one "enema syringe" per
village; these would have been very large, complex metal devices
(see, for examples, those preserved in the Gruuthuse Museum,
Bruges). Since modern Saramakas do not practice heroic purging and
no longer preserve any memory of giant enema syringes (or of the
eighteenth-century word for them, *adjuda* [Schumann 1778]), it is at
least possible that they used these contraptions for some other, possibly ritual purpose.

23. I count twenty-eight men and eleven women (all wives);
Staehelin's summary statistics for the mission exclude two of these
men, whom he considers merely "visitors" (St 3, pt. 3, 234). Because
of illness and death, there was a high turnover of mission personnel
throughout the century. Of the thirty-nine missionaries who served,
twenty-three were in Saramaka for less than one year, and the bulk of
the work fell upon the dozen or so who lasted three years or longer.

Of these latter stalwarts, only four were women, who served along-side their husbands. (Although unmarried sisters were regularly shipped out from Europe to be married off immediately to eligible Brethren, many died in the early months. One of the longer-lasting Brethren in Saramaka lost two such wives in quick succession.)

24. Throughout the eighteenth-century tropics, newly arrived Europeans died at enormous rates. In the Caribbean, West Africa, and parts of the southern United States, malaria was the principal cause. Curtin (1968) has shown that mortality rates for new arrivals in contemporary West Africa, the famous "white man's grave," ranged from 350 to 800 per thousand per annum. My own rough figures, culled from Moravian documents, give a comparable figure for the Saramaka mission of 360 per thousand for all newcomers, but over 800 per thousand for those who came directly from Europe (i.e., with less than three months' stay in coastal Suriname). These figures are obtained by dividing the number of deaths by the number of years of exposure.

I have found data on the first months of thirty-four new arrivals to the mission. (In the other five cases, the diaries are missing or incomplete.) Of these, thirty contracted "the fever" (which proved fatal for eleven of them), one contracted smallpox, and only three—all veterans of other Suriname missions—remained more or less healthy. "First-shock" mortality was clearly related to acquired immunity. Nine out of the eighteen newcomers to Suriname who were sent directly to Saramaka caught the fever and died; yet only two of the twenty-one newcomers to Saramaka who had already been in Suriname for at least three months died in this first shock. (These "seasoned" people were, of course, themselves "survivors." I count sixty-two Moravian arrivals to Paramaribo [between 1765 and 1800] who did not go to Saramaka during their first year. Of these, fifteen died in the first shock, a rate about half that of the newcomers who went directly into the interior. Those who survived and later came to Saramaka had already been through it all once.) But though seasoning mitigated mortality for those who continued on to Saramaka, it did not affect the frequency of the initial fever itself: thirty of the thirty-three new arrivals in Saramaka succumbed. The Moravians seemed to believe that women were more susceptible to the fever than men: "Practically all the European sisters suffer from this sickness when they arrive here." But my own data suggest rather that a relatively high proportion of unseasoned arrivals were women, and that this, rather than gender, was the determinant. For people who survived the first-shock fever in Saramaka, subsequent mortality rates decrease considerably, to 53 per thousand per annum. But morbidity at the mission was staggering, with debilitating malaria attacks, dysentery, smallpox, infected wounds, and dermatological complaints most common. Even a cursory reading of the Moravian diaries makes it clear that illness and death were a constant preoccupation, a seamless backdrop to mission life in Saramaka.

The diaries reveal only a little of the missionaries' theory and treatment of disease, but it is enough to suggest that the Moravians subscribed to what Sheridan calls "the humoral-climatic and miasmatic theory of medicine" (1985, 329). The "airs" were often blamed for the fever. For example, Brother Kersten wrote in 1770 that

> **the heat and the cool winds alternate with one another much more rapidly than in Paramaribo. Thus the air is much more consuming for Europeans, to the point that even the healthiest and strongest have little energy or strength here. I have been here four months now and am still sickly. A four-day fever simply does not want to leave me; I am incapable of doing anything but writing and just a little bit of gardening. (St 3, pt. 1, 139)**

At other times, the missionaries blamed the chills that accompanied the fever on having spent time in the rain or in the river: "In addition we had chills, and the reason was that while crossing a large rapids we had to spend much time wading in the water" (St 3, pt. 1, 140). There are several complaints about inadequate food and its influence in slowing recovery, but while there may be some truth to this, it is probably not in terms of the particular foods the missionaries found wanting:

> **To be sure one recovers here in a much slower manner than in Europe, especially because of a lack of the most basic provisions. For example, we no longer have either bread or sugar. And although coffee grows on our own grounds, we have to drink it without milk or sugar; and the cassava that must take the place of bread is, both for the sick and for those who are recovering, a most difficult food to digest. (St 3, pt. 2, 138)**

The missionaries made use of medications of various kinds but seemed aware of their general ineffectiveness. Indeed, a diarist, writing in 1778 of standard "first-shock fever," claims that "we have as yet found no remedy against it" (St 3, pt. 1, 348), by which he means *effective* remedy. For, entries scattered through the diaries indicate the existence of a number of standard medical ingredients and procedures, without specifying (except for bloodletting) precisely what they were. In 1779, for example, Brother Riemer wrote, nonspecifically:

> **My very kind colleague Wietz felt it necessary now to care for me during my illness, which he did with the greatest fidelity, care, and endurance. He administered the customary medicines, of which we had a great many. (St 3, pt. 2, 204)**

Nevertheless, several weeks later, Riemer contrasted this treatment to what he received back on the coast, where a Paramaribo doctor "could examine me and give me proper medication, that along with the European refreshments available here, could heal me" (St 3, pt. 2, 206).

This last comment implies a practice that is more explicitly described in other diary passages—the missionaries' common use of "negro" remedies. For example, in 1770, "Brother Rudolph became very sick, and our old [slave] housekeeper gave him a drink made from herbs which had good effect on him" (St 3, pt. 1, 140). Similarly, Brother Nitschmann's infected heel had, in 1769, been treated "in the negro way" (St 3, pt. 1, 131). And in 1792, when the missionaries were trying without great success to cure one of their own domestic slaves, they wrote, "But we are not without hope, for we have the help of some negro herbalists who are specialists in curing" (St 3, pt. 3, 51). The postholders, too, found themselves dependent on Saramaka remedies during their tours of duty.

> *22 November [1779]. This evening I [Weinhold] suddenly became sick . . . and had Soldier Bleijtner who was with me summon Captain Etja. . . . I told him [Etja] that something had come over me but that I didn't know what. . . . Etja said that since it was night, I must wait till morning and that he would then find some remedy.*

> *23 November. At 5 a.m. Etja came with an old Negro woman. He told me that she would cure me quickly but that I would have to pay her. Being in dire need, I had no choice and agreed. (Hof 108)*

From other sources, we know that Europeans in eighteenth-century Suriname were often avid followers of one or another slave "physician" (see, for example, van Lier 1971, 83–84, and R. Price 1983a, 153–59). And available evidence certainly suggests that Afro-American medicine was, at the time, at least as effective as that of the Europeans.

But just as the missionaries occasionally tried Saramaka medication, Saramakas sometimes—though I think more rarely—sought medical assistance from the missionaries. For example, a Moravian wrote in 1772 that "we are looked upon by the negroes as evangelists, doctors, and surgeons," and he added plaintively, "yet so much [knowledge] is missing; it is most unfortunate that we did not pay closer attention to learning about more kinds of things in Europe" (St 3, pt. 1, 181). And another reported that

> **on the 2nd of February [1773], a negro, whose hand had been wounded by a flintlock, came to Brother Kersten asking for help. Also, two negresses have been here for four weeks with open sores on their feet, and he is taking care of them. (St 3, pt. 1, 185)**

In general, the missionaries' faith and its attendant fatalism pushed empirical remedies into the background. They often expressed such sentiments as "Here in the jungle, the Savior is our only doctor, and He alone heals us" (St 3, pt. 2, 138); or, "We are aware that our good and dear Lord is also the Lord of life and death and has our days counted. It [all this sickness and death] may keep us in constant intercourse with Him, and bring us joy and blessings in the harmony of love while we are serving Him" (St 3, pt. 1, 348–49); or again, "I am actually a poor sinner and useless wretch, and He is using me as He wishes" (St 3, pt. 1, 195). And in many ways the most difficult burden imposed on the Moravians by pervasive sickness and death—worse even than the incredible time and effort they consumed—was the reaction to this ongoing spectacle of missionary helplessness by the empirically minded Saramakas, who constantly found it difficult to lend credence to the powers of a god who rewarded its adherents with such miseries.

25. Brother Schumann's 1778 Saramaccan-German dictionary (s.v. *bem*) makes it clear that this "description" is a bit cavalier and that houses were in fact carefully carpentered. The houseposts were interspersed with thin poles (*latta*) that supported the woven walls, and a ridgepole (*langa bem*) supported other poles (also called *latta,* as today) that in turn supported the roof. The walls were made from the tightly woven fronds of the *murru murru* (today's *mumbúu*) palm (Schumann s.v. *broko*). Roofs were made by first putting down a layer of *pinna* palm leaves, followed by prepared strips of *tassi* leaves. (*Tási* today remains the preferred roofing material, but though longer lasting than others it also requires considerably greater labor; *pína* is today more common, as it is easier to lay down; women who must do the work alone often use the still-more-available *palulú* [wild banana] or *sapatí,* neither of which lasts long [and both of which Schumann lists, but without indicating uses].) Roofing materials were difficult to obtain, even in the eighteenth century; to get *tasi* in 1781, people had to go three days' distance from the village. Binding materials used in housing were the same as today's: the forest vines *sipó* and *mandú* (see Schumann).

Houses were normally divided into a front room (*sarrakassa,* today's *sákása*) and a back room (*dindruhosso,* today's *déndMuósu*), separated by a dividing wall (*mindrihosso,* a wall of unspecified dimensions but which is now built to about shoulder height). But not all houses were thus divided; Schumann also describes a *gang* (passageway?—the word is obsolete in Saramaccan), "which many negro houses have." Lacking windows, houses served, then as now, largely as places to sleep, cook, eat, and store things. The "doorstep," extending across the front wall of the house and overhung by a long gable, was the preferred spot for socializing, food preparation, sewing, and so on.

26. In July 1766, a missionary in Paramaribo reported that two of Abini's sons, "who are quiet and fine people . . . are lodging in our house," but whether Alabi was one of the visitors is unclear from the text (St 3, pt. 1, 30). For the whole eighteen-month period between the missionaries' arrival at the end of 1765 and the middle of 1767, the only "diary" I have seen is a several-page-long summary account written retrospectively by Dehne in October 1766, while recovering

Roofing a new house in 1967

his health in Paramaribo (St 3, pt. 1, 23). After the *awainza* description and Jones's death, Dehne gives precious little detail about anything, at least in the version available to me (ibid.).

27. This account of Abini's formally presenting Alabi to the Moravians may well be part of missionary apocrypha. Christian Saramakas today maintain a similar tradition orally: that before going off to battle in 1766 (where he was, in fact, killed), Abini called Alabi to him and formally gave him the responsibility of looking after the missionaries, should anything happen to him. And other Saramakas maintain a related tradition (with several variants): that Abini's mother Yaya (who was during the wars the medium of a great fighting god, and later the "prophet" of peace—see Chapter 1, passed on to Alabi a Bible given her by the Moravians; or, in a version that fits better with the events of 1771, that Yaya persuaded other (angry) Saramakas to permit Alabi to accept "the book" from the missionaries. In any case, it was in her honor that the Moravian hospital at the Djumu Mission, which opened in the 1960s, was officially named the Jaja Dande Hospital.

Four: The Whole Land Shook

Sources for this chapter, in approximate order of use, include: for the Abini/Stoll letter, Hof 74, 2 Nov. 1766; for the Court's expedition plans, Hof 74, 24 Oct. 1766; for missionary descriptions of Musinga's Saron visit, St 3, pt. 1, 38, 46; for Musinga's testimony, SvS 333, 16 Nov. 1767; for Frick's confirming letter, Hof 74, 20 Oct. 1766; for Musinga's raid, Hof 166, 3–5 Oct. 1766; for the size of Dörig's commando and for all of the incidents described by Dörig during his expedition with Abini, SvS 331, 28 Mar. 1767; for the period that includes Abini's funeral (for which I have not seen missionary diaries), I rely on funeral descriptions elsewhere in the diaries (as well as on modern oral accounts and discussions about ritual details in the past); for the *nyanyantue* quotations, St 3, pt. 1, 184–85; cf. St 3, pt. 2, 125; for the corpse-carrying quotation, St 3, pt. 2, 55; for internal politics surrounding Abini's succession, I rely largely on oral accounts; for Dehne's characterization of Alabi, St 3, pt. 1, 77; for Alabi's gifts from Dörig, SvS 331, 28 Mar. 1767 [6 Mar. 1767]; for Alabi's Paramaribo trip, St 3, pt. 1, 49, 76–77; for Alabi's rivalry with Samsam, SvS 332, 20 June 1767; for Samsam and Etja's interventions regarding Musinga, SvS 332, 18 July 1767; for Alabi's "sitting-down" (besides the very rich oral sources), SvS 331, 28 Mar. 1767, and R. Price 1983a, 96–97, 119; for the abandoning of Sentea, St 3, pt. 1, 139, 80–81; for the schoolboys' joining the Moravians, St 3, pt. 1, 84–87, 89; for Skipio's abortive *obia,* St 3, pt. 1, 132; for Skipio's progress, St 3, pt. 1, 90; for missionary hopes, St 3, pt. 1, 90, 92–93; for the Moravians' "unpleasant situation," Holmes 1818, 276; for Stoll and Nitschmann on same, St 3, pt. 1, 75, 83–84; for the year-end report, Holmes 1818, 276; for Brother Rudolph's encounter with Samsam, St 3, pt. 1, 80; for the trunk pilferage, St 3, pt. 1, 88–89; for Thoni's activities, St 3, pt. 1, 89;

for theft from whitefolks, St 3, pt. 2, 54; for Stedman's Paramaribo melee, 1988, 181–82; for Adjagbo's Paramaribo scrape, SvS 206, 8–12 Sept. 1768; for Alabi's New Year's return, Hof 79 (see figure, p. 96 [Etja's son's letter]), St 3, pt. 1, 91; for Sister Kersten's description, *PA* 2:95; for Brother Kersten's version, St 3, pt. 1, 130–32; for Abini's "second funeral" at Baakawata, I rely on nonspecific missionary, post-holder, and oral sources, as well as rich ethnographic experience, since I have not seen missionary diaries from February to December 1769, and the postholder's reports for the period are concerned exclusively with Dörig's stay in Matawai (Hof 79, 2 May 1769); for the Matawai peace negotiations, SvS 332, 18 July 1767, SvS 333, 16 Nov. 1767, SvS 206, 20 July 1768, 11 Sept. 1768, 24–25 Apr. 1769, 28 Dec. 1770, Hof 81, 1 Feb. 1770, St 3, pt. 1, 117, 99, Wolbers 1861, 286; for Boterbalie and its aftermath, SvS 206, 11 Dec. 1770, SvS 163, 16 Jan. 1771, 22 Feb. 1771, St 3, pt. 1, 120–21, R. Price 1983a, 150–52, SvS 165, 6 July 1773, SvS 207, 3 July 1773; for developing Alabi-Musinga relations, Hof 166, 11–15 Sept. 1769; for the Moravian assessment of Alabi's spiritual state, St 3, pt. 1, 134–35.

1. A 1764 letter from Postholder's Assistant Hintze contained a plea from Musinga to the Court to permit him normal passage by this route (SvS 321, 9 Jan. 1764).

2. A letter from the former Djuka postholder, Sergeant Frick, provides a confirming hearsay report that Musinga and Planteau had indeed had some very angry words that day (Hof 74, 21 Oct. 1766). Note that it was common practice, when a planter felt threatened by Maroon attack, to arm his slaves in defense of the plantation.

3. Kinke seems to have been Alabi's half-brother, with a different mother.

4. Today, Saramakas recounting Abini's death display uncertainty about its precise circumstances, reflecting their difficulty in accepting the fact of Abini's vulnerability. Awana captain Gome's account is emblematic:

> *Alabi's father didn't go to Matawai expecting to do battle! The thing those Matawais did! As soon as he arrived, they started to fight. Well, the Saramakas hadn't gone ritually prepared. If they had been "prepared," do you think that the Matawais could have killed Abini? Abini was an* obiama. *Yet they killed him.*

A Matjau claimed, further, that "Abini arrived in the midst of a big *obia* 'play.' *Atiama* [the Matawai war *obia*] had warned them of the approach of whitefolks. So they were ready. They killed Abini at once."

5. More than two hundred years later, Tribal Chief Agbagó told me how, as a young man, he had once requested permission from the Matawai headcaptain to cut some timber in Matawai territory, not far from this very spot:

Headcaptain Kín of Matawai asked me angrily, "Whatever gave you the idea that you might be allowed to work in our part of the forest?" I answered, "Someone of mine is buried here. No one has the right to expel me from here. This land is mine. They killed and buried me here. Anything I want to do on this river [i.e., in this area] I can do!" The captain consented.

6. During the twentieth century, at least, three gunshots only are used to announce the arrival of the hair and nails of a man who has died while far from home (which, today, almost always means on the coast). It is said that firing more such salutes at that moment (as would be normal for a death in which the corpse is physically present in the village) risks calling down further deaths.

7. Here is another *nyanyantue* description, taken from a May 1781 diary entry:

On the 11th and 12th, a heathen feast was again begun, which happens often. They bring the deceased food and drink and beg him never to return to do evil to them. Whenever someone gets sick or dies, it is their belief that it was caused by sorcery or by the malice of a dead person. Recently, one of our female neighbors was stung by a wasp, and immediately the blame was placed on an aunt [or female cousin] who had died the previous year. (St 3, pt. 2, 50)

8. This type of communal hunting, done solely for ancestral feasts, exposed Saramakas not only to far richer hunting grounds than existed closer to the villages but also to the special dangers of the forest. For this reason, the women were never left alone in the camp during the day, for fear of attacks from jaguars; and for the same reason, the carefully trained and ritually prepared dogs that were so much a part of normal Saramaka hunting were never brought to such isolated spots. Such hunting also tended to be selective (though game prohibited for use in the feast itself could be served to villagers and their guests). Of the thirty-three game species (edible fauna, not counting fish or birds) that the missionaries happen to mention as being hunted by eighteenth-century Saramakas, twenty-five are today prohibited from use in *nyanyantue*s, for diverse symbolic reasons—all "animals of above" (the various monkeys and sloths), the anteaters, the armadillos, and the large lizards, as well as others that were (and are) much appreciated for normal meals. In addition, Abini's personal and idiosyncratic food prohibitions (which would have been numerous for a senior chief), would have been scrupulously respected. The season would have influenced the availability of various game as well: for example, tapirs, the largest of forest animals, would have been avoided for Abini's feast because by January or February they are so thin that their meat turns dark and

unpleasant-tasting (they begin to fatten only in March or April when the palm fruit that they feed on gets ripe); the two kinds of peccary are far rarer in the early months of the year than in the Long Dry Season (August–October); and so on. Indeed, given that it fell at the beginning of the Short Dry Season, the hunting for Abini's feast probably produced more fish and birds than large land animals. (For a more general discussion of eighteenth-century Saramaka hunting and fishing, including details on their already deep knowledge of their forest environment, see R. Price 1990.)

From a Saramaka perspective, hunting involves delicate spiritual relations between people and animals, and between animals and the gods who live in particular stretches of the forest. During the late eighteenth century, as today, the shrine of the "great *obia*" of the Dombi clan, Mafúngu, was the focus of special ritual for hunters. (Mafungu priests are responsible for purifying the forest throughout Saramaka territory from the pollution of deaths that occur in it [that is, deaths outside of villages and not on the river], and it is they who know the secrets of locating people who have become lost in the forest.) In 1792, Brother Randt witnessed a sacrifice to Mafungu, in the Dombi village:

> **To be sure, idolatry is pursued with especial vigor at this place, which is why I was forced to remain here an entire day. . . . My canoemen wished to make sacrifices, which they did in public. They cooked a tapir and a rabbit which they had shot, and presented them to their idols. The priest, who is the father of one of my canoemen . . . took the meat, cut it in small pieces, and placed it before the three idols which stood side-by-side, saying, "Look, here is the head of an animal we have shot. We give it to you! Here also is the heart and liver and lungs. All of this we give you. Do you see and hear this? Now you must assure that our people return safely from the hunt and that no wild animal kills our dogs." The people shouted out, "Yes. Yes. This you must do!" As soon as the priest had finished, the people started their meal, and they all ate the meat with great gusto, leaving the idols only the bones, which were then carried off by the dogs. (St 3, pt. 3, 47–48; cf. St 3, pt. 2, 139, as well as Riemer [1801, 281–82 = St 3, pt. 2, 274], who plagiarized this passage from Randt, claiming the experience as his own)**

9. Although rapid religious syncretisms among slaves of diverse African provenance were an earmark of colonial Suriname's first hundred years, rituals and other performances associated with Papa, Nago, Loango, Púmbu, Komanti, and other African "nations" (as they were often called in Afro-America) were still an important feature of late eighteenth-century life, among both Saramakas and plantation slaves. On Suriname plantations during this period, about 70 percent of slaves were still African-born, with some 35 percent having arrived

during the previous ten years (R. Price 1976), so the periodic assertion of African ethnicity hardly seems surprising in that setting. (A Moravian missionary in Paramaribo, describing slaves in 1745, noted that "since they do not all belong to one nation but to several, their [native] languages differ one from another. In Suriname they must all speak Negro-English in order to communicate among themselves. However, when they perform their idol worship, for example during funerals, each nation conducts it in its own native language" [St 1:91].) By the 1760s among the Saramaka, "Papa," "Luangu" or "Komanti" rites and dances would have included people and ideas of quite varied (and mixed) African ancestry. Few African-born Saramakas were still alive, and Saramaka marriage was in no sense endogamous according to place of African ancestors' origin. Nevertheless, bundles of rites or drums/dances/songs/language, which had their origin in particular African ethnicities, were kept together by eighteenth-century Saramakas (as they still are today). That is, a young Saramaka in 1760—who might well be a fourth generation Afro-Surinamer (as was Alabi, on his father's side), having, say, great-grandparents who hailed from as many as eight different African groups—would learn the bundle of "Papa" or "Komanti" or "Nago" rites not because he *was* a Dahomean or Gold Coaster or Yoruba "by origin" but because of the particular meanings and uses these rites had taken on in contemporary Saramaka life. All Saramakas, then as today, participated to some extent in all such rites, but the responsibility for keeping each bundle discrete and alive fell on its chosen adepts. And these specialists never held a strictly preservationist ethic: gradual change and creativity has always been central to Saramaka ritual, so that the *papa* drumming of one generation is modified (Saramakas would say improved) by the experts of the next. (See for further discussion, S. and R. Price 1980, Mintz and Price 1976.)

10. Saramakas have (and, by the mid-eighteenth century, had) well-elaborated beliefs and rites having to do with *neseki*s. After death, a person's *akáa* (the separable aspect of the "soul") leaves the body and, if there has been a proper burial, eventually serves as the "supernatural genitor" (*neseki*) in the conception of one or more new children. Every person has a *neseki* (almost always an ancestor but occasionally a deceased hunting dog or even a forest spirit) who, like the mother and father, contributes at the moment of conception to that person's fundamental character (see R. Price 1975, 51–52). The death of a person with whom one shares a *neseki* places a person in grave danger, and, until the "second funeral," many sorts of protective rites occur to assure that the deceased does not carry off the living *neseki*-sharer. The general notion of *neseki* was brought to Suriname by the African ancestors of the Saramaka; it is widespread from West Africa into the Kongo (see, for example, Lucas 1945, 245, 258, and Vass 1979, 35). It also played an active role in the life of eighteenth-century Suriname slaves (see, for example, van Dyk n.d.,

246–47). Brother Riemer, on the basis of his 1779/80 stay, alluded to Saramaka *neseki* beliefs without, however, mentioning the term; he also seems to have confused the concept with literal name-sharing:

> It should be noted that the free negroes hold the belief that their souls do not die with them but live on in another body, a kind of transmigration of souls. (St 3, pt. 2, 283)

> The negroes believe that the soul of the departed immediately incorporates itself into the fruit of the pregnant relative who will be next to give birth. Because of this it is not surprising that some men have women's names and some girls have men's names. Such a situation occurred here. The wife of the captain [Sialôto, Alabi's wife] bore a boy soon after the burial of its grandmother [Akoomi], and this woman had—since early childhood—been a faithful pupil of this Grang-Mama. The boy bore the name of this grandmother until he was baptized together with his mother, who was the first negro woman who was converted to Christianity. (Riemer 1801, 300; see also Schumann 1778, s.v. *nem*)

11. Saramakas believed that such "unusual" deaths posed acute dangers to the whole community. The missionaries twice mention, for example, Saramaka concerns regarding death by drowning, and its accompanying special ceremonies.

> On the third of November [1784], some heathen negroes came back from Paramaribo. Since one of them had drowned on the way and they were unable to find the corpse (and since, according to their beliefs, a soul which does not have a funeral cannot find rest), on the 4th and 5th they decided to take part in all kinds of sorcery. For this, they made a small coffin and, accompanied by many different kinds of ceremonies, the soul was summoned and placed in the coffin, and the burial was accomplished. (St 3, pt. 2, 82–83)

> On the second of September [1788], there was a great commotion here because an important conjurer had been summoned to perform with all his magic paraphernalia for a pregnant woman who had fallen into the river and drowned. (St 3, pt. 2, 135)

The few details in these descriptions, such as summoning the soul of an unfound corpse for special burial in a tiny coffin or the implied special danger of death during pregnancy (the most ritually polluting of all deaths in the twentieth century) only hint at the complex ritual activities that must actually have taken place. In the twentieth century, the corpse of a drowned person who dies anywhere in Saramaka is sought by ritual specialists from the Nasi (or, more rarely, Abaisa) clan, who cruise the appropriate stretch of river, carrying a finished coffin in their canoe, along with their *obia* paraphernalia. If found, the corpse is ritually prepared and buried not in a normal cemetery but in the riverbank, close to where it was discovered. If the *obia* fails to locate the corpse, the soul of the deceased is summoned to a special coffin back in the village, much as in eighteenth-century descriptions. Today, women anywhere in Saramaka who die while pregnant are buried with complex rites supervised by the priest of the Abaisa "great *obia,*" Bòòfángu.

Likewise, the death of a Saramaka man in whitefolks' territory (*bakáa kôndè*) on the coast—an event that was to become far more frequent by the turn of the twentieth century—had already become ritually routinized.

> **On the first of June [1785], news arrived from Paramaribo that a local negro [from here] had died, and immediately the death-shrieks rang out. The usual funeral ceremonies took place but with an empty coffin. Most of our baptized people played some part in it, causing us to call them together and tell them that we could not hold Holy Communion with them. They were sinful and promised not to do this in the future. (St 3, pt. 2, 84–85)**

This coffin may or may not in fact have been "empty." If it did not contain the hair and nails of the deceased, sent upriver from the city, it would—as in the drowning death already mentioned—have contained the man's "soul," summoned for proper burial by a ritual specialist (who would have called it into a calabash from the depths of the Suriname River). In present times, when a man dies on the coast, clippings of his hair and nails are normally sent back to Saramaka in a little metal trunk along with the message of death. There is a rigid prohibition against bringing a corpse back from whitefolks' territory: "Dead people can't be brought over Mamadan Falls," says the aphorism. As the canoe passes the villages strung along the river, the men accompanying the remains fire salutes, and, if they are answered (for example, if the deceased had kinfolk there), the men go ashore for a spontaneous "play" in his honor. (If they reach the deceased's father's matrilineal village [his *táta kôndè*] before reaching his own [matrilineal] village [his *máma kôndè*], the hair and nails are placed in a special narrow coffin, 5–6 feet long but less than a foot wide, at that time, for transport upriver. If they reach his own village first, there are three lone gunshots and a "play," and the miniature coffin is made there.) After a week-long funeral (always at the man's own village), the coffin is buried in a special shallow grave. Numerous other symbolic markers distinguish such a funeral from a normal one today—from the opening libations, which are poured from a bottle (rather than a clay jug) in front of the deceased's house (rather than at the ancestor shrine), to the construction of the special grave, done in one day (rather than the usual week or more).

Special rites are performed as well for people who have died in another especially dangerous environment, the forest (e.g., in a horticultural or hunting accident). Under the supervision of Mafungu *obia*-men from the Dombi clan, the corpse is placed in a flat (or only

Divination with a hair-and-nails coffin among the nineteenth-century Alúku Maroons. Engraving by Ch. Barbant, after a sketch by Jules Crevaux (Crevaux 1880, 36).

slightly gabled) coffin for a much smaller than usual funeral in the village. After the closing feast for the ancestors (the *báka nyanyán*) a week later, the Mafungu *obia* specialists perform rites to purify the village. In such cases, there is never a "second funeral," and the Mafungu specialists must ritually "smoke" the forest before people may resume their normal gardening and hunting activities.

12. The missionaries, in an account of a routine funeral, described how, as an alternative to carrying the coffin, divination was conducted with the hair-and-nail packet; indeed, they wrote with considerable distaste of this "spectacle with the hair" (St 3, pt. 2, 128). Such alternation continues to be an ordinary part of twentieth-century Saramaka funerals.

13. Brother Riemer provided a more generalized description of Saramaka coffin-carrying that suggests both how little the Moravians really understood of the rituals they witnessed and the extent to which they, as eighteenth-century Europeans, shared certain "supernatural" beliefs with Saramakas. Riemer is convinced that the credulous Saramakas are being "fooled" by their *obia*-men (a deception that he, as a person of superior intelligence, can easily perceive); yet at the same time he appears to believe in the spirit's power to move the coffin, seeing the "deception" largely as a matter of "tricky questioning."

The coffin is carried on the heads of two negroes to the dwelling of the deceased. There the witch doctor addresses the deceased in the presence of a crowd of people, asking, "Have you died by one or another accident? Did the Great God kill you? Did the evil gods kill you? Did the spirits of the dead kill you?" and other such questions. After each question, the observers watch to see if the coffin has moved, as such movement signifies an affirmative response. If, however, after these preliminary questions, no answer has been received, the Obia man continues his questioning: "Did someone kill you by poisoning [sorcery]?" Usually, the coffin does make some movement at this point. If this is the case, further questions are posed to determine in which village the evildoer may be found. If this is learned, then the names of all the inhabitants of that village are immediately called, and when a movement of the coffin is seen, that person whose name has been called is responsible. Even if these questions were to be repeated often for confirmation, it is easy to see that the witch doctor already has inklings of who the guilty party is and can tailor his oracular incantations accordingly. But how easy it is to make an innocent person appear to be guilty, and how easy it is for the Obia man to judge according to his passions! Such possibilities are never taken into consideration. The evildoer who is discovered during these ceremonies is immediately seized and placed in fetters. (St 3, pt. 2, 266–67)

The acceptance of the power of the dead to move the coffin would not have been unusual for a European Christian. Indeed, a twentieth-century Roman Catholic missionary to the Saramakas described coffin divination in negative terms rather like those of Riemer, but attributed the coffin's actual movements not to the soul of the deceased but rather to Satan (Donicie 1948, 180–81). (Similarly, Ariès describes an incident involving the corpse of St. Vaast, who died in A.D. 540: "When the pallbearers tried to carry him away [for burial, outside the city] they could not move the corpse, which had suddenly become too heavy. Then the archpriest begged the saint . . . [and] the body at once became light" [1974, 17].) Routine coffin divination after every death, widespread in West and Central Africa, was one of the most broadly distributed "Africanisms" in colonial Afro-America (Mintz and Price 1976, 28).

14. One afternoon would have been devoted to the coffin's distributing Abini's material legacy—his houses, guns, tools, canoe, and so on—among his close matrilineal kin.

15. During the month of February, Dörig and his troops, plus some reinforcements, remained encamped downstream from the Saramaka villages. On the twenty-fifth, Dörig sent a commando to destroy Musinga's gardens, but it was repulsed and suffered eight casualties. Three Saramakas were involved as "guides" or "scouts" for Dörig's troops and seem purposefully to have led them into ambush.

After the senior Saramaka chiefs had firmly but gently made it clear to Dörig that they would not cooperate in such efforts against the Matawai, he left with his troops in March for the city. (See SvS 28 Mar. 1767.)

16. In terms of kinship, residence, and authority, it is clear that Saramaka society, as described by mid-eighteenth-century missionaries and postholders, was already organized according to the matrilineal principles that operate today (R. Price 1975). However, these chroniclers provide little generalized description of political succession itself. The earliest normative account dates from 1828, when a postholder wrote:

> **At the death of a Chief-over-All, his surviving sons do not succeed him, but rather the firstborn son of his oldest sister. ... The same thing occurs upon the death of the other chiefs [captains], that is, [the position] goes to a male descendant of a sister. (van Eyck 1828, 11–12)**

A careful examination of a number of cases of captains' succession from the second half of the eighteenth century suggests that this pattern was by that time already in place. Yet it is important to stress that Saramaka matriliny, then as now, involved a lively tension between "paternal" and "matrilineal" sentiments.

The emergence of the institutions of political leadership—including the offices of *gaama, kabiteni,* and *basia*—are unevenly documented in the historical record. The terms used by Saramakas for these three offices are most likely borrowed from colonial sources: *gaama* from the Sranan word for (colonial) governor; *kabiteni* from Dutch *burger-kapitein* (a district military officer), though a Middle Passage nautical derivation cannot be ruled out; and *basia* from Dutch *bastiaan* and Sranan *basya* (black driver or overseer on the plantations). But it would certainly be an error to assume that these offices were largely imposed from the outside. If the treaty served to firm up or solidify the political positions of those chiefs who were now recognized as *kabiteni* by the colonial government, there was nevertheless nothing like the degree of internal political change that occurred after the signing of similar treaties in Jamaica (Kopytoff 1976). Rather, I would argue that in Saramaka, formalized political offices corresponding to chief-over-all, headman, and *basia* (the latter of which was never recognized by the colonial government during the eighteenth century) existed from early runaway times, based firmly on African models of leadership, and that the treaty simply added to them an extra measure of authority. Before the treaty, Saramaka political office was already deeply bound up with notions of sacred authority, what Africanists call "mystical values." Officeholders had special, ritually powerful stools and staffs (*basias* had only staffs), and all underwent complex ceremonies of installation. Among the literally scores of indications of the noncolonial nature of these offices, I might mention the immense aura of sacredness surrounding all activities of the *gaama*, his numerous African-style honorific titles, his power to cure illness by the laying on of hands, his personal drummer who comments in drum language on his public activities, the lengthy rituals of installation and enstoolment as well as the extraordinary rites surrounding his death and burial. Or, for a *kabiteni*, the several-week-long installation ceremonies, with visits to specific shrines and sites, complex enstoolment rites, including the designation of a *"kabiteni's* wife" (not his secular wife), who is ritually enstooled with him, and his "mystical" powers in healing. Or, for a *basia,* a similar complex of installation rites, "mystical" properties attributed to his *mása-wípi* staff, his role as village crier (see Chapter 3, note 17), and so forth. Postholder van Eyck's early nineteenth-century comment that *kabiteni*s stored their uniforms in their "idolatry-houses" (shrines) may be the earliest direct recognition by whitefolks of the sacred associations of political leadership among Saramakas (1828, 11), but these associations date from the beginnings of the society and are strongly African in form and feeling.

As regards political succession, a captain's or *basia's* staff should be understood first and foremost as a corporate possession, owned by groups (*lôs*) that, by the mid-eighteenth century, thought of themselves in matrilineal terms. However, to reconstruct the meaning of *lo*-(clan-)identity in the late eighteenth century—what it really meant to be a Matjau or a Nasi person—requires a complex effort of the imagination, holding simultaneously in mind a very large number of contemporaneously documented interactions and incidents while being constantly alert to the dangers of historical presentism or anachronistic inference. I have demonstrated to my own satisfaction (but will not recapitulate the massive amount of supportive detail here) that most of the *lo*-identities salient in twentieth-century Saramaka were already salient two hundred years before. That is, the labels "Paputu," "Abaisa," "Nasi," and so on were in common use during the eighteenth century to refer to social units similar to those of today. Nevertheless, it is important to keep in mind that, for example, the Matjaus or Dombis, while deriving their respective common identity from a combination of putative plantation origins and putative matrilineal kinship, were strongly differentiated internally. Indeed, the kinds of intra-*lo* divisions that today derive from matrilineal segmentation were, in the eighteenth century (when some *lo*s had not yet had time or genealogical depth for such segmentation to occur), often derived (at least in part) from subgroups having different plantation or African origins or different times and circumstances of arrival in Saramaka. With the passage of time, such initial internal divisions generally disappeared, to be replaced by divisions based on internal genealogical segmentation within the broader *lo*. The emergence of a system vertebrated by descent ideology makes what was a somewhat messy social reality appear, when viewed retrospectively, to have been relatively orderly and systematic. So, for example, Alabi's "Awana" *lo* actually consisted, during the second half of the eigh-

teenth century, of several subgroups, of different orders of magni-
tude: Tobiási-nêngè (descendants of the slaves who escaped from
the plantation owned by Massa Tobiasi, and others who joined them
early on), who considered themselves the Awanas proper; the Bákapáu group, who got this name during the late 1760s but who were the
descendants of slaves from Plantation Toutluy Faut who had escaped
and traveled with the Tobiasi-nenge; the Íngi-písi people, the late-
arriving "Indian" relatives of Kodjo Maata; and the children of Alabi
and Sialoto, whose matrilineal descendants during the nineteenth
century became known as Agbós. For Saramakas who did not belong
to this agglomeration, all these people were considered, for most
practical purposes, to be Awanas. Likewise, what for most purposes
was considered from the outside to be the "Langu" *lo* was divided
(residentially and politically) into Kaapátu, Kadósu, and, for much of
the century, the people who eventually became the independent *lo*
known as Kwamá. And so on. (For ethnohistorical details, see R. Price
1983a; for some theoretical considerations relating to the origins of
matriliny among Maroons—a subject which no one has adequately
treated to date—see Mintz and Price 1976, 35–36, and Hoogbergen
1985, 416–28.)

In regard to these complexities, I consider my primary responsibility throughout this book to consider, at each moment, which of
these identities would have been salient—and above all to avoid pro-
jecting backwards identities and unities that would not yet have come
into play.

17. During the roughly two-year period in which Akoomi remained
under the care of her affines in Baakawata, she had to display her
special status in various ways: as soon as she arrived in the village,
she was settled into one of Abini's houses there, given a "cape" of his
to wear (which she would do until it was little more than a rag), and,
after her head was shaved, given a mourning band made from an old
cloth to wear around her head. She was forbidden to set foot out of
the house until the sun "had fallen on the earth" of the village each
morning, nor could she be out after sunset. One of Abini's sisters
accompanied her to the river to wash each day. Back in Sentea, the
women's (nonwarrior) part of the shrine of Madanfo, for which she
was priestess, and those of any other gods she may have had in her
head, had been ritually closed for the duration of the mourning period,
by being "boarded up" with sticks of the *malêmbèlêmbè* plant. In
Baakawata, she was treated as if she were menstruating—polluted
and polluting, unable, for example, to hand any object to a man or
even to speak to certain men who had strong *obia*s. For the first
weeks, Abini's kinfolk brought her food each day. After that, they
permitted her to cook for herself and, eventually, to accompany them
to their gardens and participate in horticultural work. Likewise, with
time, they gave her greater freedom to visit around the village. Once
or twice during the mourning period, she was permitted to return
briefly to Sentea (and, when that village was abandoned, Kwama),

accompanied by her affines. But it was only after Abini's "second funeral," and the special rites performed to purify her, that Akoomi could return to her normal status as one of the most respected women, and major ritual specialists, in the Saramaka nation.

18. Throughout the period that the hair-and-nails packet hung in Abini's house, the village elders of Baakawata could consult it on any current matter of concern, whether the cause of someone's illness or a decision about moving a horticultural camp. Abini's spirit would have easy access to the other ancestors; and, as a "familiar," his relatives could ask special favors of him.

19. Samsam had been given identical gifts by Dörig on 12 January 1767, soon after Abini's death. At that time, Dörig made it clear that "their Excellencies the Honorable Chartered Society of Suriname" had sent these equivalent gift sets for the two most important chiefs, Abini and Samsam, "with the earnest resolution that they would see that the Peace is kept" (SvS 331, 28 Mar. 1767 [12 Jan. 1767]). See also the final page of Chapter 3.

20. The missionaries described another departure for Paramaribo in 1774.

> On the 23rd [June], when Kodjo prepared to go to Paramaribo with most of the villagers, the women summoned their gods. This took place with a great deal of drumming and shouting after which they made noise the entire night. Finally, Kodjo's wife became inspired [possessed]. She is the oldest sister of Johannes [Alabi], and she shouted terribly and made the most wondersome gestures. (St 3, pt. 1, 230)

It seems worth stressing that these late eighteenth-century trips were the direct successors of the immensely dangerous coastal raids that, for nearly a century, had been the focus of Saramaka war magic and the source of all guns, powder, tools, and other products necessary for survival during the period. With the coming of peace, Saramaka perceptions of the coast changed but gradually. A trading trip meant, in addition to the very real risks of river travel, entering the world of the enemy, where slavery was a ubiquitous reality. At military posts along the river, rudeness and threats were common, and a drunk soldier could easily fire shots at passing Saramakas for sport. In Paramaribo, as well as at the plantations where they had to sleep, Saramakas often met hostility and had to witness the barbarous tortures inflicted on slaves. Among the men traveling with Alabi to Paramaribo were elders who had themselves faced whitefolks along the barrel of a gun or at the wrong end of a whip.

Two hundred years later, at a time when one could reach the capital by a one-hour flight by light plane, Alabi's descendants still prepared for their trips to the coast—where they might work for a year or two as carpenters at the French Guiana space center or as day laborers for Alcoa—with complex protective rites. Ancestors, village deities, and "great obias," as well as visits to special shrines in other villages, each played a role in such preparations, which I witnessed many times in the 1960s and 1970s.

21. Some modern oral accounts of these events also place Alabi at Tutu Creek and Langa Amana with other members of his family, rather than alone.

22. A large number of archival references, dating from 1765 to 1785, list (Dondo) Kasa as the Dombi captain. These same sources indicate that, by 1780, he began occasionally to send Dóndo Ainsá (called by the whites "Heinza") to council meetings in his stead. The modern Dombis with whom I discussed eighteenth-century affairs insisted that their first post-treaty captain, Masiá, was soon succeeded by Djánti Kunduku (whom they depict as a very close friend of Alabi who, eventually, became Alabi's sister's [or sister's daughter's] husband) and was himself succeeded by Dondo Ainsa. At the same time, these Dombis insisted that Dondo Kasa was never a captain. (See also Chapter 7, note 41.)

23. The stress in these stories on Alabi's relative youth, at the time of the promise that he would one day become tribal chief, is reinforced by a remark the postholder made six years later, when he characterized Alabi as "young, well-intentioned, and shy of speech" (Hof 87, 4 Mar. 1773).

24. I have heard a number of accounts from modern Saramakas of the reasons for particular eighteenth-century village moves. I offer three examples of this distinctive type of discourse. The first two concern the move of a large Matjau village in Baakawata to nearby Pási Creek on the Upper Pikilio ca. 1770. The third concerns the mid-1770s move of the Dombi segment then led by the great *obiama* Kungooka and living (briefly) on Kudébaku Creek on the Gaanlio to the area around present-day Daume. (For additional examples and discussion, see Chapter 5 for the move from Kwama to Gwafu Bambey, and Chapter 8 for the move from Gwafu Bambey to Waná Bambey.)

> [Tebini:] The Awana person did the thing that "broke the village" [caused its abandonment]. . . . [R.P.:] What happened? [Tebini:] There was a certain place. People did not go there. There was something there. And they killed the thing. [R.P.:] Who killed it? [Tebini:] Dákwama. An Awana person. And they [the Matjaus] encountered misfortune until finally they had to flee. That's what "broke" Baakawata. Abini was already gaama. He lived in Sentea [with his wife's people, the Awanas]. There was a bird that "owned" that place. You could not kill it. And then they killed it. Andole [the kind of bird]. It was like the fowl of that place. . . . The Awana person brought the ruin of that village. Abini's own wife's people! That was Dakwama. So they went to live at Pasi Creek on the mother river [the Pikilio].

> [Peleki:] The taboo of the place. You must not kill the Andole. You can see it but you can't shoot it. [R.P.:] Was it

*a god or a bird? [Peleki:] The god-whose-place-it-was, it
was his bird, his taboo-thing. [R.P.:] So the Awana person
came along. [Peleki:] And killed the* Andole. *That's why
they had to leave there. Well, the* Andole. *It was the man
called Dakwama who killed it. Well, when he'd killed
it, he brought it [to the village]. And everyone said,
"Woooooo! So you killed the* Andole? *Well, it was not to
be killed." Then he took the [dead]* Andole *and tossed
it down. They slept till morning. Then they awoke. There
was another* Andole *on the ground there. Well, the day
before he'd killed an* Andole. *Now in the morning they see
two. So they threw the two of them away. The next morning
they see four. They tossed them away. The next day they
find five. Right on the ground there, dead. So it became a
big thing. Every time they tossed them away, the next day
there'd be more. So they were afraid. Misfortune had come.
They said [to one another] "Some thing will come out of
the forest to eat us!" So they fled. They moved their village.
But it was the Awana person who caused it.*

*[Peleki:] The creek [Kudebaku] didn't like Kungooka
to use* kusuwé *[Bixa orellana, roucou, annatto—a red* obia
ingredient]. When he mixed his obia *there. It reminded
the [god of the] creek of blood. Divination told them that.
The* apuku *was afraid of war. So they had to leave.*

25. The new village of Kwama was a five- or six-hour walk from
Sentea, and some six hours from the river (see map 3, p. 143).
"Kwama" was a common Saramaka creek name: several contempo-
raneous Langu villages were on a branch of Agamadja called Kwama
(R. Price 1983b, 166), and the original name of what became known as
Tutu Creek—in the Middle River region where many of Alabi's Awana
descendants still live—was Siliê (which Captain Gome explained was
the "Indian" name for *kwama* [bamboo]).

26. As one scholar has written of eighteenth-century Moravian
missionaries more generally, "schooling was not a priority" for them
but, rather, a tool in proselytization. Indeed, when the missionaries in
the Danish Virgin Islands realized that schooling, rather than religion,
was the slaves' main motive for approaching them, they abruptly
ended such instruction (Rupp-Eisenreich 1985, 132, 144). Similar conflicts occurred between Moravians and Cherokees, with the latter
insisting on schooling without religion (McLoughlin 1984, 43, 53).

27. The ritual use of kaolin (Saramaccan *keéti*), a chalky clay often
applied to the body in solution, or the red dye made from annatto
(Saramaccan *kusuwe*)—both used by Saramakas in a variety of rites—
was an important symbolic marker for the Moravians throughout the
history of the mission. In 1788, for example, a convert described to
one of the missionaries how

his mother-in-law, a heathen, had bedaubed his children with paint, to prevent their going to church: for as painting is considered by the free-negroes as an Obia, or charm, those who come painted to the church, are refused admittance, till they have washed themselves. However the old woman did not quite obtain her end; for the two smallest children washed the paint off the same day, and came to the children's meeting. We took this opportunity to tell them, that in these things they were not bound to obey man; and that the next time she offered to treat them in the same way, they should tell her, that they were determined to be children of god and not to serve Satan. (PA 3:50–51)

28. The missionaries report almost continual tests of these schoolboys' faith, with equivocal results.

On the 31st [March 1770], our lads witnessed a spectacle and thus missed the evening service. When they came home [they were boarding with the missionaries] Grego said, "My heart kept telling me to come home, and had I obeyed I would not have missed the service." Our lads said they had only wanted to tell their brothers and sisters about Jesus but the other people just laughed at them. We reproved them and told them to think of the Savior and how much shame he had endured on our behalf. (St 3, pt. 1, 134)

On the 23rd [December 1770] the people here became very excited because of a woman who had just received her Gado. Our Grego went there in order to see what was happening but soon returned and said that his heart had been struck sorry by his act. This gave us the opportunity to give him a sincere reproach. (St 3, pt. 1, 142)

On the 2nd of July [1770], many people went to an entertainment in Siroboeka. They asked Arrabini and also our schoolboy Skipio to go with them but were unable to persuade them. We all held a blessed evening service together. (St 3, pt. 1, 139–40)

On the 28th [October 1775] a large group of people returned from Siroboeka where they had gone to repair [renew] their gods. Our Christian [Grego] was standing by the side of the path and they called out to him to bow down, so the Gado could pass by. But he replied, "Go ahead and pass; I have nothing to do with your Gado." (St 3, pt. 1, 243)

29. As the missionaries' lifeline to the city, those Saramakas who carried their supplies were in a strong position of control and frequently took advantage of the missionaries' dependence. Brother Stoll's passivity, when Samsam's people broke into the chests they were carrying for him, was a characteristic Moravian response. Indeed, his colleague Brother Dehne, commenting on the incident,

expressed resigned satisfaction about those few things that Brother Stoll had managed to rescue and bring back to Sentea.

We were very happy and thankful to our dear Lord that this affair had now reached a conclusion. Because it is remarkably difficult, once the negroes have something belonging to someone else in their hands, to get it back. (St 3, pt. 1, 80)

Saramaka rivermen often expressed their control by refusing the missionaries simple favors or by mocking them because of their dependence.

On the 3rd of November [1770], Grego [one of the Moravians' schoolboys] returned from the city. We had hoped to receive letters and congregational news with him, but he brought nothing of the kind because the negroes who controlled the canoe would not allow him to bring anything like that along. (St 3, pt. 1, 143)

[In 1767] One of the negroes who had just returned from Paramaribo said that Brother Dehne [who had gone there on a visit] had asked that he soon be picked up, and they made great fun of this. It appeared that none other than the Power of Darkness had run rampant over them, and this continued for several days. (St 3, pt. 1, 79)

One must never forget what the Saramakas were putting up with. Indeed, the missionaries were simply bearing the brunt of the generalized hostility built up in Saramakas' interactions with whitefolks. In this particular case, for example, the Saramakas who flaunted their power by threatening to deny Brother Dehne passage had themselves been badly handled.

The people who had returned complained bitterly to their friends that nothing had been given them to eat by the Court [the government] in Paramaribo. This incensed their comrades, and many strong protests and curses were uttered. I [Brother Stoll] remained silent throughout, because they were all drunk and knew not what they were saying. (St 3, pt. 1, 79)

30. Brother Riemer, who served as missionary during 1779 and 1780, summarized Moravian understandings of theft among the Saramaka.

This crime is a rarity among the Saramaka Negroes. They have a special means by which they are able to secure all their possessions, namely: Superstition. They hang across the door of their houses a piece of tyger skull, or any other part of this animal, which they consider a god. With this object, they also hang herbs, leaves, and the like. Such a talisman is called Kandu. They also use such objects at the entrances to their gardens.

They are thus insured that nobody will touch or make use of any of their property. And thus it is common, even when they are away from the village all day, that their dwellings will be left completely open. The Kandu, which hangs across the door, serves as the only guard, because each person has such great respect for those frightening effects that the Kandu can produce. (St 3, pt. 2, 264)

It is something that one hangs up or places somewhere as a sign that no one is supposed to go there or take anything. It is similar to our straw broomheads in Germany, except that the negroes have an indescribable superstitious fear of it, as they connect it with some kind of sorcery. (Schumann 1778, s.v. *Kandu*)

Kándu in fact refers to a large class of devices (tiny bows and arrows, ritually prepared bottles, herb bundles, and so on) designed to protect property (houses, fruit trees, gardens); it also refers to venereal disease, the alleged result of violating such a guard.

31. As early as March 1767, Abini's aged mother Yaya had pleaded with Postholder Dörig for a government contribution for this ceremony, and he had agreed to give "everything in his power" (SvS 331, 28 Mar. 1767).

32. Stedman, describing Paramaribo in 1774, wrote that it

is a verry lively place, the Streets being crowded with Planters, Sailors, Soldiers, Jews, Indians, and Negroes, while the river Swarms with Canoes, barges, yoals, Ships boats &c constantly going and coming from the different Estates and crossing and passing each other like the wheries on the Thames, and mostly accompanied by bands of Musick this and all the different-colour'd flags perpetually streaming in the wind, while continually some Guns are firing in the roads from the Shipping, and whole Groops of naked Girls are playing in the water like so many mermaids, can not but have a truly enchanting appearance from the beach, and in some Measure Compensates for the many Curses that one is here dayly exposed to. (1988, 236)

33. In general, Saramaka ritual was (and remains today) event-triggered, rather than calendrically regulated. That is, rites were performed when misfortunes or other unusual events required divination, which, in turn, prescribed particular rites. The Moravians were puzzled and troubled by this lack of calendrical regularity (and, hence, from their perspective, discipline) among the Saramaka,

which allows them to give reign to all their passions. They have no regular time for religious services and no day set apart for the [true] Sabbath. . . . However, in our village, Wednesdays and Thursdays—and in some other villages Fridays—are designated as "small-" and "large sabbaths." Between these "sabbaths" and normal days they make little distinction, such as that trees cannot be felled [etc.]. . . . On these [small] days, however, peo-

ple do paint themselves with Obia [actually, *keeti*], which is a white clay that the gods supposedly have infused with special powers. (St 3, pt. 1, 137)

Although Brother Riemer refuses to consider what he calls "small days" sabbaths, eighteenth-century Saramakas certainly did. However, Riemer is correct in noting that such sabbaths (Saramaccan *sabá*) are purely local. That is, there are special sabbaths (days of the week) on which a person may not cut trees or do garden work in a particular area of the forest or on a particular stretch of riverbank, and each village has one or two days on which its residents must observe particular work-related ritual restrictions. Saramaka sabbaths commemorate local events—a hunting accident that forever makes Tuesdays inappropriate for using a certain area of forest, the words of a snake god that prohibit horticulture in a certain area on Wednesdays, and so on.

Christmas (Saramaccan *Bedáki*) and New Year's (*Yáai*) were the only exceptions to this noncalendrical regulation of rituals. (For a description of the protective rituals surrounding Christmas dangers among early twentieth-century Saramakas, see Junker 1927.)

34. In rituals as well as everyday life, Saramakas pay particular attention to the specialness, and the danger, of the first time something is done, e.g., the first time a baby tastes hot pepper, the first time a widow sleeps with a new partner, the first time a girl enters the menstrual hut. The first time the *papa* men play their drums at a funeral falls into this very broad class.

35. All of the clothes and accessories mentioned in this passage appear, often with detailed descriptions, in the missionary documents or, much more rarely, in the postholders' reports. (For further discussion of Saramaka clothing through time, and comparison with eighteenth-century slave dress, see S. and R. Price 1980, 47–95, 166.)

36. On Saramaka *adjiboto* in the early twentieth century, see Herskovits 1929 and 1932.

37. *Papa* men themselves call their music *"aladá"* and their metal instrument *"gan"* (from the same Ewe word). (Grand and Little Popo in Togo were major slave shipping ports, as was neighboring Ardra or Allada.) When *komanti* men play the identical instrument, they call it *"dáulo"* (probably from Twi *adauru*). The Matjau and Abaisa clans are considered the masters of the Saramaka music of death—Abaisas as the preeminent players of *papa* itself, Matjaus as the virtuosos of *adugba* (the drums played right after *papa* at cock's crow) and *adju* (the drums that follow at full dawn to accompany the final *sangaa*-chasing of the ghost from the village). At Abini's second funeral, his own Matjau kinsmen did the honors, as their relations with Captain Samsam's Abaisas remained rocky.

In 1978, *Basia* Tandó, a Matjau who is a pretty fair *papa* player himself, recounted a neat tale to explain this division of labor and knowledge between the clans.

*Once, an Abaisa man married a Matjau woman. A Matjau
man married an Abaisa woman. They went off, all four
of them, to make a garden together. (It was on the site of
an old cemetery but they didn't know that.) In the evening,
the two Matjaus fell asleep but the Abaisas didn't. And
the dead people began to play* papa, *all night long until
cock's crow. Then the Abaisas fell asleep and the Matjaus
awoke. The dead people began to play* adugba. *Until
full dawn. Then they began the* adju. *The Abaisas slept
right through the* adju. *Which is why each clan knows what
it does.*

Today, when Matjau *papa* players like Tando are invited as specialists to play at a second funeral and are presented with the traditional
baskets full of cloths, bottles of rum, and so on, they always transfer
the baskets' contents as well as the rum to their own containers,
brought for the purpose. But when the Abaisa *papa/alada* masters
perform, it is always their prerogative, and their practice, to go home
with baskets, rum bottles, and all. (For an account of a heroic *papa*
contest between Matjaus and Abaisas that seems to have taken
place in the 1750s, see R. Price 1983a, 148–49.)

38. Pipe-smoking was ubiquitous in eighteenth-century Suriname, among both men and women and among masters, slaves, and
Saramakas, as well as among Moravian missionaries. But Saramakas
also grew tobacco for "chewing" (holding in their cheeks) and, apparently, for a method still favored among older Saramakas today: soaking pieces of leaves in water and inhaling the dark juice through each
nostril for a quick high.

39. One of the central historical events of the war years, the (ritual) shooting of Wii by Ayako's son Dabi, occurred during such a
sangaa, early on the morning of Ayako's burial day (R. Price 1983a,
167–71). Though today *sangaa*s occur only during second funerals,
they seem to have happened both on the day of burial and at second
funerals during the eighteenth century. Indeed, Johannes King's own
description of the *sangaa*s he had witnessed as a boy, during the
second quarter of the nineteenth century, referred to the celebrations
when men returned from having received whitefolks' goods as tribute—suggesting that *sangaa*s used to occur outside of funeral contexts as well.

*They fired salutes, sang, danced, blew African trumpets,
and played* sangaa *drums. And the adults would* sangaa *all
over the place. That word, "sangaa," means many people
with guns, machetes, and spears in their hands running all
over the place exactly the way that the warriors used to
fight in Africa itself, and with many war cries. And the older
men showed the youths and young girls how they had
fought with the whites and how the warriors raided and
destroyed whitefolks' plantations, carrying off people to the*

forest. While they were running around like this, they
would shoot many, many salutes, just like the [government]
soldiers do in the city square. Then many people would
shout together: "Battle! Battle! The battle's on!" And then
they would fire guns, play drums, and blow horns, like
warriors going off to raid a plantation. And if someone were
far off who didn't know about this, he would think that
a real battle was taking place on a plantation, there were so
many cries and guns shooting. And they played drums
so! When they were finished, they would bring a bush drink
that they made from sugar-cane juice, and which is called
bush rum. They would pour a libation on the ground. That
was in order to give thanks to [the Great] God and the
ancestors. After that they would play for the obias and for
the other gods who had helped them fight. (King 1979,
303–4)

40. Because she was the widow of the *gaama,* Akoomi was prohibited from subsequent marriage or sexual relations. ("Who," asks
the Saramaka proverb, "can measure his foot against the *gaama's*?")
Therefore she did not need to undergo the ordinary rituals required for
a widow or widower, designed to prevent harm inflicted by the jealous spirit of the deceased on the new lover or spouse.

For an ordinary widow, about a year after the second funeral, a
close relative of the deceased (often a mother's brother) would come
to her for three nights and, after herbal purifications, sleep with her
"to remove the prohibition," to make her safe for other men. (Saramakas say, "That man takes the woman across the river.") Then, one
of the deceased's brothers, usually specified by the coffin before
burial, would take her as his wife. Thenceforth, they were like any
married couple—more or less—though each might feel special obligations to behave decently, for fear of punishment by the dead. In the
case of a man, the "removal of the prohibition" is today done by an
"innocent" city prostitute. Under the direction of the dead woman's
lineage, the widower is taken shortly after the second funeral to
Paramaribo, where he must have sex with a non-Saramaka woman
before he is ready to resume normal life. Although the missionaries
are silent on this subject, knowledgeable Saramakas told me that
since the Peace, Saramaka widowers have always gone to the city for
this rite. And given the existence in eighteenth-century Paramaribo of
prostitutes serving all social orders, there seems little reason to doubt
such testimony.

41. While on his way to the city to return these twelve slaves,
Musinga stopped off at the Moravian Indian mission at Saron, on the
Lower Saramacca River. A missionary reported that

these [Matawai] Free Negroes brought with them an Indian
whose name was Gottfried, who they had stolen [from Saron] in

1761. He was the only son of our Ignatius, who had often asked to see him again. He was now grown and had married a negress. The father asked for his son to be returned, and the negroes gave him hope that they would give him back if he paid them a large sum. He [Ignatius] thus went with the negroes . . . to Paramaribo, where the Government agreed to give him his son. But when the negroes brought him back a few weeks later, he was near death, perhaps because they had given him poison. (St 3, pt. 1, 117–18)

42. Matawai bounty-hunting was part of a complex and shifting set of relations that this westernmost of Saramaka village groups had developed with the various bands of Indians, maroons, and *"Karboeger*-Indians" (offspring of an Indian and an African parent) who lived in the area between the Saramacca and Coppename rivers. Though Musinga at one time had alliances with some of these groups (SvS 331, 28 Mar. 1767), in 1767 others of them joined Dörig and the Saramakas in their expedition against Musinga (Wong 1938, 324). Matawai relations with the Indians at the Saron mission, though pacific for long stretches of time, erupted periodically, as these Indians often engaged in bounty-hunting for new maroons. As a missionary complained,

The miserable thing is that they [the Indians] are given a reward for hunting down runaway negroes—forty florins for bringing them in alive but the same if they must kill them. . . . If only this miserable regulation could be suppressed! But the Government would be furious and perhaps even exile us if we tried to interfere. There is even a law here that if a white man gives or sells powder to a free negro, he gets a firebrand on his body and is thus marked forever as a rascal. (St 3, pt. 1, 14; see also Chapter 2, note 3)

In 1765, a large group of Indians fled the mission in fear of a second Matawai raid (St 3, pt. 1, 14). And there were problems again in the mid-1770s, this time actually causing the definitive closing of the post. A missionary described how

some [Matawai] Free Negroes were nearby, canoemaking in the forest, and the officer in charge of the military post "The Seven Provinces" learned that there were slaves among them who had been taken from the Coropina [Para] plantations [in 1766] and who they were supposed to return. He asked an Indian from Saron to guide his soldiers to where the negroes were. This Indian had recently been insulted by the negroes, who had stolen a Carib hammock worth 25 guilders from his son. . . . The soldiers attacked the negroes very early in the morning, while they were still asleep in their huts . . . killing two and taking two others, plus Captain Beku, prisoner. However they let Captain Beku go. One of the captured men, who had been a *Bastian*

[black overseer or driver] on his plantation but who had helped the Free Negroes destroy it [in 1766] committed suicide, out of fear. The only advantage reaped by this attack, which proved so fatal to Saron, was that the soldiers captured one live "slave" and had the three [right] hands of the dead men, which they could bring to the Government [for a bounty]. . . . The Free Negroes vented their full anger on our Indians at Saron, saying that the soldiers would never have found them in the forest had the Indian not shown them the way. . . . All of our Indians became quite frightened . . . and did not dare visit their hunting and fishing grounds, as they were scared that the negroes would come there and capture them. (St 3, pt. 1, 313–15)

This sounded the death knell for the Saron mission, which soon closed permanently, as the Indians drifted back into the forest, toward the west.

Five: To Be a Christian and a Man

Sources for this chapter, in approximate order of use, include: for the Alabi-Kodjo fight, St 3, pt. 1, 133; for the seriousness of marriage, St 3, pt. 2, 261–62; for Riemer's "duel" description, St 3, pt. 2, 263–64, Riemer 1801, 256–59; for Riemer's "reconciliation" description, St 3, pt. 2, 263; for Brother Stoll's Saramaccan sermon, PA 2:417; for Alabi's sobbing incident, St 3, pt. 1, 135; for Alabi's "passionate" proselytizing, St 3, pt. 1, 135; for Alabi's lengthy "reminiscence," St 3, pt. 3, 102–3; for the cayman killing, PA 2:96, St 3, pt. 1, 135–36; for the declaration of baptismal candidates, St 3, pt. 1, 135; for Alabi's "pouring water," St 3, pt. 1, 136; for the idol priestess, St 3, pt. 1, 136, Holmes 1818, 276; for Alabi's role at the tribute distribution, SvS 206, 11–13 Mar. 1769, St 3, pt. 1, 140; for the priestess's "slavery" speech, St 3, pt. 1, 140–41; for Alabi's hernia and its aftermath, St 3, pt. 1, 384, 141–42, PA 2:96; for the "impassioned" woman possessed, St 3, pt. 1, 142; for Antama's god and its taboos, St 3, pt. 1, 143; for Antama's request to Dörig, SvS 331, 28 Mar. 1767 [9 Jan. 1767]; for Antama's request for goods, Hof 79, 17 Dec. 1768; for the postholder's assessment of Antama, Hof 87, 4 Mar. 1773; for the postholder's "dog" speech, Hof 87, 26 Feb. 1773 [8 May 1772]; for a man's affinal duties, St 3, pt. 2, 261; 3, pt. 1, 137; for Alabi's wife's contrariness, St 3, pt. 1, 106; for Akoomi's calling the god, St 3, pt. 1, 144; for Alabi's baptism and its immediate aftermath, St 3, pt. 1, 144–46; for Abini's brother's plan and Alabi's refusal to participate, St 3, pt. 1, 147; for Alabi's urging of slave returns, Hof 84, 25 Oct. 1771 [5 Mar. 1771]; for the pregnancy divination, Hof 84, 25 Oct. 1771 [24 Jan. 1771]; for Antama's role in this same affair, St 3, pt. 1, 147–48, Hof 84, 25 Oct. 1771 [27 Mar. 1771]; for the Kwadjani-Antama accusation, Hof 84, 25 Oct. 1771 [15 May 1771]; for Samsam's sorcery threat, Hof 84, 25 Oct. 1771 [7 June 1771]; for descriptions of divorce, St 3, pt. 2, 261–62, 148; for the tribute distribution preparations, Hof 84, 1 Apr. 1771, 25 Oct. 1771; for Alabi and others at the tribute distribution, Hof 84, 25 Oct. 1771 [7 Sept. 1771], Hof 85, 22 Nov. 1771; for the postholder's comment on illness, SvS 164, 11 Nov. 1772; for the "measles" rites, St 3, pt. 1, 177–78; for the "new priest of the idol," St 3, pt. 1, 177; for Alabi's killing the anaconda, St 3, pt. 1, 177; for the duck killing, St 3, pt. 1, 181; for Alabi's siblings' request, St 3, pt. 1, 231; for the missionaries' attempt to curb Alabi, St 3, pt. 1, 231; for Alabi's "freedom" speech, St 3, pt. 1, 178; for Alabi's speech to Bambo, St 3, pt. 1, 177; for Alabi's request for the Passion, St 3, pt. 1, 179; for Adjagbo's enstoolment, SvS 207, 30 Apr. 1772; for the double murder case, SvS 164, 11 Nov. 1772; for the sorcery case, St 3, pt. 1, 184; for Alabi's becoming a communicant, St 3, pt. 1, 180; for Simon's heathen kin, St 3, pt. 1, 189; for the "soul-sacrifice" description, St 3, pt. 1, 184; for the accusation against Simon's soul, St 3, pt. 1, 189–90; for the accusation against Alabi, St 3, pt. 1, 187; for the old man's funeral, St 3, pt. 1, 188; for the Yanki-Alabi commiseration, St 3, pt. 1, 185; for Daunitz's poisoning, St 3, pt. 1, 183; for Daunitz's French orders, SvS 149, 4 Apr. 1773; for his multiple confrontations with Alabi and the other chiefs, SvS 165, 14 May 1773, 17 May 1773; for the Court's present to Daunitz, SvS 165, 13 Dec. 1773; for missionary reluctance to leave Kwama, St 3, pt. 1, 190; for the final cayman-god rite, St 3, pt. 1, 193.

1. Traces of these formalized adultery fights (*tjanga-feti*) remain alive in Saramaka collective memory, though the institution died out more than a century ago. The Matjau Peleki once told me that during his childhood, one boy would draw a circle on the ground (*tjanga* = ring, as in boxing) and call out in a rapid-fire formula, "Who with who with who? *Tjanga-feti* was a big thing! The person who's ready should come!" (And the boys played a king-of-the-mountain shoving type game to see who could stay inside the ring.) As he grew older, Peleki asked his elders what a *tjanga-feti* had really been like, and they told him. After setting a date for the battle, the combatants prepared for days with fighting *obia*s, to protect themselves against the knuckle-dusters, fighting bracelets, and so on that were the weapons of choice. (Many of these hand-to-hand combat weapons were based directly on African models—razor-sharp finger rings, wrist knives, blackjacks, and animal claws—and they had names of African origin [Schumann 1778, s.v. *malunga*] as well as descriptive names like *básu wóyo* ["under the eye," because that is where this double-pronged ring was poked].) The contest itself was an affirmation of manhood, a corollary of warrior values that played a central role during the society's first hundred years. After the early nineteenth century, for reasons that may well be related to the growing irrelevance of these particular warrior values, the cuckold no longer defended his honor in a battle between equals. Rather, he and his brothers would stage a "surprise" and thoroughly unequal beating of the wife's lover—a beating that had rules designed to prevent murder (which nevertheless did sometimes occur) but in which the same weapons were regularly

used. It was only during the first quarter of the twentieth century that *Gaama* Djankusó called in all such fighting weapons in Saramaka and attempted to ban them forever.

Modern Saramakas conceptualize adultery as "a woman's taking a lover in her husband's house." The husband's rights have been transgressed, and the woman's matrilineage must take full responsibility to see that he is adequately compensated. They palaver about whether the woman's lover should pay a fine to the wronged husband or be subjected to a collective beating by his kinsmen, and they decide exactly how heavy the punishment should be on the basis of their evaluation of how well the husband has fulfilled his marital obligations (including cutting gardens and hunting and fishing for his in-laws). In addition, a village captain (such as Alabi) pays an especially high price. If a beating is decided on, it should in theory take place with fists only, and a special effort is made to leave the man with badly swollen face and thighs. Nevertheless, abuses are common; I have been told of cases ranging from beatings with clubs to splitting open a man's skull with a chisel, and deaths do occur. Once a payment or beating has taken place, the woman is free to become the wife of her lover. Saramakas, then, continue to "take marriage very seriously," though (as I suspect was true in the eighteenth century as well) adultery is also an activity that many men and women participate in—doing their best not to get caught—throughout their active lives.

2. Brother Riemer offers an example of such treachery.

A negro who had lost his wife in the aforementioned manner and whose wife's abductor lived in Bambey got roaring drunk. He loaded his musket and hid behind the door of his enemy's house to shoot him upon his return. It so happened that the negroes of Bambey were still away in their gardens, and only a small boy was present, but he detected the hidden armed negro and came to inform me. I immediately sensed danger and went to the spot, wresting the musket out of the negro's hands. I assured him that I acted with good reason and that he would get his musket back the next day. After he had slept it off for the night, he appeared the next day accompanied by the captain [Alabi] and he thanked me on his knees for having relieved him of his loaded gun, as otherwise he would certainly have shot the negro who had stolen away his most beloved wife. (1801, 257–58)

3. Modern Moravian missionaries in Saramaka have fully understood what is at stake in such a transformation.

[Because] all everyday activities—paddling, fishing, walking in the forest, clearing a garden, planting it, harvesting it, singing, and dancing—are infused with religion, the major question for a Bush Negro who becomes a Christian is how it is possible to remain Saramaka: how can he still walk, eat, have children, and cure sickness without the old religion. It implies the beginning of a new life the shape of which he himself must create. (Vlaanderen n.d., 30)

As for providing a straightforward explanation of why Alabi eventually converted, I deliberately demur. Though I offer various hints, from different kinds of sources, of the multiple pressures upon Alabi at the time and the ways in which conversion seems to have provided a personal solution, I believe that in such cases we reach the limits of our ability as historians or social scientists to explain (retroactively) or predict (prospectively). It is perhaps banal to evoke my experience of knowing two adolescent Saramaka brothers growing up in the same family environment in the 1960s, attending the Moravian school at Djumu Mission, one of whom became a marijuana-smoking construction worker and the other a pious Moravian nurse. Sometimes, monolithic retrospective explanations do little to advance our understanding of complex social, psychological, and spiritual experiences.

4. Awana captain Gome offered this as well as the subsequent description in 1978.

5. Modern versions of Alabi's motivation for his sacrilegious acts, from non-Christian Saramakas, include Tebini's logical argument that, since Abini's murder, Alabi had lost faith in the power of Saramaka *obia*s because they had not protected his father. Indeed, Tebini's version of Alabi's conversion may well encapsulate a central psychological truth:

> *Do you know why the church really came [to Saramaka]?*
> *When the Matawais killed Abini, his son Alabi said, "The*
> obia *are no good" (since they didn't protect his father).*
> *"I'll throw them away." Because he hadn't thought that the*
> *Matawais could kill his father. So [now] he'd get rid of*
> *the* obia *and go over to the side of the whites. So he said*
> *he was ready for baptism. And he was baptized. It was*
> *all because of his father's death.*

6. Brother Riemer later provided a moving description of another "Gado stick" or *"Obia* stick":

> **While I was working today by the riverbank, a group of traveling negroes passed me in their canoe. I heard a loud prayer for a successful trip being said by one of the negroes to his Obia, which was a stick from which some animal teeth hung. The prayer was so beautiful and moving that it was truly uplifting. (But it would *really* have been uplifting had it been addressed to the true source of salvation and blessing!) The form of address to the stick was: "Oh you, my Lord, you who are my real, my true Lord." (St 3, pt. 1, 347)**

7. Years later, Sister Kersten gave her retrospective version of this period of religious conflict:

Illustrations from a twentieth-century Moravian tract that bowdlerizes the missionaries' dramatic eyewitness accounts of Alábi destroying his Madánfo staff and, soon after, shooting a cayman god (Legêne 1941, 8, 17, 22, 23).

The women, who are servants of their idols, were excessively enraged, made a great noise, and threatened that their gods would kill all those who came to us. (These gods are stones, wooden images, large trees, heaps of sand, crocodiles, &c.) The poor people being frightened by these threats came no more: Arabini alone remained steady, and faithful to his convictions. He was therefore persecuted with great malignity. In consequence of our frequent declarations, that their idols could neither help nor hurt them, being inanimate things, Arabini took his idol, which was a staff, curiously decorated with beads, and burnt it privately. (*PA* 2:96)

8. Schumann (1778, s.v. *watra*) described the ceremony as

a certain offering to the dead. A bowlful of water is sprinkled on the ground while a prayer is spoken to the deceased so that he will no longer trouble people. And afterwards there follows the entertainment.

9. Even in 1775, by which time Alabi had been a staunch Christian for several years, the force of kinship obligation, expressed through the ancestors, was still not fully resistible.

> On the 14th of November [1775], we called together our baptized
> ones in order to warn them seriously about the spectacle that
> the negroes would hold that evening in the village, in honor of
> the deceased Abini. There was to be celebrating, eating, and
> drinking until early the next morning. We warned them to take
> heed of their hearts and also to warn others of their people who
> believed in Jesus and who wanted to follow His path.
>
> On the 16th, our Johannes [Alabi] came early in the morning
> to Brother Kersten and confessed, with many tears, a sin he had
> committed the previous evening. He said that his heart had felt
> heavy the whole night, and he had begged the Savior for forgive-
> ness and had requested that it become day as soon as possible so
> he could tell us of his error. (St 3, pt. 1, 244)

It is difficult to judge to what extent Alabi's participation was motivated by filial piety and to what extent by political expediency.

10. A missionary account of Sister Kersten's 1769 arrival in Saramaka referred to Tjazimbe, who would then have been in her late
eighties.

> She [Sister Kersten] was the first sister who undertook this dan-
> gerous journey [to Kwama]. . . . She had already become famil-
> iar with the language of the negroes in Paramaribo, and it was
> hoped that she would have an easier time with the Free Negro
> women than had the male Brethren. But this was not to be, as
> long as Arabini's grandmother was alive. This octogenarian so-
> called idol priestess was known in the village as Grangmama,
> and her words were taken by the people as a divine message.
> Arabini himself got from her only continued ridicule in regard
> to his increasing inclination to follow the Brethren. (Risler 1805,
> 2, pt. 3, 188–89)

11. Other women were also giving Alabi a particularly hard time.

> On the 8th [July 1770] we had not a single negro woman but only
> negro men at the Sunday service. The Enemy holds a powerful
> influence in this land, especially among the female sex. On the
> 15th, Arrabini returned from Ouroe Creek, where he had gone
> the previous day. The people there told him that they wished to
> continue to pursue their [heathen] ways, and he was forced to
> listen to a great many lies on our account. (St 3, pt. 1, 140)

Brother Stoll reports a similar incident, dating from two years earlier.

> An old woman came to buy some beads from us. She was very
> happy when she got them and said that she had already bought
> many other things that her Gado required, such as small dishes,
> through negroes who had traveled to Paramaribo. I asked her,
> "Do you mean the God that created you, me, and everything,
> and do you think that He requires anything of the kind? All He
> requires is that you give your heart to Him, so He can take it."

She immediately answered back: "Well, he has my heart already and, as a matter of fact, he has already come into my head [possessed me]!" (St 3, pt. 1, 91)

He then comments, sadly but perceptively, on one of the reasons Saramakas had thus far failed to take Christianity seriously.

They all have ready excuses of this type, and they seem very calm in their miserable plight. They realize that we are people who have come to teach them the ways of the Great God, but they are also convinced that all this is only for us whites and does not concern blacks. (St 3, pt. 1, 91)

Meanwhile, the missionaries were becoming accustomed to more direct rebuffs to their preaching, such as Samsam's "If they love me as much as you say, why don't they send me a fine musket?" or the following reaction to Brother and Sister Wietz's departure for Para-maribo (some years later):

After Brother and Sister Wietz left, some heathen negroes said that they were very sorry. When they were asked why, they said it was because they had received so many gifts from them. I told them about the real purpose for which we had been sent here, but they would hear none of it, and departed immediately. (St 3, pt. 2, 124–25)

Reports of similar incidents dot the missionaries' journals.

When I saw a child who had cuts on his ears I asked why this had been done. His mother replied that the child was a Gado. I then tried to tell the people that this was mere superstition, but they refused to listen. Indeed, they had no ears for this at all. (St 3, pt. 3, 130)

While I was working in the garden on the 15th [January 1778], an old woman came over to me and began to chat. After she had expressed amazement at my diligence and the Europeans' skills in agriculture, she remarked, "Your big god will greatly bless your efforts and grant you a rich harvest." I instantly took up her words, asking her, "Are you not convinced that He would help not only us but would be ready to help you too?" But as soon as she heard this, she stopped talking and immediately left. (St 3, pt. 1, 345)

It seems clear that the old woman was merely trying to make polite conversation and hardly expected a "lesson." The diarist continues, candidly.

This has happened to me often with the negroes, especially with two who have shown me great love. They are always ready to chat with me, but they cause me indescribable pain and melancholy by running home as soon as I begin to speak of the Impor-

tant Story. And, after all, it is only because of them that we have
come here. (St 3, pt. 1, 345–46)

Although direct insults were a common Saramaka reaction to proselytizing, subtler verbal brush-offs—most of which the missionaries
failed to understand—also are frequently reported in the diaries. Often, Saramakas who otherwise showed not the slightest interest in
Christianity simply told the Moravians what they wanted to hear.

> On the 20th [January 1796] we visited three villages and in the
> fourth lodged with a well-known negro called Prinz. With him
> was his wife and an understanding woman from another village,
> and we had a very interesting conversation with them. They
> remembered the long story of the Redemption that Brother
> Randt had told them, and they said that they wished they could
> hear those words every single day. (St 3, pt. 3, 130)

Talk seems to have been cheap. In 1789, Captain Alando—the great
priest of Kaasi's *sooi-gadu* and the man who "purified the river" (see
Chapter 1)—played the perfect innocent to the visiting Brother Randt.
And I suspect that Alando enjoyed every moment, though for different reasons from those of the Moravian.

> In the evening I had a very nice conversation with Captain
> Alando, who confessed to me that the negroes were poor blind
> people just like their forefathers, because they simply did not
> know any better. Among other things, he asked me who it is that
> we call our Gado. I showed him the deception that their con-
> jurers were playing on them, as I felt that their people were
> robbing themselves of their reason by ingesting herbs, and that
> they could thus claim that they were possessed by the Gado. In
> addition, I told him that in the Holy Scriptures the Devil had
> performed his work in the same way. I explained how the Devil
> deliriously deceives people and is then overjoyed about this. He
> understood me, even though he was a heathen, and he showed
> that he was a reasonable man. The next day he came to me again
> and said he wanted to hear more. But unfortunately there were
> many mockers there so that I could not even open my mouth.
> (St 3, pt. 2, 140–41)

And in 1789, Captain Antama, probably the greatest living *obiama*
during that period, also contributed a notable insult in the form of
flattery:

> He asked me, among other things, why we had come to live in
> this land, saying that he had heard it from others but now
> wanted to hear it from our own mouths. I then took the oppor-
> tunity to tell all those people present about the gospel of the
> Lord. Some said it was a sweet and beautiful story. The magician
> [Antama] said, "Who could possibly not have respect for these

things once one knows that one can have an eternal life with God!" (St 3, pt. 2, 140)

Occasionally, the missionaries reported another kind of verbal reaction—light banter and joking—which must have occurred quite frequently at their expense. For example, the famous captain of Kayána, Agosu Danyei, near the end of his life, was approached by a Christian Saramaka who

> spoke about the love of the Creator for all people. . . . Captain Daniel explained that such things were too late for him. However, one of the baptized, Lydia, called out to him, "Don't say that it's too late for you. You simply don't want it!" (St 3, pt. 3, 136)

And in 1792, Brother Randt talked with people in the Dombi-clan village who

> were amazed to hear about the Creator of all things who had become a man and had shed His blood for mankind, and about how ungrateful were those who did not recognize this. I told them further that this was not simply something to ponder, because on the Day of Judgment of two people who are presented only one will be called and the other sent away. Then a young negro said, "Well, if I see the one who is being taken up to Heaven on the Day of Judgment, I'll just tie a rope around him and follow him on up!" I was moved to have a conversation with this boy. (St 3, pt. 3, 47)

A final example of Saramaka noninterest in the missionaries' message dates from 1798.

> One old man . . . expressed his dissatisfaction with the white people, meaning the government of Surinam, for ceasing [temporarily] to make presents to the free-negroes. Upon this John Arabini [Alabi] answered: Why art thou so much concerned about temporal things? seek those things rather that are eternal! and on his enquiring where he should seek them? he preached to him the only Creator and Lord of all things, and the Redeemer of mankind. He objected: that the great God had however created the other gods to be worshipped [which is standard non-Christian Saramaka theology]; and when we were beginning to give him instruction on that head, he returned for answer, that he was sleepy and must now go to bed. (PA 3:54)

12. Brother Kersten had described one cayman (or "crocodile") being shot (St 3, pt. 1, 135); Brother Stoll seems responsible for the passage quoted here, which suggests that two had been slain. A similar incident and "explanation," dating from nearly three decades later, provides an interesting comparison.

Christian [Grego] had the misfortune to tread upon a fish in the water, with two spikes upon its head (a species of the sting-ray) by which he was so much hurt, that it was some weeks before he was thoroughly restored to health. The savages who were present with him, told him, he was well served, because he spoke so much in favor of *his* God and had lately shot an alligator, considered by the negroes to be a divine being. (PA 3:50)

13. The Moravians were fascinated by Saramaka spirit possession, particularly involving women. They seem not to have questioned the reality of the phenomenon but to have attributed it, on the one hand, to the Devil and, on the other, to chemical stimuli. They consistently misread Saramaka symbolic behavior for empirical acts: they assumed that herbs, for example, must be psychotropic rather than symbolic stimuli. Yet, almost all Saramaka possession is in fact induced by symbolic (nonchemical) means. Here are some relevant Moravian observations. (The third, somewhat misogynistic passage is by Brother Kersten, who—married at the behest of the Brethren to a widow ten years older than himself—seems to have had a particular problem about strong-willed, assertive females.)

They have many idols, this one representing one thing and that one another thing. Each has its own domain. Many believe that they have theirs in their heads, and when they feel the inspiration, they gnash their teeth, snort, and make wondersome gestures so that sweat covers their whole body. When their attack is over, they open their mouth and begin to speak, and their words are taken to be those of their idol. A recent example occurred when a negress who is looked upon with great respect said that the whole negro country would perish because the Matawai negroes had done so much evil. (St 3, pt. 1, 76)

Such fooleries, however, are not the whole, or the worst part, of their superstition. Some persuade themselves, in so lively a manner, that the spirit of their gado is upon them, that, while under this delusion, their bodies are subject to the most violent and frightful agitations; and the more ghastly and horrid the contortions of such a person are, in the greater veneration is he held by the people, who repose unlimited confidence in his pretentions. (Holmes 1818, 275)

There is a law among them that is a real roadblock to our future success. In truth, the women rule the entire people, because they are the ones that have most to do with the gods and are often possessed by them. This concept is called "getting the Gado." When their words are [thus] legitimized, they are taken as pure gospel. But they talk mostly not through words but through signs and signals. So that if a prophecy does not come true, they can interpret it in another way. (St 3, pt. 1, 137)

Many women have their own special houses for idols. In these, they have many wondersome sculptures made out of clay. They enter these houses if someone is sick or in any other special circumstance, with bells, to ask things of their idols. They receive answers but no one except them hears them, and most are ambiguous. Should they not receive an answer, they call to their idol from the bush and even sacrifice a fowl. If he [the idol] comes, the women act as if a demon has possessed them and one can only believe that they are under supernatural control. In a nearby village, two negroes who we know well and are in no way sorcerers got the Gado. From that moment they began to stutter [today, a sign of *papa-gadu* = snake-god possession], something they had never done before. . . . Possession does not usually last more than an hour, and then they are as proper as before it began. (St 3, pt. 1, 137–38)

It truly hurts me a great deal when I see all these children who grow up not only in ignorance but in downright idolatry. It particularly pains me to see the poor children walking about in the gait of the Masiklaya [*sic;* see Schumann 1778, s.v. *massikabaija*]. This is a movement of the body that people here do when their god comes upon them. (St 3, pt. 1, 82–83)

When the Negroes observe anything uncommon, either in the bodily form, or in the intellectual powers, of a child, he is committed to the tuterage of an old idol-priestess who from infancy prepares him for the *inspiration of a gado,* in such a manner, that it is impossible not to discern the effects of satanic influence. And though a pupil of this discription is often dreadfully emaciated by the paroxysms, which accompany his initiation, he willingly submits, in the hope of once becoming a great man, and being respected as an *obia,* or *gado*-man, whose advice and counsel are sought in case of sickness, and on other occasions. Such persons are, in general, expert deceivers, who know how to turn the superstitious credulity of the people to their own advantage, and never fail to enrich themselves. (Holmes 1818, 275)

The 13th of September [1774] in the afternoon, we suddenly heard a shout from the women and children because a woman had fallen unconscious. Since the men were all off in the forest, the Brethren Kersten and Stoll went to help out. According to the negroes, the woman had gotten the Gado and screamed in a frightening way. We sprinkled her with vinegar until she came to. (St 3, pt. 1, 235)

On the 4th [March 1788] I came to the last of the negro villages. . . . I found that I was surrounded by heathen horrors. In one house, a woman offered me something to eat but quickly disappeared. Her husband told me, "I have a bit of work." And, since I did not think there was anything special about this, I told him, "Go do your work and don't worry about me." After a short while, however, I heard loud drumming close to the house. And someone brought me news that the woman had received her Gado. I went outside and saw that she looked like someone who had lost all reason. There were many people gathered together and all fell down before the god and said "I greet you Masra!" At which point a drink of cassava was consumed by all as they knelt. I was also offered some but refused. When this was over, I asked the husband whether he had not in fact given his wife an herb potion to drink. He refused to admit this but wanted me to believe that if he simply called the Gado it would immediately come into his wife. But later, another negro admitted to me that they have a special preparation of herbs which they buy at a high price from the Gado priests. Once, an old woman said to me in [the village of] Kayana, "Master, I want to give you something to smell, so that you will receive the Gado." Another time, an important magician told us in our house, "Give me your to-bacco pipes [to prepare] and as soon as you smoke from them, the Gado will come." We really made every effort to discover what gave this stuff its powers but could not, because their incredible skillfulness with herbs, and even mixing poisons, is a very deep secret among them. (St 3, pt. 2, 130–31)

When a woman receives her god, as they put it, she gets outside of herself and starts to speak with heavy tongue, from inside her, like someone talking in her sleep—with the only difference being that she is awake and walking about. [If] she speaks of herself as a man, the negroes then address her as a man and do not consider her utterances as her own but rather as the words of the spirit who speaks through her. Even though, as one might suspect, such a person is brought into this state of wild excite-ment by natural simples [drugs], every so often she speaks of strange things, of which I offer an example that I remember: During my stay in the village [of Wana Bambey], it happened that several children died one after another, on which occasions the heathens immediately assume that an evil spirit (or ghost) killed them. The Prince of Darkness certainly takes advantage of such situations! A woman from another negro village who had been here several times and had always behaved decently visited again but suddenly got into the aforementioned state, in which she said (among other things): "Yes, I am angry with you. Therefore, I killed your children, and I'm going to kill more. What I'd really like is to kill the children in [the other part of] the village, namely those of the believers. But I can't get there because they are so well protected." Ever since this incident, I have had a special appreciation for the baptism of children, since the Enemy himself had to confess that the baptized children are so well protected by angels that even he is unable to do them any harm. (St 3, pt. 3, 289)

14. Although Alabi had shot the core of the Madanfo shrine and had burned his personal Madanfo *obia* stick, Madanfo was still being summoned and utilized during this period by his female relatives, under the active leadership of his mother Akoomi, with the spiritual support of her own aged mother Tjazimbe. Like other *gaan obia*s ("great *obia*s"), Madanfo had various "parts" to it, several "specialties." One, involving war and male invulnerability, seems to have been moribund at this time, in the wake of Alabi's acts. But another involved pregnancy and other "women's concerns." I assume that it was this latter that was particularly active during the period following Alabi's sacrileges.

15. Sister Kersten wrote a parallel description of these events many years later.

> January 6th, 1771, my husband had the joy to baptize Arabini into the death of Jesus, as the first fruits of the Free negroes at Quama. His family were greatly enraged at this transaction, and sent for a priest [Antama] from a neighboring village, informing him that Arabini had worshipped a strange God. The priest came strait into our house, with a loaded gun and a drawn sword in his hand, which he brandished over my husband's head exclaiming, "Who has given you power to convert and baptize our people?" My husband replied with calmness and courage, "Who art thou? art thou stronger than God? canst thou hinder his work?" The priest said not another word, but instantly quitted the house. (*PA* 2:97)

16. Alabi himself linked these themes. In a sermon to his countrymen, he once said,

> "You acknowledge me for your Chief, and therefore ask my advice in all important concerns, and I freely tell you my mind. You know I have often told you, how good it is to live in peace with the white people, and that it is not good, if it be broken through our own fault. But when I tell you, that you wage war against *Him*, who has made you and the whole world, and who out of love to us, has come down from heaven to redeem us from all iniquity by his own blood and death, you pay little attention to my discourse. God hath sent the brethren, to make these things known to us: I beseech you, reflect seriously on these great truths. (Holmes 1818, 280; cf. St 3, pt. 1, 235–36)

And it would hardly have escaped Saramakas' notice that many of the twenty-four domestic slaves, brought by the missionaries from Paramaribo, were baptized during the course of the mission (St 3, pt. 3, 233). The great majority of Saramakas certainly held to what some scholars call "the dualism principle"—the idea that there were two "religions," one appropriate to outsiders, the other to them, and that they wanted to keep things that way (Berkhofer 1976, 108–9).

17. The postholder reported that

> *on the 7th [June 1771], we heard that Samsam had sent someone from his gardens to the gardens of Etja to seek some earth from under Etja's house, and that he did the same for that of Chief Kwaku [Kwadjani]. And that the earth was to be brought back to Samsam, so that he could make with this earth a certain poison [sorcery] to kill Etja and Kwaku [Kwadjani]. But the Negro who was sent to get the earth went to the wrong gardens, so that all this had no effect. (Hof 84, 25 Oct. 1771 [7 June 1771])*

18. A decade later, Alabi's brother-in-law and fellow Christian, Joshua Kodjo, made an attempt to leave his "idolatrous" wife under very similar circumstances. He had been under great pressure trying to be a Christian and still fulfill his Saramaka obligations. The Moravians, here as elsewhere, counseled reconciliation and pacifism in the face of anger and violence.

> **On the 10th [April 1780], Joshua came to Brother Wietz and complained terribly about his evil wife [Alabi's sister]. She is a highly respected sorceress here. He was planning to leave his house, wife, and children and move to Paramaribo. Brother Wietz begged him not to carry out this plan, because it was not befitting a baptized person. (St 3, pt. 2, 42)**

Another late eighteenth-century case is similar:

> **[20 August 1791] Alexander, another [baptized person], brings us great pain. He became so angry in an interchange with his wife, who is a heathen, that he took all his belongings and moved out of the house and, in heathen fashion in the middle of the street, called out to his dead father to kill him should he ever take back his wife. Such curses mean a great deal to the heathen Free Negroes and cannot be rescinded without special public ceremonies. Johannes and Andreus [Alabi's baptized brother-in-law] were very distressed by these events, and brought Alexander to Brother Wietz, where they told him very seriously, in his presence, that he had caused the Savior offense and disappointment. . . . Brother Wietz reminded him of his promise to renounce the Devil and his works and to consecrate himself forever to the realm of the Savior. This speech struck his heart, and he became gentle. (St 3, pt. 3, 36; cf. St 3, pt. 2, 276)**

In general, Moravian missionary policy worldwide was against divorce. An official statement held that "if any baptized man leaves his wife, and takes another . . . he is excluded from the fellowship of the Church" (PA 1:14). On the other hand, the church made one general exception: "If a heathen woman will not stay with a believing husband, he sinneth not if he let her depart" (Anon. n.d., 36).

19. The Moravians were consistently struck by what they viewed as a most peculiar balance of power between the sexes. They wrote, for example, that

male abuse of women is rare. Men have given women so many privileges that it would not be advisable for a man to strike his wife. . . . A group of women would undoubtedly band together and storm the man's dwelling—without first asking if he was or was not in the right. (St 3, pt. 2, 275–76)

Emblematic of the biases that their construction of gender introduced into their diaries was the Moravians' very general avoidance of women's names.

20. I have not seen documentary materials relating to this funeral or to its implications for Alabi.

21. Postholder Daunitz kept a detailed diary throughout this period, but I have not seen corresponding Moravian diaries.

22. During the course of 1770, Captain Dörig—who was then stationed at the military post of Rama in the plantation area along the Suriname River—was de facto replaced as Saramaka postholder by Ensign Daunitz, a German immigrant, who became official postholder in 1772 and who spent much of the period 1772–74 living in Saramaka. For the two decades beginning in 1775, the postholders spent relatively little time actually in Saramaka; their official residence became Post Awara, just across the river from Saánga, the Nasi village of Gaama Kwaku Etja. Close to Bambey, this location allowed the postholder, when in Saramaka, to spend considerable time with the missionaries, whose relative permanence on the scene permitted somewhat more comfortable living conditions. During the 1780s, the postholders maintained an "office" only twenty feet from the missionaries' house (St 3, pt. 3, 38, 95). Here is a list of Saramaka postholders (as complete as I have been able to reconstruct from the documents I have examined) between 1762 and 1795, when the Moravians (Horn, Wietz, and later Maehr) took over the job until shortly before their departure in 1813.

1762–72	Captain J. C. Dörig (with assistant B. F. Hintze)
1772–79(?)	Ensign J. Daunitz (began actual service in 1770, effectively retired in 1775)
[1775–76	Sergeant J.A.G. Wurzler (officially Daunitz's assistant, dismissed after Daunitz accused him of womanizing and other "shameless behavior" in Saramaka)]
1777–82	Sergeant C. G. Weinhold (began as Wurzler's replacement but by about 1780 was the official postholder with his own assistant, de Vries)
1782–86(?)	C. L. de Vries (like his predecessors, a military man)

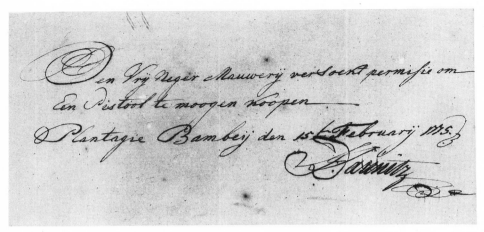

Mauweri's pistol pass. "The Free Negro Mauwery seeks permission to buy a pistol. [Plantation] Bambey, 15 February 1775. [signed] Daunitz" (Hof 91).

1786(?)–92   Beck
1792–94   Specht (and assistant Grunewald)

Note that I spell postholders' names according to their own signatures. The archival documents include diverse renderings in other people's hands.

23. Dörig later wrote that he had never had such "brutal" encounters with Saramakas as during this 1771 gift distribution (Hof 84, 29 Oct. 1771).

24. Early the next year, Dörig (in Paramaribo) signed a document outlining the government's unilateral understanding of its future relationship with the Saramakas—nearly two dozen separate items relating to matters originally sealed by the 1762 treaty. The captains would henceforth be required to come to Victoria to get their gifts; no new captains (except direct successors) would be recognized; the whites would give no further funeral gifts when a captain died; Saramakas would not be allowed to travel to the city without a pass signed by Daunitz; anyone wanting to repair a musket or buy a pistol or shot or flints would have to get a permit from Dörig; the gift distributions would henceforth take place in an orderly manner, without the Saramakas showing the least brutality toward Dörig; returned runaways would be exchanged against a bounty of fifty florins and a bottle of powder; and so on (Hof 85, 29 Apr. 1772).

This attempt by the colonial government to abrogate or modify aspects of the 1762 treaty was not unique. Such efforts were frequent during the succeeding years (see Chapter 6 for examples), and they continued not only throughout the nineteenth century (see, for example, Anon. 1916) but until the very eve of Suriname's independence from the Netherlands in 1975. Indeed, these efforts intensified in the 1960s, with the flooding of approximately half of Saramaka territory as defined in the treaty, in order to produce cheap electricity for Alcoa's new smelter near the capital, and with the forced transmigration of some six thousand Saramakas from their homes. Since Suriname's national independence, without even the nominal protection of the Dutch crown, the terms of the 1762 treaty have been yet more seriously violated, with ambitious urbanistic plans to regroup Saramakas and other Maroons in modern agglomerations (never realized) and culminating in a bloody war between Maroons and the coastal government that continues to rage as I write these lines.

Meanwhile, Saramakas, like their Maroon counterparts in Jamaica (Kopytoff 1979), have continued to see the treaty as a sacred charter and have refused to believe that it could be fundamentally altered. The whitefolks' various ultimatums, sometimes couched in legalistic language, have never been understood by Saramakas as more than arbitrary and transitory words. As Kenneth Bilby comments,

> Since independence in 1962, Jamaican Maroons, disgruntled with various governments, have constantly asserted that their primary allegiance is to the British and not Jamaican government . . . and they expect the British government to reciprocate, considering it still to be bound by the terms of the [1739] treaty. Just as Jamaican Maroons at odds with one post-independence administration or another have written letters to the Queen of England requesting intercession on their behalf, so have representatives of the [Suriname] refugees [in French Guiana] and a number of Maroon officials in Suriname (according to reports I've heard) sent letters to "Misi" (the Dutch Queen) asking for aid and intervention by the Dutch government. The contradictions following independence in the two nations are rather similar, although much more extreme in a Suriname torn by civil war. (Personal communication, 1987)

A Saramaka who had served in happier days in Suriname's parliament recently told a Dutch reporter how, in 1974 when he was in the Netherlands for the final negotiations leading to national independence, he had told the Dutch prime minister that "we [Surinamers] were not yet ready for independence . . . [because] we [Maroons] have a treaty with the Netherlands, in which it is stated that the country's interior does, and forever will, belong to us" (Ruggenberg 1986).

25. This description of Kaana awakening Madanfo was offered in 1978 by Captain Gome, who told me that Kaana was from the Bakapau (Tíifóu-nêngè) segment of the Awana group. Because of Kaana's awakening of Madanfo, it is his Bakapau descendants who, today, control this *gaan obia*.

26. Today, more than two centuries later, Alabi's sacrilegious acts are still enveloped in an aura of great danger. In 1978, the elderly Captain Gome interrupted his whispered recounting of "the two things that Alabi killed at Sentea Creek" (i.e., the cayman and the anaconda) to say:

I don't want children to hear this. The water and the shore!
[a veiled reference to the two things]. I will not tell them.
My mother's brother used to say, "Talk with them but don't
tell them. Because if you tell them, those things [the animal
gods] will rise up and come listen!"

27. I have heard a story that sounds similar to these events but
which, on the basis of the personae involved, would seem to date
from several decades later. It is remembered today, in part, because it
preserves the origin of a place-name on the Gaanlio, "Kabálo."

Ma Gobina, the sister's daughter of Musumba [an important
Matjau-clan man] lived at Kabalo, near Maáta Sándu.
There was a pond next to the village. She used to raise fowls.
There was an anaconda that used to come up out of the
pond and catch them. So the people made a pact to kill it!
Then, one day Ma Gobina called out "He he he he!" A
god had possessed her. [It said] "Kabálô f'únu" [= "(This
will be) The end of your clan!"]. The god of the pond warned
them. "Don't do the thing you're thinking of doing." That's
how that place got that name.

28. Alabi's characterization of Saramaka religion as based on fear
and countless obligations sounds by this time fully congruent with
the Moravians' conception of it (see also Chapter 7, note 42). For
example, the missionaries wrote that

the local Negroes have innumerable kinds of Tjina [taboos], that
is, superstitious fear of totally innocent things. For example,
when a woman walks by with a cooking pot, she calls out to the
men "Bielabakka," which means "turn your backs." And such
things are innumerable among them. (St 3, pt. 1, 183; cf. St 3, pt.
2, 139 and 3, pt. 3, 46)

There is no doubt that Saramaka ritual prohibitions are numerous and
complex, but they are also systematic and logical. Today, *komanti*
men (among scores of other special concerns) must be sure that,
when sitting, no one passes behind their back—which is probably the
bit of customary behavior that piqued the missionaries' interest here.

29. Gwafu, the name by which twentieth-century Saramakas remember the village, was said by the missionaries to refer to the
rapids at that point in the river where, some years earlier, a god or *obia*
by that name had fallen out of a canoe and been lost (St 3, pt. 1, 238).
However, an old man of the Awana clan claimed in 1976 that it derived, rather, from Alabi's having said, on their descending the river,
"This is the place. *U gó háfu*" ("We have come halfway [to the
coast]").

Regarding the choice of "Bambey" as a place-name, available documents are contradictory. One account states that

[the missionaries] called their new residence, Bambey, which in the language of the country signifies, *Only wait*, or *Have patience!* By this appelation, they would remind each other, that the gospel ought to be preached with patience and perseverance, and in confident expectation of the help of the Lord. (*PA* 2:418)

This version may be based on comments in St 3, pt. 1, 182, 3, pt. 2, 196, or directly on Schumann's 1778 Saramaccan-German dictionary, which gives, s.v. *bambei!*, "Geduld! warte nur! gedulde dich! (Patience! please wait! be patient!)," and as a Saramaccan example, *pakka mi hessi, mi no lobbi bambei-sani* ("pay me immediately, I don't like bambei-way-of-doing things [i.e., procrastinating]"). Since *bambei* is not a word in modern Saramaccan, it seems at least possible that Schumann was reporting normal contemporary speech in his example, but that *bambei* was being used ironically, having entered the Saramaccan vocabulary only *after* its choice as the name for the mission village. In other words, Bambey—not yet a word in Saramaccan—might have been chosen as a name for one or another reason and then become synonymous, among non-Christian speakers of the language, with "slowness" and other undesirable traits. One possible element of this scenario: there was a Moravian missionary who served in the Suriname Indian missions, died in 1761 at Saron, and whose name was Johannes M. Bambey (Blair 1984, 69). And the Moravians reported in 1773 that Saramakas, particularly women, "did not eagerly pronounce it ['Bambey']" (St 3, pt. 1, 195). (On this issue, see also Kesler 1939; 214, whose sources are not, however, clear.) Kenneth Bilby, upon reading this note, suggested a further and perhaps simpler solution—that Bambey might derive from Sranan *bambai* (or an obsolete Saramaccan cognate), itself apparently derived from English "by and by."

30. It was Captain Gome, in 1978, who offered this explanation of why Alabi's people had to leave Kwama.

31. The previous year, Alabi's people had found it necessary to abandon an extensive, already planted set of new gardens still further downstream near the Tutu Creek because of difficulties with the site. The missionaries claimed that these problems concerned drainage (St 3, pt. 1, 180); it seems more likely that difficulties with local gods were the proximate cause. Captain Gome, in 1978, described for me the domestication of the god that "owned" Tutu Creek, as it finally took place during the mid-nineteenth century, allowing his ancestors (Alabi's descendants) finally to settle in the area.

Táta Wáimáu Amósu, his wife Pelámma, and his brother Uwíi. They came into the creek to cut gardens. But the creek didn't want people to come inside it, the apuku *who lived there called Masikwékè. It fought with them. Surrounded them with a hundred [evil] things. Well, they made a shed. . . . [Waimau went hunting and returned.] He said,*

*"I went hunting and killed only one bird!" She [his wife]
said, "Go to the Afoompísi people [the people who today inhabit Tjalíkôndè, at Tutu Creek]. They have Baimbo [an
obia]. Go to them. Beg them for help." So he went. . . . They
told him what to prepare. He assembled:* nyanyán búka
nyanyán *[a combination of various raw foods used in certain
sacrifices], cane drink, parrot feathers, cowrie shells, a
white-cloth hammock sheet, a white cock. Then they "killed
the chicken." To ask whether the place would accept them
now. And they were able to come on over. . . . That* apuku
*had been so baad! If you tried to cross the creek in a canoe,
it would sink you! So, they did it all [the ceremony]. Killed
the chicken. Its testicles were pure white! [indicating that
the god was pleased]. They raised the flag [the hammock
sheet, planted on a pole]. They poured the sugar-cane libations [at its foot]. The* apuku *had said they could work
the land there.*

Techniques of site-divination, getting the *apuku* "who-has-the-place"
to agree to the use of the land and to encourage its productivity, vary
in detail. Some are as simple as placing a calabash with particular
leaves and water on a forked stick for a week, after the fields have
already been cleared, felled, and burned, for the god's final approval;
others involve the technique described for Alabi's people at Gwafu,
carried out before the land is desecrated at all. As with almost all
Saramaka ritual, different people know and use different techniques
and formulae. But every potential field site, especially in an area that
has not previously been used for gardens, must be approached with
respect and caution, and the local gods must be brought into the
process of preparing it, planting it, and harvesting it at every stage.
And the process of interaction with the local gods is a central part of
all horticultural activity.

32. R. and S. Price 1977 includes a recording of twentieth-century
Saramaka axe-songs.

33. Despite the rich crop repertoire that Saramakas had developed
by the mid-eighteenth century, periods of near famine were not rare.
Lean years might result from early rains (which prevented fields from
being properly fired), not enough rain after planting, or depredations
from leaf-cutting ants or other horticultural pests. The crunch, when it
came, usually occurred in the early months of the year, just before the
new crops were ready to harvest but when those of the previous year
had already been consumed. In early April 1780, for example, one of
the diarists wrote:

**The starvation among the local negroes has reached enormous
proportions. Yesterday evening a baptized man came to us and
asked for a meal. We could not help him as we ourselves have
nothing in the house. (St 3, pt. 2, 42)**

And the following year, a missionary on a river trip noted that he and his companions

> **came to a small village where they had nothing to eat, so we had to retire to our hammocks hungry. (St 3, pt. 2, 47)**

Noncultivated forest foods were important supplements in times of hunger: palm cabbages and various palm fruits, and different kinds of wild vegetables. For discussion of eighteenth-century Saramaka subsistence horticulture—crops, techniques, ritual, and so on, see R. Price 1990; on the eighteenth-century calendar, see R. Price 1984.

34. Divination with fowls was a common procedure in the eighteenth century. As today, such divination was frequently used during the course of larger rituals, as a means of asking a god (or the ancestors) whether the ritual was being conducted in an appropriate way, or whether there were further procedures to follow. Here is one of the fuller examples recorded by the missionaries:

> **On the 22nd [July 1788], the person I was lodging with [on a missionizing trip away from Bambey] went off into the forest to gather herbs in order to set things right for his god, whom he believed had become tainted. This [ceremony] was carried out on the subsequent days. First the god was painted red and white, then they all approached him reverentially—the children who had been painted white except for their faces, and the elders whose legs were red and who had red and white spots on their faces and bodies. In an attempt to find out what had tainted the god, a trial was performed by the killing of chickens. If the fowl fell on its back with its wings still flapping before it was fully dead, this had a different meaning than if it fell on its side and made no movement. Among the other questions asked him [the god, via the chicken] was whether he had been insulted by any of the travelers [in the village] (by which I [Brother Randt] was meant). As it turns out, the answer was the he had not been [insulted], though in truth I did despise him! They finally found another reason and prayed with bended head [faces to the ground?] and ended the whole procedure with loud shouts of joy. . . . I really had a frightening feeling about all this, and my courage completely left me. I decided not to remain with them any longer. (St 3, pt. 2, 133–34)**

35. Simon's infant son had already been the focus of religious conflict.

> **On the 2nd of August [1773] a little son was born to our Simon, but because—as is the local custom—the father has no say concerning his children, and since the mother and her brothers are faithful devotees of the idol, we could not even consider having a baptism or blessing. (St 3, pt. 1, 189)**

The Moravians' frustration at the strongly developed Saramaka system of matrilineal authority appears a number of times in the diaries. For example, Brother Kersten had noted in 1770 that

> **Grego [then a potential convert] is going with his mother's brother to Paramaribo. It is, in fact, the mother's brother who is responsible for him because among the local negroes the father has no say over his children. It is always the mother's oldest brother (or her nearest [male] relative) who is responsible for the children. (St 3, pt. 1, 132)**

36. Alabi once gave a fuller "lesson" on the Christian concept of the soul to a heathen Saramaka.

> **On the 16th [May 1777] a negro came to us to fetch some medicine, and asked Johannes Arrabini why one brother after another was coming here [to Saramaka]. Johannes told him that it was in order to preach the gospel of Jesus Christ to the negroes, and he showed him how he had set his own heart on the straight path, and how he had freed himself from sin and found bliss. We were delighted to see the beautiful way Johannes comported himself in addressing these paramount matters. . . . When he wanted to show him how the soul and body were parted at death, he took his cape and laid it on the ground, and he himself got up and walked away as if he were going home, and he said, "This is how we discard our body, just as I have left my cape here, and thus the soul leaves the body and never dies. And just as the cape rots out in the rain, while I remain healthy and unharmed, so the body decays while the soul endures." (St 3, pt. 1, 335)**

37. I am unable to identify this important old man on the basis of the missionary reports.

38. The date of Alabi's marriage to Sialoto is unclear. In the diaries that I have seen, the missionaries first allude to her by name only at the time of her baptism in 1780. She is, however, mentioned in their baptismal records as the mother of Alabi's child Izaak in 1775. He may well have married Sialoto soon after the death of his first wife in 1771; on the other hand, his religious preoccupations at the time may have caused him to delay remarrying for a year or two. Sialoto's plantation origins are unclear. Next to her name in the baptismal records, the missionaries list as her birthplace what looks to me like "Plantation Falsi," which I am unable to identify, but I may simply be misreading their difficult script. In any case, Sofi and Sialoto are conceptualized as a pair that arrived without other relatives in Saramaka. (See Jozefzoon 1959, 12, for a garbled account of some of these events.) And though Sofi was a leper and did not marry, Sialoto more than made up for her: between 1775 and 1800 she and Alabi (to whose new religion she converted after some six or seven years of marriage) had twelve

children together. In 1835 a visiting missionary reported that she was still alive, though very old (Voigt 1837).

39. In late 1772, three Saramakas were arrested and imprisoned in Paramaribo for "corrupting slaves," but, on the intervention of Daunitz, they were released back into the custody of Saramakas rather than being hanged. Daunitz personally supervised their public whipping in Etja's village, and he made it clear that it was only by the Court's special dispensation that their lives had been spared. Henceforth, he stated, offenders would be hanged. On orders from the Court, the three men were forbidden ever to travel to the coast again or to receive powder or guns (SvS 165, 31 Dec. 1772, 17 May 1773). This is one of the very few cases I know in which a government official played a role in the dispensing of Saramaka justice, and it happened only because the Saramakas were violating whitefolks' laws in whitefolks' territory.

40. The captains were "going aside" for private discussion (béndi a sê), as was—and remains today—standard procedure in what the missionaries called a "grang-kruttu: the supreme council where all the village captains meet, and over which the gaama presides" (St 3, pt. 2, 267). Saramaka gaán kuútus—tribal council meetings—are highly formalized political/oratorical events, to which a summary description cannot do justice. They begin with the summoning of various categories of participants (headmen [captains], assistant headmen [basias], senior women) on the apinti (talking) drum (see R. and S. Price 1977 for a sample recording and transcription). In the eighteenth century (and until the early twentieth century) people were also formally summoned by the tutú, a wooden signal horn (which began by "recounting its name" and calling on the Great God: Odún, odún, odún [= wándji, the wood from which horns were made]. Odún amánpong kwáu. Sasí naná. Kediamá Kedíampon.) Today, the apinti drummer still plays intermittently during the meeting itself, commenting (in drum-language proverbs) on the proceedings, and he plays appropriate rhythms (e.g., "the gaama is walking") as the meeting disperses. During the kuutu, a speaker never addresses the gaama directly. Rather, he speaks to a third party, who provides the appropriate "interruptions" to the speech, and who—when the speaker concludes—rhetorically asks the assemblage "if they have heard," to which they answer, accompanied by quiet handclapping, "We have heard." Once the two sides of a case have been presented, the council room (which is often a large, open shed) empties out (except for the gaama and a few retainers), as the parties retire to "go aside" at the edge of the village to work out a solution. Once in agreement, they return to the meeting and a spokesman relates to a third party what they have "found." The gaama may then give his final views—usually presented through elliptical proverbs.

41. Daunitz, apparently without full knowledge, had hit upon an almost foolproof strategy. For Saramakas, the surest means of re-

venge is to commit suicide (after first making clear the reason) and then to return as an avenging spirit to sicken and kill the matrilineage of the offender(s). The mere threat of such a suicide requires quick action by the person(s) accused of inspiring it in order to avoid these dreadful consequences. And the Saramaka chiefs must have responded to Daunitz's threat with this scenario very much in mind.

42. Saramakas had a long tradition, dating from the wars, of trying to send false information to the whites along with returned slaves (see R. Price 1983a, 140–43). It appears that they acted similarly with some of the 1773 returnees (though one can only guess at the sanctions or incentives they may have held over such people—e.g., keeping their relatives, as a kind of guarantee). Samsam, for example, specifically instructed Daunitz to tell the court to interrogate the returnee Quami carefully, for "he will tell all about who has more slaves [still hidden]" (SvS 165, 14 May 1773). And he indeed reported (falsely) that Samsam had none, though he said that other clans had some thirty of his fellows (SvS 165, 23 July 1773).

43. Saramakas, then as now, conceptualized their territory in linear, riverine terms: directions were "upstream"/"downstream" (and "inland [from the river]"/"toward the river"). The moves of the 1770s were radical in that they fully halved the distance from the first rapids along the Suriname River (close to the Treaty-Signing-Place, the official border between whitefolks' and Saramaka territory) and the southernmost Saramaka villages. These moves represented a conscious compromise, a "going halfway" to the land of the enemy, which was also in certain respects the land of plenty. The moves of the 1770s are far too complex to summarize on a single map, and the details would be of interest only to the most devoted of Saramaka historians. The main lines, however, may bear sketching in as they have emerged from some twenty years of oral and archival research, which would not be easy to replicate. (The following data—captains' names, village names and locations, and so forth—depend on hundreds of bits of archivally confirmed oral data, specific sources for which I cannot cite here. Refer, also, to map 3, p. 143.)

The move by Alabi and his people to Gwafu Bambey was contemporaneous with that of the Nasis, Biitus, and Dombis, who settled just upstream from them. The Dombis, led at the time by Captain Dondo Kasa, established their village of Wangania closest to Gwafu Bambey, not far from the present site of Futuná; the Nasis, led by Captains Kwaku Etja and Kwaku Kwadjani, and the Biitus settled a bit further upstream around the mouth of Muyanwoyo Creek (where they had lived and fought against the whites during the 1740s), first living in a village called Saanga, then moving around a good deal within an area of a few square kilometers, on both sides of the river. The postholder's station of Awara was established on the east bank, near the mouth of Awáa Creek.

By the late 1770s, the Abaisas, led by Apabe (also called Atje), the sister's son (or son?) of Samsam (who died in 1777), were settled in the area that still remains their homeland, on the east bank of the Suriname, not far below the confluence of the Pikilio and the Gaanlio, where Samsam had claimed a number of creeks on the southward journey during the 1730s and 1740s. It is they who gave the people of Daume their land just across the river, near Kofí Creek, and it is they who arranged for the Fandáákis, after the various wanderings described in Chapter 6, to settle in the area around Sasaaku Creek that they still inhabit today.

Beginning in the mid-1770s, the various people who inhabited Baakawata—the Matjaus and their client clans, the Watambiis, Paputus, Paati-nenges, and Kasitus (who together made up more than one-third of the Saramaka population)—also moved downstream, and before the decade was out Baakawata was largely abandoned. The great bulk of Matjaus (led by Captains Kristofel and Mbuti), accompanied by the Watambiis, first moved down the Pikilio to Háfupási ("halfway [along the] path") at the site of today's Dángogó, where the great shrine to the First-Time ancestors now stands. By the mid-1780s, they had moved a couple of kilometers farther downstream to Bèkúun, on the west bank of the Pikilio (the present-day cemetery for Pikilio Matjaus). This latter move was accompanied by the founding of Alasá by the old Matjau, Captain Adjagbo (who for several years had been having serious problems with the Paputus for whom he served as headman), for his wife Paanza and their Kasitu children, across from Bekuun, and by the settling of the Paati-nenges (who later founded Asaubasu) on a small island in the river. Meanwhile, two Matjau brothers, the quasi-captain Djaki and Awóyo, moved far downstream, just above the new postholder's residence, to establish the island village of Kúmbu, called by the Moravians "Djaki's Plantation," at Biáháti Rapids. Likewise, when Baakawata was abandoned, the Paputus (who had been living on its upstream tributary, Kanga Creek) moved down to Gaan Djumu, at the confluence of the Pikilio and the Gaanlio, and thence, before long, across the river into their present territory near Gódo (in the wake of the incident described below in Chapter 8, which led also to the founding of Soolán next door, for the descendants of Ayako's Dombi wife, Asukume).

During this period, and continuing into the 1780s, the Langu people gradually "came down to the river [the Gaanlio]" (as Saramakas today say); by the end of the century, they were the sole inhabitants of the area above Gaandan, now called simply "Langu." Agosu Danyei, one of the Langu captains mentioned occasionally by the Moravians, is today credited with bringing his people to the river, where he founded the village of Kayana (across from its present Gaanlio site) on the creek by that name. The villages of captains Alando and Antama, which figure frequently in the Moravian accounts of the Great Awakening during the 1790s, as well as that led by Bakisipambo, remained for some years inland, along the Agamadja and Kwama creeks (where the missionaries several times visited them), before finally joining Agosu's people along the Gaanlio itself—Alando's people in the area of present-day Bendiwata, Bakisipambo's people upstream, across from and a bit above old Kayana, and Antama's people still farther upstream, not far from present-day Bundjitapá. As part of this migration, the people who became known as the Kwama clan, now led by one of Alubutu's "brothers," Captain Bonio, also abandoned their villages at Agamadja and Kwama creeks for the territory that they still inhabit today, just downstream from the Abaisas (with whom they at first lived but with whom they soon had serious problems).

A final caveat regarding the reconstruction of village moves: such description runs the risk of oversimplifying, making them seem more sudden and complete than they actually were. During the lifetime of any village, whatever its core composition in terms of clan affiliation, affines were frequently moving in and out (sometimes forming important groupings), and various men were staking out gardens far away and, if they liked the place enough, deciding to stay on. Most villages were constantly sending out, as it were, such "advance guards" who, later, might be joined in the new site by other villagers. Such a process was taking place constantly in Langu during the 1770s, 1780s, and 1790s (as can be seen in the missionaries' diaries), and even the apparently linear moves of Alabi's people were, at a microscopic level, far more complex. Rather, for example, than the straightforward Sentea-Kwama-Gwafu Bambey moves chronicled by the missionaries and postholders, modern Awanas can provide details on several intermediate steps, creating the series: Sentea-Petó Dán-Libankôndè-Kwama-Ásigoón-Sofibúka-Gwafu Bambey. (Peto Dan, Libankonde, and Asigoon were "advance guard" garden sites, potential village sites on the Gaanlio that, for various reasons, never became permanent; Sofibuka, across the river from Gwafu [and named after Alabi's mother-in-law, several years after it had served as a brief residence] was, again, a trial site that did not work out.)

Six: On to Bambey

Sources for this chapter, in approximate order of use, include: for Daunitz's decision to stay with Alabi, Hof 90, 5 Aug. 1774 [18 Jan. 1774]; for the Moravian description of Etja, St 3, pt. 1, 246; for the Etja-Daunitz confrontation, Hof 90, 5 Aug. 1774 [30 May 1774]; for Etja's "excuses," Hof 90, ca. June 1774, Hof 91, 5 Dec. 1774; for Mbuti's captain's staff, SvS 167, 23 June 1775; for Etja's argument about Matawai gifts, SvS 167, 28 Aug. 1775 [12 Nov. 1774], SvS 167, 21 Oct. 1775; for the withholding of Samsam's goods, SvS 167, 10 Aug. 1775; for Samsam's "intelligence coup," SvS 167, 21 Oct. 1775, 21 Dec. 1775, passim; for Alabi's slave, Hof 90, 5 Aug. 1774 [10 May 1774]; for the nineteenth-century postholder's assessment, van Eyck 1828, 28; for the list of captains at the 1774 distribution, Hof 90, 13 Oct. 1774; for the whites' ultimatums, Hof 90, n.d. [mid-1774]; for the gift list, Hof 90, n.d. [mid-1774]; for the whites' laundry list, Hof 90, n.d. [mid-1774]; for special treatment of some Saramakas, Hof 90, 15

Oct. 1774; for accusations against Samsam, Hof 87, 26 Feb. 1773; for Adjagbo's Paputu problems, Hof 93, 13 Apr. 1776, SvS 208, 18 Feb. 1778; for the governor's comments on Alabi, SvS 207, 16 Dec. 1777; for Daunitz's questioning of Alabi, SvS 165, 17 May 1773; for Samsam's plans, SvS 207, 3 Dec. 1774; for Djuka complaints, SvS 355, 19 Nov. 1774; for Fourgeoud's delegates' visit to Saramaka, SvS 359, 9 June 1776, Stedman 1988, 558; for Etja's peanut gift, Hof 93, 22 Apr. 1776; for Fourgeoud's gifts to Alabi and others, SvS 365, 26 Mar. 1778, SvS 208, 24 Feb. 1778; for the Moravians' hopes about Bambey, St 3, pt. 1, 148; for their early Bambey activities, St 3, pt. 1, 193–94, 236, 238–39; for their dependency, St 3, pt. 1, 185, 230; for Daunitz's aiding the Moravians, St 3, pt. 1, 229; for Brother Stoll's account of his wife's sufferings, St 3, pt. 1, 236–37; for Kersten's remarks on same, St 3, pt. 1, 235; for Simon Yanki's final illness, St 3, pt. 1, 230; for his funeral, St 3, pt. 1, 230; for the flood, St 3, pt. 1, 240–41; for the statement of missionary optimism and "happiness," St 3, pt. 1, 198, 244; for Kodjo Maata and the schoolboys, St 3, pt. 1, 208, 243; for the summary of missionary "success," St 3, pt. 1, 364; for the two negative Moravian assessments, St 3, pt. 1, 355, 364–65; for the death of Alabi's child, St 3, pt. 1, 240; for the child-burial, St 3, pt. 2, 46; for the Moravian self-image quotation, McLoughlin 1984, 36; for Brother Stoll's complaint, St 3, pt. 1, 75; for the hunting sack incident, St 3, pt. 1, 242; for the old man with the pure heart, St 3, pt. 1, 90–91; for the Moravian comment on confession, St 3, pt. 1, 180; for Saramaka incomprehension and resistance to the Moravian message, St 3. pt. 1, 356, 3, pt. 2, 78–79; for the possible "danger" of Christian prayer, St 3, pt. 1, 181–82; for the Moravian descriptions of Saramaka executions, St 3, pt. 1, 337–38, 3, pt. 2, 270–72; for Brother Schumann's travails, St 3, pt. 1, 338–43, 348, 353–55, *PA* 2:419; for Alabi's help with the dictionary, St 3, pt. 1, 347; for the closing of the mission, St 3, pt. 1, 357.

1. In various documents from this period, Etja alludes in addition to the fact that he had lost two of his men in whitefolks-related incidents and that he considers the slaves he is harboring to be replacements. In a May 1774 report, Daunitz gives the background, adding that Etja claims he would turn in his two slaves if the whites would give him "two [other] good slaves" in return.

One of the two Saramakas, a man named Blantij, found himself in Paramaribo at the moment of Musinga's action [the 1766 plantation raid], and fled, on hearing the news, out of fright that he might be punished simply because he was a Saramaka. In the forest, behind Jews Savannah, he came upon a gang of slaves sawing timber, one of whom was his own son. The slaves, seeing him, shot his son dead. That makes one [person whom Etja "counts" as a personal loss].

The other had a brother who was a slave of the whites. He marooned and came to Etja's village, where his brother lived.

In the course of time, the two argued with some other Sara-
makas and . . . the Saramaka ended up killing his own brother,
who was called Cupido. That makes two. (Hof 90, 3 June 1774)

2. Etja's brother, Captain Kwaku Kwadjani, compelled Daunitz to
include a P.S. on one of his 1774 letters to the Court:

Captain Kwaku [Kwadjani] wishes to inform your Excellen-
cies that one of Etja's two slaves is married to Etja's sister, and
that this slave cannot, therefore, be turned in to the whites.

Daunitz, however, added a word of his own:

Might I suggest that as a reply Your Excellencies remind him
that Your Excellencies did not order Etja to give his sister to a
slave? (Hof 90, n.d. [May? 1774])

3. Given the state of the documents (with many volumes officially
"sealed" because of decay), my information can hardly be considered
complete. Yet it seems worth noting that I have seen definitive records of only three slaves returned in 1774, two in 1775, one in 1776,
four in 1777, one in 1778, one in 1779, a few in 1780, and so on (Hof 90,
11 May 1774, SvS 167, 4–13 Dec. 1775, SvS 207, 17 Mar. 1777, 22 Sept.
1777, SvS 208, 19 Oct. 1778, 22 Apr. 1779, 7 July 1780, 18 Sept. 1780, 4
Oct. 1780). And this in spite of the fact that negotiations between
postholders and captains continued throughout the century (see, for
example, St 3, pt. 2, 147, 3, pt. 3, 220), and that new runaways were
arriving in Saramaka, in small but steady numbers, all the time.

4. There are archival indications that the Matawais managed to
integrate into their own villages some twenty-odd slaves from the
massive 1766 liberation (Hof 105, n.d. [post-13 Apr. 1779])—about the
same number they turned back to the whites in 1769 (see Chapter 4,
and also Hoogbergen 1985, 394–95). But the great bulk of these
newcomers had, by the mid-1770s, become Saramakas.

5. Alabi's relations with his father's killers, the Matawais, remained
ambivalent throughout this period. In 1776, the Matawais were reported still to be worried about rumors of possible vengeance from
Alabi—at a time when other Saramaka chiefs, such as Kwaku Etja,
were expressing strong solidarity with them—and he was persuaded
to send a delegation to reassure them that he no longer bore a grudge
(SvS 168, 9 Apr. 1776, 21 July 1776, Hof 93, 9 Apr. 1776, Hof 94, 21 July
1776). (Almost certainly, questions of supernatural vengeance by the
ghost of Abini were involved: in 1788, as Matawai chief Beku lay
dying, he sent messengers requesting Alabi to present a "sacrifice"
on his behalf to Abini—an act that in Saramaka terms could have no
other meaning.) By 1778, Alabi was able to join other Saramaka chiefs
in intervening as a friendly party by arguing to the postholder on
behalf of one of Musinga's sons that he should be the one to succeed
his recently deceased father as Matawai chief (Hof 102, 10 July 1778).

6. The Paputus were the last substantial group of escaped slaves

to join the Saramakas before the Peace, arriving in 1759 and soon settling on an arm of Baakawata Creek, as "guests" of the Matjaus (R. Price 1983a, 161–62). Like the Fandaakis, their "whitefolks' plantation" was on the Coropina Creek in the Para region. Indeed, one of the plantations from which Musinga, in 1766, "liberated" the people who later became the Fandaakis belonged to the Widow Papot (whom Saramakas called "Paputu"). In 1978, a Fandaaki captain told a government official, "Our clan is really Paputu but we don't carry the same name as them. [Our ancestors were] Two sisters. But we don't carry the same name. Because if we did, the Paputus would be able to dominate us."

7. Several oral fragments regarding Fandaaki travels after their arrival in Saramaka involve a man from one of the established clans marrying (and protecting the kin of) one of the immigrant women. Such stories make clear that the newcomers were, in fact, spread fairly widely among Saramaka villages, even if the bulk of them traveled together. One version of the establishment of Fandaaki territoriality on lands owned by the Abaisa (the Pempé-Sémóisi area, where the Fandaaki still live today) involves such a case, here recounted by Otjutju in 1978. (Otjutju's knowledge comes directly from Kositán, his Matjau "great-grandfather" and the "brother" of *Gaama* Abgago, whose father was an Abaisa [see R. Price 1983a, 26].)

> [Someone from the village of] Daume "protected" the ancestress of [the village of] Pempe [that is, the Fandaakis].
> The Daume man married the woman's daughter. They were on their way downstream because people said the woman was a witch. The Fandaaki woman [the mother] had had a Langu husband, at Kayana. She had an obia to "prepare" the river, to "smoke" the forest. As she was on her way downstream, fleeing Langu, the Daume [Dombi-clan] man "caught" her and married the daughter.... (She had been on her way down to meet other Fandaakis, who still lived as maroons in the forest, near the plantations.).... Later, he bought her [and her kinfolk] land from the Abaisas at Sasaaku Creek [where the Fandaakis still live]. The payment for the land was 10 koósu [lengths of cloth] and 1 akôbè [= 3½ liters] of rum.

On another occasion, Fandaaki elder Tebini further specified that "the [Abaisa] man who 'sold' the Fandaakis their land was Tata Gbúnu-gbúnu."

Another means by which Saramakas protected the newcomers was to spread around their children via fosterage (a common Saramaka practice in normal times as well). One of Postholder Daunitz's 1774 letters reports his own discovery of this "ruse."

The other [anti-Samsam] Saramakas say that if the Matjaus must turn in all the "slave" children so should Samsam, and

they report that a child of Soeka is in fact a foster child whose real parent is Kwamina [a slave], who was recently turned in, and that a child of Komba is really a foster child received from Chocolade, who was turned in some time ago. Indeed they [Samsam's people] would like to make it seem that the two children are born of Free Negroes [Saramakas] but that is a lie. (Hof 90, n.d. [mid-1774])

I believe that only the fact that, in the end, the postholder remained largely powerless in forcing particular slave returns permitted rival factions of Saramakas to "disclose" the whereabouts of each other's slaves with relative impunity. They could at once gain some credit with the postholder and be fairly sure that no harm would come to the slaves they mentioned by name.

8. "Agosu Danyei," the name of a powerful Langu captain during the late eighteenth century, is being used here to stand for the Langu clan in general. Other modern Saramakas recounting who first "received" the Fandaaki refugees from Matawai used "Kaasi" (an earlier Langu leader who in fact died before the Peace) in this same metonymic fashion.

9. It seems worth emphasizing that the postholders' documents, by insistently characterizing newcomers as *slaves,* foster the illusion that this status is somehow inherent in these people's character, that they are a radically different kind of person (if it is admitted that they are "persons" at all). That Saramakas may have considered newcomers simply as people newly arrived from plantations is not allowed for in postholder discourse, making it very difficult to sort out what the relationships between newcomers and Saramakas must really have been like.

It does, however, seem clear that the status of individual newcomers varied considerably. As a rule, women were taken as wives and directly assimilated, and likewise with any man who already had ties of kinship or friendship, no matter how distant, with a Saramaka and could easily be included in his village. It was among all the others that precise status was open to negotiation: powerful Saramaka men often hosted a newcomer or two in a decidedly patron-client relationship, with the latter knowing that his continued welcome, indeed his very life, depended on his satisfactorily carrying out his end of the relationship. One frightened newcomer generally tried to stay with at least some others, as a kind of security; there was some safety (e.g., against hasty witchcraft accusations) in numbers. (When a whole group of newcomers was taken in by a Saramaka village or clan and given its own land, their generalized patron-client relationship has often continued, via their descendants, into the present.) But for individual newcomers, their negotiated status in regard to a particular patron could vary from that of a quasi-domestic servant or retainer to that of a close friend, from that of a prospective brother-in-law to that of a potential witch.

Let us briefly explore some of the implications of these generaliza-
tions for eighteenth-century Saramaka group identity and formation.
One can divide female newcomers into three categories: (1) the overwhelming majority who married into a clan (*lo*) and were simply assimilated into it, so that their offspring became members of that clan;
(2) those who were likewise assimilated but whose separate origin
(as a latecoming nonclan member) is still remembered and used, in
certain contexts, within the clan; and (3) those who became conceptualized as the founders of new clans. I have rather full information
about five women of the second category; the Matjau brothers Djaki
and Awoyo's newcomer wives, who arrived in the late 1770s (see
Chapter 7); the Matjau Musumba's newcomer wife, whom he obtained by murdering her husband (Chapter 7); Foola, the newcomer
who arrived via Matawai and who "founded" Kampu (Chapter 7); and
the early eighteenth-century Amerindian wife of the Langu leader
Kaasi. Since, in cases of latecoming women, assimilation can be
taken as the norm, it is the preservation of separate origins, in these
particular cases, that begs for explanation. And in each of these five
cases, I can document sharp intraclan conflict or violence at the
outset, memory of which the descendants of the involved parties
choose to preserve in their own interests, for occasional political use.

I have good documentation on four women in the third category,
latecomers who today are considered to have founded matrilineal
groups: Adjagbo's wife Paanza, Alabi's wife Sialoto, and two very
latecoming Djuka women, Gbagidí's wife (see Chapter 8) and the still-
later-arriving woman who is the ancestress of a large matrilineage in
Kampu. It does not seem surprising that the two Djuka women are
conceptualized as lineage founders, simply because of the extreme
lateness of their arrivals; in contrast, the cases of Paanza and Sialoto
are more complex. During her lifetime, Paanza possessed a strong
plantation identity, Kasitu (< de Kastilho), shared by her well-known
Djuka brother Kofí Tjapánda. Though he was a Djuka captain, and she
a Saramaka, they were both considered by whitefolks and Maroons
alike as (among other social identities) "Kasitu nenge" (people of the
Kastilho plantation), an identity that was based on the same principle
as that behind many Saramaka and Djuka clan names (Matjau, Abaisa,
Nasi, Dombi, and so forth). Modern Matjaus, who maintain a conflict-
ridden patron-client (father-child) relationship with the Kasitus, never
tire of recounting how Adjagbo, in his old age (unfairly, in their view),
favored the children he had with Paanza over his own sisters' children,
how he taught them all the major *obia*s he had learned from his
Matjau elders (e.g., Akwadja, Lamba) while denying this knowledge
to his own clan, how he built a separate village for them across from
the Matjau village, and so on. In short, Adjagbo's attitudes (which are
confirmed in the eighteenth-century written records) combined with
Paanza's strong Kasitu social identity, and their joint fertility, to permit
the creation—from early on—of a new clan identity for their children.

Paánza páu, the shrine built in Bêndêkôndè by the descendants of Paánza and Adjágbò, to honor the founder of the Kasitú clan (1978)

The case of Alabi's children with Sialoto appears to have a different dynamic. While their many children seem to have been assimilated conceptually into Alabi's Awana group during his lifetime, conflicts arose during the third and fourth decades of the nineteenth century between these children and Alabi's matrilineal relatives, resulting eventually in Alabi and Sialoto's descendants leaving the Middle River to found the village of Ganzê, far downstream, in 1848. In this case, then—unlike that of Paanza—it seems likely that the new clan identity (here, Agbo) did not become salient until many decades after the newcomer woman's arrival.

In cases such as this, the anthropologist's efforts to sort out social process butts up against the historian's fidelity to event-centered, particularistic detail. With few documented cases and only the most retrospective of eyes with which to behold shifting eighteenth-century social realities, it seems foolish in conclusion to do more than indicate the relevant variables: time and circumstances of arrival, the newcomer's social origins, the nature and timing of interpersonal conflict, the relative fertility over time of a couple and their (matrilineal) descendants, and so on. Because the ways these variables worked themselves out in any particular case can be imagined only in retrospect, our understandings remain, of necessity, partial and modest.

10. Tebini, in an independent discussion that same year, filled in a few details.

> My mother's clan [the Fandaaki] came here from the [Matawai] village of Tuido. But they really came from the Para region. The Matawais liberated them and brought them upstream. They kept them at Tuido. Until one day, the Matawais said, "These people are witches." And they [the Matawais] began to treat them badly. The whitefolks were still looking for them. So, one person left, and then the next followed, until they were all in Saramaka.

11. This provision would seem to contradict a 1771 Court resolution recognizing these two Matjau captains (see Chapter 5), but there are contradictions in the relevant documents. In any case, upon the death of Sentea in 1775, a kinsman, Andries, went to Paramaribo to demand that he be recognized as captain in his place. But Daunitz reported to the Court that captains Kwaku Etja and Kwaku Kwadjani (who could have had their own reasons to lie in this case) confirmed to him that Sentea was never a real captain but had nevertheless received, by the good graces of the Court, two jugs of gunpowder every three years for life plus one piece of cotton cloth. Daunitz recommended to the Court that they give Andries a "douceur" of one bottle of gunpowder and a jar of rum to compensate him for his otherwise fruitless journey (SvS 167, 23 Aug. 1775).

12. These proposals seem to have been a modified and expanded version of Dörig's 1772 list (see Chapter 5, note 24).

13. Such mourning gifts constituted an adaptation of the Saramaka practice of anyone who knew the deceased making a material contribution to the funeral celebrations. Typical examples of government contributions include: for Captain Alubutu's funeral in 1772, "a half piece of *salempuri* cloth, 3 jars rum, 1 barrel salt, and 1 bottle gunpowder" (SvS 165, 6 July 1773); and for the funeral of Tribal Chief Kwaku Etja in 1783 (note that the government never, in fact, stopped such "mourning gifts"!), "2 pieces of *salempuri* cloth, 1 piece of *platielje* cloth, 2 jars of cooking fat, 20 jars of rum, 2 jugs of gunpowder"

(SvS 175, 14 July 1783). (See, for other examples, SvS 164, 30 Apr. 1772, SvS 207, 30 Apr. 1772, SvS 208, 19 Oct. 1781.)

14. There is evidence that, during the 1770s, even the governor admitted in private that the whites were cheating on the Maroons every chance they got. In 1776 Stedman (who received his information on such matters from his good friend Governor Nepveu) allowed as he "must Acknowledge that they [the Maroons] are unfairly Dealt with, the Society of Surinam not Sending the Yearly *Presents* . . . without Which Perhaps they would be more true & faithful Allies than they have been" (1988, 510). And Stedman's diary entry for 26 July 1776 is still more explicit.

> The white peaple are the occation of it [the Free Negroes being "excedingly dangerous"]—for making an inglorious peace with them and now wanting to break their word in not Standing to their promises and feading them with trifling preasents, and [demanding] a most unmanly Submission for those black gentlemen, where ever they appear[.] The [Free] negros are no fools and in return presume impertenence trying daily to keep the whites more and more in awe of their long beards and Silver headed [captains'] Staves, whom they wil (at least at this rate) I am afraid try in futurity to extirpate all together. . . . Nb. their number is incredible and all are armd.

15. I am unable to quantify this demographic expansion, though signs of its existence pervade the contemporary documents. Even the total number of Saramakas is unclear. Given the methods used by postholders to make estimates in the three available sets of late eighteenth-century population figures, one can be certain only that there were several thousand (probably four or five thousand) Saramakas alive at the time (see, for example, St 3, pt. 2, 259). Of greater immediate relevance is information on the relative size of different groups, as presented in a village-by-village census made by Postholder Daunitz in 1773 (Hof 87, 4 Mar. 1773). (I regroup his information by clans; a comparison with various nineteenth- and twentieth-century census estimates suggests that Daunitz's list is plausible.) The large grouping of clans then living in Baakawata—the Matjau, Watambii, Paputu, Kasitu, and Paati-nenge—made up 40 percent of the Saramaka population. The next biggest group, Langu, comprised 26 percent. The Nasi, Biitu, Dombi grouping made up 12 percent. The Abaisas were 11 percent and their close allies the Kwamas 5 percent. And Alabi's Awanas accounted for only 6 percent of the total. (In 1779, Brother Riemer wrote that Bambey consisted of "fifty households [St 3, pt. 2, 196].)

16. For example, in 1775, captains Alabi, Kwaku Etja, and Kwaku Kwadjani petitioned the Court to have the village of Soni, which would soon split off from Bambey, be recognized as independent, in terms of tribute goods and a new captain. For the time being, however, the Court was able to hold the line on its desire to limit gifts and

captain's staffs. Serious arguments on these issues between Alabi and Soni continued for years (see, for example, Hof 93, 27 Dec. 1775, Hof 101, n.d. [ca. Apr. 1778], Hof 102, 3 June 1778, 20 July 1778).

17. Such accusations are not surprising in that captains were in a privileged position to ask the whites for special gifts, and the whites followed a consistent policy of cooptation. The government operated on the general principle that the loyalty of any captain could be bought, and although this was far from being true, the captains were in any case pleased to accept the gifts. The minutes of the Court are filled with references to resolutions to give one or another Saramaka captain "eeinige kleinigen" or a "douceurtje." And similar gifts from the Court to "pretenders" tended, temporarily, to defuse the explosive political/demographic situation within many villages by further cooptation.

18. I have not seen documents recording the precise date of Etja's accession to office. In 1772, Dörig's written ultimatums to the Saramakas included the stipulation that "the chiefs shall decide among themselves who will be tribal chief in place of Abini, who will have say over all" (Hof 85, 29 Apr. 1772). Postholder Daunitz's journal for 1778 records that

> *a message had [apparently] arrived from the Cottica Rebels [affirming] that they formally recognize Etja as tribal chief of the Saramakas. . . . I asked Chief Etja how the Cottica Negroes had gotten this [piece of] intelligence but he just struck his chest and laughed, giving no further answer. (Hof 103, n.d. [ca. Nov. 1778 (26, 28 Oct. 1778)])*

And in July 1783, when the Court in Paramaribo received news of Etja's recent death, they decided "to consider the choice of a [new] tribal chief at [their] next session" (SvS 175, 14 July 1783). (In December 1783, Alabi officially succeeded to the office of *gaama*.)

19. Recall the strength of missionary views about Saramakas, especially unsympathetic Saramakas, more generally: e.g., "It is, to be sure, a horrible race . . . a people who can truly be called ugly and frightening" (St 3, pt. 1, 92, 186). It is instructive to compare these frightened, distancing Moravian evaluations with some remarkably sympathetic comments made by contemporary Moravians who ministered to the slave population of the Danish Virgin Islands and who, in some of their statements, genuinely empathized with the slaves' sense of cultural and linguistic loss.

> **One would need to believe that the slaves are completely without feelings to imagine that they could be transported across the ocean, far from their native lands, their gods, their possessions, separating husbands from wives, parents from children, children from parents, one brother from another, and without giving them any idea of their destination or what kind of life or death**

awaited them—and all this by strangers whose language they could not understand—without their feeling the deepest sense of pain. (Oldendorp, cited in Rupp-Eisenreich 1985, 145)

In the Virgin Islands, the Moravians could pity the material conditions of the slaves; in Saramaka, the Moravians were genuinely dependent and afraid. These two settings, so contrastive in terms of the Moravians' power (as well as in terms of their ultimate success in producing converts) help highlight Rupp-Eisenreich's suggestion that the Moravians' appeal was strongest to the wretched of the earth, especially those who wished to assimilate to white society. Brother Riemer, a maverick missionary who lived in Saramaka in 1779–80, wrote his own evaluation of this issue some years after leaving the church:

Undoubtedly, for the Europeans who must serve there, the mission among the Free Negroes is the most difficult of all missions, as well as the most threatening to life and health. Its main purpose—the conversion of the heathen—can only be accomplished poorly compared to other missions, since the political constitution of these people renders the acceptance of Christianity very difficult, in the same way that the unfortunate submissiveness and physical misery of the negro slaves favors the work of conversion. The Free Negroes, although they are heathen, or crude savages, have in many regards a favorable situation with which they feel happy. And the character of most of them is by nature noble. Nor do they know, given their total lack of fear of others, how to dissimulate, and they have no desire to insinuate themselves to their own advantage. In contrast, the negro slaves have to make every effort to curry favor with their European tyrants and for that reason are devoid of all love-of-life, and are more ready to accept Christian religion than the others. (Riemer 1801, 429)

20. Moravian missionaries worldwide held to a strategy of isolating their mission villages from the surrounding heathen. McLoughlin describes how, in North America,

the Moravians believed that once converted, an Indian must move away from his or her heathen family and friends and come to live near the mission in a Christian environment. The pietistic separatism of the Moravians had led them to a similar choice; they separated themselves from the sinful world by forming their communes in Bethlehem and Salem, where they could keep their children free of bad influences. So must it be for the Indian converts. To expect a new convert to sustain his or her faith while continuing to live among pagans was to place an impossible burden upon him or her. The Moravians planned their mission settlements as Christian enclaves within the pagan nation. All converts were to be given Christian names at baptism, to be dressed in whiteman's clothes, and then asked to build new homes for their families at the mission station. Other heathen, seeing the superior moral, social, and economic benefits of this Christian enclave, would wish to join it. Gradually the mission compound would expand; a church and school would be built. As the compound grew, the pagan community would shrink. Ultimately the whole Indian nation would be encompassed in the ever-widening Christian circle. (1984, 43–44)

And the Moravians at Bambey shared this model sufficiently to be able to write very soon after their move, perhaps with a mixture of relief and repugnance,

> **From our [enclave of] Bambey, we hear of the horrors of idolatry and of the inhuman uproar from distant places. (St 3, pt. 1, 238)**

21. Poultry-raising was a Moravian concern, and frustration, throughout the history of the mission. In Sentea, just when it seemed that this effort would succeed,

> **on the 15th [May 1768], a wildcat came into our hen house and killed all but two of our chickens. Until that time, we had always managed to surmount our lack of provisions, but since then we have truly had to beg our dear Father in Heaven to help us survive. (St 3, pt. 1, 84)**

And a decade after Brother Stoll had constructed the new chicken house at Bambey, a diarist wrote with discouragement,

> **Our few chickens have almost all been lost [to wild animals]. The bats come at night and suck out their blood, and during the day large birds of prey and snakes attack them. (St 3, pt. 2, 86. See also St 3, pt. 1, 239, 3, pt. 3, 133, Riemer 1801, 330–31)**

22. The Moravians believed that coffee, grown on a commercial scale (one thousand trees were hoped for), might be the key to financial self-sufficiency for the Saramaka mission (St 3, pt. 1, 237). (In Paramaribo, before coming to Saramaka, Brother Kersten and others had already begun building the cloth and tailoring trades into the thriving Moravian enterprise that later became C. K. Kersten, N.V., Suriname's largest retail outlet, which contributed considerable financial security for the Moravians in the city [Helman 1968].) In 1768, they had already harvested their own coffee at Sentea (St 3, pt. 1, 84), and during the next two years they planted several hundred trees at Kwama (St 3, pt. 1, 133). Shortly before leaving Kwama, Sister Kersten planted 240 seedlings, to be taken with them to Bambey, where they were eventually planted (St 3, pt. 1, 235). By 1775, the missionaries had a total of 305 coffee trees at Bambey (St 3, pt. 1, 244), and they used their domestic slaves to work the crop (St 3, pt. 3, 133). But despite their hopes that coffee—the most valuable single plantation product of coastal Suriname in the mid-eighteenth century—would bring the mission financial independence, their crops were inconsistent and often yielded "not even enough for our own household needs" (St 3, pt. 3, 133). (A later attempt at cash-cropping, this time

with rice, went awry in 1790 when a field intended to pay for communion wine, bread, and candles was deliberately burned by Saramakas
[St 3, pt. 2, 147–48, 151].) The missionaries, especially toward the end
of the century, did receive a small cash income by gathering tonka-
beans in the forest and selling them in Paramaribo (for their essential
oil, which was used as an ingredient in snuff and scents). But it was
not easy work.

> Of all these employments, the gathering of Tonka-beans is the
> most troublesome; and attended with some danger. For it must
> be done in the midst of thick woods, where, in the long rainy
> season, it is very easy to contract disorders from the moisture
> and impure vapors. Besides the most constant care is requisite
> to avoid being wounded by serpents and scorpions. On account
> of the former, it is not easy to walk many steps, without a sword
> or hanger. These serpents, some of which are mortally ven-
> omous, are often so concealed, that in gathering the fruits of the
> earth, we are near laying hold of them with our hands; and we
> are glad to discover them in time, to avoid touching them. In the
> course of the present harvest, we killed eight serpents of various
> kinds. (*PA* 3:64 [cf. *PA* 2:69, 3:388])

23. Food shortages were commonplace at Sentea and Kwama, as
the missionaries had little success with gardening or hunting.

> On May 3 [1771] we began to drink maize instead of coffee in the
> morning, since the latter had run out, like most of our provi-
> sions, because the river is so high that no canoe has been able to
> get through from the city. (St 3, pt. 1, 148)

Throughout the history of the mission the Moravians—or, more usually, their domestic slaves imported from Paramaribo—made gardens,
planting such crops as bananas, taro, yams, *napí,* rice, and cassava,
but the harvests were inconsistent and generally meager, often ow-
ing to an insufficient knowledge of the environment. Despite occasional success in fishing (St 3, pt. 3, 190), and experiments with
importing sheep and even cows (*PA* 3:143), the Moravians, for most
of their time in Saramaka, remained largely dependent on foods sent
from Paramaribo or bartered—often for gunpowder—with Saramakas.

24. Contact between the missionaries and the city, including mail
and occasional supplies sent upriver, occurred sporadically but aver-
aged, perhaps, every three months. However, supplies rarely arrived
intact and dry, both because of difficulties with the rapids and because Saramakas frequently helped themselves (often without missionary knowledge) or allowed missionary supplies to be ruined on
purpose. Here is a representative report:

> Our Brethren in Paramaribo sent us a chest filled with bisquits
> which we received on the 3rd of September [1789]. However, on

> the way it fell in the river and the bisquits were ruined. The same month, we had a similar mishap: they had sent us a barrel of sugar. What had occurred [according to the Saramaka boatmen] was that the negroes in the canoe had decided to go ashore for some hunting, and a spiteful negro who wanted to pick a fight with them overturned their canoe, so that all of the things fell in the river and stayed there. To be sure, they tried to retrieve as many things as they could, and everything was fished out, but the things that were ruined could not be transported. They brought us the sugar barrel, but of course the sugar had simply turned into water. (St 3, pt. 2, 138)

Likewise, the missionaries' letters sent from the coast often arrived water-soaked and illegible (St 3, pt 2, 44), and many of their own diaries and outbound letters suffered a similar fate.

25. Since the move to Bambey, Captain Daunitz (who was a German Catholic) had established his official residence near Bambey at Post Awara, just across from the new Nasi village. Throughout the period, however, he actually resided with Alabi or with the missionaries (with whom he seems to have felt particularly comfortable).

> He is, according to his own confession, a man of faith, and he brings the negroes to us, at every opportunity, for which we thank God. . . . We look upon it as a dispensation from our dear Heavenly Father that this man first relates to us his suggestions about the critical situation with the negroes, before telling them to the Government, because he has such respect for us and for our Johannes. (St 3, pt. 1, 183, 192)

Daunitz was also a man after the missionaries' hearts in his outspoken contempt for Saramaka religion. In 1772, for example, he described how in Baakawata,

> *Djaki's daughter became possessed by her god and he had me called. . . . I sent a message that I recognized only the Great God and no other. Whereupon Djaki came himself and said that I needn't be afraid of the god, that it was a good god, and that now that I lived here I must do as they do and then their god will show me love. I replied, "I have no need for your god's love . . . and if you want me to stay here, you'll have to leave me in peace about this god of yours!"*

The scene ended with Daunitz shutting his door tight (Hof 87, 28 Feb. 1773 [8 Mar. 1772]).

By this time, the missionaries had already helped Daunitz through a serious illness of his own and had often been his hosts for several-day-long visits in their homes. This personal relationship may have influenced the Moravians, despite their principles regarding noninterference in government affairs, to undertake

> a trip to the Upper River region in order to investigate and report on topography for the Government, so that the local postholder would not have to do it. (St 3, pt. 2, 224)

More generally, the mission station provided a haven for postholders on tours of duty, a meeting place for Europeans who shared the feeling of being marooned among savages. In 1791, the missionaries described the postholder's office as being "only twenty paces from our house" (St 3, pt. 3, 38).

26. The previous year in Kwama, for example, a new brother had arrived from Paramaribo, "healthy and well" and filled with enthusiasm. But almost immediately

> Brother Schreyer came down with the fever on the 24th of August, though on the 27th he seemed much better. . . . On the 28th, it became so strong that the Brethren had to keep watch over him. On the 31st, our dear Lord decided to call this dear young, vigorous, twenty-seven-year-old Brother to Him. He had only been with us for three weeks and two days, as if it were a visit. (St 3, pt. 1, 191)

27. During this period, one of Alabi's brothers was feeling the same antimissionary pressures as Simon.

> [8 August 1773] A biological brother of our Johannes, Mouwkeri, who has a wife in another village, came and said that the people in his village had told him that if he continued to come to our prayer meetings, he could no longer live with them, as his deceased father [Abini] would then kill them all. He did not pay attention to this. We have hope that he will enter the Savior's realm. . . . On the 10th of March [1775], Mouwkeri told me that his mother [Akoomi, priestess of Madanfo] had become very annoyed that he was attending our meetings. She had begged him not to convert as long as she was still alive, saying that after she was dead he could do as he wished. The last time he was preparing to go to the city, she brought him, according to negro custom, a chicken to sacrifice so that no ill would befall him on the trip, but he told her that he had given his body and soul to the One who would protect him against all evil. (St 3, pt. 1, 189, 245–46)

The previous year, a friend of Alabi named Awali had suffered similar pressures.

> On the 8th [February 1772] Awali returned home, having spent a few days planting peanuts with his wife and children at a place three hours away. A year ago he was moved by the testimony of the Gospels but was later discouraged by his relatives, who for a long time have been especially strong servants of the idols. Now, however, he sees that they have deceived him and that his long-

ing is true, and he wants to open his heart. We have spent many enjoyable evenings with him recently.

On the eighteenth, a local woman went to the Priest of the Idol [Madanfo] in order to have her Gado called. Once the spirit had come over the woman, she went to the aforementioned Awali's house. Our Johannes Arrabini was sitting with him, but the spirit wanted nothing to do with him. However, it asked Awali all sorts of questions. Because Awali did not want to have anything to do with such questions, the woman grabbed him several times and tried to drag him outdoors. But each time he tore himself away until finally the woman, or the Gado, told him, "You shall die." (St 3, pt. 1, 176)

And other stories of direct threats to potential converts dot the missionary diaries for the rest of the century. Here are two representative examples.

[In 1780] A negro whose sister has been coming to our church regularly . . . has threatened that he will cut off her ears so that she can no longer hear. (St 3, pt. 2, 44–45)

[In 1792] Christian [Grego's] mother-in-law came here to say that she wants to forbid her daughter to attend church—otherwise, she will die. Christian [a convert] said to her, "My wife is no longer a child. She has already borne me five children and she knows the difference between good and evil. You will commit a great sin if you try to prevent her from following the Path of Life. And even if you continue to insist, you will not be able to stop her. As the Savior said, 'Who loves his father and mother more than me is not worthy of me.' " (St 3, pt. 3, 46)

28. A Moravian hymn, composed by Zinzendorf, expresses similar sentiments.

Whene'er I in my Chamber am, And clasp and kiss my dearest Lamb, Then have I the Wounds wholly: Deep in the Side I lay me Thus, Now in the Length, and now across, As if it were mine solely. For I Do lie In the Side's Bed, And the Hands red And the feet too Are my Cov'ring and my Pillow. And had my lamb not laid on me Some Labour, I should certainly Mind nothing else but eating; I could by the dear Wounds so red, My Office and my Brethren's Need Be easily forgetting: Since I Dearly Love to sit near Ev'ry Scar dear, Them revising, On his Body herbalizing. (*Hymns Composed . . .* , 1748)

29. Environmental hazards consistently posed special problems for the missionaries, who never fully adapted to Saramaka solutions in terms of personal cleanliness and dress, housebuilding, or gardening. Here are some illustrations to add to the Bambey flood:

At the end of the month [January 1778], I became very sick again and could not work at all. Probably the cause is the poor provisions I have been eating these last two months. We no longer have any fresh food here. I have nothing to eat but local root-crops. I try to find wild greens, as the garden is not yet ripe, and I boil them with the roots. Unfortunately, the rats and large ants have come here in the last few weeks and have damaged our garden and fruit crops greatly. It has been very difficult for us to protect our provisions from them, even in the house. In the morning, I find that the ants have made such large holes in the clothing that I laid out in the evening, that my clothes are unwearable. More than once, I have had to get up in the middle of the night to chase the rats from my bed. (St 3, pt. 1, 346)

My wife and I are content here but there are certain things I will never praise: (1) There are a kind of flies here no bigger than tiny fleas that fly in hordes and bite so terribly, leaving itching and burning all over, that one cannot help but scratch. . . . (2) There are lizards, mice, and rats everywhere, and they nest above us in all the buildings because all the roofs are made from a kind of woven leaves. The rats are so bold that in the evening they travel the walls, and when we are in bed play master of the house. All over, we hear them jumping and running about, and we even expect to be visited by them in bed. (St 3, pt. 1, 350)

We must add that we presently have a very hard life and a difficult future because we are unable to pay people for goods. The trees are very hard to fell and we are unable to do it because of illness. The wind is not strong so that unhealthy vapors linger. The insects are very numerous, particularly the big ants which come in great numbers here, so that we can hardly plant anything. (St 3, pt. 2, 82)

For a week now, I have had to struggle with a terrible plague, the large brown water rats which, especially at night, come into my dwelling in such numbers that I feel helpless. . . . I have had some traps laid that were made by a slave, and we stayed up the whole night, catching thirty of the miserable thieves and killing them. (St 3, pt. 2, 221–22)

On the 17th [July 1792] toward evening we heard a large storm outside, and before we could prevent it, half our roof was torn off. We were in the dark, and did not know what to do, awaiting the moment when everything would be destroyed. Soon, however, our neighbor [Postholder] Specht came to the rescue and we were successful, holding torches, in securing the remaining half of the roof. . . . But the rain continued and we were too busy for the entire rest of the night getting our things in order to keep ourselves dry. Nothing could remain downstairs because the earth floor was completely soaked. After we had changed our

clothes, namely our nightclothes, we lay down to rest. We were
lucky that the part of the roof that remained was over our beds;
but we had such cold drafts floating around us that my wife
became sick with fever and a cough. In the morning I tried, with
the help of a negro, to piece together the roof. . . . The next day
we had good weather and everything could dry out once more. It
took us several days to get the floor in order, and the negroes
helped us dutifully, but I was still very concerned about my
wife. On the 23rd, I believed she was gravely ill, so I opened one
of her veins. There followed a day of complete unconsciousness.
(St 3, pt. 3, 56–57)

30. This example of missionary arrogance is worth underlining,
because of the cultural presuppositions it encapsulates: two apparently childless male missionaries are presuming here to instruct a
group of Saramaka women in neonatal care—an early historical para-
digm for "development aid" in the Third World. More generally, the
missionaries' lack of children must have been one of their most striking attributes in Saramaka eyes. In addition to Mrs. Kersten, who was
past childbearing age, three youngish Moravian couples spent a total
of some twenty-eight years in Saramaka during the late eighteenth
century, apparently without bearing a single child.

31. Alabi continued for some years to waver between faith and
doubt regarding the efficacy of baptism and the meaning of prema-
ture death. And no wonder, given his own experience and the nature
of missionary explanation.

On the 6th of February [1778] I had a meaningful and blessed
conversation with Johannes, who had been going around in a
dark mood of late. He told me with tears in his eyes that he had
great temptations [to backslide] recently, since two of his children, whom he had baptized, had died. And thus he did not want
to have the one who had been born on the 8th of last month
baptized. However, when it became very sick, he prayed to the
Savior incessantly not to let the infant die. And then, when it
did, he became very upset. Now, however, he sees that the Savior
had to allow the baby to die in order to rescue it from the
heathen way of life. . . . In fact, the enemies of the gospel here
had declared loudly, with many threats, that the child, which
had not been baptized, would have its mouth stopped up by
death. (St 3, pt. 1, 346–47)

The Saramakas' prevailing interest in Christianity's efficacy was clear,
and troubling, to the missionaries. Writing of a "spectacle with the
hair" to determine the cause of a death in 1788, they noted that

in all these horrors, not only one of our baptismal candidates
but two of the baptized actually took part. And we even heard
that a third baptized brother asked a sorcerer to make him an
Obia so he would be successful at the hunt. We tried our best

during this period . . . but it is little wonder that so few heathens here convert, because they see that those who have converted . . . are no better off than they. (St 3, pt. 2, 128)

The related notion that "Christians get sicker more often" even traveled to Djuka. In 1857, the Djuka tribal chief told the local postholder that "he had always heard that it was precisely those Saramaccaners in the Upper Suriname area who had become Christians who were most suffering from and dying of diseases, which was the clearest proof that this religion was not suited to them" (de Groot 1977, 84).

32. I have seen no missionary description of this particular burial; the following quotation refers to another infant death described by the Moravians. According to the memory of the oldest living Saramakas today, funerals for infants and young children have always been marked by extreme simplicity. Today, when a small child dies, an ungabled trapezoidal-shaped coffin is quickly fashioned from a wooden crate (e.g., a White Horse Whiskey box), and the corpse laid in and buried on the day of death, without further ceremony. There is, however, a *nyanyantue* (feast for the ancestors), to inform and honor the deceased kin of the child. Children's burials always take place in a special cemetery apart from that for adults. It is said that (recently deceased) children would be terribly afraid of all the old people they didn't know, were they to be buried with adults. As one Saramaka remarked, "They are much better off with other children in their own cemetery. There, they have nothing to do but play together all day long."

33. The idea of burying a hunting dog in a coffin seemed bizarre to the older men I queried. However, the practice of special burials for such dogs was still standard in the 1970s. Here is a transcript of the late elder Asipei, recounting the instructions given him by his "mother's brother," Tribal Chief Tudéndu, ca. 1935, when he asked his advice about how to bury a much-loved hunting dog.

He told me, "Nephew, take a new length of cloth. Wrap it [the dog's corpse] in the cloth. Don't bury till the next day! Wrap it up so that it's really well wrapped. Then place it in a kokóo [a hard, rounded "tray" made from a part of the maripa palm]. Place it on a beam in a cooking shed. Let it sleep there. Make sure to leave a [kerosene] lamp burning. Let it sleep till morning. Then take it to be buried. Now, when you go to bury it, you must shoot three gunshots. When you've finished burying it, you shoot the three salutes and then get back in your canoe. That's the proper way to bury a hunting dog, man!" So, I said "yes." Well, I buried him exactly as my uncle told me. Brother, I cried and cried! That dog had brought me so much to eat! . . . He told me, "When you bury it, make sure the nose isn't plugged up. [N.B. When humans are buried, the nostrils are plugged with cotton.] Then, when something wants to come kill

Asipéi of the Wátambíi clan, 1912–1983 (photo 1968)

*you, the dog will hunt it, chase it away. That's why
you mustn't plug its nose." So I buried him. I shot the
salutes. Right there just below the mouth of Dan Creek.
That's where we bury dogs. That's the cemetery especially
for dogs.*

Many years later, Asipei's dog relaxed his vigilance: in 1983, while
walking to his gardens, Asipei—a dignified septuagenarian—was fatally bitten by a poisonous snake.

34. An early encounter between the Saramakas' "practical religion" and the Moravians' idea of ultimate salvation is particularly instructive:

> On the 24th [July 1767] some negroes came and asked if I would
> go with them to help pray that their gardens would prosper. I
> told them that it was not necessary for me to go there to pray,
> and that I could pray at home or anyplace else to my God, who
> was my Creator, not only for me but for them. I would, however,
> especially pray for the eternal well-being of their souls. One of
> them then said to the others, "Don't you see? I told you he only
> speaks about this one thing." (St 3, pt. 1, 79)

Because of the additive, eclectic, nonexclusivistic nature of Saramaka
religion, a Saramaka would find it natural to seek a blessing from the
missionaries' god, in addition to whatever rituals he had already performed for the localized gods who were believed to control the fertility of his gardens.

35. Many this-worldly/otherworldly conflicts were blunter:

> On the 30th [October 1787] we visited [the village of] Awara. I
> tried to speak a bit about the Savior but an old blind woman
> interrupted, "If you can heal my eyes, fine. But please get out of
> here with that story!" (St 3, pt. 2, 127)

By 1775, in Bambey, Alabi himself was missing no opportunity to
play on the Saramaka stress on efficacy to try to gather new converts.

> On the 2nd of August, a Gado-man came to our Johannes [in his
> role as captain] and asked for permission to do things in the
> village to assure that the children would prosper. Johannes
> asked whether he could prevent the death of a child. He an-
> swered, "No." Then Johannes said, "If you cannot even prevent
> the death of a child, you can hardly assure that the children will
> remain healthy. Your devices can hardly help us here. Do you
> remember when we felled the trees in this area [to make gardens
> and village]? I prayed to my God, the true God who made you
> and me and everything that you see, and I begged Him to spare
> us from injuries and to bless us and keep us healthy. You see that
> we have had meat and fish in abundance here and that not one of
> us has become sick. In contrast, the others who have had Obia
> performed for them have become sick." (St 3, pt. 1, 241–42)

But though Alabi used such arguments whenever he could, circumstances, such as frequent illness and death among both missionaries
and converts, lent them a somewhat hollow ring.

36. In 1773, the missionaries had merely alluded to the execution
of another accused sorcerer, said to have killed nine people, who was
burned at the stake (St 3, pt. 1, 184). And in 1776, Postholder Wurzler
reported yet another witchcraft conviction: a "slave" named Angula
was found to have killed a child in Chief Etja's family, but Etja, instead
of having him burned to death, wanted to turn him in to the whites for
a bounty (Hof 94, 21 July 1776).

37. Throughout his lifetime, Alabi continued to believe fully and

matter-of-factly in the reality of witchcraft-sorcery. In 1798, a missionary described how,

> on the 20th [February] a strange negro, with several women,
> came hither from the upper country [i.e., from upstream]. While
> we were conversing with them, Arabini came running, and with
> great authority, without ceremony, drove them away from us
> and out of the village. We were quite astonished, and knew not
> what to think of such conduct, as visitors are always well re-
> ceived. But he afterwards told us, that the above-mentioned
> negroe professed the art of mixing poison [sorcery], and boasted
> that he had already destroyed many people by it, so that he was
> everywhere to be shunned. (*PA* 3:51)

38. From yet a third perspective, that of twentieth-century social
anthropology, these accusations of *wisi* must be seen as part of a
complex social process—unfortunately, too complex to analyze on
the basis of the materials the missionaries provide. Modern studies
of witchcraft among Suriname Maroons would suggest, however,
that an understanding of the lengthy process from initial whispered
accusations to public executions or lynchings (which continued into
the 1950s in Djuka) would require a very close acquaintance with local
village politics and personalities (van Wetering 1972, 1973). It is clear
at least that eighteenth-century witchcraft helped "explain" unusual
deaths (e.g., the death of three siblings in quick succession), permitted the collective release of strong emotion, and, through scapegoat-
ing, effected the elimination of certain marginal or "difficult" individuals (largely innocent and defenseless people who were often among
the aged, the handicapped, those who had risen too far too fast, the
patronless, and so on). In one unusual late eighteenth-century witchcraft craze, among non-Saramaka Maroons belonging to the group of
Kwami, allied with Boni, twenty-eight villagers were quickly accused
and executed in a Jim Jones-like frenzy (Hoogbergen 1985, 130).

39. Brother Riemer wrote a separate description of the *kangaa*
ordeal (see also Schumann 1778, s.v. *kangraa*).

> If a crime has been committed . . . and there is a suspect, the
> person is taken to this type of Obia man for the Kangra ordeal to
> be administered. This is done as follows. The accused must
> kneel, and the sorcerer conjures him in the presence of the gods.
> He then takes several Taya [taro] leaves and burns them, reduc-
> ing them to ashes. With these ashes, he coats the tongue of the
> suspect, and takes a feather, which is as thin as possible, from
> the outermost tip of a hen's wing, and he thrusts it through the
> ashes-coated tongue. If the feather passes through without diffi-
> culty and without crumpling, then the person is held to be fully
> innocent. But if the feather breaks, there is no doubt of his guilt.
> Despite the unpredictability of this type of ordeal, the negroes
> submit themselves to it readily and voluntarily. Indeed they go

> so far as to submit themselves to the feather when a friend
> of theirs is a suspect, to demonstrate his innocence. But the
> feather ordeal does not always prove satisfactory, and if the
> friend submits and is proven guilty, the suspect himself is
> brought before the court and if he is unwilling to subject him-
> self to the punishment meted out to him, he must himself sub-
> mit to the Kangra ordeal. (St 3, pt. 2, 265–66)

Today, the *kangaa* ordeal, which remains the ultimate arbiter of guilt or
innocence in Saramaka, is in the sole hands of the Abaisa clan. Its
techniques, including the thrusting of a ritually prepared feather
through the tongue of the accused, seems directly traceable to the
eighteenth-century Kingdom of Benin (Lindblom 1924, 92–93; Barbot
1732, 373).

Brother Riemer described another ordeal as well.

> A person accused of manslaughter or poisoning, or suspected of
> murder, may be forced to drink the oath-poison. The witch doc-
> tor takes some water in which the body of the victim, or any
> other corpse, was washed, and mixes in a bit of earth from the
> grave of the deceased, as well as sundry herbs that are kept
> highly secret. From these he mixes a drink which the accused
> must then swallow, while the witch doctors conjure and pray
> with the most awesome and frightening oaths to their gods. If
> the suspect is really the murderer, then—according to the super-
> stitions of these ignorant people—he will immediately begin to
> swell up. However, if he is not guilty, the drink will have no
> harmful effects on him at all. (St 3, pt. 2, 266)

40. Brother Riemer described what happens when a person found
by the *kangaa* ordeal to be guilty of murder still refuses to confess.

> In this case, certain customary tortures are performed. . . .
> They tie the man's thumbs together and hang him by them from
> the branch of a tree, with his feet bound together and weighted
> with a heavy stone, so that he is just off the ground. He remains
> in this position while two close relatives of the victim, usually
> the two strongest, flog him continually until he confesses why
> and in what manner he killed the deceased. If the criminal
> admits his deed, which happens most of the time, then the
> Grang-Kruttu [*gaan kuutu*]—the supreme council of all village
> captains, presided over by the tribal chief—formally pronounces
> the death sentence of the confessed criminal, and a day is desig-
> nated for the execution. The carrying out of the sentence, as
> well as the mode of execution, is left to the discretion of the
> close relatives of the murder victim.
>   The conjuring of the witch doctors can lead to the conviction
> of an innocent man, since the torture itself is almost as bad as
> the death penalty, and the two men doing the whipping do not

stop until the person has confessed. But, fortunately, it is only rarely that an innocent man is convicted because the Obia man, insofar as he is not a scoundrel, has already gained exact knowledge of who is guilty through his own research, by means of private, secret investigations. He uses this knowledge plus his magical incantations to make a spectacle out of it. And those men who carry the coffin [to determine the cause of death] have been informed in advance as well. Moreover, the supreme council goes about its work cautiously when dealing with the death sentence and never forgets the presence of the Obia man, for whoever has the misfortune to get to the stage of torture [to force a confession] will die either from the whippings or at the stake. (St 3, pt. 2, 267–68)

In April 1778, a convicted sorcerer was again brutally executed— the third man to be so killed in or near Alabi's village during less than a year. His "confession" seems to have been exacted in one of the ways described by Riemer. Here is Brother Schumann's description:

During the following days, we again had a very unpleasant murder case here in the village [of Bambey]. After yet another child had died, the murderer was discovered by means of a Satanic spectacle. And based only on those malicious lies, this negro who was supposed to be the murderer was so terribly tortured that he confessed to having killed the child. The father of the child was our only baptismal candidate. This one plus a baptized person who had been excluded [from the congregation] were the leaders of this abominable Devil's play. All of our reproaches had no effect and did not prevent their evil vindictiveness nor lessen their lust to kill. Only Johannes Arrabini, who was involved in the case, paid the slightest attention to our advice and managed to extricate himself from the affair. The presumed murderer was executed here after being tortured for six days with their customary inhuman tortures. (St 3, pt. 1, 355)

Schumann's 1778 dictionary gives a description of another Saramaka means of exacting a confession in such cases (a technique identical to one used widely in seventeenth-century Europe and called there "the rosary").

Asempreh. Kind of torture; a knotted rope is tied around the head and very strongly tightened, to wring a confession out of the criminal.

In 1967, I overheard a Saramaka who had a bad headache saying "they're doing *asêmpè* to my head" (*a tá náki asêmpè a mí hédi*), showing that memories of this long-obsolete ordeal are collectively preserved in everyday speech. And in 1978, Otjutju—after ritually spraying a mouthful of rum to the ancestors—revealed knowledge of

more specific esoteric details, when he told me that *asempe* was the
personal *obia* of his Matjau forebear Musumba Kokoko.

> *You know what "Father" Musumba used to do when some-*
> *one refused to confess? He would tie their heads with a*
> *band made from the* kwatíi *tree. Then he'd place the drum*
> *pegs [wedged between the person's head and the band].*
> *Then he'd hammer them down! That's* asempe. *Now, when*
> *he knocked one* gán! *[intensifier], the person would say,*
> *"ÓÓÓ, AAÍÍÍÍ! This is what I did . . ." Until it [the interroga-*
> *tion] was over. Nothing more to it. The person would just*
> *keel over. Some died from it, some lived.*

And Otjutju went on to complain at length about the supernatural
punishments that these activities of Musumba had visited on his
matrilineal descendants.

A Moravian historian summarized the missionaries' understandings of such Saramaka practices:

> **Their custom on such occasions is shocking to humanity. The**
> **sorcerers pretend they have discovered the murderer, and, fixing**
> **on some miserable wretch, apply the most cruel tortures to**
> **extort confession from him of the alleged crime, and then put**
> **him to death in the most barbarous manner. (Holmes 1818, 282)**

41. Brother Riemer wrote a generalized description of Saramaka
witchcraft executions that complements this case.

> **The relatives of the deceased, with the help of some associates,**
> **take the criminal by canoe to a distant place where they had**
> **already constructed a funeral pyre the previous day. Here, they**
> **bind him to a prickly [awara] tree right next to the pyre, and first**
> **cut off his nose and ears which they fry over the fire and then**
> **force him to eat. They then cut open his back and rub the**
> **wounds with [hot] pepper and salt, and then rub his open back**
> **up and down against the prickly tree, during which his cries of**
> **misery can be heard at a great distance. In addition, they carry**
> **out many other kinds of barbaric acts from which human na-**
> **ture shrinks, and which decency prevents me from describing.**
> **Finally, they light up the funeral pyre near him, and allow him**
> **to burn little by little, and the victim, who is bound to the tree,**
> **suffers greatly before the fire fully reaches the tree. All this**
> **takes place without in the least bit moving the observers or the**
> **executioners to show the slightest bit of pity. (St 3, pt. 2, 268−69)**

It may be worth recalling that in the very same years the missionaries were witnessing these Saramaka "barbarities," colonial courts
in coastal Suriname were handing down capital sentences for marronage and other "crimes" against whites that were carried out

"A Negro hung alive by the Ribs to a Gallows" and "The Execution of Breaking on the Rack." Engravings by William Blake after 1770s drawings by John Gabriel Stedman (1988, 105, 548).

through similar torture and mutilation in the public square of Paramaribo. Indeed, Brother Riemer himself left a chilling description of such an execution.

> When I returned I found out that there would be an execution in which seven slaves would lose their lives. Such executions take place once a month and are normally scheduled for a half hour past sunrise. I felt it my duty to attend and was there at quarter to six. . . . Soon, six negroes were brought, bound with ropes to one another. The seventh, who was old and sick, was brought in a handcart. Of the six, only one looked melancholy. The others seemed cheerful and kept trying to humour the other who finally became a bit happier. The judicial officials were on a special structure for their use, in front of which the delinquents were made to stand in a row. Each was made to say what he had done wrong, and their death sentences were read out to them in their own language. But while their crimes or sentences were being pronounced, they just kept talking and laughing together. To their comrade who was so sad, they said "Fie! Shame on you. You're not a brave negro."
>
> After all the formalities, the delinquents were unbound from one another by the executioner, who is also a negro. Then the

sick man was pulled with great difficulty from the cart and had to be bound with ropes. Then came the four others, including the melancholy one, who shared the same fate. This last was temporarily released from the bonds tying his hands behind his back and said [to the one who untied him] "You are a good negro. You've given me back my freedom," and he clapped his hands. But this freedom of course was short-lived since the executioner and his assistant soon bound his hands with thin cord and ordered him to lie on his back on the ground. Under his head they placed a piece of wood. The executioner wanted to bind the negro's eyes but he did not want this. He said he was a negro and brave, so then the executioner cut off his right hand, after which the negro raised his bloody arm and said, "Well, at least I am free again, even though my arm is too short." The other negro who was to suffer the exact same fate, commented with humor, "Well, your head will soon become too short as well." Quickly, they turned to him, so that the piece of wood was placed under his chin, and they cut off his head with an axe. When it was time for the last one to be executed, he turned out to be the most frivolous of them all. He was at most seventeen years old and had poisoned his mistress called Missi, and he looked as if he were facing death with complete defiance. After he had lost his hand he screamed out at the executioner, "Your axe works wonders! I hardly feel anything!" (Riemer 1801, 103–6)

42. Brother Schumann's sufferings clearly included smallpox. In a letter written to his aunt, he described how

from the end of July until the end of November . . . on my whole body, from my skull to the soles of my feet, there was not one healthy spot, and the pain I felt both day and night was indescribable. In addition, another terrible sickness followed so that I had a four-day fever, then a three-day fever, then a terrible colic, awful stomach cramps, terrible diarrhea, a foul fever and gall fever with constant vomiting and retching, further attacks of high fever often with stretches of unconsciousness, legs swollen with sores and open wounds, and such awful hands that I was unable to touch anything. (St 3, pt. 1, 359–60)

But through it all, Schumann's faith remained secure.

I certainly would have gone completely astray in this pain and suffering had the Savior not shown His love, and comforted me through His strength, so that my heart remained naively faithful. . . . All this strength gradually brought back my courage and faith. (St 3, pt. 1, 358–59)

43. Brother Schumann's upbringing, living in the forest as the child of a Moravian missionary couple serving Suriname Arawak Indians,

prepared him better than most of the Moravians at Bambey for the difficulties he would experience. Nevertheless, by this time, his faith and vocation had been sorely tested. He wrote, in June 1778,

I have been here in Bambey for an entire year and have found more than sufficient opportunity to test myself in the service of the Savior among the local heathens. And I have so badly failed this test that I feel shame and pain and could simply crawl around on the earth. I see that I am completely useless and helpless for such work. Oh, what tears I have already shed because during my whole time here, I have been unable to win people to the cause of the Savior. I hesitate now and even doubt, though not completely, whether the Savior has really called me for this particular task, and I question whether His mercy and love have in fact sustained me in this mission. (St 3, pt. 1, 358)

44. The principal weaknesses of Schumann's 1778 dictionary lie in the domains of Saramaka ritual, political authority, and sexuality, which receive almost no coverage at all—reflecting Moravian lack of comprehension of these central aspects of Saramaka life more generally. (These same weaknesses are found in the best twentieth-century Saramaka dictionary, also compiled by missionary-linguists [Donicie and Voorhoeve 1963].) Compiled with Alabi's close collaboration, Schumann's dictionary also built upon the occasional previous linguistic work of his confreres in Saramaka. Some of the Moravians had eased into Saramaccan from the syntactically similar Sranan (the creole of the coast); others had learned it directly, in the field. Brother Kersten, for example, found Saramaccan "much more difficult" than Sranan (which he already knew) but learned it well enough "to explain to the negroes our reason for being here . . . in a short period of time" (St 3, pt. 1, 383). By at least 1772, some of the mission services were being held in Saramaccan (St 3, pt. 1, 176). In 1768 and 1771, with the help of Alabi, the missionaries undertook translations of liturgical texts and hymns, and in 1772, 1775, and 1776—again working closely with Alabi—they translated portions of the New Testament (St 3, pt. 1, 147, 244, and see Voorhoeve and Donicie 1963, 102). While working on his dictionary, Schumann also translated portions of the Old Testament, as did Brother Randt some years later (St 3, pt. 1, 357; Voorhoeve and Donicie 1963, 107–8). But in 1779, while the mission was temporarily closed, most of Schumann's books and papers were destroyed, and previous translations into Saramaccan were apparently ruined (Voorhoeve and Donicie 1963, 108). Later Moravians picked up the translation work again. In 1792, Brother Wietz wrote that he had finished correcting the translation of the Easter story, which he had begun eight years before, "because I now have a better command of the language" (St 3, pt. 3, 57–58). And in 1793, the Brethren were using "the new church litany which has now been translated into the local language" (St 3, pt. 3, 98), and they had

> decided on the lesson of the Epistles, which have already been
> translated into Saramaccan, and Brother Wietz will now under-
> take the translation of the Acts of the Apostles, which we have
> always missed. We are now also in the process of improving the
> Saramaccan hymnal since the present one is poor both in songs
> and verses. (St 3, pt. 3, 99–100)

In 1799, Brother Wietz undertook a full translation of the four gospels
(St 3, pt. 3, 187), and similar occasional liturgical translation work
marked the whole history of the eighteenth-century mission (Voorhoeve and Donicie 1963, 103–9).

   45. This final sentence constitutes a signal observation, less because it tells us what can, in any case, be read into so many of the
Saramaka-Moravian interactions as described in the diaries than because Brother Schumann found it possible to be so frank. One brief
comment five years earlier displayed similar candor:

> There is a big difference between the present mood of the local
> heathens toward us and what it was two years ago. At that time,
> right after the baptism of Johannes [Alabi], they could actually
> have killed us. (St 3, pt. 1, 183)

The very great majority of Saramakas had always wished that the
missionaries would leave. Only a handful of political leaders, and the
very few converts, had anything to gain from their presence, and
most Saramakas wanted to keep their territory pure and unsullied,
unpolluted by whitefolks. Saramakas, then even more than now, simply did not *like* whitefolks and, with very good historical justification,
feared them.

Seven: Ringer of Bells

   Sources for this chapter, in approximate order of use, include: for
Heydt's reopening of the mission, St 3, pt. 1, 363–64; for Musumba's
slave harboring and return, Hof 90, 11 May 1774, Hof 94, 16 June 1776,
Hof 101, 19 Feb. 1778, Hof 102, 3 June 1778, Hof 103, ca. Nov. 1778 [12
Oct. 1778], Hof 104, 10 Jan. 1779 [11 Jan. 1778], Hof 108, ca. Dec. 1779
[13 Oct. 1778], Hof 111, 12 Dec. 1780; for the similar Matjau case, Hof
104, 10 Jan. 1779 [11 Jan. 1778]; for buying slave women, Hof 103, ca.
Sept. 1778 [13 Nov. 1778], Hof 106, 6 July 1779; for Gáu's death in
Djuka, Hof 101, 19 Feb. 1778, Hof 102, 3 June 1778, Hof 104, 12 Dec.
1778, 10 Jan. 1779 [11 Aug. 1778, 10 Nov. 1778], Hof 111, 28 Aug. 1780;
for Wietz's arrival in Bambey, St 3, pt. 1, 365, *PA* 3:383–84; for Riemer's river trip, Riemer 1801, 125–223, St 3, pt. 2, 173–203; for the
Mosers' arrival, St 3, pt. 2, 205; for Riemer's downstream voyage, St
3, pt. 2, 206, 207; for Riemer's loneliness, St 3, pt. 2, 211; for his
dependence on Alabi, St 3, pt. 2, 211–12; for the jaguar encounter, St
3, pt. 2, 224–25, Riemer 1801, 389–90; for Riemer's ringworm, St 3,
pt. 2, 226; for Riemer's encounter with the local women, St 3, pt. 2,

212–14, Riemer 1801, 351–56; for Riemer's encounters with the sorcerer and tribal chief, St 3, pt. 2, 214–21; for Wietz's report on the dream, St 3, pt. 2, 35; for the baptism of Kwaku and others, St 3, pt. 2, 35–36; for the report on Bébi, St 3, pt. 2, 39–40; for Bebi (and others) becoming baptismal candidates, St 3, pt. 2, 40; for Sialoto's (and others') baptism, St 3, pt. 2, 44; for dates of baptisms and places of birth of the baptized, AEB, Inv nr 198; for Alabi's letter, St 3, pt. 2, 36–37; for Riemer's comment on Sialoto's conversion, St 3, pt. 2, 278; for Wietz's account of Akoomi's funeral, St 3, pt. 2, 40–41; for Riemer's account, St 3, pt. 2, 276–79; for the negotiations surrounding Tutuba's release, SvS 370, 17 Dec. 1779, SvS 208, 28 Dec. 1779, Hof 113, 26 Mar. 1781; for the Saramakas' role in the Djuka-whitefolks dispute, Hof 110, 8 July 1780, Hof 111, 28 Aug. 1780; for the death of Kwaku Kwadjani, St 3, pt. 2, 51–52, SvS 208, 9–13 Oct. 1781; for Weinhold's discussion with Kristofel, Hof 111, 6 Nov. 1780; for Kwadjani's request, Hof 111, 25 Nov. 1780; for the chiefs' collective requests, Hof 112, 4 Jan. 1781; for the 1781 gift list, Hof 112, 12 Feb. 1781; for the birth of the god-child, St 3, pt. 2, 46–47; for the compromise burial, St 3, pt. 2, 78; for Wietz's visit to Kungooka, St 3, pt. 2, 48; for his visit with Yaya, St 3, pt. 2, 48–49; for Alabi's intervention in a "spectacle," St 3, pt. 2, 51; for the dance-lover's speech, St 3, pt. 2, 55; for New Year's 1777, St 3, pt. 1, 332; for the food-and-drink orgy, St 3, pt. 2, 45; for Simeon's death, St 3, pt. 2, 52; for New Year's at church, St 3, pt. 2, 46, 3, pt. 3, 44; for Riemer's description of Alabi, St 3, pt. 2, 217–18, Riemer 1801, 370–71.

1. In 1779, the postholder was still trying to maintain pressure on Musumba and the Matjaus to return Musumba's woman and a handful of other slaves they were holding.

> *Awanu [another name for the Matjau, Adjagbo] told me that it was not his fault that the slaves [several of whom he had originally "found" in the forest] had not been turned in. Because I must ask for the slaves from his captain, Kristofel. I told him that this was just more Matjau-clan deception, because whenever I ask Kristofel about the slaves, he says I must ask Kokroko [Musumba] and Awanu. And when I come to ask Kokroko and Awanu, I am told I must ask Kristofel. They must think I'm an idiot while in the meantime they are all conniving together! (Hof 108, ca. Dec. 1779 [13 Oct. 1778])*

And by the next year, as part of the postholder's almost routine threats to the Matjaus about returning whitefolks' slaves, Musumba was specifically ordered to give back "his slave woman and two children"—which he never did.

2. Publicly, this clan segment is called "Matjau" and counted as such for all official purposes. But the story of this 1770s event, and the eternal curse it brings upon other Matjaus, makes this group significantly different. Children of a female stranger whose husband was "killed" by the Matjaus, this group continues to hold considerable

power over their Matjau protectors, for it is they who must pray and make offerings, on behalf of the Matjaus, to their slain ancestor, requesting that he not wreak further vengeance on the Matjaus, the people of Musumba.

3. The names of the slave man and woman are well known to local Saramakas, albeit highly dangerous to utter (which is why I do not repeat them here). This clan segment is normally called by the name of one of the daughters of Musumba and the slave woman. Some versions of this story claim that Musumba, rather than turning the slave back to the whites, murdered him on the spot. The documentary record, as discussed in the text, is not conclusive, but it seems possible that these latter versions are less well-informed, stemming from people who know only the results (the avenging spirit) and have falsely inferred the cause (not being aware of the practice of turning back slaves for a bounty).

4. These accounts, plus the traces in the archives, suggest to me that (like skyjackings and certain other terrorist tactics in our own time) practices such as keeping a newly arrived slave woman and turning back, or killing, her husband may well have become a vogue during this particular period, until other means of dealing with the problem of getting wives became more advantageous.

5. Etja added that Djaki "is quite old and his five wives are all sick and can do him no service. And he cannot live without a [healthy] wife. And here in the forest he can no longer get a young girl because of his age" (Hof 106, 16 July 1779). In fact, five wives was a most unusual number for the eighteenth century, when most men—for demographic, not ideological reasons—were limited to one or two. Djaki, like some equally nonconformist twentieth-century Saramaka counterparts, seems to have been particularly preoccupied with acquiring more: in 1780 he traveled to Djuka to bring back a new wife (Hof 111, 15 Nov. 1780), and he and his brother Awoyo are said to have founded the village of Kumbu with two escaped slave women whom they had "caught" downriver, near Remoncourt and Victoria, several years earlier.

Brother Riemer wrote of Saramaka polygyny in general:

Each negro is allowed to take as many wives as he is able to support in a respectable manner. Thus, one rarely finds one who has more than three wives, and a man who has three is looked upon by the members of his nation as being a very skillful provider. Such a man must go to three different places at least an hour apart from one another, and for each of the three families he must clear and later harvest gardens, as the dwellings of these wives must be kept as separate from one another as possible. They call each other Gambossa [*kambosa*], which means "co-wife," and they try to avoid face-to-face meetings, as between them a lethal enmity is constantly nourished. Most negroes have only two wives, but between them the enmity is equally

great. There are also poor providers who are only able to support one wife at a time, and who are therefore looked upon with a certain disdain. (St 3, pt. 2, 262)

I believe that Brother Riemer, here as elsewhere, was overgeneralizing from a small number of cases, and that the common Saramaka practice of ridiculing a man who fails at "managing" two or more wives (something like an American "henpecked husband") may have led him to the false conclusion that most men were polygynous at any time. My reconstructions of eighteenth-century marriage patterns would place the proportion of adult men who, at any given time, had two or more wives at closer to 20 percent.

6. I deduce his age from the fact that in 1739, Gau was married and old enough to have participated in a famous raid (R. Price 1983a, 107).

7. Kofi Tjapanda was the brother of Paanza, female founder of the Saramaka Kasitu clan, and he often visited Saramaka. (See R. Price 1983a, 129–34, for discussions of their 1739 escape from their Suriname River plantation, and how they separated.) In 1772, for example, he was reported to be in Saramaka "to drink an oath" (undergo an ordeal) in front of six Djuka witnesses who had accompanied him; Djuka chief Pambo had apparently accused him of witchcraft, and he had come to Saramaka to clear his name (which he was evidently able to accomplish) (Hof 87, 26 Feb. 1773 [22 May 1772]). (I suspect that this ordeal was connected to the Abaisa clan's *kangaa* oracle; for, that same year, Postholder Daunitz reported that four other Djukas were on their way to Captain Samsam's [Abaisa] village to "drink the oath" [Hof 87, 26 Feb. 1773 (22 May 1772)]. It appears that *kangaa* may, at the time, have been the supreme "ordeal" for Djukas as well as Saramakas.) And Kofi Tjapanda remained involved in Saramaka politics during the subsequent years as well (see below).

8. Saramaka-Djuka ties were by this time truly multiplex—political negotiations regarding whites and Bonis, the clandestine shunting back and forth of escaped slaves wanted by the whites, numerous kinship and marriage relations, ritual exchanges of several kinds, and even recreational and artistic interchange. For example, in 1772, a number of Saramakas and Djukas participated (illegally) in a large "play" (drumming/dancing/singing performance) on a Jews Savannah slave plantation; some of the slaves were later punished and the Saramakas and Djukas sent home with a warning (SvS 164, 12–14 Sept. 1772).

9. Staehelin, the early twentieth-century Moravian chronicler, wrote of Riemer that "as a missionary, he did not accomplish much, as neither his character nor his disposition was well suited to this vocation" (St 3, pt. 2, 173). Certainly, Riemer's Stedmanesque romanticism set him clearly apart from his confreres. He once wrote of the Saramakas, for example:

It is a great pleasure to see a people who are so content with their fate. They enjoy the fruits of their labor and are unacquainted

**with the poison of hatred. Nor do they know calumny, selfish-
ness, or pride. They act always like real _"menschen,"_ who fulfill
their happy duty of loving their neighbors more than many
people who call themselves Christians. (Riemer 1801, 333)**

10. Eighteenth-century Saramaka canoes were more crudely constructed (e.g., less finely hollowed out before being "opened" by fire)
than modern craft, which range from about ten to fifty feet in length.
Indeed, there has been notable technical refinement in Saramaka
canoe-building even during the past hundred years (R. Price 1970).
The Nasi clan is generally credited with having constructed the first
Saramaka canoes during the early eighteenth century (R. Price 1983a,
105). By the time of the Peace, such canoes were already highly
serviceable, and they fetched a good price when Saramakas brought
them for sale to the coast.

11. Brother Riemer later wrote that such paddling songs were
characterized by "a sprightly melody and countless repeats, and their
content consists mainly in asking the gods for protection on the trip,
as well as for luck in fishing, hunting, and so forth" (St 3, pt. 2, 185).
During these same years, John Gabriel Stedman wrote of slave singing in a similar vein:

> It is much practiced by the barge rowers or boat negroes on the
> water, especially during the night in a clear moonshine; it is to
> them peculiarly animating, and may, together with the sound of
> their oars, be heard at a considerable distance. (1988, 659)

Slave song, he also noted, was characterized by a call-and-response
structure,

> melodious but without Time; in Other respects it is not unlike that
> of some Clarks reading to the Congregation, One Person Pro-
> nouncing a Sentence Extemporary, which he next hums or Whis-
> tles, when all the others Repeat the Same in Chorus, another
> sentence is then Spoke and the Chorus is Renew'd a Second time
> & So ad perpetuum. (1988, 516)

12. For discussion of contemporary racialist ideas regarding differences of skin color, body form, and constitution—and their putative
biological origins—see the Introduction and Editors' Notes in Stedman 1988.

13. "Directeur" was the term used by the Dutch for the position
that the British in the Caribbean called "bookkeeper"—the resident
white manager who took care of a Suriname plantation while the
absentee owner was elsewhere—either in Paramaribo or Europe.

14. Riemer explains in a footnote that "Missi means _Frau,_ not only
in the sense of Mistress [owner] but also in the sense of concubine.
In the first case, every Mistress is called that by her slaves; but in the
latter case, she keeps that title only as long as it pleases her master"
(1801, 133). Riemer apparently chose not to mention the fact that
the "charms" of such mulatto slave women were not kept hidden.

"Missi," it seems, like her sisters in bondage who were "privileged" to wait on Massa's table, would have been "drest in the finest India Chintses—but all naked above [her] Middle, according to the Custom of the Country, and adorned in the richest manner with Golden Chains–Medals–Beads–Bracelets–and sweet smelling flowers" (Stedman 1988, 42).

15. Throughout the history of slavery in Suriname, planters and their white administrators and plantation managers, fearing eventual loss of their slave property, attempted, without success, to limit contact between their slaves and visiting Maroons.

16. By the time of Riemer's visit, the white population of Suriname, unusually heterogeneous for a plantation colony, numbered some three thousand (as compared to some fifty thousand slaves). Jews (mostly Sephardim) comprised about one-third, with the other two-thirds divided among Dutch, French, Germans, and a much smaller number of English.

17. Stedman, Riemer's contemporary in Suriname, described in even richer detail the extremes of planter luxury. Whites were routinely served at table by nearly nude house slaves, who fanned them not only during their naps but sometimes all night long, put on and removed all of their clothes each morning and evening, bathed their children in imported wine, and so on. Wealthy planters in Paramaribo had forty or fifty such hand-picked domestic slaves.

18. Governor Nepveu of Suriname, who died in 1779, left his own chilling description of the *spaans bok:*

The hands are tied together, the knees drawn up between them, and a stick inserted through the opening between the knees and the hands and fixed firmly to the ground, around which they then lie like a hoop and are struck on the buttocks with a guava or Tamarind rod; one side having been struck until the skin is completely broken they are turned over to have the other side similarly injured; some use hoopsticks for this, although this is an extremely dangerous practice as it generally results in the slave's death, even though the chastisement is less than with the abovementioned rods. (Cited in R. Price 1983b, 7–8)

Stedman, writing of the same period, offers a very similar account, adding that slaveowners rather than bothering to inflict the punishment on their own premises often sent "the Victim to the Fortress [in Paramaribo], With a Line [letter] to the Publick Executioner & to whom is Paid some Trifle in money for taking the Trouble" (Stedman 1988, 556). This latter practice is commemorated in a bitterly ironic slave proverb, recorded in the mid-nineteenth century: *Tangi vo spansi boko mi si binfoto* ("Thanks to the *spaans bok,* I got to see the inside of the fort") (Lichtveld and Voorhoeve 1980, 288).

19. Saramaka trade with the coast, guaranteed by the treaty, became institutionalized within the first decade after the Peace. In addi-

tion to rice, Saramakas sold substantial amounts of peanuts and quantities of canoes (plus other diverse items such as tame birds [St 3, pt. 1, 119]) on plantations or in the city itself. Brother Schumann's dictionary lists as linguistic examples, s.v. *munni, monni,* "in Paramaribo, peanuts bring a lot of money," "canoes bring more money than peanuts," and "sometimes rice brings little money." Saramaka purchases on the coast, which formed crucial supplements to the whitefolks' goods they received as biennial tribute, were truly varied. The documents mention large quantities of salt, various sugar products, cooking oil (to supplement that which their women produced from palm nuts), several kinds of alcoholic drinks (used largely for ritual libations), candles, soap, pots, many kinds of tools (including a number not appearing in the tribute lists, such as hammers, planes, pliers, and claspknives), various kinds of cloth, cowrie shells, beads, earrings, combs, scissors, mirrors, and of course, firearms and ammunition (the acquisition of which the government tried desperately but with little success to monitor and control throughout the century). Brother Riemer, writing of such trading trips, noted, "Their stay in Paramaribo usually lasts from four to six days, and through their transactions they spend as much as they have earned" (1801, 332–33).

20. Log rafts had played a role as transportation for Saramakas since the war years (R. Price 1983a, 66). But from the time of the Peace until well into the twentieth century, commercial logging became a major source of income for Saramakas (as well as for Djukas), who floated large rafts for sale down to the border with the whites. De Groot describes the enormous scale of such activity during the nineteenth century (1977).

21. Such concern about slaves stealing from Saramakas, and vice versa, was not misplaced. The archives contain mention of a number of such incidents. For example, in 1779, Captain Alando of the Langu clan complained to the postholder that one of his canoes, loaded with all sorts of goods (rice, peanuts, rum, guns, powder, machetes, meat, and other valuables) was stolen from a plantation landingplace while its owners (who had gone ashore for a moment) were on their way upstream (Hof 105, 24 Feb. 1779, 10 Mar. 1779). And soon after, Alando complained that two of his men had been badly beaten with a stick, without provocation, by the director of Plantation Nieuw Star (Hof 110, 5 June 1780).

22. Saramaka libations were normally intended not for gods but for ancestors, who are often addressed collectively as *gádukôndè* (literally, "god-country")—whence, perhaps, the confusion on the part of Brother Riemer.

23. Like the postholders, the missionaries wore strictly European clothes when in Saramaka. The engravings in Brother Riemer's book show missionary men consistently dressed in a kind of stovepipe hat, dress shirt (and, apparently, vest) and jacket, trousers, shoes and stockings, and their wives in long dresses, jackets, bonnets, and shoes and stockings. And their diary entries repeatedly make it clear

Mamádan shrine, ca. 1955 (Jozefzoon 1959, 28).

that the correctness of their clothes, no matter how ill-suited to the humid tropics, was an important mark of distinction to separate them from heathens and slaves.

24. Riemer is referring to the *nyumaa* (*Hoplius macrophthalmus*), the largest fish in the Suriname River, which is carnivorous.

25. Mamadan was the greatest of the Suriname River falls, and it was my privilege to see it once, in 1966, before it was forever flooded over by Alcoa's artificial lake. An island in the midst of the awesome Mamadan scenery housed an impressive shrine to the god of the falls, where offerings were made for safe passage.

Brother Langballe's 1797 description of his passage through the falls reflects something of its evocative power.

> [The water] spreading into four arms, [fell] about eighteen feet, nearly perpendicular, where was a portage. We were much struck with the scenery about this dam. The noise of the water was tremendous, and we could not hear each other speak. A rocky island, overgrown with brushwood, upon which we landed, divides the middle portion of the cataract into two streams of amazing rapidity. Standing close to the swiftest of them I felt the rocks trembling beneath me; the heavens were overcast with thunder clouds, and every now and then awful claps, and rolling of thunder above, seemed to overpower the noise of the rushing waters beneath. The impression made on

> my senses nearly amounted to dread, and I represented to my-
> self that scene of majesty, when the law was given on Mount
> Sinai. (*PA* 2:427–28)

26. The practice of collectively celebrating the return of *bakáama*
(men who have been to *bakaa konde*—whitefolks' territory) dates
from the war years, when large celebrations, replete with ritual, took
place for warriors returning from raids on plantations. (For a story that
vividly captures the emotional pitch of such wartime returns, see R.
Price 1983a, 147.) Just as every peacetime departure for whitefolks'
territory—whether in the 1760s or the 1960s—required complex protective rites, so each return was an occasion for thanksgiving and joy.
Late eighteenth-century returns, according to the missionary diaries,
were also characterized by wild drunkenness, something that I neither witnessed nor was able to elicit any memory of among the
oldest living Saramakas.

> On the 7th of August [1777] a group of negroes came back from
> Paramaribo and brought a great deal of liquor. For several days,
> both day and night, they drank, danced, drummed, fired shots,
> and shouted wildly. It is really indescribable how painful this
> noise has become for us. (St 3, pt. 1, 338; cf. St 3, pt. 2, 45, 136,
> 197; 3, pt. 3, 45)

But, apart from New Year's, these return-from-the-coast celebrations
seem to have been the only occasions for drunkenness. Although the
missionaries—not surprisingly, given their general neglect of female
concerns—are silent regarding the attitudes and reactions of Saramaka women to these returns, modern Saramakas stress the excitement of their eighteenth-century female ancestors on such occasions. These women, who were the recipients of cloth, pots, knives,
and other whitefolks' items when men returned from the coast, engaged in special celebration, "cutting" a dance called *bandámmba,*
which is rarely seen today but which until recent decades was especially associated with returns from the coast. As the canoes of the
returnees approached, men stood on shore firing salutes of welcome, and women broke into *bandammba,* grinding their lower tor-
sos sinuously, hands on hips (see, for a recording of *bandammba*
drums, R. and S. Price 1977).

27. This youth was probably the missionaries' favorite pupil, Christian Grego (see note 32, below).

28. Because Saramakas spend days (and at some seasons
weeks) at a time in their gardens, which are often several hours' walk
or canoe trip from their village, housing is substantial and often resembles a small village. For discussion of twentieth-century garden
settlements, see S. Price 1984, 28–31. The missionary diaries make it
clear that eighteenth-century garden settlements were equally extensive.

29. By the middle of the eighteenth century, Saramaka cuisine was already rich and varied, and thoroughly Afro-American in its blending of Old and New World procedures and ingredients. For detailed discussion, see R. Price 1990.

30. As S. Price has written,

> Today . . . visual isolation [of men and women eating] continues to be the critical variable. To Saramakas, one of the most exotic features of western culture is the custom of women eating within sight of their husbands. The segregation of the sexes is as strongly embedded in Saramaka concepts of propriety for meals as it is in western notions about public bathrooms. (1984, 45)

For Riemer's more general discussion of eighteenth-century Saramaka meals see 1801, 276–78; for S. Price's twentieth-century counterpart, 1984, 46, passim.

31. Today, the entrance of *bakaama* canoes continues to be carefully choreographed. I have witnessed a string of several outboard-motor-driven canoes execute triple loops, to the cheers of onlookers, in their final approach.

32. The identity of the horn player is unclear. It was not Christian Grego, since he seems to have accompanied Brother Riemer on the voyage (see note 34, below), but he did know the instrument. (In 1791, when two missionaries arrived at the mission station, "Christian [Grego] took his hunting horn and blew the melody 'Sing Praises unto God on High'" [St 3, pt. 2, 150].) Given Saramaka musical skills more generally, as well as the eighteenth-century importance of wooden signal trumpets, many youths may well have learned to play the Moravian horn.

33. Brother Riemer's musicianship was part of a more generalized Moravian pattern. (For example, an impressed Benjamin Franklin wrote from Bethlehem, Pennsylvania, in 1756, "I was at their church, where I was entertain'd with good music, the organ being accompanied with violins, hautboys, flutes, clarinets, etc." [Franklin 1948, 747].) In 1770, Brother Kersten had already used his zither to attract a Saramaka crowd, which then "gave us the opportunity to praise the love of our Creator" (St 3, pt. 1, 133), and Saramakas were intrigued by his other musical talents as well.

In the evening we sang a song which Brother Kersten had recently composed, and in which the brothers' and sisters' voices alternated. This pleased our people greatly, as they had never heard anything like this before. (St 3, pt. 1, 244–45)

A few years later, Brother Schumann charmed Saramakas with his violin.

On the 20th [May 1777] I began to play a song on the violin, which made a strong impression on the negroes, who derived great pleasure from it. They were very surprised that I had

> learned so quickly to play their negro language on the violin, as
> they expressed it, because the melody of the violin was in har-
> mony with the words that they sang. (St 3, pt. 1, 335)

(A Saramaka *adunke* song, dating from the nineteenth century, uses
the phrase "violin language" to mean "sweet, seductive talk," but it is
unclear whether the metaphor initially sprang from hearing a Moravian play [R. and S. Price 1977].) Moravian skills served as curiosities
and entertainment for Saramakas in other realms as well.

> This month Brother Kersten made a spinning wheel for his wife
> so that she could spin cotton and enjoy the diversion of knitting
> and sewing. The negroes were truly amazed about this way of
> spinning [as Saramakas knew only hand-held spindles] and they
> could not take their eyes off her. (St 3, pt. 1, 143)

But even in such apparently innocent encounters, fundamental cultural differences between Moravians and Saramakas often came to
the fore.

> When Brother Wietz was playing the zither one evening [in
> 1780], a whole lot of frivolous negroes came into the house to
> dance to it. Brother Wietz explained that the music was not
> meant for dancing, and that we would not tolerate such behavior
> in our house. They became angry and asked why it was wrong to
> do this, since there are Europeans in Paramaribo who do the
> same. Then Brother Wietz explained to them that our joys come
> from different experiences and that these experiences last for an
> eternity whereas their own last only an instant. They were
> moved, asked for forgiveness, and departed. (St 3, pt. 2, 43)

34. Brother Wietz reports that "On 7 January Brother Riemer returned [from Paramaribo] with four baptized negroes" (St 3, pt. 2, 35).
There were, at this time, only five Saramaka converts—Alabi, Joshua
Kodjo, Christian Grego, David Skipio, and Simon Aduku (who had
been baptized only two weeks before, probably too recently to have
made the trip).

35. Though Brother Riemer spent barely six months in Saramaka,
he had two other close encounters with jaguars as well.

> After Johannes left [my house], at midnight, I lay down in my
> hammock to get some rest. But by the bright moonlight I saw
> through the open door, near which my sleeping dog lay, that a
> large tyger was slowly approaching the house. I did not show the
> slightest fear, since my freshly loaded musket was standing in
> the doorway and I imagined that this beast, like all animals,
> would therefore show respect for me, as even lions are said to be
> afraid and have this instinct. So, I lay quiet in my hammock. I
> was, however, afraid for my dog, lying just outside the door and
> in grave danger. The tyger paced back and forth until, finally, he
> struck the dog on the head with his paw, knocking him uncon-

"Help Massa! I'm dead" (Riemer 1801, pl. 14).

scious and grabbing him in his jaws. As this dog was one of my dearest possessions, and I needed him for hunting, I ran after both the tyger and the dog with my musket. But unfortunately, I could not find a trace of either one, so I returned feeling sad. The following morning, I told the negroes of the incident and they immediately began to fashion a tyger trap in which they hoped to catch him the next night, employing an old, useless dog as bait. However, the uninvited guest had been sufficiently sated by the booty from my house that he did not show up until the third night. But he was indeed trapped this time!

The negro who was standing watch immediately sent word to the other negroes, and they sent word to me. It was truly frightening to see this angry animal run around the trap in pure rage. The older negroes claimed that they had never seen such a large tyger in this area. . . . After I had fired the first shot at the [trapped] tyger, the other negroes followed suit. Although, after the second shot he lay there dead, they all continued to shoot anyway, to vent their anger. They were all the more angry because they had prized my dog as the best hunting dog in the village. Finally, they carved up the animal into small pieces and returned to their hammocks singing. (St 3, pt. 2, 222–23)

This type of jaguar trap, called seéka (see Schumann 1778, s.v. sekra), has long been obsolete in Saramaka, but its memory is preserved in an obscure proverb, "The jaguar's in the seeka trap!" As an old man explained to me,

> It [a seeka] must have been set something like a bákisi [fishtrap]. Let's say you had been an important person but then you get chronically ill; you're all washed up. People will say, "The jaguar's in the seeka trap!" Anyone who wants to can come and shoot you with an arrow. Even little kids! You once were so powerful but now you're helpless: "The jaguar's in the seeka trap!"

Brother Riemer's third encounter, in which he played the hero, is depicted in a contemporary engraving.

Riemer's jaguar tales are not fantasies: postholders several times matter-of-factly report the death of Saramakas from jaguar attacks (e.g., that of Captain Samsam's adult son—Hof, 25 Oct. 1771 [8 Sept. 1771]).

36. Here is an early example of Saramaka men showing contempt for the Moravians through stylized, ironic "tomming":

[Today,] two negroes came to eat with us. After we had eaten, we sang a verse as usual. One negro asked the other what we had sung. The other told him that we had just thanked the Great God for the meal that we had enjoyed. To which the first responded, "What these people do is surely correct. We negroes know nothing about that. We are just like the beasts in the

forest who eat and drink and simply go their way. We are just like that!" (St 3, pt. 1, 92)

Here is a more direct, more characteristically female put-on from some years later:

A negro woman came to me while I [Schumann] was suffering from my lingering sickness and offered to help me. [Some time later] When she heard that I felt better, she asked in all serious-ness for compensation, because she had prayed to God for my recovery! (St 3, pt. 1, 347)

37. The Moravians tried to confront and deny widespread Sara-maka beliefs in their wealth, but without success.

We made the suggestion to our church Brethren that they con-tribute a bit of money to buy a crate of candles for the church, suggesting that since they previously spent so much money on their idolatry, they now could spend just a little for the church. Unfortunately, this suggestion did not meet with much fa-vor. . . . Part of the reason is that they have grown accustomed to receiving things free from the Government. They themselves say that whitefolks have plenty of excess, and they are unable to understand how we [Moravians], who are white people, could be so poor. When we tell them we have only those funds put to-gether by our Brethren and Sisters [in Europe and North Amer-ica] . . . they simply cannot believe it. (St 3, pt. 2, 135)

Fundamental Saramaka ideas about the world of the whites as a world of boundless material wealth—fostered during slavery, nur-tured by raiding parties during the years of war, and confirmed by government largess (and, even, occasional withholding of same) fol-lowing the Peace—remain powerful today. Nearly every anthropolo-gist who has lived with Suriname Maroons has commented upon the personal difficulties such ideas engendered, and relations with the government in Paramaribo (or, for Alukus, Cayenne) remain very much conditioned by them. (See, for discussion of this theme, Ver-non 1985.)

38. Brother Riemer's account of his triumph over the "witch doc-tor" was an early example of one kind of discourse about outsider-Saramaka relations that continues into the twentieth century. For example, the North American physician Morton Kahn, describing his art-collecting trips on behalf of the American Museum of Natural History during the 1920s, reported that

the women . . . laugh, giggle, put their finger coyly in their mouths, joke bashfully with bystanders, and cannot make up their minds as to the price. . . . Sometimes, they will mention a preposterous figure, hoping like a naive child that the strange bahkra [white man] will pay that much. But on such occasions a rebuke will make them more reasonable. Once an arrogant witch doctor intervened in a transaction with a Bush Negro woman, demanding angrily that she receive an exorbitant payment. His anger was squelched with a few sharp words, and, contrite, he sat up all night to carve an ornate implement to present to the bahkra as a peace-offering. Cunning Adjobo, the medicine man! (Kahn 1931, 196)

For another similar (eighteenth-century) example, see Stedman 1988, 510.

39. Elderly Saramakas told me that to touch one's index finger to another's forehead (tjòkô fínga) used to be a sign of great seriousness, something like an oath. The practice has been obsolete for many decades.

40. This dream seems to date from nine years earlier. In January 1771, immediately after Alabi's conversion, the missionaries reported that

> in the afternoon, Abini's widow [Akoomi], who had been possessed by the Gado on the first, visited Brother and Sister Kersten. Brother Kersten asked her what she thought about [Alabi's] baptism. She said that she did not understand any of it. However, as she seemed willing to hear about the gospel, he told her about the Savior's love unto death for her and all negroes, and told her that she should not remain behind. He told her further that her children were seeking in all earnestness to find the way which is pure and right, and he asked her why she would wish to continue on the path of darkness. One could see her discomfort at this speech, and the unrest in her heart, and after she had promised to visit us often, she told us of a dream that her daughter [Bebi], who had always been very hostile to us, had had. She dreamt that she had seen us pray together, and a person came down from Heaven and remained. Her daughter interpreted the dream to her by saying, "Mother, I believe we are doing these people an injustice. They are teaching the correct path." The negroes have great respect for their dreams and think a great deal about them. (St 3, pt. 1, 146–47)

In 1788, the Moravians reported that the bulk of the inhabitants of a certain village had moved because of a dream (St 3, pt. 2, 128–29), and in 1791 they described a witchcraft trial, based on evidence in a dream (see also note 45 below, and Chapter 8). Today, dreams continue to be taken as omens, and many of the minor divinatory séances that take place each day in a Saramaka village are aimed at interpreting a troubling dream of the previous night.

41. The converts included Alabi, his wife Sialoto, their infant daughter Helena, his sister Bebi and her husband Kwaku Andreus, his sister's husband Joshua Kodjo and their son David Skipio, plus Simon Aduku, who later married Alabi and Sialoto's daughter Rosina—as well as the youthful Christian Grego and two very old African-born men. (It seems possible that the man known to the Moravians as

Simon Aduku is the man called by modern Saramakas Djanti Kunduku. Saramakas recall that he was, like Alabi, born at Timba, and that he remained throughout his life a very special friend of Alabi; some Saramakas insist that he was a Dombi captain, others that he was a member of the Paputu clan. See Chapter 4, note 22.)

42. Two years earlier, during Brother Schumann's difficult stay at Bambey, Alabi had dictated another letter, in answer to one he had received from a certain Brother Weiss in Germany. Its lurid imagery—Negroes as "slaves of the Devil" who were "living under the power of Satan"—combines with his specification (in the 1780 letter) of the heart as the seat of thought to suggest how far Alabi may have come, by this time, in internalizing Moravian rhetoric and categories of thought (if we accept the hypothesis—which seems reasonable to me here—that the missionaries were recording Alabi's words with something like their intended meanings [cf. Chapter 5, note 28]).

"My dear Brother Jonas Paulus Weiss, I would like to talk to you now as if you were standing right in front of me and I were here with you. I received your letter from dear Brother Hans and his wife, who have just come to us. I cannot say how happy I am that they arrived here safely because I had been terribly saddened that the Savior took Brother Rudolph [Stoll] and all the other Brethren who had come here, and that only Brother Schumann remained with us, and for many months he has been so sick I thought that he would pass on, as well. This has pained me a great deal and I prayed to the Savior the whole time that He should send us new Brethren to make us truly happy. Now that He has truly sent them to us, I do not know how to thank Him enough. I beg Him now that He should keep them here for a long time, for as long as Brother Rudolph was with us [= 22 years]!

It was Brother Rudolph who first told us the great story of how He came down from heaven to earth. When I first heard the story I had to think about it for some time until I understood it. I realized that the world itself did not care whether I enjoyed it or not. And now I see that by myself I cannot make a joyful life in this world but that all my wishes depend on following the good path of Jesus Christ. I pray to Him each day that He will sustain me until I can come to Him, and I would even be happy were this to take place right away, but until He calls me I will always love Him because He so loves me. The Devil used to plague me greatly, but when I got to know the Savior I became free. After I had asked the Savior for redemption, He freed me from the Devil and from the slavery of sin. And I know that as long as man remains in the hands of the Devil he is as much his slave, as the [plantation] negro is the slave of his master. I beg the Savior that my compatriots will also find the joy of his presence, but until now they do not want to take Him on but want to remain in the power of the Master of Evil. When I see

this it causes me great pain and grief. I often tell them the sweet words about what God has done for us. I call them and invite them but they never come and take up my invitation. It really pains my soul that they act this way, but I think that I have been part of the reason for this and thus am not tired of begging the Savior, with resignation and a faithful heart, that the hour soon strike when they will free themselves from the slavery of the Master of Evil, the Devil, and place themselves in the arms of our good and dear Lord, who died out of love for us. I will try to help out the new brother and sister with advice, and if I can help them in any way to remain healthy it will give me great pleasure. [N.B. Both died within weeks.]

My dear brother, to be sure I do not see you with my eyes but when I see the letter you have sent me it gives me indescribable joy. . . . I want to talk with you, and once I go to the Savior I will see you and talk with you there. You have told me that you are very old and that you do not expect to remain in this world much longer. . . . Now I take my leave from you. Farewell, farewell, farewell, my dear friend, my dear brother. Please think often of me and I will think of you until the Savior takes you to Him, and then I will follow in order to see you by His side. Then we will kiss one another and will enjoy each other's company eternally.

Now I am kissing Brother Schumann, who is standing up and embraces and kisses me so sweetly that the tears are falling from his eyes. And I would like to kiss you and the other Brethren but I cannot reach you! . . . Farewell, farewell, I am your brother Johannes Arrabini."

(This letter was written during a strong thunder storm, as the heavens sent down heavy rainsqualls on Sunday 21 March 1778, at Bambey.) (St 3, pt. 1, 350–53)

For comparison, it is worth citing a letter written by the much younger Christian Grego to accompany Alabi's letter of 1780.

"I have a great desire to write a letter to my dear brother Gerstorf in Europe because I want to report on the state of affairs in my country. From this letter you will be able to see that my progress is good. I hope that you are well, too. I also want to tell you that the Great God has done wonders among my people. He has died for my sake, and I have found a good life in His realm which will never cease as long as I wander His path, because He loves me greatly. This is why I place my entire confidence in Him and only want to live for Him and remain in His hand and be His servant with my entire heart, body, and soul. If I do something for myself, it cannot be good, but through Him, I have found *the* good. Thus when my body dies my soul will live on in Jesus, and I will truly be able to thank Him for having sent teachers to us in this great forest. They have told us how God

loved mankind so much that He became a poor person, to redeem us from the Devil's hand and to lead us into eternal life.
My dear Brother Gerstorf, it has really hurt me that God decided
to take away Brother Moser, whom He had sent to this country
in order to speak the good word to us. God has taken him to
Himself so that he may find some rest. It is there near his Lord
Jesus that he will find eternal joy. I am, nevertheless, sad about
this, but comfort myself with the knowledge that God has done
it all Himself, and that He truly knows what is good for us.

I know that you do not understand my language and thus
would not understand this letter, so my Brother will translate it
into your language and he will translate your [return] letter into
my language. I say farewell to all the Brethren and Sisters and
am your black Brother Christian Grego." (St 3, pt. 2, 37–38)

These letters—again, if they are read as translations of what Alabi
and Grego actually intended—seem to confirm Harding's argument
about the role of rhetoric in certain kinds of Christian conversion, that
"embracing a narrative tradition that rewords" the convert's experience is at the heart of the process, and may well be more generally
true (1987, 167, 169; see also Chapter 5, note 28).

43. Brother Wietz wrote of the second sick woman:

The other woman was pregnant and cried out loud to her Gado
day in and day out—so loud that we could hear her all the way
over here. An old woman was called to help her, who was highly
respected as a sorcerer. She immediately began to practice her
diabolical tricks. The sick woman improved somewhat, but as
soon as the sorcerer left she began to scream again, worse than
before. In such situations, the powers of darkness and Satan,
under which especially the old women live, can only evoke our
amazement and compassion. (St 3, pt. 2, 40–41)

I have not seen records indicating what happened to this patient.

44. An eight-day-long funeral seems to have been standard, at
least as far as missionary understandings went, during the eighteenth century. For example, in 1771, Brother Kersten described how,
upon the death of a Matjau woman in Baakawata, "for a period of
eight days, her closest relatives had to stay in the house of mourning,
as is the custom, howling, shooting, and shrieking day and night" (St
3, pt. 1, 150). And in 1778, when a woman died, "for a week long, both
day and night, there was incessant noise and commotion, with shooting, drumming, and singing" (St 3, pt. 1, 356).

45. Brother Riemer explains, with characteristic enthusiasm, that

the title of Grang-Mama or grandmother is given only to those
women who have reached old age and have made a name for
themselves in the arts of magic, and who have a sizeable number of great-grandchildren. . . . To be sure, there are also younger
women [who practice these arts], and the older ones had them-

> selves been introduced to these mysteries in their youth, but
> it is those who are oldest who gain the most respect. These
> women not only receive great respect from members of their
> own sex but hold strong influence over the minds of the men as
> well. Yes, there are even cases when their dreams and conjurings
> play a major role before a court [of law]. If, for example, such an
> old conjuress—called Grang-Mama—dreams that one or an-
> other negro who she knows enters her house with a firebrand,
> she deems this to be suspicious and reports it to the village
> captain. At first, such a report is kept secret, but the Krutto
> [*kuutu*, village council] keeps a watchful eye on the negro in
> question. If, however, this Grang-Mama or another woman
> dreams the same situation a second time and reports it again,
> then this Krutto declares the poor negro without hesitation to
> be a suspect who should be gotten rid of. (St 3, pt. 2, 269)

46. This is a standard Saramaccan verbal formula, *"mi bái helú,"*
publicly denying, to higher authorities, personal responsibility for an
act.

47. Using independent evidence, I would place Akoomi's age at
closer to eighty at the time of her death.

48. That the baptized men—apparently with missionary approval—celebrated Akoomi's funeral separately, with a kind of music
not otherwise associated with Saramaka funerals, suggests the development of parallel, syncretic rites, neither strictly "Herrnhuter" nor
Saramaka. Fife and drum music disappeared from Saramaka before
the memory of the oldest people with whom I have spoken.

49. My reconstruction of Akoomi's funeral is based on Moravian
records, discussions with modern Saramakas about funerals in the
past, and personal participation in a number of modern funerals. Like
the evocation/reconstruction of Abini's second funeral in Chapter 4, it
at once stays strictly within the bounds of what is known and fills in
the gaps with the best educated guesses I can muster. Although, like
all historical writing, it runs the risk of presentism, it is written with
special attention to preserving every shred of difference that has left
traces in the records.

50. The missing sister was Tutuba, held in slavery by the whites
since her capture during the wars. The missing brother was Jan van
Abini (also called Djákuabíni), the official "hostage" in Paramaribo.

51. What outside observers, from eighteenth-century Moravians
to twentieth-century anthropologists, have considered "chaos,"
"noise," and "confusion" at Saramaka public events deserves to be
placed in the broader context of Afro-American cultural patterns. As I
have written elsewhere (1975, 160):

> In Antigua, for example, Reisman noted that "people take great joy
> in 'making noise' [the local term for argument and speaking Cre-
> ole]," and that it is "the basis of the symbolism of most village
> rituals. Meetings begin with a call for Conduct, and descend into

'noise' and Creole via argument" (1970, 141). Here, "the oscillation between noise and order" is tied to fundamental values (ibid.). And Abrahams, referring primarily to Nevis, arrives at a very similar interpretation of the "organized mayhem" or "organized chaos" which marks public meetings on that island (1970).

52. Until the middle of the twentieth century, all graves, except those of tribal chiefs, were "vaulted." By the 1960s, only the particularly conservative village of Daume still retained the practice.

53. Staggered or syncopated entries in dance (as well as in instrumental and vocal music) remain one of the hallmarks of Saramaka style (S. and R. Price 1980, 168). During the twentieth century when an especially old and important woman dies, it is a special kind of *adunke* dancing/singing—to commemorate times gone by—that is performed as women circle the coffin three times.

54. Currently, on the day of burial, kinfolk witnessing the final rites of preparation of the coffin in the village make a similar show of wildly clinging to it and must be bodily dragged away, before undergoing a final ritual of formal separation of their *akaa* ("soul") from that of the deceased, as the coffin leaves the village.

55. From what the Moravians report, eighteenth-century Saramakas seem routinely to have buried their dead within a day or two—one of the most striking of all ethnographic differences from the present or the currently remembered past, and a change I am at a loss to explain. Since at least the late nineteenth century, Saramakas (except, of course, Christians) have kept the coffin above ground for periods of one to several weeks, the length varying directly with the social importance of the deceased. Today, even the most ordinary burials take one to two weeks and burials of important people some forty to sixty days. The bodies of twentieth-century tribal chiefs have been kept above ground before burial for a full three months (with city-bought chemical preparations, as well as local herbs, being used as preservatives in the coffin).

56. Men born in the first and second decades of the present century described to me having seen coffins circling the house three times in this fashion, but the practice has fallen into disuse.

57. Brother Riemer does not appear to be describing coffin divination in this account, though he elsewhere discusses this practice (see notes to Chapter 4).

58. Before the start of what Brother Riemer calls "the funeral procession," Akoomi's canoe-bottom had been loaded up with all the detritus of death—the sweepings from the floor of the mourning house, the poles that had held the platform on which Akoomi's corpse had rested, the banana leaf-head pads on which the canoe-bottom itself had been carried for divination—and, carried on the shoulders of two men, it had been borne before the coffin to the cemetery. Along the way, at the edge of the village, there was a final rite of separation, with whitened *sangaafu* as before, to separate Akoomi from the village as a whole. As Kaana sliced the plant in two,

gunshots from the men and wails from the women rent the air. And only then did the procession enter the forest.

59. Asking for offspring, game, and protection against evil continues to be among the standard formulae in such Saramaka prayers today. The twentieth-century Saramaka belief that the very recently dead possess special powers to encourage game to be plentiful may have roots in the eighteenth century: one missionary reports that when a tapir ran into the village and was killed during a funeral, the people "believed that the spirit of the deceased had sent the animal so that they would have food for the ceremonies" (St 3, pt. 2, 151).

60. The music played in Saramaka cemeteries is *papa,* but in contrast to the special drums used when *papa* is played on the night before burial in the village, the sole accompaniment to singing in the cemetery—as while the coffin is being built—is the *gan,* an old piece of machete blade struck with another piece of metal. However, messages for the living and the dead—proverbs and other commentary on the proceedings—played on the *apinti* ("talking drum") were a crucial part of all eighteenth-century funerals. Indeed the promise to play the *apinti* at the head of a parent's grave is one of the most frequently mentioned ways, in Saramaka folktales, for a son to promise to honor his father or mother.

61. Before leaving the cemetery, the gravediggers overturned Akoomi's canoe-bottom on the heaped earth and placed her favorite stool at the head of the grave, and each purified himself with a cloth by three times brushing Akoomi's *akaa* (soul) toward the sunset and his own toward the sunrise. With three parting gunshots and some final rhythms on the *apinti* drum, bidding adieu to the ancestors, they headed for home. Back in the village, they took the axe, machetes, and shovels used in digging the grave and quickly sank them near the landing in an old canoe—to be removed and purified by fire the next day.

62. Very little is known about eighteenth-century Saramaka folktales, as neither missionaries nor postholders showed any interest in them. Here and there in the written records, however, tales are mentioned, and in one case, at least, recorded (see Chapter 3, note 15). Comparing today's corpus to those tales recorded during the nineteenth century, there seems little reason to doubt that most of the characters, plots, and situations in eighteenth-century tales would be familiar to a twentieth-century Saramaka. For a number of examples of tales told at wakes by Alabi's descendants, see R. and S. Price 1990.

63. It appears that in the eighteenth century, the house of the deceased was often destroyed at the end of the eight-day period of deep mourning as part of the ritual of keeping the ghost away from the village. A missionary reports that once, while visiting Kayana, "the inhabitants of the village left for another village where an old woman had died the previous week. On the ninth day after her death, as is customary, they would either clean out or tear down her house and

hold a memorial service for her" (St 3, pt. 2, 133). (This memorial service would have been the *baka nyanyan,* the "last feast.") Today in Saramaka, only the front of the house is removed (at the time of death), and the rest of the structure is left standing to be used during the second funeral, a year or more later.

64. In fact, when important Saramakas died, mourning goods from the government were solicited not for the funeral/burial (which would not have been practical, given time constraints) but for the "second funeral" that followed burials by about a year. In the case of Akoomi, a month after her death, Captain Alabi formally solicited both mourning goods and the presence of his hostage brother, Jan van Abini (who was normally kept in Paramaribo), for the second funeral. Both wishes were granted, after the Saramaka emissary reminded the Court that "she was the wife of the deceased Tribal Chief Abini, who had done a great deal for the whites, yes, even given his life for them" (Hof 110, 22 May 1780). The goods given by the Court included "one case of candles, one length of *salempuri* cloth, and six jars of rum" (ibid.).

65. For comparative purposes, it may be worth quoting here a little-known 1745 eyewitness description by Brother Zander of a funeral among Suriname slaves.

> **Their funerals consist of various ceremonies, and the more respect a person had amongst them, the more elaborate the ceremonies. I once saw a [slave] funeral in which the deceased was of the Popo nation in Guinea, and was highly respected amongst them. The corpse was carried by negroes and everyone who was able came along, but especially the family and friends of the deceased. Walking in front of the corpse was the most distinguished negro nation, the Coromantines, who carried a flag and made music with drums and fifes. At the burial ground, they placed the corpse near the grave, which had been quite beautifully bedecked with all kinds of expensive cloths and pieces of silk. As soon as the coffin was lowered into the grave, a large number of negro women came and each threw a piece of this cloth into the grave. After this, earth was thrown onto the coffin until the grave was half filled, and then all of the friends came together and stood in a circle around the grave. A woman then came with a calabash and passed it around to all the friends in the circle. There was a drink in it and everyone had some, and then the grave was closed, after which one of the sorcerers or conjurers came with a big jug of liquor. This he placed on the grave, and while speaking many earnest words, poured it intermittently on the grave, as he jumped up and down, repeating all this until nearly all the liquor had been used up and he had stepped on every part of the grave. Afterwards, everyone went home.**
>
> **After this ceremony I asked a negro whom I trusted about its**

meaning. He told me: "The woman had washed the sweat of death from the deceased and put it in the calabash, mixed with liquor, eggs, and lemon juice. The assembled friends drank it as a sign of love. But the main point is that should anyone refuse to partake of the drink, it would be a sign that he was responsible for the person's death. The sorcerer poured the liquor to the deceased to strengthen him for his journey, while saying the following words: 'I now order you to leave the land [of the living] and never to return again,' and each time he repeated these words, he poured out liquor and jumped around the grave. When all this was finished, the wife of the deceased brought him his freshly-prepared meals at the grave each day for six weeks, and the grave was often visited by the deceased's friends as well. And finally, when the deceased begins to be forgotten by his friends, a white chicken will be placed on his grave and burned and sacrificed in his honor." (St 1:91–93)

This final comment would seem to be referring to the "second funeral," which we know from other sources was practiced by Suriname slaves as well as maroons. Note also that although coffin-carrying for divination is not included in this particular description, it was standard practice on Suriname plantations at that time (see the illustration in Chapter 4).

66. Although I have not examined all of the relevant documents on this case, I have indications of its outline. In 1767, Etja asked Postholder Dörig why the whites had not yet turned over to them "the woman Baba, who was promised to us at the time we faithfully returned the runaways from plantations Boxel and LaRencontre," and Dörig promised to look into the matter (SvS 331, 28 Mar. 1767 [5 Feb. 1767]). Almost a decade later, she had not yet been returned, as Andries—an Abaisa who had split off from Samsam's village in 1773—was reported to have requested from the postholder that "his mother, Baba" be permitted to come upstream to live with him (SvS 168, 2 July 1776). The previous year, this same Andries had asked the Court for permission for his brother, who was a freed slave serving in the Vrij Corps military unit, to retire and come live with him in Saramaka, and he made a similar request—refused by the Court—for his slave sister, Seraphina (Hof 90, 5 Aug. 1774 [19 June 1774], SvS 167, 22 Dec. 1775, 9 Feb. 1776). Finally, sometime in the late 1770s, Baba was freed to rejoin her kinfolk, as indicated by Etja when making his plea for Tutuba's release (see also Hof 105, 13 Apr. 1779).

67. The name Sofi Creek has kept generations of Saramakas aware of Alabi's mother-in-law's illness, since everyone knows that lepers (like madmen) must receive special burial. Rather than being interred in the cemetery, they are buried at the water's edge, in the riverbank, and their houses are immediately destroyed.

68. Captain Gome, whose father's matrilineage descends from

these Indian women, told me that they were "Aluángo" (Arawakans) who had fled from a war on the Tapanahoni River, to the east. In his version of their arrival at the Matjau village, they tossed three balls of spun cotton rather than *awaa* pits, and the Matjaus said to each other, "It must be human beings. Because evil (*ógi*) does not know how to spin."

Relations between Saramakas and Amerindians ran the gamut from limited friendship and solidarity to bitter enmity. After initially making acquaintance with Indians as fellow plantation slaves, some early Saramakas sought them out in the forest, and it was a group of Indians who initially harbored the early nucleus of the Matjaus (R. Price 1983a, 45). During that early period, individual Indians served as occasional advisers and spouses for Saramakas (ibid., 80). By the time of the Peace, one Saramaka village in Matawai included about a dozen Akurio Indians (R. Price 1983b, 189) as well as the several Arawak captives from the Saron mission (see Chapter 2), and the Nasi village included the famous "Tufinga" group (see note 77, below). Much of Saramaka material culture and horticultural technique—everything connected with the growing and complex processing of cassava, many local fishing and hunting techniques, the art of hammock-weaving and certain kinds of basketry, and much else—was learned from Indians.

But these (and other) occasional cases of solidarity and cohabitation should not mask the more generalized fear that Saramakas had of those Indians (most often Caribs) who served the government as the most effective of jungle scouts and bounty hunters against them. The government's military expeditions of the early eighteenth century were often led by Indian pathfinders, and many Indians served as private and redoubtable maroon-hunters. The story I have dubbed "Adugwé's Indian," recounted in *First-Time,* captures some of the emotional tone of Saramakas' feelings toward these manhunters (R. Price 1983a, 145). After the Peace, the area to the west of the Saramacca River remained dotted with Indian and "Karboeger" (mixed Indian-African) villages, and for a time Musinga maintained secret military treaties with some of them; others of these Indians fought with the government against him in 1767 (see Chapter 4, note 42). For other Saramakas, along the Suriname River, it was only rarely after the Peace that an Indian was encountered. Unlike the Djukas, who dealt regularly with Indians for trade (passing along, for example, whitefolks' goods in return for specially trained Indian hunting dogs), Saramakas lived in an area that had, by the second half of the eighteenth century, been pretty much emptied out of its original Indian inhabitants.

During Suriname's civil war, which began in 1986, the government's use of coastal Indians (Caribs—Galibi) against Maroons has once again become frequent. Suriname military have depended heavily upon Indian scouts in their recent operations along the Cottica and inland in Eastern Suriname. And in the refugee camps across the border in French Guiana, relations between Galibi and Maroons continue to pose serious problems.

69. For details of this complex incident, very revealing about relations among the Djuka, the Boni, and the colonial government, see Hoogbergen 1985, 241–52.

70. Although it had been explicitly prohibited in the peace treaty of 1762, Saramakas and Djukas had, in 1776, drunk a formal oath of eternal friendship and alliance (Hof 110, 22 May 1780). Now, in 1781, about ten Saramakas (including the two "hostages," Alabi's brother Jan van Abini and Samsam's son Christoffel) and some thirty-five Djukas were actually serving together as supplementary troops at outlying government military posts, as part of the government effort to contain further maroon depredations and marronage. They received "the usual private's pay" plus a gun, sword, and scabbard, "an ordinary slave hat, a *bussel* [knapsack?], a shirt, and blue pants"—taken together, serious inducements for cash-poor people (Hof 113, 29 Mar. 1781).

71. One of the most strongly forbidden of all sexual partners is the wife of a *mati* (formal friend), since between *mati*s there should be absolute trust. As an oft-cited Saramaka proverb states, *máti ganyá i, án o láfu* (when your *mati* cheats you, he won't smile—that is, he'll be deadly serious).

72. This dramatic version, including the anachronistic kerosene, comes from *Basia* Bakaa of Botopasi. The elder Aseedu of Kambaloa, characteristically far more reticent with me (see R. Price 1983a, 20), said in response to my asking about Kwadjani's death:

> They raised the coffin. It said "a person killed him." They went to kangaa [the ordeal]. [It said:] "Yes, a person killed him" [i.e., he died from sorcery]. They went and caught him and brought him back. And they burned him. We know where they did it [but aren't telling].

It may be worth noting that the missionaries recorded at least one sorcery case in which the *kangaa* ordeal yielded a verdict of innocent. Only two months before Kwadjani's death,

> **On the 21st of May [1783] a child died whose father was a Communicant but whose mother was still a heathen. Because the child had not been ill for long, the people here became suspicious that someone had poisoned it [killed it by sorcery], which is always the first thought when someone has died. The next day, they began to investigate the situation [through divination]. An old woman was accused, but after she had submitted to an ordeal, she turned out to be innocent. This superstitious ordeal is conducted in the following way: as the suspect kneels on certain leaves, a hen's feather is thrust through his tongue. If it goes through without difficulty, the person is innocent; however, if it breaks, then he is guilty. (St 3, pt. 2, 78)**

73. During roughly this same period—though probably closer to the end of the century—there was another Djuka-Saramaka witch-craft execution, but in the opposite direction. My information comes solely from oral sources. I had asked Tebini, in 1976, about the origin of a place-name, A-gé-(or A-ké-)bófo, near the site of Kampu at the confluence of the Pikilio and the Gaanlio.

Tata A-ke of the Paputu clan, he killed a tapir [bófo] there. He's the one the Djukas killed. His kúnu [avenging spirit] is bigger than all other kunus! They [the Djukas] took the skin from his back and sewed it into an apinti drum! They were playing agubaa [one of the rhythms of death] on it . . . taku môò híí sóni ["really baaad"] . . . coming along Djukápási [the footpath leading from Djuka to the Upper Pikilio]. Then they got to Afíngasándu where they met Gbagidi [an important Matjau, who had his gardens there]. He said, "What's this?" They explained until they had fin-ished. He took a stick and smashed it right through the drumhead dzuluu [intensifier], as it was being played, right between the man's legs!

They had killed him [A-ke] at Djuka. He had gone there and they had said he was a witch. After Gbagidi broke the drum, he went to the Paputus. (Tata A-ke, he was a Paputu.) He told them, "Don't you go to them! I am going to help you take care of this. I will help you with my wife's people" [because Gbagidi was married to a Djuka]. Then he brought them [the Djukas] to a big open shed in the gardens at Gaán Goón [on the Lower Pikilio]. He said, "You're my wife's people. When I used to visit you [in Djuka], I saw how you lived. Well, now, I will give you punishment. Then he boiled plantains and asubusúbu [a kind of banana] and poured it [the gruel] out onto banana leaves [set out on the ground]. He'd cut palulu [wild banana] leaves, cook the mess in a big kerosene drum, pour it out, and say "Here, this is your food!" They stayed for one whole year. Then they [the Saramakas] held a council meeting. And Gbagidi ended their punishment and took them back to Djuka.

These two executions, one in each direction, undoubtedly stand for a number of others whose traces I no longer could find. And they serve as testimony to what must have been an extremely active and varied intertribal intercourse.

74. For example, in a 1780 tribal council meeting, Postholder Weinhold announced that henceforth only twenty-five guilders would be paid as bounty for an escaped slave who was dead, and that a certificate from the postholder plus the right hand of the deceased would have to be turned in to obtain the bounty; the usual bounty, which since 1698 had stood at 50 florins (according to Hartsinck 1770,

756–57, Hof 85, 29 Apr. 1772, and Stedman 1988, 387) or 150 florins (according to Hoogbergen 1985, 394), would remain in effect for slaves turned in alive (Hof 110, 8 Aug. 1780; cf. Stedman 1988, 387).

75. By this time, the captain-by-captain list was at least lightly adjusted to account for population differences among villages. For example, the captains with the two largest constituencies (the Matjaus and the Langus) received ten iron pots each, Alabi received nine, most captains received eight, and the captain with the smallest village received but three. Most items, however, continued to be given out uniformly, regardless of village size.

I have seen a very similar list of goods destined to be distributed during the dry season of 1783. (Apparently, the 1781 distribution was a year later than planned, and the next "triennial" occurrence was 1783.) The only differences from the 1781 list were the following slightly different quantities of three items: 40 pieces of cotton cloth, 300 (quantities) beads, and 900 (quantities) shot (Hof 118, 26 Aug. 1782).

76. During the initial months of missionization, one of the Moravians described Saramaka beliefs about albinos.

> **[At Captain Etja's village of Dosu Creek] I saw a little negro lad with rather white skin and with hair that resembled white sheep's wool, although his father and mother were black. The negroes regard such children as young gods and they let them do whatever they want, in order not to hinder them and so that they do not leave them. I have heard that such poor creatures are born rarely and almost never live to be old. When they do become a little older and something dreadful occurs, then they commit suicide. They are then not buried like other people but are thrown into deep water, so that they can return unhindered to the place whence they came. (St 3, pt. 1, 87–88)**

Saramakas call albinos *wéti-gádu* (literally, "white gods") and consider them, as well as children with "red" hair, to be closely associated with *tone* water spirits. Brother Riemer described how some of these children were prepared to be ritual specialists:

> **If nature distinguishes a youth by something special, for example unusual facial features, a long nose, a pointy chin, unusual height, red hair, or something of the like, then he is destined for special training, and from childhood he will be put under the supervision of a famous witch doctor, who will teach him the art of herbs and all the other great mysteries of his art. Such a man [is like] a born miracle worker. (St 3, pt. 2, 265)**

Saramakas also distinguished other "special births." For example—as throughout West and Central Africa—twins were considered gods and (along with their parents, as well as the child who followed in the birth order) were subjected to complex rituals from birth to death (see R. Price 1983a, 60–61).

77. Some hint of the complexities with which eighteenth-century non-Christian Saramakas dealt with "monstrous" births may be gleaned from Postholder Daunitz's 1774 journal, in which he describes (if through a glass darkly) the role of Antama's *tone* god in one such case.

3 March. I have heard that toward the end of last year . . . in a certain village there had been a miscarriage. But afterwards, the woman still seemed pregnant, so her family called on Captain Antama, who was the biggest god-maker, to ask him to "make" the gods so the woman would not bring another stillbirth into the world. Antama said "Yes, I shall do it," but first sought payment. Such lads say that if they are not well paid, the gods will not work. The fee for such godwork or obia is 40 lengths of cloth. He took his payment and began his work. Then he said to the person who had hired him, "You needn't be afraid any more. The girl will no longer have miscarriages nor bring into the world unnatural fruit." Some time later, the woman's time arrived. She was duly delivered of a child which was half human and half monkey or ape. Then was the good Antama, along with his god, in some difficulty. They summoned him immediately and asked him what kind of a child this was. He was more than a little embarrassed by all this, and afraid that he would lose his good name and the earnings he got from them. He called his gods together and begged them to make him [the child] normal, but his pleas were in vain. Antama told the people that the time had not yet come for the gods' powers to transform him into a natural human posture. "I have never seen such a thing. The gods cannot help with it." I was not told what they did with that child but I will try to find out more. (Hof 90, 5 Aug. 1774)

The strange case of the "Twofinger Indians," who were eventually assimilated into the Nasi clan, provides another example. Soon after their arrival in Saramaka, the missionaries wrote that

some negroes also live here [Dosu Creek] who have but two fingers on each hand and two toes on each foot. Their origin is a negro who, with his biological sister, fled to the bush, and who together conceived only such children. They were found by the negroes near Dossu Creek, and since then have had intercourse with other people and have had normal children. (St 3, pt. 1, 88)

Saramakas and Dutch officials described these people rather as Indians, and their complex story fascinated both eighteenth-century whitefolks and Saramakas for some years. (See, for details as well as illustrations, R. Price 1983a, 162–65, 1983b, 128, 233.)

78. Kungooka was never, in terms of government recognition, a captain. But he was the de facto political headman as well as the spiritual leader of the village at Kofi Creek (see R. Price 1983a, 121–22,

147–48). In 1788, a missionary on an upriver proselytizing trip noted, "We spent the night in Dagome in a house where a woman was inspired [possessed] by her Gado and danced about with loud roaring" (St 3, pt. 2, 130).

Only a year or two before Brother Wietz's visit, the elderly Kungooka was involved in an incident that is still preserved by Saramaka historians. (I can date the incident so closely because [1] the Matjau quasi-captain Djaki had already founded his middle-river village of Kumbu [which occurred in the mid- to late 1770s]; [2] the village of Daume [then called Kofi Creek] had already moved to near its present site [which occurred contemporaneously]; and [3] Mbuti, who died in mid-1779, was still alive.) The speaker is Tebini, the great historian who is descended, on his father's side, from Foola, one of the story's protagonists.

> *Dungí [= Mbuti, the Matjau captain] saw them at the creek across from Lafánti, at Dungíkiíki [not far upstream from Bambey]. He had come down to visit Djaki [the founder of Kumbu, just upstream]. He had come down to make a peanut garden there. That's when he saw them, Foola and her husband Bentóla. He said, "I thought runaway slaves were a thing of the past, but now I've 'caught' myself two!" She said, "You haven't caught us. We're looking for my brother. Have we come to the right river? Do you know the man called Kungooka?" She continued, "We've done a terrible thing. It is driving us crazy. But if we can get to Kungooka, he will be able to fix it up." Dungi said, "I can bring you to Kungooka. I know where he lives. He is at Daume [Kofi Creek]." Then he brought them to Djaki, at Kumbu. They discussed it inside and out. (You see, the terrible thing that they did, the thing that had stopped up the mouth of the husband, that made him unable to speak, it was that they had killed a man. With a dêsè [a curved, iron adze]. His ghost was troubling them. It wouldn't leave them in peace. It was a Dumukúku [a newly arrived maroon] they killed. In Matawai. The woman was very pregnant.) They went to Kungooka. As soon as he saw them, he went into his obia house. Then he came out and said "that thing."* Those words cured them. The man spoke! Then Dungi said, "We want them [these people], because we were the ones who found them." Kungooka said, "I can't give them away to you.*

---

*Before beginning the story of Foola and Bentola, Tebini had discussed with Peleki, who was also present at this evening session in 1976, how until recently he and only one other living man still knew the words that Kungooka had spoken upon seeing his long-lost sister. The other man, Tebini said, had just died suddenly, and Tebini himself could no longer remember them. Together, they lamented the loss, "It's lost, it's finished!" exclaimed Tebini.

But the thing you've done by bringing them here is big! So, when she gives birth, if it's a boy, he'll be your mati [formal friend], if a girl, when she comes of age, she'll be your wife." Then, the woman gave birth to a child that died soon after.*

But when she next gave birth, the child was Pikí Kwasíba [the apical ancestress of the village of Kampu]. Kungooka spoke with his sister, saying, "When I am no longer here [i.e., when I am dead], if these people here [in Daume] don't treat you well, go to the Matjaus. They're the ones who found you."

When Kungooka died, the Daume people did not live well with the children of Foola. They fought with them, accused them of stealing things. So they went to the Matjaus, at Bekuun. They said, "We've come to you just as we promised." The Matjaus held a council meeting and concluded, "We don't have enough land for you here." But Tjibidó [a Matjau man] argued, "We cannot talk this way. Look at the captain's staff we have in this village. It once belonged to Dungi [Mbuti]! Well, what's this I am hearing about not accepting these people? We own this whole area all the way to Asigoon [on the Gaanlio]." Then he took the footpath behind the village and went to "cut" [the site of] Kampu for them. He brought them there, saying, "Let's live here together. I will go back and forth between here and Bekuun." And they lived there [for a long time]. They really produced children! So many people! And they never left that area again.

Note that this story, the heart of which is about the founding of Kampu and the Matjaus' role in it, contains two widely separated temporal incidents: the first sequence in the late 1770s, the second long after Mbuti's death. Genealogically, Tjibido is two generations below Dungi, and Foola's "children" had already become a sizeable group. A reasonable guess might place the founding of Kampu between 1810 and 1820, some thirty to forty years after Kungooka's initial intervention.

79. Three decades later, New Year's still retained this special flavor, with "heathen" Saramakas making churchgoing part of their general celebrations.

January 1st, 1809, an unusual number of heathen negroes attended the forenoon's-service, so as to fill our new church. We should feel more encouraged by this appearance of a desire to hear the gospel, if it were not their annual custom. Many come

---

*This is a standard Saramaka gift, the most precious that can be offered by one man to another.

Gaamá Djankusó (tribal chief, 1898–1932) wearing his ceremonial gorget and his *lôndò* (Kahn 1931, facing p. 106).

on New-Year's Day, who afterwards do not enter the church doors all the year round. . . .

We supposed, that the heathen in the village would, according to custom, make it a day of riot. Early, about four o'clock, we were waked by the firing of muskets and shouting, and immediately after the morning service, the heathen began to drum

and make other noises, intending to set about it in good earnest in the afternoon; but at 3 o'clock, a report was spread that an old negroe man had just died. Thus their sport was speedily ended, each sneaking off to his own hut. (PA 4:461–62)

80. Brother Riemer, even while poking fun at Alabi, understood that it was his preference to go barefoot. In Suriname, the right to wear shoes was an important symbol: shoes were strictly forbidden to slaves by contemporary law (see, for example, Schiltkamp and de Smidt 1973, 927), but those (apparently rare) Saramakas who wished were allowed to use them when visiting the capital. However, Alabi, like most Saramakas, seems to have been uncomfortable in shoes. His twentieth-century successor *Gaama* Agbago compromises by wearing whenever possible an unlaced pair of high-top basketball sneakers. (At least one case of a *gaama*'s death during the twentieth century is attributed by Saramakas to witchcraft having to do with a pair of shoes.)

Before its general shape was altered during the twentieth century, the *gaama*'s cocked hat was called by Saramakas *lôndò,* the more usual meaning of which is "cunt," because the shape of its orifice resembles the female genitalia. Tebini described to me how *Gaama* Djankuso (who died in 1932) proudly told him that Queen Wilhelmina herself had sent him his, and he noted that, "like a woman's private parts, it's good forever."

Eight: Chief-over-All

Sources for this chapter, in approximate order of use, include: for Alabi's accession to the office of *gaama,* SvS 175, 8 Dec. 1783, Wong 1938, 341; for Alabi's visit to Paramaribo and de Vries' report, SvS 175, 17 Dec. 1783; for Alabi's official requests, SvS 175, 17 Dec. 1783; for the 1785 tribute distribution, Hof 125, 16 Apr. 1785 [7 Apr. 1785]; for Alabi's council meeting activities, St 3, pt. 2, 126–27, 147–48, 3, pt. 3, 136; for Antama's pretensions, St 3, pt. 3, 59; for the 1800 slave returns, St 3, pt. 3, 192, PA 3:146; for Alabi's attempted abdication, St 3, pt. 3, 45–46; cf. St 3, pt. 3, 21; for Alabi's handling of the Djuka sorcery case, St 3, pt. 3, 136; for the discussions of moving, St 3, pt. 2, 53, 79; for the noise and earthquake, St 3, pt. 2, 83; for the Moravians' move, St 3, pt. 2, 86, 123–24; for descriptions of New Bambey, St 3, pt. 2, 54, 124, 126, 3, pt. 3, 95–56, 146; for Sister Randt's death, St 3, pt. 2, 126–27; for Brother Randt's bats, St 3, pt. 2, 127; for his melancholy, St 3, pt. 2, 132–33; for his repulsion, St 3, pt. 2, 133; for his new wife's death, St 3, pt. 2, 136–37; for the difficulties with slaves, St 3, pt. 2, 141–42, 149, 143; for Brother Wietz's summary, St 3, pt. 3, 51, 55; for the chronicle of illness and death, PA 3:386–87; for school reports, St 3, pt. 3, 36; cf. 3, pt. 2, 142, 3, pt. 3, 101; for congregational numbers, St 3, pt. 2, 142; for Christmas, St 3, pt. 2, 142; for the "choir" division, St 3, pt. 3, 98; for Alabi in Kayana, St 3, pt. 2, 134; for the national brotherhood, St 3, pt. 3, 51–52; for Christian participation in memorial rites, St 3, pt. 2, 135; cf. St 3, pt. 2, 136; for further backsliding, St 3, pt. 2, 128; for the death of Yanki's wife, St 3, pt. 2, 128; for Alabi's intervention in a funeral, St 3, pt. 2, 137–38; for Alabi's intervention in an execution, Holmes 1818, 282; for the Easter Monday "conversation," *PA* 2:70–71; for Moravian sternness, *PA* 1:11–12; for New Bambey "exclusions," St 3, pt. 3, 63, 3, pt. 2, 137, *PA* 4:463 (cf. St 3, pt. 1, 343 for two exclusions in Gwafu Bambey); for Moravians' unwillingness to compromise, *PA* 1:13; for the proclivities of the "pagans," Holmes 1818, 282; for the message from Beku, St 3, pt. 2, 129; for the "Awakening," Weiss 1911, 69; for "prophetic move-ments," de Beet and Thoden van Velzen 1977; for Randt's 1788 and 1789 Kayana visits, St 3, pt. 2, 133, 135–36; for visits by Puli and his fellows to Bambey, St 3, pt. 2, 135–36; for Puli's god, St 3, pt. 2, 144; for his baptism, St 3, pt. 2, 144; for the woman's amazement, St 3, pt. 2, 145; for the Bambey Christians' upriver visit, St 3, pt. 2, 148; for Pikinkoyo's visit to Bambey, St 3, pt. 3, 35; for Wietz's upriver trip, St 3, pt. 3, 40–43; for Puli's Bambey visit, St 3, pt. 3, 45; for Randt's 1792 upriver trip, St 3, pt. 3, 48–50; for Antama's wrath, St 3, pt. 3, 54; for the back and forth visits, St 3, pt. 3, 57; for Alabi's visit, St 3, pt. 3, 59–60; for Grego's trip, St 3, pt. 3, 62; for Alabi's follow-up, St 3, pt. 3, 62; for Andreus's report, St 3, pt. 3, 101; for Alabi's confrontation with Antama, St 3, pt. 3, 186, *PA* 3:53–54; for Wietz's 1801 visit, St 3, pt. 3, 194–95, *PA* 3:260; for Domósi's conversion, St 3, pt. 2, 144–46, 3, pt. 3, 188, *PA* 3:60–62; for Djemi's conversion, St 3, pt. 3, 93; for Skipio's death, *PA* 3:62–63, St 3, pt. 3, 188–89; for Cornelius's tale, *PA* 1:341, *PA* 2:65–67; for Brother Wietz's 1794 report, *PA* 2:69; for the Mora-vians' sentimental journey, *PA* 2:433, St 3, pt. 3, 141; for the con-cerned diarist, *PA* 3:58; for Alabi as tender father, *PA* 2:432–33; for Alabi's bloody speech and verses, *PA* 3:147–49 (cf. St 3, pt. 3, 191); for Andreus's departure, *PA* 3:264–65; for the 1803 report, *PA* 3:306; for Brother Wied's report, St 3, pt. 3, 208; for the 1805 diary fragment, *PA* 3:427–29; for the year-end prayer, *PA* 3:431; for the discouraged diarist, St 3, pt. 3, 217, 222; for Joshua Kodjo's death, St 3, pt. 3, 214–15; for Alabi's final reported sermon, St 3, pt. 3, 225–26; for the letters to Germany, *PA* 5:78–79, 243; for the closing of the mission, St 3, pt. 3, 233.

1. The history of Saramaka *gaama* succession has not yet been written, and I know of no published list that is complete and correct. Without delving into details here—for most successions have been just as politically complex as that of Alabi (with promises of the office being held in trust by one clan until a chosen candidate from another comes of age, and so on)—I nevertheless present a complete sche-matic chart, indicating names, dates, clans, and genealogical re-lations. (Note that during Alabi's *gaama*ship, Antama and Gbagidi served as de facto *gaama*, for many purposes, for the Gaanlio and Pikilio areas respectively, and that during the *gaama*ship of Alabi's grandson, the Christian Frans Bona, Bongoótu served similarly for

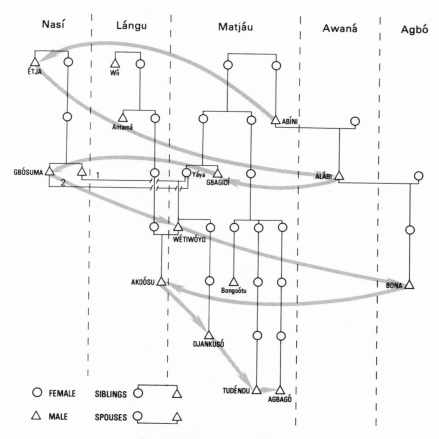

Saramaka *Gaamás* since 1762

Kokokú ABÍNI, 1762–1767
Kwakú ÉTJA, 1770s–1783
ALÁBI Pantó, 1783–1820
GBAGIDÍ Gbagó, 1821 (died before city installation)
Kofí GBÓSUMA, 1822–1835
Abraham WÉTIWÓYO, 1835–1869

Frans BONA, 1870–1886
AKOÓSU, 1888–1897
Moana DJANKUSÓ, 1898–1932
TUDÉNDU, 1932–1948
AGBAGÓ (ABÓIKÓNI), 1951–1989

non-Christian Saramakas. Note also that dates of accession to office in different sources vary in part depending on whether the Saramaka or city installation was used.)

2. In 1835, the government provoked a crisis by demanding the return of several new maroons harbored by the Saramakas. This violent if temporary confrontation eventually resulted in the deposing of the Nasi-clan *gaama,* Kofí Gbósuma, in favor of the Matjau Wétiwóyo, an event unique in Saramaka history. (See, for details, Hoeree and Hoogbergen 1984, Junker 1932/33, Morssink 1934/35, Oudschans Dentz 1948.) The internal drama was played out among the same four

power blocs—Matjaus, Nasis, Langus, and Awanas (Agbos)—who figure in every *gaama* succession.

3. Because I rely largely on the compilation of Moravian manuscripts made by Staehelin (1913–19) (and to a lesser extent on the very selective English translations made from the German originals and published during the early nineteenth century in *Periodical Accounts,* and some limited ancillary manuscript materials from Utrecht), rather than on the diverse surviving manuscript diaries themselves (which are dispersed among Herrnhut, Paramaribo, and Utrecht), I cannot be sure that there are not additional significant data in the originals. It seems clear that Staehelin himself made the judgment that the diaries postdating the early 1780s were less interesting for his own (Moravian history) purposes, and that he therefore severely abridged the later documents. Perhaps Dr. Peter Neumann, who has been working for years with the Herrnhut collection, will someday flesh out the picture that I sketch in here. The same holds true for Dutch archival materials: my own work in the government archives gave relatively short shrift to materials postdating the early 1780s.

4. It is not clear whether Alabi in fact met the governor on this trip. In early 1785, the governor noted in his journal that Alabi had visited him in order to receive official congratulations on his accession to office (SvS 209, 18 Mar. 1785).

5. Tjapanda was the brother of Adjagbo's wife Paanza and escaped slavery contemporaneously with her (R. Price 1983a, 129–33). He himself had a Nasi wife and frequently visited Saramaka. In 1776, he sought permission to live permanently in Saramaka, but the Djuka tribal chief refused. His continuing problems with the Djukas, and the intervention of his Saramaka kinfolk and friends, are the subject of many postholder letters and reports during the 1780s (e.g., Hof 121, 14 May 1783, Hof 123, 6 Mar. 1784, 26 May 1784); I have not examined these materials in sufficient detail to summarize the complex affair. There is a missionary passage, clumsily rendered in English in *Periodical Accounts,* that seems to refer to Tjapanda's end.

December 17th [1793], a peculiar circumstance occurred here with an old heathenish negro, called *Pansa*. He belonged to the Okamish [Djuka] tribe of free negroes, inhabiting the banks of the Moravina [Marowijne], and was accused of being a mixer of poison [sorcerer], for which he was to have been burnt alive. He therefore fled, and came into these parts, when his fears operated so strongly upon him, that he grew raving mad, and ran to and fro in the neighborhood of our settlement by day and night, till at last he was found dead, about a hundred paces from our house. A report prevailing here, that *Pansa* had vowed to the god of the Okamish negroes, that he would not quit his own country, the heathen now believed, that the god in great wrath had followed him hither and killed him for not performing his vow.

> They were therefore exceedingly frightened, and not one of them would touch the corpse to bury it. Many women and children fled into the woods to hide themselves for a season from this angry god. At length, a conjurer undertook to appease the angry god for the proper fees, and as the people believed in his skill, they ceased to fly. The deceased had a good house, well built and furnished after the manner of the negroes, which was pulled down, and as no one durst venture to touch any thing belonging to him, the conjurer was well paid. (*PA* 2:67–68)

6. I have seen records of Alabi's attendance at the 1788 tribute distribution, but the subsequent reports available to me are silent about these periodic events.

7. This ordeal-by-fire may have been a kind of *kangaa.*

> In this ordeal-by-fire, conducted by an old woman, a red-hot piece of iron is passed over the leg of the accused negro (or of a person who is his representative, if he cannot be present), after the area had been smeared with banana juice. Whether he is judged innocent or guilty depends on whether or not the skin is singed. If it is singed, then the accused is seized and executed in a most cruel manner. (St 3, pt. 3, 136)

8. Alabi's adjudication of an Upper River dispute in 1798 is characteristic. He intervened only at his daughter's specific behest, and the procedures did not pose any conflict with his Christian ideals.

> We lodged with [Alabi's] daughter [by his first wife], and she greatly rejoiced once more to see her father. She told us of a disagreement which had lately arisen among their friends, and which the [local] Chief had not as yet been able to settle. [Alabi] undertook the business, and held a council on the 4th, in which he heard the complaints of both sides, and then pronounced sentence according to equity. After this, all who had been engaged in the dispute filled their mouths with water, and then spat it out again, to signify that their hearts were now freed from all bitterness. Yet some was probably left behind: for we found not that entrance with the gospel, which we could have wished. (*PA* 3:54–55)

9. This appears to be a reference to the same old woman who was accused of sorcery several months earlier, in connection with a child's death. Though the *kangaa* ordeal proved her innocent at that time (St 3, pt. 2, 78), gossip about her guilt apparently continued. Saramakas then, as now, took a practical stance about findings of innocence in such sorcery accusations: if innocent people continued to die, the *kangaa* might have been mistaken (e.g., the operator of the ordeal might not have properly observed a ritual prohibition), so the woman might still be guilty.

10. Brother Riemer wrote of the silk-cotton tree,

The negroes designate it as their greatest idol, using the branches and leaves on various important occasions and making staffs out of the wood which they hang with tyger teeth and various Obia herbs, and they worship such decorated staffs as a travel-Gado. (1801, 322)

The tree-felling prohibition is confirmed by Stedman, writing of contemporaneous slaves in Suriname, who "bring their offerings to the *Wild Cotton tree* Which they Adore With high Reverence."

this Proceeds /Said an Old Black Man to Me/ from the following Juditious Cause, having no Churches on the Coast of Guinea and this Tree being the largest and most beautiful Growing there. Our People Assembling often under its branches to keep free from the Heavy Show'rs of rain and Schorching Sun Shine, when they Are Going to be instructed; do not You Christians Pay the Same homage to Your bibles &c. We well know that our tree is but A Wooden Logg Covered With Leaves of Green, Nor is your book Assuredly any more than a Piece of Lumber Composed of Leaves of Paper— Under this tree the Gadoman or Priest Delivers his Lectures and for which the Vulgar Negroes have much Veneration, that they Will not Cut it down upon any Consideration Whatever—(1988, 520–21)

11. For the first time since Kaana "awakened Madanfo [*obia*]" and since Alabi and Kodjo's adultery fight, serious internal dissension seems to have split the tiny Christian community. The missionary diaries leave only traces of what must have been a very troubling conflict:

After the sermon on the 28th [April? 1784], which dealt mostly with brotherly love, some baptized people asked me to stay with them at church because in my absence there had been a great many disagreements among them, and they now wished to settle them in my presence. (St 3, pt. 2, 81)

On the 13th [August] . . . we were unable to hold Communion because the negroes are having too much strife amongst themselves. (St 3, pt. 2, 82)

And my field information is little better, simply because I did not pursue the matter. But my fieldnotes and tapes from 1978 do record Captain Gome's alluding to a serious fight about a woman.

[It was a] Man-and-wife thing. It had begun before the whitefolks cut down the tree. It would have ruined them no matter what, but they wouldn't have had to move. They'd have divided up into two groups. It was their own people. They didn't live well. A man took his brother's wife. They wanted to whip him.

Several years later, the Moravians again report serious fights within the Bambey community. On the way back from Kayana in 1788, we were traveling with 18 people in four canoes when a terrible fight erupted. Axes and muskets were used! But thank goodness it was soon over. (St 3, pt. 2, 134–35)

And a year later, in New Bambey,

on the 6th of July a big fight took place in the village, and some of our baptized Brethren, in spite of being innocent, came away with black eyes. (St 3, pt. 2, 137)

Presumably, these fights, too, were about women, though the documents I have seen are mute on the subject.

12. During the course of the mission, the Moravians were intermittently successful in extracting free labor from Saramakas, but only from members of the congregation. For example,

I suggested to our church Brethren that we set aside a field in order to grow rice. With the sale of this rice [on the coast], we could get money to buy various provisions: wine and bread for communion, candles, and suchlike. However, it is very hard to make such a suggestion to them, though I spoke most earnestly. I said, "When I hear how at other missions even the poor slaves have the responsibility of defraying the costs of the church, then I ask myself what kind of people the Saramaka Negroes are. You do not have to pay for our subsistence, and even when our provisions are picked up from Paramaribo, you do not have to pay anything. What I am asking for is not for ourselves but for you and for the use of the church. It is your obligation to do this. Do not be rebellious." This address had such a good effect that during the next two days, they were all very busy felling trees and cutting undergrowth to get a garden ready for planting. Also, the church and our house were repaired. (St 3, pt. 2, 147–48)

(Incidentally, this is the same field that was completely destroyed, some weeks later, by a mysterious fire.) Years later, such a church field was fully functioning, and the six male members of the congregation received twenty-two guilders for the crop when they sold it on the coast (St 3, pt. 3, 45). But a close reading of the missionaries' diaries makes it clear that their labor needs, over and above what their own slaves (imported from the coast) could do, were largely met by hiring Christian Saramakas, as in the case of the new field at Wana Bambey, or on other occasions.

[In 1772] We asked them [Alabi, Kodjo and other friends] to fell trees to make a garden for us, in return for a small payment. (St 3, pt. 1, 180; cf. St 3, pt. 1, 195, 239)

13. All whites in eighteenth-century Saramaka, whether soldiers, postholders, or missionaries, traveled there with slaves. (Indeed, until

our own arrival in Saramaka in 1966, all outsiders—including Melville and Frances Herskovits—had traveled with non-Saramaka cooks/ servants/interpreters brought from the city.) The Moravians' slaves were often their only companions in Saramaka, and the Brethren's dependence was very real. During the forty-eight-year-long course of the mission, at least twenty-four slaves served in Saramaka, many of them children (St 3, pt. 3, 233). I know very little about these slaves' relations with Saramakas, but it seems not to have been close. Almost all of the Moravians' slaves became converts and underwent name changes (e.g., Kwobangu to Abraham), and there was at least one married couple, who had a number of children. Between missionaries and slaves the cultural gap remained almost as wide as with Saramakas.

> **[1778] We have a negro and negress who are our own [slaves]. They and I are responsible for running the whole household. . . . The negro woman, besides doing field labor, also takes care of the washing and cooking. Because she understands just about as much as I about cooking European food [i.e., almost nothing], you can imagine what delicious meals we prepared together. I often did not know whether to become angry or laugh. I do know that there was one dish, which some people would not even have touched, that I had for over half a year, even during my severe illness! (St 3, pt. 1, 360)**

In general, Moravian views on slavery contained a fundamental contradiction, one that affected every aspect of their missions among plantation slaves, whether in coastal Suriname, South Carolina, or the Danish Virgin Islands, and that certainly affected their work in Saramaka as well. Their personal acceptance of the institution, as part of the divine plan, led them to preach a message to slaves of passive submission—a message that one powerful Suriname planter noted "is not only of benefit to the slaves but enhances the masters' profits as well" (St 3, pt. 1, 253). But their treatment of slaves as human beings (in the eyes of God), in every way equal (except for their secular situation) to their masters, created an ideological breech in the slave system and, however indirectly, encouraged rebellion. On a personal level, the Moravians fully accepted slavery, criticizing only "inhuman" abuses by sadistic masters. (Such a position was standard, among Europeans of varied middle-of-the-road political stripes, almost until the end of the eighteenth century—see Stedman 1988, Introduction.) Brother Riemer, characteristically, waxed eloquent about the pleasures of being rocked to sleep by a plantation slave on his outward journey from Saramaka (St 3, pt. 2, 176). (Other references to mission slaves in the diaries include St 3, pt. 1, 241, 242, 3, pt. 2, 141, 151, 222, 224, 3, pt. 3, 133, 190. For the Moravians' dependence on slaves in their Paramaribo business enterprises, as well as for their special purchases of slaves for the Saramaka mission, see Helman 1968, 85, 99, passim.)

14. The ongoing tension between Alabi and the Matawais came to the fore again several years later, when several Matawai men and women left their people to settle with the Saramakas. One such man, Adosu, married Lena, a daughter of Alabi and Sialoto, and in 1800 he was baptized Adam (*PA* 3:145). (In 1870, Adam and Lena's son Frans, born in 1799, became the only Christian *gaama* in Saramaka history other than Alabi.) In January of 1799, Alabi had presided at a day-long council meeting with a Matawai leader, an important woman sent as emissary, who demanded that Alabi relinquish the Matawais.

[Three Matawai women] had fled thence to this neighborhood, as their husbands—having abandoned their responsibilities there—live on the Surinam [River]. The lady now required, that these women should be given up to her; as no woman, according to the customs of the free-negroes, is to leave the place of her residence for the sake of her husband. In order to settle this dispute, John Arabini held a council on the 10th., in which the debates continued from morning till night. As at the conclusion the three fugitives declared, they would rather die than surrender themselves: they were no longer troubled about returning, and the lady was under the necessity of returning home, without having succeeded. (*PA* 3:59)

I suspect that these events are the origin of an account I heard several times from Matjaus during the 1970s: that Alabi called some Matawais "with *obia*" as a way of avenging his father's death; that they arrived in Saramaka, where they were at first received by the Dombi clan; but that they soon settled permanently with Alabi, where they helped "make" a portion of Wana Bambey.

15. Since oral traditions stress that Sialoto and her mother Sofi came to Saramaka without other kinfolk, it seems possible that Hwéte (the Agbo-clan woman accused, in the story, of killing her husband) was a latecoming relative who came to live with them in Bambey. The possibility that she was a daughter of Alabi and Sialoto, remembered today by a non-Christian name, seems to me unlikely, though it cannot be ruled out simply on chronological grounds. One folk etymology relates the name of the Agbo clan to an *obia* of that name owned by the Kwama clan, one of whose members is said to have participated in the original "finding" of Sofi and Sialoto (Jozefzoon 1959, 12). Yet another possibility, which I heard occasionally voiced (though vigorously denied by Tebini and others), is that—unlike other clans—the Agbo do not have a single putative origin (e.g., an ancestress or a plantation). Rather (and this is said, in this version, to explain their geographical dispersion), the Agbo consist of several unrelated groups each descended from an ancestress designated "Agbo" because she, or a male relative, had murdered someone. (This would seem to fit for both the Agbo groups in Bundjitapa and Soolan [see below] but not, as far as I know, for Alabi's affines.)

16. Other oral sources recount that Ngwete himself had loaded

the powder into his kinsman Abaansi's gun but that a recently arrived runaway, Adeabaka, surreptitiously added the fatal ball. After divination had shown that Adeabaka was responsible, he was beaten to death by a group of Abaansi's distant matrilineal kinsmen. And he became a redoubtable avenging spirit for them, one that operates to this day.

17. I do not have explicit information on the death of Yaya, which probably occurred during the early 1780s. (There is an indication that she was still alive in 1781 [St 3, pt. 2, 48].) It is just possible that it was she whom the missionaries described as "the great priestess of the idols . . . very closely related to Johannes," who died in 1789. In any case, her death prior to these events would have been necessary for the "succession."

18. I have heard several versions of Gbagidi's bringing back a wife from Djuka. One, at once rich and obscure, deserves recording here, for it is one of those rare Saramaka narratives I have heard that was told neither for my benefit nor in my presence. One day during the early 1970s, at cock's crow, the Matjau Abáteli, then about forty, visited his mother's mother's brother, Captain Kala (Dangasi)—the successor to the staff once held by Bongoóto, son of Gbagidi's son— to hear the highly charged story of Gbagidi's trip to Djuka. (Abateli recorded this cock's crow encounter on tape; I later obtained permission from him and Kala to use it here.) Before launching into his account, the elderly captain offered a historiographical note as a means of adding weight to his words.

> Just the other week, when we did the thing at the shrine
> of Gaán Táta [a ceremony recently held at Kala's village of
> Dangogo], Tebini and [Gaama] Agbago and I tied our
> hammocks in a single house. I went there expressly to sleep
> with them [and learn things]. And that [the story he is
> about to tell Abateli] is the first thing I asked them about.
> . . . "Well," Tebini said to me, . . . "Man, you have asked
> well. But tell me what you have heard. [After all,] you knew
> Asapampia, so tell me what you've heard. If it's not
> correct, I will tell you where the truth is." And then I really
> told them!

Kala then launched into his account of Gbagidi's voyage for Abateli.

> Now, Gbagidi went to Djuka! Gbagidi [was the one who]
> cut the path here, the Djuka Path. Well, when he got to
> Djuka he saw the woman called Yoyo. When he got to Djuka
> he saw her by the riverside just sitting there. He stared at
> her for a long while and then turned away. (Now, she was
> goodlooking, man! According to what I've heard, she was
> one beautiful woman!) So he stared at her until he went on.
> He went until he returned. She was still there. So he
> asked her, "Woman, what's wrong?" She said, "Who, me?"

He said yes. "They are planning to kill me." He said, "What
did you do?" "They say I have evil [i.e., I'm a witch]." (Man,
the thing you're hearing here, stick-behind-your-ear! [I.e.,
it's very dangerous, so be careful with it.] Never tell it
to anyone with whom you might have bad relations [so
they can't use it against you].) She said, "They want to kill
me." "What did you do to make them want to kill you?"
She said, "They say I have evil and that they will burn me
[to death]." "Really? Right now?" She said, "Yes. They've
already gathered the wood for the fire. They already put me
through the ordeal. They said I can't be with people any
more. That's why I'm all alone here." He said, "Yes. Well,
woman, do you really have evil?" She said, "No. I don't
have evil." He said, "You do! If you do, you'd better tell me."
She said, "I don't." "Ah! Well, given how much I love you,
if you don't have evil, you're going to be all mine." She said
yes. She said, "But however you know to get me out of
here, do it. I don't have witchcraft." He said, "Yes. Let's go.
If you know you really don't have evil, I will help you.
I came here to Djuka on some business but I won't stay
any more. I'll take on your problem." She said, "It's yours."

So they agreed. Then Gbagidi took his canoe and gave
it to her. He told her to get her things ready. "When night
falls, we'll make our escape. I'll leave with you." So the
woman got ready. Night fell. She took all her things and she
loaded up the canoe. Gbagidi stole another canoe there.
And they loaded the first one up until they were all finished.
They traveled downstream [with the two canoes] all night
long until dawn. Then he said to the woman he would head
back up. But she should keep going. "When it's full
daylight, then hide. Make sure no one sees you. You know
this river well. Hide yourself whenever someone comes.
Then, when they're out of sight, keep on going. Me, I'll
return to Djuka." She said yes.

So, Gbagidi went back. (He didn't accompany the woman
to the mouth of Djuka Creek, man. That's what Asapampia
told me!) So, Gbagidi went back. And the woman
continued on. Gbagidi finally arrived [at Djuka]. They said,
"Gbagidi, where did you go?" He said, "My canoe 'went'
[was cut loose and drifted downstream]. My canoe left so
I had to go after it." "So [they said] Gbagidi's boat left!"
Well, the woman. Since they had already given her the
ordeal [and found that she was a witch], they didn't pay
attention to her, didn't even go to say good morning
anymore. Except for her sister's daughter Agooto. She was
the only one who still went to greet her each morning.
That morning, she went to her. But she didn't see her. She
thought, "Oh! She's dead! Just as we said. She's drunk

*poison!" Just then Gbagidi returned. He brought the other
person's canoe he had taken and said that his own had
disappeared. That's how he arrived back in Djuka. Meanwhile, the woman had already gotten as far as the mouth of
Adjai Creek, right at the head of the [Djuka] Path. She
took out all the baggage and sunk the canoe right there.
. . . Gbagidi prepared to leave [Djuka]. He said that the thing
that had happened to him [his canoe's disappearance] was
a bad omen. He shouldn't stay. So, he made the necessary
social rounds and they gave him a canoe. And he left.*

*Did he go fast! He didn't know if the woman was alive
or dead. So he really paddled! All the way to the mouth
of Adjai Creek and on up that creek. And then he saw her.
He said, "Woman, I've come." She said, "No problem." Well,
they slept there. Till morning. Then they took the path
all the way to the mouth of Tukusí Creek [on the Upper
Pikilio]. That's where they hit the river. That's where the
woman swore her oath. She washed her face. Then she
swore an oath to the river. Then they took a canoe and
came downstream, man. They came to the village. Gbagidi
had brought a woman back from Djuka!*

*He came and told his kinfolk the whole story, just as
it happened. So they lived together, as man and wife. The
woman swore to them that she didn't have evil. And the first
child she bore, that was Akondiá. Then after Akondia, it
was Yaisí. When Akondia grew up, he was just as big as his
father! He took Adísi [a Matjau] as his wife. They said
that they wouldn't give him a wife elsewhere, they didn't
want his children to be born elsewhere. They wanted
his offspring for themselves. Because the children he
would beget would be large [strong]! And he begat Bongootu.
Bongootu was as big as his father! Then he begat those
children, Alimátipína, Tutúabêè, Yabíkoósu, Mmágoósu.
Those are the ones he begat with Adisi. (The things of
our lineage you ask me about sometimes. That is what I'm
telling you here!) Then they gave him a wife, Ayaiso [another
Matjau]. And he begat Mandéa. . . . Now that lineage, that's
us. The children of Gbagidi that he made on this river
[the Pikilio], the first one he begat took Adisi and together
they made all of us you see here [in this section of Dan-
gogo] . . . enough people to fill ten giant canoes!*

19. See, for example, Hof 967, 26 Mar. 09, where he is referred to
by his "whitefolks'-name," Sadda. This archival entry also refers to
Gbagidi's close relations with the Abaisa clan; in fact, his father was
Awansi, an Abaisa.

20. Likewise, seven decades later, when Alabi's daughter's son—
Frans Bona, a Christian—was official *gaama,* Gbagidi's son's son,

Bongootu, a Matjau, served as de facto *gaama* for the whole Upper River region. Today, Gbagidi himself is remembered not only as a political leader but as a powerful ritual specialist. Matjau Basia Tando, himself a serious *komanti* man, once described to me how Gbagidi ritually prepared his son Akondia so effectively with Kaamósu (*gaan obia*) that he could eat vulture meat!

21. This narrative, unlike others in this book, was reconstructed from notes rather than recorded on tape. I make no attempt here to imitate Saramaka speech style. The speaker was the Matjau Peleki.

22. Among the gifts the whitefolks gave Gbagidi were three large iron griddles for baking cassava cakes, which Gbagidi divided among three Matjau matrilineages. By the 1960s, those in the villages of Kampu and Dangogo had been broken (though Kampu still kept a rusting piece in the village council house—according to Tebini, "to show little children what had happened on that long-ago day when the whites offered Peace to Gbagidi"). But the third griddle still stands where Gaama Djankuso had it placed during the early 1930s, in front of the tribal council house in Asindoopo, as a reminder of his "great-grandfather" Gbagidi's miraculous feats.

23. Indeed, Puli consistently asked for a missionary to come live in his village. In August 1791, it was reported that

> **a group of negroes visited us from the Upper Region. One of them, Primo, brought us greetings from our baptized Paulus who, like others at that place, are deeply stirred by salvation and sorely want a brother to stay with them there. This Primo showed us that nothing was more dear to him than to hear the story of Jesus. He said that Paulus had called together those people in his house who had wanted to become believers, and the feeling that they had about the Savior was such as he could not describe. . . . The confessions of Paulus are accompanied by spirit and life. . . . It is through him that the Awakening in the Upper Region has taken place. (St 3, pt. 3, 36–37)**

24. Puli was the first convert since Alabi who seems to have been at all comparable in terms of personal commitment—a militant rejection of Saramaka religion combined with a true zeal for proselytizing.

25. The "interruptions" that annoyed Brother Wietz are but one illustration that contrapuntal Saramaka speech style, so pervasive today, was important during the eighteenth century as well. Sally Price and I, apropos of modern Saramaka, have written of

> certain stylized contrapuntal patterns that structure everyday speech and gossip, the formal rhetoric of ritual and judicial sessions, and public song/dance/drum performances. Normal conversations are punctuated by one of the listeners, who offers supportive comments such as "That's right," "Yes indeed," or "Not at all." Even when men living on the coast send tape-recorded messages back to their villages, pauses are left after each phrase, and the "conversation" assumes its proper two-party form once it is

played. In formal settings, stylized responses become more frequent. . . . Prayers also assume an antiphonal structure, as participants periodically support the speaker's words in unison with slow handclapping and a specially intoned declaration of "Great thanks!" (1980, 167–68)

26. It is worth noting that such missionary trips to the Upper Region were not common, in ordinary times. Many years often went by without a missionary visiting the villages around Kayana.

27. It seems clear, as early as several years previous, that Christianity was being used in the Upper Region as additional protection, to be called on whenever a person—choosing among his other gods or medicines—wished.

> On the 7th of July [1793], Andreus [Alabi's brother-in-law] came back from a visit to the village of Kayana. He said that he had spoken to various people there who wanted to hear about the Savior. Also, he had seen the baptized woman Elizabeth at a heathen celebration, but she claimed that she still valued her love for the Savior, and gave as evidence that recently, when she had become sick and her relatives had wanted to perform sorcery over her, she told them that she could handle the sickness without this because her soul belonged to the Savior. (St 3, pt. 3, 101)

A less subtle example dates from 1788.

> In the evening we arrived at Awara where I stayed with the postholder, H. Beck. I had a conversation with two of our communicant-candidates who live here. A famous old magician wanted to show me that he knew how to pray the Ave Maria on his knees, using those gestures he had seen the Catholics making. [He may have learned this from a previous postholder, Daunitz, who was a devoted Catholic.] I took the opportunity to explain to him the meaning of the Savior but he soon fled. (St 3, pt. 2, 129)

28. By the 1790s, few of the men who had fought in the wars were still alive. The missionaries did, however, record one final, touching encounter with one of these wartime heroes, the Matjau Adjagbo, at the very end of his life.

> [On 20 January 1796] We visited old Captain Adjagbo on the other side of the river. He was completely blind, had Obias hanging all over him, and was painted all over with white, red, and black colors. He was very pleased with our visit and said he remained only partly in this world, since all he had left was his skin. He also said that God had created all creatures properly except for man, who is plagued with so many ills. A snake, for example, always gets a new skin when it needs one, but people do not have this advantage. At this, we immediately told him

the story of the Fall of Man and his Redemption. He thanked us for the good instruction but said he really did not want to hear any more about it. However, he did have one request for me, that I send him a bit of salt. (St 3, pt. 3, 130–31)

29. The idea of praying directly to the Great God reappears periodically in moments of Saramaka religious intensification during the succeeding decades. (See, for example, de Beet and Thoden van Velzen 1977, 108–11.)

30. Domosi's testimony, together with the diary entry about the death of Simon Yanki's widow in 1788 (cited earlier in this chapter), makes it clear that at the time of his baptism Simon had two wives, both "heathens." It was standard Moravian practice to permit baptized men to retain all their wives, following the explicit advice of the apostle Paul (1 Cor. 7:21). Monogamy was strictly enforced, however, in terms of taking additional wives.

Missionaries should keep strictly to the following resolutions: 1. That they could not compel a man who had, before his conversion, taken more than one wife, to put away one or more of them without her or their consent. 2. But yet that they could not appoint such a man to be a Helper, or servant, in the Church. 3. That a man, who believeth in Christ, if he marry, should take only one wife in marriage, and that he is bound to keep himself only to that woman, till death part them. . . . If any baptized man leaves his wife, and takes another, or takes one or more wives besides the first, or in case he has had two, and one dies, marries another, he is excluded from the fellowship of the Church. (PA 1:14)

31. This offhand Moravian allusion to Saramaka menstrual beliefs and practices confirms the early existence of a central cultural institution, one that affected every person's daily life. Brother Riemer provides details.

In regard to certain physical conditions of women, there is among the Free Negroes a unique and remarkable custom. Because they leave the company of their husbands during this critical moment and must avoid all kinds of social interaction, it was decided to establish an institution by which some of the families get together and build for their wives and young women a certain communal house for this purpose, and they are obliged to maintain it in a liveable condition. As soon as a negress notices that such a female condition is coming on, she must leave her house and family immediately, even in the middle of the night, and go to this designated *kay*-house. She takes along her cookware, some food, and her hammock, and a mother can take along her very small children. On the way to this house of quarantine, she must very carefully avoid showing her back to any man she happens to meet, nor can anyone pass

> behind her. She must stop still when anyone approaches, and wait till the person has passed by. If it happens that a man or woman comes toward her, and it appears they want to speak to her, then she immediately stands still and says, in a fearful voice, *mi kay, mi kay,* I am unclean! She is not allowed to reenter the house of her husband until everything is over with. If she needs something from her house during this time . . . she must stand in front of the doorway and whatever she needs must be handed out to her. And then she must scurry back to her shelter. Furthermore, she is not allowed, during this time, to have dealings even with her very best female friend. These rules must be observed to the letter by all negro women, and even the wives of the village captain are no exception to the rule. (1801, 278–80)

From a modern Saramaka perspective, the single most important difference in conduct between Christians and non-Christians involves menstruation. All *obia*s, gods, and other spiritual powers are vulnerable, and a man's ability to hunt or fish, not to mention his sexual prowess, depends on his staying unpolluted. Modern Saramaka women, like Alabi's contemporaries, spend their several days per month of menstruation in a small hut at the edge of the village (see, for an early nineteenth-century description, van Eyck 1828, 18). A menstruating woman may not cook for a man, or even speak to men who have certain *obia*s. During the 1960s, it was still considered a serious communal danger for an Upper River man to marry a Christian woman, because on her visits to his village people could never be certain that she was not "cheating" (as any observance of the rules on her part would represent a courtesy to her hosts, not a matter of belief). Domosi's act of accepting food from Alabi's wife Sialoto in effect signaled that she was willing to risk the vengeance of her gods and ancestors. (For a discussion of menstrual pollution in modern Saramaka, which, when compared with Brother Riemer's description, shows remarkable cultural continuities, see S. Price 1984, 21–24.)

32. According to the missionaries, their stress on a joyous afterlife held strong appeal for at least some Saramakas. As early as 1768, Brother Stoll told Saramakas that

> our job is to tell you [Samsam] and all the negroes that the Creator loves you and truly wishes to help you, so that when you die, you will go to a wonderful place where dwells the Lord, and no longer remain in the clutches of the Devil. (St 3, pt. 1, 80)

An early Saramaka reaction to such preaching seems to presage the several deathbed conversions of later years.

> On Maundy Thursday [1772] there was special emotion in greeting the suffering of Jesus. The negroes who were assembled could hardly express themselves enough about how well the

story related to them and how much they delighted in hearing it. They said, among other things, "If we truly understand this in our hearts, we will never again need to be afraid of death." (St 3, pt. 1, 177)

Brother Wietz's 1793 observations lend further support to such an argument:

The celebration of the Passion Week and Easter was attended with much blessing. Several of our people declared, that the history of our Savior's sufferings appeared to them as new as if they had never heard it before, and they found more than ever, that nothing could save them but his precious blood, shed for the remission of their sins. In one instance particularly, the great change wrought in them is apparent. Whereas a heathen negro dreads the idea of death so much, that he would not on any account approach the grave of a deceased friend, our people meet with pleasure on Easter-Sunday morning, according to the custom of the Brethren's Church, in the burying ground to pray the Easter morning litany, and declare that they feel comfort in considering that they shall also once rest with their Brethren in the grave, till the Lord shall call them again by the power of his resurrection. (PA 2:70)

Christian Grego stressed the same theme in 1798.

When Brother Mahr visited the men who were making the coffin, he found them engaged in conversation, [about] how unfortunate it was, when death came upon one so unexpectedly, as in the case of the deceased. Upon this the assistant, Christian, replied: "I am not afraid of death, should it even come to-day: for I know, that my soul will go to Jesus Christ, my Saviour." (PA 3:57)

Alabi himself occasionally used this theme to frighten others into contemplation of conversion:

On another occasion, when the subject of the sermon had been the final judgment, Arabini, overhearing some of the heathen converse together and remarking, that then they would hide in the wood, or kill themselves, stepped forward and addressed them thus: "The Lord will know where to find you, even those who have died many years ago; all, all must appear before him; and those, who have loved him in this world, he will bring with him into eternal joy, but all the rest he will consign to the torments of everlasting fire." Some replied, that as so many would share in the punishment, it would not be so severe to each individual. Arabini shrewdly answered: "Try the experiment, and all of you put your fingers together into the fire, let us see, whether each individual will not feel the same degree of

pain, as if he were alone." Struck dumb by this remark, the whole assembly broke up with a heavy sigh. (Holmes 1818, 280–81)

And in 1800, a Matawai chief visiting New Bambey specifically asked Brother Mahr "whether the believers, when they left this world, would know each other again in heaven" (*PA* 3:146).

It is worth stressing, however, that the intense fear of death imputed to Saramakas by the Moravians represented a distortion of Saramaka beliefs and practices. Most Saramakas, clearly preferring life on earth, found it hard to understand the Moravians' insistence on the joys of falling asleep in Jesus. (They themselves believed matter-of-factly that the dead lived in their own land [*dede-konde*] but exercised considerable power over the living.) It is less that Saramakas especially feared death than that they actively preferred life. Missionary ideas about the existence of two destinations after death—an "everlasting fire" and a joyous Heaven—in a sense served mainly to change the stakes for those few Saramakas who paid attention.

33. Apparently, in 1784, Skipio had become the first Saramaka to journey to Amsterdam, having been taken there by Brother Kersten, as a kind of living exhibit (Helman 1968, 89).

34. It would not have occurred to the Moravians that their form of memorializing the dead might be as exotic as that of the Saramakas.

35. During the whole history of the mission, from 1765 to 1813, only twenty-nine Saramaka adults and fifty-nine children (almost all belonging to these adults) had been baptized. (For comparison: during thirty-seven years of eighteenth-century Moravian proselytizing in the Danish Virgin Islands, some seven thousand slaves were baptized [Rupp-Eisenreich 1985, 154].) As one Moravian historian summed up Saramaka soul-saving,

[Among the Saramakas] the general desire after the word was not of long continuance. In most of the hearers it bore no fruit, the allurement and cares of the world choaked the good seed, and few attained the vital experience of the salvation, purchased by Jesus Christ. (*PA* 2:418)

Saramaka conversion was most definitely a family affair. Two Christian couples, Alabi and Sialoto (who had twelve children of their own) and Alabi's sister and brother-in-law, Bebi Rebecca and Andreus Kwaku, accounted for forty-two of the fifty-nine baptized children, counting their own children, grandchildren, and great-grandchildren. And at least fifteen of the twenty-nine people baptized as adults fit onto a single genealogy with Alabi at its center. (N.B. My figures for baptisms come from Moravian documents now at Utrecht; Staehelin, based on materials at Herrnhut, gives slightly different totals [St 3, pt. 3, 233]. Note also that it is possible that the husband and children of two of Alabi's sisters [Yoyo (= Yoyome) and Bosi] may be reversed on the genealogy; my sources are contradictory.)

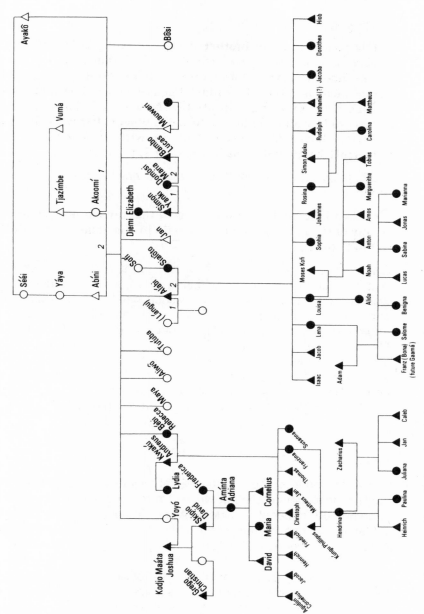

Alábi's Christian relations. Darkened symbols represent the baptized.

36. On 20 August 1791,

Old Joshua came to Brother Wietz and said, "Although I have been sick and you have visited me, I did not attend the last communion service and that has been bothering me. I am now old and do not know how much longer I have to live, and I have done many evil things in my life. Now I really have no more time to lose and would like to spend what is left with the dear Savior who has cleansed me of my sins with His blood." One can be truly happy with this brother. (St 3, pt. 3, 36)

37. Missionary sources report Alabi's final words to Christian Grego:

"When I die, make certain above all that my children learn the Way of the Lord, so that they remain in His hand." (Ledderhose 1847, 30)

Since Grego outlived Alabi by only four years, and no missionaries visited Saramaka during the period, it may be that this "quotation" was passed along orally until it reached newly arrived Moravians some fifteen years later. (In 1835, Alabi's daughter's son Frans Bona, a future *gaama* born in 1799 and brought up in part by Alabi, served as the main Saramaka guide for Brother Voigt, then on the reconnaissance trip that led to the reopening of the Saramaka mission several years later [Voigt 1837].) It is, however, possible that the report was included in one of the letters sent during the early 1820s from Gingee Bambey to Paramaribo by a literate Saramaka—probably Grego himself (Steinberg 1933, 245).

Epilogue

1. Not long after the missionaries abandoned Wana (New) Bambey, its inhabitants moved downstream to Kambaloagoon, where a large number of people, including Alabi, died one after another, precipitating the abandonment of the site and the move a few miles back upstream to Gingee (or Djendjen) Bambey, where they remained until 1848.

2. Matjaus recount that well before Gbagidi's succession, Saa's medium Yaya—while married to Gbosuma's brother—had had an affair with Gbosuma; after the brother's death, she married Gbosuma. The means by which Saa is alleged to have effected the transfer of the *gaama*ship from Yaya's Nasi husband to her Matjau son in 1835 forms the core of a complex tale, ultimately involving the death of Gbosuma and his transformation into an avenging spirit that continues to plague the Matjaus to this day.

In 1976, although Saa had not possessed anyone since Yaya's death well over a century before, a piece of cloth belonging to the god, and worn by Yaya when possessed, was still preserved in *Gaama* Agbago's storehouse. Consisting of a thick, navy blue weave with cowrie shells and a small bell sewn onto its border, the cloth was used as a means of speaking to Saa in time of need.

The Moravians left an 1801 description of a Matjau-clan "house of idols," which, to judge from its ritual paraphernalia, may well have belonged to Saa.

> **They [the idols] consisted of two water pitchers, covered, and painted with divers colors; bows and arrows of a white color; some painting-brushes, some crooked sticks, and a little black water-pot covered. (PA 3:260)**

3. The late Aleks de Drie, one of Suriname's premier Creole raconteurs, related the tale sometime in the 1970s (de Drie 1985, 198–200); among Creoles, such tale-telling (*ananstori-prey*) forms part of the memorial ceremonies for the deceased a year after the death, roughly equivalent to Saramaka "second funeral" rites. This tale apparently relates to historical incidents that occurred during the early 1860s, involving a group of maroons who lived on the Surnau Creek. That many of the descendants of the tale's protagonists later became Christians only increases the poignancy of the encounter. For details and additional references, see de Drie 1984, 91–93, 130–31, and 1985, 358–60.

4. A further history of Saramaka Christianity, attending to multiple perspectives, has yet to be written. Suffice it to say here that the reopening of the Moravian mission in 1840, and the 1848 move far downstream (led by Alabi's and Sialoto's descendants) to found the Christian village of Ganze, permitted the maintenance and gradual expansion of Christianity in Saramaka. Several chroniclers, associated with the Moravian (or, later, the Roman Catholic) mission efforts, have sketched in many of the details from their own points of view (see, for example, Beck 1914, Doth et al. n.d., Morssink n.d., Schneider 1893, Steinberg 1933, van der Veer 1969, and Weiss 1911, and for additional references, R. Price 1976, 63). Missionary perspectives have remained remarkably stable. In the twentieth century, Moravian spokesmen refer to "the unknown numbers of heathen, who still swarm in the southern woods and jungles" (Hutton 1923, 250) and write of "the most powerful bulwark of Satan in the interior of Suriname" (Koorndijk n.d., 65). With much the same optimism and patience that bolstered their German predecessors, Dutch and Creole Moravian leaders in our own time maintain the confidence that "the complete collapse of Satan's fortress in the Suriname bush is, in our opinion, only a question of time" (Koorndijk n.d., 66). Meanwhile, across the Marowijne River in Aluku Maroon villages, the anthropologist Kenneth Bilby reports that Jehovah's Witnesses (and similar groups) are conducting heavy proselytization—as, I am told, has also been occurring in Saramaka during the 1980s—with results very similar to those in Alabi's day: a recently converted captain killing sacred snakes to show his invulnerability and the superiority of his new faith; attempts by this same man to suppress coffin-carrying, praying at

ancestor shrines, and so on; and virulent resistance, often expressed in a "supernatural" idiom, by other members of the community. As Bilby wrote from the field in 1987, after reading a draft of this book, "The spirits of both Alabi and Akoomi are alive in Aluku."

5. In a report from a reliable source in Suriname, I learned that some Saramaka warriors, fighting on the side of Ronnie Brunswijk's "Jungle Commandos" against the Bouterse regime, have actually carried copies of *First-Time* (which they could not read but the message of which they knew) into battle with them.

References Cited

Archival references are abbreviated as follows:

AEB   Archief der Evangelische Broedergemeente in Suriname vanaf 1764, Archief Rijksprovintie Utrecht (Utrecht).

ARA   Algemeen Rijksarchief (The Hague).

Hof   Archieven van het Hof van Politie en Crimineele Justitie, Algemeen Rijksarchief, Eerste Afdeling (The Hague).

SvS   Archieven van de Sociëteit van Suriname, Algemeen Rijksarchief, Eerste Afdeling (The Hague).

Two frequently cited sources are abbreviated as follows:

PA   *Periodical Accounts relating to the Missions of the Church of the United Brethren Established among the Heathen.* London, 1790–1834.

St   Staehelin 1913–19. See below for full reference.

Abrahams, Roger D.

1970   "Patterns of Performance in the West Indies." Reprinted in R. D. Abrahams, *The Man-of-Words in the West Indies,* 1–20. Baltimore: Johns Hopkins University Press, 1983.

Anonymous (in order of publication date)

1748   *A Collection of Hymns: Consisting Chiefly of Translations from the German Hymn-Book of the Moravian Brethren.* Part 3. London.

1749   *Hymns Composed for the Use of the Brethren.* London [apparently by Zinzendorf].

433

1776   *A Concise Account of the Present State of the Missions of the United Brethren (Commonly Called Moravians) in 1776.* [London?]

n.d. [ca. 1784] *Instructions for the Members of the Unitas Fratrum Who Minister in the Gospel among the Heathen.* London: Brethren's Society for the Furtherance of the Gospel among the Heathen.

1793   *Liturgic Hymns of the United Brethren.* Translated from the German. London.

1916   "Politieke contracten met de Boschnegers in Suriname." *Bijdragen tot de Taal-, Land- en Volkenkunde* 71:371–411.

Ariès, Philippe

1974   *Western Attitudes toward Death.* Baltimore: Johns Hopkins University Press.

Barbot, John

1732   "A Description of the Coasts of North and South-Guinea." In *A Collection of Voyages and Travels,* edited by Awnsham Churchill. Vol. 5. London.

Beck, Siegfried

1914   *Die wirtschaftlich-soziale Arbeit der Missionsgeschäfte der Brüdergemeine in Suriname.* Herrnhut.

de Beet, Chris, and H.U.E. Thoden van Velzen

1977   "Bush Negro Prophetic Movements: Religions of Despair?" *Bijdragen tot de Taal-, Land- en Volkenkunde* 133:100–35.

Beidelman, T. O.

1982   *Colonial Evangelism.* Bloomington: Indiana University Press.

Berkhofer, Robert F., Jr.

1976   *Salvation and the Savage.* New York: Atheneum.

Blair, Barbara L.

1984   "Wolfert Simon van Hoogenheim in the Berbice Slave Revolt of 1763–1764." *Bijdragen tot de Taal-, Land- en Volkenkunde* 140:56–76.

Boon, James

1982   *Other Tribes, Other Scribes.* Ithaca: Cornell University Press.

Bubberman, F. C., A. H. Loor et al., and C. Koeman, ed.

1973   *Links with the Past: The History of Cartography in Suriname, 1500–1971.* Amsterdam: Theatrum Orbis Terrarum.

Burridge, K.O.L.

1975   "Other Peoples' Religions Are Absurd." In *Explorations in the Anthropology of Religion*, edited by W.E.A. van Beek and J. H. Scherer, 8–23. Leiden: Koninklijk Instituut voor Taal-, Land- en Volkenkunde.

Clifford, James

1986   "Partial Truths." In *Writing Culture*, edited by James Clifford and George E. Marcus, 1–16. Berkeley and Los Angeles: University of California Press.

Crevaux, Jules

1880   "Erste Reise im Innern von Guayana (1876 bis 1877)." *Globus* 37:1–7, 17–23, 33–38, 49–55, 65–72, 81–83.

Curtin, Philip D.

1961   "'The White Man's Grave': Image and Reality, 1780–1850." *Journal of British Studies* 1:94–110.

1968   "Epidemiology and the Slave Trade." *Political Science Quarterly* 83:190–216.

Dening, Greg

1980   *Islands and Beaches. Discourse on a Silent Land: Marquesas, 1774–1880.* Honolulu: University Press of Hawaii.

1986   "Towards a Pale Blue Book on Producing Histories." Paper.

1989   "A Poetic for Histories: Transformations That Present the Past." In *Clio in Oceania*, edited by Aletta Biersack. Washington, D. C.: Smithsonian Institution Press.

Dittelbach, Petrus

1692   *Verval en val der Labadisten.* Amsterdam: Daniel van den Dalen.

Donicie, Antoon

1948   "Sterfhuis en begravenis bij de Saramakkanen." *West-Indische Gids* 29:175–82.

Donicie, Antoon, and Jan Voorhoeve

1963   *De Saramakaanse woordenschat.* Amsterdam: Bureau voor Taalonderzoek in Suriname van de Universiteit van Amsterdam.

Doth, R.E.C., E. M. Koorndijk, R. Schimdt, W. Vlaanderen, and Jan Voorhoeve

n.d. [1965?]   *Kondre sa jere.* Zeist: Seminarie der Evangelische Broedergemeente.

de Drie, Aleks

1984   *Wan Tori fu mi Eygi Srefi*. Samengesteld door Trudi Guda.
                Paramaribo: Afdeling Cultuur Studies van het Ministerie
                van Onderwijs, Wetenschappen en Cultuur.

1985   *Sye! Arki Tori!* Samengesteld door Trudi Guda. Parama-
                ribo: Afdeling Cultuur Studies van het Ministerie van
                Onderwijs, Wetenschappen en Cultuur.

Dyk, Pieter van

n.d.   *Nieuwe en nooit bevooren gezien onderwyzing in het Bas-*
                tert Engels, of Neeger Engels. Amsterdam. Reprinted in
                Suriname: Spiegel der Vaderlandse Kooplieden, edited by
                Ursy M. Lichtveld and Jan Voorhoeve, 219–49. The Hague:
                Martinus Nijhoff, 1980.

Edel, Leon

1984   *Writing Lives: Principia Biographica.* New York: Norton.

Eyck, J.W.S. van

1828   Algemeen verslag van den tegenwoordige staat en huis-
                selijke inrigtingen, benevens de levenswijsen der bevre-
                digde boschnegers binnen deze kolonie. MS [at Koninklijk
                Instituut voor de Tropen, Amsterdam].

Franklin, Benjamin

1948   *Benjamin Franklin's Autobiographical Writings.* Edited
                by Carl Van Doren. New York: Viking Press.

Furley, Oliver W.

1965   "Moravian Missionaries and Slaves in the West Indies."
                Caribbean Studies 5(2):3–16.

Geertz, Clifford

1976   " 'From the Native's Point of View': On the Nature of An-
                thropological Understanding." In *Meaning in Anthropol-*
                ogy, edited by Keith H. Basso and Henry A. Selby, 221–37.
                Albuquerque: University of New Mexico Press.

Gollin, Gillian Lindt

1967   *Moravians in Two Worlds.* New York: Columbia Univer-
                sity Press.

de Groot, Silvia W.

1977   *From Isolation towards Integration.* The Hague: Marti-
                nus Nijhoff.

Hamilton, J. Taylor

1900   *A History of the Church Known as the Moravian Church.*
                Bethlehem, Pa.: Times Publishing.

Harding, Susan F.

1987   "Convicted by the Holy Spirit: The Rhetoric of Funda-
            mental Baptist Conversion." *American Ethnologist* 14:
            167–81.

Hartsinck, Jan Jacob

1770   *Beschrijving van Guiana of de Wilde Kust in Zuid-Ame-
            rika.* Amsterdam: Gerrit Tielenburg.

Helman, Albert

1968   *Zaken, Zending en Bezinning.* Paramaribo: C. Kersten.

Herskovits, Melville J.

1929   "Adjiboto, an African Game of the Bush-Negroes of Dutch
            Guiana." *Man* 29:122–27.

1932   "Wari in the New World." *Journal of the Royal Anthro-
            pological Institute* 62:23–38.

Hoeree, Joris, and Wim Hoogbergen

1984   "Oral History and Archival Data Combined: The Re-
            moval of the Saramakan Granman Kofi Bosuman as an
            Epistemological Problem." *Communication and Cogni-
            tion* 17:245–89.

Holmes, John

1818   *Historical Sketches of the Missions of the United Breth-
            ren for Propagating the Gospel among the Heathen, from
            Their Commencement to the Present Time.* Dublin: R.
            Napper.

Hoogbergen, Wim

1985   *De Boni-Oorlogen, 1757–1860: Marronage en guerrilla
            in Oost-Suriname.* Utrecht: Centrum voor Caraibische
            Studies.

Hurault, Jean

1961   *Les Noirs Réfugiés Boni de la Guyane Française.* Dakar:
            Institut Français d'Afrique Noire.

1970   *Africains de Guyane: La vie matérielle et l'art des Noirs
            Réfugiés de Guyane.* Paris and The Hague: Mouton.

Hutton, J. E.

1909   *A History of the Moravian Church.* 2d ed. London: Mora-
            vian Publication Office.

1923   *A History of Moravian Missions.* London: Moravian Pub-
            lication Office.

Jozefzoon, O.J.R.

1959   *De Saramaccaanse wereld.* Paramaribo: Varekamp.

Junker, L.

1927   "Kerstfeest bij de Boschnegers." In H. G. Steinberg, *Ons Suriname*, 235–37. The Hague: Algemeene Boekhandel, 1933.

1932/33   "Het einde van een dynastie: de dood van Jankosoe." *West-Indische Gids* 14:49–58.

Kahn, Morton C.

1931   *Djuka: The Bush Negroes of Dutch Guiana.* New York: Viking Press.

Kesler, C. K.

1939   "Een Moravische Zuster uit de 18e Eeuw, Anna Maria Kersten geb: Tonn." *West-Indische Gids* 22:206–17.

King, Johannes

1979   Skrekiboekoe. MS (1885). [Fragment translated in *Maroon Societies: Rebel Slave Communities in the Americas*, edited by Richard Price, 298–304. Rev. ed. Baltimore: Johns Hopkins University Press.]

Koorndijk, E. M.

n.d. [1965?]   "De Boslandzending in 1965." In R.E.C. Doth et al., *Kondre sa Jere*, 61–66. Zeist: Seminarie der Evangelische Broedergemeente.

Kopytoff, Barbara Klamon

1976   Jamaican Maroon Political Organization: The Effects of the Treaties. *Social and Economic Studies* 25:87–104.

1979   Colonial Treaty as Sacred Charter of the Jamaican Maroons. *Ethnohistory* 26:45–64.

Ledderhose, Karl Friedrich

1847   *Die Mission unter den freien Buschnegern in Surinam und Rasmus Schmidt.* Heidelberg: Universitäts Buchhandlungen von Karl Winter.

Legêne, P. M.

1941   *Waar is uw broeder? Een verhaal uit het donkere oerwoud van Suriname.* Zeister Tracktaten no. 4. Zeist: Zendingsgenootschap der Evangelische Broedergemeente.

Lichtveld, Ursy M., and Jan Voorhoeve, eds.

1980   *Suriname: Spiegel der Vaderlandse Kooplieden.* 2d ed. The Hague: Martinus Nijhoff.

van Lier, R.A.J.

1971   *Frontier Society: A Social Analysis of the History of Surinam.* The Hague: Martinus Nijhoff [orig. 1949].

Lindblom, Gerhard

1924   *Afrikanische Relikte und Indianische Entlehnungen in der Kultur der Busch-Neger Surinams.* Gothenburg: Elanders Boktryckeri Aktiebolag.

van der Linde, Jan Marinus

1956   *Het Visioen van Herrnhut en het Apostolaat der Moravische Broeders in Suriname, 1735–1863.* Paramaribo: C. Kersten.

1963   *Heren, slaven, broeders: Momenten uit de geschiedenis der slavernij.* Nijkerk: G. F. Callenbach.

Lucas, J. Olumide

1945   *The Religion of the Yorubas.* Lagos: C.M.S. Bookshop.

McLoughlin, William G.

1984   *Cherokees and Missionaries, 1789–1839.* New Haven: Yale University Press.

Marcus, George E., and Michael M. J. Fischer

1986   *Anthropology as Cultural Critique.* Chicago: University of Chicago Press.

Mintz, Sidney W., and Richard Price

1976   *An Anthropological Approach to the Afro-American Past: A Caribbean Perspective.* Philadelphia: ISHI.

Morssink, F.

1934/35   "Nogmaals: de dood van Jankoeso en: nog niet het einde van een dynastie." *West-Indische Gids* 16:91–105.

n.d. [1934?] "Boschnegeriana (misschien beter: Silvae-nigritiana?). Eenige gegevens omtrent geschiedenis en missioneering onzer Surinaamsche Boschnegers." MS.

Nassy, David de Ishak Cohen, et al.

1788   *Essai historique sur la colonie de Surinam.* Paramaribo.

Oldendorp, C.G.A.

1987   *History of the Mission of the Evangelical Brethren on the Caribbean Islands of St. Thomas, St. Croix, and St. John.* Edited by Johann Jakob Bossard. Translated by Arnold R. Highfield and Vladimir Barac. Ann Arbor: Karoma [orig. 1777].

Oudschans Dentz, Fred.

1948   "De afzetting van het Groot-Opperhoofd der Saramaccaners Koffy in 1835 en de politieke contracten met de Boschnegers in Suriname." *Bijdragen tot de Taal-, Land- en Volkenkunde* 104:33–43.

Philipp, June

1983 "Traditional Historical Narrative and Action-oriented (or Ethnographic) History." *Historical Studies* 20:339–52.

Polimé, T. S., and H.U.E. Thoden van Velzen

1988 *Vluchtelingen, Opstandelingen en andere Bosnegers van Oost-Suriname, 1986–1988.* Utrecht: Centrum voor Caraibische Studies.

van de Poll, Willem

1959 *Suriname.* Paramaribo: Varekamp; & The Hague: W. van Hoeve.

Pratt, Mary

1986 "Fieldwork in Common Places." In *Writing Culture,* edited by James Clifford and George E. Marcus, 27–50. Berkeley and Los Angeles: University of California Press.

Price, Richard

1975 *Saramaka Social Structure.* Rio Piedras: Institute of Caribbean Studies.

1976 *The Guiana Maroons: A Historical and Bibliographical Introduction.* Baltimore: Johns Hopkins University Press.

1983a *First-Time: The Historical Vision of an Afro-American People.* Baltimore: Johns Hopkins University Press.

1983b *To Slay the Hydra: Dutch Colonial Perspectives on the Saramaka Wars.* Ann Arbor: Karoma.

1984 "To Every Thing a Season: The Development of Saramaka Calendrical Reckoning." *Tijdschrift OSO* 3:63–71.

1990 "Subsistence on the Plantation Periphery: Crops, Cooking, and Labor among Eighteenth-Century Suriname Maroons." *Slavery and Abolition* (in press).

Price, Richard, and Sally Price

1977 *Music from Saramaka: A Dynamic Afro-American Tradition.* New York: Folkways FE 4225.

1990 *Two Evenings in Saramaka.* Chicago: University of Chicago Press.

Price, Sally

1984 *Co-wives and Calabashes.* Ann Arbor: University of Michigan Press.

Price, Sally, and Richard Price

1980 *Afro-American Arts of the Suriname Rain Forest.* Berkeley and Los Angeles: University of California Press.

van Raalte, J.

1973   *Secularisatie en Zending in Suriname.* Wageningen: H. Veenman en Zonen.

1986   "Kerk en staat in Suriname." *Tijdschrift OSO* 5:43–53.

Ranger, Terence

1987   "An Africanist Comment." *American Ethnologist* 14: 182–85.

Reisman, Karl

1970   "Cultural and Linguistic Ambiguity in a West Indian Village." In *Afro-American Anthropology,* edited by Norman E. Whitten, Jr., and John F. Szwed, 129–44. New York: Free Press.

Riemer, Johann Andreus

1801   *Missions-Reise nach Suriname und Barbice.* Zittau and Leipzig.

Risler, Jeremias

1805   *Geschichte der Mission in Sud-Amerika.* Barby: Conrad Schilling.

Rosaldo, Renato

1986   "From the Door of His Tent: The Fieldworker and the Inquisitor." In *Writing Culture,* edited by James Clifford and George E. Marcus, 77–97. Berkeley and Los Angeles: University of California Press.

Ruggenberg, Rob

1986   "Suriname is doodsbang." *De Stem,* 20 December, "Weekend," 1.

Rupp-Eisenreich, Britta

1985   "Les frères moraves, ethnologues de la condition esclave? (Iles Vierges, Petites Antilles, 1731–1768)." In *Naissance de l'ethnologie? Anthropologie et missions en Amérique, XVIe–XVIIIIe siècles,* edited by Claude Blanckaert, 125–72. Paris: Cerf.

Sack, Baron Albert von

1821   *Reize naar Surinamen.* Haarlem: Erven F. Bohn.

de Salontha

1778   *Précis de deux lettres.* Nimmegue: Isaac van Campen.

Schiltkamp, J. A., and J. Th. de Smidt

1973   *Plakaten, Ordonnantiën en Andere Wetten, Uitgevaardigd in Suriname, 1667–1816.* Amsterdam: S. Emmering.

Schneider, H. G.

1893   "Die Buschneger Surinames." *Allgemeinen Missions-Zeitschrift* 20(1):1–16; (2):17–30; (3):33–48; (4):49–64; (5):72–80.

Schumann, C. L.

1778   "Saramaccanisch Deutsches Wörter-Buch." In *Die Sprache der Saramakkaneger in Surinam*, edited by Hugo Schuchardt, 46–116. Verhandelingen der Koninklijke Akademie van Wetenschappen te Amsterdam 14(6), 1914. Amsterdam: Johannes Müller.

Schwartz, Stuart B.

1986   "The Challenges of Ethnohistory." In *Proceedings of the 1986 Meeting of the Rocky Mountain Council on Latin American Studies*, edited by Garth M. Hansen, 3–13. Las Cruces, N.M.: New Mexico State University.

Sheridan, Richard B.

1985   *Doctors and Slaves: A Medical and Demographic History of Slavery in the British West Indies, 1680–1834.* Cambridge: Cambridge University Press.

Shweder, Richard A.

1988   Review of Clifford Geertz, *Works and Lives. The Anthropologist as Author. New York Times Book Review,* 28 February, 13.

Staehelin, F.

1913–19   *Die Mission der Brüdergemeine in Suriname und Berbice im achtzehnten Jahrhundert.* Herrnhut: Vereins für Brüdergeschichte in Kommission der Unitätsbuchhandlung in Gnadau.

Stedman, John Gabriel

1988   *Narrative of a Five Years Expedition against the Revolted Negroes of Surinam. Transcribed for the First Time from the Original 1790 Manuscript.* Edited, and with an Introduction and Notes, by Richard Price and Sally Price. Baltimore: Johns Hopkins University Press.

Steinberg, H. G.

1933   *Ons Suriname: De zending der Evangelische Broedergemeente in Nederlandsch Guyana.* The Hague: N. V. Algemeene Boekhandel voor inwendige en uitwendige Zending.

Taussig, Michael

1987   *Shamanism, Colonialism, and the Wild Man: A Study in Terror and Healing.* Chicago: University of Chicago Press.

Vass, Winifred Kellersberger

1979   *The Bantu Speaking Heritage of the United States.* Los Angeles: Center for Afro-American Studies, UCLA.

van der Veer, Johan J.

1969   *De daad bij het woord: zendingswerk in Suriname.* Baarn: Bosch en Keuning.

Vernon, Diane

1985   *Money Magic in a Modernizing Maroon Society.* Tokyo: ILCAA Tokyo University of Foreign Studies.

Vlaanderen, W.

n.d. [1965?]   "Het begin van de boslandzending." In R.E.C. Doth et al., *Kondre sa Jere,* 16–32. Zeist: Seminarie der Evangelische Broedergemeente.

Voigt, J.H.P.

1837   "Verhaal van Broeder J.H.P. Voigt, aangaande zijne reize onder de vrije Auka- en Saramakka-negers aan de boven-Suriname, in September en October 1835." *Berigten uit de Heiden-Wereld* (1):8–16; (2):17–29; (3):33–34.

Voorhoeve, Jan

1959   "An Orthography for Saramaccan." *Word* 15:436–45.

Voorhoeve, Jan, and Antoon Donicie

1963   *Bibliographie du Négro-Anglais du Surinam.* The Hague: Martinus Nijhoff.

Walsh, John, with Robert Gannon

1967   *Time Is Short and the Water Rises.* New York: Dutton.

Weiss, H.

1911   *Ons Suriname.* The Hague: Boekhandel van den Zendings-studie-raad.

Wekker, Just B. Ch.

1986   "Historische fragmenten rond 18e-eeuwse zendingsposten in Suriname." *Tijdschrift OSO* 5:171–90.

van Wetering, W.

1972   "Witchcraft among the Tapanahoni Djuka." In *Maroon Societies: Rebel Slave Communities in the Americas,* edited by Richard Price, 370–88. Rev. ed. Baltimore: Johns Hopkins University Press, 1979.

1973   "Hekserij bij de Djuka: een sociologische benadering." Ph.D. diss., University of Amsterdam.

Whitten, Norman E., Jr.

1986   Review of R. Price, *First-Time* and *To Slay the Hydra.*
                Ethnohistory 33:91–94.

Wolbers, J.

1861   *Geschiedenis van Suriname.* Amsterdam: H. de Hoogh.

Wong, E.

1938   "Hoofdenverkiezing, stamverdeeling en stamverspreiding
                der Boschnegers van Suriname in de 18e en 19e eeuw."
                Bijdragen tot de Taal-, Land- en Volkenkunde 97:295–
                362.